Lecture Notes in Information Systems and Organisation

Volume 72

Lecture Notes in Information Systems and Organization—LNISO—is a series of scientific books that explore the current scenario of information systems, in particular IS and organization. The focus on the relationship between IT, IS and organization is the common thread of this collection, which aspires to provide scholars across the world with a point of reference and comparison in the study and research of information systems and organization. LNISO is the publication forum for the community of scholars investigating behavioral and design aspects of IS and organization. The series offers an integrated publication platform for high-quality conferences, symposia and workshops in this field. Materials are published upon a strictly controlled double blind peer review evaluation made by selected reviewers.

LNISO is abstracted/indexed in Scopus

Alessio Maria Braccini • Francesca Ricciardi •
Francesco Virili
Editors

Digital (Eco) Systems and Societal Challenges

New Scenarios for Organizing

Springer

Editors
Alessio Maria Braccini
Department of Economics, Society and Business Organisation
Università degli Studi della Tuscia
Viterbo, Italy

Francesca Ricciardi
Department of Management "Valter Cantino"
University of Turin
Turin, Italy

Francesco Virili
Department of Economics and Social Sciences
Catholic University of the Sacred Heart
Piacenza, Italy

ISSN 2195-4968 ISSN 2195-4976 (electronic)
Lecture Notes in Information Systems and Organisation
ISBN 978-3-031-75585-9 ISBN 978-3-031-75586-6 (eBook)
https://doi.org/10.1007/978-3-031-75586-6

Business and Management
IT in Business
Business Information Systems
Organization
Business and Management, general
Organizational Studies, Economic Sociology

This Springer imprint is published by the registered company Springer Nature Switzerland AG
The registered company address is: Gewerbestrasse 11, 6330 Cham, Switzerland

Contents

Digital Eco-Systems, Change, and Organising

Alessio Maria Braccini, Francesca Ricciardi, and Francesco Virili

Abstract In digital ecosystems, connected objects interact with each other and humans to create dynamic and adaptive environments. The proliferation of devices beyond personal computers and mobile phones has given rise to smart entities such as smart homes, factories, and cities. These interconnected systems exhibit complex behaviours and blurring boundaries between organizational and institutional spheres, thus raising challenges for research and practice. This chapter focuses on the definition and origin of the concept of digital ecosystems in the information systems, ecology, and economics literature and introduces the book's contributions to the research in this domain: 22 chapters that provide an interdisciplinary and multi-focal perspective on this topic. The chapters address different aspects of digital ecosystems, including their role in agrifood systems, the design and analysis of specific artefacts for solving wicked problems, and environmental and societal implications.

Keywords Digital ecosystems · Smart organising · Smart entities

The original version of the chapter has been revised. A correction to this chapter can be found at https://doi.org/10.1007/978-3-031-75586-6_24

A. M. Braccini (✉)
Department of Economics Engineering Society and Business Organisation, University of Tuscia, Viterbo, Italy
e-mail: abraccini@unitus.it

F. Ricciardi
Department of Management "Valter Cantino", University of Turin, Torino, Italy
e-mail: francesca.ricciardi@unicatt.it

F. Virili
Department of Economic and Social Sciences, Catholic University of the Sacred Hearth, Piacenza, Italy
e-mail: francesco.virili@unicatt.it

A. M. Braccini et al. (eds.), *Digital (Eco) Systems and Societal Challenges*, Lecture Notes in Information Systems and Organisation 72,
https://doi.org/10.1007/978-3-031-75586-6_1

1 Introduction

It is common to say that digital technologies are widespread, ubiquitous, and continuously diffusing. Data about the number of people connected to the Internet show steadily but continuously growing numbers that will eventually get closer to the population of the earth. However, the number of connected devices has already exceeded that digit [1]. From smartphones and wearable gadgets to smart home appliances and autonomous vehicles, digital devices have become integral to everyday life and professional activities. Projections talk of 75.44 billion devices connected by 2025 because of the pervasive adoption of digital technologies [2].

This diffusion extends beyond the realm of personal computers and mobile phones. Today, many objects– from industrial machinery and medical equipment to household items and agricultural tools—are equipped with sensors and connectivity capabilities, giving rise to smart entities, such as smart homes, smart platforms, smart factories, and smart cities [3, 4]. These connected objects communicate with each other and communicate with people, exchanging data and performing coordinated actions, either without human intervention or in partnership with humans.

The connected objects interact based on different mechanisms: programming logic, institutional logic, or sociotechnical interplay [5–7]. Regardless of the logic, the interplay of these entities creates a dynamic and adaptive digital environment that extends well beyond the traditional concept of a socio-technical system and approaches living entities [8]. While sociotechnical systems primarily emphasise the interaction between human actors and technology within a specific context [9, 10], the integration of connected objects introduces a new layer of complexity, giving rise to what is now recognised as a *digital ecosystem*.

2 The Rise of Digital Ecosystems

A *digital ecosystem* is a set of co-evolving components playing any role in a specific area and can generate complementarities within a digital network platform by affecting each other and the entire environment, forming a modular, self-contained system with proper boundaries [11]. The concept of a *digital ecosystem* originates around three conceptual origins: information systems, ecology, and economics. From the ecology literature, digital ecosystems borrow the focus on the systemic coevolution process of actors and objects [12]. From the information systems literature, digital ecosystems inherit the centrality of digital artefacts and digital platforms [13, 14]. Finally, from the economics literature, digital ecosystems borrow the mechanisms by which digital technologies activate benefit generation and enable the joint evolution of actors, actions, products, and services, which is considered today a central tenet of digital ecosystems' value production [15].

The components of digital ecosystems are represented mainly by digital artefacts and their connected living and non-living entities. Due to this nature, a digital ecosystem has both a physical (traditional/material) and a digital manifestation, embodying the peculiarities of cyber-physical systems [16, 17]. Being interconnections of both living and non-living entities, digital ecosystems raise both technical and organising issues [18], around the collective action of interlinked organisational actors that interact with the common interest of developing digital technologies for materialising shared benefits [19]. Digital ecosystems often present dynamic and blurring boundaries, spanning across organisational and institutional boundaries, giving the impression of complex and interdependent self-organising entities [18], giving rise to new forms of collaboration, new sources of value creation, and new approaches to solving wicked problems. Digital ecosystems present opportunities and challenges for individuals, organisations, and society.

3 Researching Digital Ecosystems

In line with this way of reasoning, the chapters of this book provide an up-to-date overview of the research on digital ecosystems performed by scholars animating the interdisciplinary and international community of information systems in Italy. The chapters represent a selection among the best papers presented at the 2023 edition of the annual conference of the Italian Chapter of AIS and underwent a double-blind peer review. They were selected and included in this book because they provide an interdisciplinary and multi-focal perspective on digital ecosystems. In total 22 papers are published in this book, addressing different aspects of the interdisciplinary research of digital ecosystems. The book's papers tackle four perspectives on digital ecosystems: the role of digital technologies in the agrifood system; digital technologies for smart cities, urban mobility, and smart tourism; the modelling, design, analysis, and testing of artefacts in digital ecosystems; and the sustainability perspective, exploring the role of digital technologies for the environment and society.

3.1 Digital Technologies in the Agrifood System

Four chapters deepen the perspective of digital ecosystems within the agrifood systems domain. This domain is not usually targeted by the information systems literature, yet it retains significant implications for the nutrition and well-being of the earth's population and for the sustainable management of such industries.

In this regard, with their study, Chiara Cagnetti and Alessio Maria Braccini in Chap. "Exploring the Connection Between Enabling Factors and Digital Technology Adoption in Agricultural Industries" contribute to the viable academic debate on the digitalization of agricultural industries by delving in-depth into the Italian context. They find some pivotal enabling factors that are instrumental in adopting digital technologies in agriculture.

Chapter "The Covid-19 Impact on Food Digital Transformation: A Bibliometric Analysis of Academic and Practitioners' Perspectives" by Canio Forliano, Paola De

Bernardi and Martina Panero explores the relationship between the Covid-19 pandemic and the digital transformation of the food industry. Based on a bibliometric analysis and the analysis of practitioners' documents, the study identifies five thematic clusters and specific real-world insights on the ongoing debate.

In Chap. "Digital Technologies for Sustainable Value in the Food Sector" Haiat Perozzo, Aurelio Ravarini, Emanuele Gabriel Margherita, Alessio Maria Braccini and Giorgio Occhipinti conduct a multiple case study on six leading Italian companies in the food sector to explore whether, how and to what extent the adoption of digital technologies is a driver for the pursuit of sustainability objectives. Based on the academic literature on the technology-sustainability nexus, the findings highlight a lower level of maturity in the real world than one could have expected.

Finally, Laura Roma, Chiara Cagnetti, Alessio Maria Braccini and Rocco Agrifoglio focus in Chap. "The Non-Adoption of Digital Technologies in the Agricultural Industries: A Systematic Literature Review" on the adoption and patterns of adoption of digital technologies in the agriculture sector. Based on a systematic literature review, the study identifies the leading digital technologies in this industry and the main barriers to technology adoption.

3.2 Digital Technologies for Smart Cities, Urban Mobility, and Smart Tourism

Six chapters are dedicated to the digitalization of urban ecosystems and the emergent role of smart cities and smart tourism in designing new patterns of mobility and tourism.

Filippo Marchesani, Francesca Masciarelli and Andrea Bikfalvi propose in Chap. "International Promotion Patterns in the Smart City Literature: Exploring the Role of Geography in Affecting Local Drivers and Smart Cities' Outcomes" a study motivated by the recent rise of smart cities, a significant trend in contemporary urban development. While academic discussions on the impact of smart city development continue, global recognition remains uncertain due to their multidisciplinary nature. The authors conducted a systematic literature review of top-tier peer-reviewed articles from 2008 to December 2021 to address this. They highlight local drivers and smart city outcomes across different contexts by focusing on geographical location as a driver of cities' international promotion strategies. The proposed literature analysis contributes to smart city debates by emphasizing the role of geographical location in shaping smart city trajectories.

The study by Ludovica Antenozio, Daniela Di Berardino and Augusta Consorti in Chap. "Intercepting Smart Policies to Foster High-Tech SMEs in Regional Environment" investigates smart city urban policies and high-tech Italian SME localization over an 8-year period (2013–2020). Analyzing a heterogeneous sample of 250 SMEs, the authors find that location choices are influenced by smart urban policies emphasizing innovation and competitiveness. Additionally, SMEs play a pivotal role in transforming urban entrepreneurial traits. These insights contribute to ongoing debates on spatial distribution and offer guidance for policymakers and urban planners aiming to foster innovation-driven economic development.

Chapter "The Influence of Physical and Virtual Servicescapes on Public Transportation Choices" by Sina Zimmermann, Thomas Schulz, Andreas Hein, Heiko Gewald and Helmut Krcmar is motivated by the widespread use of private cars, contributing to global traffic congestion and air pollution in cities. While mobility apps within smart city initiatives are believed to influence public transport choices, empirical evidence is scarce. Using choice-based conjoint analysis, their study examined mobility decisions among 185 private car commuters. By analyzing physical and virtual servicescapes, the authors found that factors like overcrowding and app layout influenced commuters' choices. Surprisingly, even when provided with public transport information via apps, many commuters continued to favor private cars.

In Chap. "Smart Inclusive Cities Advancing" Mauro Romanelli focuses on the concept of "smart inclusive city" and argues that a smart city strategy should leverage high technologies and urban planning to promote and shape inclusive urban growth and communities.

Chapter "Microfounding Urban Big Data Infrastructure Through Multiplex Networks" by Edgardo Bucciarelli, Alessia Regnicoli and Aurora Ascatigno explores urban big data infrastructure (UBDI) within the context of complex adaptive systems. The study outlines the intricate nature of today's urban areas by considering multileveled frameworks and emergent properties. It aims to understand dimensions emerging from state-of-the-art literature on UBDI and methodological challenges. Additionally, a novel approach is introduced, by representing UBDI as a hybrid organizational form, emphasizing the pivotal role of people in the urban ecosystem.

Chapter "Emerging Paradigms in Tourism Industry: Smart Tourism and Local Development" by Francesco Russo, Alessia Munnia, Angelo Bonfanti, Melita Nicotra and Marco Romano explores recent evolutions of destination management, which has undergone a profound transformation under the wave of the shift toward smart tourism. The aim of the study is to provide an overview this emerging change and, adopting a deductive approach, derive propositions to enhance the overall understanding of the phenomenon. The originality of their contribution lies in the attempt to relate smart tourism to local development.

3.3 Modelling, Design, Analysis, and Testing of Artefacts in Digital Ecosystems

The third group of six chapters addresses the modelling, design, analysis, and testing of artefacts in digital ecosystems, exploring how digital artefacts help address wicked societal problems.

In Chap. "Layer Upon Layer: Developing Layered Modular Architectures for Data-Driven Health Platform", Bjarki Freyr Sveinbjarnarson, Erna Sif Arnardottir, and Anna Sigridur Islind present a layered-modular architecture for a digital platform aimed at data extraction and representation for data-driven health platforms. The study describes the process of testing said architecture and highlights its advantages.

In Chap. "Drivers from Extended Institutional Theory Supporting the DPP as a Tool of CE", Luca Balzani and Katia Corsi develop a critical analytical review of the academic literature and available professional materials on the EU's Digital Product Passport. The DPP's role and potential effectiveness are conceptualized in the light of the New Institutional Theory to highlight its usefulness for harmonizing economic development and environmental protection.

In Chap. "Local Digital Twin Ecosystems: A Human-Centric Approach", Oleg Missikoff explores the growing importance of the human component in Digital Twin (DT) design and implementation. The study proposes an extension of the DT legacy paradigm and discusses it in the light of epistemological justifications, international case studies, enabling methodologies, and ongoing pilot projects.

Chapter "A Systems Integration view on Data Ecosystems" by Federica Ceci and Andrew Davies takes into consideration models of digital ecosystems as intricate networks of interconnected entities, characterized by multilateral connections that extend beyond bilateral relationships. Participants within these ecosystems collaborate, innovate, and generate knowledge through resource dependencies and product/service offerings. Drawing insights from systems integration literature, the study by Ceci and Davies explores managing interdependencies and complexities in data ecosystems, using the Gaia X project as an empirical context. By leveraging this knowledge, successful data-driven innovation can be achieved. A key aspect is the continuous exchange of data, which has become a pervasive resource for knowledge acquisition and action.

The last two chapters of this group are proposing simulation models for the analysis of digital ecosystems.

Chapter "Studying the Distribution of Strategies in the Two-Scenario Snowdrift Game" by Edgardo Bucciarelli, Shu-Heng Chen, Aurora Ascatigno and Alfredo Colantonio contributes to the longstanding debate on the dynamics of cooperation among individuals. Their study delves into the Snowdrift game, a strategic construct used to explore conflict situations. By conducting computer simulations, they examine variations in expected payoffs for fictitious players under different conditions. Their findings align with the mixed strategy Nash Equilibrium, revealing distinct patterns of cooperation in two scenarios. The subtle manipulation of payoff parameters significantly impacts the expected payoffs, shedding light on the game's intricate dynamics.

In Chap. "Bargaining, Inequality, and Willingness to Bribe: A Novel Experimental Design" Edgardo Bucciarelli, Umberto Masotti and Aurora Ascatigno propose a novel experimental design addressing collective action problems. These problems arise when individuals face bargaining and cooperation situations, leading to issues like free-riding and corruption. Unequal initial resources exacerbate these challenges. In the proposed experimental design, the authors combine three games to explore the endogenous creation of initial endowments. The Ultimatum Bargaining

Game's payoff serves as an initial endowment for the Public Goods Game, which is a real-effort task. Subsequently, the total payoff from the Public Goods Game becomes the initial endowment for the Bribery Game. This design offers new insights into existing explanations to produce local and global public goods.

3.4 Digital Technologies for Environment and Society

A final group of six chapters addresses research on the impact of digital technologies on the environmental and societal dimensions of digital ecosystems. This is a highly relevant stream of studies that addresses sustainability issues in a broad sense [20].

Chapter "Green Recommendation Systems for Smart and Sustainable Cities: A Proof-of-Concept on the City of Milan" by Matteo Spinazzola, Dario Cottafava and Marco Pironti contributes to the field of Green Information Systems (GIS). While previous work has primarily focused on sensory data, this study introduces the concept of Green Recommendation Systems (GRS) for smarter and more sustainable cities. An original framework presenting the functioning of a GRS for Smart and Sustainable Cities (GRS3C) was designed. This framework, tested in the context of Milan, recommends academic knowledge and relevant actors specializing in air pollution. Preliminary results suggest that GRS3C can aid policymakers and entrepreneurs in understanding complex issues and identifying local expertise, potentially fostering innovation and entrepreneurship in smart cities.

Michele Cipriano, Stefano Za and Francesco Virili develop a bibliometric analysis and describe in Chap. "Exploring the Evolution of the Circular Economy Debate" the existing research and main topics around the circular economy debate. This study paves the way to developing a theoretical and methodological position on the organizational and HR factors that may support the circular economy.

Alessia Zoppelletto, Sabrina Bonomi, and Paolino Fierro conduct an in-depth longitudinal case study to explore how networked SMEs use information systems to support the sustainability transition in Chap. "Sustainability-Oriented Information Systems toSupportaNetwork's Sustainability Transition:Lights and Shadows". The results highlight the role of information systems as a key driver for sustainability in network organizations; on the other hand, the results also shed light on the network-level negative dynamics that implementing a sustainability-oriented information system may foster.

The last three chapters in this group are dealing with societal aspects of sustainability in digital ecosystems, considering gender issues, privacy issues, and even issues connected with the religious sphere raised by the adoption of digital and AI-based technologies.

In Chap. "Does AI Reflect Human Behaviour? Exploring the Presence of Gender Bias in AI Translation Tools", Marco Smacchia, Stefano Za and Álvaro Arenas investigate gender bias in translations by large language model tools. By comparing human and artificial translations of Italian sentences related to specific jobs, where gender is not explicitly mentioned, into English, the study reveals significant gender bias, particularly favoring male-associated occupations. The findings highlight the need to explore the origins of bias in artificial intelligence tools and their reflection of societal gender distributions.

Chapter "To Ban, or Not to Ban, this Is the D(AI)lemma: An Analysis of Ecosystem Landscapes" by Francesco Bolici, Alberto Varone and Gabriele Diana is inspired by a recent episode, when the Italian Data Protection Authority (GPDP) suspended ChatGPT in Italy due to illicit data collection and processing practices. Using the Twitter debate as a proxy, their study examines the Italian response to the suspension, focusing on the innovation-privacy trade-off. Findings indicate an active reaction, with both popular and less popular users participating. While negative sentiment predominated, mentions of VPNs and ChatGPT alternatives showed more positive sentiment, suggesting that inaccessibility drove negativity rather than privacy concerns. The GPDP intervention was perceived as a restriction, prioritizing innovation over privacy.

In Chap. "How Social Communication and New Media Have Reshaped the Way People Deal with Religion? A Systematic Literature Review", Johana Hajdini and Lea Iaia investigate the drivers of the adoption of digital interactive communication and new media in the religious context, as well as the positive and negative consequences of such adoption. The study is based on a systematic analysis of two databases covering technologies and social science and a literature review.

References

1. Carillo, K., Scornavacca, E., & Za, S. (2017). The role of media dependency in predicting continuance intention to use ubiquitous media systems. *Information & Management, 54*, 317–335. https://doi.org/10.1016/j.im.2016.09.002
2. Report, S.R.: Number of connected devices worldwide 2015–2025. (2016).
3. Shim, J. P., Sharda, R., French, A. M., Syler, R. A., & Patten, K. P. (2020). The internet of things: Multi-faceted research perspectives. *Communications of the Association for Information Systems, 45*, 511–536. https://doi.org/10.17705/1CAIS.04621
4. Margherita, E. G., & Braccini, A. M. (2021). Managing industry 4.0 automation for fair ethical business development: A single case study. *Technological Forecasting and Social Change, 172*, 121048. https://doi.org/10.1016/j.techfore.2021.121048
5. Hesse, A., Kreutzer, K., & Diehl, M. R. (2019). Dynamics of institutional logics in a cross-sector social partnership: The case of refugee integration in Germany. *Journal of Business Ethics, 159*, 679–704. https://doi.org/10.1007/S10551-017-3775-0/FIGURES/7
6. Baptista, J., & Baptista, J. (2009). Institutionalisation as a process of interplay between technology and its organisational context of use. *Journal of Information Technology, 24*, 305–319. https://doi.org/10.1057/JIT.2009.15
7. Wang, P. (2021). Connecting the parts with the whole: Toward an information ecology theory of digital innovation ecosystems. *MIS Quarterly, 45*, 397–422. https://doi.org/10.25300/MISQ/2021/15864
8. vom Brocke, J., Braccini, A. M., Sonnenberg, C., & Spagnoletti, P. (2014). Living IT infrastructures — An ontology-based approach to aligning IT infrastructure capacity and business needs. *International Journal of Accounting Information Systems, 15*, 246–274. https://doi.org/10.1016/j.accinf.2013.10.004

9. Emery, F. E., & Trist, E. L. (1969). Socio-technical systems. In F. E. Emery (Ed.), *Systems thinking*. Penguin.
10. Trist, E. L., Murray, H., Trist, E. L., & Miller, E. J. (1993). *The socio-technical systems perspective*. University of Pennsylvania Press.
11. Schaeffer, D. J., Herricks, E. E., & Kerster, H. W. (1988). Ecosystem health: I Measuring ecosystem health. *Environmental Management, 12*, 445–455. https://doi.org/10.1007/BF01873258
12. Moore, J. F. (2006). Business ecosystems and the view from the firm. *The Antitrust Bulletin, 51*, 31–75. https://doi.org/10.1177/0003603X0605100103
13. Ceccagnoli, M., Forman, C., Huang, P., & Wu, D. J. (2012). Cocreation of value in a platform ecosystem: The case of enterprise software. *Management Information Systems Quarterly, 36*, 263–290.
14. Gawer, A. (2014). Bridging differing perspectives on technological platforms: Toward an integrative framework. *Research Policy, 43*, 1239–1249. https://doi.org/10.1016/J.RESPOL.2014.03.006
15. Hou, H., & Shi, Y. (2021). Ecosystem-as-structure and ecosystem-as-coevolution: A constructive examination. *Technovation, 100*, 102193. https://doi.org/10.1016/j.technovation.2020.102193
16. Kim, J. H. (2017). A review of cyber-physical system research relevant to the emerging IT trends: Industry 4.0, IoT, big data, and cloud computing. *Journal of Industrial Integration and Management, 02*, 1750011. https://doi.org/10.1142/s2424862217500117
17. Leitão, P., Colombo, A. W., & Karnouskos, S. (2016). Industrial automation based on cyber-physical systems technologies: Prototype implementations and challenges. *Computers in Industry, 81*, 11–25. https://doi.org/10.1016/j.compind.2015.08.004
18. Lazazzara, A., Ricciardi, F., & Za, S. (2020). Introduction to digital ecosystem. *Lecture Notes in Information Systems and Organization, 33*, 1–7. https://doi.org/10.1007/978-3-030-23665-6_1
19. Selander, L., Henfridsson, O., & Svahn, F. (2013). Capability search and redeem across digital ecosystems. *Journal of Information Technology, 28*, 183–197. https://doi.org/10.1057/JIT.2013.14
20. Kotlarsky, J., Oshri, I., & Sekulic, N. (2023). Digital sustainability in information systems research: Conceptual foundations and future directions. *Journal of the Association for Information Systems, 24*, 936–952. https://doi.org/10.17705/1jais.00825

Exploring the Connection Between Enabling Factors and Digital Technology Adoption in Agricultural Industries

Chiara Cagnetti and Alessio Maria Braccini

Abstract The digitalisation of agricultural industries brings about significant organisational, technological, and societal transformations. Despite the predominantly traditional nature of the agricultural sector, the adoption of digital technologies has witnessed a recent upsurge, fostering heightened productivity and efficiency. While the literature has seen more studies focusing on the digitalisation of agricultural industries, these investigations encompass diverse countries and contexts. Notably, studies that examine a specific context, such as Italy, and discern the pivotal enabling factors instrumental in adopting digital technology are absent. Hence, the primary objective of our study is to survey agricultural industries and unearth the enabling factors. These factors are subsequently subjected to non-parametric testing aimed at substantiating the existence of a consequential nexus between these factors and the adoption of digital technologies in the Italian agricultural sector. Our findings illuminate the significance of specific factors over others. These initial results enrich an understanding of the intricate interplay between enabling factors and digital technology adoption in agricultural industries. These insights deepen our comprehension and chart a course for prospective research endeavours.

Keywords Digitalisation · Agricultural industries · Enabling factors

1 Introduction

The agricultural industry is transforming digitally, bringing about significant organisational, technological, and societal changes. This has resulted in a complete overhaul of business models [1, 2]. To achieve this, structural changes are being implemented that modify production, processes, and individual operations, leading

C. Cagnetti · A. M. Braccini (✉)
Department of Economics, Engineering, Society and Business Organization, University of Tuscia, Viterbo, VT, Italy
e-mail: chiara.cagnetti@unitus.it; abraccini@unitus.it

A. M. Braccini et al. (eds.), *Digital (Eco) Systems and Societal Challenges*, Lecture Notes in Information Systems and Organisation 72,
https://doi.org/10.1007/978-3-031-75586-6_2

to heightened planning, organisation, and management [3, 4]. This evolution has created a more complex and dynamic working environment, which profoundly impacts the social and institutional context [5].

The agricultural industries are mainly traditional and have a low penetration of digital technologies. Hence, they are not frequently studied in the literature, but they represent a relevant industry for economies because they meet the need to ensure the nutrition of a growing world population and are intensely focused on sustainability [6, 7]. Consequently, exploring how digitalisation in agricultural industries may contribute to improving practices and outcomes in different countries and contextual conditions is a relevant area of research [8, 9]. Studies that explore a specific context, such as Italy, and discern the pivotal enabling factors instrumental in adopting digital technologies are absent in the literature [5, 8–12].

This paper aims to explore the factors contributing to the adoption of digital technology in the agricultural industry. Through empirical research, we aim to explore meaningful connections between individual factors and technology adoption. Using data collected through a questionnaire, our methodology uses the chi-square test (chi^2) to identify links between these enabling factors and digital technology adoption in agriculture. The results highlight differences in the links between various technologies and the factors involved.

This paper explores the following research question: *What is the connection between enabling factors and digital technologies*? In this regard, we use the concept *factor* to refer to any element that can influence the digitalisation process within the agricultural industry. We particularly consider enabling factors, which we define as pre-adoption elements, that can help industries start the digitalisation process, leading to the adoption of digital technologies [13–15].

The paper is divided into several sections. Section 2 provides context on digitalisation in agriculture, specifically from the perspective of the Italian agricultural industry. In Sect. 3, we introduce our methodology for collecting and analysing data, followed by the presentation of our results in Sect. 4. Section 5 explores the discussions and implications of our findings, and we conclude in Sect. 6 with this study's limitations and future research.

2 The Theoretical Framework

This paper combines two streams of literature: digitalisation in the agricultural industries and enabling factors in such a digitalisation process. The related literature concerning the two streams is summarised in the following two sub-sections.

2.1 Digitalisation in Agricultural Industries

In this article, we look at the concept of digitalisation. Although the term digitalisation has many definitions in the literature, in this work, we use *digitalisation* to refer to the adoption of modern digital technologies in organisations to transform analogue-based practices—i.e. adopting non-digital technologies for information collection and processing—into *digital* ones—i.e. leveraging on digital technologies for information collection and processing [16].

Implementing modern digital technologies in agriculture industries, known as digitalisation, can enhance decision-making, efficiency, and automation of business processes [4, 17]. Adopting digitalisation in agriculture makes it possible to address societal issues pertaining to the industry, such as product traceability and environmental impact [1, 5, 18].

Various digital technologies, such as the Internet of Things (IoT) infrastructure, blockchain platforms, drones, automated agricultural machinery, Business Management Information Systems, and business intelligence for data analysis, are often integrated to form complex systems [17]. For example, the IoT infrastructure can be combined with blockchain platforms to track products and locate them or with sensors to gather data [19].

Digital technologies serve different purposes and have significant economic and environmental impacts. Economically, they improve productivity and profitability in various sectors. In terms of sustainability, they promote environmentally friendly production techniques [3].

In Italy, the adoption of digital technologies in agricultural industries still needs to grow. In 2021, the digitalisation investments in the Italian agriculture industry summed up to 1.6 billion €, but digital technologies were used only in 6% of the total area cultivated in the country [20]. According to ISTAT data, 26.1% of digitalised agricultural industries carry out production and livestock activities, 18.4% carry out livestock activities, and 13.1% carry out agricultural activities [21]. Therefore, the agricultural industry's digitalisation has growth margins and may benefit from support for producing and distributing products to make them fast, functional, and safe [22].

Considering the context of the digitalisation of agricultural industries, we see that adopting digital technologies depends on a heterogeneous set of enabling factors, which we have classified into the three dimensions of the Technology Organisation and Environment framework [23] (see Sect. 2.2). There are already studies in the literature exploring the factors associated with the digitalisation of the agricultural industry, but only some in the Italian context. Moreover, the literature still needs to clarify whether the enabling factors are generalisable to all digital technologies in agricultural industries. For this reason, it is necessary to verify the significance of each enabling factor concerning each digital technology, considering the context of Italian agricultural sectors. Figure 1 summarises the research gap.

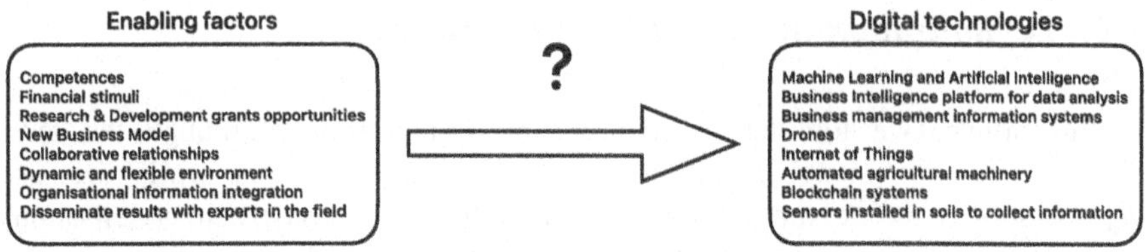

Fig. 1 Gap of analysis

2.2 *Contextualisation of Enabling Factors*

The enabling factors we consider in this paper emerged from the literature analysis and are described below: competencies, financial stimuli, R&D funding opportunities, collaborative relationships, organisational information integration, and dissemination of results with experts in the field.

The first factor is the *competencies* that individuals inside and outside the organisation must have to adopt technologies [24]. Competences acquired through specific learning [25] and by completing education levels [26] help businesses adopt technologies, contributing to the success and development of innovations [27].

Financial stimuli represent the economic basis that incentivises agricultural industries to adopt technologies [28]. Financial stimuli are opportunities [27] that help initiate programs to digitalise agricultural industries and improve production activities [29]. Financial stimuli provide agricultural industries with an economic basis to stimulate transformation and introduce innovations in the sector [28, 30]. The government agrees that financial stimuli, considered opportunities, help implement programmes and improvements in agricultural production activities [29].

Research and development (R&D) funding opportunities allow agricultural industries to participate in publicly financed projects that incentivise research activity and a strategic approach [2]. Universities and research centres, in collaboration with agricultural industries, propose research and development activities and implement a set of practices and mechanisms to promote knowledge and technology transfer.

Research & Development grants opportunities enable the testing of new ideas and the development of know-how but also provide feedback on the applicability and relevance of new technologies [31].

Another factor is *new business models*, i.e., creating innovative business models that can improve agricultural industries revenues and reduce costs [24]. New business models depend on the ability to perceive change and adopt innovations [32].

The *collaborative relationship* creates a collaborative working environment between industries [33]. Through collaboration, operations can be carried out following the strategies and objectives set by the industries [34].

Another enabling factor is a *Dynamic and flexible environment*, where the adoption of digital technologies is increasingly dynamic, impacting the social and institutional environment [5].

Table 1 Classification enabling factors with TOE framework

Environmental	Organisational	Technology
Financing and Incentives	Competences	Disseminating results with experts in the field
R&D funding opportunities	New business model	
	Collaborative relationship	
	Dynamic and flexible environmental	
	Organisational information integration	

Another enabling factor is the possibility of organisational information integration. Access to information contributes to the widespread adoption of technology, using reliable and timely information [35, 36] and reducing industry isolation by increasing relations, including commercial relations, and the efficiency of agricultural industries [24, 36].

Finally, the last enabling factor is *disseminating results with experts in the field.* Information dissemination facilitates the adoption of technology by introducing new skills and knowledge that can improve farming practices, farm management, and decision-making [37]. Dissemination can also influence agricultural industries' skills, attitudes, beliefs, and convictions, helping them overcome various production-related obstacles [38].

As indicated in Table 1, the identified factors pertain to different dimensions of the TOE theoretical framework [39].

3 Methodology

The research method adopted is quantitative and allows us to test the connections between various elements. In this study, we used an empirical approach and a questionnaire for data collection, on which we then carried out non-parametric tests [35, 40].

We used the X^2 test because it allows us to determine the relationship between two variables. In our study, the X^2 test allows us to verify the existence of a relationship between a set of enabling factors and the adoption of digital technologies, considering the same enabling factors for a group of different technologies.

3.1 Data Collection

The questionnaire has 28 main sections. The first section contains questions about knowledge of digital technologies and adoption, and the second section includes reasons for non-adoption. Then, we find sections 3–26 for the digital technologies listed in Sect. 2 above. The sections are the same for each technology, with questions on the degree of adoption and the assessment of enabling factors. Finally, the last section consists of questions on the demographic data of the individual respondents and the industry size.

The questionnaire items are constructed with Likert scales of 1–5 points (1—strongly disagree, 2—disagree, 3—neutral, 4—agree, 5—strongly agree). They are derived from items identified in the literature review, often extrapolated from previous studies that tested similar study contexts [8, 24, 25].

The questions that comprise the demographic data section are all closed-ended, not allowing exclusive answers but the possibility of choosing from a defined list of options. To obtain many re-answers, we used an existing database available at www.maiload.com. The database includes demographic information of 3286 Italian agricultural industries with their e-mail addresses. We sent the questionnaire to all 3286 agricultural industries in the database.

The questionnaire underwent two revision phases before being administered to the total sample. In the first phase, with the help of experts in the field, we tested the questionnaire internally for functionality and correctness. In the second phase, we tested the pilot questionnaire on 193 agricultural industries in the Lazio region, extrapolating from the total sample from March to April 2023. We selected the region of Lazio, which is a sufficiently large and diverse sample and representative of the complete population. The objective was to observe the interpretation of the questions, the concepts used, and the detection of errors. From the pilot test, we obtained 14 responses, with a response rate of 7%. We improved the questionnaire through feedback received from the pilot questionnaire respondents through an interaction via email. We then sent the defined questionnaire to the total sample using the CAWI (Computer-assisted Web Interviewing) technique, using Google Modules as the diffusion and data collection software. We used web-based questionnaire administration because it is a well-known method that allows for creating a computerised database to avoid errors in the transfer of information, reduce costs, and increase anonymity [41]. The questionnaire administration started in April 2023 and is still ongoing. To date, we have obtained 171 responses, with a response rate of 5%.

3.2 Chi-Square Test

At this exploratory stage of the research, we merely hypothesise a connection between enabling factors and adopted technologies. We used the χ^2 test to verify this hypothesis. This test measures the association between two categorical variables by testing two hypotheses: null and alternative.

$\mathbf{H_0 = 0}$ (Independence between two variables)
$\mathbf{H_1 \neq 0}$ (Dependence between variables)

Table 2 Enabling factor testing

Factor	Name	Authors
Factor 1	Competences	[3, 5, 15, 26, 30, 36, 38, 42–45]
Factor 2	Financing & Incentives	[6, 9, 17, 28]
Factor 3	R&D funding opportunities	[2, 6, 46, 47]
Factor 4	New business Model	[6, 19, 45, 48]
Factor 5	Collaborative relationships	[2, 17, 24, 28, 32–34, 40, 45, 49–52]
Factor 6	Dynamic and flexible environment	[10, 26, 32, 36, 50, 53, 54]
Factor 7	Organisational information integration organisation	[32, 50]
Factor 8	Disseminate results with experts in the field	[10, 15, 19, 30, 33, 34, 36–38, 45, 50, 55–57]

The factors used in the χ^2 test were derived from the questionnaire administered to agricultural industries, selecting the question concerning the assessment of enabling factors for adopting technologies [14, 15]. Table 2 summarises the enabling factors derived from the literature review.

To test the relationship between the factors, we considered a significance level of 0.05 and accepted/rejected the test according to the p-value. If the p-value <0.05, we rejected the null hypothesis and therefore stated that there is a significant relationship between the variables considered. If the p-value >0.05, we accepted the null hypothesis and considered the presence of independence between the variables [58, 59].

4 Findings

Table 3 summarises the individual descriptive characteristics of the respondent, while Table 4 describes the industry's size.

4.1 Data Analysis

The results show that the respondents are mainly men (71% of the sample) with an age range between 31–40 and 41–50 years of age (27% of the sample; 24% of the sample) and with a high school diploma as a qualification (43% of the sample). The industries have a turnover of ≤200,000 € (69% of the sample) and a size of 0–19

Table 3 Summary of demographic characteristics

Demographic characteristics		Frequency	Percentage
Gender	Male	121	71%
	Female	50	29%
	Sub total	**171**	**100%**
Age	18–30 years	17	10%
	31–40 years	46	27%
	41–50 years	41	24%
	51–60 years	37	22%
	>60 years	30	18%
	Sub total	**171**	**100%**
Qualification	Middle certificate	9	5%
	Higher Diploma	74	43%
	Bachelor's degree	27	16%
	Master's degree	49	29%
	PhD/Master	12	7%
	Sub Total	**171**	**100%**

Table 4 Summary of industry characteristics

Industry characteristics		Frequency	Percentage
Turnover	≤200,000 €	118	69%
	200,001–700,000 €	31	18%
	700,001–1.800,000 €	11	6%
	>1,800,001 €	11	6%
	Total	**171**	**100%**
Size	0–19 employees	158	92%
	20–49 employees	8	5%
	50–249 employees	4	2%
	250–499 employees	0	0%
	>500 employees	1	1%
	Total	**171**	**100%**
Production	Agricultural	134	78%
	Livestock	7	4%
	Either	30	18%
	Total	**171**	**100%**
Experience	<5 years	20	12%
	5–10 years	40	23%
	>10 years	111	65%
	Total	**171**	**100%**

employees (92% of the sample). This observation is compatible with the general characteristics of the Italian context. Finally, respondents state that they have more than 10 years of experience (65% of the sample), and agricultural production characterises the most significant number of industries involved in the study (78%).

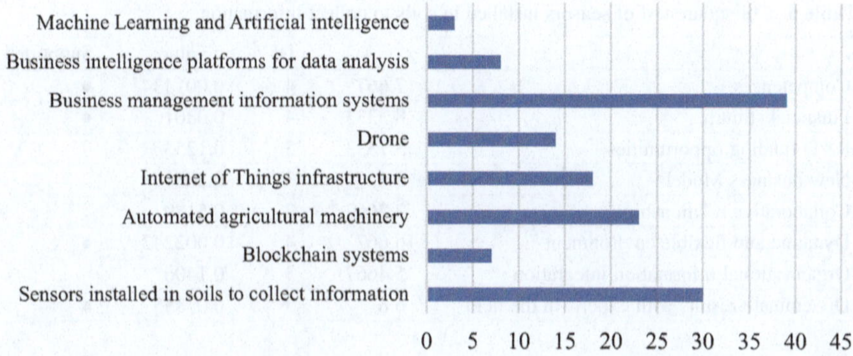

Fig. 2 Digital technologies adoption

Table 5 Chi-square test of business management information systems

	χ^2	Df	p-value	Supported
Competences	14.974	4	0.004755	•
Financial stimuli	4.7179	4	0.3175	
R&D funding opportunities	10.359	4	0.0348	•
New business Model	5.4872	4	0.2409	
Collaborative relationships	6.7692	4	0.1486	
Dynamic and flexible environment	10.103	4	0.03873	•
Organisational information integration	3.6923	4	0.08094	•
Disseminate results with experts in the field	3.6923	4	0.4492	

Regarding the technologies in the questionnaire, only 66 of 171 respondents adopted digital technologies in agricultural industries. Figure 2 shows the list of technologies adopted by the respondents. The most widely used digital technologies relate to Business Management Information Systems, sensors installed in soils to collect information, and automated agricultural machinery.

4.2 *Exploring the Connection Between Enabling Factors and Digital Technologies*

We conducted the χ^2 tests on adoption technologies in agricultural industries by making a practical choice for our analysis. Before conducting the test, we decided to consider, based on the answers obtained to the questionnaire administered, only the most adopted digital technologies so as not to bias the analysis. We created three different databases, where the columns were represented by the eight enabling factors to be analysed, and the rows represented the questionnaire respondents. The χ^2 test was conducted using R software, using specific packages.

Below, in Tables 5, 6, and 7, we have reported the value of each test χ^2.

Table 6 Chi-square test of sensors installed in soils to collect information

	χ^2	Df	p-value	Supported
Competences	17.667	4	0.001434	•
Financial stimuli	8.3333	4	0.0801	•
R&D funding opportunities	5.7333	3	0.1253	
New business Model	3.6	3	0.308	
Collaborative relationships	2.2667	3	0.5189	
Dynamic and flexible environment	16.667	4	0.002243	•
Organisational information integration	5.4667	3	0.1406	
Disseminate results with experts in the field	6.8	3	0.07855	•

Table 7 Chi-square test of the automated agricultural machinery

	χ^2	Df	p-value	Supported
Competences	10.565	3	0.01432	•
Financial stimuli	4.6522	3	0.1991	
R&D funding opportunities	2.5652	3	0.4636	
New business Model	5.6957	3	0.1274	
Collaborative relationships	4.6522	3	0.1991	
Dynamic and flexible environment	5.6957	3	0.1274	
Organisational information integration	2.2174	3	0.5285	
Disseminate results with experts in the field	1.8696	3	0.5999	

In Tables 5, 6 and 7, χ^2 represents the value of the test obtained. *Df* indicates the degrees of freedom, *p-value* represents the probability of the null hypothesis, and finally, *supported* indicates, based on the results obtained, whether the factors connect with the digital technologies analysed.

5 Discussion

The results of the χ^2 tests show differences between the three technologies. While testing the same enabling factors, not all technologies show links to the same factors. The results of the ties can be found in Tables 5, 6, and 7 in the column called "supported". While testing the same enabling factors, not all technologies show ties to the same factors. We note that factor 1, *competencies,* is relevant in all three technologies. Factor 2, *Financial stimuli* and *Disseminating results with experts in the field,* have ties only with sensors installed in soils to collect information. Factor 3, *R&D funding opportunities*, and factor 7, *Organisational integration information*, have ties only with business management information systems. Factor 6, *Disseminate results with experts in the field,* has ties with business management information systems and sensors installed in soils to collect information. Finally, factor 4, the *New Business Model*, and factor 5, *Collaborative relationships*, have no ties to the three digital technologies.

From the tables above, we note that only Factor 1, *competencies*, is significantly associated with the adoption factors for all three technologies. *Competences* enable agricultural industries to improve their production practice. With the adoption of digital technologies, there is a need to increase educational content and training courses, including customised ones, for stakeholders inside and outside the agricultural industries to generate a competitive advantage in agricultural industries [24, 25, 48]. Factor 2, *Financial stimuli*, is significantly associated with adopting sensors installed in soils to collect information for ground data collection. Financial stimuli enable the transformation of agriculture [17] by increasing the use of digital technologies, thus creating increasingly digitalised agricultural infrastructure [28].

Factor 3: R&D funding opportunities are significantly associated with adopting Business Management Information Systems. Participation in research and development activities stimulates knowledge and technology transfer [2], possibly using technologies, such as Business Management Information Systems, to collect data and information to optimise business processes [33].

Factor 6, *dynamic and flexible environment*, is significantly associated with adopting Business Management Information Systems and sensors installed in soils to collect information. A flexible organisational environment makes it possible to identify changes and opportunities that influence the performance of agricultural industries [26, 48, 54]. Soil data collection sensors are installed in soils to collect information, and business management information systems need an environment that can adapt to transformation and innovation [26] to take advantage of all the opportunities technologies can offer [54].

Factor 7, organisational information integration, is significantly associated with adopting business management information systems. An organisation where hierarchical levels have diminished allows for more straightforward and more integrated dissemination of information, developing a single and integrated communication throughout the organisation, avoiding possible risks [32, 60]. Factor 8, *Disseminating results with experts in the field*, is only significantly associated with sensors installed in soils to collect information. The sensors can acquire a large amount of varied data (moisture temperature, planting) and disseminate the collected data with experts in the field [61].

Finally, factors 4 and 5, the *new business model* and *collaborative relationship*, have no significant relationship with adopting the three technologies. The analysis shows that the enabling factors of the three digital technologies have different levels of significance: factor 1, *competencies* and factor 6, *dynamic and flexible environment.*

The significance of one factor over another highlights the importance of the factor for the technology. Whereas for sensors installed in soils to collect information, it is essential to have funding and loans to adopt the technology, for Business Management Information Systems, it is more significant to participate in research and development, i.e., to be part of projects where the in question are tested and adopted. The same argument can be made about the significance of disseminating the results obtained through sensors installed in soils to collect information rather than having

Table 8 Classification results with TOE framework

Environmental	Organisational	Technology
Financial stimuli	Competences	Disseminating results with experts in the field
R&D funding opportunities	Dynamic and flexible environmental	
	Organisational information integration	

the organisational information integration in adopting Business Management Information Systems.

The results show that the *competencies* factor is significant in all three technologies, while the *dynamic and flexible environment* is a peripheral factor combined with the factors of *R&D funding opportunities* and *organisational information integration*. Finally, we find *financial stimuli* and *disseminating results with experts in the field*.

The equation below summarises the results.

$$adoption = f\left(Capabilities + \left\{Dynamic\ environment + \left\{\begin{array}{c} R\&D\ opp + Integration \\ Financial\ stimuli + Experts \end{array}\right\}\right\}\right)$$

Considering the TOE model, we note that the factors in the equation can be classified in the three dimensions of the theory, as shown in Table 8.

According to the TOE model, *competencies* are sufficient for adopting automated agricultural machinery, especially when there is no need for systemic integration with other technologies. Considering business management information systems and sensors installed in soils to collect information, according to the results predicted by the TOE model, suggests that *competencies* must be combined with a *dynamic and flexible environment*.

However, the *dynamic and flexible environmental* factor requires two further combinations of factors. The first case combines *organisational information integration* and *R&D funding opportunities* (for business management information systems adoptions). The second case combines *Financing stimuli* and *Disseminating results with experts in the field* (for sensors).

The analysis highlights mainly theoretical implications. First, since the factors have been extrapolated from the literature, they may need to be completed, given the increasing number of studies concerning the digitalisation of agricultural industries. It is, therefore, necessary to continuously update the literature to identify new factors that can be tested through new analyses using methodologies other than the questionnaire. Secondly, since the χ^2 test only allows for a significance test between factors, proposing a new model that considers the significant factors for each digital technology is necessary. Thirdly, given that the questionnaire is still in the submission phase, it may be necessary to repeat the administration phase to obtain more responses that allow for increasingly significant results. Finally, the propositions will have to be tested on a larger sample to see if they are meaningful only for the types of technology we have considered in this article or if they are abstract to any digital technology.

The analysis also has practical implications. First, the results show that digitalisation in the agricultural industry depends on competencies, which are an organisational factor, so managers should seek to develop them inside organisations. A second practical implication concerns organisations' need to leverage contextual environmental factors to adopt specific digital technologies (business management information systems and sensors).

Finally, the analysis also brings policy implications. If governments want to modernise agricultural industries, they must make *financial stimuli available* and allow agricultural industries to participate in *R&D funding opportunities*. Since it is also necessary to have a stock of knowledge capital on the ground (*Disseminating results with experts in the field*), and since this factor is beyond the reach of individual agricultural organisations, government policies may also attract or facilitate the building of knowledge capital stock on the territory to stimulate innovation through digitalisation in the agricultural industry.

6 Conclusion

Our study aims to identify a significant connection between enabling factors and adopting digital technologies in agricultural industries. Using a non-parametric test of χ^2, we tested the significance level between the factors in the questionnaire and extrapolated from the literature with agricultural industries adopting digital technologies. The test was conducted on the technologies most adopted by the respondents because they offered a higher significance level of the results. The results show different levels of significance between the factors of the technologies analysed, showing that some factors are more significant in some technologies than others.

The article has limitations. Firstly, the research is ongoing; therefore, the number of responses could increase and change the analysis. Secondly, the non-adoption of specific technologies influenced the analysis, which only considers a small part of the digital technologies currently adopted in agricultural industries. Finally, the low response of agricultural industries to the questionnaire limits the possibility of obtaining numerous answers.

This article is the first exploratory step that needs further investigation. In the next steps of the research, we will further explore the connections between the enabling factors and the adoption of digital technologies by exploring multiple variables models, aiming to contribute to the literature on the adoption of digital technologies in the agricultural industry. The idea is to build a multiple regression model that allows us to define, for all eight digital technologies, the enabling factors, barriers, and adoption outcomes for each of the technologies.

References

1. van der Burg, S., Bogaardt, M. J., & Wolfert, S. (2019). Ethics of smart farming: Current questions and directions for responsible innovation towards the future. *NJAS—Wageningen Journal of Life Sciences, 90–91.*
2. Regan, Á. (2021). Exploring the readiness of publicly funded researchers to practice responsible research and innovation in digital agriculture. *Journal of Responsible Innovation, 8*, 28–47. https://doi.org/10.1080/23299460.2021.1904755
3. Zscheischler, J., Brunsch, R., Rogga, S., & Scholz, R. W. (2022). Perceived risks and vulnerabilities of employing digitalisation and digital data in agriculture—socially robust orientations from a transdisciplinary process. *Journal of Cleaner Production, 358*. https://doi.org/10.1016/j.jclepro.2022.132034
4. Valiyev, A. (2022). The digitalization effectiveness as an innovative factor development of the agriculture in Azerbaijan. *Journal of Eastern European and Central Asian Research, 9*, 194–205.
5. Giua, C., Materia, V. C., & Camanzi, L. (2022). Smart farming technologies adoption: Which factors play a role in the digital transition? *Technology in Society, 68*. https://doi.org/10.1016/j.techsoc.2022.101869
6. Aivazidou, E., & Tsolakis, N. (2022). Transitioning towards human–robot synergy in agriculture: A systems thinking perspective. *Systems Research and Behavioral Science*. https://doi.org/10.1002/sres.2887
7. Zavhorodnii, A., Ohiienko, M., Biletska, Y., Bondarenko, S., Duiunova, T., & Bodenchuk, L. (2021). Digitalization of agribusiness in the development of foreign economic relations of the region. *Journal of Information Technology Management, 13*, 123–141. https://doi.org/10.22059/JITM.2021.82613
8. Pivoto, D., Barham, B., Waquil, P. D., Foguesatto, C. R., Corte, V. F. D., Zhang, D., & Talamini, E. (2019). Factors influencing the adoption of smart farming by Brazilian grain farmers. *International Food and Agribusiness Management Review, 22*, 571–588. https://doi.org/10.22434/IFAMR2018.0086
9. Bitrus, S., Vajjhala, R., & Strang, K. D. (2019). Factors impacting farm management decision making software adoption. *International Journal of Sustainable Agricultural Management and Informatics, 5*, 1. https://doi.org/10.1504/ijsami.2019.10019819
10. Navimipour, N. J., Milani, F. S., & Hossenzadeh, M. (2018). A model for examining the role of effective factors on the performance of organizations. *Technology in Society, 55*, 166–174. https://doi.org/10.1016/j.techsoc.2018.06.003
11. Ibrahim, A. M., Hassan, M. S., & Gusau, A. L. (2018). Factors influencing acceptance and use of ICT innovations by agribusinesses. *Journal of Global Information Management, 26*, 113–134. https://doi.org/10.4018/JGIM.2018100107
12. Yoon, C., Lim, D., & Park, C. (2020). Factors affecting adoption of smart farms: The case of Korea. *Computers in Human Behavior, 108*, 106309. https://doi.org/10.1016/j.chb.2020.106309
13. Cagnetti, C., & Braccini, A. M. (2023). La digitalizzazione delle organizzazioni nel settore dell'agricoltura- un'analisi esplorativa su fattori abilitanti, barriere e risultati dell'adozione delle tecnologie digitali. Prospettive in Organizzazione.
14. Tolentino, T. R., & Hernandez, A. A. (2020). User acceptance of agricultural market information system with analytics: Insights from the Philippines. *International Journal of Enterprise Information Systems, 16*, 39–57. https://doi.org/10.4018/IJEIS.2020100103
15. Singh, S., Haneef, F., Kumar, S., & Ongsakul, V. (2020). A framework for successful IoT adoption in agriculture sector: a total interpretive structural modelling approach. *Journal for Global Business Advancement, 13*, 382. https://doi.org/10.1504/jgba.2020.10033252
16. Reis, J., Amorim, M., Melão, N., Cohen, Y., & Rodrigues, M. (2020). Digitalization: A literature review and research agenda. In *Lecture notes on multidisciplinary industrial engineering* (pp. 443–456). Springer Nature.

17. Lioutas, E. D., Charatsari, C., & De Rosa, M. (2021). Digitalization of agriculture: A way to solve the food problem or a trolley dilemma? *Technology in Society, 67*, 101744. https://doi.org/10.1016/j.techsoc.2021.101744
18. Klerkx, L., Jakku, E., & Labarthe, P. (2019). A review of social science on digital agriculture, smart farming and agriculture 4.0: New contributions and a future research agenda. *NJAS—Wageningen Journal of Life Sciences, 90–91*, 100315. https://doi.org/10.1016/j.njas.2019.100315
19. Maffezzoli, F., Ardolino, M., Bacchetti, A., Perona, M., & Renga, F. (2022). Agriculture 4.0: A systematic literature review on the paradigm, technologies and benefits. *Futures, 142*. https://doi.org/10.1016/j.futures.2022.102998
20. Osservatorio Smart AgriFood. (2022). Smart agrifood: raccogliamo i frutti dell'innovazione digitale.
21. ISTAT. (2022). Digitalizzazione e innovazione delle aziende agricole italiane.
22. ANITEC-ASSINFORM. (2022). Il digitale e l'innovazione tecnologica a supporto del settore agrifood italiano.
23. Cagnetti, C., & Braccini, A. M. (2021). Exploring digitalisation in agriculture through socio-technical perspectives. In: *CEUR workshop proceedings*.
24. Carmela Annosi, M., Brunetta, F., Capo, F., & Heideveld, L. (2020). Digitalization in the agri-food industry: the relationship between technology and sustainable development. *Management Decision, 58*, 1737–1757. https://doi.org/10.1108/MD-09-2019-1328
25. Valsamidis, S., Kazanidis, I., Petasakis, I., & Kontogiannis, S. (2015). An adaptive prototype system for ubiquitous learning in agriculture. *International Journal of Sustainable Agricultural Management and Informatics, 1*, 317–332. https://doi.org/10.1504/IJSAMI.2015.075029
26. Aubert, B. A., Schroeder, A., & Grimaudo, J. (2012). IT as enabler of sustainable farming: An empirical analysis of farmers' adoption decision of precision agriculture technology. *Decision Support Systems, 54*, 510–520. https://doi.org/10.1016/j.dss.2012.07.002
27. Khanh Chi, N. T. (2022). Driving factors for green innovation in agricultural production: An empirical study in an emerging economy. *Journal of Cleaner Production, 368*. https://doi.org/10.1016/j.jclepro.2022.132965
28. Rijanto, A. (2020). Business financing and blockchain technology adoption in agroindustry. *Journal of Science and Technology Policy Management, 12*, 215–235. https://doi.org/10.1108/JSTPM-03-2020-0065
29. Kidd, P. T. (2012). The role of the internet of things in enabling sustainable agriculture in Europe. *International Journal of RF Technologies: Research and Applications, 3*, 67–83. https://doi.org/10.3233/RFT-2011-017
30. Vargas-Canales, J. M., Palacios-Rangel, M. I., Aguilar-Ávila, J., Camacho-Vera, J. H., Ocampo-Ledesma, J. G., & Medina-Cuellar, S. E. (2018). Efficiency of small enterprises of protected agriculture in the adoption of innovations in Mexico. *Estudios Gerenciales, 34*, 52–62. https://doi.org/10.18046/j.estger.2018.146.2811
31. Regan, Á. (2019). 'Smart farming' in Ireland: A risk perception study with key governance actors. *NJAS—Wageningen Journal of Life Sciences, 90–91*, 100292. https://doi.org/10.1016/j.njas.2019.02.003
32. Galliano, D., & Orozco, L. (2013). New technologies and firm organization: The case of electronic traceability systems in French agribusiness. *Industry and Innovation, 20*. https://doi.org/10.1080/13662716.2013.761379ï
33. Sibona, F., Chiavarini, L., Bortoletto, A., & Mainiero, S. (2020). Innovation in farming: An engaging and rewarding business model to foster digitalization. *CERN IdeaSquare Journal of Experimental Innovation, 4*, 9–15. https://doi.org/10.23726/cij.2020.1052
34. Spanaki, K., Karafili, E., & Despoudi, S. (2021). AI applications of data sharing in agriculture 4.0: A framework for role-based data access control. *International Journal of Information Management, 59*. https://doi.org/10.1016/j.ijinfomgt.2021.102350

35. Aarthi Dhakshana, J. D., & Rajandran, K. V. R. (2018). Effectiveness of ICTs in dissemination of agricultural information among farmers in Cauvery Delta, Thanjavur. *International Journal of Supply Chain Management, 7*(5), 933–938.
36. Dannenberg, P., & Lakes, T. (2013). The use of mobile phones by Kenyan export-orientated small-scale farmers: Insights from fruit and vegetable farming in the Mt. Kenya region. *Economia Agro-Alimentare, 15*, 55–75. https://doi.org/10.3280/ECAG2013-003005
37. Armstrong, L. J., Diepeveen, D. A., & Tantisantisom, K. (2010). An eAgriculture-based decision support framework for information dissemination. *International Journal of Human Capital and Information Technology Professionals, 1*, 1–13. https://doi.org/10.4018/jhcitp.2010100101
38. Gerli, P., Clement, J., Esposito, G., Mora, L., & Crutzen, N. (2022). The hidden power of emotions: How psychological factors influence skill development in smart technology adoption. *Technological Forecasting and Social Change, 180*. https://doi.org/10.1016/j.techfore.2022.121721
39. Tornatzky, L. G., & Fleischer, M. (1990). *The processes of technological innovation*. Lexington Books. Retrieved March 13, 2023, from https://www.scirp.org/(S(351jmbntvnsjt1aadkozje))/reference/referencespapers.aspx?referenceid=1771512
40. Razilan Abdul Kadir, M., Shahrul Nizam Mohd Danuri, M., & Sazili Shahibi, M. (2019). Transforming smallholder farmers business towards agribusiness: A framework using ICT. *Social Sciences & Humanities, 27*, 1635–1658.
41. Couper, M. P. (2000). *Review: Web surveys: A review of issues and approaches*. Winter.
42. Giua, C., Materia, V. C., & Camanzi, L. (2021). Management information system adoption at the farm level: evidence from the literature. *British Food Journal, 123*, 884–909. https://doi.org/10.1108/BFJ-05-2020-0420
43. Moga, L. M., Constantin, D. L., & Antohi, V. M. (2012). A regional approach of the information technology adoption in the Romanian agricultural farms. *Informatica Economica, 16*(4), 29.
44. Kountios, G., Bournaris, T., Papadavid, G., Michailidis, A., & Papadaki-Klavdianou, A. (2018). Exploring educational needs of young farmers in precision agriculture in Serres, Greece, and the perspective of innovative agricultural educational programs. *Journal for International Business and Entrepreneurship Development, 11*.
45. Wolfert, S., Ge, L., Verdouw, C., & Bogaardt, M. J. (2017). Big Data in smart farming—a review. *Agricultural Systems, 153*, 69–80.
46. Ruffoni, E. P., & Reichert, F. M. (2022). Capabilities and innovative performance in the Brazilian agricultural machinery industry. *Revista Brasileira de Gestao de Negocios, 24*, 275–293. https://doi.org/10.7819/rbgn.v24i2.4168
47. Weber, R., Braun, J., & Frank, M. (2022). How does the adoption of digital technologies affect the social sustainability of small-scale agriculture in South-West Germany? *International Journal on Food System Dynamics, 13*, 275–293. https://doi.org/10.18461/ijfsd.v13i3.C3
48. Cannas, R. (2021). Exploring digital transformation and dynamic capabilities in agrifood SMEs. *Journal of Small Business Management*. https://doi.org/10.1080/00472778.2020.1844494
49. Zeng, M., & Lu, J. (2021). The impact of information technology capabilities on agri-food supply chain performance: the mediating effects of interorganizational relationships. *Journal of Enterprise Information Management, 34*, 1699–1721. https://doi.org/10.1108/JEIM-08-2019-0237
50. Rijswijk, K., Klerkx, L., Bacco, M., Bartolini, F., Bulten, E., Debruyne, L., Dessein, J., Scotti, I., & Brunori, G. (2021). Digital transformation of agriculture and rural areas: A socio-cyber-physical system framework to support responsibilisation. *Journal of Rural Studies, 85*, 79–90. https://doi.org/10.1016/j.jrurstud.2021.05.003
51. Hassan, S. Z., Jajja, M. S. S., Asif, M., & Foster, G. (2020). Bringing more value to small farmers: a study of potato farmers in Pakistan. *Management Decision, 59*, 829–857. https://doi.org/10.1108/MD-12-2018-1392

52. Chaudhuri, B., & Kendall, L. (2021). Collaboration without consensus: Building resilience in sustainable agriculture through ICTs. *Information Society, 37*, 1–19. https://doi.org/10.1080/01972243.2020.1844828
53. Ronaghi, M. H., & Forouharfar, A. (2020). A contextualized study of the usage of the Internet of things (IoTs) in smart farming in a typical Middle Eastern country within the context of Unified Theory of Acceptance and Use of Technology model (UTAUT). *Technology in Society, 63*. https://doi.org/10.1016/j.techsoc.2020.101415
54. Lin, J., Li, L., Luo, X. (Robert), & Benitez, J. (2020). How do agribusinesses thrive through complexity? The pivotal role of e-commerce capability and business agility. *Decision Support Systems, 135,* 113342. https://doi.org/10.1016/j.dss.2020.113342
55. Kudryavtseva, T., & Skhvediani, A. (2020). Effectiveness assessment of investments in robotic biological plant protection. *International Journal of Technology, 11*, 1589–1597. https://doi.org/10.14716/ijtech.v11i8.4528
56. Shen, Z., Wang, S., Boussemart, J. P., & Hao, Y. (2022). Digital transition and green growth in Chinese agriculture. *Technological Forecasting and Social Change, 181*. https://doi.org/10.1016/j.techfore.2022.121742
57. Aleke, B., Ojiako, U., & Wainwright, D. W. (2011). ICT adoption in developing countries: Perspectives from small-scale agribusinesses. *Journal of Enterprise Information Management, 24*, 68–84. https://doi.org/10.1108/17410391111097438
58. McHugh, M. L. (2012). The Chi-square test of independence. *Biochemia Medica (Zagreb), 23*, 143–149. https://doi.org/10.11613/BM.2013.018
59. Ugoni, A., & Walker, B. F. (1995). The chi square test: An introduction. *COMSIG Review, 4*(3), 61–64.
60. Chen, Y., Li, Y., & Li, C. (2020). Electronic agriculture, blockchain and digital agricultural democratization: Origin, theory and application. *Journal of Cleaner Production, 268*. https://doi.org/10.1016/j.jclepro.2020.122071
61. Rijswijk, K., Klerkx, L., & Turner, J. A. (2019). Digitalisation in the New Zealand Agricultural Knowledge and Innovation System: Initial understandings and emerging organisational responses to digital agriculture. *NJAS—Wageningen Journal of Life Sciences, 90–91*. https://doi.org/10.1016/j.njas.2019.100313

The Covid-19 Impact on Food Digital Transformation: A Bibliometric Analysis of Academic and Practitioners' Perspectives

Canio Forliano, Paola De Bernardi, and Martina Panero

Abstract The Covid-19 pandemic has brought about significant disruptions and challenges for businesses, including those in the food sector. This paper presents a bibliometric analysis exploring the relationship between the pandemic and digitalization in the food industry analyzing both academic and practitioners' documents for a comprehensive understanding of the post-pandemic digital landscape.

The analysis of scientific articles reveals a growing interest in the effects of Covid-19 on the food industry. Five thematic clusters emerge from the analysis: the impact of Covid-19, food production and supply, digital transformation and business model innovation, employees' well-being, and consumer behavior. These clusters demonstrate the interconnections between various aspects influenced by the pandemic and the role of digital technologies in addressing the challenges.

The study also examines practitioners' documents from Nexis Uni to complement the academic analysis. The content analysis of these documents provides real-world insights into current debates and practices related to digital transformation in the food industry. This dual perspective offers a holistic view of the research topic. Overall, this study contributes to the existing literature by illuminating the evolving relationship between the pandemic and digitalization in the food sector. The research captures the state of digital technology adoption in the food industry after the pandemic outbreak, and the findings provide valuable insights for academics, practitioners, and policymakers interested in understanding the implications of digitalization in the post-pandemic food industry.

Keywords Food sector · Digital technologies · Covid-19 · Food supply chain

C. Forliano (✉) · P. De Bernardi · M. Panero
Department of Management "Valter Cantino", University of Turin, Turin, Italy
e-mail: canio.forliano@unito.it; paola.debernardi@unito.it; martina.panero@unito.it

A. M. Braccini et al. (eds.), *Digital (Eco) Systems and Societal Challenges*, Lecture Notes in Information Systems and Organisation 72,
https://doi.org/10.1007/978-3-031-75586-6_3

1 Introduction

The contemporary business scenario is increasingly characterized by rapid changes and uncertainty [1] presenting companies with numerous challenges in their entrepreneurial environment [2]. The recent pandemic that our society experienced, forced firms to adapt to a disruptive atmosphere that exacerbated current challenges and triggered new problems. One of the crucial takeaways from the Covid-19 pandemic is the recognition that digital solutions play a pivotal role in addressing the challenges associated with disruptive events, such as sudden pandemics. However, it is important to acknowledge that while digital technologies can be instrumental in mitigating and managing crises, they can also expose vulnerabilities and risks [3]. Nowadays, most companies' success and competitiveness are increasingly dependent on the adoption of digital technologies (DT). In this fast-paced economy, it is expected that enterprise and global prosperity growth will be contingent upon investments in DT that foster an interconnected and dynamic world [4, 5].

The pandemic significantly impacted the food sector, forcing companies, restaurants, and producers to adapt to fluctuations in both demand and supply, while confronting increased difficulties related to safety measures, food availability [6], and worsening working conditions in the labor market [7]. Readiness and flexibility have been key to firms' survival [8]. Covid-19 changed how food is produced and consumed, accelerating pre-existing trends towards automation, e-commerce, and contactless delivery, stressing also the utmost importance of food security and resilience in the supply chain [9]. In this vein, the pandemic fostered the digital transformation of the food industry; but at the same time, this turbulent environment is redefining the way we experience food and might as well open the door to innovations and developments in this industry [10]. Scholars have extensively studied the global impact of the pandemic on business management, particularly in the food sector, highlighting disruptions in supply chains [11–13] and the subsequent changes in working [7, 14]. Indeed, as businesses faced unprecedented challenges, traditional work patterns were disrupted, and many individuals turned to remote or gig work for income opportunities. However, the gig workers themselves faced increased economic uncertainty and health risks, as they often lacked job security, benefits, and adequate social protection [15, 16]. Additionally, the literature unveils that Covid-19 also triggered relevant changes in consumers' behavior, accelerating trends like home delivery and e-commerce for food, potentially shaping long-term market preferences [17]. However, academic contributions also point out that despite the tragic consequences, this event prompted profound shifts in how the food sector operates, revealing new opportunities for the development of innovations for the supply and demand of food [10].

Despite some existing studies [18, 19], further research is needed to understand the effect of DT adoption and Covid-19 in the food industry. While global business management consequences have been explored, the specific effects of DT adoption in the context of the food sector remain understudied. Additionally, since several years have passed, new investigations are required to capture the state of DT in the food industry after the pandemic outbreak. In particular, the literature still does not bring evidence of practitioners and public debates. Practitioners have established their reservoir of knowledge and frequently struggle to incorporate robust theoretical frameworks from academia [20]. Nevertheless, they continue to be the ones actively observing the progress of DT, business models, and real-life trends.

Using a bibliometric approach, this study examines the relationship between the pandemic and digitalization in the food industry. The Covid-19 outbreak and its consequences likely hastened this digital transformation [21]. To achieve this, we reviewed scientific articles that explore the nexus between the digitalization of the food sector and the pandemic's effects and we analyzed practitioners' documents to understand the actual integration of digital technologies in the food sector post-Covid-19. This dual approach combines academic perspectives with real-world insights, aiming to expand the research scope and capture realistic cases and implications from multiple stakeholders [20]. Therefore, the research question (RQ) that we want to respond to is: What are the impacts of Covid-19 on the processes of digital transformation of the food sector from the practitioners' and academics' perspectives?

The analysis reveals contrasting trends between practitioners' publications and scientific papers, with the latter showing continued growth in interest regarding the pandemic's impact on the food sector. Both academic and public debates converge on five thematic clusters identified in our findings.

Our bibliometric offers a dual perspective, synthesizing insights from academic and practitioner sources to enhance understanding of digitalization in the food sector post-pandemic. This study contributes by shedding light on emerging trends in digitalization within the industry and revealing novel research directions. The intended target for this study includes researchers, practitioners, and policymakers in the fields of food industry, digital technologies, and innovation. Academics seeking to deepen their understanding of the digitalization trends in the food sector after the pandemic will find valuable insights from this study, revealing thematic areas of interest. For practitioners and policymakers, the examination of these documents can offer real-world insights and knowledge from those actively observing the progress of digital transformation and business models.

2 Research Design and Methods

Bibliometric analysis examines publications like scientific articles to uncover trends and relationships in a field. This method allows us to delve into the evolutionary aspects of the field, while also illuminating the emerging areas [22–24]. Clustering techniques are used to group related themes [22–24], making it suitable for analyzing academic and practitioner documents in this study on digital transformation in the food sector post-pandemic [25, 26].

2.1 Bibliometric Data Collection

The bibliometric data collection began with selecting Scopus as the primary database, the largest in social sciences [26–28]. To validate the choice, the query was also run in Web of Science, which yielded 45% fewer results. Then, to collect data from Scopus, we had to select keywords relevant to our RQs. So, we used the generic keyword "food*", as done in previous studies on similar topics [29, 30]. Then, to grasp studies related to the topic of DT, following previous systematic literature reviews [31–33], we combined both general words such as "digiti*" and "digital*" with keywords related to Industry 4.0 and digital technologies.

Following Scopus' syntax, wildcards enabled us to capture different variants of the selected keywords. At the same time, we could combine the strings associated with the three interrelated topics under investigation through Boolean operators. So, the final string we developed to search within documents' titles, abstracts, and keywords was the following: TITLE-ABS-KEY (food*) AND TITLE-ABS-KEY (digiti* OR "digital*" OR "Internet of Things" OR "IoT" OR "Big data" OR "artificial intelligence" OR "industry 4.0" OR "cloud comput*" OR "augmented realit*" OR "virtual realit*" OR drone* OR robot* OR blockchain* OR "additive manufactur*" OR "autonomous vehicle*")

Finally, using Scopus' feature of searching in any field of results, we restricted our search to studies investigating the post-pandemic scenario by adding the following string: ALL ("covid*" OR "coronavirus" OR "corona-virus"). Moreover, we excluded all studies published before 2020, to investigate the effects of the Covid-19 outbreak on the food industry. The initial search was conducted in November 2022 and then updated in January 2023. This initial search led to 1952 results. Then, we applied several exclusion and inclusion criteria to select only relevant and reliable scientific studies [34, 35]. The study filtered 185 papers by excluding non-English documents, non-journal articles, and those outside the business and management fields. Further refinement included selecting articles from journals ranked in the 2021 Academic Journal Guide for Business and Management (formerly Chartered Association of Business Schools) [36, 37], and obtaining 134 documents. The full paper of those documents was thus retrieved, and its content was analyzed through Leximancer to identify the conceptual structure of the theme under analysis. The full text of the articles was read by the authors to delve deeper into the academic literature. Only three documents had to be excluded from this step since we could not retrieve their full text (Fig. 1).

2.2 Collecting and Analyzing Practitioners' Documents

To investigate the discussion in practitioners' documents and the public debate, we used Nexis Uni (formerly Lexis Nexis), which includes documents such as newspaper articles, periodicals, financial and industrial information, business cases,

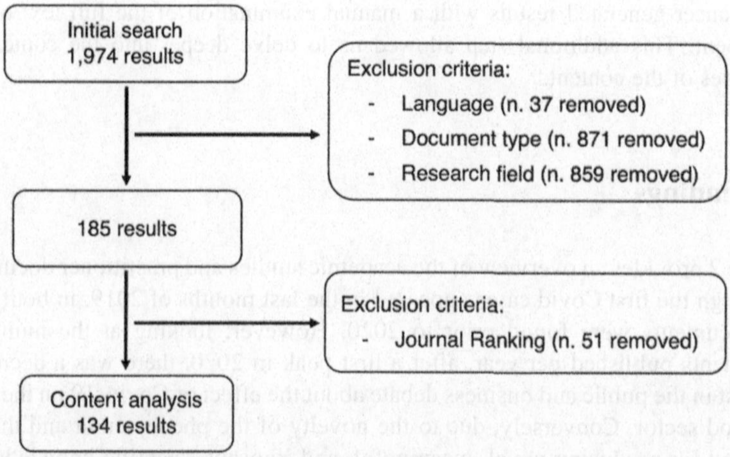

Fig. 1 The academic data collection. Source: the authors

market reports, and legal documents [38, 39]. Since Nexis Uni does not provide records' abstracts or keywords, we used the same string adopted in Scopus to search whether the keywords appeared anywhere in the article, not only in the title. However, since the first search led to more than 465,000 documents, to restrict to the most relevant ones, we only considered those registered within the "Food and beverage industry" category and where the selected keywords were present at five words of distance from each other [40, 41]. This method yielded 385 results. After further screening for duplicates, 125 results were removed, leaving 260 unique results. The full text of each result was then retrieved, read, and downloaded for processing with the content analysis.

2.3 *Data Analysis*

We utilized Leximancer software (ver. 4.5) for content analysis, leveraging its capability in text mining and conceptual mapping [40–42]. Leximancer employs a Bayesian learning algorithm to identify frequent terms and their relationships, facilitating systematic and unbiased concept extraction [42, 43]. However, since Leximancer should be used as a supporting tool to guide researchers in conducting the content analysis and coding activities [44], we manually analyzed the initial, automatic concept proposal and grouped similar concepts related to word variants (e.g., related to singular and plural forms) or removed meaningless concepts related to general words (e.g., https, doi, pp).

Finally, using the software features, we aggregated the list of concepts into themes. To ensure a more comprehensive analysis, we complemented the

Leximancer-generated results with a manual examination of the full text of each document. This additional step allowed us to delve deeper into the context and subtleties of the content.

3 Findings

Figure 2 provides an overview of the academic studies and practitioner documents. Although the first Covid cases appeared in the last months of 2019, in both cases, no documents were found prior to 2020. However, looking at the number of documents published per year, after a first peak in 2020, there was a decreasing interest in the public and business debate about the effect of Covid-19 on the DT of the food sector. Conversely, due to the novelty of the phenomenon and the time required for producing novel, meaningful, and rigorous scientific knowledge, the academic debate shows an inverse trend, with the number of publications still increasing over the years. Moreover, it must be noted that around 33% of papers published in 2020 dealing with Covid-19 were in the form of pre-prints or with accelerated peer-review processes due to the necessity of fast information sharing [45]. However, many of them had to subsequently be retreated [46]. Thus, as recent studies and calls for papers are asking, there is still the necessity to explore the innovation processes characterizing food companies in the post-pandemic global scenario [41, 47, 48].

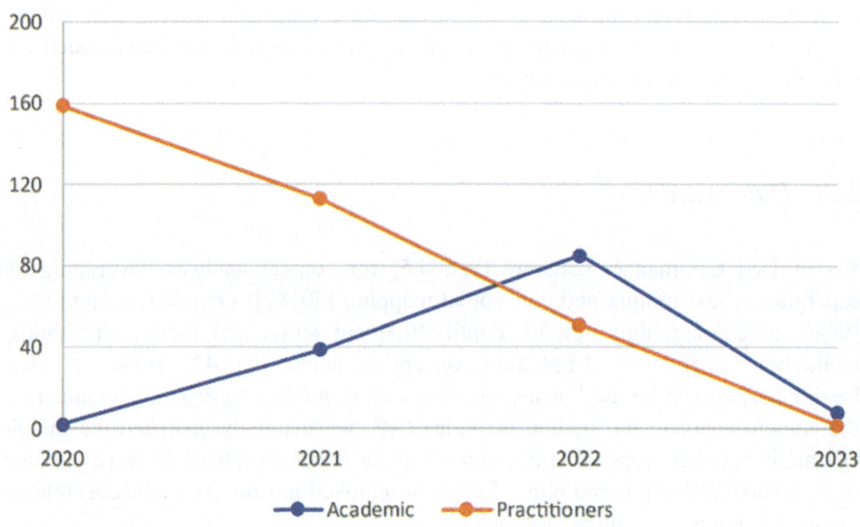

Fig. 2 Publication trends of scientific and practitioners' documents. Source: the authors

3.1 *Digital Transformation in the Food Sector in Academic Sources from the Business and Management Field*

In this paragraph, we present the results of the co-occurrence analysis that we performed to investigate the scientific debate on the topic. As shown in Fig. 3, we structured the data by identifying the following five different themes: (1) the impact of Covid-19; (2) food production and supply; (3) digital transformation and business model innovation; (4) employees' wellbeing; (5) consumer behavior. Notably, all these clusters show some interconnections and overlap with each other, with DT playing a transversal role among them.

The first cluster that emerged analyzing the academic debate about the (post) pandemic scenario of food companies is related to assessing the Covid-19 impact, and the subsequent measures taken by governments to mitigate the spread of the virus while avoiding disproportionate economic downturns. Covid-19 has indeed usually been framed as a trade-off between public health, personal freedom, and economic growth. This is captured by keywords such as "public", "health", "lock-down", "impact", and "risk". As a result of governments restricting measures and media coverage of the pandemic, which resulted in difficult access to food markets and consumers' panic buying and stockpiling activities, some companies tried to mitigate the people's perceived vulnerability through targeted social media campaigns as done in crisis management [49]. Furthermore, to compensate for the higher

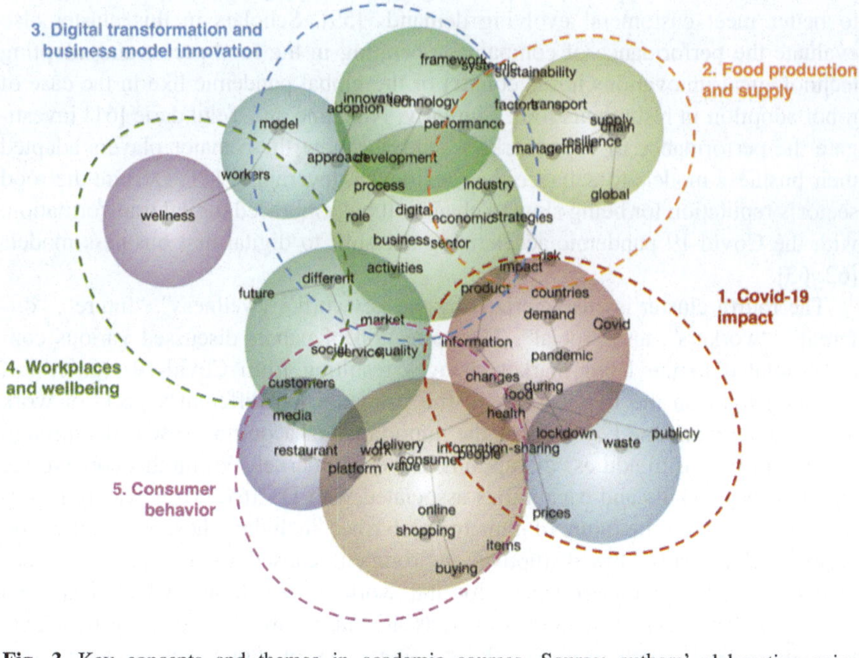

Fig. 3 Key concepts and themes in academic sources. Source: authors' elaboration using Leximancer

amount of food loss and waste generated as a result of the disruption of the supply and value chains [50], the prices of different food products raised abruptly. For instance, Cariappa et al. [50] investigated the lockdown effects on distribution and consumption of agricultural goods, discussing the consequences of this disruptive event on food prices. Various other studies have advocated the role that big data analytics can play in supporting managers to forecast food inflation or set effective pricing strategies [51, 52].

With keywords such as "supply chain", "global", "transport", "resilience", and "strategies", the second cluster focuses on the effects of the pandemic on the food supply chain's robustness and resilience. Indeed, Covid-19 has shown the high interdependence of modern supply chains and their fragility when exposed to severe disruptions [53, 54]. For instance, Singh et al. [55] identified how logistical issues like clogged production and distribution channels, labor shortages, and customer panic buying as the root cause of insufficient food supplies. As suggested in several studies investigating the post-pandemic scenario, the increasing integration of DT such as IoT, machine learning, big data, and blockchain can improve trust-based relationships with customers and other stakeholders, and support data-driven decision-making processes to lessen risks and uncertainties [56, 57]. For example, Joshi and Sharma [58] highlight DT's role in ensuring food security in developing economies during crises.

A third cluster emerged highly interconnected with all the other thematic areas. The digital transformation has brought about profound improvements in food companies' operations and productivity, managing their supply chain, and allowing them to better meet customers' evolving demands [59]. Scholars in this cluster also evaluate the performance of companies operating in the food sector and adopting technological innovations in the context of the global pandemic like in the case of robot adoption in restaurants [60]. Similarly, Njomane and Telukdarie [61] investigate the performance of supermarkets, studying how these major players adapted their business models to enhance their resiliency, leveraging IoT. Despite the food sector's reputation for being slow to change, it has embraced digital transformation, with the Covid-19 pandemic accelerating the shift to digital-first business models [62, 63].

The fourth cluster is characterized by the keyword's "wellness", "future", "different", "workers", and "social". The collection of papers discussed various concerns related to the labor market changes resulting from Covid-19 restrictions, shedding light on the implications of the pandemic on different aspects of work and employment. One key focus is the importance of acquiring new skills through training programs to address disruptions in the job market. Within this context, the significance of skills and capabilities associated with DT [64, 65] is widely recognized as crucial for the future of numerous job roles, including those within the food sector. Additionally, the disruptive environment caused by the pandemic has resulted in adverse consequences for the working conditions, which has been investigated by several authors. Concerns are raised also in the study by Gupta and Gupta [16] which examines the consequences of digital advancements that contribute to the emergence of the gig economy.

The analysis highlights significant issues in the food delivery sector, where gig workers often face dehumanizing conditions amidst the rise of app-based employment. This underscores the need for a thorough examination of the social impacts linked to the proliferation of DT and gig work systems. Similarly, Muszyński et al. [66] reveal that the pandemic caused high volatility in the demand for these workers, amplifying imbalances within an unregulated and precarious employment arrangement typical of platform workers.

The fifth cluster encompasses keywords such as "customers", "consumer", "buying", "shopping" and "delivery". This thematic group is primarily focused on consumers' behaviour [50]. Researchers have explored food consumption patterns to understand their fluctuations during the pandemic [67, 68] revealing a growing trend of purchasing groceries through e-commerce channels, necessitating an increased utilization of DT by consumers as well [69, 70]. In this cluster, buying behaviours are also investigated in relation to the panic effect generated by the pandemic [49]. Customer experience is also investigated in relation to technological advancements and automation [60, 71]. In this context, Alfalih [72] investigates how automation might enhance customers' engagement in the food sector, revealing opportunities to gain customers' trust. Similarly, Ma et al. [71] explored how technological advancement emerged during the pandemic, like robotic services, affect the customer experience in restaurants.

3.2 *Digital Transformation in the Food Sector in Practitioners' Sources*

We now display the results emerged during the co-occurrence analysis of practitioners' documents related to the landscape of DT in the food industry after the pandemic. Figure 4 depicts five thematic clusters linked to (1) public response to the pandemic, (2) workplaces and well-being (3) consumer behavior and business model innovation (4) food supply chain (5) digital technologies and food production.

The first cluster "public response to the pandemic", including keywords like "health", "public", "virus", governments", "contact" and "measures", focuses on global health crisis management, emphasizing digital technology deployment. For instance, the EU Reporter [73] discusses measures such as the EU Digital Covid-19 Certificate, facilitating safe mobility and Covid-19 testing across EU member states [74]. The use of digitalization has emerged as a crucial factor in addressing health-related concerns, revealing the enhanced value of DT in navigating crises; notably, the deployment of QR codes, online certificates, and digital platforms has been instrumental in facilitating the implementation of effective measures for safeguarding public health [75]. In the realm of the food sector, distinct measures have been implemented. Initiatives highlighted by FoodNavigator illustrate technological advancements tailored to food production challenges [76]. Noteworthy entities such as the Food and Agriculture Organization and the African Union have

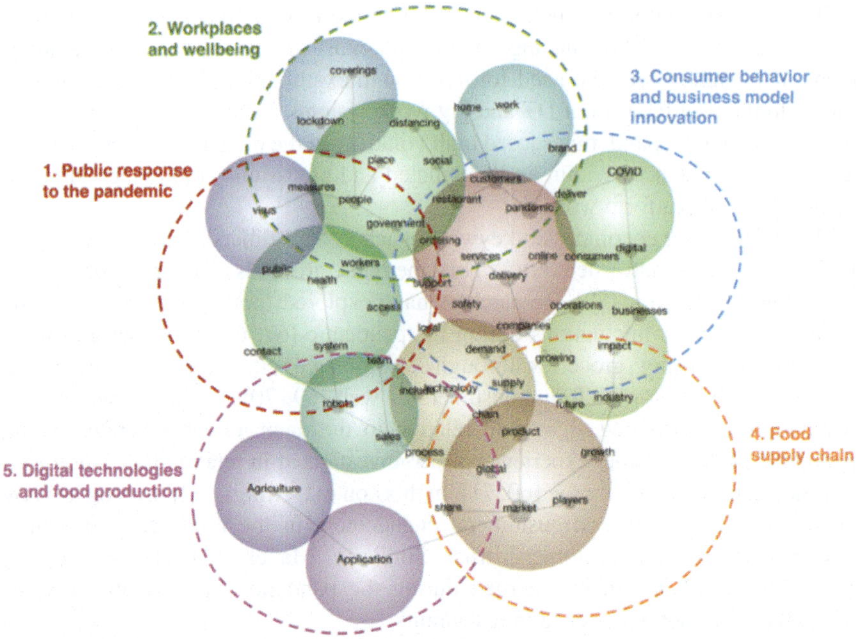

Fig. 4 Key concepts and themes in practitioners' sources. Source: authors' elaboration using Leximancer

similarly undertaken endeavors to safeguard food security on an international scale [77].

The second cluster involves topics related to workplaces and well-being. Businesses have been compelled to reassess their workspaces and embrace remote solutions [78]. However, the food sector, dependent on physical presence, faced significant disruptions, including temporary closures in Europe due to infections and health concerns. Companies prioritized employee health and safety, leading to new measures within facilities. Many individuals became unemployed due to restaurant closures. As the report by EIT Food [79] highlights, various companies needed to prioritize employees' health and implement new measures to maintain safety inside the facilities. Furthermore, a significant number of individuals were also left unemployed as a consequence of the mandated closures imposed on restaurants [80]. The integration of technology has helped monitor work areas and reduce contamination risks [81]. Non-contact procedures were widely adopted, with delivery companies like Deliveroo implementing measures to limit contagion. DT like artificial intelligence has also found application in assisting businesses in monitoring the risk associated with Covid-19. For instance, Delfin Health and DocHQ developed AI tools to assess workforce health and safety in the food sector. However, the digitalization of economies has also widened disparities between less digitally connected and highly digitalized societies, and the rise of gig workers highlighted the need for equal rights and protections [82, 83].

The third cluster developed in practitioners' documentation deals with consumers' preferences and business model innovations. Disclosures have highlighted the influence of the pandemic on individuals' relationship with food, unveiling a heightened inclination towards food-related interactions within the realm of social media, alongside an augmented aspiration for cultivating and undertaking baking endeavors autonomously [84]. In parallel, the public discourse has also highlighted that consumers exhibited an increasing level of ease in engaging with the practice of online grocery shopping. Remarkably, this crisis period witnessed a substantial surge in the growth of major entities such as Walmart and Amazon [78]. The study conducted by EIT Food [79] reveals that the pandemic has significantly influenced customer behavior and food consumption patterns, particularly due to the widespread adoption of remote work arrangements, leading individuals to consume meals within their households. This lifestyle change has consequently prompted a notable shift in people's purchasing habits, favoring e-commerce orders of food. Food retailers like Carrefour largely adapted their business models, accordingly, switching to digital platforms and investing in digital marketing [85]. This inevitably involved adopting strategies to improve the customer experience through DT to meet both the increased demand for food and the customers' expectations [86]. Moreover, the pandemic catalyzed the emergence of innovative business models, exemplified by the advent of "digital-only kitchens" such as Chipotle in New York. These establishments eliminated indoor dining facilities and minimized contact with employees. In response to the growing consumer demand for digital accessibility, various food chains like Burger King, reconfigured their business models to address the emerging need to avoid personal contact [87]. Overall, these documents point out that changes in consumer trends that emerged during the pandemic, such as food delivery, are anticipated to persist even after the conclusion of the crisis and DT is expected to play a key role in the development of new solutions [88].

Keywords like "market", "product", "growth", "share" characterize the fourth cluster, which focuses on the alterations observed in the Food Supply Chain (FSC) amidst the pandemic. As highlighted by the Wall Street Journal, the pandemic initially saw a surge in grocery demand alongside restaurant closures, leading to increased distribution complexity [89]. This period marked significant shifts, notably heightened food demand; for instance, the Great Boston Food Bank distributed 56% more food in 2020 compared to previous years [89]. Data analytics played a crucial role in managing this demand surge and optimizing supply chain operations. Warehouse operations used DT to enhance operational efficiency and optimize processes in response to the increased demand [86]. Also, partnerships emerged along the supply chain; for instance, GBFB formed a partnership with McKinsey to assess the organization's existing technological infrastructure and develop a strategic plan to embrace digitalization. The pandemic necessitated a general enhancement of efficiency across the FSC, which involved improving communication with food distribution partners, facilitating the sharing of resources, and organizing digital orders, adapting to the evolving circumstances. Along with that, there has been a substantial surge in demand for robotics companies that offer machinery capable of harvesting, handling, and delivering food and managing the challenges of the FSC. This surge has accelerated the ongoing trend toward automation that was already underway [90, 91].

The last cluster depicted in Fig. 4 is characterized by a thematic area of DT and food production. As anticipated in an article in Forbes [92], the effects of the crisis are expected to perdure necessitating, for instance, grocery stores to adapt to revised operational patterns, using online platforms; indeed, the most substantial transformation will occur in the realm of online platforms. This health has also underscored the imperative of ensuring food security. Within this context, food production, particularly in the realm of agriculture, has the potential to achieve notable efficiency gains [93, 94]. The agricultural sector, in particular, has been portrayed as highly promising for the integration of artificial intelligence applications. Such solutions present opportunities to curtail waste, optimize resource use, and effectively manage inventory, providing a potential approach to avoid the risk of disruptions hindering the food system [95–97]

4 Discussion

4.1 The Impact of Covid-19

First of all, we found several studies investigating the general impacts of the Covid-19 outbreak. Declaring a pandemic has indeed impacted every economic sector, at a direct or indirect level and both locally and globally [10], requiring the need to make trade-offs between public health, personal freedom, and economic growth during the pandemic. From what emerges in the academic and practitioner documents we can observe how research and public debate have mainly centered on discussing the negative impacts of the pandemic and the weaknesses of our economy, pointing out some of the main downturns: the sudden shuttering of businesses and imposition of lockdowns have led to job losses and economic contractions [98]. Sectors such as tourism, hospitality, and retail have been hit hard as people are unable or unwilling to travel or gather. Another issue relates to supply chain disruptions, as factories and production facilities have been closed and transportation has been disrupted. This has led to shortages of certain goods and increased prices for others [50]. Additionally, many small businesses have been forced to close permanently due to a lack of customers and financial difficulties. Thus, the safety measures adopted to reduce the spread of the virus, including the use of protective gear and masks, quarantining, lockdowns, and restrictions to social activities, have had a detrimental effect on business operations and supply chains in all sectors [99].

Governments have implemented a variety of economic stimulus measures in an attempt to mitigate the economic impact of the pandemic, like direct payments to individuals, loan guarantees or financial assistance to businesses, also tax deferrals and other forms of relief. In this context, the examined documentation has discussed the employment of DT solutions as a means for overcoming the challenges brought about by the protracted lockdown and the forced halt of transportation activities. This is notably exemplified by the observable surge in online retailing and doorstep deliveries facilitated through digital applications [100, 101]. In this vein, the documents reveal how the pandemic has also led to some positive changes, supporting the adoption of technologies and a shift towards more sustainable consumption patterns. However, it is noteworthy to mention that this cluster of analysis has contributed to the examination of short-term impacts of the Covid-19 pandemic, and little is known or forecasted about how the consequences of this period will impact in a longer period. For this reason, future research might still explore the long-term effects of the pandemic on the food sector and consumers, reasoning on how DT is evolving to meet the changed production and consumption patterns.

4.2 Food Production and Supply

For what concerns the production of food, the robustness and resilience of the food supply chain appeared to be the key topics in this cluster. The articles in this group highlighted how Covid-19 has shown the high interdependence and complexity of modern supply chains and their fragility when exposed to severe disruptions such as those imposed by governments for responding to the pandemic [53, 54]. This also resulted in higher food scarcity and subsequent food-panic-buying behaviors [49, 98]. For instance, Singh et al. [55] identified how logistical issues such as clogged production and distribution channels, labor shortages, and customer panic buying as the root cause of insufficient food supplies.

Notwithstanding the difficulties of predicting such disasters, research suggested that companies can and should take preventive measures to lessen uncertainties in the FSC, and DT adoption might be a strategy [56]. Accordingly, to avoid further shortages and chaotic behaviors, Ivanov [102] suggested strengthening supply chains' viability by pursuing four different strategies aimed at increasing their robustness and resilience. The four strategies are (1) intertwining; (2) scaling; (3) substituting; and (4) repurposing.

The first strategy, intertwining, seek synergies between typically non-cooperative supply chains, exemplified by circular businesses that upcycle food waste into new products [29, 103]. The second strategy, scaling, involves enhancing supply chain infrastructure to manage lockdowns and restrictions. For instance, Too Good To Go expanded operations by partnering with food producers to sell surplus food, while Canadian food processors scaled down by closing 12.5% of their plants due to decreased supply [82, 104]. Then, the strategy of substituting entails adapting the supply chain by replacing products with alternatives or finding new partners to overcome closures [56]. Short supply chains and local markets were advantageous during the pandemic due to their reliance on transportation and consumer preferences shifts for authenticity, safety, fresh foods, and home-cooked meals [105–107]. Finally, repurposing supply chains involves making structural changes to seize new opportunities during transitions [64]. Literature and practitioners highlight the potential of digital transformation and data-driven decision-making to enhance proactive planning and reduce risks and uncertainties [53, 54, 58].

4.3 Digital Transformation and Business Model Innovation

Overall, the COVID-19 pandemic has accelerated the food sector's shift towards a digital-first approach, compelling rapid adaptation despite the industry's reputation for slow change [62, 63]. This digitization has profoundly enhanced food companies' operations, productivity, and supply chain management, enabling them to better meet evolving customer demands [47, 48, 59]. The transformation has driven companies to innovate their business models and invest in new technologies and channels [53, 108]. Notably, digital technologies foundational to Industry 4.0, such as blockchain, big data, IoT, and robots, have significantly impacted competition and consumer experience. This shift has made the competition more data-driven and consumer experiences more user-centric, enabling customized mass production of goods and services [101].

Given the many applications of DT to adapt food companies' business models, Fig. 5 maps the extent to which each technology has been investigated in post-pandemic academic discourse regarding different aspects of a company's operations. Some studies addressed various disruptive technologies; thus, the general category "digital transformation" is included. Since multiple categories are often mentioned, the total number of mapped technologies and business activities exceeds the sample size. Most studies (17) focus on how companies had to adapt or rethink their supply chains by investigating the broader digital transformation or Industry 4.0 without concentrating on specific technologies. Industry 4.0's core principles encompass increasingly decentralized, interoperable, virtualized, and modular business processes, enhancing decision-making capabilities [59]. So, most of the attention was posed to the role played by the blockchain in increasing the transparency and traceability of information and material flows [109, 110], reducing risks and transaction costs [65, 111, 112], while enhancing trust among different stakeholders [53],

	Supply Chain	Marketing	Food Production	Decision Support Systems	Workplace	Relational Governance
Digital transformation	17	1	7	7	2	1
Blockchain	16	1	0	0	0	1
Mobile app/Digital platform	9	15	1	0	3	2
ICT / Social media	3	11	1	1	0	1
Robots and Drones	8	3	2	0	1	0
Big Data Analytics (BDA)	6	3	0	3	0	0
Internet of Things (IoT)	6	0	2	1	0	1
Artificial Intelligence (AI)	2	3	0	1	0	0
Augmented (AR) or Virtual Reality (VR)	0	3	0	0	0	0
Cloud Computing	0	0	1	0	0	0

15+ 10 5 0

Fig. 5 Research focus heatmap per number of contributions. Source: the authors

reducing food waste and frauds [111]. For similar purposes, scholars have also explored the drivers and barriers to adopting the Internet of Things and big data analytics [108, 113], as well as integrating them to plan customers' demand and organize pick-up points [61]. Regarding the supply chain, most of the studies have also explored new ways for companies to sell and deliver food to customers, leveraging mobile apps [70, 114], e-commerce [115, 116], or drones and robots for reducing time, costs, and social contacts [117, 118].

Another well-debated area is related to experiential and/or digital marketing, with scholars mainly focusing on the role played by digital platforms and social media in fostering information-sharing processes between consumers [119] or increasing their willingness to pay for some products or services [120, 121]. Big data analytics have been sometimes considered to conduct such analysis [122, 123]. So, for example, Thongsri et al. [101], the authors investigated food friend application, finding that psychological variables (i.e., alertness to distinction, openness to novelty, and orientation in the present) impact consumers' choices differently than technologically related variables such as digital tool's design and information quality. Moreover, DT has been investigated as a tool to better meet customers' expectations by innovating some aspects of companies' business models [59]. Some studies have further considered to what extent the inclusion of robots into companies' operating activities, especially in the touristic or food service industries, can increase customers' experience or be perceived as detrimental [124, 125]. Finally, fewer studies were found investigating the impact of DT in enhancing companies' food production activity (e.g., increasing crops' yields) or in supporting the decision-making systems (e.g., through big data analytics, IoT) [108, 126], suggesting a possible avenue for future research. Also, the way workplaces are changing, or novel relations can be established and managed with partners [127] are promising areas to be explored. At the same time, there is still space for exploring the potentialities of technologies such as artificial intelligence, augmented or virtual reality, and cloud computing systems.

4.4 Workplace and Well-Being

As discussed in the previous paragraph, one of the most significant impacts of the pandemic on the food industry has been the shift toward automation and e-commerce. With social distancing measures, many food businesses have turned to online platforms to reach customers [58, 128], increasing demand for contactless delivery and online ordering [70, 114]. Automation has become more prevalent in warehouses and distribution centers, with robots picking and packing orders, and some restaurants using automation to prepare food [108, 117]. However, this digitization has social implications, often linked to a fifth industrial revolution paradigm: in Secundo et al. [48] the authors show how food companies, as essential businesses that could not stop their activities, implemented crisis management committees to guarantee employees' health or promoted remote working policies, investing in training to foster employees' technological literacy. Despite these efforts, the increased use of technology has exacerbated issues of technostress and digital surveillance, particularly among remote workers, who report higher levels of stress. Accordingly, Farrish [129] found that remote workers reported higher levels of technostress due to the increased use of technology for communication, collaboration, and information sharing, affecting work-life balance. To mitigate these negative effects, employers should support employee well-being by providing training on managing information overload, setting clear availability boundaries, and offering mental health support [130]. Delving into the dark side of digital transformation, Parwez and Ranjan [131] questioned to what extent the digital boom and the platform-based economy have lowered companies' transaction costs at the expense of workers' safety. So, the authors continue asking policymakers and digital platforms to deal with the uncertainty typical of the so-called gig economy, embracing the novel jobs created by the digital revolution while recognizing fair salaries and welfare measures for workers. Similar concerns have also been raised in other studies investigating how Covid-19 has shaped the future of the food service industry or the set of skills required for workers to adapt to a digital world [15]. Given the complexity of this phenomenon and its continuous evolution [132], the authors suggest that future research might explore how the digitalization of jobs in the food sector is progressing, studying the new professions emerging and the normative scenario of the gig economy.

4.5 Consumer Behavior

The examined documents have also discussed the fact that the Covid-19 pandemic has impacted the way that consumers behave when it comes to food. In the early days of the pandemic, there were widespread reports of panic buying and empty store shelves as consumers stockpiled essential goods. This was particularly true for items such as non-perishable foods like canned goods and dried pasta [67]. DT played a key role also in the realm of food consumption: as the pandemic progressed and lockdowns were put in place, many consumers turned to online grocery shopping and home delivery services as a way to avoid going to physical stores [70]. Food consumption changed too, with many people turning to home cooking and meal delivery services. With lockdowns and social distancing measures in place, people have been spending more time at home, and have been looking for ways to make home cooking easier and more convenient [107]. This has led to a surge in demand for meal kits, online grocery delivery, and meal delivery services. Many food companies have responded by launching new products and services, and by investing in new technologies to make home cooking easier and more convenient [118]. The trend of increased home cooking and meal planning is expected to continue as people spend more time at home. Urban farming is also on the rise, with individuals growing food in small gardens or on balconies. However, there is a lack of research on consumer engagement and loyalty in online food services. Future studies should explore consumer engagement strategies using digital technologies in the food sector, examining the relative advantages and disadvantages.

5 Conclusion

This study shows that the pandemic accelerated the digitalization of the food industry, with companies adopting technologies like blockchain, big data analytics, IoT, and e-commerce. This shift was driven by the need to adapt business models and meet changing consumer demands. DT has improved supply chain transparency, reduced risks and transaction costs, enhanced customer experiences, and optimized production and delivery processes. However, the increased adoption of DT has also raised concerns about technostress, digital surveillance, and the impact on workers' well-being.

This study primarily provides practical contributions through the exploration of a burgeoning theme that has garnered interest in our society. This research holds substantial value for companies seeking to address the challenges arising from the post-Covid-19 landscape. Additionally, policymakers could find this study pertinent in formulating business support measures. In general, the findings suggest that companies in the food industry need to continue investing in DT and innovating their business models to remain competitive and resilient in the face of future disruptions. They should prioritize supply chain optimization, diversification, and collaboration to strengthen their robustness and resilience. Additionally, they should focus on addressing the social and well-being aspects of digital transformation, providing support and training to employees to manage technostress, and maintaining work-life balance. In addition to that, this study points out the fragilities of FSC, underscoring the absolute need to support innovative and resilient business models; this may involve exploring alternative distribution channels, implementing personalized marketing strategies, or exploring new revenue streams.

Concerning limitations, we recognize that the document database depends on the keywords chosen for the retrieval of articles and practitioners' documents. We excluded non-business and management documents and restricted the sample to English-only documents, possibly missing significant information. The thematic analysis might be influenced by the author's experience and knowledge. One additional point to mention is that Covid-19 is still unfolding, preventing a global balance needed for conclusive outcomes, and the digital transformation of the FSC is in its early stages. For this reason, we acknowledge that also the subsequent digital transformation of the FSC is just in its early stages. Further investigation is needed to explore best practices and DT applications. As new technological developments emerge, a fruitful area of research related to the impact of automation on job displacement, workforce skills, and the overall socio-economic implications is crucial. Future studies might also explore how artificial/virtual reality technologies can enhance customer experiences, support virtual product demonstrations, improve training programs, and facilitate immersive dining experiences. In addition to that, our study does not consider the implications of DT adoption and Covid-19 on the sustainability of the FSC. Therefore, we also suggest delving into the sustainability implications of the digital approach in the food industry, weighing the environmental impacts of e-commerce, for instance.

Acknowledgments This study was carried out within the Agritech National Research Center and received funding from the European Union Next-GenerationEU (PIANO NAZIONALE DI RIPRESA E RESILIENZA (PNRR)—MISSIONE 4 COMPONENTE 2, INVESTIMENTO 1.4—D.D. 1032 17/06/2022, CN00000022). This manuscript reflects only the authors' views and opinions, neither the European Union nor the European Commission can be considered responsible for them.

Disclosure of Interests The authors have no competing interests to declare that are relevant to the content of this article.

References

1. Santoro, G., Vrontis, D., Thrassou, A., & Dezi, L. (2018). The Internet of Things: Building a knowledge management system for open innovation and knowledge management capacity. *Technological Forecasting and Social Change, 136*, 347–354. https://doi.org/10.1016/j.techfore.2017.02.034
2. Ferraris, A., Mazzoleni, A., Devalle, A., & Couturier, J. (2019). Big data analytics capabilities and knowledge management: impact on firm performance. *Management Decision, 57*(8), 1923–1936. https://doi.org/10.1108/MD-07-2018-0825
3. European Commission. (2021). Communication from the Commission to the European Parliament, the Council, the European Economic and Social Committee and the Committee of the Regions 2030 Digital Compass: the European way for the Digital Decade [Online]. Available: https://eur-lex.europa.eu/homepage.html
4. International Data Corporation. (2019). IDC FutureScape: Worldwide IT Industry 2020 Predictions [Online]. Available: https://www.statista.com/statistics/1134766/nominal-gdp-driven-by-digitally-transformed-enterprises/
5. Donthu, N., & Gustafsson, A. (2020). Effects of COVID-19 on business and research. *Journal of Business Research, 117*, 284–289. https://doi.org/10.1016/j.jbusres.2020.06.008
6. Messabia, N., Fomi, P.-R., & Kooli, C. (2022). Managing restaurants during the COVID-19 crisis: Innovating to survive and prosper. *Journal of Innovation and Knowledge, 7*(4), 100234. https://doi.org/10.1016/j.jik.2022.100234
7. Tagliacozzo, S., Pisacane, L., & Kilkey, M. (2021). The interplay between structural and systemic vulnerability during the COVID-19 pandemic: migrant agricultural workers in informal settlements in Southern Italy. *Journal of Ethnic and Migration Studies, 47*(9), 1903–1921. https://doi.org/10.1080/1369183X.2020.1857230
8. Kazancoglu, I., Ozbiltekin-Pala, M., Kumar Mangla, S., Kazancoglu, Y., & Jabeen, F. (2022). Role of flexibility, agility and responsiveness for sustainable supply chain resilience during COVID-19. *Journal of Cleaner Production, 362*, 132431. https://doi.org/10.1016/j.jclepro.2022.132431
9. Chen McCain, S.-L., Lolli, J., Liu, E., & Lin, L.-C. (2022). An analysis of a third-party food delivery app during the COVID-19 pandemic. *British Food Journal, 124*(10), 3032–3052. https://doi.org/10.1108/BFJ-03-2021-0332
10. Apostolopoulos, N., Ratten, V., Petropoulos, D., Liargovas, P., & Anastasopoulou, E. (2021). Agri-food sector and entrepreneurship during the COVID-19 crisis: A systematic literature

review and research agenda. *Strategic Change, 30*(2), 159–167. https://doi.org/10.1002/jsc.2400
11. Liu, Y., Lee, J. M., & Lee, C. (2020). The challenges and opportunities of a global health crisis: the management and business implications of COVID-19 from an Asian perspective. *Asian Business and Management, 19*(3), 277–297. https://doi.org/10.1057/s41291-020-00119-x
12. Farooq, M. U., Hussain, A., Masood, T., & Habib, M. S. (2021). Supply chain operations management in pandemics: a state-of-the-art review inspired by COVID-19. *Sustainability, 13*(5). https://doi.org/10.3390/su13052504
13. Aday, S., & Aday, M. S. (2020). Impact of COVID-19 on the food supply chain. *Food Quality and Safety, 4*(4), 167–180. https://doi.org/10.1093/fqsafe/fyaa024
14. Parwez, S. (2022). COVID-19 pandemic and work precarity at digital food platforms: A delivery worker's perspective. *Social Sciences & Humanities Open, 5*(1), 100259. https://doi.org/10.1016/j.ssaho.2022.100259
15. Voipio, V., Vilko, J., Elfvengren, K., & Korpela, J. (2023). The future of work: skills and knowledge perspective on service automation in the foodservice industry. *Technology Analysis & Strategic Management*. https://doi.org/10.1080/09537325.2023.2165440
16. Gupta, R., & Gupta, R. (2022). Lost in the perilous boulevards of gig economy: Making of human drones. *South Asian Journal of Human Resources Management*. https://doi.org/10.1177/23220937221101259
17. Cavallo, C., Sacchi, G., & Carfora, V. (2020). Resilience effects in food consumption behaviour at the time of Covid-19: perspectives from Italy. *Heliyon, 6*(12), e05676. https://doi.org/10.1016/j.heliyon.2020.e05676
18. Varese, E., Cesarani, M. C., Kabaja, B., Sołtysik, M., & Wojnarowska, M. (2024). Online food delivery habits and its environmental impact during the COVID-19 pandemic: an Italian and Polish study. *British Food Journal, 126*(1), 191–204.
19. Mancuso, I., Petruzzelli, A. M., & Panniello, U. (2023). Innovating agri-food business models after the Covid-19 pandemic: The impact of digital technologies on the value creation and value capture mechanisms. *Technological Forecasting and Social Change, 190*, 122404.
20. Secinaro, S., Dal Mas, F., Massaro, M., & Calandra, D. (2022). Exploring agricultural entrepreneurship and new technologies: academic and practitioners' views. *British Food Journal, 124*(7), 2096–2113. https://doi.org/10.1108/BFJ-08-2021-0905
21. Penco, L., Profumo, G., Serravalle, F., & Viassone, M. (2023). Has COVID-19 pushed digitalisation in SMEs? The role of entrepreneurial orientation. *Journal of Small Business and Enterprise Development, 30*(2), 311–341.
22. Donthu, N., Kumar, S., Mukherjee, D., Pandey, N., & Lim, W. M. (2021). How to conduct a bibliometric analysis: An overview and guidelines. *Journal of Business Research, 133*, 285–296. https://doi.org/10.1016/j.jbusres.2021.04.070
23. Mortazavi, S., Eslami, M. H., Hajikhani, A., & Väätänen, J. (2021). Mapping inclusive innovation: A bibliometric study and literature review. *Journal of Business Research, 122*, 736–750. https://doi.org/10.1016/j.jbusres.2020.07.030
24. Fahimnia, B., Sarkis, J., & Davarzani, H. (2015). Green supply chain management: A review and bibliometric analysis. *International Journal of Production Economics, 162*, 101–114.
25. Ranjbari, M., Shams Esfandabadi, Z., Gautam, S., Ferraris, A., & Scagnelli, S. D. (2023). Waste management beyond the COVID-19 pandemic: Bibliometric and text mining analyses. *Gondwana Research, 114*, 124–137. https://doi.org/10.1016/j.gr.2021.12.015
26. Bargoni, A., Ferraris, A., Bresciani, S., & Camilleri, M. A. (2024). Crowdfunding and innovation: a bibliometric review and future research agenda. *European Journal of Innovation Management, 27*(4), 1109–1133.
27. Singh, V. K., Singh, P., Karmakar, M., Leta, J., & Mayr, P. (2021). The journal coverage of web of science, scopus and dimensions: A comparative analysis. *Scientometrics, 126*(6), 5113–5142.

28. Forliano, C., De Bernardi, P., & Yahiaoui, D. (2021). Entrepreneurial universities: A bibliometric analysis within the business and management domains. *Technological Forecasting and Social Change, 165*. https://doi.org/10.1016/j.techfore.2020.120522
29. De Bernardi, P., Bertello, A., & Forliano, C. (2023). Circularity of food systems: a review and research agenda. *British Food Journal, 125*(3), 1094–1129.
30. Petrolo, D., Manesh, M. F., Pellegrini, M. M., & Flamini, G. (2022). Agri-food entrepreneurship. Harvesting, growing and reseeding the orchard through a bibliometric study. *British Food Journal, 124*(7), 2396–2426.
31. Guandalini, I. (2022). Sustainability through digital transformation: A systematic literature review for research guidance. *Journal of Business Research, 148*, 456–471.
32. Feliciano-Cestero, M. M., Ameen, N., Kotabe, M., Paul, J., & Signoret, M. (2023). Is digital transformation threatened? A systematic literature review of the factors influencing firms' digital transformation and internationalization. *Journal of Business Research, 157*, 113546.
33. Chauhan, C., Parida, V., & Dhir, A. (2022). Linking circular economy and digitalisation technologies: A systematic literature review of past achievements and future promises. *Technological Forecasting and Social Change, 177*, 121508.
34. Baima, G., Forliano, C., Santoro, G., & Vrontis, D. (2020). Intellectual capital and business model: a systematic literature review to explore their linkages. *Journal of Intellectual Capital*. https://doi.org/10.1108/JIC-02-2020-0055
35. Kraus, S., Ribeiro-Soriano, D., & Schüssler, M. (2018). Fuzzy-set qualitative comparative analysis (fsQCA) in entrepreneurship and innovation research—The rise of a method. *The International Entrepreneurship and Management Journal, 14*(1), 15–33. https://doi.org/10.1007/s11365-017-0461-8
36. Bertello, A., Battisti, E., De Bernardi, P., & Bresciani, S. (2022). An integrative framework of knowledge-intensive and sustainable entrepreneurship in entrepreneurial ecosystems. *Journal of Business Research, 142*, 683–693.
37. Battisti, E., Christofi, M., Vrontis, D., & Nirino, N. (2021). Past, present, and future of mergers and acquisitions in the MENA region: a systematic review and integrative framework. *International Studies of Management and Organization, 51*(3), 276–296.
38. Kim, N., Lee, H., Kim, W., Lee, H., & Suh, J. H. (2015). Dynamic patterns of industry convergence: Evidence from a large amount of unstructured data. *Research Policy, 44*(9), 1734–1748.
39. Cook, L., LaVan, H., & Zilic, I. (2018). An exploratory analysis of corporate social responsibility reporting in US pharmaceutical companies. *Journal of Communication Management, 22*(2), 197–211.
40. Massaro, M., Secinaro, S., Dal Mas, F., Brescia, V., & Calandra, D. (2021). Industry 4.0 and circular economy: An exploratory analysis of academic and practitioners' perspectives. *Business Strategy and the Environment, 30*(2), 1213–1231.
41. Dal Mas, F., Massaro, M., Ndou, V., & Raguseo, E. (2023). Blockchain technologies for sustainability in the agrifood sector: A literature review of academic research and business perspectives. *Technological Forecasting and Social Change, 187*, 122155. https://doi.org/10.1016/j.techfore.2022.122155
42. Randhawa, K., Wilden, R., & Hohberger, J. (2016). A bibliometric review of open innovation: Setting a research agenda. *Journal of Product Innovation Management, 33*(6), 750–772.
43. Biesenthal, C., & Wilden, R. (2014). Multi-level project governance: Trends and opportunities. *International Journal of Project Management, 32*(8), 1291–1308.
44. Bandara, W., Furtmueller, E., Gorbacheva, E., Miskon, S., & Beekhuyzen, J. (2015). Achieving rigor in literature reviews: Insights from qualitative data analysis and tool-support. *Communications of the Association for Information Systems, 37*(1), 8.
45. Watson, C. (2022). Rise of the preprint: How rapid data sharing during COVID-19 has changed science forever. *Nature Medicine, 28*(1), 2–5.
46. Capodici, A., Salussolia, A., Sanmarchi, F., Gori, D., & Golinelli, D. (2022). Biased, wrong and counterfeited evidences published during the COVID-19 pandemic, a systematic review of retracted COVID-19 papers. *Quality and Quantity*, 1–33.

47. Chatterjee, S., Chaudhuri, R., Vrontis, D., & Galati, A. (2022). Digital transformation using industry 4.0 technology by food and beverage companies in post COVID-19 period: from DCV and IDT perspective. *European Journal of Innovation Management*. https://doi.org/10.1108/EJIM-07-2022-0374. Ahead-of-print.
48. Secundo, G., Schena, R., Russo, A., Schiavone, F., & Shams, R. (2022). The impact of digital technologies on the achievement of the sustainable development goals: Evidence from the agri-food sector. *Total Quality Management and Business Excellence*, 1–17. https://doi.org/10.1080/14783363.2022.2065981
49. Zaky, A., Mohamed, H., & Saxena, G. (2022). Conceptualising the panic buying phenomenon during COVID-19 as an affective assemblage. *European Journal of Marketing, 56*(12), 3313–3346. https://doi.org/10.1108/EJM-11-2020-0796
50. Cariappa, A. G. A., Acharya, K. K., Adhav, C. A., Sendhil, R., & Ramasundaram, P. (2022). COVID-19 induced lockdown effects on agricultural commodity prices and consumer behaviour in India—Implications for food loss and waste management. *Socio-Economic Planning Sciences, 82*, 101160. https://doi.org/10.1016/j.seps.2021.101160
51. Jaworski, K. (2021). Measuring food inflation during the COVID-19 pandemic in real time using online data: a case study of Poland. *British Food Journal, 123*(13), 260–280. https://doi.org/10.1108/BFJ-06-2020-0532
52. Kayikci, Y., Demir, S., Mangla, S. K., Subramanian, N., & Koc, B. (2022). Data-driven optimal dynamic pricing strategy for reducing perishable food waste at retailers. *Journal of Cleaner Production, 344*. https://doi.org/10.1016/j.jclepro.2022.131068
53. Bechtsis, N., Tsolakis, E. I., & Vlachos, D. (2022). Data-driven secure, resilient and sustainable supply chains: gaps, opportunities, and a new generalised data sharing and data monetisation framework. *International Journal of Production Research, 60*(14), 4397–4417. https://doi.org/10.1080/00207543.2021.1957506
54. Burgos, D., & Ivanov, D. (2021). Food retail supply chain resilience and the COVID-19 pandemic: A digital twin-based impact analysis and improvement directions. *Transportation Research Part E Logistics and Transportation Review, 152*(March), 102412. https://doi.org/10.1016/j.tre.2021.102412
55. Singh, S., Kumar, R., Panchal, R., & Tiwari, M. K. (2021). Impact of COVID-19 on logistics systems and disruptions in food supply chain. *International Journal of Production Research, 59*(7), 1993–2008.
56. Erboz, G., Abbas, H., & Nosratabadi, S. (2022). Investigating supply chain research trends amid Covid-19: a bibliometric analysis. *Management Research Review*. https://doi.org/10.1108/MRR-05-2021-0408
57. Kazancoglu, Y., Ozbiltekin-Pala, M., Sezer, M. D., Luthra, S., & Kumar, A. (2022). Resilient reverse logistics with blockchain technology in sustainable food supply chain management during COVID-19. *Business Strategy and the Environment*. https://doi.org/10.1002/bse.3251
58. Joshi, S., & Sharma, M. (2022). Digital technologies (DT) adoption in agri-food supply chains amidst COVID-19: an approach towards food security concerns in developing countries. *Journal of Global Operations and Strategic Sourcing, 15*(2), 262–282. https://doi.org/10.1108/JGOSS-02-2021-0014
59. Barile, D., Secundo, G., & Del Vecchio, P. (2022). Food 4.0 for competing during the COVID-19 pandemic: experimenting digitalization in family firms. *European Journal of Innovation Management*. https://doi.org/10.1108/EJIM-07-2022-0373
60. Byrd, K., Fan, A., Her, E. S., Liu, Y., Almanza, B., & Leitch, S. (2021). Robot vs human: expectations, performances and gaps in off-premise restaurant service modes. *International Journal of Contemporary Hospitality Management, 33*(11), 3996–4016. https://doi.org/10.1108/IJCHM-07-2020-0721
61. Njomane, L., & Telukdarie, A. (2022). Impact of COVID-19 food supply chain: Comparing the use of IoT in three South African supermarkets. *Technology in Society, 71*(July), 102051. https://doi.org/10.1016/j.techsoc.2022.102051

62. Brem, A., Viardot, E., & Nylund, P. A. (2021). Implications of the coronavirus (COVID-19) outbreak for innovation: Which technologies will improve our lives? *Technological Forecasting and Social Change, 163*, 120451.
63. Troise, C., Corvello, V., Ghobadian, A., & O'Regan, N. (2022). How can SMEs successfully navigate VUCA environment: The role of agility in the digital transformation era. *Technological Forecasting and Social Change, 174*, 121227.
64. Kumar, M., Raut, R. D., Sharma, M., Choubey, V. K., & Paul, S. K. (2022). Enablers for resilience and pandemic preparedness in food supply chain. *Operations Management Research*, 1–26.
65. Sharma, M., Joshi, S., Luthra, S., & Kumar, A. (2022). Managing disruptions and risks amidst COVID-19 outbreaks: role of blockchain technology in developing resilient food supply chains. *Operations Management Research, 15*(1–2), 268–281. https://doi.org/10.1007/s12063-021-00198-9
66. Muszyński, K., Pulignano, V., Domecka, M., & Mrozowicki, A. (2022). Coping with precarity during COVID-19: A study of platform work in Poland. *International Labour Review, 161*(3), 463–485. https://doi.org/10.1111/ilr.12224
67. Chenarides, L., Grebitus, C., Lusk, J. L., & Printezis, I. (2021). Food consumption behavior during the COVID-19 pandemic. *Agribusiness, 37*(1), 44–81. https://doi.org/10.1002/agr.21679
68. Ismajli, A., Mustafa, A., Velijaj, F., & Dobrunaj, L. (2022). The impact of Covid-19 on consumer behaviour and online shopping: the case study in the developing country. *Corporate Governance and Organizational Behavior, 6*(3), 34–43. https://doi.org/10.22495/cgobrv6i3p3
69. Gomes, S., Lopes, J. M., & Oliveira, J. (2023). Online food shopping: determinants and profile of Portuguese buyers in the pandemic context. *Innovar, 33*(87), 73–91. https://doi.org/10.15446/innovar.v33n87.105507
70. Fuentes, C., Samsioe, E., & Östrup Backe, J. (2022). Online food shopping reinvented: developing digitally enabled coping strategies in times of crisis. *The International Review of Retail, Distribution and Consumer Research, 32*(2), 130–150. https://doi.org/10.1080/09593969.2022.2047758
71. Ma, E., Bao, Y., Huang, L., Wang, D., & Kim, M. (2021). When a robot makes your dinner: a comparative analysis of product level and customer experience between the U.S. and Chinese robotic restaurants. *Cornell Hospitality Quarterly*. https://doi.org/10.1177/19389655211052286
72. Alfalih, A. A. (2022). Customer engagement design during the COVID 19 pandemic, mutual trust and intelligent automation: a conceptual perspective. *Journal of Innovation and Entrepreneurship, 11*(1). https://doi.org/10.1186/s13731-022-00222-7
73. Newstex Blogs EU Reporter. (2021). Coronavirus: Commission proposes to strengthen co-ordination of safe travel in the EU.
74. Impact News Service. (2021). State aid—EU Digital COVID Certificate: Commission awards €95 million to boost access to tests.
75. Thai News Service. (2021). European Union: EU Digital COVID Certificate: EU Gateway goes live with seven countries one month ahead of deadline.
76. Food Navigator. (2020). Leveraging AI to reduce COVID-19 risk: It's not enough to rely on test and trace.
77. Impact News Service. (2020). COVID-19 updates from the GEF partnership.
78. Mercer Islands Reporter (Washington). (2021). Bracing for bigger changes in a COVID world | Brunell.
79. IT Food. (2020). EIT food foresight: The impact of COVID-19 on the food sector in Southern Europe.
80. Sequim Gazette (Washington). (2021). Guest opinion: Bracing for bigger changes.
81. Southey, F. (2020). AI drives COVID-19 detection and tracking tech for food manufacturing plants. www.FoodNavigator.com.
82. Impact News Service. (2020). The dark side of digitalization—and how to fix it.

83. CE Noticias Financiarias English. (2021). EU opens consultation on collaborative economy workers for future legislation.
84. Down to Earth. (2021). Food in good times and bad: What did 2020 teach us about the way we eat?.
85. FD (Fair Disclosure) Wire. (2021). Q4 2020 Atacadao SA Earnings Call—Final.
86. McKinsey & Company. (2021). Digital transformation comes to food banks.
87. Mail Online. (2020). Chipotle to open its first digital-only restaurant in New York which has no counter employees or seating, and offers pick-up and delivery only.
88. Newstex Blogs. (2021). Dinner date with data: How F&B retailers can use retail data to drive sales in a post-pandemic world.
89. Gasparro, A., Kang, J., & Stamm, S. (2020). Two months that tore apart the food chain. *The Wall Street Journal* [online]. Available: https://www.wsj.com/articles/two-months-that-tore-apart-the-food-chain-11588174236
90. Financial Times. (2020). Robots ease the strain on US food supply chain; Technology. Artificial intelligence; Coronavirus has heightened demand for machines that can harvest, handle and deliver.
91. Askew, K. (2021). Robotics, AI and the future of food: 'The COVID-19 pandemic is a crisis that robots were built to address'. www.FoodNavigator.com.
92. Viswanathan, V. (2020). Will this crisis change the world of grocery shopping forever? *Forbes* [online]. Available: https://www.forbes.com/sites/forbestechcouncil/2020/06/03/will-this-crisis-change-the-world-of-grocery-shopping-forever/
93. CE Noticias Financieras English. (2020). Ricardo Negri: 'The Covid accelerated digitization in food production'.
94. Down to Earth. (2021). Why healthy food and its local production should be part of the COVID-19 response.
95. Morrison, O. (2020). AI key to safeguarding food systems amid coronavirus: tech firm. www.FoodNavigator.com.
96. Impact News Service. (2020). Helping agri-food businesses with Canada Brand digital marketing during COVID-19.
97. Business Wire. (2022). Global artificial intelligence (AI) market trajectory & analytics, 2020-2021 & 2022-2027: Accelerating pace of digital transformation to benefit demand for AI. www.ResearchAndMarkets.com.
98. Alabi, M. O., & Ngwenyama, O. (2022). Food security and disruptions of the global food supply chains during COVID-19: building smarter food supply chains for post COVID-19 era. *British Food Journal, 125*(1), 167–185. https://doi.org/10.1108/BFJ-03-2021-0333
99. Srivastava, A. (2022). Challenges for evaluation practices and innovative approaches: Lessons during COVID-19 pandemic. *Evaluation and Program Planning, 92*(April), 102095. https://doi.org/10.1016/j.evalprogplan.2022.102095
100. Chotigo, J., & Kadono, Y. (2022). Are there any key factors that encourage food delivery applications use during the COVID-19 pandemic in Thailand and the role of HRM? *Human Systems Management, 41*(2), 177–198. https://doi.org/10.3233/HSM-201140
101. Thongsri, N., Warintarawej, P., Chotkaew, S., & Seksan, J. (2022). A novel extended design thinking approach and predicting antecedents of food friend application acceptance during the COVID-19 outbreak. *Foresight, 24*(3–4), 408–428. https://doi.org/10.1108/FS-01-2021-0021
102. Ivanov, D. (2021). Supply chain viability and the COVID-19 pandemic: a conceptual and formal generalisation of four major adaptation strategies. *International Journal of Production Research, 59*(12), 3535–3552.
103. Kayikci, Y., Kazancoglu, Y., Lafci, C., Gozacan-Chase, N., & Mangla, S. K. (2022). Smart circular supply chains to achieving SDGs for post-pandemic preparedness. *Journal of Enterprise Information Management, 35*(1), 237–265. https://doi.org/10.1108/JEIM-06-2021-0271
104. Vo-Thanh, T., Zaman, M., Hasan, R., Rather, R. A., Lombardi, R., & Secundo, G. (2021). How a mobile app can become a catalyst for sustainable social business: The case of Too Good To Go. *Technological Forecasting and Social Change, 171*, 120962.

105. Bartoli, C., Bonetti, E., & Mattiacci, A. (2022). Marketing geographical indication products in the digital age: a holistic perspective. *British Food Journal, 124*(9), 2857–2876. https://doi.org/10.1108/BFJ-03-2021-0241
106. Schimperna, F., Lombardi, R., & Belyaeva, Z. (2021). Technological transformation, culinary tourism and stakeholder engagement: emerging trends from a systematic literature review. *Journal of Place Management and Development, 14*(1), 66–80. https://doi.org/10.1108/JPMD-03-2020-0028
107. Manika, D., Iacovidou, E., Canhoto, A., Pei, E., & Mach, K. (2022). Capabilities, opportunities and motivations that drive food waste disposal practices: A case study of young adults in England. *Journal of Cleaner Production, 370*(August), 133449. https://doi.org/10.1016/j.jclepro.2022.133449
108. Cricelli, L., Mauriello, R., & Strazzullo, S. (2022). Technological innovation in agri-food supply chains. *British Food Journal.* https://doi.org/10.1108/BFJ-06-2022-0490
109. Sumarliah, E., Li, T., Wang, B., Khan, S. U., & Khan, S. Z. (2023). Blockchain technology adoption in Halal traceability scheme of the food supply chain: evidence from Indonesian firms. *International Journal of Emerging Markets.* https://doi.org/10.1108/IJOEM-05-2021-0678
110. Pandey, V., Pant, M., & Snasel, V. (2022). Blockchain technology in food supply chains: Review and bibliometric analysis. *Technology in Society, 69.* https://doi.org/10.1016/j.techsoc.2022.101954
111. Li, K., Lee, J. Y., & Gharehgozli, A. (2021). Blockchain in food supply chains: a literature review and synthesis analysis of platforms, benefits and challenges. *International Journal of Production Research.* https://doi.org/10.1080/00207543.2021.1970849
112. Ali, M. H., Chung, L., Kumar, A., Zailani, S., & Tan, K. H. (2021). A sustainable Blockchain framework for the halal food supply chain: Lessons from Malaysia. *Technological Forecasting and Social Change, 170.* https://doi.org/10.1016/j.techfore.2021.120870
113. Aamer, A. M., Al-Awlaqi, M. A., Affia, I., Arumsari, S., & Mandahawi, N. (2021). The internet of things in the food supply chain: adoption challenges. *Benchmarking, 28*(8), 2521–2541. https://doi.org/10.1108/BIJ-07-2020-0371
114. Vilalta-Perdomo, E., Salinas-Navarro, D. E., Michel-Villarreal, R., & García Bustamante, R. (2022). Digitalization of the logistics process in short food supply chains. An online viable system model application during the COVID-19 pandemic. *Systemic Practice and Action Research.* https://doi.org/10.1007/s11213-022-09619-7
115. Talamini, G., Li, W., & Li, X. (2022). From brick-and-mortar to location-less restaurant: The spatial fixing of on-demand food delivery platformization. *Cities, 128*(May), 103820. https://doi.org/10.1016/j.cities.2022.103820
116. Lin, J., Li, L., (Robert) Luo, X., & Benitez, J. (2020). How do agribusinesses thrive through complexity? The pivotal role of e-commerce capability and business agility. *Decision Support Systems, 135.* https://doi.org/10.1016/j.dss.2020.113342.
117. Koshta, N., Devi, Y., & Patra, S. (2021). Aerial bots in the supply chain: A new ally to combat COVID-19. *Technology in Society, 66*(March), 101646. https://doi.org/10.1016/j.techsoc.2021.101646
118. Nigro, C., Iannuzzi, E., di Santo, N., & Sisto, R. (2022). Food delivery, ghost kitchens and virtual restaurants: temporary or long-lasting game changers? *British Food Journal, 2021.* https://doi.org/10.1108/bfj-02-2022-0095
119. Sumaedi, S., Sumardjo, A. S., & Syukri, A. F. (2022). Factors influencing millennials' online healthy food information-sharing behaviour during the Covid-19 pandemic. *British Food Journal, 124*(9), 2772–2792. https://doi.org/10.1108/BFJ-06-2021-0656
120. Liu, H., Feng, S., & (Simon) Hu, X. (2022). Process vs. outcome: Effects of food photo types in online restaurant reviews on consumers' purchase intention. *International Journal of Hospitality Management, 102.* https://doi.org/10.1016/j.ijhm.2022.103179
121. Michael, N., & Fusté-Forné, F. (2022). Marketing of luxurious gastronomic experiences on social media: The visual storytelling of luxury hotels. *International Journal of Tourism Research, 24*(6), 827–838. https://doi.org/10.1002/jtr.2548

122. Horng, J. S., Liu, C. H., Chou, S. F., Yu, T. Y., & Ng, Y. L. (2022). Modelling competitive advantage using the concepts of big data and social media to develop a sustainability strategy. *Tourism Review*. https://doi.org/10.1108/TR-01-2022-0012
123. Nilashi, M., Ahmadi, H., Arji, G., Alsalem, K. O., Samad, S., Ghabban, F., Alzahrani, A. O., Ahani, A., & Alarood, A. A. (2021). Big social data and customer decision making in vegetarian restaurants: A combined machine learning method. *Journal of Retailing and Consumer Services, 62*. https://doi.org/10.1016/j.jretconser.2021.102630
124. Wu, L., Fan, A., Yang, Y., & He, Z. (2021). Robotic involvement in the service encounter: a value-centric experience framework and empirical validation. *Journal of Service Management, 32*(5), 783–812. https://doi.org/10.1108/JOSM-12-2020-0448
125. Fusté-Forné, F. (2021). Robot chefs in gastronomy tourism: What's on the menu? *Tourism Management Perspectives, 37*. https://doi.org/10.1016/j.tmp.2020.100774
126. Shams Esfandabadi, H., Ghamary Asl, M., Shams Esfandabadi, Z., Gautam, S., & Ranjbari, M. (2022). Drought assessment in paddy rice fields using remote sensing technology towards achieving food security and SDG2. *British Food Journal, 124*(12), 4219–4233. https://doi.org/10.1108/BFJ-08-2021-0872
127. Alalwan, A. A., Baabdullah, A. M., Dwivedi, Y. K., Rana, N. P., Lal, B., & Raman, R. (2021). Et-moone and marketing relationship governance: The effect of digital transformation and ICT during the COVID-19 pandemic. *Industrial Marketing Management, 98*(September), 241–254. https://doi.org/10.1016/j.indmarman.2021.09.001
128. Ardolino, M., Bacchetti, A., Dolgui, A., Franchini, G., Ivanov, D., & Nair, A. (2022). The impacts of digital technologies on coping with the COVID-19 pandemic in the manufacturing industry: a systematic literature review. *International Journal of Production Research*, 1–24. https://doi.org/10.1080/00207543.2022.2127960
129. Farrish, J., & Edwards, C. (2020). Technostress in the hospitality workplace: is it an illness requiring accommodation? *Journal of Hospitality and Tourism Technology, 11*(1), 83–92.
130. Esposito, B., Sessa, M. R., Sica, D., & Malandrino, O. (2022). Service innovation in the restaurant sector during COVID-19: digital technologies to reduce customers' risk perception. *TQM J, 34*(7), 134–164. https://doi.org/10.1108/TQM-01-2022-0016
131. Parwez, S., & Ranjan, R. (2021). The platform economy and the precarisation of food delivery work in the COVID-19 pandemic Evidence from India. *Work Organisation, Labour & Globalisation, 15*(1), 11–30. https://doi.org/10.13169/WORKORGALABOGLOB.15.1.0011
132. Milkman, R., Elliott-Negri, L., Griesbach, K., & Reich, A. (2020). Gender, class, and the gig economy: The case of platform-based food delivery. *Critical Sociology, 47*(3), 357–372. https://doi.org/10.1177/0896920520949631

Digital Technologies for Sustainable Value in the Food Sector

Haiat Perozzo, Aurelio Ravarini, Emanuele Gabriel Margherita, Alessio Maria Braccini, and Giorgio Occhipinti

Abstract In this paper, we analyse how and to what extent the adoption of digital technologies in the food and retail sector is a driver for the pursuit of sustainability objectives, and therefore for the creation of sustainable value. The in-depth analysis of the literature presents a scenario that scarcely corresponds to the picture drawn by the empirical study. Thanks to a multiple case study on six companies, leaders in the food sector in Italy, it was possible to highlight a general immaturity of the relationship between digital technology decisions and sustainability strategies in this sector. The paper identifies possible reasons for the current state as a basis for future improvements.

Keywords Digital technology · Sustainability · Food industry · Triple bottom line · Industry 4.0

1 Introduction

In parallel with the evolution of the topic of digital transformation, due to the worsening phenomenon of climate change, many companies around the world have paid more attention to environmental sustainability issues [1]. In recent years, in particular, sustainability and digital transformation have seen a strong intersection, assuming particular relevance in society and now becoming one of the most important business elements for both governments and companies [2], as drivers for the achievement of sustainable value creation. The literature makes it

---

H. Perozzo (✉) · A. Ravarini · G. Occhipinti
LIUC Università Carlo Cattaneo, Castellanza-Varese, Italy
e-mail: hperozzo@liuc.it; aravarini@liuc.it; giorgio.occhipinti@bip-group.com

E. G. Margherita · A. M. Braccini
Department of Economics Engineering Society and Business Organisation, Università degli Studi della Tuscia, Viterbo, Italy
e-mail: emargherita@unitus.it; abraccini@unitus.it

A. M. Braccini et al. (eds.), *Digital (Eco) Systems and Societal Challenges*, Lecture Notes in Information Systems and Organisation 72,
https://doi.org/10.1007/978-3-031-75586-6_4

clear that sustainable value can be created through the achievement of 17 Sustainable Development Goals (SDGs) of the 2030 Agenda [3].

The triple bottom line (TBL) is a framework introduced in the late 90s [4] that expands the traditional reporting framework to include environmental and social performance in addition to financial performance, often summarized as "people, planet, profit." This approach underscores that businesses can only thrive long-term when they act responsibly towards society and the environment [5]. As such, the triple bottom line represents a pivotal tool for integrating sustainability into the business agenda. Together, the TBL and SDGs serve as complementary frameworks guiding businesses and governments toward sustainable practices and objectives.

While the UN Agenda calls for the achievement of these objectives by companies of any industry and size, it is evident that even only pursuing them can impact the reputation of any organization: presenting itself as a "sustainable business" helps protecting and promoting the corporate image, as well as creating a potential competitive advantage. However, the question remains whether this approach turns out to be not an actual effort aiming at a "green transition" but merely a façade policy, thus falling—rather—into the so-called "greenwashing phenom".

In parallel with the complex and ambitious changes required by the SDG Agenda, companies of any kind are undergoing a so-called "digital transition", the transformation of the organizations enabled (if not even forced) by the adoption of digital technologies to support an increasingly broad range of activities. According to Vinuesa [3], digital transformation and sustainability initiatives are strongly correlated phenomena. In fact, digital technologies—and Artificial Intelligence in particular [3]—can contribute to the creation of sustainable value.

Not all industrial sectors have been equally committed to undertaking projects aimed at achieving the SDGs. Among those that appear to be most actively engaged is the retail sector, and particularly the food sector. In this sector the critical variables of sustainable value, coherently with those de-fined in general by the 2030 Agenda are: food safety, waste reduction and ethics [2]. At the same time, companies in the food sector see the adoption of digital technologies as a valuable means for pursuing sustainability goals. In fact, the food sector is constantly being affected by the advancement of digital technologies, thus influencing the competitive landscape [6].

Recent research findings show that companies in the food sector are both engaged in sustainability issues and invest in digital technology. However, there in the scientific literature there is scarce evidence about "how" such investments impact the fulfilment of sustainability objectives, and consequently "how much" companies are committed to internalizing technologies for sustainable purposes [2, 3, 7, 8]. To deal with this research gap, in this paper we explore the following re-search meta question: how and in what terms are investments and the adoption of digital technologies in the food sector drivers for the pursuit of sustainability objectives, and therefore for the creation of sustainable value?

This work aims to analyze and discuss the current characteristics and the possible future scenarios of sustainability enabled by digital transformation initiatives in the food sector. In particular, it focuses on the role of Industry 4.0 digital technologies, as potential tools to accelerate their techno-logical evolution and contribute to sustainability objectives, presenting an overview of the current situation of Italian companies operating in the sector, excluding from the analysis all those activities carried out upstream in the supply chain. This is because those activities introduce variables, such as food-lost, on which it is difficult to have visibility, especially for the customer. In this sense, it's difficult to look at sustainable goals, such as social impact.

The paper is structured as follows. We introduce the two main research streams of sustainable value creation and I4.0 technologies enabled digital transformation. The research gap deriving from this literature review is presented as a trigger for an empirical investigation through a multi-case study on five companies, leaders in the Italian food sector. The outcomes of semi-structured inter-views are then discussed, and a general picture of the role played by digital technology to support sustainability in this sector is proposed.

2 Literature Review and Research Gap

2.1 Defining Sustainability: The Triple Bottom Line and the Agenda 2030

Within the academic and practitioners' contexts there is no universally accepted definition of sustainability, and there are numerous synonyms that are often misleading. It is then not surprising that the term "sustainability" is increasingly becoming a "buzzword" adopted in many sectors, thus generating a notional and consequently practical gap. Without a standardized definition, it is also difficult for research to define the perimeter in terms of sustainability and proceed with the classification of the same [9]. In this paper we will use a definition of sustainability based on the Triple Bottom Line and the 2030 Agenda as an action program aiming to achieve a series of sustainable objectives (the Sustainable Development Goals, SDGs).

The Triple Bottom Line is a framework to evaluate organisational sustainability. It was developed by John Elkington in his book titled "Cannibals with Forks" in 1997.

[4] and describe sustainability as a multi-dimensional concept composed by [10–12]:

- Economic dimension: organisational orientation to generate profits that ensure the organisation's financial success in the long run. This dimension is achieved when revenues are greater than costs.
- Environmental dimension: the organisational orientation to mitigate the environmental impact of production activities. This dimension is achieved when the organisation use of resources is compatible with the natural regeneration cycle of the same resources.

- Social dimension: the organisational orientation to improve workforce conditions and the community where the organisation operates. This dimension is achieved when the organisation provides safer workplaces and training to improve workers' competencies.

The further sustainability framework we will use is the 2030 Agenda for Sustainable Development proposed by the United Nations in 2015. It is a global framework that sets 17 SDGS and 169 associated targets. These goals cover a wide range of social, environmental, and economic challenges and opportunities that society may address to achieve sustainability [13]. For instance, the SDG 12 relates to the food and retail sector because it reports objectives to ensure sustainable consumption and production patterns.

Although the SDG framework is a sustainability framework at society level and the triple bottom line at the organisational level, both frameworks conceptualise sustainability composed by three dimensions (economic, environmental and social).

Moreover, both frameworks emphasize the importance of integrating social, environmental, and economic considerations in everyday activities and the strategic orientation of the firms.

Therefore, in this paper, we use these sustainability frameworks to define sustainability as a multi-dimensional concept composed by three dimensions (economic, environmental, social) and Such dimensions can be achieved by following the specific objectives of SDGs.

2.2 The Reference Sector: Food & Retail

Sustainability in the retail trade sector, and more precisely in the food sector, can be seen as a set of ideas, attitudes, intentions and actions that strategically consider economic, environmental and social resources for the betterment of present and future generations [6]. In other words, a sustainability-oriented retailer considers not only short- term economic goals, but also environmental and social concerns for the benefit of present and future generations [6].

The current literature does not provide an exhaustive picture on this issue. The available studies show that sustainability in the retail sector is an emerging theme, linked to multiple business processes and issues such as logistics, transport, cleaner production, elimination of waste from the production process, eco-efficiency. As stated by Ruiz-Real et al. [2], incorporating sustainability into supply chain management requires the integration of sustainable practices along the entire chain to mitigate damage to the environment and society, while generating benefits for the latter. In addition to the placement of recycling bins in retail stores, sustainability includes a comprehensive consideration of the environmental and social impact of the business: from the acquisition of raw materials to the disposal, reuse or recycling of products; from the safety and well-being of employees to the safety and well-being of society at large [2]. Besides the obvious ethical implications, sustainable management offers numerous other benefits to retailers and consumers [2].

Increasingly, companies intend to cope with the competition by changing their supply chain strategies, aiming to make them more sustainable, investing more in supply chain management technology such as Blockchain, AI, analytics, robotic process automation and data control centres [7]. In particular, the growing influence of artificial intelligence in various sectors has given rise to the need to examine its impact on achieving the SDGs. AI has the potential to improve productivity, equality, and environmental outcomes in both the short and long term. Although positive and negative potential impacts of AI on sustainable development have been identified [3], there is no published study that systematically assesses the extent of the impact on all 17 internationally agreed SDGs in the 2030 Agenda. This gap in research is critical, as this leads to overlook one of artificial intelligence's most important sustainability potentials: examination of relevant evidence reveals that AI can facilitate most goals (79%) across all SDGs, mainly through technological improvements that can overcome current limitations [3]. In the face of a consistent competition that began with the advent of discounter retailers, in recent time there has been an exponential growth of investments in digital technology, starting from food-retail stores up to the supermarket chains to the point that technology has become a key and central element to withstand the comparison. Currently it is possible to notice a development of the technologies used for in-store and logistics operations, with the aim of increasing the effectiveness and efficiency of all retail channels. Interestingly, even as the traditional food retail sector becomes more technologically advanced, there has been a parallel resurgence of farmers' markets and street markets [8].

2.3 *Factors Influencing the Creation of Sustainable Value in the Food Sector*

The concept of sustainability is dynamic over time, taking on different nuances in terms of profitability, efficiency and social justice. Despite evolving notions of sustainability, the idea of the consumer remains relevant in the discussion of sustainable production and consumption, since it is seen as a driving force in the market. When it comes to sustainable food production and consumption, the consumers are often portrayed as an obstacle to achieving more sustainable practices, due to their desires and preferences focused on factors often far removed from sustainability. Indeed, companies are therefore encouraged to take the lead in educating consumers and promoting sustainable practices [14]. As mentioned by ASviS [15], the literature shows that the food sector in Italy dedicate a specific attention to SDG 12. This SDG is inherent to sustainable production and consumption and is in turn characterised by a series of sub-targets, each of them referring to a specific factor, the subject of a goal. We can consider such factors as variables that influence the creation of sustainable value in production and consumption.

With regards to the food sector, the sustainability goals can be fulfilled by leveraging on some of these factors (or variables):

- Food safety, which can be traced back to the SDG 12.6 e 12.4;
- Food waste, which corresponds to the SDG 12.3;
- Ethic, which corresponds to the SDG 12.8, 12.a, 12.7, 12.1.

According to studies on food waste, although research and technological development related to food waste is increasing, there is a gap in the study of waste valorisation [2]. Not surprisingly, in addition to minimizing waste, forecasting, stock control and supply chain coordination, the use of waste is often neglected. In this context, the impact of the retail sector is significant and concerns the economy, society and the environment: it represents 10% of global consumer spending, employs 40% of the global workforce and produces 30% of all greenhouse gas emissions. Moreover, according to Naido and Gasparatos (2018) [16], food waste is a social, nutritional and environmental issue of primary importance that affects the sustainability of the food distribution sector as a whole. The reduction of food waste, in the literature, is often associated with the achievement of a circular economy that includes three principles, also known as or the 3Rs: Reduce, Reuse, Recycle [2]. For example, the meat industry is responsible of a significant environmental impact due to the increase in the production of residues, which are often incinerated, landfilled or sent to the smelting process [17].

A factor contributing to food waste is the need to ensure that food is safe for human consumption. From the manufacturers' point of view, contaminated or otherwise unsafe food must be discarded to avoid harm to consumers.

In addition, the retail industry's emphasis on high quality standards for fresh products (in terms of size, shape, weight, colour, and appearance) can lead to products that do not meet those standards being discarded [17]. This is why a well-documented traceability system is needed for quality control in the food chain. Given the challenges of feeding a growing population and the need for a well-documented traceability system for quality control in the food chain, it is urgent to move from the current approach that focuses solely on increasing productivity to prioritizing sustainability.

In some cases, sustainability blends with ethics under the broader category of "green." The ideal of responsible consumer choice is emphasized in this framework of sustainability as an opportunity rather than a challenge. Moreover, there is an increase in the complexity and requests for clarification of the meaning of the term "sustainability", to which, as seen above, it does not yet seem possible to give a clear and concise universal definition. However, even if these strong trends hint at a reconfiguration of the meaning of sustainability, consumers are presented as bearers of sustainability values and attitudes that fail to translate into action. The idea of the sovereign consumer suggests that consumers are asking companies, particularly retailers, to make sustainable choices for them, thus reinforcing the notion of the consumer as a driving force in the market.

2.4 Digital Technologies in the Food Sector

Technological advances have brought relevant benefits to industrial realities, especially since the identification of a set of emerging digital technologies for modernisation of industry named Industry 4.0 technologies [18]. As noted by Rüßmann et al. [19], companies from different industries embrace Industry 4.0 technologies in different ways and at different times. According to the authors, the food industry is one of those that benefits from a greater degree in terms of productivity (Fig. 1).

According to Ferreira et al. [19], digital transformation is a procedure that seeks to improve an organization using communication, computing, connectivity and information technologies to make substantial changes to its characteristics. Organizations are faced with two alternatives: adapt to changing market conditions or risk being

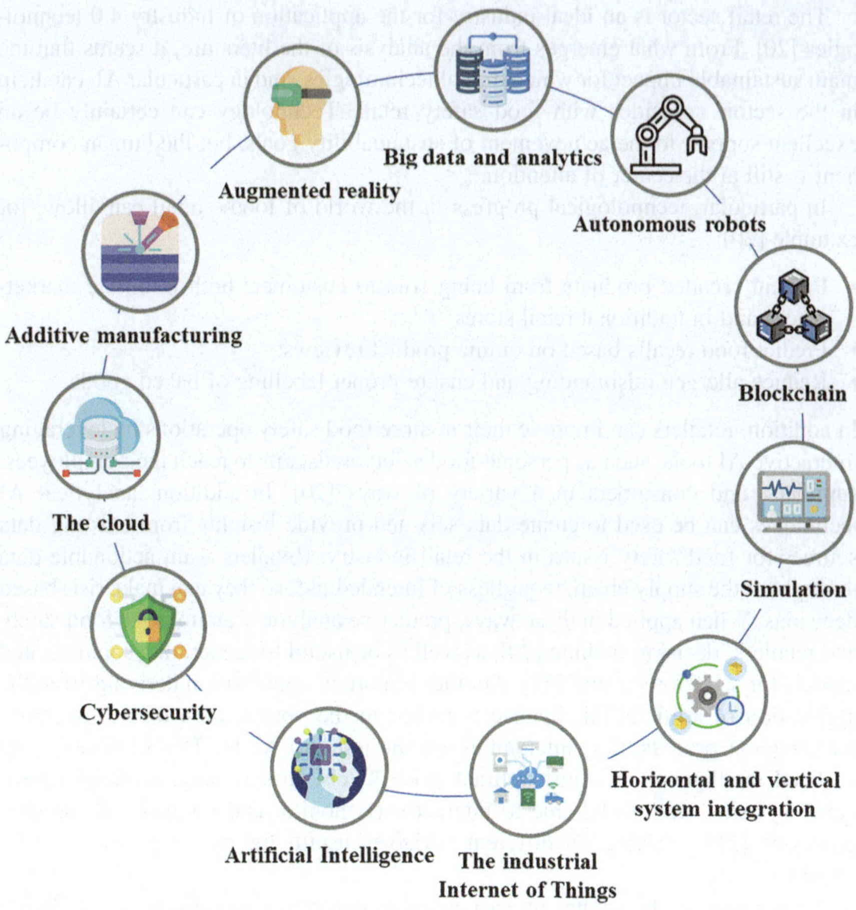

Fig. 1 The technologies of the Industry 4.0 [18]

overtaken by competitors due to reliance on outdated and outdated business strategies, as well as legacy software that can be binding. As a result, organizations must urgently assess their technology architecture and operating model to adapt to the changing landscape. Digital technology has emerged as a crucial enabler for all industries, especially the food-retail sector. The latter, in particular, has seen the most extensive applications of emerging technologies, and its companies recognize the importance of a strong technology presence to remain competitive: some have developed mobile friendly apps and websites to ensure an easy and seamless shopping experience, while others have introduced in-store features such as QR codes that connect to consumers' smartphones to improve the customer experience. It is therefore recognised that a strong technology foundation has the potential to improve retailers' overall performance; however, most organizations have not yet made significant progress in this area, thus missing out on relevant opportunities [19].

The retail sector is an ideal industry for the application of Industry 4.0 technologies [20]. From what emerges from the analysis of the literature, it seems that the main sustainable impact for which digital technologies, and in particular AI, can help in the sector, coincides with food safety retail. Technology can certainly be an excellent support to the achievement of sustainability goals, but the human component is still at the center of attention.

In particular, technological progress in the world of food—retail can allow, for example [20]:

- Prevent recalled products from being sold to customers both in online marketplaces and in traditional retail stores;
- Predict food recalls based on online product reviews;
- Reduce allergen misbranding and ensure proper labelling of baked goods.

In addition, retailers can improve their in-store food safety operations by leveraging interactive AI tools, such as personal food safety assistants to reach their employees, suppliers, and consumers in a variety of ways [20]. In addition, analytical AI techniques can be used to create data sets and provide insights from existing data sources for food safety issues in the retail industry. Retailers want actionable data throughout the supply chain, regardless of intended use, so they can make risk-based decisions. When applied in these ways, predictive analytics can improve food safety and retailers' decision-making [20], as well as be useful for generating sophisticated models for sales forecasting [21]. Another important contribution deriving from the application of artificial intelligence is linked to the optimization of the inventory management process, thus intervening on the issue of waste. This involves using artificial intelligence to adjust optimal stock levels. In summary, artificial intelligence systems seem to be able to interactively monitor and optimize all logistics processes [21], insisting on different variables useful for pursuing sustainability objectives.

To summarize, the studies on sustainability describe a scenario in which digital technology has a great potential as a leverage to enable fulfilling sustainability goals. On the contrary, there is little empirical evidence (and, in particular, within the food-retail sector) about how this potential is put at work and if and how such goals are being achieved. To explore the gap between the current state of sustainability in the food retail sector and the picture portrayed by the literature we developed two research questions: RQ1: to what extent the digital technologies adopted by companies in the food-retail sector have an impact on the variables that influence the creation of sustainable value?; RQ2: to what extent investments in digital technologies in the food-retail sector are driven by the pursuit of sustainability goals?

3 Research Methodology: Multicase Case Study Approach

A qualitative research approach is suitable because it allows researchers to "comprehend those under study from their viewpoint" [22]. Indeed, such an approach is "designed to assist researchers in grasping the perspectives of individuals and the societal and cultural contexts that shape their lives" [23].

We adopt the multiple-case-study approach, consistent with the fact that "the case study method explores a contemporary limited system (one case) or multiple time-limited systems (cases), through detailed and in-depth data collection involving multiple sources of information and reports a description of the case and themes of the case" [24]. The purpose of adopting a case study approach is the ability to explore a specific phenomenon in a limited system, such as multiple time-limited systems, "within its real-life context" [25] and seek an in-depth understanding of the people and cultural and social contexts in which they live.

Data collection was mainly carried out through six semi-structured interviews lasting 45 min on average. Each interview was transcribed and annotated. We interviewed six key informants of six companies, belonging to the food-retail sector in Italy, took part in the study. These companies have different sizes, different approaches regarding the adoption of digital technologies useful for the pursuit of sustainability goals.

Participants were selected based on their role, knowledge of the subject of study and experience. We aimed to interview people from different business functions to understand different perspectives; those who are directly involved in IT and sustainability, and those who are far from it (but may be indirectly affected by decisions and/or changes). We further collected secondary data in form of internal documentation of the studied organisations.

The interview track was developed starting from the literature. Main themes are related to the analysis of the implemented digital technologies and the sustainable value described under a triple bottom line approach (see Table 1).

Table 1 Interview canvas

ID	Question
Analysis of technology and context of use	
1	What are the industry 4.0 technologies you use?
2	What are the features of technology 4.0?
3	In which working practices is technology 4.0 used?
4	How did you do the same work practices before?
5	Did technology 4.0 create problems during the adoption phase?
6	Does technology 4.0 have any critical issues when it is in use?
7	Is the Industry 4.0 updated over the time?
Creation of economic value	
9	What are the operational advantages of technology 4.0? (get practical examples)
10	What costs have been reduced?
Creation of environmental value	
11	Is the aspect of environmental sustainability taken into account?
12	Do technologies allow the reduction of the use of raw materials and energy?
13	Using the circular economy framework of 3-Rs (reduce, reuse, recycle), what practices have started and does the technology support any of them? Do you recycle products? Or do you reuse products?
Creation of social value	
14	Who uses the new technology 4.0?
15	Has the worker been retrained?
16	Or, have you hired new staff to use technology 4.0?
17	What training activities have been put in place to prepare the worker for the use of 4.0 technologies?
18	Has a new organizational unit been opened to manage technology 4.0?
19	What other organizational units are involved in the use of artificial intelligence?
20	What are the benefits that technology 4.0 has brought to workers?
21	Has the adoption of technology 4.0 improved any aspect of security in the company?

4 The Case Studies

The sample interviewed consisted of six companies, which have the characteristics summarized in the following Table 2.

4.1 Company A

Company A is a contemporary meat distribution platform that supports meat processing and processing operations. The subject interviewed was the Plant Manager.

The company declares that the main driver in terms of sustainability is the protection of the environment. With regard to the technologies used, we see the

Table 2 Characteristics of the interviewees

Company	Description	Interviewed
A	Modern meat distribution platform.	Plant manager
B	System of supermarkets, hypermarkets and superettes managed by Italian cooperatives.	Supply chain manager
C	Leading Italian company in the sector that manages supermarkets and super stores in northern and Central Italy.	IT manager
D	Mobile application for retailers and restaurateurs.	P&C business partner
E	On-demand courier service that buys, collects and delivers the products ordered through its application.	Head of micro fulfillment centers
F	Italian company that owns brands related to the food sector, especially meat and animal feed.	CIO

use of SKIN technology, a packaging system characterized by a support of a protective film, and RFID, an automatic identification technology based on the propagation of electromagnetic waves in the air, especially in logistics, with the aim of reducing any waste.

4.2 *Company B*

Company B is a system of supermarkets, hypermarkets and superettes managed by Italian cooperatives. The interviewee held the role of head of the fresh supply chains. The company aims above all to reduce waste, mainly using information deriving from the use of technologies such as RFID and QR code.

4.3 *Company C*

Company C is a leading Italian company that manages supermarkets and superstores in northern and central Italy. The IT Manager interviewed claims to use AI primarily to make sales forecasts. In addition to this, it claims to use RFID and Blockchain to improve traceability along the supply chain.

4.4 *Company D*

Company D is a courier service on request that buys, collects and delivers the products ordered through its application. The interviewee was a P&C Business Partner.

The company is active above all in terms of raising awareness of sustainability. At the technology level, the company is exploring the use of artificial intelligence, but so far there is no actual use. In addition, as a demonstration of its commitment to sustainability, the company is initiating numerous collaborations with third parties in order to reduce waste downstream of the supply chain.

4.5 Company E

Company E is a technological platform that operates in food and home service.

The interviewee, who held the role of Head of Micro-fulfillment centers, declares that the company is attentive to the use and use of sustainable packaging, as well as in the recovery of surplus food. In terms of technologies, the company claims to use innovative technologies to improve delivery efficiency and to optimize waste management.

4.6 Company F

Company F is a leading company in the production and distribution of meat and feed.

Regarding digitization, the CIO of the company declares to use mainly functional technologies, for example, to achieve the labeling part of the products, or for weighing, or for handling, as well as 3D printing. In particular, the CIO declares that it uses the machines mainly upstream of the production process.

The introduction of these technologies has led to the emergence of two categories of problems in the company: technological and social. About the latter, the company declares itself attentive to the creation of social value within the company, especially with regard to the well-being of employees, using technologies to facilitate repetitive activities, and the training of the same. At the environmental level, Company F is committed to ESG and the Digital Supply Chain.

Finally, the CIO declares that Industry 4.0 technology adoption deliveries practices that improve production efficiency that simultaneously support environmental sustainability with a reduction of raw materials and scraps.

The creation of economic value, and therefore the reduction of costs, is a natural consequence of the use of Industry 4.0 technologies.

It is important to highlight that interviews were performed in different points in time, and the interview canvas was improved through time based on the theoretical sampling performed on the data collected so far. Regarding the data analysis, we followed established guidelines to ensure rigor in our analysis [26]. More specifically, we employed as a sensitive device the sustainable value of digital technologies on the triple bottom line [27]. Our analysis went through numerous iterations to formulate a consensus of coding among authors a coherent story [28].

5 Research Outcomes and Discussion

The interviews revealed that companies operating in the food-retail sector are aware of the emergency in terms of food waste: the food industry is facing a series of complex challenges, ranging from soil degradation and water scarcity to climate change and food waste. In this context, all the companies interviewed say they are working to promote sustainability in the food industry, from a social, economic and environmental point of view. To pursue these objectives, the companies show commitment to integrating digital technologies into processes. As with the commitment to achieving sustainability goals, also about the level of digitalisation, some companies surveyed were more mature and others less so. The following is a summary of the results and a merger of these.

Comparing the profile just presented with the characteristic one of the companies interviewed, it is possible to observe how the one most overlapping with that defined by the literature is that of Company B. It is no coincidence that this is a company that represents an intermediate situation compared to all the others interviewed: Company C turns out to be the most advanced in terms of digital technologies, while the rest seem to chase the latter. From an environmental point of view, all companies, in particular Company D and E, are founded on a business that focuses on sustainability, while Company C seems to be very active to put the latter at the center of its business model.

Also, considering the main variables identified starting from the 2030 Agenda, with reference to SDG 12, it is possible to report a clear result obtained from the interviews conducted with the five companies operating in the reference sector.

The commitment of companies is not limited to the human and social aspect, but also sees the attempted use of some technologies such as blockchain, AI and RFID, to reduce waste. More specifically, most of the companies, except Company C, have begun to explore or have already experimented with the use of RFID to track inventory in real time and reduce waste.

At the level of digitalization, it emerged that only Company C recognizes the potential of technology, in particular blockchain, to promote transparency and food safety in the supply chain. It therefore emerges that it is a variable for which end consumers increasingly require attention from companies, but upstream of the chain the companies in question do not make important investments to meet this demand from the end user. It is important to highlight how, in this case, the traceability of the products remains rather internal, but it is not given visibility to the end customer.

Another important aspect of sustainability in the food industry is the need to raise awareness and promote consumer and stakeholder education. Companies such as Company B and Company D stress the importance of educating young people about the environmental impact of food waste and promoting sustainable food practices. Company B emphasizes the role of education in fostering a culture of sustainability and empowering consumers to make informed choices. By promoting sustainable food practices and educating consumers, companies can help reduce the environmental impact of the food system.

After analysing the interviews, it is evident that artificial intelligence (AI) is a rapidly growing field, which seems to have significant potential to contribute to sustainability efforts in various sectors. Companies interviewed talked about using AI to promote sustainability by reducing waste and increasing the efficiency of their operations. Company C is the only one to claim to use artificial intelligence within its processes, especially about demand forecasting, declaring, in fact, that it is possible to buy it from external suppliers or develop it internally. Probably this gap is due once again to the different sizes that companies present and the consequent investment power in technologies with a high cost of implementation. On the other hand, the fact that in other companies AI is only in the incubation phase does not allow us to be objective and prepared about whether to consider the technology sustainable or not, even if companies seem to be quite sure of the positive impacts that could derive from its introduction into business processes. The only reliable testimony in this regard is that of the C company which, as seen above, claims to use AI to perform a better demand forecast and reports that it is sustainable both from a cost point of view and regarding the containment of food waste and the consequent environmental impact.

To conclude, our study shows that digital technologies are a valid strategy for pursuing sustainability goals, especially when applied in production. Indeed, we show in Company F that adopting digital technologies may support environmental sustainability even if it is not considered an objective of the technologies. Therefore, in order to exploit the full potential of digital technologies for sustainability, managers should have a more comprehensive vision tailormade sustainable value creation of digital technologies and not only focus on economic sustainability [29].

6 Conclusions and Further Research

The diffusion of digital technologies within Italian companies in the food sector is constantly growing, even if mainly used within specific business processes. It emerged that the adoption of digital technologies within food companies is often not directly functional to the pursuit of sustainability objectives.

Moreover, the empirical investigation conducted allows us to observe how reality is not aligned with what is reported in the literature. Indeed, if on the one hand the literature states that the Italian food-retail sector has an excellent investment potential in digital technologies to pursue sustainability objectives, it would seem rather that companies are not committing themselves to this sense. Moreover, this study proposes future research avenues. First, since Industry 4.0 is mainly adopted in production, it is interesting to investigate how the chief operating officer cooperates with CIO to manage the digital transformation. Second, the study pinpoints the variety of digital technologies adopted for sustainable development. Thus, further studies should investigate this relationship using a multisectoral perspective or compare different digital transformation paths for sustainable development in different countries.

References

1. de Freitas Netto, S. V., Sobral, M. F. F., Ribeiro, A. R. B., & Soares, G. R. D. L. (2020). Concepts and forms of greenwashing: A systematic review. *Environmental Sciences Europe, 32*(1), 1–12.
2. Ruiz-Real, J. L., Uribe-Toril, J., Gázquez-Abad, J. C., & de Pablo Valenciano, J. (2019). Sustainability and retail: Analysis of global research. *Sustainability, 11*(1), 14. https://www.mdpi.com/2071-1050/11/1/14/htm
3. Vinuesa, R., Azizpour, H., Leite, I., Balaam, M., Dignum, V., Domisch, S., et al. (2020). The role of artificial intelligence in achieving the sustainable development goals. *Nature Communications, 11*(1), 233.
4. Elkington, J. (1997). *Cannibals with forks: The triple bottom line of 21st century business*. Capstone.
5. McDonough, W., & Braungart, M. (2002). Design for the triple top line: New tools for sustainable commerce. *Corporate Environmental Strategy, 9*(3), 251–258.
6. Vadakkepatt, G. G., Winterich, K. P., Mittal, V., Zinn, W., Beitelspacher, L., Aloysius, J., et al. (2021). Sustainable retailing. *Journal of Retailing, 97*(1), 62–80.
7. Gong, S. (2023). Digital transformation of supply chain management in retail and e-commerce. *International Journal of Retail & Distribution Management*. https://www.emer-ald.com/insight/content/doi/10.1108/IJRDM-02-2023-0076/full/html?skipTracking=true
8. Stanton, R. L., Morrissey, C. A., & Clark, R. G. (2018). Analysis of trends and agricultural drivers of farmland bird declines in North America: A review. *Agriculture, Ecosystems & Environment, 254*, 244–254.
9. Moore, J. E., Mascarenhas, A., Bain, J., & Straus, S. E. (2017). Developing a comprehensive definition of sustainability. *Implementation Science, 12*(1), 1–8.
10. Alhaddi, H. (2015). Triple bottom line and sustainability: A literature review. *Business and Management studies, 1*(2), 6–10. https://doi.org/10.11114/bms.v1i2.752
11. Braccini, A. M., & Margherita, E. G. (2019). Exploring organisational sustainability of industry 4.0 under the triple bottom line: The case of a manufacturing company. *Sustainability, 11*(1), 36. https://doi.org/10.3390/su11010036
12. Hartmann, B. (2020). Triple bottom line. In *Accounting for sustainability* (pp. 101–110).
13. Delle Nazioni Unite, O. (2015). Risoluzione adottata dall'Assemblea Generale il 25 settem- bre 2015. Trasformare il nostro mondo: l'Agenda 2030 per lo Sviluppo Sostenibile, n. 70/1.
14. Ehgartner, U. (2018). Discourses of the food retail industry: Changing understandings of 'the consumer' and strategies for sustainability. *Sustainable Production and Consumption, 16*, 154–161. https://www.sciencedirect.com/science/arti-cle/abs/pii/S2352550918301386
15. ASviS, L. (2021). *'Italia e gli obiettivi di sviluppo sostenibile* (Rapporto ASviS 2020). Asvis.
16. Naidoo, M., & Gasparatos, A. (2018). Corporate environmental sustainability in the retail sector: Drivers, strategies and performance measurement. *Journal of Cleaner Production, 203*, 125–142.
17. Lagorio, A., & Pinto, R. (2021). Food and grocery retail logistics issues: A systematic literature review. *Research in Transportation Economics, 87*, 100841.
18. Rüßmann, M., Lorenz, M., Gerbert, P., Waldner, M., Justus, J., Engel, P., & Harnisch, M. (2015). Industry 4.0: The future of productivity and growth in manufacturing industries. *Boston Consulting Group, 9*(1), 54–89. https://inovasyon.org/images/Haberler/bcgperspectives_Industry40_2015.pdf
19. Ferreira, J. J., Fernandes, C. I., & Ferreira, F. A. (2020). Technology transfer, climate change mitigation, and environmental patent impact on sustainability and economic growth: A comparison of European countries. *Technological Forecasting and Social Change, 150*, 119770.
20. Friedlander, A., & Zoellner, C. (2020). Artificial intelligence opportunities to improve food safety at retail. *Food Protection Trends, 40*(4), 272–278.
21. Weber, F. D., & Schütte, R. (2019). *State-of-the-art and adoption of artificial intelligence in retailing*. Digital Policy, Regulation and Governance.

22. Gorman, G. E., Clayton, P. R., Shep, S. J., & Clayton, A. (2005). *Qualitative research for the information professional: A practical handbook*. Facet Publishing.
23. Myers, M. D. (1997). Qualitative research in information systems. *MIS Quarterly, 21*, 241–242. https://doi.org/10.2307/249422
24. Creswell, J. W. (2013). *Research design: Qualitative, quantitative, and mixed methods Approaches* (4th ed.). SAGE Publications, Inc.
25. Yin, R. K. (2013). *Case study research: Design and methods*. Sage Publications.
26. Strauss, A. L., & Corbin, J. (1990). *Basics of qualitative research: Grounded theory procedures and techniques*. Sage.
27. Margherita, E. G., & Braccini, A. M. (2020). Organizational impacts on sustainability of industry 4.0: A systematic literature review from empirical case studies. In R. F. Agrifoglio, R. Lamboglia, & D. Mancini (Eds.), *Digital business transformation* (Lecture notes in information systems and organisation). Springer. https://doi.org/10.1007/978-3-030-47355-6_12
28. Glaser, B. G., & Strauss, A. L. (2017). *Discovery of grounded theory: Strategies for qualitative research*. Routledge. https://doi.org/10.4324/9780203793206
29. Kamble, S. S., Gunasekaran, A., & Gawankar, S. A. (2018). Sustainable Industry 4.0 framework: A systematic literature review identifying the current trends and future perspectives. *Process Safety and Environmental Protection, 117*, 408–425.

The Non-adoption of Digital Technologies in the Agricultural Industries: A Systematic Literature Review

Laura Roma, Chiara Cagnetti, Alessio Maria Braccini, and Rocco Agrifoglio

Abstract Digital transformation (DT) entails radical and continuous organisational changes, including agricultural sector. Agricultural industries are in a phase of constant evolution in which traditional production techniques are becoming increasingly digitised. Recently, studies on DT and digital technologies in agricultural industries have increased. Studies focus only on the adoption of digital technologies and patterns of adoption. There is a lack of studies exploring the reasons for the non-adoption of digital technologies in agricultural industries. In this study, we present the result of a systematic literature review (SLR) that identifies the leading digital technologies and the factors to the non-adoption of digital technologies in agricultural industries. The main factors of non-adoptions are identified in technological organizational and environmental contexts. The article presents implications for research and practice.

Keywords Digital technologies · Non-adoption technologies · Agricultural industries · Agriculture 4.0 · Digital transformation

1 Introduction

Digital transformation (DT) has gained immense importance in recent years in industries as it brings about change and boosts productivity and opportunities for value creation [1]. With the reliance on modern digital technologies, industries are altering their production processes to become more automated, improving

L. Roma (✉) · R. Agrifoglio
Department of Business and Economics, University of Naples "Parthenope", Naples, Italy
e-mail: laura.roma001@studenti.uniparthenope.it; rocco.agrifoglio@uniparthenope.it

C. Cagnetti · A. M. Braccini
Department of Economics, Engineering, Society and Business Organization, University of Tuscia, Viterbo, Italy
e-mail: chiara.cagnetti@unitus.it; abraccini@unitus.it

A. M. Braccini et al. (eds.), *Digital (Eco) Systems and Societal Challenges*, Lecture Notes in Information Systems and Organisation 72,
https://doi.org/10.1007/978-3-031-75586-6_5

production management, planning and business organisation [2]. Like all other industries, agriculture is also engaged with DT, but, with peculiar contextual conditions.

The agricultural sector is vital to any economy as it provides the raw materials necessary for human nutrition [3]. Agricultural production processes are complex and heavily influenced by natural factors. Improving agricultural industries processes is crucial to addressing wicked problems and relevant societal challenges such as famine, sustainability and economic and social development [4]. DT of the agricultural industries can help address these challenges, introducing transformation in how labour, technology and organisation are enacted in organisations in the industry [2, 5, 6]. Indeed, the industry has been on an evolutionary path concerning DT, exploring increasingly digitalised production systems [7], but on average, the level of digitalisation in the industry is still low. For instance, according to national statistics, in Italy, the digitalisation of the agricultural industries interests 26.1% of organisations but only 6% of the total cultivated land in the country [8]. Despite its relevance and evolution, DT in agricultural industries is mostly addressed in agroeconomic studies [9, 10], focusing on the enabling factors of emerging digital technologies [9–13].

We find that the debate on DT in agricultural industries is mostly neglected in the information system literature and the debate on agroeconomic studies mostly focuses on the factors favouring the adoption of digital technologies in agriculture. Considering that digitalisation in the industries is emerging, we believe it is relevant to explore the factors motivating the lack of adoption of digital technologies in the industries rather than the enabling factors. In this regard, in this paper, we run a systematic literature review (SLR) to identify the factors to the non-adoption of digital technologies in agricultural industries. Consequently, this paper addresses the following research question: *What are the factors influencing to the non-adoption of digital technologies in agricultural industries?*

The paper is structured as follows. Section 2 contextualises the concept of digitisation of agriculture within the TOE framework to explain the barriers to non-adoption. Section 3 introduces the methodology used to conduct an SLR and Sect. 4 presents the results. Section 5 introduces the discussion and finally, Sect. 6 reports the conclusions and implications of the study.

2 Digital Transformation in the Agricultural Industries

Agricultural industries have slowly adopted digital technologies and the transition is taking longer than other sectors [14]. However, pieces of evidence show that through the implementation of such technologies, the industries stand to gain numerous benefits. These include collecting valuable data for decision-making and environmental impact, streamlining processes, exchanging knowledge and learning, addressing wicked societal problems and ultimately replacing strenuous human work with machines [15–19]. The adoption of digital technologies in agriculture began with Precision Agriculture in the 1980s, which used information technology to gather data to support decision-making. With the onset of the Industrial Revolution, the agricultural industries shifted from machine-drive production to a more quasi-digital production.

In literature, various terms describe digital technologies used in agriculture, such as agriculture 4.0, digital agriculture, smart agriculture and e-farming [11, 19–23]. This paper will use Agriculture 4.0 to integrate modern digital technologies into agricultural production processes to reduce production costs, increase productivity and minimise environmental impacts [21, 24]. The idea of Agriculture 4.0 is to use data collected from soil and livestock with digital sensors to inform decision-making [20, 23, 25]. This approach aims to assist organisations in the agricultural industries in effectively managing crops and livestock [20]. Agriculture 4.0 uses a varied set of digital technologies for such needs.

2.1 *Digital Technologies Portfolio*

Agricultural industries use many emerging digital technologies. Digital technologies stimulate process automation by using specialised labour that can increase the efficiency and profitability of agricultural industries [4, 9, 26] and reduce environmental impacts [27]. Several digital technologies used are the Internet of Things (IoT), sensors, blockchain, machine learning and artificial intelligence [16].

Technologies can collect data in real-time, analyse them and process information useful for decision-making [18, 28].

Each technology has many applications, frequently used in a systemic integration with other technologies. For instance, the IoT infrastructure integrates the blockchain platform for tracking and tracing products or with sensors for collecting data directly from the fields [29]. There are many technologies used in agricultural industries and identified in the literature.

For a simpler view, Table 1 below summarises the most relevant digital and, in some cases, automated technologies in agriculture. We have divided the technologies into four groups for simplicity [30].

Table 1 Summary of digital technologies

Aims of technology	Technology
Data collection	Radio Frequency Identification (RFID), Sensors, Mobile phones, GPS, GNSS, Microcontroller, Mechanised machines, Autonomous vehicles, Machinery navigation systems, Drones, E-commerce, Mobile apps
Data transmission	Bluetooth, Wi-Fi, Satellite, Cable internet connection, Internet, 2G/3G/4G//5G
Data storage	Cloud computing, Big data, Blockchain, Excel
Data processing	Machine learning, AI, Data analytics, FMIS, GIS, DSS, Virtual and Augmented reality, Image processing

2.2 Theoretical Framework: Technology, Organisation, Environment (TOE)

Considering that factors associated with the lack of adoption of digital technologies in agricultural industries can span different domains (individual, organisational, environmental), in this paper, we adopt the Technology Organisation and Environment (TOE) as the main theoretical framework [31]. Tornatzky and Fleischer, in 1990, proposed the TOE framework to explain technology adoption in organisations. Compared to rival theoretical models, the TOE acknowledges that internal and external factors influence adoption [32]. The model posits that the process of adoption is influenced by the technological context *(technology)*, organisational context (*organisation)* and environmental context (*environment*).

The *technology* in the model refers to the characteristics of the technologies in use, including their functional characteristics and perceived complexity and easiness of use. The *organisation* in the model refers to the focal entity adopting the technology and its internal context in which it will be used, including factors such as size, structure, culture and resources [33]. Finally, the *environment* refers to the organisational context and encompasses social and cultural norms, market structures and regulatory conditions [34].

Many studies use the TOE framework thanks to it is substantially abstract, encompasses high-level variables and considers the combined effects of individual factors on the adoption process [35]. Concerning alternative models explaining factors influencing the adoption process, the TOE disregards the individual perspective used, e.g. the theory of reasoned action or the technology acceptance model. The TOE model avoids the individual biases present when an individual respondent has to report on organisational phenomena [36]. For this reason, we are using it in the current paper [37].

The TOE model has already been used in the literature to classify the barriers to digital technology adoption in Industry 4.0 projects [38] or identify and rank specific technologies' adoption factors [39]. Also, in the context of DT in agricultural industries studies, the TOE model was used to classify digital technology adoption factors [40]. In our work, TOE assumes that the same theoretical understanding explaining factors influencing the adoption process also holds validity for non-adoption [34, 41]. Therefore, this paper will use the TOE model to inform the literature review results to explore the impacts of the relationships between barriers to non-adoption of digital technologies. We classify the emerging factors into the three domains of the TOE model.

3 Methodology

We conduct a systematic literature review (SLR) to understand the non-adoption in the agricultural sector. SLR is a "methodology that locates existing studies, selects and evaluates contributions, analyses and synthesises data and reports the evidence in such a way that allows reasonably clear conclusions to be reached about what is and is not known" ([42], p. 671). Scholars such as Elsbach and van Knippenberg [43] have recognised the usefulness of such reviews in providing a comprehensive understanding of existing literature. According to Snyder [44], a systematic literature reviews can tackle research questions that no single study can address by integrating perspectives from various empirical findings. Furthermore, Hulland and Houston [45] and Paul and Criado [46] suggested that systematic literature reviews create value by providing readers with a state-of-the-art understanding of extant knowledge, identifying gaps and inconsistencies and signalling avenues for future research to advance knowledge in the review domain.

SLR is "less of a discussion of the literature and more of a scientific tool" ([47], p. 10) because answering test hypotheses and theories needs defined and rigorous criteria of SLR to avoid emerging and recursive errors or biases [47–49].

Our research based on the PRISMA (Preferred Reporting Items for Systematic Reviews and Meta-Analyses) model [50], which is illustrated by a flow diagram that outlines the stages of identification, screening and eligibility. Such model was recognised as critical to conduct a thorough and comprehensive literature search in order to ensure that all relevant studies are included in the analysis.

The phases of our SLR are (1) data collection, in which the dataset is made of records selected by one database and (2) data analysis, in which the final dataset is descriptively analysed [51].

3.1 Data Collection

The first step in collecting data was to find a suitable source covering scientific journals, books, and peer-reviewed conference proceedings for a systematic literature search. We decided to choose SCOPUS, one of the most widely used academic literature search and selection research engines. To define a comprehensive dataset, we determined a search string by using some subject terms, such as "barrier to adoption" (alternatively, "barrier to use," "barrier to acceptance," "barrier to usage," "no adoption," "non-adoption," and "not to adopt"), "technology" (alternatively "ICT" and "IT") and "agrifood" (alternatively "agriculture") in title, abstract or among keywords. Bibliometric methods [52] suggest using wild cards to include both singular and plural expressions of keywords. The subject terms were based on the mentioned managerial literature related to organisation adoption. The subject terms allowed us to have 125 results corresponding to papers published from the starting date to May 2023.

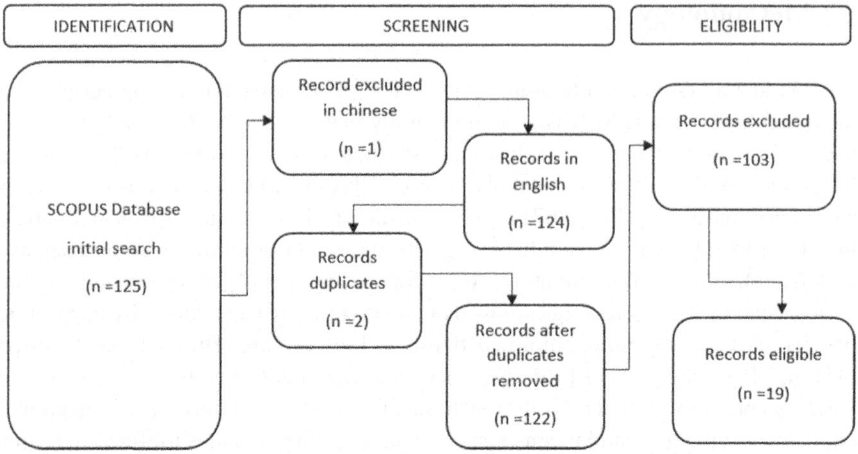

Fig. 1 Flow diagram for the selection of literature reviewed based on PRISMA

We used the PRISMA method to select the results of interest in the flowchart (Fig. 1). The inclusion and exclusion criteria avoid search mistakes. The Scopus database allows us to obtain 125 records. Then, we excluded (a) two results because they are duplicated and (b) one result because it is not written in English (Chinese), so we obtained a dataset of 123 records. Finally, we checked publications for eligibility. This way, papers that did not match our research aims were excluded (n. 103). After the screening and eligibility processes, the final dataset for the subsequent analysis consisted of 19 publications.

3.2 Data Analysis

The second step, Dataset Analysis, is a descriptive examination of the sample of 19 publications to obtain information on publication trends over the years (Fig. 2), document by type (Fig. 3), documents by subject area (Fig. 4) and documents by country (Fig. 5).

The research field of technology non-adoption in agricultural industries has the first publications in 2007 and 2008 (Fig. 2); however, the interest in this research field increased since 2016.

Figure 3 shows the sources in the original dataset: mainly journal articles (89.5%), followed by conference proceedings (10.5%).

The final dataset is composed of a few records, which belong to different sub-area, such as Agricultural and Biological Sciences (28.2%), Social Sciences (17.9%), Computer Science (10.3%), Engineering (7.7%), Environmental Science (7.7%), Economics, Econometrics and Finance (5.1%), Energy (5.1%), Multidisciplinary (5.1%), Business, Management and Accounting (2.6%), Chemical Engineering (2.6%) and in other (7.7%) Materials Science, Medicine and Veterinary

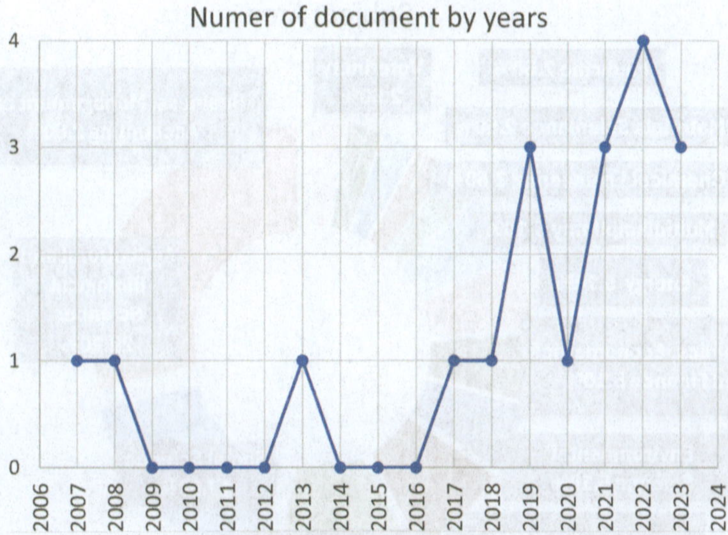

Fig. 2 Document by years

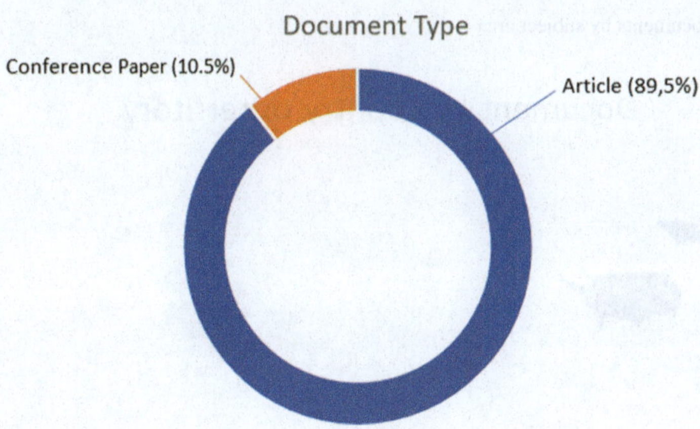

Fig. 3 Document by type

(Fig. 4). For this not homogeneous final dataset, it is difficult to identify the main authors who wrote about this research field.

In the SLR, the main countries or territories analysed in the non-adoption technologies in agriculture industries are the USA (in 5 studies), the UK (in 3 studies) and China, Australia, Netherlands and New Zealand in 2 studies (Fig. 5).

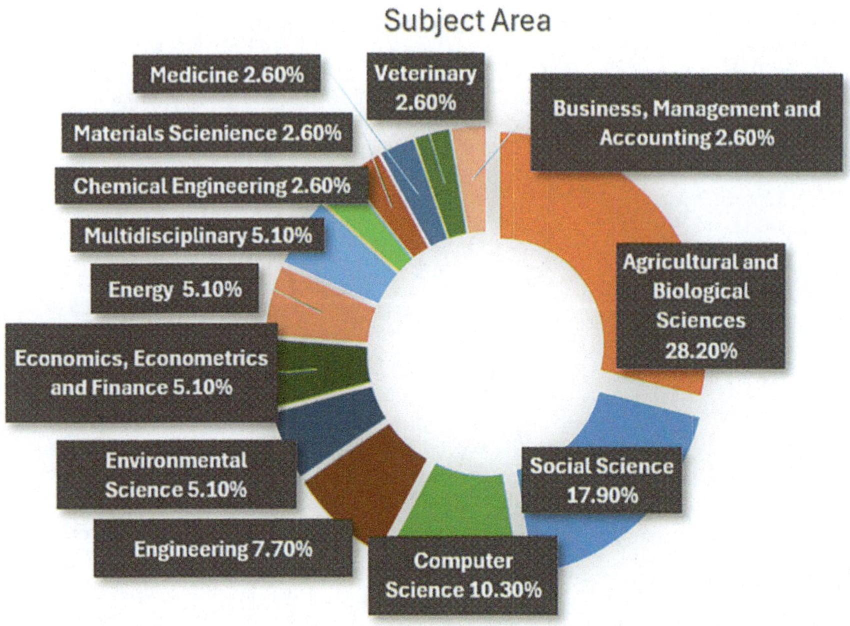

Fig. 4 Documents by subject area

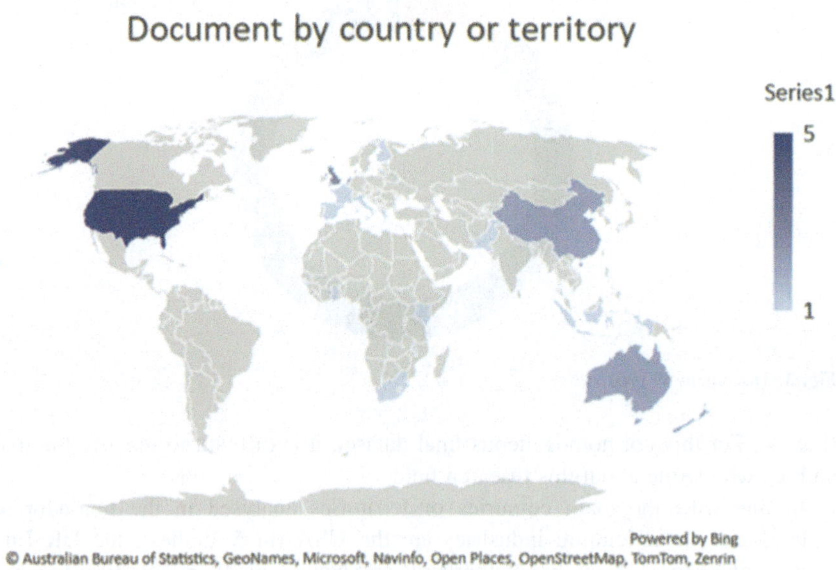

Fig. 5 Documents by country

4 Results

The final dataset was also analysed to obtain information about (1) the main technology adopted and (2) the technology adoption barriers in agricultural industries.

Table 2 shows a list of the digital technologies used in agricultural industries.

Table 3 lists technology adoption barriers in the agricultural industries we identified by analysing the final dataset results. The barriers are classified in the three dimensions of the TOE framework.

4.1 Organisational Barriers

The organizational structure of such farms is heavily influenced by several factors, including gender, age, education and work experience of the farmer. One significant factor in the non-adoption of technologies is gender, which found to be relevant with respect to both knowledge of technologies and propensity to use them. Women, for example [61, 66], tend to be more cautious when it comes to the use of technology. However, some studies have suggested that gender may not actually have any impact on the non-adoption of technology [54] Interestingly, there are also studies that suggest men may be more reluctant to use technology compared to women who may be more inclined to embrace it [63, 69].

Age is a significant determinant of potential innovation, considering that the elderly demographic tends to be more hesitant to change [54] and less inclined to prioritize long-term economic benefits [61, 69] Conversely, the dearth of young people [54] influences non-adoption of technologies in agricultural sector due to the fact that younger people are typically more familiar with and have greater access to the latest technological advancements and information [66, 68]. However, young people have less experience in the field and, therefore, less knowledge of the agricultural environment. Moreover, the lack of experience is a barrier in adopting technologies because farmers learn by doing [61]. Low levels of education are barriers to adoption [61, 69], but studies show that work experience provides comparable skills [61]. Instead, another study has shown that education variables do not have a significant impact on the adoption process [56].

Entrepreneurial orientation influences the reluctance to invest financial resources in adopting technologies due to uncertain economic returns [55, 57, 59]. Non-adoption is due to the time asymmetry between costs and benefits, especially regarding sustainable benefits. Moreover, the non-adoption of emerging technologies is influenced by lack of ownership, which dissuades investors to allocate resources in the medium to long term.

Table 2 A list of most used technologies in agricultural industries

Technologies	Description	Reference
ICT	Set of technologies to integrate telecommunications system with the aim to detect, store and communicate data between devices	[53]
Precision agriculture	Management system detects and processes temporal and spatial data, so supporting management decisions	[54–57]
Global position system (GPS)	Network of satellites and receiving devices connected to determine the location on earth	[54, 55]
Remote sensing technologies	Uses electromagnetic radiation to reveal the spatial distribution and spatiotemporal changes in objects on the Earth's surface qualitatively and quantitatively transmitting and processing information	[54, 55]
Colorimeter	An indicator of soil mineral content thought identifies soil colour	[58]
Soil moisture sensor	Placed in the soil that measure the soil water content and transmit measurements	[58]
Irrigation pump flow meter	Linked to an irrigation water pipe measures the volume of water flowing through the pipe and transmits data to an irrigation controller	[58]
Variable rate applicators	a control system calculates the application rate to match actual need for fertiliser of the soil or plants and transfers the information to a controller	[55, 59, 60]
Machine guidance	Pilot machinery using global navigation satellite systems (GNSS) integrated in the tractor's hydraulics can directly take over steering operations	[54]
Data processing and decision-making technologies	Provide operational solutions based on useful information extracted from raw data and documents for specific requests and issues.	[54]
Irrigation technology	Decide the appropriate amount of water to be applied at a certain time to maintain healthy plant growth	[54, 59, 61]
Nanotechnology	Improve characteristics of foods, absorption of nutrients and food supplements, obtain new packaging materials to preserve product conservation and to trace foods along the supply chain.	[62]
Internet and mobile phone	Tools to search for information about new agricultural innovations and specifical issues	[63, 64]
Agricultural technical assistance providers	Where farmers have assistance to use emerging technologies	[65]
Agricultural consulting platform	Where farmers can have advice about operative issues	[66]
Social media	Facebook and twitter are platform where people can create network to ask information and share experience.	[67]
e-commerce	A sales channel that allows firms to have customers from all over the world.	[60]

Table 3 Technology adoption barriers in agricultural industries

Barriers	Factors	Description	References
Organizational	Gender	Men are more exposed to agricultural technologies than women.	[63]
	Age	Older people are less inclined to new technology adoption.	[53, 54, 56, 58, 60, 61, 67, 68]
	Level of education	People with low levels of education are less inclined to new technology adoption.	[53, 54, 56, 58, 61, 64, 66, 68, 69]
	ICT experience	People with less ICT experience ignore new technologies potential benefits.	[60, 61, 65, 69, 70]
	Training	Lack of training	[55]
	Financial resource	Lack of financial resources and difficult to have bank credit due to lack of economic guarantee	[61]
	Entrepreneurial orientation	Skepticism on ROI of emerging technologies	[55, 57]
		Lack of ownership disincentivizes investments in middle-long term	[70]
Technology	Unequal access to technology	Gender and salary influence the emerging technology adoption.	[66, 70]
		High cost of purchase and maintenance emerging technologies	[55, 57–59, 61, 64, 65]
	Technical complexity	Emerging technologies are perceived as difficult to use.	[60, 66]
	Insubstantial advantages	Low level of utility perceived	[57, 59, 60, 63, 64, 66, 67]
Environmental	Infrastructures	Lack of infrastructures such as broadband, fundamental in smart technologies uses.	[53, 58, 63]
	Country regulation	Lack of legislation about use of emerging technologies creating uncertain environment	[62, 65]
	Public policies and funding	Lack of policies and public funding to increase the adoption of emerging technologies.	[65, 66]
	National culture	Lack of influencer or marketing strategies to reduce social skepticism on emerging technologies	[62, 68, 69]

4.2 *Technology Barriers*

An element of the technology non-adoption is the unequal access conditioned by the culture on gender role and financial resources. The cultural influence on the gender role in agricultural organization is evident, whereby in certain countries women tend to be less inclined to utilize technology due to low level of use and possession of technologies [66, 70] because they have not decision-making autonomy from male subjects [65]; conversely, the females adoption increases when their husbands seek alternative income sources [65] and women assume responsibility for agricultural activities.

In technology barriers it is important the financial constraint able to influence and limit adoption [58, 65]. Emerging technologies have high purchase, installation and maintenance costs [55, 57–59, 61, 64, 65]. In addition, small and medium-sized agri-food companies have no financial resources and it is difficult to access credit due to a lack of guarantees [61].

The main technology barriers is insubstantial reduction of cost because raw materials sold have a price set by market demand [63] and there is a lack of scale economy due to small surface of the land [59].

Moreover, the complexity of using technologies depends on lack of practical expertise and skilled labour [60, 66] However, the lack of perceived usefulness leads farmers not to inform themselves and not to train themself according to complexity perception influenced by the anxiety of use and previous negative experiences.

4.3 Environmental Barriers

One of the main factors of non-adoption is the lack of infrastructure [53, 58, 63], such as broadband provision and scarce transportation networks [70] in rural areas. Not accessing the Internet or having a slow connection [63] prevents farmers from taking advantage of the emerging technologies. The lack of infrastructure investment leads to the non-adoption of technologies in rural areas such as mountain areas of Wales [67] and rural areas in Pakistan [63].

The lack of regulations and policies promoting advantages of technologies in the agricultural industries leads to non-adoption. Indeed the presence of uncertainty hinders adoption [65] or, as seen with nanotechnology, the presence of heterogenic legislations across different countries tend to create confusion [62]. The inadequacy of policies is underscored by the insufficiency of public funds allocated to encourage the adoption of technologies in agrifood sector. Consequently, this results in the non-adoption, for example, of sustainable innovations as farmers are unable to gauge the potential future benefits of investing in environmentally friendly practices [70, 71].

The emerging technologies in the agricultural sector is inadequately promoted due to insufficient marketing [66], which would otherwise facilitate the dissemination of knowledge concerning benefits associated with these technologies. The non-existence of proficient professionals or influencer [62] in the propagation of emerging technologies, such as nanotechnology, in the agrifood sector impedes the eradication of preconceived notions that generate mistrust and fear. Consequently, the skepticism of society with respect to the actual benefits of technology culminates in its non-adoption.

5 Discussion

The research explores the reasons for the non-adoption of digital technologies in agricultural industries. Using a qualitative and quantitative methodology conducted through an SLR on the Scopus database, we identified the main digital technologies used in agricultural industries and the barriers to their non-adoption. Concerning digital technologies, results show: the Internet and smartphones, social media, e-commerce channels, platforms for technical assistance and professional consulting are tools that are easy to apply and have significant usefulness for those involved in agriculture. Other technologies identified as Information and Communication Technologies (ICT) are useful for detecting, storing and communicating data between devices. Several of these technologies could be strictly related to the agricultural sector. Agriculture 4.0 is a management system (vehiculated by technology) aimed at detecting soil conditions, air temperature, moisture levels and hydro-stress of plants through the Internet of Things (IoT). In this sense, data processing is functional to support management decisions, especially in a sector such as the agricultural one, underestimated in terms of technology-driven approaches. Another technology identified in the final dataset was a specific example of precision agriculture, such as the Global Positioning System (GPS), which uses satellites to define location; remote sensing technologies, detect crop conditions in a small way, communicating data; variable rate applicators, define plan fertilisation based on crop condition detected, machine guidance, determines machine itinerary through GPS and irrigation technology, regulates the use of water-based on processing data. These last three technologies are examples of data processing and decision-making technologies (DPDM).

Agricultural industries adopt the technologies identified in the dataset, excluding nanotechnology. Even though these technologies are not new in the agricultural industries, their adoption is still limited. Regarding the barriers to digital technology non-adoption, our results showed that there are organizational, technological and environmental barriers. The organizational structure in the agrifood constitutes middle-small size and for this reason management is more influenced by gender, age and level of education of farmer. The agricultural sector is characterized by advanced seniority of people involved in and their strong aversion to change. Indeed, younger people are uninterested to work in the agrifood sector. Therefore, agricultural business do not adopt emerging technologies due to the lack of young generation, who has greater propensity to innovate and invest resource on uncertain future.

Insufficient knowledge and inadequate ongoing training following the initial adoption of technologies are the primary causes for the dispersion of users, ultimately leading to the perpetuation of traditional organizational processes [56]. Indeed, farmers exhibit a preference for seeking guidance from agricultural experts, who provide hands-on guidance with live demonstrations and constructive feedback [61], rather than resorting through technology utilization and relying on online consultation or video tutorials. In terms of the skepticism on economical returns on investments is strongly dependent on entrepreneurial orientation.

In technology barriers unequal access is the result of low level of devices used by women, higher initial and maintenance costs and difficulties of middle- small farm in accessing credit. Among technological factors is widely spread the perception of technologies as complex to use and with irrelevant advantages due to low level of technical knowledge and technological experiences.

Referring to environmental barriers the insufficiency of infrastructure connections is compounded by the impacts of climate change, resulting in the hindrance of transportation routes as a consequence of landslides, inundations and other phenomena brought about by environmental calamities. Climate change has significant impacts on the agri-food sector, as prolonged droughts or sudden heavy rainfall events can lead to crop failure. The depletion of soil nutrients, scarcity of water and the rise of plant pathogens can be mitigated by employing various technologies in operational management. However, it is crucial to invest in medium and long-term sustainable innovations that may not have immediate economic returns and hence may not be readily adopted by farmers [58]. Indeed, others environmental barriers are the lack of policies promoted by public fund and homogeneous and complete legislation in adoption of emerging technology in agrifood. Internal aspects of organizational structure are linked to external environmental factors and both are influenced by technology factors. To overcome the non-adoption, arising from the lack of knowledge, the implementation of policies can be incentivized training courses or adoption of technologies. External factors. Such as information scarcity shared through mass media, sustain the deficiency in comprehension of technological advancements, thereby perpetuating the skepticism of farmers towards investing in innovation technologies.

6 Conclusion

Our study presents a SLR that identifies the main technologies and barriers related to the non-adoption of digital technology in agricultural industries. We classified the barriers by the SLR according to the TOE model: organisational, technology and environmental.

On the organisational side, mainly individual and economic barriers prevail. On the technological side, we find mainly cultural barriers. Finally, from the environmental point of view, the main barriers concern infrastructural and political elements.

For future research, it is important to use the classification of barriers to non-adoption for structuring a model built through the TOE theory. The model can be tested through quantitative or qualitative studies to verify the validity of the theory.

The model will allow a better understanding of the barriers and the exploration of a still limited field of research.

References

1. Ronaghi, M. H., & Forouharfar, A. (2020). A contextualized study of the usage of the internet of things (IoTs) in smart farming in a typical middle eastern country within the context of unified theory of acceptance and use of technology model (UTAUT). *Technology in Society, 63*, 101415. https://doi.org/10.1016/j.techsoc.2020.101415
2. Zscheischler, J., Brunsch, R., Rogga, S., & Scholz, R. W. (2022). Perceived risks and vulnerabilities of employing digitalization and digital data in agriculture—Socially robust orientations from a transdisciplinary process. *Journal of Cleaner Production, 358*, 132034. https://doi.org/10.1016/j.jclepro.2022.132034
3. Chen, Y., Li, Y., & Li, C. (2020). Electronic agriculture, blockchain and digital agricultural democratization: Origin, theory and application. *Journal of Cleaner Production, 268*, 122071. https://doi.org/10.1016/j.jclepro.2020.122071
4. Shen, Z., Wang, S., Boussemart, J. P., & Hao, Y. (2022). Digital transition and green growth in Chinese agriculture. *Technological Forecasting and Social Change, 181*, 121742. https://doi.org/10.1016/j.techfore.2022.121742
5. Rijswijk, K., Klerkx, L., Bacco, M., Bartolini, F., Bulten, E., Debruyne, L., Dessein, J., Scotti, I., & Brunori, G. (2021). Digital transformation of agriculture and rural areas: A socio-cyber-physical system framework to support responsibilisation. *Journal of Rural Studies, 85*, 79–90. https://doi.org/10.1016/j.jrurstud.2021.05.003
6. Regan, Á. (2021). Exploring the readiness of publicly funded researchers to practice responsible research and innovation in digital agriculture. *Journal of Responsible Innovation, 8*, 28–47. https://doi.org/10.1080/23299460.2021.1904755
7. Vargas-Canales, J. M., Palacios-Rangel, M. I., Aguilar-Ávila, J., Camacho-Vera, J. H., Ocampo-Ledesma, J. G., & Medina-Cuellar, S. E. (2018). Efficiency of small enterprises of protected agriculture in the adoption of innovations in Mexico. *Estudios Gerenciales, 34*, 52–62. https://doi.org/10.18046/j.estger.2018.146.2811
8. Osservatorio Smart AgriFood. (2022). Smart agrifood: raccogliamo i frutti dell'innovazione digitale.
9. Pivoto, D., Barham, B., Waquil, P. D., Foguesatto, C. R., Corte, V. F. D., Zhang, D., & Talamini, E. (2019). Factors influencing the adoption of smart farming by Brazilian grain farmers. *International Food and Agribusiness Management Review, 22*, 571–588. https://doi.org/10.22434/IFAMR2018.0086
10. Bitrus, S., Vajjhala, R., & Strang, K. D. (2019). Factors impacting farm management decision making software adoption. *International Journal of Sustainable Agricultural Management and Informatics, 5*, 1. https://doi.org/10.1504/ijsami.2019.10019819
11. Giua, C., Materia, V. C., & Camanzi, L. (2022). Smart farming technologies adoption: Which factors play a role in the digital transition? *Technology in Society, 68*, 101869. https://doi.org/10.1016/j.techsoc.2022.101869
12. Yusoff, Z. Y. M., Ishak, M. K., & Alezabi, K. A. (2021). The role of RFID in green IoT: A survey on technologies, challenges and a way forward. *Advances in Science, Technology and Engineering Systems, 6*, 17–35. https://doi.org/10.25046/aj060103
13. Navimipour, N. J., Milani, F. S., & Hossenzadeh, M. (2018). A model for examining the role of effective factors on the performance of organizations. *Technology in Society, 55*, 166–174. https://doi.org/10.1016/j.techsoc.2018.06.003
14. Sibona, F., Chiavarini, L., Bortoletto, A., & Mainiero, S. (2020). Innovation in farming: An engaging and rewarding business model to foster digitalization. *CERN IdeaSquare Journal of Experimental Innovation, 4*, 9–15. https://doi.org/10.23726/cij.2020.1052
15. Valiyev, A. (2022). The digitalization effectiveness as an innovative factor development of the agriculture in Azerbaijan. *Journal of Eastern European and Central Asian Research, 9*, 194–205.

16. Lioutas, E. D., Charatsari, C., & De Rosa, M. (2021). Digitalization of agriculture: A way to solve the food problem or a trolley dilemma? *Technology in Society, 67*, 101744. https://doi.org/10.1016/j.techsoc.2021.101744
17. Aivazidou, E., & Tsolakis, N. (2022). Transitioning towards human–robot synergy in agriculture: A systems thinking perspective. *Systems Research and Behavioral Science, 40*(3), 536–551. https://doi.org/10.1002/sres.2887
18. van der Burg, S., Bogaardt, M. J., & Wolfert, S. (2019). Ethics of smart farming: Current questions and directions for responsible innovation towards the future. *NJAS – Wageningen Journal of Life Sciences, 90*, 90–91.
19. Klerkx, L., Jakku, E., & Labarthe, P. (2019). A review of social science on digital agriculture, smart farming and agriculture 4.0: New contributions and a future research agenda. *NJAS – Wageningen Journal of Life Sciences, 90–91*, 100315. https://doi.org/10.1016/j.njas.2019.100315
20. Krishnan, S. S. R., & Arun Kumar, T. (2019). A practical implementation smart farming using recommendation routing in WSN 336. *Journal of Recent Technology and Engineering (IJRTE), 7*.
21. Zavhorodnii, A., Ohiienko, M., Biletska, Y., Bondarenko, S., Duiunova, T., & Bodenchuk, L. (2021). Digitalization of agribusiness in the development of foreign economic relations of the region. *Journal of Information Technology Management, 13*, 123–141. https://doi.org/10.22059/JITM.2021.82613
22. Armstrong, L. J., Diepeveen, D. A., & Tantisantisom, K. (2010). An eAgriculture-based decision support framework for information dissemination. *International Journal of Human Capital and Information Technology Professionals, 1*, 1–13. https://doi.org/10.4018/jhcitp.2010100101
23. Spanaki, K., Karafili, E., & Despoudi, S. (2021). AI applications of data sharing in agriculture 4.0: A framework for role-based data access control. *International Journal of Information Management, 59*, 102350. https://doi.org/10.1016/j.ijinfomgt.2021.102350
24. Carmela Annosi, M., Brunetta, F., Capo, F., & Heideveld, L. (2020). Digitalization in the Agri-food industry: The relationship between technology and sustainable development. *Management Decision, 58*, 1737–1757. https://doi.org/10.1108/MD-09-2019-1328
25. Ibrahim, A. M., Hassan, M. S., & Gusau, A. L. (2018). Factors influencing acceptance and use of ICT innovations by agribusinesses. *Journal of Global Information Management, 26*, 113–134. https://doi.org/10.4018/JGIM.2018100107
26. Singh, S., Haneef, F., Kumar, S., & Ongsakul, V. (2020). A framework for successful IoT adoption in agriculture sector: A total interpretive structural modelling approach. *Journal for Global Business Advancement, 13*, 382. https://doi.org/10.1504/jgba.2020.10033252
27. Weber, R., Braun, J., & Frank, M. (2022). How does the adoption of digital technologies affect the social sustainability of small-scale agriculture in South-West Germany? *International Journal on Food System Dynamics, 13*, 275–293. https://doi.org/10.18461/ijfsd.v13i3.C3
28. Liu, Y., Ma, X., Shu, L., Hancke, G. P., & Abu-Mahfouz, A. M. (2021). From industry 4.0 to agriculture 4.0: Current status, enabling technologies, and research challenges. *IEEE Transactions on Industrial Informatics, 17*, 4322–4334. https://doi.org/10.1109/TII.2020.3003910
29. Maffezzoli, F., Ardolino, M., Bacchetti, A., Perona, M., & Renga, F. (2022). Agriculture 4.0: A systematic literature review on the paradigm, technologies and benefits. *Futures, 142*, 102998. https://doi.org/10.1016/j.futures.2022.102998
30. Qi, Q., Tao, F., Hu, T., Anwer, N., Liu, A., Wei, Y., Wang, L., & Nee, A. Y. C. (2021). Enabling technologies and tools for digital twin. *Journal of Manufacturing Systems, 58*, 3–21. https://doi.org/10.1016/j.jmsy.2019.10.001
31. Giua, C., Materia, V. C., & Camanzi, L. (2021). Management information system adoption at the farm level: Evidence from the literature. *British Food Journal, 123*, 884–909. https://doi.org/10.1108/BFJ-05-2020-0420
32. Nguyen, T. H., Le, X. C., & Vu, T. H. L. (2022). An extended technology-organization-environment (TOE) framework for online retailing utilization in digital transformation:

Empirical evidence from Vietnam. *Journal of Open Innovation: Technology, Market, and Complexity, 8*, 200. https://doi.org/10.3390/joitmc8040200
33. Tornatzky, L. G., & Fleischer, M. (1990). The processes of technological innovation. In: Lexington. Accessed March 13, 2023, from https://www.scirp.org/(S(351jmbntvnsjt1aadkozje))/reference/referencespapers.aspx?referenceid=1771512
34. Khanh Chi, N. T. (2022). Driving factors for green innovation in agricultural production: An empirical study in an emerging economy. *Journal of Cleaner Production, 368*, 132965. https://doi.org/10.1016/j.jclepro.2022.132965
35. Zhu, K., & Kraemer, K. L. (2005). Post-adoption variations in usage and value of e-business by organizations: Cross-country evidence from the retail industry. *Information Systems Research, 16*, 61–84. https://doi.org/10.1287/isre.1050.0045
36. Li, J. C. F. (2020). Roles of individual perception in technology adoption at organization level: Behavioral model versus toe framework. *Journal of System and Management Sciences, 10*, 97–118. https://doi.org/10.33168/JSMS.2020.0308
37. Bryan, J. D., & Zuva, T. (2021). A review on TAM and TOE framework progression and how these models integrate. *Advances in Science, Technology and Engineering Systems Journal, 6*, 137–145. https://doi.org/10.25046/aj060316
38. Senna, P. P., Ferreira, L. M. D. F., Barros, A. C., Bonnín Roca, J., & Magalhães, V. (2022). Prioritizing barriers for the adoption of industry 4.0 technologies. *Computers and Industrial Engineering, 171*, 108428. https://doi.org/10.1016/j.cie.2022.108428
39. Chatterjee, S., Rana, N. P., Dwivedi, Y. K., & Baabdullah, A. M. (2021). Understanding AI adoption in manufacturing and production firms using an integrated TAM-TOE model. *Technological Forecasting and Social Change, 170*, 120880. https://doi.org/10.1016/j.techfore.2021.120880
40. Sood, A., Bhardwaj, A. K., & Sharma, R. K. (2022). Towards sustainable agriculture: Key determinants of adopting artificial intelligence in agriculture. *Journal of Decision Systems*, 1–45. https://doi.org/10.1080/12460125.2022.2154419
41. Van Looy, A. (2021). A quantitative and qualitative study of the link between business process management and digital innovation. *Information and Management, 58*, 103413. https://doi.org/10.1016/j.im.2020.103413
42. Denyer, D., & Tranfield, D. (2009). Producing a systematic review. In D. A. Buchanan & A. Bryman (Eds.), *The Sage handbook of organizational research methods* (pp. 671–689). Sage Publications Ltd.
43. Elsbach, K. D., & van Knippenberg, D. (2020). Creating high-impact literature reviews: an argument for 'integrative reviews'. *Journal of Management Studies, 57*, 1277–1289. https://doi.org/10.1111/joms.12581
44. Snyder, H. (2019). Literature review as a research methodology: An overview and guidelines. *Journal of Business Research, 104*, 333–339. https://doi.org/10.1016/j.jbusres.2019.07.039
45. Hulland, J., & Houston, M. B. (2020). Why systematic review papers and meta-analyses matter: An introduction to the special issue on generalizations in marketing. *Journal of the Academy of Marketing Science, 48*, 351–359.
46. Paul, J., & Criado, A. R. (2020). The art of writing literature review: What do we know and what do we need to know? *International Business Review, 29*, 101717. https://doi.org/10.1016/j.ibusrev.2020.101717
47. Petticrew, M. Systematic reviews in the social sciences: A practical guide By Mark Petticrew PDF: Systematic reviews in the social sciences: A practical guide by Mark Petticrew Doc: Systematic reviews in the social sciences: A practical guide by Mark Petticrew ePub: Systematic reviews in the social sciences: A practical guide by Mark Petticrew if searching for a ebook by Mark Petticrew systematic reviews in the social sciences: A practical guide in pdf format.
48. Cronin Bsc, P., & Cronin, P. Undertaking a literature review: A step-by-step approach. *British Journal of Nursing, 17*(1), 38–43.

49. The Campbell Collaboration. (2019). Campbell collaboration systematic reviews: Policies and guidelines.
50. Moher, D., Liberati, A., Tetzlaff, J., & Altman, D. G. (2009). Preferred reporting items for systematic reviews and meta-analyses: The PRISMA statement. *BMJ (Online), 339*, 332–336.
51. Gundolf, K., & Filser, M. (2013). Management research and religion: A citation analysis. *Journal of Business Ethics, 112*, 177–185. https://doi.org/10.1007/s10551-012-1240-7
52. Zupic, I., & Čater, T. (2015). Bibliometric methods in management and organization. *Organizational Research Methods, 18*(3), 429–472.
53. Purnomo, S. H., & Kusnandar. (2019). Barriers to acceptance of information and communication technology in agricultural extension in Indonesia. *Information Development, 35*, 512–523. https://doi.org/10.1177/0266666918767484
54. Berthold, T. A., Ajaz, A., Olsovsky, T., & Kathuria, D. (2021). Identifying barriers to adoption of irrigation scheduling tools in Rio Grande Basin. *Smart Agricultural Technology, 1*, 100016. https://doi.org/10.1016/j.atech.2021.100016
55. Robertson, M., Isbister, B., Maling, I., Oliver, Y., Wong, M., Adams, M., Bowden, B., & Tozer, P. (2007). Opportunities and constraints for managing within-field spatial variability in Western Australian grain production. *Field Crops Research, 104*, 60–67. https://doi.org/10.1016/j.fcr.2006.12.013
56. Vecchio, Y., De Rosa, M., Pauselli, G., Masi, M., & Adinolfi, F. (2022). The leading role of perception: The FACOPA model to comprehend innovation adoption. *Agricultural and Food Economics, 10*, 5. https://doi.org/10.1186/s40100-022-00211-0
57. Barnes, A. P., Soto, I., Eory, V., Beck, B., Balafoutis, A., Sánchez, B., Vangeyte, J., Fountas, S., van der Wal, T., & Gómez-Barbero, M. (2019). Exploring the adoption of precision agricultural technologies: A cross regional study of EU farmers. *Land Use Policy, 80*, 163–174. https://doi.org/10.1016/j.landusepol.2018.10.004
58. Hatzenbuehler, P., & Peña-Lévano, L. (2022). Adoption potential of sustainability-related agriculture Technologies for Smallholder Farmers in the global south. *Sustainability (Switzerland), 14*, 13176. https://doi.org/10.3390/su142013176
59. Rihn, A. L., Velandia, M., Warner, L. A., Fulcher, A., Schexnayder, S., & LeBude, A. (2023). Factors correlated with the propensity to use automation and mechanization by the US nursery industry. *Agribusiness, 39*, 110–130. https://doi.org/10.1002/agr.21763
60. Cloete, E., & Doens, M. (2008). B2B e-marketplace adoption in south African agriculture. *Information Technology for Development, 14*, 184–196. https://doi.org/10.1002/itdj.20105
61. Koech, R., Haase, M., Grima, B., & Taylor, B. (2021). Barriers and measures to improve adoption of irrigation technologies: A case study from the Bundaberg region in Queensland, Australia*. *Irrigation and Drainage, 70*, 909–923. https://doi.org/10.1002/ird.2583
62. Siimes, N., Sharp, E. L., Lewis, N., & Kah, M. (2022). Determining acceptance and rejection of nano-enabled agriculture: A case study of the New Zealand wine industry. *NanoImpact, 28*, 100432. https://doi.org/10.1016/j.impact.2022.100432
63. Khan, N. A., Qijie, G., Ali, S., Shahbaz, B., & Shah, A. A. (2019). Farmers' use of mobile phone for accessing agricultural information in Pakistan: A case of Punjab province. *Ciencia Rural, 49*, e20181016. https://doi.org/10.1590/0103-8478cr20181016
64. Shutske, J. M., Trechter, D., Luck, B. D., Drewry, J. L., DeWitte, M. J., Pitman, L., Kluz, M., & (ASABE) AS of A and BE. (2018). Assessment of digital capacity, needs and access barriers among crop, dairy and livestock producers. In *ASABE 2018 Annual International Meeting*. American Society of Agricultural and Biological Engineers.
65. Johnson, D., Parker, L. E., Pathak, T. B., Crothers, L., & Ostoja, S. M. (2023). Technical assistance providers identify climate change adaptation practices and barriers to adoption among California agricultural producers. *Sustainability (Switzerland), 15*, 5973. https://doi.org/10.3390/su15075973
66. Mahata, C., & Mhagama, P. (2023). Factors affecting adoption of mobile phone applications among farmers in Lilongwe, Malawi: The case of Mchikumbe 212. In *3rd International*

Conference on Multidisciplinary Research, MyRes 2022 (pp. 358–373). Society for Research and Knowledge Management.

67. Morris, W., & James, P. (2017). Social media, an entrepreneurial opportunity for agriculture-based enterprises. *Journal of Small Business and Enterprise Development, 24*, 1028–1045. https://doi.org/10.1108/JSBED-01-2017-0018
68. Mahama, A., Awuni, J. A., Mabe, F. N., & Azumah, S. B. (2020). Modelling adoption intensity of improved soybean production technologies in Ghana – A generalized Poisson approach. *Heliyon, 6*, e03543. https://doi.org/10.1016/j.heliyon.2020.e03543
69. Kendall, H., Clark, B., Li, W., Jin, S., Jones, G. D., Chen, J., Taylor, J., Li, Z., & Frewer, L. J. (2022). Precision agriculture technology adoption: A qualitative study of small-scale commercial "family farms" located in the North China plain. *Precision Agriculture, 23*, 319–351. https://doi.org/10.1007/s11119-021-09839-2
70. Autio, A., Johansson, T., Motaroki, L., Minoia, P., & Pellikka, P. (2021). Constraints for adopting climate-smart agricultural practices among smallholder farmers in Southeast Kenya. *Agricultural Systems, 194*, 103284. https://doi.org/10.1016/j.agsy.2021.103284
71. Cullen, R., Forbes, S. L., & Grout, R. (2013). Non-adoption of environmental innovations in wine growing. *New Zealand Journal of Crop and Horticultural Science, 41*, 41–48. https://doi.org/10.1080/01140671.2012

Layer Upon Layer: Developing Layered Modular Architectures for Data-Driven Health Platform

Bjarki Freyr Sveinbjarnarson, Erna Sif Arnardottir, and Anna Sigridur Islind

Abstract Data collection is a foundational aspect of research, as most research projects ultimately rely on their data. Quick and effective data overview is crucial, especially when working with extensive datasets. This paper seeks to add to the ongoing discourse about designing and developing layered-modular architectures for data-driven health platforms. We particularly emphasize data representation and address the research question: *How can layered-modular architecture be used to present and filter research data in a digital platform?* We designed and developed a layered-modular architecture for a digital platform aimed at data extraction and representation. We argue that this approach renders digital platforms more reusable, resilient to changes, and easily extendable. To evaluate its effectiveness, we evaluated the layered-modular architecture of the platform with ten experts and collected data on user experience and usability, along with semi-structured interviews. Furthermore, we examined the system's scalability with increasing data loads. The paper's key contribution revolves around the layered-modular architecture and design principles tailored for digital platforms, aiming to function effectively in socio-technical environments, particularly within intricate multidisciplinary research projects.

Keywords Digital platform · Design principles · Layered-modular architecture · Data-driven health platforms · Sleep revolution

B. F. Sveinbjarnarson (✉) · E. S. Arnardottir · A. S. Islind
Department of Computer Science, Reykjavik University, Reykjavik, Iceland

Reykjavik University, Sleep Institute, Reykjavik, Iceland
e-mail: bjarkis@ru.is; ernasifa@ru.is; annasi@ru.is

A. M. Braccini et al. (eds.), *Digital (Eco) Systems and Societal Challenges*, Lecture Notes in Information Systems and Organisation 72,
https://doi.org/10.1007/978-3-031-75586-6_6

1 Introduction

The modern world greatly depends on information, as we gather various types of data in larger quantities each year across society. This is evident in how swiftly we are collecting data. According to Statista [1], from 2010 to 2020, the total data created, captured, copied, or used grew from about 2 to 59 zettabytes (59 trillion gigabytes). Since then, global data has continued to grow, and it is expected to keep growing in the coming years [1]. As research intensifies its dependency on data, some fields find themselves in need of varied data types due to the broadening spectrum of available data [2–4]. Sleep research show this trend, since a sleep study utilizes various sensors to capture brain activity, oximetry, movement, snoring, breathing difficulty, heart rate, and more, resulting in a wide variety of data [4, 5]. Additionally, sleep has a large impact on multiple factors while awake, which enlarges the data variety of sleep research. Therefore, data for sleep research can be both of objective and subjective nature from different sources, collected at different times, including physiological signals from wearables, cognitive tests, digital self-assessments, questionnaires, and more [5]. However, when the data is collected at first, it is rarely in a format that can be used right away and requires organization [6, 7], meaning the data is not usable until it has been processed into information [8].

The Sleep Revolution project, a sizable initiative funded by the European Union and conducted at Reykjavik University in partnership with 38 collaborators across Europe, collects a wide variety of sleep data [9]. The collected data is consolidated within a single digital platform. Here, the diverse data sources are transformed into a consistent structure and displayed for participants. In the digital platform's backend, filters are crucial to researchers to navigate and comprehend the gathered data. Moreover, as the Sleep Revolution project progresses, the types of data, extraction methods, and the requirements of the platform will evolve. This underscores the need for adaptability in the platform's extraction and filtering features.

The main goal of this paper is to illuminate the socio-technical perspective during the design and development phase of the digital platform. This focus is particularly on extracting metadata from multiple sleep measurements, aiming to make it easier for end-users within the digital platform context to understand the data's content. To achieve this effectively, considering the different origins and characteristics of available data, end-users should be able to examine the data in a manner that lets them recognize the information it holds, using variables like statistical power, correlation, and information coverage. Consequently, the paper outlines the design and development of the digital platform, which facilitates the extraction of various data into a standardized structure. This structure showcases the data's information and enables the isolation and effective visualization of data with specific traits. Given the future research purposes that remain undiscovered, a highly adaptable architecture is necessary for the digital platform's data exploration. Furthermore, an adaptive architecture simplifies future designs for expanding and integrating the digital platform. In this paper, we leverage a layered-modular architecture to achieve adaptability in design and development. This raises the following question: *How can layered-modular architecture be used to present and filter research data in a digital platform*? The paper's key contribution revolves around the layered-modular architecture and design principles tailored for digital platforms, aiming to function effectively in socio-technical environments, particularly within intricate multidisciplinary research projects.

2 Related Research

2.1 Data and Data-Driven Healthcare

Collecting data forms the foundation of every research project. However, researchers often employ multiple methods for data collection, leading to the accumulation of diverse data types [10]. Common systematic data collection approaches encompass questionnaires, interviews, focus groups, observations, extraction of data from sensors, and utilization of secondary data sources such as electronic health records [10]. Moreover, when research necessitates substantial volumes of both subjective and objective data, as seen in studies involving sensor data (objective data) and sleep diaries (subjective data), comprehending the data's underlying information can pose challenges [4]. Similarly, individuals might encounter difficulties in understanding information when dealing with extensive data entries or complex data formats. Additionally, if data originates from various sources, it can adopt multiple formats. In such instances, the organization and comprehension of information within the data can be enhanced using modular metadata structures [11]. Consequently, in digital platforms that accommodate diverse or new data types, adaptability, extensibility, and scalability become imperative [11]. During metadata creation, two valuable refinements contribute to improving metadata quality [11]. Firstly, consolidating various elements that signify the same entity can enhance clarity. For instance, different data sources might use terms like "participant," "patient," and "ID," all referring to the same subject's identifier. Such elements can be unified, using "ID" universally. Secondly, defining the range or format of a data type can be beneficial. For example, time encoding could include formats such as "yyyy-mm-dd," "dd/mm/yy," or "July 5th, 2002, 15:30." Additionally, certain types of metadata, like name order or dates, might be interpreted differently across cultures. For instance, 01/02/2020 signifies February first in some countries and January second in others, highlighting the importance of addressing multicultural considerations [10]. Combining diverse formats into a unified element enhances the usability of the digital platform [11]. Consequently, the method of associating metadata with collected data is pivotal, as its effectiveness may vary based on the association model [11].

Data structures categorize data collections into three types: (i) unstructured, (ii) semi-structured, and (iii) (fully) structured. Unstructured data, such as texts, images, and videos, lacks relational database descriptions, leading to challenging navigational control [12]. Semi-structured data incorporates tags as markers, straying from structured data models while retaining flexibility and the potential for transformation into structured data through schemas [13]. Fully structured data is organized beforehand, as commonly found in relational databases. This setup ensures better performance and navigation but comes with less flexibility and scalability [12].

2.2 Data-driven Health Platforms for Sleep Data

Sleep constitutes a fundamental activity, accounting for roughly a third of human lives [3]. Remarkably, the endurance limit for sleep deprivation is shorter than for food, with the record being about 11 days [14]. Our evolving understanding of sleep has revealed an array of sleep disorders, characterized by frequent interruptions, diminished duration, and compromised quality, which is often without the individual's awareness [4, 15]. Among these, obstructive sleep apnea, a prevalent disorder in which breathing ceases periodically throughout the night, stands out. Although approximately 20% of the general population is affected while a mere 15% of the people affected are aware of their condition [15, 16]. Insufficient and poor-quality sleep is linked to impaired cognitive function, reduced quality of life, heightened disease susceptibility, including cancer, hindered physical recovery and growth, weakened immune response, anxiety, depression, and numerous other repercussions. Sleep studies encompass the collection and analysis of multiple parameters, including oxygen saturation, sleep fragmentation, sleeping position, duration across different sleep stages, heart rate, and more [3, 4, 15, 17]. Over time, researchers have crafted various instruments like questionnaires, sleep diaries, and cognitive tests to pinpoint those at risk of sleep disorders and gauge their impact on daily life. For instance, questionnaires can assess symptoms and frequency of sleep disturbances, sleep diaries provide insights into individual sleep habits and disruptions, and cognitive tests measure the effects of sleep loss on attention and memory [4, 18, 19].

Organizing components within a digital platform is essential for several key reasons. These reasons encompass: (i) substantiating the reasoning behind implementations and choices made, (ii) offering a more comprehensive understanding and defining clear objectives, (iii) simplifying the complexity of the platform, (iv) improving the reusability of code and its adaptability to alterations, and (v) possibly attaining scalability, flexibility, and enhanced performance based on the selected framework. For instance, a well-structured platform can streamline updates, facilitate easier maintenance, and optimize user experience by improving load times and responsiveness [20, 21]. Hence, selecting an architecture that aligns with the platform's design is essential to meet its requirements. Modular architecture is a widely used approach in software design and development that involves creating independent modules as part of a larger system [22]. This approach aims to decrease system complexity while increasing flexibility [22]. Additionally, due to the ease of replacing, updating, or removing components in modular architecture, it is considered adaptable [20, 22].

Likewise, layered-modular architecture divides code modules into distinct layers or packages [21]. Each layer serves a specific purpose within the system, forming a collection of components [21]. The three common layers in layered-modular architecture are the presentation/contents layer, business/service layer, and database/device layer [20, 21]. The presentation layer handles user interaction and request communication [21]. The business layer processes these requests into logical actions, often involving communication with the database layer [21]. The database layer manages data queries and access [21]. Layers are considered 'open' if the layer above can communicate with layers below them; conversely, if layers above cannot directly communicate with those below, the layer is 'closed' [21]. Generally, designers and developers aim to maintain closed layers to minimize dependencies within the system [21]. Another notable architecture is the Microkernel Architecture, featuring a core application with plug-in components that extend the core system's capabilities [23]. The design focus for the core digital platform is to make minimal adjustments necessary to seamlessly integrate added plugins [23].

3 Research Approach

Action Design Research (ADR) constitutes a research approach aimed at assessing digital products [24]. The ADR process involves four distinct phases: (i) Problem Formulation, (ii) Building, Intervention, and Evaluation, (iii) Reflection and Learning, and (iv) Formalization of Learning [24]. During the Problem Formulation phase, aspects like design creation, research question formulation, and role definition are addressed for subsequent evaluation [24]. The second phase encompasses design implementation, intervention, and evaluation. The third phase, executed concurrently with the first two, involves ongoing reflection and observation [24]. Ultimately, the last phase formalizes the acquired insights from the design process [24]. In this study, the ADR framework is applied as continuous learning informed and refined the design, akin to the third ADR stage. Moreover, the design was developed with evaluation as a core consideration, aligning with the pivotal aspects of the first ADR stage. Additionally, usability tests and evaluations were crafted to contribute to future system enhancements, which resonates with the essence of the second ADR stage. Lastly, design principles were formulated to guide analogous problem-solving endeavors, mirroring the purpose of the fourth ADR stage. However, it is worth noting that this research method does not encompass all the tasks and principles outlined in ADR. For instance, tasks such as identifying the initial knowledge-creation target and creating mutually influential roles are not explicitly incorporated in this study.

3.1 Research Context

The primary objective of the Sleep Revolution project is to amass a comprehensive collection of sleep data, enabling researchers to extract insights into fundamental aspects of sleep, sleep disorders, and alternative methods of measurement [9]. The core focus of the project lies in the collection and processing of sleep data, necessitating certain key considerations for delivering dependable results [9]. These critical factors include: (i) the ability to select relevant parameters to characterize data, (ii) comprehending data coverage across various subjects, and (iii) recognizing the significance of coverage for subject-specific characteristics. Typical parameters used to describe sleep data encompass biometric data such as age, gender, height and weight, as well as processed sleep study parameters like sleep apnea events per hour (apnea-hypopnea, AHI), sleep profile across different sleep stages and total sleep time [3].

The central idea of the project is to use specific parameters to segregate the accumulated data into research, training, and testing datasets for exploratory analysis. To achieve efficient results and avoid ineffective outcomes, it is crucial to conduct a detailed examination of the data. Additionally, assessing the informational value of the data is essential, as it might not always hold statistical relevance. This approach also helps in pinpointing dependent and independent variables. For example, collecting data across variables like gender, age, and conditions such as obstructive sleep apnea could reveal biases; perhaps participants with apnea are predominantly of a certain age or gender, which could skew the research findings. Understanding the importance of these parameters can greatly enhance the creation of meaningful training and testing datasets. Furthermore, developing a measure of coverage can identify gaps in the data not captured in the initial datasets, guiding such data towards human-in-the-loop processing for practical application. As the raw data is refined to unearth additional parameters, new types of data are incorporated into the database. However, it's important to understand that the database's primary function is not to directly solve research questions but to facilitate the retrieval of relevant sleep studies for further analysis. Therefore, the design of new database parameters should focus on enhancing search capabilities rather than trying to preempt every potential research question.

The primary users of this platform include researchers from varied disciplines such as psychology, sports science, and machine learning [9]. Rather than limiting the platform's functionalities to cater exclusively to specific research groups and objectives, we ensure that all users have a comprehensive understanding of the value and limitations of the collected data. This knowledge supports their future project planning and enhances their grasp of potential data constraints. For example, a sports scientist studying athlete performance and a psychologist examining behavioral patterns can both benefit from clear insights into what the data can and cannot provide, helping them to tailor their research methods and expectations accordingly.

In clinical research, employing inclusion and exclusion criteria is a fundamental method for ensuring data samples correspond with specific research objectives. This process is supported by data overviews and filtering techniques. Such filtering not only helps researchers eliminate irrelevant data but also aids in obtaining crucial insights applicable to current and future projects. In this field, the credibility of results often hinges on diversity, making it essential to include a wide range of ages and genders. As the project encompasses multiple disciplines, it naturally involves various pertinent data types. Consequently, study coordinators can utilize data filtering and overviews to confirm that the participants accurately reflect the necessary diversity of data types, thus improving the overall distribution and quality of the data. This approach allows for more representative and reliable outcomes across different research areas.

3.2 *Scalability Test to Technically Evaluate the Architecture*

Every digital platform requires performance evaluation to identify its operational limits. Given that data filtering is the most time-intensive aspect of our architecture, the objective of our performance tests was to determine the time needed to filter progressively larger datasets. We anticipated that the MySQL database would handle the largest set of filters on the maximum expected data volume within a few seconds. We began our testing with a dataset of 100 rows and 50 columns, measuring filtering speed. In each subsequent test, we added 100 rows and timed the process again. Testing continued until we reached 1000 iterations, culminating in a dataset of 100,000 rows—significantly more than the expected volume of data. The scalability tests were performed under two conditions: once with a database filled exclusively with text, and once with only numerical data. For text data, the filter used was "%z% z%", targeting strings containing two "z" characters, with each string formatted as "column_x_row_y," where "x" and "y" denote specific row and column numbers. For numerical data, the filter aimed to identify values between 49.0 and 50.0, with simulated numbers ranging from 0.0 to 99.9 and deliberately excluding any numbers between 49 and 50. In both scenarios, we used the "OR" operator across all 50 columns to ensure comprehensive filtering of each row.

3.3 *User Experience and Usability Test to Evaluate the Architecture*

We executed a usability and user experience test to evaluate the functionality of the digital platform, involving ten potential end-users. The main goal was to assess the effectiveness of the user interface, particularly its capacity to support end-users' tasks through filterable results. To maintain a controlled test environment, we used simulated rather than real data, as some participants had restricted access to the full dataset. The interface tested included 100 simulated rows and 10 columns, mirroring

Number of results: 27

Table for Average

recording_length	recording_id	recording_type	recording_AHI	recording_AI	recording_HI	subject_height	subject_weight	subject_age	subject_gender
NA	NA	NA	31.6	15.85	15.75	174.2	74.57	41.56	NA

Queried Database

recording_length	recording_id	recording_type	recording_AHI	recording_AI	recording_HI	subject_height	subject_weight	subject_age	subject_gender
5:24:39	10162	PSG	26.75	23.78	2.96	184.14	79.53	32	Male
8:01:45	10165	PSG	35.53	15.89	19.64	183.96	80.32	41	Male
6:02:05	10189	PSG	30.52	15.75	14.76	172.43	72.67	42	Female
6:11:20	10191	PSG	28.88	11.65	17.23	169.27	77.3	49	Male
6:54:37	10212	PSG	27.44	23.33	4.11	172.9	74.23	49	Male
8:52:23	10226	PSG	25.74	14.67	11.07	185.03	64.28	31	Male

Fig. 1 Illustrates the tables used in the user interface during the usability test. The "Queried Database" table displays rows that match specified filtering criteria, while the "Average Table" below it shows the calculated averages from the queried data. At the top of the tables, there is a display showing the total number of database entries that meet the filters applied by the participants. This layout helps users directly compare filtered data and their corresponding averages, facilitating a comprehensive analysis within the testing framework

real-world data scenarios. This setup included seven sleep-related result parameters and three body measurement parameters selected for their relevance to the project.

The user interface was designed for ease of use, allowing participants to input values to filter data, as shown in the referenced figures. We provided a brief tutorial on the system's functionalities before the test. Participants were tasked with answering four specific questions using the interface and table data:

1. The number of male and female subjects in the database.
2. Whether the severity of the Apnea-Hypopnea Index (AHI) was higher in individuals aged 40 and above or those under 40.
3. The count of male participants with a severe AHI score of 30 or higher.
4. The average weights for males and females with moderate apnea (AHI 15 to 30).

Participants documented their responses using Google Forms. We also measured the time each task took, which helped assess the complexity level of the tasks (Fig. 1). Visual aids of the table and the filter interface were provided in Figs. 2 and 3 to enhance understanding and navigation of the platform.

After finishing their tasks, participants underwent a reflective evaluation of their experience with the system. This involved completing two user experience questionnaires: the System Usability Scale [25] and AttrakDiff [26], both administered via Google Forms. Following the questionnaires, a semi-structured interview of about 20 min was conducted, primarily to delve into aspects of the system that participants found less satisfactory. This comprehensive feedback process was designed to gather insights into user satisfaction and areas of the system that may require improvement.

Fig. 2 Depicts the filters available in the user interface used during the usability test. This example includes six numerical filters and one selection filter, demonstrating the types of data inputs that participants could manipulate during the test. The filters are designed to allow users to precisely adjust their search criteria, enhancing the user's ability to explore and interact with the dataset effectively during the evaluation

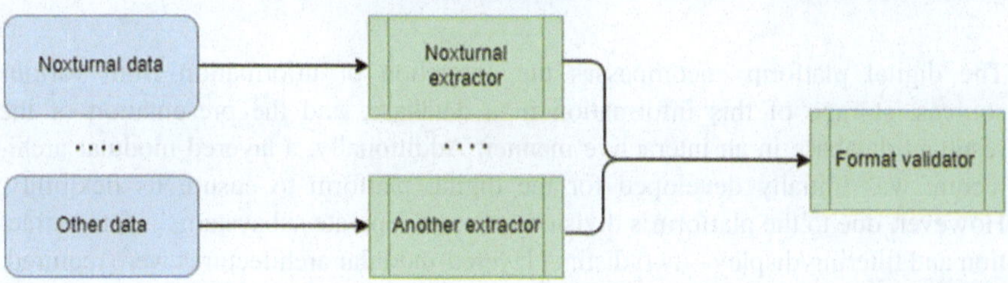

Fig. 3 Illustrates the sequential stages of data extraction followed by validation. For each unique data source, a dedicated extraction component is developed. Despite this individualized approach, all extraction components share a common format validation module. This module ensures that the data extracted from various sources is standardized and adaptable, maintaining consistency across the system. This arrangement facilitates the integration of data into the overarching database management system, optimizing both usability and reliability

4 Results

4.1 Architectural Constraints

In the designed database management system for extracted data, a relational database was selected to manage information from more than 10,000 sleep studies, offering robust search and filtering capabilities. The development of this database-driven information extraction system heavily relied on a suitable software architecture. A layered-modular architecture was chosen for its versatility across different applications and systems [21]. This architecture is particularly effective for presenting, reading, and filtering data, making it appropriate for use across various platforms including websites, desktop applications, and mobile apps. Other architectures like microkernel and modular were considered but did not offer the necessary flexibility for this project.

The architecture supports the extraction of information from a wide range of data sources, converting them into useful parameters. Extractors play a key role in processing and standardizing data formats, producing result sets that deliver detailed insights. An essential function is the creation of descriptive results that address specific research questions. For instance, a specialized extractor was developed for data from Noxturnal (sleep scoring software, Nox Medical, Reykjavík, Iceland) as part of the Sleep Revolution project. The system also needs to handle diverse data inputs such as those from smartwatches and sleep diaries, which necessitate independent components within the architecture. Format validation is critical to ensure that the extracted data conforms to the database format required by the architecture. The interplay between data sources, extractors, and the format validator is illustrated in Fig. 1.

4.2 Layered-Modular Architecture

The digital platform encompasses the extraction of information from various sources, storage of this information in a database, and the presentation of the resultant database in an interactive manner. Additionally, a layered-modular architecture was initially developed for the digital platform to ensure its flexibility. However, due to the platform's division into two separate subsystems—data extraction and filtering/display—two distinct layered-modular architectures were required. These layered-modular architectures are visualized in Figs. 4 and 5.

In the architecture, the presentation layer is designed to generate visual representations of data for applications. While each application may have its unique presentation layer, they all interact with a common secondary presentation layer. This secondary layer provides shared functionalities that are used across different presentation components enabling reusability between applications. For example, a function that converts filtered results into JSON (JavaScript Object Notation) format, which is commonly used by web and mobile applications for data interchange.

The decision to place a function in the primary presentation layer or the secondary presentation layer hinges on its utility and potential for reuse across multiple components or applications. This ensures that frequently used functions are centrally available, enhancing efficiency and reducing redundancy.

Simultaneously, the business layer contains a suite of logical functions essential for processing and managing data. This layer's reusability is critical, especially when new software solutions or external datasets need to integrate directly with the system. Functions are allocated to the business layer or the secondary presentation

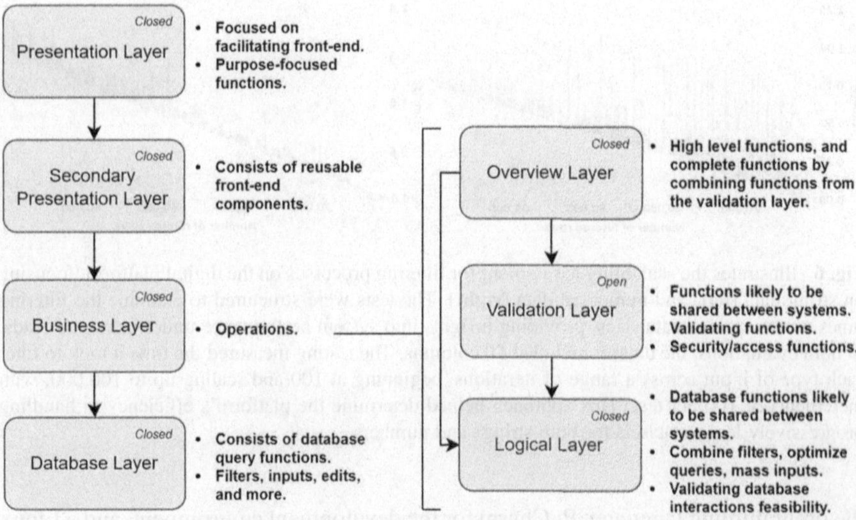

Fig. 4 Demonstrates the layered-modular architecture of the data filtering and display system, detailing the function of each layer. The architecture is divided into several layers, each designed to handle specific aspects of the system's functionality

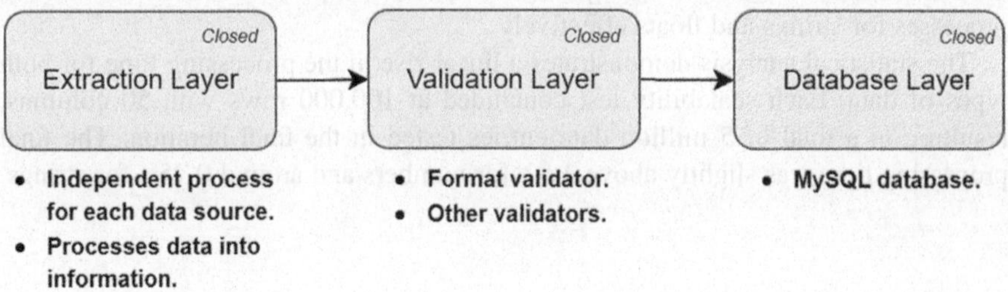

Fig. 5 Presents the layered-modular architecture used for extracting information from various data sources into the database

layer based on their specific contributions to the overall system operations. This strategic placement ensures that each functionality is positioned in the layer best suited to its role, maximizing the system's efficiency and adaptability.

4.3 Scalability

To evaluate the scalability of our digital platform, we assessed its performance, particularly focusing on the backend's ability to handle filters. We conducted tests using both floating-point numbers and string entries to understand how the system performs with our two most common data types. For the testing, we used Python as

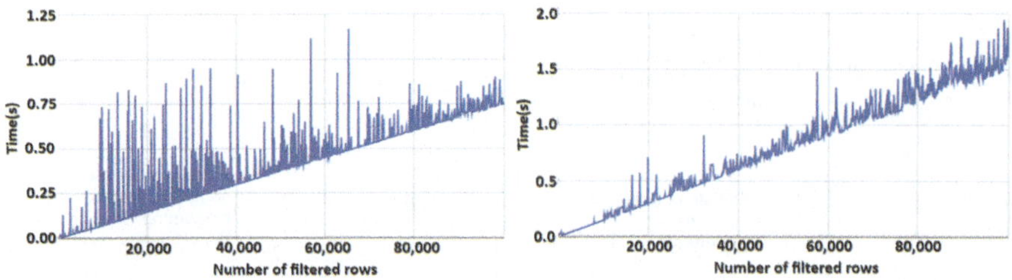

Fig. 6 Illustrates the scalability assessment for filtering processes on the digital platform, focusing on string data (**left**) and numerical data (**right**). The tests were structured to examine the filtering times across various data sizes, providing insights into system performance under increased loads. In both evaluations, the dataset included 50 columns. The testing measured the time it took to filter each type of input across a range of iterations, beginning at 100 and scaling up to 100,000, with increments of 100 per test. This approach helped determine the platform's efficiency in handling progressively larger datasets for both strings and numbers

the programming language, PyCharm for the development environment, and a Linux operating system. The hardware included a Z270X-Gaming K5 motherboard, an Intel(R) Core(TM) i7-7700K CPU at 4.20GHz with 4 cores and 8 logical processors, and an NVIDIA GeForce RTX 2080 TI graphics card. Figure 6 shows the results from these scalability tests, highlighting the system's capability to manage filtering processes for strings and floats effectively.

The statistical analysis demonstrates a linear rise in the processing time for both types of data. Each scalability test concluded at 100,000 rows with 50 columns, resulting in a total of 5 million data entries tested in the final iteration. The final processing time was slightly above 1.5 s for numbers and around 0.75 s for strings.

4.4 Usability and User Experience

During the usability and user experience testing of our digital platform, ten participants engaged in a series of evaluations to assess the system's effectiveness. These included:

1. **Performing Four Timed Tasks**: Each participant completed four specific tasks, with the time taken to finish each task recorded. The tasks were designed to evaluate their ability to navigate and utilize the system efficiently.
2. **System Usability Scale (SUS) Questionnaire**: Participants responded to a series of 10 questions using a Likert scale from 1 (strongly disagree) to 5 (strongly agree), intended to measure the usability of the system. However, due to a setup error in Google Forms, one question related to identifying system irregularities was accidentally omitted.

Table 1 Displays the results from the System Usability Scale questionnaire completed by participants during the usability testing. This table lists each question from the questionnaire along with the average rating and the standard deviation for each, reflecting how much participants agreed or disagreed with the statements. The scale for ratings ranged from 1 (strongly disagree) to 5 (strongly agree). Each question aimed to evaluate different facets of the system's usability, such as ease of use, satisfaction, and efficiency. Note that one question was inadvertently omitted due to an error in setting up the Google Forms, which pertained to identifying any irregularities in the system

Question	Average rating	Standard deviation
I think I would like to use the system frequently	4.1	0.8
I found the system to be simple	4.7	0.5
I thought the system was easy to use	4.8	0.4
I think that I can use the system without the support of a technical person	4.9	0.3
I found the various function in the website were well integrated	4.2	0.6
I would imagine that most people would learn to use the system very quickly	4.5	0.5
I found the system very intuitive	4.1	0.7
I felt very confident using the system	4.3	0.6
I could use the system without having to learn anything new	4.6	0.5

3. **AttrakDiff Questionnaire**: This questionnaire gauged the aesthetic and functional appeal of the user interface, providing insights into the user's emotional response to the system.
4. **Semi-structured Interview**: Each participant also took part in a semi-structured interview focusing on their subjective experiences and any negative aspects they encountered while using the system.

The group of participants comprised six members from the Sleep Revolution project, two sleep experts, and two novice users with a background in research and databases. Of these, eight completed the test in person, while two participated remotely using screen-sharing tools on Discord and Messenger. All participants successfully completed the tasks, except for one who confused the AHI (Apnea-Hypopnea Index) and AI (Arousal Index) parameters during one of the tasks. The average time to complete each task was under 30 s, except for the final task, which took about 45 s on average.

The findings from these activities, including the detailed results from the SUS (with the noted omission), are presented in Table 1.

The testing results revealed that participants found the system user-friendly and expressed an inclination to use it again in the future. The overall usability score reached 90 on the System Usability Scale, which is well above the benchmark score of 68 that indicates high usability. This high score reflects a strong endorsement of the system's user interface and its operational functionality.

Regarding the AttrakDiff questionnaire, it consists of 25 questions designed to gauge the emotional and aesthetic appeal of the user interface. Each question pairs two contrasting attributes, and participants indicate their preference using a scale represented by seven radio buttons. These function like a slider, allowing users to

Table 2 Compiles the results from the AttrakDiff questionnaire administered during the usability test. It presents the average score and standard deviation for each of the 25 questions. This table helps to quantitatively assess the system's appeal and usability from an aesthetic and functional perspective, highlighting areas where the user interface meets or falls short of user expectations

Question	Average rating	Standard deviation
Human (1) or technical (7)	4.0	1.2
Isolating (1) or connective (7)	4.4	1.0
Pleasant (1) or unpleasant (7)	2,1	0.8
Inventive (1) or conventional (7)	4.3	1.8
Simple (1) or complicated (7)	1.6	0.7
Professional (1) or unprofessional (7)	1.7	0.9
Ugly (1) or attractive (7)	4.9	1.4
Practical (1) or impractical (7)	1.7	0.5
Likeable (1) or disagreeable (7)	1.6	0.7
Cumbersome (1) or straightforward (7)	6.3	0.6
Stylish (1) or tacky (7)	3.7	1.3
Predictable (1) or unpredictable (7)	1.9	1.2
Cheap (1) or premium (7)	4.5	1.0
Alienating (1) or integrating (7)	6.0	0.9
Brings me closer to people (1) or separates me from people (7)	3.5	1.0
Unpresentable (1) or presentable (7)	5.6	0.9
Rejecting (1) or inviting (7)	5.5	1.1
Unimaginative (1) or creative (7)	4.5	1.1
Good (1) or bad (7)	2.1	1.1
Innovative (1) or conservative (7)	2.1	1.6
Dull (1) or captivating (7)	4.5	1.3
Undemanding (1) or challenging (7)	2.4	1.0
Motivating (1) or discouraging (7)	3.2	1.2
Novel (1) or ordinary (7)	4.0	1.3
Unruly (1) or manageable (7)	6.4	0.7

select a point closer to the attribute that best matches their experience, with 1 corresponding to the attribute on the left and 7 to the one on the right (Table 2).

Some participants faced difficulties with the AttrakDiff questionnaire due to the ambiguity of certain questions or because the questions did not precisely reflect their experiences. Despite these challenges, the majority of responses tended toward the more positive option among the two presented for each question, indicating a generally favorable perception of the system.

During the semi-structured interviews, the conversation centered around identifying gaps within the current system and discussing additional features necessary for participants to effectively use it for their specific tasks. A common point raised was the need for improved system overview and navigation, which participants found to be cumbersome and time-consuming in its current state. Moreover, there was a unanimous call for the integration of more data sources, parameters, and functionalities. Participants indicated that these enhancements were essential before they could consider adopting the system for regular use in their research or professional activities. This feedback is invaluable for guiding further development and ensuring the system meets the real-world needs of its users.

5 Discussion

Our world is becoming increasingly information-centric, collecting a myriad of data types and expanding volumes across society. The rise of data-driven research, especially in healthcare settings, necessitates the development of systems capable of extracting meaningful insights from abundant and diverse data [2–4].

Our evaluation primarily concentrated on the backend of the digital platform, utilizing a filterable database and an extraction mechanism. Our approach employs fully structured data due to its performance advantages, albeit at the expense of some flexibility [12]. This choice aligns with the importance of performance and usability in our context. Furthermore, unstructured data, like raw sleep measurements, poses storage and navigation challenges [12].

Our findings illustrate the applicability of layered-modular architecture in designing complex digital platforms suitable for socio-technical and multidisciplinary scenarios. The layered structure enhances adaptability and integrates validation layers, facilitating the incorporation of new features while maintaining system credibility. Usability tests and performance evaluations confirm the expandability, utility, and scalability of the architecture, highlighting its strong usability and user experience aspects. Insights from the semi-structured interview prompted various enhancements, including additional data types, more engaging visualization options, and improved interactions.

Prior research on platforms has explored various facets of platform dynamics [27]. Some studies have delved into platform architecture [28, 29], platform economics [30], leadership within platforms [31], and the generative nature of digital platforms [32]. Additionally, digital platforms have found applications across diverse industries, including finance [33], healthcare [34, 35], transportation [36], and electricity distribution [37]. A recent wave of research has emerged concerning data-driven digital health platforms [7, 18, 38], resulting in an expanding literature encompassing different application domains and scopes [39]. Nonetheless, scant attention has been directed toward identifying suitable architectures for intricate research projects that are both multidisciplinary and socio-technical in nature.

Furthermore, we acknowledge the limitations of our evaluation. The architecture's testing was confined to a subset of data sources and volumes, and its performance with larger datasets requires further exploration. Scalability tests demonstrated efficient filtering of entries, yet participant feedback indicated potential resource-intensive functionality gaps. A more comprehensive user-centric assessment is necessary to thoroughly gauge scalability and potential bottlenecks.

While the AttrakDiff and System Usability Scale surveys affirmed the platform's positive aspects, feedback from semi-structured interviews introduced concerns about missing functionalities and dataset limitations, influencing usability perceptions. Moreover, the predefined tasks might not accurately reflect real-world scenarios, potentially leading to differing usability insights. In summary, the design, development, and utilization of data-driven digital health platforms significantly rely on architectural choices. Our exploration of layered-modular architecture underscores its value in managing intricate data requirements. However, further research is essential to fully unravel its real-world usability implications.

6 Conclusion

In conclusion, the designed layered-modular architecture holds substantial promise. This architecture, defined by distinct code layers or packages, has been successfully applied in our study. The results confirm that our layered-modular approach establishes a resilient framework, crucial in complex multidisciplinary environments. Creating data-driven digital health platforms hinges on factors like robust data availability, diverse filtration capabilities and responsive hosting. Our architecture's validation via usability tests, surveys, and interviews demonstrates its competence in effectively handling data. Furthermore, its linear scalability makes it adaptable for larger datasets. However, the architecture's application to more extensive datasets remains unexplored, and pre-determined tasks in usability tests could introduce bias. While promising, further research is needed for real-world usability insights. From these findings, three design principles emerge: First, the design and development of digital platforms should center around components with singular purposes, fostering easier replacement, updates, or removal of elements in the future. Second, the integration of validation layers simplifies additions to the platform, enhances result credibility, scalability, and reliability. Lastly, the utilization of usability tests in tandem with semi-structured interviews emerges as a valuable methodology for evaluating products, identifying user challenges, and gaining insights into prospective enhancements and expansions. Addressing our research question, we successfully created an architecture for extracting sleep data, optimizing modularity and enhancing usability. This layered-modular approach significantly improves data presentation and filtering, ensuring usability, scalability, and performance.

References

1. Statista: Volume of data/information created, captured, copied, and consumed worldwide from 2010 to 2020, with forecasts from 2021 to 2025. Accessed April 28, 2024, from https://www.statista.com/statistics/871513/worldwide-data-created/
2. Raghupathi, W., & Raghupathi, V. (2014). Big data analytics in healthcare: Promise and potential. *Health Information Science and Systems, 2*, 1–10.

3. Pevernagie, D. A., Gnidovec-Strazisar, B., Grote, L., Heinzer, R., McNicholas, W. T., Penzel, T., Randerath, W., Schiza, S., Verbraecken, J., & Arnardottir, E. S. (2020). On the rise and fall of the apnea–hypopnea index: A historical review and critical appraisal. *Journal of Sleep Research, 29*, e13066. https://doi.org/10.1111/jsr.13066
4. Arnardottir, E. S., Islind, A. S., & Óskarsdóttir, M. (2021). The future of sleep measurements: A review and perspective. *Sleep Medicine Clinics, 16*, 447–464. https://doi.org/10.1016/j.jsmc.2021.05.004
5. Mehra, R., Stone, K. L., Varosy, P. D., Hoffman, A. R., Marcus, G. M., Blackwell, T., Ibrahim, O. A., Salem, R., & Redline, S. (2009). Nocturnal arrhythmias across a spectrum of obstructive and central sleep-disordered breathing in older men: Outcomes of sleep disorders in older men (MrOS sleep) study. *Archives of Internal Medicine, 169*, 1147–1155. https://doi.org/10.1001/archinternmed.2009.138
6. Agrawal, D., Bernstein, P., Bertino, E., Davidson, S., Dayal, U., Franklin, M., Gehrke, J., Haas, L., Halevy, A., Han, J., Jagadish, H. V., Labrinidis, A., Madden, S., Papakonstantinou, Y., Patel, J., Ramakrishnan, R., Ross, K., Shahabi, C., Suciu, D., Vaithyanathan, S., & Widom, J. (2011). Challenges and opportunities with big data 2011-1. Cyber Center Technical Reports.
7. Sveinbjarnarson, B. F., Schmitz, L., Arnardottir, E. S., & Islind, A. S. (2023). The sleep revolution platform: A dynamic data source pipeline and digital platform architecture for complex sleep data. *Current Sleep Medicine Reports, 9*(2), 91–100. https://doi.org/10.1007/s40675-023-00252-x
8. Bellinger, G., Castro, D., Mills, A.: Data, information, knowledge, and wisdom, (2004).
9. Arnardottir, E. S., Islind, A. S., Óskarsdóttir, M., Ólafsdóttir, K. A., August, E., Jónasdóttir, L., Hrubos-Strøm, H., Saavedra, J. M., Grote, L., Hedner, J., Höskuldsson, S., Ágústsson, J. S., Jóhannsdóttir, K. R., McNicholas, W. T., Pevernagie, D., Sund, R., Töyräs, J., Leppänen, T., & Revolution, S. (2022). The sleep Revolution project: The concept and objectives. *Journal of Sleep Research, 31*, e13630. https://doi.org/10.1111/jsr.13630
10. Harrell, M. C., & Bradley, M. (2009). Data collection methods: Semi-structured interviews and focus groups.
11. Duval, E., Hodgins, W., Sutton, S., & Weibel, S. L. (2002). Metadata principles and practicalities. *D-lib Magazine, 8*, 1–10.
12. Sint, R., Schaffert, S., Stroka, S., & Ferstl, R. (2009). Combining unstructured, fully structured and semi-structured information in semantic wikis. In *CEUR workshop proceedings* (pp. 73–87). Citeseer.
13. Buneman, P. (1997). Semistructured data. In *Proceedings of the sixteenth ACM SIGACT-SIGMOD-SIGART symposium on Principles of database systems* (pp. 117–121).
14. Coren, S. (1998). Sleep deprivation, psychosis and mental efficiency. *Psychiatric Times, 15*, 1–3.
15. Chokroverty, S. (2010). Overview of sleep & sleep disorders. *Indian Journal of Medical Research, 131*, 126.
16. Epstein, J. B., Rea, G., Wong, F. L., Spinelli, J., & Stevenson-Moore, P. (1987). Osteonecrosis: Study of the relationship of dental extractions in patients receiving radiotherapy. *Head & Neck Surgery, 10*, 48–54. https://doi.org/10.1002/hed.2890100108
17. Rundo, J. V., & Downey, R. (2019). Chapter 25 – Polysomnography. In K. H. Levin & P. Chauvel (Eds.), *Handbook of clinical neurology* (pp. 381–392). Elsevier. https://doi.org/10.1016/B978-0-444-64032-1.00025-4
18. Schmitz, L., Sveinbjarnarson, B., Gunnarsson, G., Davíðsson, Ó., Davíðsson, Þ., Arnardottir, E., Óskarsdóttir, M., Islind, A.: Towards a digital sleep diary standard. (2022).
19. Jóhannsdóttir, K. R., Ferretti, D., Árnadóttir, B. S., & Jónsdóttir, M. K. (2021). Objective measures of cognitive performance in sleep disorder research. *Sleep Medicine Clinics, 16*, 575–593. https://doi.org/10.1016/j.jsmc.2021.08.002
20. Yoo, Y., Henfridsson, O., & Lyytinen, K. (2010). Research commentary—The new organizing logic of digital innovation: An agenda for information systems research. *Information Systems Research, 21*, 724–735. https://doi.org/10.1287/isre.1100.0322
21. Richards, M. (2015). *Event-driven architecture. Software architecture patterns* (pp. 18–19). O'REILLY.

22. Simon, H. A. (2019). *The sciences of the artificial, reissue of the third edition with a new introduction by John Laird*. MIT press.
23. Gubser, R., Schulte-Althoff, M., Heinemann, N., Pohle, J., & Fürstenau, D. (2023). Data governance strategies for data platforms—A multiple case study in nursing care. ECIS 2023 Research-in-Progress Papers.
24. Sein, M. K., Henfridsson, O., Purao, S., Rossi, M., & Lindgren, R. (2011). Action design research. *MIS Quarterly, 35*, 37–56. https://doi.org/10.2307/23043488
25. Bangor, A., Kortum, P. T., & Miller, J. T. (2008). An empirical evaluation of the system usability scale. *International Journal of Human–Computer Interaction, 24*, 574–594. https://doi.org/10.1080/10447310802205776
26. Hassenzahl, M., Burmester, M., & Koller, F. (2003). AttrakDiff: Ein Fragebogen zur Messung wahrgenommener hedonischer und pragmatischer Qualität. In G. Szwillus & J. Ziegler (Eds.), *Mensch & Computer 2003: Interaktion in Bewegung* (pp. 187–196). Vieweg+Teubner Verlag. https://doi.org/10.1007/978-3-322-80058-9_19
27. de Reuver, M., Sørensen, C., & Basole, R. C. (2018). The digital platform: A research agenda. *Journal of Information Technology, 33*, 124–135. https://doi.org/10.1057/s41265-016-0033-3
28. Gawer, A. (2011). *Platforms, markets and innovation*. Edward Elgar Publishing.
29. Tiwana, A., Konsynski, B., & Bush, A. A. (2010). Research commentary—platform evolution: Coevolution of platform architecture, governance, and environmental dynamics. *Information Systems Research, 21*, 675–687. https://doi.org/10.1287/isre.1100.0323
30. Gawer, A. R., & Srnicek, N. (2021). Online platforms: Economic and societal effects. Panel for the future of science and technology (STOA) European Parliament.
31. Leong, C., Pan, S., Leidner, D., & Huang, J.-S. (2019). Platform leadership: Managing boundaries for the network growth of digital platforms. *Journal of the Association for Information Systems, 20*, 1. https://doi.org/10.17705/1jais.00577
32. Fürstenau, D., Baiyere, A., Schewina, K., Schulte-Althoff, M., & Rothe, H. (2023). Extended generativity theory on digital platforms. *Information Systems Research, 34*(4), 1686–1710. https://doi.org/10.1287/isre.2023.1209
33. de Reuver, M., Verschuur, E., Nikayin, F., Cerpa, N., & Bouwman, H. (2015). Collective action for mobile payment platforms: A case study on collaboration issues between banks and telecom operators. *Electronic Commerce Research and Applications, 14*, 331–344. https://doi.org/10.1016/j.elerap.2014.08.004
34. Bahmani, A., Alavi, A., Buergel, T., Upadhyayula, S., Wang, Q., Ananthakrishnan, S. K., Alavi, A., Celis, D., Gillespie, D., Young, G., Xing, Z., Nguyen, M. H. H., Haque, A., Mathur, A., Payne, J., Mazaheri, G., Li, J. K., Kotipalli, P., Liao, L., Bhasin, R., Cha, K., Rolnik, B., Celli, A., Dagan-Rosenfeld, O., Higgs, E., Zhou, W., Berry, C. L., Van Winkle, K. G., Contrepois, K., Ray, U., Bettinger, K., Datta, S., Li, X., & Snyder, M. P. (2021). A scalable, secure, and interoperable platform for deep data-driven health management. *Nature Communications, 12*, 5757. https://doi.org/10.1038/s41467-021-26040-1
35. Islind, A. S. (2018). *Platformization: Co-designing digital platforms in practice*
36. Svahn, F., Lindgren, R., & Mathiassen, L. (2015). Applying options thinking to shape generativity in digital innovation: an action research into connected cars. In *2015 48th Hawaii international conference on system sciences* (pp. 4141–4150). https://doi.org/10.1109/HICSS.2015.497
37. Kiesling, L. L. (2015). Implications of smart grid innovation for organizational models in electricity distribution. https://papers.ssrn.com/abstract=2571251
38. Sigurðardóttir, S. G., Islind, A. S., & Óskarsdóttir, M. (2022). Collecting data from a mobile app and a smartwatch supports treatment of schizophrenia and bipolar disorder. In *Challenges of trustable AI and added-value on health* (pp. 239–243). IOS Press.
39. Islind, A. S., Lindroth, T., Snis, U. L., & Sørensen, C. (2016). Co-creation and fine-tuning of boundary resources in small-scale platformization. In U. Lundh Snis (Ed.), *Nordic contributions in IS research* (pp. 149–162). Springer International Publishing. https://doi.org/10.1007/978-3-319-43597-8_11

Drivers from Extended Institutional Theory Supporting the DPP as a Tool of CE

Luca Balzani and Katia Corsi

Abstract Purpose: To facilitate a circular economy (CE) transition, the European Union (EU) introduced digital product passports (DPPs) as useful tools for providing information on products' compositions, origins and disposal. DPPs enable product-related information and processes to be electronically registered and shared amongst supply chain businesses, consumers and authorities.

In this work we aimed to integrate findings from the available literature to offer insight into the conceptual framework of DPPs as circularity tools and their roles in companies in terms of legitimacy, compliance and relevance to the many sustainability variables.

Design: This work conceptualizes DPPs based on theoretical frameworks for promoting companies' sustainability and outlines prospects for using DPPs. A critical analytical review of the academic literature and available professional documents has been conducted to investigate DPPs' connotations. Then the new institutional theory and its extended version has been applied to DPPs to enhance conceptualization.

Originality/value: Although some authors have analysed DPPs, most works offer an engineering and IT point of view. In this work we attempt to enhance the descriptive conceptualization of DPPs by focusing on their influence on organizations' behaviour and the relationship between organizations and the social context, thus offering a business perspective.

Research implications: DPPs facilitate the harmonization of economic development (efficiency) and environmental protection (legitimacy). The application of DPPs could be explored with a focus on additional devices and technologies, such as blockchains.

The original version of the chapter has been revised. A correction to this chapter can be found at https://doi.org/10.1007/978-3-031-75586-6_24

L. Balzani (✉) · K. Corsi
University of Sassari, Sassari, Italy
e-mail: l.balzani@phd.uniss.it; kcorsi@uniss.it

A. M. Braccini et al. (eds.), *Digital (Eco) Systems and Societal Challenges*, Lecture Notes in Information Systems and Organisation 72,
https://doi.org/10.1007/978-3-031-75586-6_7

Keywords Digital product passport · Circular economy · Digitalization · Traceability · Extended institutional theory

1 Introduction

The European Union (EU) is taking a great interest in the circular economy (CE), and the aim of achieving a transition from a linear economy to one in which resources continue their life cycles is evident in many acts issued by the European Commission (EC). In recent years, among the most important regulatory acts is the European Green Deal (EGD), which promotes the EU's transition towards more sustainable models through a so-called twin transition: an energy transition using renewable energy sources to produce electricity and a digital transition that involves adopting digital technologies to make pre-existing models more efficient [1].

The EGD was issued in 2019, but the sustainability objectives can be traced back to previous documents issued internationally by the United Nations (UN), such as the sustainable development goals (SDGs), which clearly indicate the direction, at an international level, for achieving environmental, social and economic sustainability in the coming years. A CE is vital for achieving the SDGs, since SDG 12 aims to ensure sustainable consumption and production models [2].

SDGs have many aspects, including the incorporation of high levels of renewables into the energy mix, the reduction of greenhouse gas (GHG) emissions in the environment, the reduction of waste and the promotion of material recycling systems, which raise important issues related to the recovery of strategic raw materials, such as rare earth.

To support the EGD and the commitment to reaching a sustainable system, the Circular Economy Action Plan (CEAP) has been formulated [3], representing a fundamental step towards defining structural measures for the transition to a CE, including the Eco-Design for Sustainable Product Regulation (ESPR) [4] The ESPR aims to enhance consumer empowerment, offer solutions to the EU's dependence on raw materials and promote new circular business models [5]. Moreover, it draws attention to the impact of product life cycles on the environment [5].

From a CE perspective, the attention is on managing resources, products and waste, improving the product life cycle loop and recovering materials with strategic value. Digitization has been proposed as a means to achieve these objectives and thus support the transition towards sustainable systems [5].

Digitization opens the door to effectively managing the data and information generated by business activities. As explained in the next section, the efficient exchange of information throughout supply chains is the basis for efficient material recovery and product reuse processes, the aim of which is to overcome the deficiencies of these operations, such as a lack of information transparency, product traceability and information access, enabling companies to make decisions oriented towards sustainability and seize the opportunities of new business models. In this context, the ESPR indicates that digital product passports (DPPs) are effective tools for supporting the transition to a CE. However, to date, few academic and professional works have offered univocal interpretations of these tools, with most studies relating them to specific cases and/or contexts without attempting theoretical abstraction regarding their roles.

The novelty of the subject, which is still embryonic, means that the researchers have largely listed a series of characteristics and possible variations of DPPs, aiming to provide answers to questions regarding the functions of DPPs and their operational characteristics. These researchers have analyzed various types of product passports (PPs), material passports (MPs), digital battery passports (DBPs) and so on without necessarily considering their general connotations.

Based on these considerations, we aimed to integrate findings from the available literature to offer insight into the conceptual framework of DPPs as circularity tools and their roles in companies in terms of legitimacy, compliance and relevance to the many sustainability variables. For these reasons, this paper has two goals. First, by analyzing selected works, we aim to identify the different characteristics that DPPs must have to be effective and to support a CE. Second, we aim to provide a theoretical conceptualization of DPPs by adopting a sustainability framework based on institutional theory and its subsequent developments. In Sect. 2, we introduce DPPs, considering the definition and purpose of a DPP (2.1), and explain the theoretical framework used for our analysis of DPPs (2.2). Section 3 presents the methodology and a flowchart of the research process. Finally, we present the findings and discussion and draw conclusions.

2 Digital Product Passports

2.1 Definition and Purposes

Herein, we situate DPP development in the context of the transition towards a CE based on current examples of DPP-related projects. There is no single definition of a CE since the topic is vast and embraces many sectors; however, many works have followed the Ellen MacArthur Foundation, seeing a CE as "a systems solution framework that tackles global challenges like climate change, biodiversity loss, waste and pollution" based on three key factors: "eliminate waste and pollution, circulate products and materials, regenerate nature" [6].

Kohronen et al. 2018 [7], to define a CE, reported several definitions of a CE based on the indications provided over the years by the Ellen MacArthur Foundation. Among these various definitions, due to their relevance to the DPP theme, we highlight the one given by Hobson 2016 [8]:

> A CE has been defined as an industrial system that is restorative or regenerative by intention and design. It replaces the end-of-life concept with restoration, shifts towards renewable energy, eliminates toxic chemicals, which impair reuse and return to the biosphere, and aims to eliminate waste through the superior design of materials, products, systems and business models.

Recycling is just one way to improve the circularity of resources through a circular design and extend product life spans; another is to introduce new business models to facilitate the exchange of quality data and information [9].

The EU proposes, through the ESPR, using DPPs to facilitate supply chain management, sustainable resource flows and consumer empowerment [10]. The scope of ESPR is focused on waste reduction and aims to guarantee that products made or sold in the EU are eligible to be included in a CE, climate neutral and efficient in terms of resource consumption [5]. Although we have no clear definition of a DPP, several authors have attempted to define the concept through the functions and characteristics of DPPs.

According to Plociennik et al. 2022 [11], a DPP allows exchanges of information relating to product materials, such as hazardous materials, material flows and disassembly instructions. As reported by Gotz et al. 2022 [5], the European Commission (EC) considers a DPP to be an electronically accessible product-specific data set that registers and processes information about a product through a data carrier and shares it among consumers, supply-chain businesses and authorities. Based on this definition, Gotz et al. 2022 [5], also explained that a DPP can provide information about a product, its origin and composition to facilitate its repair or disassembly and the recovery of its components for recycling or disposal. Adisorn et al. 2021 [12], also mentioned another DPP element: 'trace and track' information. The objectives of this digital tool are clear: to promote transparency throughout the product life cycle and among stakeholders [12] by digitalizing the product life cycle [13] and to alleviate the lack of relevant information among the various actors involved [12].

DPPs are a novelty that has fostered debate and comparisons among scholars and professionals to establish the information a DPP must contain. According to some authors, a DPP should report manufacturing, usage, end-of-life and life-cycle data [11, 14]. Plociennik et al. 2022 [11], pointed out that the requirements for DPPs are influenced by various criteria, including the complexity of the product and its life cycle, the value of the product or its fractions and its harmful potential. Moreover, from a CE perspective, it is necessary to ask what information favours second-hand purchases [12].

Issues still remain regarding the possibility of having different DPPs for different stakeholder groups, which raises the question of who should manage the DPP system while respecting the recognition of intellectual property and knowledge [5]. According to Adisorn et al. 2021 [5], manufacturers are the main providers of product-related information; however, to determine which subjects will be able to access this information, the type of provided information, the type of interaction with the DPP and the goals of the interaction should be considered.

It may be helpful to analyze other types of passports to clarify some of their common aspects, but it is important to specify that although the product groups covered by DPPs are unclear, the World Business Council for Sustainable Development (Wbcsd) prioritized the industries recognized as priorities by the CEAP regulation:

- Electronics and Information and Communication Technologies (ICT)
- Batteries and vehicles
- Textiles

- Plastics
- Furniture
- Construction and buildings
- Chemicals [9].

Notably, some industries have been excluded, such as food, human and veterinary medicinal products, products of human origin, living plants, plant and animal products relating directly to their future reproduction, animals and micro-organisms [9]. Researchers have analyzed various passports adopted by other sectors for different product types, but the most relevant for this study is the DBP, which is a passport required by the EC and is expected to be introduced in 2026 [15]. Regarding the CEAP, the EU Sustainable Battery Regulation supports a CE in its intention to standardize the battery sector to guarantee the sustainability and safety of its products and allow for the recovery of raw materials from them [14]. Applying information technology (IT) is expected to increase transparency in the battery market and the safe sharing of data [10].

Berger et al. 2022 [15], analyzed a DBP and determined four categories of information that should be considered:

- Battery information
- Sustainability and circularity information
- Diagnostic and maintenance information
- Value chain actors' information.

Each of these categories has sub-categories relating to battery information, as follows:

- General product information (manufacturing information, battery application type and identifier, battery chemistry employed)
- Specific product information (information about performance properties, specifications related to materials, electrical engineering and battery structure) [15].

Walden et al. 2021 [13], listed the benefits of applying a DBP, supported by the Global Battery Alliance, highlighting the possibility of validating and tracing information across the value chain, transparency related to practices and impacts throughout the battery life cycle and the opportunity to standardize and benchmark sustainability and responsibility across batteries.

Besides the EU battery regulation, other regulations state information requirements for specific sectors in various initiatives, such as End-of-Life Vehicles for dismantling, testing and storage information regarding the reused parts of vehicles [16]; Registration, Evaluation, Authorisation and Restriction of Chemicals (REACH) for safety data sheets and further information on chemicals [17]; and Waste Electrical and Electronic Equipment (WEEE) for information on electrical and electronic equipment [18]. There are still other regulations that require information to be provided on products, the phases of the product life cycle and defined subjects who operate during the life cycle. Other passport types allow for the extension of analysis of a PP as an instrument for providing product information, enhancing transparency along the value chain and sharing information to achieve sustainability and a CE.

Adisorn et al. 2021 [12], highlighted different product information initiatives, such as MPs, the Maersk cradle-to-cradle (C2C) passport containing material information for recycling products at the end of their lives and the Asset Administration Shell (AAS).

MPs can be understood as digital information systems that enable value-chain stakeholders to share material information and improve life-cycle transparency [19]. The construction sector appears to be the main user of MPs. They boost clarity related to building materials' circularity features and provide information based on environmental product declarations (EPDs) or technical data sheets [19]. Building information modelling (BIM) supports MPs by collecting information on building materials and evaluating their environmental impact, particularly whether and to what extent they can be recycled [13]. BIM is recognized as a building-level inventory database [12] that represents the phases of the building life cycle [20].

According to Plociennik et al. 2022 [11], the AAS supports DPP implementation. The AAS creates a digital twin or digital image of a product, connecting the physical object (asset) to the digital one [11, 12]. It includes an abstraction layer, and its model structure is articulated via sub-models that contain the asset's characteristics, technical aspects and functionalities [11].

Buildings as a Material Bank (BAMB) is a European initiative involving several institutes and countries in the building sector. It aims to create a circular solution and proposes a new approach by considering buildings as temporary material storage units using a digital platform that comprises more than 300 MPs [20, 21].

Numerous projects and initiatives aim to record product information to favour a CE. The study of digital passports shows that differences between the various types of passports relate to their design and scope, which differ because the problems they are intended to solve vary [22]. However, we can list some of the benefits associated with DPPs.

DPPs enhance the availability of information related to the entities, locations, certificates and product composition [10], providing transparency for product users [12] and facilitating sustainable choices [5]. Moreover, DPPs increase traceability and consistency for value-chain players, providing potential new business models to underpin sustainable investment decisions and resource optimization [5]. In this context, various issues emerge that require solutions, such as data management and infrastructure characteristics.

The Boston Consulting Group asked whether DPPs must or should concern certain product groups, company sizes, application levels, data storage, data carrier, access, requirements and governance to be feasible [9]. Similar questions were raised by Adisorn et al. 2021 [12], who asked how a synergetic data flow should be organized and highlighted the challenge of producing data and information during the use phase. Gotz et al. 2022 [5], questioned how and 'whether social sustainability data should be part of a DPP'. Many such open questions and challenges remain unresolved.

2.2 *Dpp Through the Lens of Institutional Theory*

Institutional theory [22] focuses on the behaviours of social actors (individuals and organizations) influenced by their surrounding institutions. A new version of this theory, labeled 'new-institutionalism', considers institutions 'composed of cultural-cognitive, normative and regulatory elements which, together with the associated activities and resources, provide stability and meaning' [23], thereby influencing decision-making and organizational practices. The pioneering work of new institutional theorists explains that organizations are forced by different pressures to make very similar decisions and to adopt similar practices and processes [24].

In recent years, this theory has been used by many scholars to analyze corporate sustainability issues, such as sustainable disclosure [25, 26], sustainable supply chains [27, 28] and sustainable models [29, 30]. Since the theme of CE has recently gained attention within the corporate sustainability field, several researchers have used this theory to interpret different strategies, models and tools for facilitating a CE [31–33]. Hence, applying institutional theory to DPPs as a new tool to support a CE could help in better characterizing these instruments and theoretically substantiating the effect of external pressures on their adoption and diffusion.

Different forces encourage sustainable practices to legitimate organizations and make them desirable and appropriate within social norms, values and beliefs. Research regarding this legitimacy has driven organizations towards isomorphism. In fact, according to more traditional institutional theory frameworks [24, 34], three isomorphic mechanisms can explain sustainable behaviour. Coercive isomorphism is based on compliance with the rules and laws of governments and institutions, such as the EU, which influence good practices by imposing penalties. Normative isomorphism relates to pressures encouraging organizations to be more conscious of new models and new social rules, which call for a commitment to resolving environmental problems. Normative pressures arise from professional and educational institutions, such as universities and professional networks, that provide education and standards. Mimetic isomorphism is linked to cognitive factors, which, to reduce uncertainty, lead firms to copy the best practices of other firms that have demonstrated success. These pressures allow firms to gain and/or maintain legitimacy by imitating successful behaviours and minimizing the risk of being first movers. Through mimetic isomorphism, firms could obtain legitimacy and efficiency; conversely, through coercive and normative isomorphism, compliance with rules helps firms to become legitimate, but not necessarily to increase their efficiency and performance.

These considerations opened the way for the extended version of neo-institutional theory applied by some scholars [35, 36] to conceptualize CE practices. This theory proposes two forms of isomorphism: the traditional form is the sociological variant oriented towards legitimacy seeking, based on three mechanisms of isomorphism, and the economic variant is based on forms of imitation (recalling mimetic isomorphism), which can operate collectively among organizations to help them achieve efficiency objectives. A CE can be defined as follows:

A production and consumption model that involves reusing, repairing, refurbishing and recycling existing materials and products to keep materials within the economy, wherever possible. A CE implies that waste will itself become a resource, consequently minimizing the actual amount of waste'.[1]

The extended institutional theory, including the economic variant, is appropriate for conceptualizing CE practices, including DPPs.

The economic variant adds three more mechanisms of isomorphism based on imitation:

1) Frequency-based imitation, which refers to the mimicking of actions that reach a critical mass of adopters.
2) Trait-based imitation, which involves the adoption of the practices espoused by prestigious firms.
3) Outcome-based imitation, which entails copying actions that provide salient positive outcomes [36].

Kauppi 2013 [35], emphasized the social and economic variants of neo-institutional theory and highlighted that, in mimetic theory, there is an orientation towards efficiency and legitimacy: the three types of mimicking of the economic variant have commonalities with mimetic isomorphism, which is evident if we consider benchmarking, which borrows best practices from organizations seen as leaders or 'best in class' [35, 37]. Benchmarking is a typical behaviour related to mimetic pressures and an 'outcome-based imitation' compliant with the economic variant; it allows firms to gather legitimacy and reduce costs and risks linked to uncertain strategies and practices based on profit-maximization logic. According to these double variants of institutional theory, Do et al. 2022 [36], proposed a different taxonomy for influencing factors (as shown in Fig. 1). Among the sociological variants, they identified two types of factors that should guarantee the legitimacy of adopted practices: (1) regulatory factors related to coercive isomorphism and (2) socio-cognitive factors related to normative and mimetic isomorphism, compliant with Scott's model [34]. Among the economic variants, the authors highlighted two other factors: (3) economic factors corresponding to outcome-based imitation to ensure cost containment and economic advantages in procurement and other processes management and (4) technological factors corresponding jointly to frequency-based imitation and trait-based imitation, which attribute to a wide range of technological options the possibility of facilitating the role of mimickers in achieving economic advantages: '*frequency-based imitation*, which refers to the mimicking of actions that reach a critical mass of adopters; *trait-based imitation practices, which involve the endowed of* the practices espoused by prestigious firms'.'

[1]From the European Parliament: https://www.europarl.europa.eu/thinktank/infographics/circulareconomy/public/index.html.

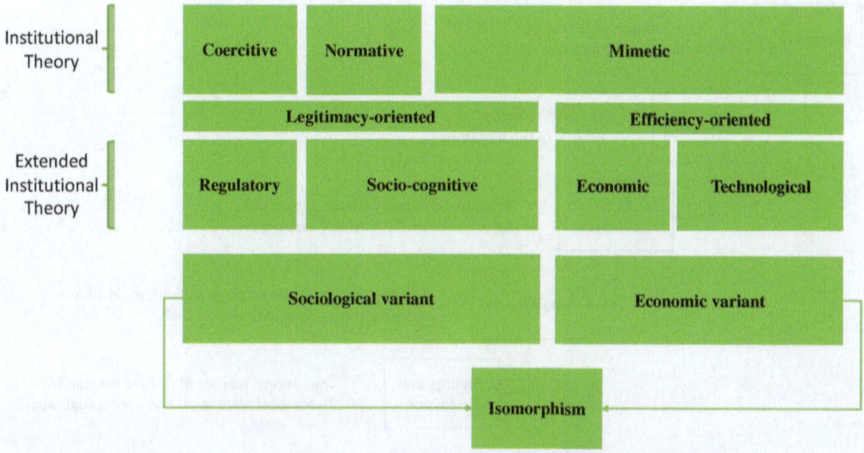

Fig. 1 Isomorphic drivers based on extended institutional theory

3 Methodology

This work is based on a literature review regarding DPPs as a specific and novel topic. We considered different sources to collect a wide range of works that dealt explicitly with the DPP theme. We conducted our literature review following traditional protocols, such as those developed by Tranfield et al. (2023) [38]. Considering the specificity and novelty of the research theme, we collected papers using recognized databases, such as Scopus and Web of Science (WoS), at the end of March 2023. We searched for 'digital product passport' (in the titles, abstracts and keywords) without any filter relating to time, language, product type or scientific area, with the objective of considering all the information necessary to deepen the topic. In Scopus, we identified 48 works, and by reading the abstracts, we selected 17 articles—the only ones that centered on our research topic. The same search was conducted in WoS, through which we obtained a list of 22 works and selected 12 of them, 8 of which duplicated those found in the previous Scopus search.

Since the CE and DPP concepts have received considerable attention from professionals and organizations outside academia, we also considered the grey literature, searching for reports or articles from the professional world on the internet. This enabled us to find nine other relevant documents. Finally, we created a list of 30 documents that the authors read fully to determine the aims of their work. The selection resulted in articles and documents published between 2019 and 2023 that were consistent with the topic's novelty.

To conduct a critical analysis of the literature, we prepared an Excel grid with 30 rows (one for each selected paper) and as many columns as there were relevant aspects, in addition, of course, to columns containing the articles' master data (such as authors, years, journals, titles, etc.). In particular, the first group of columns included the connotations and characteristics of DPPs: the name of the passport

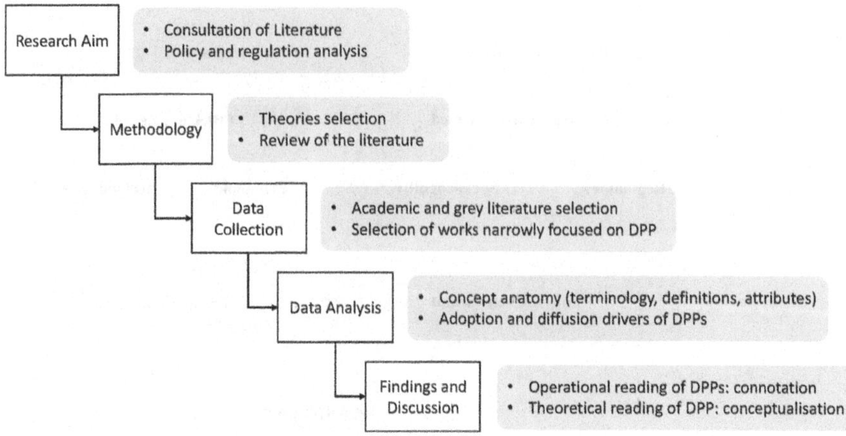

Fig. 2 Flowchart of the research process

under study, the reference sector, the technological aspects and the specific EC purposes. A second group of columns contained elements that could allow us to conceptualize DPPs, particularly the characteristics of and attention to specific theoretical frameworks that recalled neo-institutionalist theory, in its traditional and extended forms, as well as legitimacy and stakeholders.

The grid was completed independently by each researcher. Subsequently, the data collections were compared to arrive at convergence in a single grid, making it possible to clarify the results (Fig. 2).

4 Findings and Discussion

The analysis showed that DPPs are a new topic that has recently attracted increasing interest from academics and professionals, given that the selected works were all published in the last 4 years, particularly in 2022 and 2023. No consensus emerged from the critical analysis regarding the definition of DPPs due to widespread descriptive heterogeneity, as shown in Table 1.[2]

DPPs have various nuances determined by, for example, the product type to which they refer, their functions and scopes and the sectors for their application. However, certain elements commonly recur. First, in the analysed literature, about half of the research referred to DPPs in general terms involving all sectors within the

[2]The following are the acronyms used in the literature to indicate the different types of digital passports: digital product passport (DPP); MP, material passport (MP), digital product passport ecosystem (DFFE), Digital Battery Passport (DBP), Product Material Passport (PMP), digital life-cycle passport (DLCP), property passport (PrP), and building material passport (BMP).

Table 1 DPP's valuable elements

Authors	Document type	Title	Year	Pass. type	Valuable elements	Focus
Jensen S.F. et al.	Article	Digital product passports for a circular economy: Data needs for product life cycle decision-making	2023	DPP	Decision making enabler, transparency, high-quality data, product life cycle decision-making.	CE
van Capelleveen et al.	Review	The anatomy of a passport for the circular economy: a conceptual definition, vision and structured literature review	2023	MP	Digital, interface, certified identity, single identifiable object describes part of object' identity represented by life cycle data.	CE
Jansen M. et al.	Article	Stop guessing in the dark: Identified requirements for digital product passport systems	2023	DPP	Contains product's components information and their origin; should carry information for environmental and social impact assessment around production, use, and transformation phases of a product.	ALL
King M.R.N et al.	Article	A proposed universal definition of a Digital Product Passport Ecosystem (DPPE): Worldviews, discrete capabilities, stakeholder requirements and concerns	2023	DPPE	Socio-technical system of systems; evidences sustainable business practice and product design values; encourages change in consumer and disposer behaviour.	CE/ALL
Koppelaar R.H.E.M. et al.	Article	A digital product passport for critical raw materials reuse and recycling	2023	DPP	Integrates various datasets about all life cycle phases of products; ability to trace and track a products life-cycle history as features.	Recycling
Berger K. et al.	Article	Digital battery passports to enable circular and sustainable value chains: Conceptualization and use cases	2022	DBP	Instrument capable of facilitating more sustainable and circular value chains through the battery life-cycle phases data.	Battery
Panza L. et al.	Conference paper		2022	MP	Digitized information system contains material information which will flow	CE/ALL

(continued)

Table 1 (continued)

Authors	Document type	Title	Year	Pass. type	Valuable elements	Focus
		A collaborative architecture to support circular economy through digital material passports and internet of materials			together with physical material. Each receiver stakeholder will update the MP according to its working information.	
Plociennik C. et al.	Conference paper	Requirements for a digital product passport to boost the circular economy	2022	DPP	Aims to create transparency along a product's lifecycle and to enable the product-related data collection and sharing among various stakeholders.	CE
Schaubroeck S. et al.	Conference paper	Circularity of building stocks: Modelling building joints and their disassembly in a 3D city model	2022	PMP	Records useful information for disassembly and reuse	Buildings
Plociennik C. et al.	Conference paper	Towards a digital lifecycle passport for the circular economy	2022	DLCP	Optimizes product' lifecycle, reduces natural resources' demand and contributes to the circular economy.	E-waste
Walden J. et al.	Review	Digital product passports as enabler of the circular economy	2021	DPP	Dataset of product components, materials, and chemical substances; contains information on reparability, spare parts, and proper disposal instructions.	Battery
Adisorn T. et al.	Article	Towards a digital product passport fit for contributing to a circular economy	2021	DPP	Provides track and trace information on the product origin, composition, repair and dismantling options.	ALL
Paramatmuni, C., et al.	Article	Extending the capability of component digital threads using material passports	2023	MP	Unique identification documents of corresponding components recorded by data collected within the DThs during manufacturing.	Manufactures
Gligoric, N. et al.	Article	SmartTags: IoT product passport for circular economy based on printed sensors and unique item-level identifiers	2019	PP	Enables updates and insight by all stakeholders. Enables monitoring of changes during the product lifecycle.	Item level identifiers

Saull, A. et al.	Article	Can digital technologies speed up real estate transactions?	2020	PrP	Stores all the individual property information and its own unique digital data file.	Real Estates
Munaro, M R. et al.	Conference paper	'Proposal of a Building Material Passport and Its Application Feasibility to the Wood Frame Constructive System in Brazil'	2019	BMP	Set of data and indicators that describe materials or systems characteristics; aims to give recovery and reuse value.	Buildings
Çetin et al.	Article	'Circular Digital Built Environment: An Emerging Framework'	2021	MP	Refers to digitally registered data sets of an object describing its characteristics, location, history and ownership status, in a varying level of detail.	Built environment
Holger Berg et al.	Professionals	Overcoming information asymmetry in the plastics value chain with digital product passports	2022	PP	May increase trust and transparency along the entire supply chain creating new forms of recycling.	Recycling
Thomas Götz et al.	Professionals	Digital product passport: The ticket to achieving a climate neutral and circular European economy?	2022	DPP	Provides origin, composition, repair and disassembly possibilities of a product information; includes how recycle or dispose of at end of life.	ALL
Maike Jansen et al.	Professionals	Current approaches to the digital product passport for a circular economy	2022	DPP	Product information data set; refers to all product life cycle phases; used for various purposes of all stages.	CE
Saari, Leila et al.	Professionals	Digital product passport promotes sustainable manufacturing	2022	DPP	Composed by MP concept, data carrier and a unique product identifier.	CE/ALL
Deloitte	Professionals	Impact of international, open standards on circularity in Europe	2022	DPP	Provides product's characteristics and origin—Data which is required to identify, track and manage resources across a product's value chain.	CE/ALL
WBCSD)and Boston Consulting Group	Professionals	The EU digital product passport shapes the future of value chains: What it is and how to prepare now	2023	DPP	Makes products environmental impact visible, traceable, and easily accessible to relevant VC actors. Increases transparency and circular VC collaboration that facilitate circular designs and closed-loop activities.	CE/ALL

purview of a CE. In this case, two nuances of DPPs were reported: MPs, also present in other sectors [39], and the DPP ecosystem [40].

Overall, descriptions of the DPPs focused on their features, generally referring to information about products' origins, characteristics and components in terms of their life cycles, which provided transparency, favouring collaboration across the value chain and supporting decision-making processes [5, 9–12, 14, 19, 41]. All other works focused on analyzing the application of DPPs and their nuances to specific sectors. For example, the construction sector is evidently a prominent sector for applying DPPs [20, 21, 42].

MPs have been identified as supporting a CE system by closing the life-cycle loop of the products used for construction [12, 20, 42]. MPs contain information about specific materials, their characteristics and their histories [21]. The recognized purpose of an MP is to facilitate recovery, disassembly and reuse [20, 42]. MPs are often referred to in connection with BIM, which supports MPs by providing data related to building life cycle assessment (LCA), building materials and environmental impact [13]. BAMB was also mentioned as a tool in relation to MPs [20]. A sector that is heavily involved in the application of DPPs is the electric battery sector. In this case, interest was generated by the European Directive, which foresees the imminent application of DBPs [43]. The value of the information in DBPs is that they facilitate a sustainable and circular value chain by providing information about the components and substances products contain [13, 20], which facilitates their repair and correct disposal [13]. The waste and recycling sector has also received considerable attention in terms of DPPs and their nuances [11, 44, 45]. These sectors and their contexts are covered by the CEAP [3].

The life-cycle concept has been fundamental for determining DPPs' ability to collect information for tracing products' histories [44]. Plociennik et al. (2022) [11], introduced the concept of a digital life-cycle passport (DLCP), which recognizes the contribution to a CE by reducing the demand for natural resources and optimizing the product life cycle. Berg et al. (2022) [45] further highlighted the role of PPs in improving transparency and trust throughout the supply chain.

Finally, the various nuances of DPPs have other applications, including manufacturing MPs [46] and their integration with other technologies, such as the Internet of Things (IoT), the application of PPs [47], and the introduction of property passports (PrPs) in the real estate sector [48].

Among the articles analyzed, two presented helpful literature reviews for a comparison with our work. Van Capelleveen et al. (2023) [39] tried to formalize the concept of passports for a CE using a descriptive research approach and considering nine dimensions of passports to formalize a definition based on their characteristics, boundaries and relationships with other concepts. Also, Walden et al. (2021) [13] conducted a literature review regarding DPPs, highlighting their contribution to the transparency and traceability of products but indicating that some challenges remain.

From this perspective, a possible conceptualization of DPPs emerges based on their roles in companies, their influence and the opportunities they offer organizations. Almost all the examined works were highly technical and sometimes closer to the engineering than the managerial field since they often assumed an operational rather than a conceptual character. Although there was no homogeneity in the descriptions of DPPs in these works, common shared and recurring characteristics became evident in the various sectoral applications relating to specific product groups. Above all, transparency, traceability of the product life cycle, collaboration throughout the value chain and information about products' origins, histories and compositions were highlighted as supporting recovery, reuse and/or recycling processes.

The different characteristics and attributes that emerged from the analysis also allowed us to apply the chosen theoretical neo-institutionalist approach to explain the adoption and diffusion of DPPs and to highlight their primary purposes. The analyzed articles identified several drivers of organizations' behaviour in adopting DPPs, as follows:

- Clear mandatory information sharing, laws and regulations: the regulations indicate requirements that influence an organization's behaviour. Regulations may overcome organizations' reluctance to share certain important information [39]. The mandatory information in DPPs might refer to a product's characteristics and life cycle, clearly showing the product components and every life-cycle stage.
- Product compliance requirements encourage organizations to pursue the path towards a CE, which, through the use of DPPs, could increase the compliance and sustainability of products [13].
- Expected sustainability: considering, for example, electric battery manufacturers, the social and regulatory pressure is probably leading them to improve their products' sustainability and life cycles by intervening in their value chain; the use of DBPs aims to reduce the social and environmental impacts of products and maximise circularity without compromising sustainability [15].
- Strategy-oriented actors: entities such as authorities, education institutions, etc., may be interested in and affected by the availability of information provided by DPPs [11]. These actors are important stakeholders and thus influence the adoption of DPPs.
- Transparency has valuable effects on decision-making regarding products' life cycles. The high-quality information and data provided by DPPs can improve transparency [49].
- Awareness of product life-cycle stages: sharing information and sustainability data about product life-cycle stages facilitates an aware decision-making process for consumers and organizations [12].
- High sustainability performance contributes to improving an organization's reputation [19, 50], strengthening its pursuit of legitimacy.
- Successful DPP adoption: organizations could be encouraged to disseminate *success stories* to foster other operators' adoption of DPP [38].
- Supply-chain efficiency: DPPs contain information provided by product value-chain stakeholders [14]; a well-designed DPP makes information accessible to all

supply-chain actors and can support businesses in their transition to decarbonization, providing an opportunity to make their products sustainable [5].
- Cost-saving and expansion of the secondary materials market: applying a CE might increase the availability of secondary materials, contributing to secondary materials market growth. It might increase preferences for secondary materials over others, thus reducing the need for primary resources, eliminating unnecessary processes and/or reducing primary resource consumption [44].
- Decentralization: information collection could involve many supply-chain operators in entering information that might refer to several phases of the product life cycle, which would require collaboration between several actors to access information [14].
- Technology as a motivator: technologies might function as vehicles for increasing the motivation of manufacturers to provide circular information; both business models and new technologies could generate motivation for producers to provide circular information. Several technologies for enhancing the traceability of products, such as blockchain and IoT technologies, could boost and improve the adoption of DPPs.
- Information access: accessing certain information through a well-designed DPP could provide an important source of information for organizations, policymakers and consumers, which would enhance access to comparable and reliable information about product sustainability [5].

Deeply analyzing these listed drivers allowed us to note their relevance to the three types of isomorphism identified in neo-institutional theory, thanks to the categories of drivers proposed by Do et al. (2022) [36] regarding the application of extended institutional theory to CE issues.

The drivers 'clear mandatory information sharing' and 'product compliance requirements' could be included in the regulatory drivers' category [36] and related to the coercive isomorphism influenced by the pressure of the policies and regulations with which companies must comply. Indeed, the adoption of DPPs and precise product conformity requirements would oblige companies to adapt.

'Expected sustainability', 'strategy-oriented actors', 'transparency', 'awareness of product life-cycle stages', 'high sustainability performance enhancing an organization's reputation' and 'successful DPP adoption' are strong socio-cognitive drivers linked to companies' and stakeholders' attitudes and awareness that encourage them to use and share relevant information. For example, 'strategy-oriented actors' refers to the presence of actors interested in the available information contained in DPPs, who could exert pressure for adaptation.

Also, the 'transparency' driver could play a role in companies' decision-making processes and satisfy the information needs of several institutional or supervisory subjects and consumers. This links to 'expected sustainability' and 'awareness of product life-cycle stages' because it would provide significant information clarity, particularly for responding to social expectations.

The socio-cognitive category includes drivers with characteristics associated with normative isomorphism [35] and some drivers with features resembling mimetic

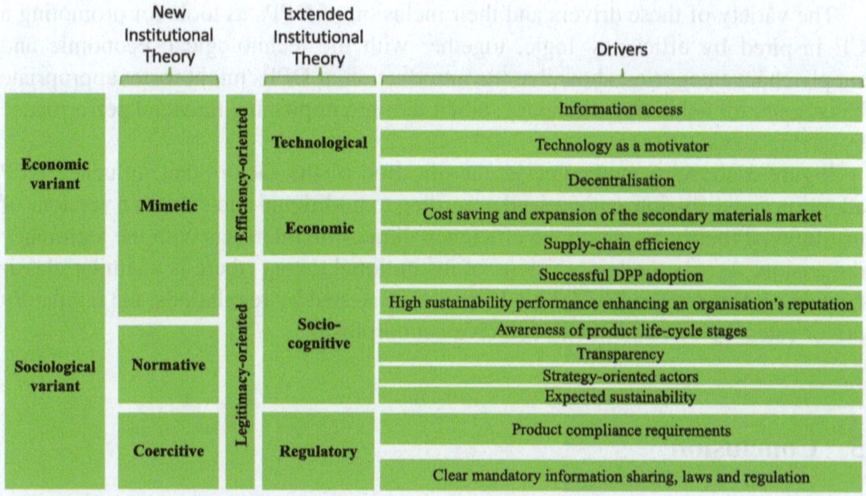

Fig. 3 Drivers of new institutional and extended institutional theory

isomorphism. In fact, concerning the latter, consistent with Fig. 1, which shows the sociological and economic variants of institutionalism theory, we assert that mimetic behaviours could enhance legitimacy and efficiency. However, the socio-cognitive category can be totally aligned with the social factor of legitimacy because the drivers included in it facilitate legitimacy but do not necessarily reduce costs. In fact, 'successful DPP adoption' and 'high sustainability performance' reflect the mimicking of other organizations in the adoption of DPPs: this is only narrowly linked to mimetic isomorphism and, including the attempt to reach high sustainability performance, reflects organizational legitimacy-seeking behaviours.

Other drivers aligned with mimetic isomorphism also emerged. They highlighted the tendency of organizations to take actions already taken by other organizations to improve efficiency, as shown in Fig. 3, involving the 'cost saving and the expansion of the secondary materials market' and the 'supply-chain efficiency' drivers.

The economic category refers to the drivers that influence efficiency and push organizations to improve their supply chains. Efficiency can be achieved by seizing opportunities to enhance strictly economic performance, as in the cases of cost-saving and secondary materials market drivers.

Finally, drivers are consistent with the technological category [36]. These drivers are closest to an influence generated by access to technology, which also responds to dynamics focused on efficiency. The remaining drivers present a move towards new business models that would increase motivation for the CE realization.

The 'decentralize', 'technology as a motivator' and 'information access' drivers can support DPPs by encouraging technology adoption and helping companies achieve a high reputation and performance.

The variety of these drivers and their inclusion of DPPs as tools for promoting a CE inspired by efficiency logic, together with the technological, economic and supply chain categories, show that the introduction of DPPs might foster appropriate behaviours for achieving efficiency, albeit through improving financial performance by saving costs.

Figure 3 shows a more precise classification of the factors that influence DPP adoption and diffusion, categorized according to traditional and extended versions of institutional theory by which the efficiency dimension intersects with the legitimacy dimension. Across the two versions of institutional theory, there is a similar classification of drivers associated with the pressure exerted by regulations: the regulatory driver category corresponds to coercive isomorphism.

5 Conclusion

This analysis has fulfilled the task of shedding light on DPPs, which are destined to become increasingly relevant in supporting the sustainability of organizations and a CE. DPPs could be a source of punctual information generated throughout a product's life, intended to communicate its environmental impact. Above all, DPPs allow for the planning of a product's future use by reducing environmental and social impacts. They would incorporate the most important principles underlying the ecological transition aspired to by the EU because they would comprise a strong digital component. They would also contribute to reducing GHG emissions by enhancing recycling processes and saving consumed materials, with social consequences, such as the reduction of landfills and pollution. Many terminologies are currently applied to DPPs, depending on the reference sector and the technological platforms adopted. Still, beyond these differences, the digital passport typologies considered in this analysis have common attributes and purposes.

The inclusion of multiple product categories in DPPs would require the definition of specific sets of information, which should not be seen as an obstacle, but as an opportunity to embrace sustainability challenges and open up new business models. DPPs strengthen the social component of organizations through their collaborative nature by involving various subjects in sharing information that is not often disclosed, thereby enhancing the logic of trust. Different technology applications could support this logic of trust, and DPPs would require in-depth reflection on the adopted platform's governance and architecture.

Another purpose of our analysis was to apply a theoretical approach to DPPs since an operational approach, often based on the technological perspective, prevailed in the documents we examined. Among the selected documents, only some dealt with the topic non-operatively, and they were limited to offering a general overview of the DPP concept, focusing on the descriptive aspects and retracing the historical background of the passport concept [13, 39]. Our work attempts to enhance the descriptive conceptualization of DPPs by focusing on their influence on organizations' behaviour and the relationship between organizations and the social context.

To achieve this aim, we adopted an institutional theory framework that has been widely used to address sustainability issues. Specifically, we have worked on the extended version of this theory, combining the sociological factors of traditional institutional theory, inspired by research on legitimacy, with economic factors, inspired by efficiency. DPPs are closely related to a CE [13] and oriented towards sustainability because they reduce environmental pressures and improve efficiency by 'minimizing waste through reusing, refurbishing and recycling existing materials products'. A CE is oriented towards improving economic development while alleviating environmental resource depletion; it can harmonize economic development (efficiency) with environmental protection (legitimacy). In this philosophy, DPPs linked to supply-chain management, waste management and recycling processes are pivotal in safeguarding the environment, reducing waste and increasing efficiency.

It is, therefore, correct to consider DPPs as helpful tools, on the one hand, for limiting environmental damage and the waste of resources through sustainable behaviours that can enhance the relationship between companies and the surrounding society, enabling them to acquire legitimacy; on the other hand, they are tools for improving the management of supply chain operations by increasing the dissemination of information and coordination among various operators to achieve higher levels of efficiency and performance.

DPPs are destined to become increasingly widely adopted due to mimetic pressures. Indeed, mimicking is linked to adopting behaviour that increases an organization's reputation and performance through various imitative logics, which refer to companies copying practices already widely adopted and used by other prestigious companies.

To provide an extensive overview of the possible development and application of DPPs, some critical issues should be more deeply addressed. However, only a few works among the analyzed documents indicated critical elements that companies should consider. Instead, their main attention was on the limitation of DPP technical development oriented towards data requirements, storage, carrier and integration [9], the creation of standards and their related costs [10]. Attention to critical issues such as difficulties applying DPPs by firms came mostly from grey literature rather than academic literature.

These critical issues include the costs of DPPs, system development, and difficult collaboration within the global value chain. In addition, a critical factor concerns the requirements for products subject to DPPs, which should also apply to products from non-EU countries [10]. Based on the analysis conducted by Deloitte, producers are the main actors on which these costs fall. These issues and the other open questions reported in this article still need to be addressed in future studies [10].

The novelty of the topic necessitates further insight into possible practical applications involving the value chain for a certain category of products. Moreover, the role played by DPPs in terms of the communication of information on emissions could be analyzed more deeply referring to the GHG emissions generated along a value chain. Furthermore, the application of DPPs could be explored with a focus on additional devices and technologies, such as blockchains.

Finally, our analysis represents exploratory work on the topic of DPPs. Future research should deepen knowledge of this topic thanks to the academic literature produced in the intervening years and to a greater diffusion of DPPs in support of CE. Future research could evaluate the theoretical framework presented in this work by adopting different types of digital passports with different scopes to verify the coexistence of pressures and determine which ones prevail.

References

1. European Commission. (2019a). Brussels, Belgium, European Green Deal. Accessed April 25, 2023, from https://eur-lex.europa.eu/legal-content/IT/TXT/?uri=CELEX:52019DC0640
2. United Nations, Department of economic and social affairs, 12 Ensure sustainable consumption and production patterns. Accessed April 25, 2023, from https://sdgs.un.org/goals/goal12
3. European Commission. (2020a). Brussels, Belgium, circular economy action plan: For a cleaner and more competitive Europe. Accessed April 25, 2023, from https://ec.europa.eu/environment/pdf/circulareconomy/new_circular_economy_action_plan.pdf
4. European Commission. (2022). Brussels, Belgium, Proposal for a Regulation of the European Parliament and of the council establishing a framework for setting ecodesign requirements for sustainable products and repealing directive. Accessed April 25, 2023, from https://eur-lex.europa.eu/legal-content/EN/TXT/HTML/?uri=CELEX:52022PC0142
5. Götz, T. (2022). *Digital product passport: The ticket to achieving a climate neutral and circular European economy? University of Cambridge Institute for sustainability leadership (CISL) and the Wuppertal institute*. CLG Europe (GOTZ).
6. Ellen MacArthur Foundation: What is a circular economy. Accessed April 25, 2023, from https://ellenmacarthurfoundation.org/topics/circular-economy-introduction/overview
7. Korhonen, J., Nuur, C., Feldmann, A., & Birkie, S. E. (2018). Circular economy as an essentially contested concept. *Journal of Cleaner Production, 175*, 544–552.
8. Hobson, K. (2016). Closing the loop or squaring the circle? Locating generative spaces for the circular economy. *Progress in Human Geography, 40*(1), 88–104.
9. Beanland, A. (2023). *The EU digital product passport shapes the future of value chains: What it is and how to prepare*, World Business Council for Sustainable Development. Switzerland. Accessed April 25, 2023, from https://policycommons.net/artifacts/3379437/the-eu-digital-product-passport-shapes-the-future-of-value-chains/4178369/. CID: 20.500.12592/zxb5mn.
10. Deloitte. (2022). Impact of international, open standards on circularity in Europe. Accessed April 25, 2023, from https://www2.deloitte.com/content/dam/Deloitte/pl/Documents/Reports/pl_Impact_of_international_open_standards_on_circularity_in_Europe_April2022_2.pdf
11. Plociennik, C., Pourjafarian, M., Saleh, S., Hagedorn, T., Carmo Precci Lopes, A. D., Vogelgesang, M., Baehr, J., Kellerer, B., Jansen, M., Berg, H., et al. (2022). Requirements for a Digital Product passport to boost the circular economy. In Proceedings of the INFORMATIK 2022, Hamburg, Germany, 26–30 September 2022.
12. Adisorn, T., Tholen, L., & Götz, T. (2021). Towards a digital product passport fit for contributing to a circular economy. *Energies, 14*, 2289.
13. Walden, J., Steinbrecher, A., & Marinkovic, M. (2021). Digital product passports as enabler of the circular economy. *Chemie Ingenieur Technik, 93*, 1717–1727.
14. Jansen, M., Meisen, T., Plociennik, C., Berg, H., Pomp, A., & Windholz, W. (2023). Stop guessing in the dark: identified requirements for digital product passport systems. *Systems, 11*, 123.

15. Berger, K., Schöggl, J.-B., & Baumgartner, R. J. (2022). Digital battery passports to enable circular and sustainable value chains: Conceptualization and use cases. *Journal of Cleaner Production, 353*, 131492.
16. European Commission. (2019b). Brussels, Belgium, Registration, End-of-life vehicles directive. Accessed April 25, 2023, from https://eur-lex.europa.eu/legal-content/EN/TXT/HTML/?uri=CELEX:32000L0053
17. European Commission. (2006). Brussels, Belgium, Registration, Evaluation, Authorization and Restriction of Chemicals (REACH); Accessed April 25, 2023, from https://eur-lex.europa.eu/legal-content/EN/TXT/HTML/?uri=CELEX:32000L0053
18. European Commission. (2012). Brussels, Belgium, Waste of Electrical and Electronic Equipment (WEEE). Accessed April 25, 2023, from https://eur-lex.europa.eu/legal-content/EN/TXT/HTML/?uri=CELEX:02012L0019-20180704
19. Panza, L., Bruno, G., & Lombardi, F. (2022). A collaborative architecture to support circular economy through digital material passports and internet of materials. *IFAC-PapersOnLine, 55*, 1491–1496.
20. Munaro, M. R., Fischer, A. C., Azevedo, N. C., & Tavares, S. F. (2019). Proposal of a building material passport and its application feasibility to the wood frame constructive system in Brazil. *IOP Conference Series: Earth and Environmental Science, 225*, 012018.
21. Çetin, S., De Wolf, C., & Bocken, N. (2021). Circular digital built environment: An emerging framework. *Sustainability, 13*, 6348.
22. Selznick, P. (1957). *Leadership in administration: A sociological interpretation*. Harper and Row.
23. Scott, R. W. (2001). *Institutions and organizations* (2nd ed.). Sage.
24. Di Maggio, J., & Powel, W. W. (1983). The iron cage revisited: Institutional isomorphism and collective rationality in organizational fields. *American Sociological Review, 48*(2), 147–160.
25. Cormier, D., Magnan, M., & Van Velthoven, B. (2005). Environmental disclosure quality in large German companies: Economic incentives, public pressures or institutional conditions? *European Accounting Review, 14*(1), 3–39.
26. Bebbington, J., Higgins, C., & Frame, B. (2009). Initiating sustainable development reporting: Evidence from New Zealand. *Accounting, Auditing and Accountability Journal, 22*(4), 588–625.
27. Sarkis, J., Zhu, Q., & Lai, K. (2011). An organizational theoretic review of green supply chain management literature. *International Journal of Production Economics, 130*(1), 1–15.
28. Govindan, K., & Hasanagic, M. (2018). A systematic review on drivers, barriers, and practices towards circular economy: A supply chain perspective. *International Journal of Production Research, 56*(1–2), 278–311.
29. Liu, J., Feng, Y., Zhu, Q., & Sarkis, J. (2018). Green supply chain management and the circular economy. *International Journal of Physical Distribution & Logistics Management, 48*(8), 794–817.
30. Caldera, H. T. S., Desha, C., & Dawes, L. (2019). Evaluating the enablers and barriers for successful implementation of sustainable business practice in 'lean' SMEs. *Journal of Cleaner Production, 218*, 575–590.
31. Ranta, V., Aarikka-Stenroos, L., Ritala, P., & Mäkinen, S. J. (2018). Exploring institutional drivers and barriers of the circular economy: A cross-regional comparison of China, the US, and Europe. *Resources Conservation and Recycling, 135*, 70–82.
32. Shooshtarian, S., Caldera, S., Maqsood, T., Ryley, T., Wong, P. S. P., & Zaman, A. (2022). Analysis of factors influencing the creation and stimulation of the Australian market for recycled construction and demolition waste products. *Sustainable Production and Consumption, 34*, 163–176.
33. Fuchs, M., & Hovemann, G. (2022). Homogeneity or heterogeneity: An institutional theory view on circular economy practices in the outdoor sporting goods industry. *Sustainability, 14*(10), 6279.

34. Scott, W. R. (2008). *Institutions and organizations: Ideas and interests* (3rd ed.). Sage Publications.
35. Kauppi, K. (2013). Extending the use of institutional theory in operations and supply chain management research. *International Journal of Operations & Production Management, 33*(10), 1318–1345.
36. Do, Q., Mishra, N., Colicchia, C., Creazza, A., & Ramudhin, A. (2022). An extended institutional theory perspective on the adoption of circular economy practices: Insights from the seafood industry. *International Journal of Production Economics, 247*, 108400.
37. Huang, X., Gattiker, T. F., & Schroeder, R. G. (2010). Do competitive priorities drive adoption of electronic commerce applications? *Testing the contingency and institutional views, Journal of Supply Chain Management, 46*(3), 57–69.
38. Tranfield, D., Denyer, D., & Smart, P. (2003). Towards a methodology for developing evidence-informed management knowledge by means of systematic review. *British Journal of Management, 14*, 207–222.
39. van Capelleveen, G., Vegter, D., Olthaar, M., & van Hillegersberg, J. (2023). The anatomy of a passport for the circular economy: A conceptual definition, vision and structured literature review. *Resources, Conservation & Recycling Advances, 17*, 200131.
40. King, M. R. N., Timms, P. D., & Mountney, S. (2023). A proposed universal definition of a digital product passport ecosystem (DPPE): Worldviews, discrete capabilities, stakeholder requirements and concerns. *Journal of Cleaner Production, 384*, 135538.
41. Jansen, M., Gerstenberger, B., Bitter-Krahe, J., Berg, H., Sebestyén, J., & Schneider, J. (2022). *Current approaches to the digital product passport for a circular economy (Wuppertal Paper no. 198)*. Wuppertal Institute.
42. Schaubroeck, S., Dewil, R., & Allacker, K. (2022a). Circularity and LCA—Material pathways: The cascade potential and cascade database of an in-use building product. *IOP Conference Series: Earth and Environmental Science, 1122*, 012040.
43. European Commission. (2020b). Brussels, Belgium, Batteries and waste batteries regulation. Accessed April 25, 2023, from https://www.europarl.europa.eu/RegData/docs_autres_institutions/commission_europeenne/com/2020/0798/COM_COM(2020)0798_EN.pdf
44. Koppelaar, R. H. E. M., Pamidi, S., Hajósi, E., Herreras, L., Leroy, P., Jung, H.-Y., & others. (2023). A digital product passport for critical raw materials reuse and recycling. *Sustainability, 15*(2), 1405.
45. Berg, H., Kulinna, R., Guth-Orlowski, S., Stöcker, C., Müller, J., Thiermann, R., & Porepp, N. (2022). *Overcoming information asymmetry in the plastics value chain with digital product passports (Wuppertal paper no. 197)*. Wuppertal Institute.
46. Paramatmuni, C., & Cogswell, D. (2023). Extending the capability of component digital threads using material passports. *Journal of Manufacturing Processes, 87*, 245–259.
47. Gligoric, N., Krco, S., Hakola, L., Vehmas, K., De, S., Moessner, K., Jansson, K., Polenz, I., & van Kranenburg, R. (2019). SmartTags: IoT product passport for circular economy based on printed sensors and unique item-level identifiers. *Sensors, 19*, 586.
48. Saull, A., Baum, A., & Braesemann, F. (2020). Can digital technologies speed up real estate transactions? *JPIF, 38*, 349–361.
49. Jensen, S. F., Kristensen, J. H., Adamsen, S., et al. (2023). Digital product passports for a circular economy: Data needs for product life cycle decision-making. *Sustainable Production and Consumption, 37*, 242–255.
50. Ashby, M. F. (2020). *Materials and the environment materials and the environment* (3rd ed.). Elsevier. https://www.elsevier.com/books/materials-and-the-environment/ashby/978-0-12-821521-0

Local Digital Twin Ecosystems: A Human-Centric Approach

Oleg Missikoff

Abstract This work explores the growing importance of the human component in Digital Twin design and implementation, challenging the validity of the legacy, purely cyber-physical paradigm. In fact, recent advancements in key enabling technologies have expanded Digital Twin applications to encompass complex socio-technical ecosystems, such as smart cities, highlighting the ever-increasing relevance of humans in these contexts. Consequently, the traditional mechanistic bipolarity of the physical twin/Digital Twin paradigm, derived from industrial engineering, is proving inadequate to model highly anthropogenic landscapes. Therefore, it is necessary to align the Digital Twin model with the prevailing trend of a human-centric digital transformation. In this paper, we propose an extension of the Digital Twin legacy paradigm from a pair-based to a triple-based model that formally includes the human component. This proposal is supported by epistemological justifications, international case studies, enabling methodologies, ongoing pilot projects, and future research directions. The model presented in this paper fosters a human-centric approach to improve decision-making processes and enhance user engagement in Local Digital Twin Ecosystems.

Keywords Local Digital Twin Ecosystems · Human-centric digital transformation · Systems thinking · Socio-technical systems · Stakeholder engagement

1 Enhancing the Legacy Digital Twin Paradigm

The concept of a digital representation dynamically connected to the physical world has a history dating back to the early 1990s [1] but it wasn't until the early 2000s that the first industrial applications of this concept emerged [2]. However, the term

O. Missikoff (✉)
Sapienza University, Rome, Italy

Earth 3.0 Foundation, London, UK
e-mail: oleg.missikoff@uniroma1.it

A. M. Braccini et al. (eds.), *Digital (Eco) Systems and Societal Challenges*, Lecture Notes in Information Systems and Organisation 72,
https://doi.org/10.1007/978-3-031-75586-6_8

"Digital Twin" was officially coined in 2010 when NASA included it in its technology roadmap [3]. The traditional conception of Digital Twin (DT), still in use today, consists of creating a virtual replica of a physical asset, process, or system to which it is coupled through a live digital connection for a specific purpose. The coupling between the physical and the digital components is kept live through a constant flow of data collected autonomously from inhomogeneous sources (i.e. IoT sensors, the Web and large datasets) or manually entered by human operators. The refresh time of a DT varies according to the specific purpose for which it has been designed: In the case of monitoring the melting speed of a glacier, for example, the refresh rate will be very different than in checking the functionality of an aeroplane engine. Collected data are then processed using big data analytics, advanced statistics and artificial intelligence algorithms, such as machine learning (ML), deep learning (DL), and neural networks (NN), to be transformed into meaningful information. Finally, the DT leverages that knowledge and provides recommendations to humans or, in cases of need for an immediate response (e.g. autonomous driving vehicles, fire extinguishing systems, etc.), operates direct unmanned interventions. Once changes are made on the physical plane, the Digital Twin will automatically align itself, closing a loop which is continually iterated [4]. As we will see in more detail below, the Digital Twin paradigm originated in the field of Product Lifecycle Management (PLM) [2] and has been used for years as an advanced form of Computer Aided Engineering (CAE) and Manufacturing (CAM) to develop components or devices. Due to the mechanistic epistemological perspective characterising industrial engineering, the human component hasn't been included in the loop that connects the physical and Digital Twins. Consequently, the original model has been conceived as a binary system of exclusively cyber-physical nature [5], and this legacy perspective still influences today's vision. However, the growing complexity of socio-technical systems, such as smart cities, highlights the limitations of this approach. Therefore, traditional models often fail to adequately account for human behaviour and social dynamics, leading to a lack of user engagement. This can significantly impact the success of these systems.

Concerning the methodological approach, this concept paper adopts a qualitative research method based on an epistemological analysis and real-world case studies, to address the following research questions: (i) What are the key factors driving the need for a human-centric approach in Local Digital Twin Ecosystems? (ii) How can a human-centric approach be effectively integrated into the design and implementation of Local Digital Twin Ecosystems? By exploring these research questions, the present study seeks to uncover the motivations behind the need for a shift towards a human-centric Digital Twin model and provide insights into effective strategies for its implementation.

1.1 Recognising the Centrality of the Human Factor

Despite the traditional focus on the cyber-physical aspects, a closer look reveals that the human component has always been central to the development of DTs. Indeed, even in industrial applications, designers, engineers, and maintainers have always had a key role in selecting the sources of information and deciding whether and when to carry out a recommended intervention on the physical twin. This perspective also highlights the value of DTs as advanced decision support systems, as their ability to harness the power of real-time data collection and advanced analytics provides valuable insights for informed decision-making [6]. By continuously monitoring and analysing a physical asset, process, or system, DTs offer recommendations based on predictive modelling, anomaly detection, and optimization algorithms, enabling stakeholders to make proactive and data-driven decisions to enhance performances, mitigate risks, and ensure operational efficiency [7].

Moreover, thanks to the availability of increasingly performing Key Enabling Technologies (KETs) such as storage space, computational power, and AI algorithms, Digital Twins have recently gained momentum and crossed the boundaries of laboratories and industrial plants to be applied in practically all sectors of human activity: from building design and construction to urban planning, from Supply Chain Management (SCM) to energy and telecommunication grids, from agriculture to healthcare, from climate adaptation to circular economy, and more.

As it is easy to deduce, with the extension of the scope from mechanical engineering to socio-technical systems, the relevance of the human component has been growing exponentially. However, the basic DT model has remained limited to only considering the physical and digital dimensions [4].

1.2 Digital Twins and Socio-Technical Systems

The objective of this work is therefore to stimulate a reflection on the need to update the Digital Twin model, shifting from a pair-based paradigm, that exclusively considers the digital and physical dimensions, to a triple-based model that explicitly includes the human element. By fostering this enhancement of the legacy DT paradigm, the aim is to strengthen the understanding, design, and implementation of Digital Twins, particularly in the context of complex socio-technical systems such as smart cities.

Applying the same logic, the term "smart city", although prevalent for more than a decade now, also appears inadequate to recognize the importance of the human component. In this work, it is suggested to adopt the notion of a "smart community" to shift the focus from the infrastructure, the "smart city", to the people that live therein. This notion also broadens the scope beyond urban centres to include smaller and more decentralized contexts, including suburbs, towns, villages, and rural settings. Furthermore, this notion reinforces the human-centric perspective, emphasizing the importance of considering the specific needs, aspirations, and social dynamics of the people who live and work in target areas.

A human-centric approach is fostered by the European Commission that, through the Declaration on European Digital Rights and Principles, promotes a digital transition shaped by European values, the first of which is "putting people and their rights at the centre of the digital transformation" [8].

To effectively address the needs and aspirations of local communities, this paper focuses on the concept of Local Digital Twin Ecosystem (LDTE). This scope matches with the EU Local Digital Twin initiative launched within the LIVING-IN.EU movement, which is part of the Digital Europe programme. The goal of the community growing around this initiative is to discuss and find common ground to resolve challenges related to local governance, ecosystem data management (data collection and sharing, data governance and stewardship, data models and standards), cybersecurity, privacy, ethics, interoperability and skill gaps [9]. Within this initiative, aiming to increase the engagement of local communities, the Directorate General for Communications Networks, Content and Technology has recently launched a project to "Co-design the Local Digital Twins (LDT) toolbox technical specifications for advancing the transformation of Smart Communities" [10].

Indeed, according to the epistemological perspective on which this study is based, the barriers to the widespread adoption of innovation projects are predominantly human rather than technological in nature. Therefore, to allow them greater chances of success, local digital innovation projects should be guided by a deep understanding of the socio-cultural, socio-economic, and socio-technical dimensions that characterize the communities with which they will be co-designed and co-developed (see Sect. 6.2).

In the next chapter, a brief historical background will be provided to outline how the evolution of the relationship between humans and digital technologies, also referred to as the "digital journey", has progressively shifted from machine-oriented to human-oriented [11], enabling the expansion of the DT scope.

2 Towards a Human-Centric Digital Transformation: The Digital Journey

The term "digital journey" refers to the ongoing process of integrating human beings with digital technologies. This transformative journey has significantly influenced our way of life and will be examined in relation to the technological revolutions that have shaped its various stages, ultimately enabling the emergence of Digital Twins.

The roots of the digital journey can be traced back to the Third Industrial Revolution (Industry 3.0 or IR3), also known as the Digital Revolution, that began in the 1970s. This period marked a crucial turning point as it witnessed the transition from mechanical and analogue electronic technologies to digital electronics, laying the foundation for the digital age [12].

2.1 Stages of the Digital Journey

The digital journey unfolded through three interconnected stages: digitization, digitalization, and digital transformation [13]. Each stage built upon advancements in digital technologies and brought about significant changes in various aspects of society, the economy, and everyday life [14]. Despite their widespread use, the terms digitization, digitalization, and digital transformation are often used interchangeably, requiring a disambiguation of their meaning by briefly specifying the role that each played in the digital journey.

Digitization The first stage marked the initial step and is concerned with the conversion of analogue information into digital format, enabling basic automation and computation of existing processes. This stage gained momentum from the 1970s onwards, driven by advancements in Information and Communication Technology (ICT). Key Enabling Technologies (KETs), such as larger storage devices, smaller microchips, and increased computational power, played a crucial role in facilitating the digitization process [15]. By converting analogue data into digital form, organizations were able to enhance information accessibility, management, and sharing, leading to increased productivity in various industries [16].

Digitalization The second stage, which is still ongoing for most players, involves a broader application of digital technologies to streamline and optimize existing business processes [17]. Digitalization goes beyond digitization by leveraging the power of digital technologies to increase organizations' efficiency and effectiveness, and enhance user experiences. This stage is characterized by the integration of digital technologies into various aspects of society, reshaping the way human activities are carried out. KET evolution continues to play a significant role, as the Internet, mobile networks, computing power, and sophisticated algorithms enable the development of new digital services, platforms, and data-driven decision-making processes. Digitalization leads to streamlined operations, enhanced connectivity, and the creation of innovative products, services, organizational configurations, and business models [18]. Digitalization enables better decision-making processes, opening up new avenues for entrepreneurship and innovation [19].

Digital Transformation (DX) The latest stage of the digital journey represents a comprehensive and strategic shift towards a digitally enabled and innovative society [12]. DX requires a more profound and holistic approach, driven by a pervasive adoption of digital technologies across all human activities, with the goal to achieve Industry 4.0 and ultimately pave the way for Industry 5.0 and Society 5.0 [20].

Leveraging the full potential of digital transformation involves reimagining business processes, reconfiguring organizations, and creating new value propositions

[21]. DX goes beyond incremental improvements and aims to radically reshape mindsets, organizational culture, and business strategies to seize new opportunities and address emerging challenges. KETs such as AI, cloud computing, big data analytics, and the Internet of Things, are instrumental in driving digital transformation efforts [22]. By harnessing these technologies, organizations can embrace innovation to improve agility, optimize performances, and deliver personalized experiences to customers, thus gaining a competitive advantage over competitors [23]. However, due to the difficulties in changing the work and enterprise culture, the vast majority of organizations are still going through the digitalization phase.

While the digital journey has brought significant advancements, limiting the focus solely on technology can present challenges. A primary concern lies in the potential for neglecting the human element in the relentless pursuit of technological innovation. Emerging technologies offer immense capabilities, but their sustainability hinges on their successful integration into human workflows and their ability to augment human capabilities rather than replace them altogether. Chip-scale miniaturization, ever-increasing internet speeds, storage capacity, computing power and AI algorithms, enabled the current, disruptive explosion of Generative AI, with conversational chatbots built on top of Large Language Models (LLMs), such as OpenAI ChatGPT, Google Gemini and Microsoft Copilot [24], opening up opportunities to be reaped but also risks to be mitigated.

In the next chapter, by analysing their evolutionary trajectory, impact and capacity to integrate various technologies, DTs emerge as powerful enablers that facilitate the achievement of a full-fledged digital transformation.

3 Evolution of the Digital Twin Paradigm

This chapter traces the evolutionary trajectory of the twin concept, starting before the advent of digital technologies with its first practical use during the Normandy landings in June 1944. At that time, the war room at Southwick House utilized a real-time representation of Allied forces' positions using a large map and movable model ships, updated with radio-transmitted data from the front line.

Another milestone is marked by the Apollo 13 accident in April 1970 when, after an explosion on board, the astronauts radioed the famous phrase "Houston, we have a problem." This expression, made famous by the homonymous 1995 film, would have entered popular culture to describe the emergence of an unforeseen problem. On that occasion, engineers at NASA's Manned Spacecraft Center employed a replica of the Apollo 13 Lunar Module Simulator they had in the hangars, to simulate conditions and devise solutions for the astronauts' safe return to Earth.

These historical examples illustrate the early, analogue applications of dynamic real-world reproductions for planning, monitoring, and simulations.

3.1 Mirroring Worlds: Digital Representations of Reality

The concept of a digital representation dynamically connected to the physical world was introduced by David Gelernter in his 1991 book, "Mirror Worlds" [1]. A decade later, in 2002, Michael Grieves presented the "Mirrored Spaces Model" at a conference of the Society of Manufacturing Engineers, focusing on Product Lifecycle Management (PLM). The model consisted of three elements: real space, virtual space, and a bidirectional connection mechanism for data/information flow between the two [2]. However, due to a lack of enabling technologies, a widespread adoption of Digital Twins was hindered at that time.

3.2 Coining the Term: NASA's Digital Twin

The term "Digital Twin" (DT) was finally introduced by NASA in its 2010 technology roadmap, where it is referred to as the "Virtual Digital Fleet Leader." They defined DT as an integrated multi-physics, multi-scale, probabilistic simulation of a vehicle or system that mirrors the life of its flying twin. NASA's contribution played a pivotal role in solidifying the definition and understanding of the DT concept [3].

Since its initial definition by NASA, DTs have been described by various authors in different terms, reflecting their diverse applications. The definitions of Digital Twins in the literature have encompassed virtual or digital models or counterparts, simulations, and information constructs representing their physical counterparts [4].

3.3 The Final Chapter: Recent Trends and Applications of the Digital Twin

From the second half of the 2010s, the availability of enhanced digital technologies has allowed for an evolution and adoption of Digital Twins across various industries. The Digital Twin concept, initially focused on non-living entities and industrial products, expanded to encompass biological systems such as the human body [25], and even complex natural ecosystems such as a forest [26].

However, the key aspect shared by most definitions of a DT is the bidirectional transfer or sharing of quantitative and qualitative data related to material, manufacturing, process, historical trends, and environmental data, at a predetermined frequency between a physical asset and its Digital Twin. Furthermore, the integration of GIS, satellites, and drones has facilitated the capture and delivery of terrain models and geospatial data, enhancing the accuracy and detail in the digital representations of territories. As a result of these technological advancements, Digital Twins have gained traction and have been adopted by public authorities and private organizations at local, national, and international levels to support sustainable development in territorial systems (see Chap. "The Non-adoption of Digital Technologies in the Agricultural Industries: A Systematic Literature Review").

4 Conceptual and Terminological Disambiguation

Before proceeding to analyse the case studies in Chap. "The Non-adoption of Digital Technologies in the Agricultural Industries: A Systematic Literature Review", it is worth clearing up some common misconceptions about the Digital Twin concept by highlighting its differences from four widely used technologies that are often mistaken for Digital Twins. These are Computer-Aided Design (CAD), Computer-Aided Manufacturing (CAM), Computer-Aided Engineering (CAE), Geographic Information Systems (GIS), and Building Information Modelling (BIM) and Digital Threads. Indeed, rather than a technology, a DT can be seen as an integrated environment where these technologies can operate synergistically, along with others such as IoT, AI algorithms (ML/DL/NN) and graphic renderings such as Virtual, Augmented and eXtended Reality (VR/AR/XR).

The two main differences between these technologies and Digital Twins are that the digital models they produce do not have a live connection to a specific real-world asset or the context that surrounds it, and are only used in specific industries, while DTs are dynamic, contextualised and allow for broader applicability across multiple fields [27]. Digital Twins, indeed, go beyond static models by incorporating real-time data and enabling continuous monitoring, analysis and simulation, facilitating real-time decision-making and predictive maintenance.

We will now proceed to look at the specific differences between Digital Twins and each of these technologies, while also pointing out some similarities that may contribute to the confusion.

Digital Twins vs. CAD/CAM/CAE. Traditional computer-aided models are digital representations of physical objects or systems designed as blueprints to produce multiple instances, disconnected from a specific real-world asset or process throughout its lifecycle. Digital Twins are instead connected to their physical counterparts through real-time data, allowing for continuous monitoring. Additionally, these technologies are confined to the field of product design and manufacturing [28].

Digital Twins vs. Geographic Information Systems. GIS are used to acquire, manage, analyse, and visualize geospatial data and can generate digital maps, spatial representations, various analytical tools, and digital terrain models. However, as their name suggests, GIS focus primarily on geographic information and do not incorporate other perspectives as those provided by Building Information Modelling (BIM) or Supply Chain Management (SCM). In addition, Digital Twins can also integrate real-time information about dynamic objects or systems such as infrastructures and human activities [29].

Digital Twins vs. Building Information Modelling. BIMs aim to create and manage digital representations of buildings and allow for collaboration and coordination between different stakeholders. BIMs provide a complete digital representation of a building or infrastructure project, focusing primarily on the design, construction and maintenance phases. However, BIMs cannot incorporate real-time data or allow for continuous monitoring and evaluation of the operational performance of the physical asset, which is a key feature of Digital Twins. Also, unlike BIM models, DTs are aware of their surrounding context [30].

Digital Twins vs. Digital Threads. A Digital Thread achieves this by capturing and seamlessly integrating data flows associated with the product, from design and production to operation and service. In essence, while a Digital Twin is a snapshot in time of a physical object, a Digital Thread serves as the object's storyline, capturing its entire history and lifecycle. Digital Threads and Digital Twins can be combined by connecting traditionally siloed elements across manufacturing processes. This allows for an integrated view of an asset throughout its entire lifecycle. These complementary concepts, when used together, can significantly enhance our understanding, monitoring, and optimization of complex systems [31].

4.1 Digital Twins as Enablers of Territorial Development Plans

As previously mentioned, Digital Twin should not be considered a technology, but rather a paradigm that fosters the development of integrated and synergistic environments where diverse technologies can converge and combine.

Because of its capacity to integrate multiple technologies, the DT paradigm is a powerful enabler for territorial development plans. To support this statement, in the next chapter several case studies and best practices will be analysed [32].

5 From Local to Global: Scaling the Digital Twin Paradigm

To understand the global impact Digital Twins are having as a means of planning and managing complex spatial systems, some of their most recent and significant applications worldwide will be examined in the following sections. As anticipated at the end of the last chapter, very diverse case studies have been selected to allow for a deeper understanding of the power and versatility of the DT paradigm: from small towns to megacities, nations, continents and up to the entire planet Earth.

5.1 Small-Town DT: The House of Emerging Technologies of Matera

This project aims to transform Matera (Italy) into an international reference centre for the development and application of emerging technologies in urban, creative, and cultural fields. Emerging technologies include Artificial Intelligence (AI), Blockchain, Internet of Things (IoT), and 5G. The project encompasses several coordinated actions to establish an integrated system for open innovation, benefiting citizens, businesses, institutions, and the research community. Furthermore, the project seeks to position the local economic and knowledge system within national and international contexts, providing innovation tools, promotion opportunities, growth prospects, and skills development [33].

Aligned with Matera's primary development vocations, the project focuses on the following areas of innovation: the supply chain of cultural and creative industries, the management of cultural and environmental heritage, and services for sustainability and sustainable tourism.

Coordinated by the Department of Engineering, ICT and Technologies for Energy and Transport of the Italian National Research Council (ICAR-CNR), the project aims to create a DT of a large geographical area within the city of Matera. The project also involves the development and testing of hardware and software technologies within the urban context, including the implementation of sensors and innovative approaches to their use. ICAR's final objective is to design and develop a data platform capable of securely representing the vast amount of structured, semi-structured, and unstructured data acquired from existing sensors and databases.

5.2 Megacity DT: Virtual Singapore's Smart Nation Initiative

Singapore's well-established position in urban innovation and digital transformation makes it an ideal example to showcase the scalability and applicability of Digital Twin technology across diverse urban contexts. By delving into Singapore's experiences, we can gain valuable insights into the implementation of Digital Twins in a highly developed urban environment and understand their role in shaping the future of megacities. Under the Smart Nation Initiative, Singapore has been leveraging Digital Twins to enhance urban management, optimize resource allocation, and improve citizen services.

The Singaporean government has implemented a comprehensive strategy for adopting Digital Twins across various sectors such as transportation, utilities, buildings, and public services. Through the integration of real-time data from sensors, IoT devices, and other sources, Digital Twins provide a holistic and dynamic representation of the city's infrastructures, processes and systems.

DTs have enabled Singapore to achieve significant advancements in urban sustainability, efficient transportation management, and responsive citizen services.

They facilitate data-driven decision-making, predictive analytics for urban planning, and the optimization of energy consumption and waste management.

Moreover, the Singaporean government has leveraged DTs to foster a collaborative ecosystem, engaging public and private stakeholders, research institutions, and the community. This approach promotes innovation, co-creation, and the development of Digital Twin applications that address diverse urban challenges.

By showcasing Singapore's Smart Nation Initiative, we highlight the potential of Digital Twins as catalysts for urban innovation, citizen-centric services, and sustainable development in megacities. The Singapore case study exemplifies how a proactive and comprehensive Digital Twin strategy can transform a city into a smart and future-ready urban environment [34].

5.3 *Country-Scale DT: The National Digital Twin Programme UK*

The National Digital Twin programme (NDTp) in the United Kingdom is a significant initiative focused on driving the digital transformation of an entire country [35]. Launched in July 2018 by HM Treasury, the NDTp aims to deliver key recommendations outlined in the National Infrastructure Commission's "Data for the Public Good" report. Designed and deployed by the Centre for Digital Built Britain at the University of Cambridge, the program aims to establish an ecosystem of connected Digital Twins (CDTs) across various infrastructures, assets and organizations, collectively forming the National Digital Twin (NDT).

The NDTp offers several benefits to stakeholders, including transparent engagement, improved customer satisfaction, increased national productivity, enhanced business efficiency, and positive environmental impacts.

Since its inception, the NDTp has achieved significant milestones. These include the development of the Gemini Principles [36] and the prioritized Path Towards the Information Management Framework (IMF) outlined in the NDTp roadmap [37]. The establishment of the Digital Twin Hub provided a collaborative platform for early adopters to share knowledge and progress in Digital Twin implementation [38].

The UK NDTp offers a large number of use cases that demonstrate the program's impact across different sectors, such as the implementation of smart infrastructures to enhance safety and reliability within the rail network or the utilization of digital technologies to innovate service provision and hospital design in the "Smart Hospital of the Future" project. The "Smart Mobility Living Lab" in London provides an example of designing and testing solutions for a complex real-world transportation system. The "Climate Resilience Demonstrator" (CReDo) is a pioneering climate change adaptation Digital Twin project that provides a practical example of how connected data can improve climate adaptation and resilience across a system of systems. Lastly, the NDTp investigates how Digital Twins can drive business model innovation in the B2B sector, enabling organizations to leverage digital transformation for enhanced operations and customer insights. Through its comprehensive approach and diverse case studies, the National Digital Twin Programme UK plays a pivotal role in advancing the Digital Twin paradigm and facilitating sustainable development in the country.

5.4 Cross-Border DT: The Australia | New Zealand Blueprint

Introducing the collaboration between Australia and New Zealand in creating a shared Digital Twin expands the scope of our exploration to an international level. Inspired by the UK National Digital Twin programme, this joint effort represents a significant milestone in advancing Digital Twin technology and highlights the power of cross-border collaboration in shaping regional development.

The Australia | New Zealand Blueprint for Cross-border Digital Twins aims to enhance shared infrastructure planning, resource management, and disaster preparedness. This comprehensive Digital Twin model will encompass multiple cities, regions, and critical infrastructure across both countries and aims to facilitate information exchange, decision-making, and coordinated actions using advanced technologies and data integration. Expected benefits include cross-border integration, data-driven decision-making, and enhanced regional planning and resilience. A robust governance framework ensures effective knowledge sharing, stakeholder engagement, and data privacy considerations. This cross-border initiative sets an example for leveraging DTs in regional development and highlights the importance of international partnerships. The Australia | New Zealand Blueprint provides a valuable reference model for holistic and integrated territorial management [39].

5.5 Planet-Wide DT: The EU/ESA Destination Earth Initiative

Destination Earth (DestinE) is a flagship initiative of the European Commission and the European Space Agency (ESA), aiming to develop a Digital Twin of the whole planet Earth. This project integrates scientific and industrial excellence to leverage digital technologies for monitoring and predicting climate change, supporting sustainable development, and more. Key aspects of DestinE include continuous monitoring and simulation of Earth's ecosystems, anticipation of disasters and promotion of resilience, scenario development for sustainable development, collaboration and data sharing, user benefits and applications, a cloud-based platform to host DTs, and a roadmap with milestones for implementation. DestinE will revolutionize our understanding of Earth's systems, enabling informed decision-making, proactive measures, and a collaborative approach to address global environmental challenges [40].

6 Final Considerations and Methodological Approach

The scaling of the Digital Twin paradigm, as observed in the previous chapter, has led to its application in increasingly complex contexts, heavily influenced by anthropic activities. This trend has increased the relevance of the human component within the model, exposing the limitations of the mechanistic approach underlying the rigid digital-physical model inherited from early applications in industrial engineering. As reiterated throughout the article, in the writer's opinion humans represent a clearly distinct element both from the physical component, which constitutes the target of applications, and the digital one, represented by technological tools. To support this statement, the emerging discussion regarding the need to develop a human-centric Digital Twin model that aligns with the principles of digital transformation, though still limited to the industrial sector, has been thoroughly analysed [41]. Key reference methodologies for developing Local Digital Twin Ecosystems (LDTEs) and ongoing pilot projects will then be presented.

6.1 The Relevance of Human-Centricity

However, the term "human-centric" itself hides a dangerous ambiguity that gives rise to two very different interpretations and can also lead back to a mechanistic approach [42]. A legacy interpretation would see a Local Digital Twin (LDT) as a consumer product, to be designed by collecting information on recipients and trying to guess their preferences by analysing historical data or users' behaviours and sentiments. Over the years, this type of strategy has proven to be extremely valid for creating and marketing "off-the-shelf" products. However, developing the Digital Twin of a territory, whether rural, suburban or urban, is the furthest away from serial production.

While recognizing the human being as having greater centrality in an LDT compared to an industrial application, this approach implies a substantially top-down vision which sees the communities benefiting from the interventions as just commercial targets.

In the writer's opinion, however, this approach could not produce optimal results in designing an LDT because it would fail to capture in detail the specificities of each territory and the communities that inhabit them, together with their aspirations and needs. These specificities can indeed only be known by those who are in daily contact with the reality of a territory as they live, study or work there permanently, or just visit it temporarily for leisure. Each territory and each community is characterized by a unique blend of socio-cultural, socio-economic and socio-technical systems, geomorphological characteristics and eco-cultural resources, which is impossible to grasp in its entirety without the strong involvement of local stakeholders.

On the other end, a purely bottom-up, grassroots approach is generally difficult to implement due to the stakeholders' lack of time, skills, vision and organizational capacity, especially in the case of smaller-sized territories or activities. For this reason, the enhanced model proposed in this study adopts an inside-out approach, placing the LDT in a barycentric position for easily interacting with all the elements that compose the ecosystem and binding them together [43].

In this study, the concept of user-centricity redefines the role of the human component from a passive recipient to an integral and actively engaged participant throughout the entire LDTE's lifecycle, from planning to operation. By sitting at the centre of local ecosystems, the LDTE facilitates the collection, processing and redistribution of information and services within and beyond their boundaries.

6.2 Supporting Methodologies and Ongoing Pilots

The first step in creating a sustainable LDTE infrastructure consists of mapping the actual ecosystem, which is typically composed of natural, cultural, infrastructural and human resources. To facilitate this operation, it has been chosen to leverage the Quintuple Helix Model of innovation which organizes the main elements of an ecosystem into five categories: (1) academia, (2) business, (3) government, (4) civil society and (5) the territory [44]. The engagement and active participation of all categories of stakeholders should start from the earliest stages of the LDTE implementation process and go through four phases: (1) co-design, (2) co-creation, (3) co-deployment and (4) co-management. In addition to the advantage of greater accuracy in the final result, this approach produces another effect of primary importance, as it will allow the beneficiary community to develop a sense of ownership both towards the LDTE and the local resources, representing the best guarantee of the project's success and long-term sustainability.

In line with the Agile methodology, after an early engagement of local stakeholders, each phase of the implementation process will be characterized by periodic meetings to check if the development is in line with their expectations and, if needed, activate improvement loops to adjust. This approach allows to spare time and resources as possible issues and potential conflicts are identified and fixed as they arise [45].

According to this approach, the very first concrete action to engage the stakeholders consists in the submission of a sketchy outline of the project and the administration of a questionnaire drawn from the SWOT analysis, composed of the following questions:

- Expected achievements (Opportunities): What would your institution/organization aim to achieve through this project and how would you like your world to change through it?
- Expected barriers during implementation (Threats): What kind of barriers and wicked problems do you think the project might encounter in pursuing its goals?
- Reasons for failure of previous similar efforts (Weaknesses): Why have previous similar efforts not produced the expected results?
- Contribution to the project (Strengths): How do you think your institution/organization can contribute to overcoming problems and achieving project goals?

In addition to its value in mapping the ecosystem, administering a questionnaire demonstrates a listening attitude, which represents the best start to establishing with local stakeholders a relationship based on mutual understanding and trust.

The responses are then used to identify an initial core of participants who show a predisposition to adopt new solutions. This nucleus will form a team of "innovation champions" and will have three tasks: participate in co-designing the system, act as a catalyst to engage other local stakeholders, and set up the first hubs in the area. An LDTE is indeed composed of a network of DT Hubs distributed throughout the territory and integrated into a territorial network of interoperable hubs. These hubs will draw from both the European Digital Innovation Hubs (EDIHs) [46] and the UK Digital Twin Hub (DT Hub) [38].

As regards the topological configuration of the network, in the initial phase it is suggested to adopt a "hub and spoke" model that provides a more streamlined and manageable structure, easier to set up and maintain [47]. This model can also help to establish the basic communication and coordination between the first nodes of the ecosystem. However, as the LDTE grows, becomes more complex and achieves sufficient stability, a more flexible and self-managed "hubs of hubs" model [48] will be progressively adopted to improve its efficiency, resilience, and scalability over time. Migrating from a hub and spoke model to a hubs of hubs model as the system stabilizes, ensures that the ecosystem grows in a controlled and sustainable way and that the structure of the system is optimized for its specific needs and characteristics.

Three more key elements are needed to ensure Local Digital Twin Ecosystems a successful adoption and long-term sustainability: (i) an emic perspective, (ii) non-linear ecosystem thinking, and (iii) semantic technologies.

Firstly, the adoption of an emic perspective allows for achieving a deep understanding of the stakeholders' sentiments and worldviews, which is where the most significant barriers usually lie. The emic approach, drawn from anthropology, is based on the principle that to understand a culture or a community it is necessary to be able to look at the world from their perspective [49].

Secondly, as LDTEs are confronted with highly complex scenarios, they require non-linear ecosystem thinking to grasp all the dependencies and intricacies [50]. This approach emphasizes the complexity and interconnectedness of inhomogeneous vertical sector systems, and the importance of considering multiple factors and perspectives to produce a higher integration between them. This approach to problem-solving is needed to create resilient knowledge-based socio-economic ecosystems, as it recognizes that the behaviour of subsystems cannot be predicted through linear cause-effect relationships, because of the complex relationships between multiple variables and their interactions over time.

Finally, the use of federated ontologies [51] and semantic mapping methods [52] will enable interoperability, both within and across sectors, paving the way for the breaking of data silos and the diffusion of open innovation [53]. These topics will be the subject of a follow-up paper.

As part of this research, pilot projects are currently being co-designed with local stakeholders in an Italian rural area (the Tuscia), as well as in two suburban areas of sub-Saharan Africa, namely Kampala (Uganda) and Bujumbura (Burundi). These initiatives are already generating real-world feedback, providing valuable insights into the practical application and effectiveness of the proposed approach. The first consolidated results will be published as soon as they are available, helping to refine the model and enhance its viability.

7 Conclusions

This concept paper aims to stimulate a discussion on the need to update the current Digital Twin paradigm and align it with the well-established trend towards a human-centric digital transformation. Employing a qualitative research method, the proposal draws on epistemological justifications and the analysis of case studies from diverse global contexts, providing insights that address the first research question. Additionally, this work dispels common misconceptions surrounding Digital Twins and sheds light on a potential ambiguity inherent in the notion of "human-centricity."

Furthermore, in response to the second research question, the methodology for creating LDTEs is introduced, presenting a practical framework for integrating the human component into the Digital Twin paradigm. Future directions of this research are also outlined, emphasizing the importance of promoting open innovation and knowledge sharing among LDTE members and beyond.

To demonstrate the feasibility and potential of this approach, three ongoing pilot projects will yield valuable feedback to further enhance the proposed model and showcase the practical applications and tangible benefits of human-centric Digital Twins across various domains.

In summary, this work provides a foundation for advancing the Digital Twin paradigm by acknowledging the significance of the human component and formally incorporating it into the model. By embracing a human-centric perspective, Digital Twins are better equipped to address the complexities of socio-technical systems, opening up new avenues for sustainable development in different types of contexts.

Acknowledgements We would like to express our gratitude to the Centre for Digital Built Britain (CDBB) at the University of Cambridge for having allowed us to follow the establishment of the UK NDTp in the making. We're also grateful for their enthusiastic support in creating and hosting an Italian Network within the UK DT Hub, a vibrant international community that comprises over 3400 members representing more than 1600 organizations from 77 countries worldwide.

References

1. Gelernter, D. (1993). *Mirror worlds*. Oxford University Press.
2. Grieves, M. W. (2005). Product lifecycle management: The new paradigm for enterprises. *International Journal of Product Development, 2*(1–2), 71–84.
3. Le Moigne, J. (2022). Earth system Digital Twins (ESDT) workshop. In *2022 earth system Digital twins (ESDT) workshop*.
4. Singh, M., Fuenmayor, E., Hinchy, E. P., Qiao, Y., Murray, N., & Devine, D. (2021). Digital Twin: Origin to future. *Applied System Innovation, 4*(2), 36.
5. Jones, D., et al. (2020). Characterising the Digital Twin: A systematic literature review. *CIRP Journal of Manufacturing Science and Technology, 29*(Part A), 36–52.
6. Abdoune, F., Cheutet, V., Nouiri, M., & Cardin, O. (2023). Digital Twin for decision-support: An insight into the integration of simulation models into Digital Twin architectures. In *International workshop on service orientation in Holonic and multi-agent manufacturing* (pp. 15–25). Springer Nature Switzerland.
7. Kao, L. J., et al. (2014). Service innovation and smart analytics for industry 4.0 and big data environment. *Procedia CIRP, 16*, 3–8.
8. European Commission. (n.d.). Europe fit for the Digital age. Accessed May 28, 2023, from https://commission.europa.eu/strategy-and-policy/priorities-2019-2024/europe-fit-digital-age_en
9. Local Digital Twin. (n.d.). Accessed June 03, 2023, from https://living-in.eu/groups/solutions/local-digital-twin
10. Co-design the Local Digital Twin Toolbox (n.d.). Accessed June 04, 2023, from https://living-in.eu/news/co-design-local-digital-twins-ldt-toolbox
11. Morakanyane, R., O'Reilly, P., McAvoy, J., & Grace, A.A. (2020). Determining Digital transformation success factors. Hawaii International Conference on System Sciences.
12. Rifkin, J. (2011). *The third industrial revolution: How lateral power is transforming energy, the economy, and the world* (pp. 5–15). Palgrave Macmillan.
13. Vrana, J., & Singh, R. (2021). Digitization, digitalization, and digital transformation. In N. Meyendorf, N. Ida, R. Singh, & J. Vrana (Eds.), *Handbook of nondestructive evaluation 4.0*. Springer. https://doi.org/10.1007/978-3-030-48200-8_39-1
14. Verhoef, P. C., et al. (2021). Digital transformation: A multidisciplinary reflection and research agenda. *Journal of Business Research, 122*, 889–901.
15. Johnson, L., et al. (2019). *NMC horizon report: 2019 higher education edition*. The New Media Consortium.
16. Frey, C. B., & Osborne, M. A. (2017). The future of employment: How susceptible are jobs to computerization? *Technological Forecasting and Social Change, 114*, 254–280.
17. Westerman, G., Bonnet, D., & McAfee, A. (2014). *Leading digital: Turning technology into business transformation*. Harvard Business Review Press.
18. Bharadwaj, A., et al. (2013). Digital business strategy: Toward a next generation of insights. *MIS Quarterly, 37*(2), 471–482.
19. McQuivey, J. (2013). *Digital disruption: Unleashing the next wave of innovation*. Forrester Research, Incorporated.
20. Zengin, Y., Naktiyok, S., Kaygın, E., Kavak, O., & Topçuoğlu, E. (2020). An investigation upon industry 4.0 and society 5.0 within the context of sustainable development goals. *Sustainability, 13*(5), 2682.

21. Gupta, A., Mithas, S., & George, G. (2020). *Transforming digital business models: A guide to digital innovation and disruption with case studies*. Routledge.
22. Lacity, M. C., Willcocks, L. P., & Craig, A. (2019). Robotic process automation and cognitive automation: Opportunities and challenges for shared services and outsourcing. *Journal of Information Technology, 34*(4), 329–345.
23. Berman, S. J., Lyytinen, K., & Pentland, B. T. (2019). Digital transformation: From driving change to ongoing transformation. *MIS Quarterly Executive, 18*(2), 87–100.
24. Agarwal, V., Garg, M. K., Dharmavaram, S., & Kumar, D. (2024). "Which LLM should I use?": Evaluating LLMs for tasks performed by undergraduate computer science students. ArXiv. /abs/2402.01687.
25. Hassani, H., Huang, X., & MacFeely, S. (2022). Impactful Digital Twin in the healthcare revolution. *Big Data and Cognitive Computing, 6*(3), 83.
26. Buonocore, L., Yates, J., & Valentini, R. (2022). A proposal for a Forest Digital Twin framework and its perspectives. *Forests, 13*(4), 498.
27. Guo, J., & Lv, Z. (2022). Application of digital twins in multiple fields. *Multimedia Tools and Applications, 81*(19), 26941–26967.
28. Grieves, M., & Vickers, J. (2017). Digital Twin: Mitigating unpredictable, undesirable emergent behavior in complex systems. In *Transdisciplinary perspectives on complex systems: New findings and approaches* (pp. 85–113).
29. Gama, J., et al. (2020). Digital twins for smart cities: A survey. In *Proceedings of the 2020 IEEE international smart cities conference (ISC2)* (pp. 1–6).
30. Lee, G., Lee, J., & Song, Y. (2019). A systematic review of the Digital Twin: A disruptive technology for manufacturing, supply chain, and sustainability. *Journal of Cleaner Production, 233*.
31. Lehner, C., Padovano, A., Zehetner, C., & Hackenberg, G. (2023). Digital twin and digital thread within the product lifecycle management. *Procedia Computer Science, 232*, 2875–2886. https://doi.org/10.1016/j.procs.2024.02.104
32. Destination Earth (DestinE). (n.d.). Accessed May 28, 2023, from https://www.esa.int/Applications/Ob-serving_the_Earth/Destination_Earth
33. Castelli, G., et al. (2022). Urban intelligence: Toward the digital twin of Matera and Catania. In *In 2022 workshop on blockchain for renewables integration (BLORIN)* (pp. 132–137). IEEE.
34. Myers, J., Larios, V., & Missikoff, O. (2023). Thriving smart cities. In *The Digital Twin* (pp. 901–969). Springer International Publishing.
35. Akroyd, J., Mosbach, S., Bhave, A., & Kraft, M. (2020). The National Digital Twin of the UK–a knowledge-graph approach. *Preprint, 264*.
36. Bolton, A., et al. (2018). *The Gemini principles: Guiding values for the national Digital Twin and information management framework*. Cambridge University Press.
37. Information management Framework. (n.d.). Accessed May 28, 2023, from https://digitaltwinhub.co.uk/archive/imf/what-is-the-imf/
38. UK Digital Twin Hub. (n.d.). Accessed May 28, 2023, from https://digitaltwinhub.co.uk/
39. The Australia | New Zealand Digital Twin Blueprint. (n.d.). Accessed May 28, 2023, from https://www.digitaltwinhub.org/blueprint
40. Nativi, S., Mazzetti, P., & Craglia, M. (2021). Digital ecosystems for developing digital twins of the earth: The destination earth case. *Remote Sensing, 13*(11), 2119.
41. Asad, U., Khan, M., Khalid, A., & Lughmani, W. A. (2023). Human-centric Digital Twins in industry: A comprehensive review of enabling technologies and implementation strategies. *Sensors, 23*(8), 3938.
42. Ivanov, D. (2023). The industry 5.0 framework: Viability-based integration of the resilience, sustainability, and human-centricity perspectives. *International Journal of Production Research, 61*(5), 1683–1695.
43. Frau, M., Moi, L., & Cabiddu, F. (2020). Outside-in, inside-out, and blended marketing strategy approach: A longitudinal case study. *International Journal of Marketing Studies, 12*(3), 1–13.

44. Carayannis, E. G., & Campbell, D. F. (2018). *Smart quintuple helix innovation systems: How social ecology and environmental protection are driving innovation, sustainable development and economic growth*. Springer.
45. Gaborov, M., et al. (2021). Comparative analysis of agile and traditional methodologies in IT project management. *Journal of Applied Technical and Educational Sciences, 11*(4), 1.
46. Hervas-Oliver, J. L., et al. (2021). Emerging regional innovation policies for industry 4.0: Analyzing the digital innovation hub program in European regions. *Competitiveness Review: An International Business Journal, 31*(1), 106–129.
47. An, Y., et al. (2015). The reliable hub-and-spoke design problem: Models and algorithms. *Transportation Research Part B: Methodological, 77*, 103–122.
48. Delaney, P., & Pettit, C. (2014). Urban data hubs supporting smart cities. *Research@ Locate, 14*, 07–09.
49. Morey, N. C., & Luthans, F. (1984). An emic perspective and ethnoscience methods for organizational research. *Academy of Management Review, 9*(1), 27–36.
50. Carayannis, E. G., et al. (2018). 'Mode 3' universities and academic firms: Thinking beyond the box trans-disciplinarity and nonlinear innovation dynamics within coopetitive entrepreneurial ecosystems. *International Journal of Technology Management, 77*(1–3), 145–185.
51. Tu, Z., Zacharewicz, G., & Chen, D. (2016). A federated approach to develop enterprise interoperability. *Journal of Intelligent Manufacturing, 27*, 11–31.
52. Bartalesi, V., et al. (2023). Using semantic story maps to describe a territory beyond its map. *Semantic web (Preprint)*, 1–18.
53. Bakshi, S. (2020). 'Breaking the silos' of innovation methods. *International Journal of Systematic Innovation, 6*(2), 36–41.

Emerging Paradigms in Tourism Industry: Smart Tourism and Local Development

Francesco Russo, Alessia Munnia, Angelo Bonfanti, Melita Nicotra, and Marco Romano

Abstract Destination management has undergone a profound transformation under the wave of the shift toward smart tourism. The aim of the paper is to provide an overview of this emerging change and, adopting a deductive approach, derive propositions to enhance the overall understanding of the phenomenon. The originality of our contribution lies in the attempt to relate smart tourism to local development.

Social Media, and the enormous amount of data generated (Big Data) are crucial factors in increasing the degree of smartness of a destination as well as in providing a smart touristic experience. Furthermore, low-cost carriers have further revolutionised destination management. They have established novel approaches to the booking process from the point of view of tourists, and a smarter approach in the interaction with tourists themselves. Their presence further increases the smartness of a destination and its attractiveness toward different segments of travellers, including digital nomads and potential start-uppers, who can act as key drivers of local growth and development.

Keywords Social media · Destination choices · Low-cost airlines · Local development · Smart cities · Start-ups creation

1 Introduction

Local development is strongly dependent not only on tourism but also on investment attraction and start-up creation. Attracting touristic flows as well as creating a productive environment for new venture creation is therefore strategically relevant and may act as an accelerator of territorial wealth.

F. Russo (✉) · A. Munnia · M. Nicotra · M. Romano
Department of Economics and Business, University of Catania, Catania, Italy
e-mail: francesco.russo@phd.unict.it

A. Bonfanti
Department of Management, University of Verona, Verona, Italy

A. M. Braccini et al. (eds.), *Digital (Eco) Systems and Societal Challenges*, Lecture Notes in Information Systems and Organisation 72,
https://doi.org/10.1007/978-3-031-75586-6_9

In this perspective, the destination management organisations (DMO) and transportation infrastructures (such as airports) play a crucial entrepreneurial role: their strategic decisions and actions are able to impact territorial competitiveness and attractiveness. We aim to examine some elements that, if adequately exploited by destination decision-makers, are able to make a destination smarter and exert an influence on its attractiveness to tourists, potential investors, digital nomads, or start-uppers. Moreover, we explore how local attractiveness may benefit from a strategic collaboration between destination managers and low-cost airline carriers, in a context where the exploitation of digital technologies contributes to make both the destination and the transportation infrastructure smarter (i.e. smart airports).

Travel and tourism industry has undergone a profound shift as a result of the advent of the Internet, which led to the emergence of the new paradigm of what is called e-tourism. The Internet as a primary source of information has indeed fostered the creation of a very dynamic and complex digital ecosystem in which a wide network of tourists interacts with each other to exchange useful information, and companies try to connect to tourists and engage with them. Various components from this electronic network facilitate interactions among different stakeholders. These components are: social media platforms, travel review websites (such as TripAdvisor), general search engines (such as Google), online travel agencies (OTAs) (such as Booking and Expedia), communication exchange channels (such as YouTube), sites that allow tourists to compare prices (such as Trivago), tour operator websites, blogs and microblogs, and the various major tourism service providers (e.g. airlines, hotels, etc.) [1]. A high degree of adoption of Information and Communication Technologies is what determines the emergence of a smart city, which in turn drives tourism toward smart tourism. The paradigm of smartness has been applied to a wide range of concepts, from technological devices to physical infrastructures, cities, and, as anticipated, to tourism. It generally entails the idea of technology integration while leveraging the hidden power of the huge quantity of data available.

As clarified by [2], embracing smartness in tourism entails a reorientation of the entire industry toward a pervasive adoption of ICTs in all the activities performed by the different actors, together with an extensive usage of social media and a proper exploitation of big data as a precious source of insights to guide business decisions. In particular, according to the authors, smart tourism is characterised by three main pillars, all of which are fuelled by the collection, exchange, and processing of data: smart experience, smart business ecosystem, and smart destination. The first one is an augmented tourism experience facilitated by the integration of technological solutions as well as by personalised offerings. The second one refers to the ecosystem of interconnected actors and processes empowered by digitalization that co-create value for tourists, thus enhancing their experience. Eventually, smart destinations represent a particular type of smart cities where effort to improve the quality of life is addressed not only to residents but also to tourists during their stay, incorporating ICTs into physical infrastructures.

In a smart tourism ecosystem, the consumer community and a supplier network interact in a digitalised and data-driven environment where mobile and wireless technologies, sensor technologies, social media, and intelligent systems are key enablers of these valuable relationships [3]. Consistently, also [4] list the internet, social media and big data among the factors that are determining relevant changes in tourism.

These factors are indeed enablers of the smart interaction between consumers and suppliers and of the finer alignment between demand and offer due to the real-time data available that feeds a constantly updated knowledge base on tourists and their experiences.

However, given the undeniable importance of transportation as an enabler of tourism and given the constant growth of air transportation, a focus on the aviation industry is also helpful for a broader understanding of emerging challenges in the tourism industry. The evolution of the air market had indeed led to the emergence and empowerment of low-cost carriers, which not only have disrupted the market itself, but they are also impacting the mechanisms underlying tourism demand and destination choices. Furthermore, their contribution is also extended to the creation of a more attractive environment for established businesses as well as for new ventures. This effect is amplified by the offer to tourists of a satisfying customer experience in a smart destination. Indeed, among tourists, there may be the so-called "digital nomads", who decide to work digitally while travelling around exotic destinations [5] as well as individuals interested in contributing to the development of the area, such as start-uppers.

The aim of the paper is to provide an overview of these three disrupting factors that have been influencing the tourism industry toward smart tourism in the last decades and to derive propositions on the topics investigated. The remaining of the paper is organised as follows: the first section briefly explains the methodology adopted, the second one provides a brief overview of the tourism industry, the third and fourth sections respectively examine the emergence of Social Media and Big Data as innovations that redefine the paradigm of destination management in influencing tourists' destination decisions as well as their decisions made during the trip. The fifth section explores the effect of the evolved aviation market, characterised by growing market share of low-cost airline companies, on the development of the local airport and, as a consequence, on destination decisions. In the sixth and last section we present the propositions as result of our deductive investigation on the three main objects of analysis.

We eventually present the main conclusions of our work, pointing out also the main managerial implications of the propositions we derived.

2 Methodology

The present work employs a deductive approach to theory building. The purpose is to derive novel propositions to advance existing theory on smart tourism, suggesting relationships between existing concepts. Generating new emerging knowledge through a deductive process starting from existing knowledge is indeed a prominent trend in management literature: [6] refer to "conceptual deduction" and list it among the methodologies that can lead to the elaboration of a conceptual framework and, therefore, to an advanced understanding of phenomena. Specifically, one way of contributing to existing theory is explicating the way constructs and relationships interact at different levels, thus generating new insights on existing knowledge [7].

For the aforementioned purpose, we studied the state of the art concerning two factors that the literature has identified as crucial for the shift toward smart tourism: social media and big data. Furthermore, we focused our attention on an emerging factor whose impact is still understudied in academic literature, namely the rise of low cost carriers.

Building on this overall picture, we deduced some propositions to shed light on the possible impact of the identified factors and advance the current understanding of smart tourism as an emerging phenomenon.

3 Brief Overview on Tourism Industry

Tourism has a significant impact on economic growth [8]. Given its remarkable role, it becomes interesting to investigate the changes that are currently affecting the industry, and in particular tourism destinations, tourist experience, and the activity of businesses operating in it.

A tourism destination (TD) is referred to as a geographical area that provides visitors with the chance to participate in a diverse range of activities and attractions, as well as an area that is supported by all the hospitality and other services that the visitor might need during their stay. It is essentially represented by a collection of physical sites in which tourists spend their time for the purposes of sightseeing both man-made and natural attractions, performing activities, such as swimming, skiing, and learning, and, more generally, spending their time by visiting bars, events, shops, restaurants, and other local services [9].

According to [10], a destination can also be intended as a perceptual concept, which can be subjectively interpreted by customers. In this perspective, it can be dependent on a variety of factors, such as prior travel experience and the aim of the visit, as well as psychographic and demographic characteristics of the destination. This term therefore refers to both the location with all its physical features and attractions and to the way these aspects are perceived and evaluated by tourists.

In the context of smart cities, destinations are likely to undergo a shift toward smart destinations, essentially defined as innovative destinations that largely rely on advanced technologies to facilitate tourists' interaction with the surrounding areas, thus enhancing the overall quality of their experience as well as the quality of life of residents [2], while enabling tourism stakeholders to access and exploit relevant information in real time [11]. Technology and stakeholders are indeed two key components of a smart destination [12].

However, for the development and management of a smart destination, a central role is attributed to destination marketing officers since they are responsible for spreading smart vision and smart leadership that drive the destination's stakeholders to implement smart initiatives [13].

Smart destinations aim to offer a smart experience, leveraging the pervasive adoption of ICTs by both tourism stakeholders and travellers themselves; such experiences are personalised and exploit enhanced context awareness and the possibility to perform real-time monitoring [14]. Therefore, in the current world, permeated by technology, especially ICTs, even tourism has become an information-intensive industry. In such a context, Internet of Things devices and IT infrastructures create an ecosystem where tourism stakeholders 'decisions are guided by the collective knowledge [15] generated and shared by both tourists and businesses. Therefore, an effective integration of ICTs in the activities performed by tourism businesses enhances tourist experience, which becomes ICT-assisted, but also improves the overall destination attractiveness and competitiveness [16].

4 Social Media: Definition and Impact on Tourism Industry

The focus in this section concerns the components that fall under the umbrella of what are referred to as social media, with the final goal to explore the role they play in smart tourism.

The term "Social Media" (SM) was originally used in 1994 on a Tokyo online media environment known as Matisse. The first social media platforms were developed and introduced to the public during that period, which coincided with the early stages of the commercial use of the Internet. Both the variety of social media platforms and the number of people actively using them have expanded dramatically over the course of time, establishing social media as one of the most prominent uses of the Internet [17]. Social media, in its broadest sense, refers to the set of web-based apps and interactive platforms that enable users to create, discuss, modify, and share user-generated content (UGCs). Therefore, social media do not just refer to social networking sites like Facebook; they also include blogs (e.g., The Huffington Post), business networks (e.g., LinkedIn), collaborative projects (e.g., Wikipedia), enterprise social networks (e.g., Social Cast), forums, microblogs, photo sharing (e.g., Photobucket), product/service reviews (e.g., Amazon), social bookmarking (e.g., Pinterest), social gaming (e.g., World of Warcraft), video sharing (e.g., Youtube), and virtual worlds (Aichner & Jacob, 2015) (e.g. Metaverse). The expression SM therefore refers to the various forms of social interactions taking place on a variety of digital media and technologies that enable users to produce and share contents as well as to collaborate with each other. The advent of these new media has revolutionised the way we create information and communicate, but also our consumption habits. The power of social media lies in the fact that they allow people to instantaneously spread knowledge to a potentially worldwide audience, in the form of tweets, posts, and other types of web documents, by means of social networking sites, and this information is released, received, and shared by peers. This gives rise to innovative ways of collaborating, such as the so-called "collective intelligence", which refers to the intelligence produced by the interplay of interconnected people who discuss and communicate with each other [18].

A new and extensive global society of always-connected people who are glad to share, interact, and collaborate has been created as a result of the widespread growth of social media sites, which are based on the voluntary public sharing of such information [9].

The role played by social media in the tourism industry has been widely investigated in tourism literature and, among SM, social networks deserve particular attention due to their growing popularity.

The increasing adoption of social media, especially social networks, has changed and is still transforming the way tourism companies interact and communicate with tourists and potential tourists. In this evolved environment, traditional communication approaches based on the use of mass media are indeed partially outdated and less effective since tourists now have access to all the information they need on destinations, attractions, and accommodation alternatives through the Internet. Therefore, tourism companies and destination managers need to adopt new channels to reach their potential customers.

The availability of credible information on social media helps travellers develop reasonable expectations and eliminate uncertainty. Because tourism products are intangible, potential tourists require as much information as possible before booking their trip. They trust other travellers' recommendations more than official tourist organisations. This form of online interpersonal influence is referred to as electronic Word of Mouth (WoM), which can lead to increased customer satisfaction since it allows to learn what travellers think and feel about their experiences, thus enabling tourism companies to improve their service (for example, by finding solutions to issues and questions previously emerged or doubts that tourists have during the travel). WoM allows companies to track their reputation and rivals' strategies. Since tourists increasingly rely on SM as a source of information, these media have become an increasingly strategic, unbiased, and low-cost way to collect data on tourists (see the following section on Big Data) and deliver tailored marketing communications, such as recommendations based on their interests and experiences. This allows to deliver a personalised and unique value proposition [19].

The use of social media and the consequent proliferation of user-generated contents, in addition to being a strategic source of information for tourism companies, has then unquestionably had an effect on the travel process in its entirety, including pre-travel, during travel, and post-travel stages. In the pre-purchase step, as mentioned above, UGCs represent an instant and reliable source of precious information that guide tourists in the development of their travel plan and also contribute to shaping their expectations, which will be fundamental also in the post-travel stage, affecting the formative process of tourists' satisfaction; during the travel, UGCs are instead relevant in influencing perceptions on the tourist experience [20].

Furthermore, social media are nowadays a strategic imperative for destination branding strategies, aiming at promoting specific tourism destinations.

The concept of destination branding originates from a mix of tangible and intangible components. The idea of branding a location indeed encompasses much more than just a well-known name, distinctive logo, slogan, or symbol. The process of branding a destination is far more sophisticated. It represents a marketing strategy that incorporates practical, emotional, relational, and strategic aspects that, in their entirety, contribute to producing in the minds of customers a distinctive network of associations [21].

Because of the unique qualities that destinations possess as brands, it can be challenging to successfully transfer marketing strategies to locations such as cities, regions, or even countries. The branding process applied to tourist destinations has been considered even more challenging than the one of consumer goods [22].

Blain, Levy, and Ritchie [23] define it as the "set of marketing activities that (1) support the creation of a name, symbol, logo, word mark, or other graphic that readily identifies and differentiates a destination; that (2) consistently convey the expectation of a memorable travel experience that is uniquely associated with the destination; that (3) serve to consolidate and reinforce the emotional connection between the visitor and the destination; and that (4) reduce consumer search costs and perceived risk. Collectively, these activities serve to create a destination image that positively influences consumer destination choice" [23, p. 337].

This process is made even more complicated by the fact that tourists themselves, by means of social media, actively participate in the co-creation process of experiences, and, by sharing them, they also contribute to shaping the destination's identity. Therefore, tourists play a crucial role in the construction of a destination's image. The risk is that, as a result of this process, the final brand identity may not coincide with the intended one. Destination managers can then analyse tourists' behaviour on social media and consequently take actions.

Therefore, social media clearly represent both a precious source of information on tourist experiences [24] and a revolutionary communication tool for all the players operating in the tourism industry, for the purposes of marketing promotion, destination branding, community management, and consumer interaction [25].

5 Big Data: Definition and Impact on Tourism Industry

This section presents an overview of the concept of Big Data (BD), of which social media represent a key source, and then clarifies the role it plays in the tourism industry and, specifically, on destination branding and marketing.

The term "Big Data" has been one of the most popular buzzwords for several years. Data is abundant in the era of the Internet of Things (IoT), and for years, academics and industry professionals have been investigating the implications of Big Data for various domains of development, including business [26]. In the seminal paper that Bryson et al. wrote and published in 1999 in the Communications of the Association for Computing Machinery (ACM), the term BD was introduced for the very first time. In particular, applications built for the Web 2.0 platform and the proliferation of mobile devices further contributed to the increase in data volumes [27, 28]. The concept was later resumed by Doug Laney, an analyst working for META, which is now known as Gartner, who used a model called the 3Vs (further explained below) to describe the opportunities and difficulties resulting from the increase in data [29].

A widely accepted definition of big data is the following: "Big data is high-volume, high-velocity, and high-variety information assets that demand cost-effective, innovative forms of information processing that enable enhanced insight, decision-making, and process automation". This definition places an emphasis on the three "Vs": volume, velocity, and variety. Therefore, Big Data refers to datasets whose size is beyond the capability of typical database software tools to capture, store, manage, and analyse. Hence, Big Data has been originally defined and identified in terms of volume (it cannot be stored with ordinary tools since it exceeds the space limits), variety (data can take different forms, such as text, images, videos etc.) and velocity (data are created, modified, and spread at unprecedented speed) [30, 31].

However, there is no unique and universally accepted definition of Big Data linked to their size, and this is mainly due to the constant advances in technology that lead to continuous changes in the sizes of datasets to be considered and identified as "big". In point of fact, Big Data continues to expand around the globe on a daily basis, even on a second-by-second basis, primarily as a consequence of the growing number of Internet of Things devices in use.

Nevertheless, the definition of the 3Vs has been later expanded to include other additional Vs. A broader definition by [32] includes 6 Vs: volume, variety, velocity, veracity, visibility, and value. More recent contributions have identified 5 additional Vs which constitute a comprehensive definition including 11Vs: Volume, Variety, Velocity, Veracity, Value, Visibility, Variability, Validity, Volatility, Viscosity, and Viability [33–39].

Big data are playing a vital role in the evolution of global travel in this era of digital transformation, bringing significant opportunities for organisations operating in the tourism industry and for the territories in general.

Indeed, the shift toward smart tourism largely depends on the ability of both businesses and destinations to effectively gather, manage, and leverage huge volumes of data to improve tourism activities [15].

Big data applications for the hospitality and tourism industries have been rapidly developing as a result of recent technological advancements in database management systems and analytical tools. Companies have always had their own internal data, but with the introduction of new technology and additional external data, they are now able to obtain insights into how they may enhance their relationships with customers as well as their operations. Therefore, Big Data supplies more detailed and precise information on travellers who nowadays leave electronic traces of most of their travel activities (such as their searches, plans, bookings, and reviews) [40].

Big Data analytics are, for example, frequently used to acquire insights on hotel guests from user-generated contents posted on social media. In the current era, customers are indeed willing to share copious amounts of feedback regarding their positive and negative experiences at hotels, restaurants, and other travel destinations

[41]. These reviews, if adequately analysed, can represent a good starting point to improve customer satisfaction.

Another advantage of Big Data is represented by the possibility for managers to use it to improve effectiveness and efficiency of operations. [42] explore how Big Data on monthly electricity and water consumption can be exploited by hotel chains that have access to it to increase energy efficiency dynamics.

Another interesting application of big data adoption in tourism is linked to destination marketing, which leverages the local attractiveness of territories indented as tourism destinations.

Indeed tourists, throughout their trips, as well as in their processes of decision-making and communication, actively contribute to the generation of a large flow of data that is generated by sensors, micro-devices, and cameras. The data is spread on urban and extra-urban sites that are of interest to tourists and can be used as a valid starting point for both the creation of what are considered "smart destinations" and the enhancement of the capacity of tourism businesses to tailor the products and services they supply to customers [43]. TDs are commonly managed and advertised by destination management organisations (DMOs), who also interact with the local tourist industry and plan several development initiatives. The vast amount of data generated by tourists on the Internet may provide extremely useful insights to DMOs to improve their activity. This precious information on tourists' behaviour shared on social media and on other websites, that is particularly difficult for local authorities to collect, holds a great potential since they can reveal to destination managers which locations are preferred by tourists, which factors mostly attract them, and what are their future travel intentions [9]. Tourists express their opinions on the destinations they visit on the internet, thus producing user-generated contents which, to some extent, shape the overall image and reputation of the location and have also the power to influence the perception of future visitors about a certain location in the process of selecting their vacation destination. The internet is therefore frequently adopted by tourists to acquire information. As a result, the existence of a tourist attraction within the context of the digital environment is of the utmost importance. Destination marketers should then place a great deal of emphasis on the contents they produce to advertise a location, since they are an increasingly powerful tool. A key aspect of this mechanism is that the above-mentioned UGCs may be leveraged to increase the efficiency of marketing of tourism destinations by means of Big Data Analytics, which enables better management of online reputation and, consequently, provides insights to increase the online competitiveness of destinations [44].

Del Vecchio, Mele, Ndou and Secundo [45] summarise the four main ways in which Big Data, especially Social Media Big Data, can create value in the context of smart tourism: (1) improving the decision-making process that can rely on real-time information on tourist experiences; (2) enhancing and enriching tourists' experiences, being able to predict and anticipate their needs; (3) developing new business models and new products or services, thanks to the improved interaction between stakeholders (4) enhancing interconnectedness within the business ecosystem, facilitating collaboration and enhancing trust between actors operating in the ecosystem.

Therefore, in this Big Data environment, the effect of investing in Big Data Analytics can be seen as twofold. All the different businesses involved in the tourism industry (from hotels to airline companies) can benefit from it to implement enhanced marketing strategies, particularly relevant in those contexts characterised by intense competition and exacting and experienced customers. Big Data Analytics may support these businesses in improving their strategic and operational decision-making, and in the value-generation process [28]. These companies, by leveraging tourist experience, mainly shared on social media, as customer knowledge, become more competitive and contribute to the creation of a smart destination [46]: they are indeed able to deliver the best service possible, with respect to customer requirements, at the right place and at the appropriate time [47]. This huge transformation taking place in a smart tourism environment entails changes from both tourists and marketers points of view since it gives rise to an interactive bilateral flow of information. On the one hand, it changes travellers information search behaviours, guaranteeing increased flexibility in the arrangement of touring plans; on the other hand, it allows destination marketers to access precious real-time information on tourists' demand and, at the same time, to improve the quality of communication and services [48].

Adopting the lens of knowledge management, this type of customer knowledge is therefore strategic to better respond to customer needs, improve service delivery, and orient marketing activities [49].

Enlarging the scope from the single businesses operating in a certain location to the location itself, BDA benefits can be extended to the competitiveness of the overall tourism destination. If TDs perform the appropriate analysis on big data dataset containing, for example, information in the form of tourists' feedbacks, reviews, photos, and messages (which are unstructured data), the results may be of help for tourism destination managers to construct consumer-metrics-based frameworks that are useful to classify tourist segments, track tourists' perceptions and attitudes and make predictions on future strategic patterns. Furthermore, as a result of BDA, destinations that rely on tourism can now offer enhanced and personalized services to visitors, in line with the idea of smart tourist destinations [44].

6 The Emerging Role of Low-Cost Carriers

As stated by [50], "transport plays an important role in the successful creation and development of new attractions as well as the healthy growth of existing ones. Provision of suitable transport has transformed dead centers of tourist interest into active and prosperous places attracting multitudes of people."

When it comes to comparing transportation choices made by tourists worldwide, considering air, road, water and train as alternatives, 59% of tourists decided to travel by airplane in 2019. Air transportation is therefore crucial for worldwide touristic flows [51]. It raises relevant considerations on the relationship between the transportation mode and the destination choice.

The selection of a tourism destination and airline is not a simple process. Such selection process nowadays requires the analysis and evaluation of numerous options before deciding on the best solution. Various factors are transforming this process, making it particularly complicated on the one hand, but also simpler on the other hand. A first factor is represented by the dramatic increase in the number of destinations competing with each other's for the attention of potential visitors. Secondly, travellers are becoming more and more autonomous in the selection and booking process without resorting to the help of traditional intermediaries (i.e. travel agencies and incoming tour operators), thus relying on direct sales channels and online booking websites. This happens as a result of the significantly enhanced digitally enabled accessibility to travel information. Other factors are the following: the emergence of several forms of tourism (i.e. urban, rural, nature, historic, and luxury), lowered travel costs, and the consequent increased travel frequency. However, it should be kept in mind that the selection process always begins with two major constraints: time and money budgets for the upcoming journey [52, 53].

Tourism literature has investigated how travellers make their choices in light of the above-mentioned renewed characteristics of tourists' decision-making process, recently focusing also on the influence of airline companies, which are gaining increasing market power because of the tendency of travellers to directly book from their websites. For this reason, airlines also started to collaborate with online travel agencies (i.e. Booking) and other online service providers (i.e. rental car agencies) offering combinations of travel and accommodation solutions.

A recent contribution studies the sequencing effect in a choice experiment and finds out that, depending on the order in which travellers receive information about airlines and tourist destinations, visitors may assess tourism destinations differently when confronting a decision. In particular, they suggest that having chosen the airline option, passengers are more likely to select the same tourist alternative in the second stage, while the opposite is not true [54].

From the tourism demand point of view [55], transport accessibility is strongly influential. Airline companies mainly rely on the existing demand pattern to define their future plans and schedules, thus contributing to further reinforce the existing demand pattern. This planning mechanism, typically adopted by the incumbent companies, is consistent with a hub-and-spoke approach and negatively impacts peripheral destinations. However, it has been raised the idea that the availability of flights to reach peripheral locations may cause an increase in tourism demand for that destination, considering aviation as a supportive factor for international tourism.

This is consistent with the point-to-point business model adopted by low-cost companies.

In this perspective, another factor not to discard in the attempt to describe the transformation of tourism industry is the evolution of the aviation market, with the growing market share of low-cost airlines. This growth was envisaged in the past [56] and has been confirmed by ex-post data [57]. This is the result of a modernisation process within the air market in conjunction with the emergence of digital platforms. Before the twentieth century, international aviation was dominated by flagship airlines—mostly public-owned and part of airline alliances—also called full-service airlines (FSC), which offer differentiated cabin classes and originally linked capital cities. Charter carriers (CCs) were developed to serve destinations located far from capital cities, but they were characterised by low profitability and severe demand volatility, but they provided some additional services such as accommodation and excursions. Low-cost (LCC) airlines emerged as a solution to connect regional airports with low frequency by offering a single type of cabin class and no additional services. A critical and innovative feature of LCCs is that they used websites as major distribution channel, cutting costs deriving from travel agency intervention. Lower costs are the main advantage of online booking, and this is true not only for transportation but also for accommodation, whose market has been disrupted by the use of online booking portals [58]. Focusing on the destination decision-making process, the *sieving concept* [53] represents the modern approach to such process, which is nowadays a fast and easy traveller journey experience based on the use of several digital touchpoints. This new paradigm is the result of some renewed contextual conditions (availability of a greater number of destinations, lowered costs) as well as of the transformed tourists' habits (booking by themselves and more frequently). The sieving tourism destination process is described as a simplified and fast step-by-step process, made less risky by the information available online and by the willingness of travellers to consider the discarded destination as an option for a future trip.

LCC leverage this changed pattern in the booking behaviour because they are digital by inception and therefore exploit modern media to communicate with customers. They also exploit Big Data as a precious customer knowledge base, thus acting as smart businesses in the smart tourism industry.

Since tourism researchers agree upon the idea that the attractiveness of a destination toward visitors strongly depends on the availability of affordable transportation [59], and given the idea in tourism literature that air transport accessibility can support the touristic development of an area (even peripheral locations), in light of the empowerment of low-cost airlines, we argue that the availability of low-cost flights is able to determine an increase in tourism demand of the relative destination. A market overlap between destination management and low-cost airlines management can lead to more efficient strategic behaviours for both actors, adopting a shared value approach [60] to create value from a customer-centric perspective.

The presence of LCC contributes to making the local airport much more competitive. However, the evolution of the aviation industry is a broader phenomenon, driven by changes in demographic trends, and the advent and development of communication technologies, which necessitate the creation of novel business models and strategies. The turbulence in this market enhances the wants and needs of passengers, who are becoming more and more accustomed to new technology in all aspects of their lives, especially in a smart city context. Some examples of customers' expectations from the aviation industry are receiving real-time information about aircraft delays, gates, and special offers from airlines and airports. In particular, higher levels of expectations are being placed by passengers on the workflow processes that are responsible for the supply of personalised services, as well as cargo and transportation [61]. To come up with renewed travellers' expectations and with the growing travel volumes, many airports in developed areas, such as smart cities, started their digital transformation journey by adopting cutting-edge innovations in the Information Technology & Telecommunication field [62].

All these factors contribute to enhancing the notoriety of the destination. This, in turn, creates opportunities to attract not only leisure tourists, but also business tourists or, in general, individuals who are interested in finding places where their wellbeing may grow, living distant from their chaotic hometowns, especially in the smart working era. This is a widespread phenomenon known as Digital Nomadism, which leverages the flexibility of work allowed by the use of digital technologies. Digital nomads are able to both work and travel, thus improving their work-life balance and adopting a work-leisure lifestyle [5, 63]. In doing this, they tend to prefer smart destinations.

As a result of this phenomenon, in the south of Italy the "Make in South" movement emerged. Make in South leverages the idea that the south itself has the potential to become a production centre of value through the retention and attraction of talents, the emergence of digital infrastructures, and the new distribution of development opportunities among territories due to smart working. This perspective refers to the future of innovation and work as a frontier to explore and experiment for the growth of an area or country. However, apart from potential workers, the increased attractiveness of an area may also make it more appealing to potential start-uppers, who would end up playing their part in economic growth, thus contributing to a virtuous circle. Furthermore, smart tourist destinations are characterised by an intense effort made by both authorities and businesses for the creation of incubators and accelerators. Therefore, the tourism industry is conducive and supportive to start-up creation [64].

7 Propositions

As emerged from the literature, both Big Data and Social Media contribute to the creation of smart tourist destinations in smart cities, which results from a broader digital transformation process concerning many aspects of everyday life. Indeed, thanks to the possibility to leverage these applications, tourism is becoming a more and more information-intensive phenomenon. The potential of tourism to become smart is strongly dependent on the level of dissemination of IT applications to everyday aspects of life, which characterises smart cities as intelligent and hyperconnected cities able to exploit and take advantage of information and communication technologies (ICT) [65, 66]. Therefore, a smart city where ICT is highly exploited is likely to become a smart destination. Its smartness has a positive effect on tourists' experiences, making it as memorable, seamless, pleasurable, and stress-free as possible. However, tourists may travel for different purposes and, in addition to those who are known as leisure tourists, business tourist may also occur, as well as employees who are interested in working in a smart mode, from a peripheral and relaxing location. Finally, some of the satisfied tourists may also be potential start-uppers with the intention to invest in a new venture creation. This is an additional potential positive effect of the empowerment of smart destinations in the context of smart cities.

Proposition 1a Social Media empowered by Big Data increases the degree of smartness of the destination, making it more attractive. A proper exploitation of the two factors increases the effectiveness of destination management actions to attract tourists by influencing travellers' decision-making process.

Proposition 1b Social Media empowered by Big Data enable the adoption of a customer-centric view, thus enhancing the quality of the smart touristic experience. The increased quality is due to the possibility for tourists to optimize the experience itself by spending their limited time in those activities they find enjoyable.

Furthermore, we have focused our attention on the growing power gained by low-cost carriers, which may play a crucial role in influencing tourism demand and in increasing the overall attractiveness of the served airports and territories. These companies, digital by inception, generally tend to engage with customers in a smart way. Positioning them in a broader picture characterised, as mentioned above, by digital nomadism led us to elaborate two additional propositions.

Proposition 2 Low-cost airlines, digital by inception and empowered by the use of social media and big data, with their decisions on which destination to serve, influence the attractiveness of both already served and popular destinations and less popular destinations. The increased attractiveness may concern different actors: leisure tourists, digital nomads, and potential start-uppers interested in contributing to territorial development.

Proposition 3 The collaboration between decision makers acting on the destination and low-cost carriers' sides, in a smart tourism environment, boosts attractiveness and the growth of local touristic flows, including again both leisure tourists and digital nomads and potential start-uppers. The adoption of such a complementarity approach increases the overall efficiency of their decision-making process.

8 Conclusion and Implications

In the last decades, several challenges have affected the travel and tourism industry, leading toward the emerging paradigm of smart tourism. We derive some propositions on Social Media, Big Data, and the emergence of Low-Cost carriers, plying a relevant role for the attractiveness of a smart touristic destination. On one hand, we suggest that Social Media, empowered by Big Data for the development of tailored messages, positively affects a destination's attractiveness by making it smarter and enriching the smart touristic experience from a customer-centric perspective. On the other hand, we state that low-cost airlines' decisions on destinations influence local demand of both served popular destinations and less popular ones, attracting different types of tourists, including leisure tourists, digital nomads, and potential start-uppers, thus contributing to increasing local attractiveness. In the digital era, a smart destination is indeed more attractive, not only toward leisure tourists but also toward digital nomads and/or potential start-uppers.

Moreover, we propose that the collaboration between decision makers acting on destination and low-cost carriers' sides, in a smart environment, leads to efficient strategic behaviours in developing territorial wealth, which may also be fostered by new venture creation.

The work has some relevant managerial implications. First of all, it provides insights to destination managers and marketers on the strategic importance to migrate toward the smart tourism paradigm by integrating ICTs at all levels and by investing in Social Media and Big Data. These managers, especially those acting in peripheral locations with a relevant growth gap in terms of attractiveness, may benefit from an increased awareness concerning the benefits provided by a synergic adoption of Social Media and Big Data Analytics. These tools are indeed necessary to enter the digital bilateral exchange of information between tourists and destinations or businesses, which is crucial to successfully engaging with tourists themselves. This enhanced interaction with tourists and a proper exploitation of the insights hidden in the data also allows managers to offer an improved smart experience to tourists. In addition, greater clarity on the crucial role played by LCC in increasing the smartness and accessibility of a destination can better orient managers in their interaction with these companies.

Considering that, in addition to leisure tourists, there can be also other targets such as digital nomads and/or start-uppers, the increased attractiveness toward these categories would result in a greater boost in local wealth and development.

From an academic point of view, our work can represent a useful starting point to further enrich theory on the emerging topic of smart tourism, with a specific focus on its impact on local development.

References

1. David-Negre, T., Almedida-Santana, A., Hernández, J. M., & Moreno-Gil, S. (2018). *Understanding European tourists' use of e tourism platforms. Analysis of networks* (Vol. 20, pp. 131–152). Information Technology & Tourism.
2. Gretzel, U., Sigala, M., Xiang, Z., & Koo, C. (2015). Smart tourism: Foundations and developments. *Electronic Markets, 25*, 179–188.
3. Gretzel, U., Werthner, H., Koo, C., & Lamsfus, C. (2015). Conceptual foundations for understanding smart tourism ecosystems. *Computers in Human Behavior, 50*, 558–563.
4. Ivars-Baidal, J. A., Celdrán-Bernabeu, M. A., Mazón, J.-N., & Perles-Ivars, Á. F. (2019). Smart destinations and the evolution of ICTs: A new scenario for destination management? *Current Issues in Tourism, 22*, 1581–1600.
5. Dal Fiore, F., Mokhtarian, P. L., Salomon, I., & Singer, M. E. (2014). "Nomads at last"? A set of perspectives on how mobile technology may affect travel. *Journal of Transport Geography, 41*, 97–106.

6. Meredith, J. (1993). Theory building through conceptual methods. *International Journal of Operations & Production Management, 13*, 3–11.
7. Shepherd, D. A., & Suddaby, R. (2017). Theory building: A review and integration. *Journal of Management, 43*, 59–86.
8. Lee, C.-C., & Chang, C.-P. (2008). Tourism development and economic growth: A closer look at panels. *Tourism Management, 29*, 180–192.
9. Miah, S. J., Vu, H. Q., Gammack, J., & McGrath, M. (2017). A big data analytics method for tourist behaviour analysis. *Information & Management, 54*, 771–785.
10. Buhalis, D. (2000). Marketing the competitive destination of the future. *Tourism Management, 21*, 97–116.
11. Buhalis, D., & Amaranggana, A. (2013). Smart tourism destinations. In *Information and Communication Technologies in Tourism 2014: Proceedings of the International Conference in Dublin*, Ireland, January 21–24, 2014 (pp. 553–564). Springer.
12. Shafiee, S., Rajabzadeh Ghatari, A., Hasanzadeh, A., & Jahanyan, S. (2021). Smart tourism destinations: A systematic review. *Tourism Review, 76*, 505–528.
13. Sorokina, E., Wang, Y., Fyall, A., Lugosi, P., Torres, E., & Jung, T. (2022). Constructing a smart destination framework: A destination marketing organization perspective. *Journal of Destination Marketing & Management, 23*, 100688.
14. Buhalis, D., & Amaranggana, A. (2015). Smart tourism destinations enhancing tourism experience through personalisation of services. In *Information and Communication Technologies in Tourism 2015: Proceedings of the International Conference in Lugano*, February 3–6 (pp. 377–389). Springer.
15. Xiang, Z., & Fesenmaier, D. R. (2017). Big data analytics, tourism design and smart tourism. *Analytics in Smart Tourism Design: Concepts and Methods, 299–307.*
16. Cimbaljević, M., Stankov, U., & Pavluković, V. (2019). Going beyond the traditional destination competitiveness–reflections on a smart destination in the current research. *Current Issues in Tourism, 22*, 2472–2477.
17. Aichner, T., Grünfelder, M., Maurer, O., & Jegeni, D. (2021). Twenty-five years of social media: A review of social media applications and definitions from 1994 to 2019. *Cyberpsychology, Behavior, and Social Networking, 24*, 215–222.
18. Schoder, D., Gloor, P. A., & Metaxas, P. T. (2013). Social media and collective intelligence—Ongoing and future research streams. *KI-Künstliche Intelligenz, 27*, 9–15.
19. Živković, R., Gajić, J., & Brdar, I. (2014). The impact of social media on tourism. *Singidunum Journal of Applied Sciences* 758–761.
20. Narangajavana Kaosiri, Y., Callarisa Fiol, L. J., Moliner Tena, M. A., Rodríguez Artola, R. M., & Sanchez Garcia, J. (2019). User-generated content sources in social media: A new approach to explore tourist satisfaction. *Journal of Travel Research, 58*, 253–265.
21. Ruiz-Real, J. L., Uribe-Toril, J., & Gázquez-Abad, J. C. (2020). Destination branding: Opportunities and new challenges. *Journal of Destination Marketing & Management, 17*, 100453.
22. Pike, S. (2005). Tourism destination branding complexity. *Journal of Product & Brand Management, 14*, 258–259.
23. Blain, C., Levy, S. E., & Ritchie, J. B. (2005). Destination branding: Insights and practices from destination management organizations. *Journal of Travel Research, 43*, 328–338.
24. Simeon, M. I., Buonincontri, P., Cinquegrani, F., & Martone, A. (2017). Exploring tourists' cultural experiences in Naples through online reviews. *Journal of Hospitality and Tourism Technology, 8*, 220–238.
25. Chu, S.-C., Deng, T., & Cheng, H. (2020). The role of social media advertising in hospitality, tourism and travel: A literature review and research agenda. *International Journal of Contemporary Hospitality Management, 32*, 3419–3438.
26. Sheng, J., Amankwah-Amoah, J., & Wang, X. (2017). A multidisciplinary perspective of big data in management research. *International Journal of Production Economics, 191*, 97–112.
27. Bryson, S., Kenwright, D., Cox, M., Ellsworth, D., & Haimes, R. (1999). Visually exploring gigabyte data sets in real time. *Communications of the ACM, 42*, 82–90.

28. Mariani, M., Baggio, R., Fuchs, M., & Höepken, W. (2018). Business intelligence and big data in hospitality and tourism: A systematic literature review. *International Journal of Contemporary Hospitality Management, 30*, 3514–3554.
29. Laney, D. (2001). *3D data management: Controlling data volume, velocity and variety* (pp. 1–4). Meta Group. Lakshen.
30. Chen, M., Mao, S., & Liu, Y. (2014). Big data: A survey. *Mobile Networks and Applications, 19*, 171–209.
31. Manyika, J., Chui, M., Brown, B., Bughin, J., Dobbs, R., Roxburgh, C., & Hung Byers, A. (2011). *Big data: The next frontier for innovation, competition, and productivity*. McKinsey Global Institute.
32. Wu, C., Buyya, R., & Ramamohanarao, K. (2016). Big data analytics= machine learning+ cloud computing. arXiv preprint arXiv:1601.03115
33. Khan, N., Alsaqer, M., Shah, H., Badsha, G., Abbasi, A. A., & Salehian, S. (2018). The 10 Vs, issues and challenges of big data. In *Proceedings of the 2018 international conference on big data and education* (pp. 52–56).
34. Owais, S. S., & Hussein, N. S. (2016). Extract five categories CPIVW from the 9V's characteristics of the big data. *International Journal of Advanced Science and Computer Applications, 7*.
35. Villars, R. L., Olofson, C. W., & Eastwood, M. (2011). Big data: What it is and why you should care. *White paper, IDC, 14*, 1–14.
36. AGCOM. (2020). *Indagine conoscitiva sui Big Data—AGCOM.*
37. Emani, C. K., Cullot, N., & Nicolle, C. (2015). Understandable big data: A survey. *Computer Science Review, 17*, 70–81.
38. Bresciani, S., Ferraris, A., Romano, M., & Santoro, G. (2021). *Digital transformation management for agile organizations: A compass to sail the digital world.* Emerald Group Publishing.
39. Verma, J. P., Agrawal, S., Patel, B., & Patel, A. (2016). Big data analytics: Challenges and applications for text, audio, video, and social media data. *International Journal on Soft Computing, Artificial Intelligence and Applications (IJSCAI), 5*, 41–51.
40. Hu, Y.-H., Chen, Y.-L., & Chou, H.-L. (2017). Opinion mining from online hotel reviews–a text summarization approach. *Information Processing & Management, 53*, 436–449.
41. Bowen, J., & Whalen, E. (2017). Trends that are changing travel and tourism. *Worldwide Hospitality and Tourism Themes, 9*, 592–602.
42. Kahn, M. E., & Liu, P. (2016). Utilizing "big data" to improve the hotel sector's energy efficiency: Lessons from recent economics research. *Cornell Hospitality Quarterly, 57*, 202–210.
43. Ardito, L., Cerchione, R., Del Vecchio, P., & Raguseo, E. (2019). *Big data in smart tourism: Challenges, issues and opportunities* (Vol. 22, pp. 1805–1809). Taylor & Francis.
44. Cillo, V., Rialti, R., Del Giudice, M., & Usai, A. (2021). Niche tourism destinations' online reputation management and competitiveness in big data era: Evidence from three Italian cases. *Current Issues in Tourism, 24*, 177–191.
45. Del Vecchio, P., Mele, G., Ndou, V., & Secundo, G. (2018). Creating value from social big data: Implications for smart tourism destinations. *Information Processing & Management, 54*, 847–860.
46. Muniz, E. C. L., Dandolini, G. A., Biz, A. A., & Ribeiro, A. C. (2021). Customer knowledge management and smart tourism destinations: A framework for the smart management of the tourist experience–SMARTUR. *Journal of Knowledge Management, 25*, 1336–1361.
47. Centobelli, P., & Ndou, V. (2019). Managing customer knowledge through the use of big data analytics in tourism research. *Current Issues in Tourism, 22*, 1862–1882.
48. Li, Y., Hu, C., Huang, C., & Duan, L. (2017). The concept of smart tourism in the context of tourism information services. *Tourism Management, 58*, 293–300.

49. Anand, A., Shantakumar, V. P., Muskat, B., Singh, S. K., Dumazert, J.-P., & Riahi, Y. (2022). The role of knowledge management in the tourism sector: A synthesis and way forward. *Journal of Knowledge Management*.
50. Kaul, R. N. (1985). *Dynamics of tourism: A trilogy—Transportation and marketing: Vol. III*. Sterling Publishers.
51. Statista. (2019). *Inbound tourism worldwide by mode of transport 2019*.
52. Jacobsen, J. K. S., & Munar, A. M. (2012). Tourist information search and destination choice in a digital age. *Tourism Management Perspectives, 1*, 39–47.
53. Krakover, S., & Corsale, A. (2021). Sieving tourism destinations: Decision-making processes and destination choice implications. *Journal of Tourism, Heritage & Services Marketing (JTHSM), 7*, 33–43.
54. Keshavarzian, P., & Wu, C.-L. (2021). Exploring the effect of sequentially receiving airline and destination information on the choice behavior of tourism destinations. *Journal of Travel Research, 60*, 251–266.
55. Koo, T. T., Rashidi, T. H., Park, J.-W., Wu, C.-L., & Tseng, W.-C. (2017). The effect of enhanced international air access on the demand for peripheral tourism destinations: Evidence from air itinerary choice behaviour of Korean visitors to Australia. *Transportation Research Part A: Policy and Practice, 106*, 116–129.
56. Passport: World Overview for Travel Transportation (2019).
57. EUROCOTROL. Data Snapshot #34 on the rise of Low Cost Carriers in Europe. EUROCONTROL Data Snapshot #34 | EUROCONTROL
58. Eugenio-Martin, J. L., & Perez-Granja, U. (2021). Have low-cost carriers crowded out full services and charter carriers in tourism destinations? A trivariate structural time series analysis. *Journal of Travel Research, 60*, 810–832.
59. Álvarez-Díaz, M., González-Gómez, M., & Otero-Giráldez, M. S. (2019). Low cost airlines and international tourism demand. The case of Porto's airport in the northwest of the Iberian peninsula. *Journal of Air Transport Management, 79*, 101689.
60. Porter, M. E., & Kramer, M. R. (2011). Creating shared value. *Harvard Business Review, 89*, 62–77.
61. Alansari, Z., Soomro, S., & Belgaum, M. R. (2019). Smart airports: Review and open research issues. In: *Emerging Technologies in Computing: Second International Conference, iCETiC 2019*, London, UK, August 19–20, 2019, Proceedings 2 (pp. 136–148). Springer.
62. Rajapaksha, A., & Jayasuriya, N. (2020). Smart airport: A review on future of the airport operation. *Global Journal of Management and Business Research, 20*, 25–34.
63. Hensellek, S., & Puchala, N. (2021). The emergence of the digital nomad: A review and analysis of the opportunities and risks of digital nomadism. *The flexible workplace: Coworking and other modern workplace transformations*, 195–214
64. Gusakov, A. A., ul Haque, A., & Jogia, A. V. (2020). Mechanisms to support open innovation in smart tourism destinations: Managerial perspective and implications. *Polish Journal of Management Studies, 21*, 142–161.
65. Harrison, C., Eckman, B., Hamilton, R., Hartswick, P., Kalagnanam, J., Paraszczak, J., & Williams, P. (2010). Foundations for smarter cities. *IBM Journal of Research and Development, 54*, 1–16.
66. Jasrotia, A., & Gangotia, A. (2018). Smart cities to smart tourism destinations: A review paper. *Journal of tourism intelligence and smartness, 1*, 47–56.

The Influence of Physical and Virtual Servicescapes on Public Transportation Choices

Sina Zimmermann, Thomas Schulz, Andreas Hein, Heiko Gewald, and Helmut Krcmar

Abstract The predominant use of private cars is the root of several problems like traffic congestion and air pollution in cities worldwide. While it is generally believed that mobility apps as part of smart city initiatives can help influence mobility choices in favor of public transport, there is not much empirical evidence for this. This study used a choice-based conjoint analysis to examine mobility choices among 185 private car commuters. By adopting a service-dominant logic perspective, we analyzed the influence of physical and virtual servicescapes on public transportation choices for the commuters. In contrast to previous servicescape literature, we found that the physical (e.g., overcrowding of a vehicle) and the virtual servicescape (e.g., app layout and functionality) influenced commuters' mobility choices. Our study also found that commuters who had no information about travel times by public transport before using apps continued to choose private cars for commuting.

Keywords Servicescapes · Choice-based conjoint analysis · Mobility behavior · Smart City · Mobility apps

1 Introduction

The abundant use of private cars, especially in developed countries, leads to numerous ecological problems, such as air, and noise pollution. A significant source of emissions can be attributed to commuting to and from work. For example,

S. Zimmermann (✉) · T. Schulz
University of Applied Sciences Neu-Ulm, Neu-Ulm, Germany

Technical University of Munich, Munich, Germany
e-mail: Sina.zimmermann@hnu.de

A. Hein · H. Krcmar
Technical University of Munich, Munich, Germany

H. Gewald
University of Applied Sciences Neu-Ulm, Neu-Ulm, Germany

A. M. Braccini et al. (eds.), *Digital (Eco) Systems and Societal Challenges*, Lecture Notes in Information Systems and Organisation 72,
https://doi.org/10.1007/978-3-031-75586-6_10

commuters account for one-fifth of the total traffic in Germany, and 69% of commuter travel makes use of a private car [1]. Scholars agree that public transport has significant potential to contribute to a more sustainable mobility concept than other services such as car- and ride-sharing [2], especially in countries, and regions where the public transport infrastructure is well developed. In the past, various actions on part of the authorities and the government have helped shift people's mobility choices from private car use to public transport use. For example, public transport timetables have been optimized to reduce waiting times, and intelligent traffic lights have been installed to minimize travel time in public transport [3].

The widespread use of smartphones and the availability of mobility apps (hereafter referred to as *apps*) as part of smart city initiatives can also support this shift by making public transport information available to (potential) customers anytime and anywhere. For instance, a recommendation is adjusted whenever a vehicle (e.g., buses, trains, trams) included in the suggested route is delayed. However, despite the promise of new technology promoting a switch from private to public transport, private cars are still the predominant mode of transport. One reason for this is a knowledge gap about how information technology (IT) solutions like apps influence people's mobility choices and behavior. Khan, Habib [4, p. 934] summarized the inability of science to guide the efforts of practitioners as follows: "the existing literature investigated the relationship between ICT and travel, [but] it is not evident how the usage of smartphone applications influences individuals' daily mobility choices" (similar [5]). Moreover, the current literature lacks an understanding of how attributes of the physical and virtual servicescapes influence mobility choices [6, 7]. In our case, the physical servicescape refers to the environment in which a public transport service is provided, such as the available vehicle seating capacity. The virtual servicescape refers to the virtual aspects of a public transportation ride, such as mobility apps. In contrast to previous literature on servicescapes [6, 7], we argue that in hybrid customer interaction scenarios where (potential) customers are present in the physical and virtual world simultaneously [8], such as when a private car commuter (hereafter *commuter*) uses a app mobility for a public transportation ride, an analysis of both servicescapes is required to understand app users' choices.

Therefore, we pose the following research question: *Which attributes of physical and virtual servicescapes influence commuters' choices regarding the use of public transportation?* To answer this question, we adopted a service-dominant (S-D) logic perspective [9] and performed a choice-based conjoint (CBC) analysis with 185 commuters in Germany [10, 11]. Our survey design, in which different public transport options were presented to each participant, resembled the virtual servicescape of an app. The results provide insights into the mobility choices of commuters when using an app and their underlying preference structures. In particular, we show how the difference in travel times using private cars and public transport affects the relationship between the servicescapes and commuters' mobility choices as a moderating variable. Our study contributes to the literature on transportation, especially to the relationship between app usage and mobility choices. In addition, this study contributes to further establishing the S-D logic perspective by showing how physical and virtual servicescape influence value co-creation among app providers and users.

2 Theoretical Background

2.1 *Service-Dominant Logic Perspective*

The service-dominant (S-D) logic perspective, with its three main concepts of service ecosystem, service platform, and value co-creation, was introduced by Vargo and Lusch [9]. A **service ecosystem** is "a relatively self-contained, self-adjusting system of mostly loosely coupled social and economic (resource-integrating) actors connected by shared institutional logic and mutual value creation through service exchange" [12, p. 161]. According to Schulz, Zimmermann [13], mobility providers (e.g., public transport and car-sharing companies) that make their service available to potential customers via an app also constitute a service ecosystem. An app represents a **service platform**, which is defined as "a modular structure that consists of tangible and intangible components (resources) and facilitates the interaction of actors and resources (or resource bundles)" [12, p. 162]. A service platform makes the exchange of services among the actors of a service ecosystem more effective and efficient [12]. For example, Zimmermann, Schulz [14] show that an app can provide (potential) public transport customers with dynamic information like the location of the next stop or ticket prices, anywhere, and anytime. Finally, **value co-creation** is defined as resource integration and service exchange among actors [15].

The S-D logic perspective differs from the goods-dominant (G-D) logic perspective by assuming "that value is fundamentally derived and determined in use—the integration and application of resources in a specific context—rather than in exchange—embedded in firm output and captured by price" [16, p. 145]. Accordingly, the S-D logic perspective assumes customers are also engaged in service exchange [9]. For example, in the case of an app, customers can improve the quality of the recommendations by using their smartphone to provide real-time information about how crowded their vehicle is [17]. Moreover, value co-creation depends on the context it is applied [16]. For instance, app recommendations from a mobility app are more useful right before using public transport instead of receiving the same recommendations after a trip. The service encounter represents the interaction between a company and a customer and is part of the service context [18]. A service encounter can be physical or virtual, such as ticket control in public transportation or the use of a mobility app. The **servicescape** is the physical and social environment of such a service encounter and influences commuters' experience with public transportation [18].

2.2 *Physical and Virtual Servicescapes*

According to Ballantyne and Nilsson [19, p. 226], the "servicescape concept adds meaning to a service provider's [such as a public transport company] value-proposition by modifying customer [i.e., commuter] expectations and customer experience." For the most part, the extant literature on the servicescape concept assumes that the servicescape of a customer is either physical or virtual. Numerous studies, especially from the marketing field (as well as [6], for an overview see [7]), have examined the physical servicescape.

With the advent of the internet, more and more scholars have shifted their attention from the physical to the virtual servicescape [7]. Ballantyne and Nilsson [19] defined a company's website as its virtual servicescape. Based on this definition, an app, such as a smart city or mobility app, can also be regarded as a virtual servicescape. A mobility app can be offered by public transportation companies or by companies offering additional mobility services, like Google maps, and they can supplement offline mobility services. For instance, mobility apps can be used to buy public transportation tickets, for navigational purposes, or to receive current information on construction sides or delays.

According to Harris and Goode [20], the virtual servicescape has three aspects: (1) aesthetic appeal (e.g., originality of design), (2) layout and functionality (e.g., usability, the relevance of information), and (3) financial security (perceived security and ease of payment). Kim and Koh [21] have provided an alternative conceptualization that includes four dimensions: (1) aesthetics (e.g., design of a site), (2) ambient (e.g., sound effects), (3) spatial layout and functionality (convenience in use, ease in browsing, etc.), and (4) symbols and artifacts (e.g., icon design). As compared to the physical servicescape, a key characteristic of the virtual servicescape is that "the linear time and place assumptions [...] are called into question. It becomes possible to move from one place to another within a 'click'." [19, 21].

Based on these definitions, we found that analyzing the physical ([22], e.g., [23]) and virtual servicescapes separately and independent of each other (e.g., [19, 20, 21]) is inadequate because commuters that use an app are embedded in a so-called hybrid interaction scenario. According to Nüesch, Alt [8], a hybrid customer interaction scenario is characterized by the fact that a customer is simultaneously present in the virtual and the physical world. For instance, a commuter receives information about the available public transport services in a mobility app. The commuter then purchases a mobile ticket via the app and, simultaneously, is part of the physical world, using information from the manifestation of the virtual world, i.e., the app, such as distance, and directions to the public transport stop and the degree of crowding in the vehicle. In other words, "siloed interaction points are overcome and individual interaction points merge so that the customer [i.e., commuter] perceives the interaction in the online and offline world as a 'no-line system'." [8, p. 77].

Under the term 'smart servicescape', initial studies [24, 25] argue that technological progress is increasingly changing the virtual servicescape and that the boundary between the virtual and physical servicescape is blurring. Roy, Singh [25] examined how the smart servicescape affects co-creation, and their results show, for example, that superior functionality, and perceived personalization increase value co-creation. In addition to looking at what shapes customers' choices, previous studies have examined the influence of the servicescape on issues like customer expectations, customer satisfaction, and customer well-being [19, 26].

The relationship between the servicescape and customer behavior can be modulated by moderation factors such as the competitive intensity, which is defined as "the availability of substitutes or switching opportunities open to customers" [27, p. 398]. In the present study, the difference in travel times between the use of public transport and the private car serves as a measure of the competitive intensity between the two modes of transportation, as this difference will most likely influence the choice of public transportation options. For instance, if the difference in travel times between a private car and public transportation was 1 h, less people would choose the public transportation option compared to a difference of 10 min. In summary, the servicescape literature is limited as it focuses on either the physical or virtual servicescape. Therefore, in the case of hybrid customer interaction scenarios (such as when using a mobility app and using public transportation), interactions, and dependencies between the two servicescapes are so far not considered.

3 Methodology

3.1 Choice-Based Conjoint Analysis

Conjoint analysis was first developed in the field of psychology [28]. Since then, this method has been applied in numerous fields, including information systems (IS) (see [29] for an overview). Choice-based conjoint (CBC) is considered the preferable variant of conjoint analyses for understanding participant choices [10, 11]. In this variant, participants are presented with several choice sets of products/services and choose one product/service at a time. These different products/services pose several trade-off scenarios containing different attributes to participants, which allows a conclusion on the importance of each of these attributes.

CBC analysis is based on the assumption that the usefulness of a product/service attribute can be determined based on its overall evaluation [11, 30]. For example, an attribute of a public transport service is its price, and possible attribute levels are 2.50 €, 3.50 €, and 4.50 €. Based on the product/service choices of the participants, the part-worth for each attribute level of the attributes can be estimated. Subsequently, the importance of each attribute can be determined by calculating the difference between the lowest and the highest part-worths of its attribute levels. The relative importance of each attribute is calculated by putting this difference concerning the sum of the differences between all attributes [11, 30]. Finally, the total value of a product/service can be determined by adding up the part-worths of the attribute levels present [30].

3.2 Survey Design and Data Collection

To keep the participants' complexity manageable, it is recommended to limit CBC analysis to six attributes of the product/service examined [30]. Hence, we conducted a preliminary study with 29 participants to identify the six most important attributes (respectively, their attribute levels) of a public transport service and its physical servicescape. First, we created a pool of 14 attributes based on prior literature [31, 32] and apps available on the market (e.g., DB Navigator, Reach Now). Then, we presented these attributes to the participants, asking them to select the attributes relevant to their public transportation choices for commuting and rank them in order of importance. The participants were also allowed to add any additional attributes. The participants were randomly selected at different train stations at Germany to obtain a diverse sample. The participants conducted the study on a tablet that we used to present the different attributes.

Afterwards, we defined three attribute levels for each of the six most important attributes from the pre-test. According to Hair Jr., Black [30, p. 363], "the range (low to high) of the [attribute] levels [should be] set somewhat outside existing values but not at an unbelievable level." To gain insight into 'existing values', we used a route between two city districts of Berlin (Pankow and Mitte) as the basis for defining the attribute levels. The six most important attributes of a public transport service and their attribute levels are shown in Table 1.

The attribute waiting time reflected the waiting time until the departure of a public transport vehicle after arriving at the station. The attribute travel time defined the overall commuting time when using public transport. The price attribute indicated the overall cost of a trip, and the attribute number of transfers referred to how many times a person would have to change between different means of transport (e.g., from a bus to a train) or within a means of transport (e.g., from train A to train B). The attribute crowding provided information on how crowded a specific vehicle was. The last attribute, greenhouse gas emissions, reflected the environmental pollution that could be attributed to one person when choosing a public transport service.

We created the choice sets using the software QuestionPro. In addition to these choice sets, the questionnaire included questions about the participants'

Table 1 Attributes and their attribute levels for the characterization of a public transportation service used in the CBC analysis

Attributes	Attribute levels		
Waiting time (in min)	≤5	6–10	11–15
Travel time (in min)	≤15	16–30	31–45
Price (in euros)	2.50	3.50	4.50
Number of transfers	0	1	2
Crowding	Low (free seats)	Medium (possibly free seats)	High (no free seats)
Greenhouse gas emissions (in grams)	≤150	151–300	≥301

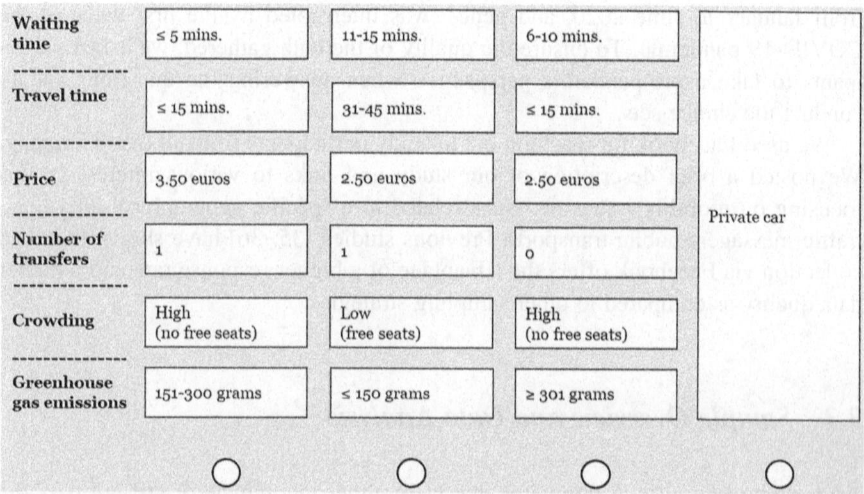

Fig. 1 Exemplary choice set of the CBC analysis (translated), which corresponds to the Virtual Servicescape

demographic (e.g., age, income), their current commuting behavior (means of transport used in the last month, travel time by private car and public transport), and their app usage (e.g., frequency of app use). Twelve choice sets were presented to each participant. The first four choice sets were used to ensure the data's quality and assess the validity and reliability of the obtained results. They were not used for estimating the part-worth of each attribute level. Two of the four choice sets were identical to facilitate an attention check. The other two choice sets were used to calculate the hit rates, to determine how well the mobility choices by the participants can be predicted based on the estimated part-worths [10, 11].

The other eight choice sets were used to estimate the part-worth of each attribute level. An example choice set is shown in Fig. 1. The choice sets were complemented by briefly describing the choice situation (conducting a mobility choice in an app before commuting) and explaining the attributes. The travel time for the private car option was assumed to be equivalent to the average travel time by car for each participant (queried in the questionnaire). The choice sets represent the virtual servicescape in the case of app use by commuters [20, 21]. Therefore, each of the attributes can be part of the virtual and the physical servicescape. For instance, a mobility app can provide a commuter with the information on the expected crowding of a train (virtual servicescape), while the actual crowding during the ride is part of the physical servicescape.

Before starting data collection, a pre-test was conducted with six participants to check if the questions, attributes, and attribute levels of the choice sets were clearly described. We collected data from commuters living in Germany, as Germany has an extensive public transport infrastructure that can support the desired shift to a non-private car-based mobility system [33, 34]. Data collection was conducted from January to June 2020, and hence, was interrupted by the first wave of the COVID-19 pandemic. To ensure the quality of the data gathered, we asked participants to take a pre-pandemic perspective when answering the questions and to conduct the choice sets.

We used Facebook for reaching out to study participants from all over Germany. We posted a brief description of our study and links to various interest groups focusing on mobility issues or issues related to a specific geographical area (e.g., traffic messages, public transport). Previous studies [35, 36] have shown that data collection via Facebook offers the advantage of a higher response rate and a higher data quality as compared to other sampling strategies.

3.3 *Sample Overview and Data Analysis*

After discarding all questionnaires that were either incomplete or did not pass the attention check test, we were left with 310 questionnaires. We performed CBC analysis on data from the questionnaires of participants who commuted to and from work primarily by private car in the previous month (n = 185). A few participants (7.03%) also used their private bicycles for commuting on one or more days. 49.19% of the participants were female, 50.27% are male, and 0.54% were diverse. The average age of the participants was 34.81 years and thus less than the average age of the population of Germany in 2019 [37]. The largest proportion (31.89%) of participants were in the group of those with a net monthly income of 2001–2600 €, which agrees with the average net income of gainfully employed adults living in Germany in 2018 (1948 €) [38]. Most participants (67.03%) commuted 30 min or less by private car, which is also true for 72% of people living in Germany [1]. In contrast, if using public transport, most participants (49.73%) reported needing more than 60 min for their commute. Despite the relatively low average age of the participants, a relatively high proportion of them (47.03%) did not use an app for commuting.

We performed the data analysis with SPSS. Based on our assumptions (drawing on [27]), the difference between travel time by private cars and by public transport is a measure of the competitive intensity that moderates the relationship between the physical and virtual servicescapes. We created several groups based on the commuters' mobility choices. Participants from the group marked '?' had no information about the average travel times by public transportation. The travel time was approximately the same either by private car or public transport for participants from the group '='. The time advantage due to the use of a private car rather than public transport increased steadily between the groups '−1' to '−4.' The travel time saved by using the private car was particularly high for participants from group '−4'. Participants in the group '+1' had a travel time advantage by using public transport rather than private cars. For further data analysis, we assumed a normally distributed sample for groups with 30 or more participants [39]. For groups with fewer participants, we conducted a Kolmogorov-Smirnov test to check for a normal distribution.

Following the recommendation of Backhaus, Erichson [11], we carried out a Cox regression analysis to estimate the part-worth of each attribute level for the CBC analysis. In the case of the two groups '+1' (n = 1) and '−4' (n = 3), the regression coefficients (i.e., the estimated part-worths) did not converge, so these groups were excluded from further analysis. To assess the quality of all other regression models, we carried out a likelihood-ratio test [11]. In addition, we calculated the hit rates using the logit choice model [11]. With four different options in a choice set (three public transport options, and one option of using a private car), the probability of choosing any option by random selection is 25%. Previous studies ([40–42], etc.) could reach a hit rate of approximately 50%, which indicates a good prediction quality of the estimated part-worths. Furthermore, we performed a Mann-Whitney U test to check whether the part-worths of the two groups differ significantly.

4 Results

The likelihood-ratio test performed for each group resulted in a p-value of 0.000. This means that the regression models were highly statistically significant. Furthermore, we calculated the hit rate for each group to obtain information about the predictive validity of the estimated part-worths (i.e., regression coefficients). The hit rates of groups 1 to 4 ranged between 58.67% and 83.33%, indicating high predictive validity. The hit rate is below 50% only for group 5 (36.73%), which is considered in some studies [40–42] to indicate an insufficient degree of predictive validity. Nevertheless, it was more than 25%, the hit rate of random selection.

Table 2 provides an overview of the choice rates for each group. To compare whether the choice rates were statistically different between two groups, group 1 was always chosen as the reference group. It can be observed that the choice rates for any of the public transport options were non-zero and positive in all groups. This means that despite any perceived travel time disadvantages associated with choosing a public transport option, some commuters still opted for public transport. Surprisingly, as compared to group 1 (81.94%), in which the commuters have no information about travel times by public transport, the percentage of participants choosing to use a private car was statistically lower in groups 4 and 5 (63.17% and 49.23%). In

Table 2 Choice Rates (in %) (* $p < 0.10$; ** $p < 0.05$; *** $p < 0.01$)

Option	Group 1: '?' (n = 18)	Group 2: '=' (n = 11)	Group 3: '−1' (n = 28)	Group 4: '−2' (n = 75)	Group 5: '−3' (n = 49)
Public transport service 1	6.25	13.64	9.38	15.67**	20.41***
Public transport service 2	9.72	12.5	12.05	12.83	18.37*
Public transport service 3	2.08	6.82*	6.25**	8.33***	11.99***
Private car	81.94	67.05	72.32	63.17**	49.23***

Table 3 Relative importance of attributes (in %)

Attribute	Group 1: '?' (n = 18)	Group 2: '=' (n = 11)	Group 3: '−1' (n = 28)	Group 4: '−2' (n = 75)	Group 5: '−3' (n = 49)
Waiting time	2.78	5.10	8.43	9.59	7.41
Travel time	22.35	27.97	30.66	37.11	39.03
Price	26.81	17.51	15.15	15.18	14.82
Number of transfers	15.26	26.27	27.55	18.63	23.29
Crowding	16.06	13.09	15.94	11.27	11.40
Greenhouse gas emissions	16.74	10.06	2.28	8.22	4.05

other words, a lack of information about the travel times by public transport promoted the use of private cars even more than knowing that public transport would take longer when considering the difference between travel time using a private car and public transport as a moderator.

In groups 1 to 3, the proportion of commuters who chose a private car in all choice sets ranged between 63.64% and 60.71%. In contrast, only a small proportion of the commuters from groups 4 and 5 always chose to use a private car (44.00% and 30.61%). In other words, most of these commuters demonstrated flexibility in their mobility choices. As compared to group 1, the choice rate for public transport service 3 was statistically higher in all other groups. For groups 4 and 5, this also applied to the choice rate for the public transport service 1. In the case of group 5 (18.37%), the choice rate for public transport service 2 is also significantly higher than in group 1 (9.72%).

The relative importance of each attribute, shown in Table 3, provides information on which attributes were particularly relevant for the observed mobility choices by commuters (see Table 2). The attribute 'travel time' occupies a prominent position, having the highest relative importance in groups 2 to 5, with values between 27.97% and 39.03%, and the second highest in group 1 (22.35%). In addition, the relative importance of the attribute increased with increasing differences in travel times between public transport and private cars (groups 2 to 5). In group 1, the attribute 'price' had the highest relative importance (26.81%), while in other groups, it was ranked in the middle with values between 14.82% (group 5) and 17.51% (group 2). In summary, either 'travel time' or 'price' had the highest relative importance in all groups.

The relative importance of the attributes of the physical servicescape paints a relatively consistent picture. The attributes 'waiting time' and 'greenhouse gas emissions' have the lowest and second lowest relative importance in all groups, except for the attribute 'greenhouse gas emissions' in group 1. However, an exclusive focus on the ranks might miss the fact that in some cases, there were significant differences in the relative importance of the attributes between the groups. For example, the relative importance of the attribute 'greenhouse gas emissions' is more than four times higher in group 2 (10.06%) than in group 3 (2.28%). The relative importance of the attribute 'crowding' was at a similar level in all groups, varying between 11.27% (group 4) and 16.06% (group 1). Somewhat surprisingly, the relative importance of the attribute 'number of transfers' was lower in group 4 (18.63%) than in the group with the same travel duration either by public transport or by private car, and in other groups with shorter travel times using a private car (with values between 23.29% and 27.55%).

Table 4 provides an overview of the estimated part-worth for each attribute level (and thus into the value co-creation on part of the commuters), as well as on their standard deviation (SD) and mean difference (MD) in comparison to reference group 1. Only the part-worth for the attribute level '31–45 min.' of the attribute 'travel time' was statistically significant in all groups and varied between −1.485 (group 1) and −2.326 (group 5). In other words, as compared to public transport with a travel time of 15 min or less (the basis attribute level, see Table 1), a commuter from group 5 lost a value of 2.326 if the travel duration by public transport service was between 31 and 45 min (respectively, gained a value of 2.326 for public transport travel durations of 15 min or less). However, the Mann-Whitney U test each carried out shows no statistically significant difference between the part-worth of groups 2 to 5 and the reference group 1 (as in the case of all other attribute levels).

It can be further observed that the part-worths for the attribute levels '1' and '2' of the attribute 'number of transfers' are statistically significant in all groups with a current travel time advantage for the private car (groups 3 to 5). In the other two groups, the part-worth for the attribute level '2' (−1.750) is statistically significant only in group 2. Similarly, the part-worth for the attribute level 'high' of the attribute 'crowding' is statistically significant only in groups 4 and 5 (−0.600 and −0.680). The greenhouse gas emissions caused by commuting had a statistically significant negative influence on mobility choices only among the participants in groups 1 and 4. A peculiarity of group 5 was that the attribute level 'none' (i.e., no presented public transport service option chosen, but rather a private car instead) has a statistically significant negative part-worth (−0.837). This meant that the choice of a private car was associated with a loss of value.

5 Discussion

5.1 Theoretical Implications

Our study has three main theoretical implications. First, our results generated new insights into how using a mobility app influences commuters' mobility choices [4, 5], and, in turn, their mobility choices regarding public transport. In our study, we focused on the mobility choices of short-distance commuters using private cars in Germany, where commuter traffic accounts for a fifth of total traffic and where most trips are made using a private car (69%) [1]. We demonstrated how scholars can use CBC analysis to examine the influence of app use on mobility choices when commuters have a choice between public transport and private cars. For instance,

Table 4 Part-Worths for the attribute levels (*$p < 0.10$; **$p < 0.05$; ***$p < 0.01$)

	Group 1: '?' (n = 18)		Group 2: '=' (n = 11)			Group 3: '−1' (n = 28)			Group 4: '−2' (n = 75)			Group 5: '−3' (n = 49)		
Attribute level	Part-worths	SD	Part-worths	SD	MD	Part-worths	SD	MD	Part-worths	SD	MD	Part-worths	SD	MD
6–10 min	−0.117	0.550	0.340	0.585	0.457	−0.244	0.374	−0.127	0.099	0.190	0.216	0.095	0.215	0.213
11–15 min	−0.185	0.551	0.260	0.622	0.445	−0.469	0.406	−0.284	−0.411*	0.233	−0.226	−0.346	0.255	−0.161
16–30 min	−0.294	0.497	−0.305	0.473	−0.012	−0.470	0.323	−0.176	−0.707***	0.173	−0.413	−0.756***	0.190	−0.462
31–45 min	−1.485*	0.826	−1.863**	0.844	−0.378	−1.704***	0.572	−0.219	−1.975***	0.293	−0.490	−2.326***	0.358	−0.841
3.50 euros	−0.287	0.510	−0.253	0.545	0.034	0.108	0.356	0.395	0.053	0.194	0.339	0.203	0.221	0.490
4.50 euros	−1.782*	0.946	−1.166	0.812	0.616	−0.734	0.515	1.048	−0.755***	0.255	1.026	−0.681**	0.293	1.101
1	−0.144	0.580	−0.872	0.551	−0.728	−1.340***	0.367	−1.196	−0.692***	0.201	−0.548	−0.874***	0.217	−0.730
2	−1.014	0.829	−1.750**	0.786	−0.735	−1.531***	0.465	−0.517	−0.992***	0.234	0.023	−1.388***	0.265	−0.374
Medium	0.611	0.593	−0.124	0.584	−0.735	0.549	0.371	−0.062	−0.306	0.218	−0.917	−0.285	0.235	−0.896
High	−0.456	0.699	−0.872	0.711	−0.415	−0.337	0.436	0.119	−0.600***	0.217	−0.144	−0.680***	0.252	0.223
151–300 g	−0.446	0.506	−0.670	0.618	−0.224	−0.127	0.416	0.319	−0.365*	0.219	0.081	−0.016	0.260	0.430
≥ 301 g	−1.113**	0.568	−0.475	0.499	0.638	−0.010	0.355	1.102	−0.438**	0.184	0.675	−0.241	0.216	0.871
None	0.854	1.039	−0.242	1.042	−1.096	0.374	0.626	−0.480	−0.273	0.323	−1.128	−0.837**	0.366	−1.691

our results show that the provision of information on public transportation services can promote its use compared to private cars, even if the information contains that the use of public transportation will exceed the travel time with a private car.

Second, we contributed new perspectives on smart servicescapes by drawing on the S-D logic literature in combination with literature on the physical ([22], e.g., [23]) and virtual servicescapes (e.g., [20, 21) in our study. On one hand, the S-D logic perspective encompasses the assumption that companies can only make value propositions to potential customers [16]. In other words, there is a value-in-use, or more precisely value-in-context [15, 43]. Although earlier works ([18], see also [43]) defined the servicescape as one component of context and argued that they are important to an understanding of value co-creation, the majority of former studies focused exclusively on service ecosystems. On the other hand, based on earlier literature, we conclude that the previous mode of analysis considering the physical and virtual servicescapes separately in the case of choosing a mobility service via an app is inadequate, as potential customers are simultaneously embedded in the online and offline worlds. Our conclusion is in line with Kang, Kim [24] and Roy, Singh [25] who highlighted that the virtual servicescape is changing due to technological progress, and it is insufficient to focus solely on a website or an app. Instead, the physical, and virtual servicescape are increasingly interlinked, for example, by using sensors inside vehicles. We complemented these two studies by identifying relevant characteristics of the physical space (e.g., number of transfers) and by analyzing the influence of the virtual servicescape in form of a mobility app on peoples' choices.

Third, we proposed the use of CBC analysis to simultaneously investigate the influence of the physical and virtual servicescapes on peoples' choices. The attributes and their attribute levels can represent the techno-economic characteristics of a product or service [29]. In the context of our study, the attributes described the public transport service, and the physical servicescape (e.g., number of transfers, degree of vehicle overcrowding), focusing on the six most important attributes determined in a preliminary study. In our work, we also showed how a moderation effect on the relationship between the servicescapes and peoples' choices, as postulated by Harris and Ezeh [27] for the competitive intensity (in the present study covered in form of the current travel time difference between private car and public transport use), can be analyzed through an appropriate grouping of the participants.

5.2 *Practical Implications*

Our work has three important practical implications. First, we show that using an app reduces the proportion of commuters' choosing to use private cars for commuting. We provided empirical evidence that app use can promote the choice of public transport among commuters by providing certain relevant information. This behavior change can mitigate problems associated with the predominant use of private cars, such as environmental pollution. Practitioners can use our results on choice rates (see Table 2) in guiding and preparing for expected changes in the mobility behavior of car commuters.

Second, by categorizing participants based on the difference in travel durations between public transport and using a private car, we also accounted for a moderation effect on the relationship between the servicescapes and commuters' choices. Initially, our results complement the work by van Exel and Rietveld [44], showing that the provision of public transport information via an app shortly before the commute is not sufficient in itself to change mobility choices significantly among all commuter groups. Commuters who have no information about commuting time by public transport prior to app use have significantly more likely chosen to use a private car than commuters who have information that using a private car would lead to a shorter commute. Hence, commuters who lack information about public transport travel times must be attracted through other actions, for example with offers that combine public transport and additional mobility services such as car- and ridesharing.

Third, our results highlight that actions taken to reduce public transport travel durations and increase its competitiveness as compared to private cars, such as optimizing timetables, introducing bus lanes, and installing intelligent traffic lights [3] can significantly contribute to influencing commuters' mobility behavior. Contrary to what one might expect, our results show that the choice rate for the private car was the lowest in groups 4 and 5, where commuters needed more time to commute by public transport than by private cars. However, one reason could be that these commuters can often reduce their travel time using public transport by choosing one of the public transport services presented in the choice sets. This conclusion is supported by the high relative importance of the attribute 'travel time' in both groups (see Table 3). Furthermore, our analysis of the relative importance of the attributes illustrate that practitioners can motivate commuters from all groups to switch to public transport, particularly by reducing the number of transfers and offering cheaper rates.

5.3 Limitations and Future Research

Our work has some limitations, which future studies should address. Initially, there were some limitations concerning the generalizability of our results. CBC analysis is the best method for analyzing people's choices. However, we have examined only one specific virtual servicescape. For comparison, future research should examine additional virtual servicescapes to better understand their influence on public transport and private car choices. The virtual servicescapes may differ, for instance, in terms of the number and design of options presented and the use of graphical elements.

In addition, the location, timing, and the individuals selected for data collection could potentially limit the generalizability of our results. We collected the data in line with previous studies, which consider Germany a suitable target for data collection due to its pre-existing infrastructure and legal conditions. However, this study could have had different results in other countries due to various factors such as differences in the public transport system and mobility culture, which make further studies necessary.

Furthermore, the data collection focused on the mobility choices of commuters in a pre-COVID-19 environment. It is, however, possible that commuter preferences and mobility choices might have changed permanently because of the pandemic due to reasons such as an increased aversion to crowding. Our study was also limited to private car commuters who have short travel durations. Previous research reveals that the preferences for an app that provides access to different mobility services, such as public transport and car-sharing, vary between participants from a big city or a rural area [45], and we therefore expect that the preferences of commuters with a long travel time will also differ.

6 Conclusion

Reducing private car use to mitigate related problems such as air and noise pollution is one of the most important challenges of our time. In science and practice, it is assumed that apps can contribute to adopting more sustainable mobility behaviors, such as switching from private cars to public transport use. However, extant research does not provide much empirical evidence for how mobility app usage influences daily mobility choices among individuals. The present study fills this gap by using CBC analysis to examine the mobility choices of 185 private car commuters. Following a S-D logic perspective, CBC analysis allows us to simultaneously analyze the influence of the physical (e.g., overcrowding of a vehicle) and virtual servicescapes (e.g., app layout and functionality) on commuters' mobility choices. Our results show that while the use of a mobility app reduces the proportion of commuters choosing to use private cars, commuters who have no information about public transport travel durations continue to predominantly choose the private car.

References

1. Bauer-Hailer, U. (2019). Berufspendler im Bundesländervergleich. *Statistisches Monatsheft Baden-Württemberg, 1*, 10–14.
2. Wright, S., Nelson, J. D., & Cottrill, C. D. (2020). MaaS for the suburban market: Incorporating carpooling in the mix. *Transportation Research Part A: Policy and Practice, 131*, 206–218.
3. Nesmachnow, S., et al. (2019). Traffic lights synchronization for bus rapid transit using a parallel evolutionary algorithm. *International Journal of Transportation Science and Technology, 8*(1), 53–67.
4. Khan, N. A., Habib, M. A., & Jamal, S. (2020). Effects of smartphone application usage on mobility choices. *Transportation Research Part A, 132*, 932–947.

5. Cellina, F., et al. (2019). A large scale, app-based behaviour change experiment persuading sustainable mobility patterns: Methods, results and lessons learnt. *Sustainability, 11*(9).
6. Rosenbaum, M. S., & Massiah, C. (2011). An expanded Servicescape perspective. *Journal of Service Management, 22*(4), 471–490.
7. Mari, M., & Poggesi, S. (2013). Servicescape cues and customer behavior: A systematic literature review and research agenda. *The Service Industries Journal, 33*(2), 171–199.
8. Nüesch, R., Alt, R., & Puschmann, T. (2015). Hybrid customer interaction. *Business & Information Systems Engineering, 57*(1), 73–78.
9. Vargo, S. L., & Lusch, R. F. (2004). Evolving to a new dominant logic for marketing. *Journal of Marketing, 68*(1), 1–17.
10. Berger, B., et al. (2015). It is not just about competition with "free": Differences between content formats in consumer preferences and willingness to pay. *Journal of Management Information Systems, 32*(3), 105–128.
11. Backhaus, K., Erichson, B., & Weiber, R. (2015). *Fortgeschrittene Multivariate Analysemethoden: Eine anwendungsorientierte Einführung*. Springer Gabler.
12. Lusch, R. F., & Nambisan, S. (2015). Service innovation: A service-dominant logic perspective. *MIS Quarterly, 39*(1), 155–175.
13. Schulz, T., et al. (2021). Value co-creation and co-destruction in service ecosystems: The case of the reach now app. *Technological Forecasting & Social Change* – work in progress.
14. Zimmermann, S., Schulz, T., & Gewald, H. (2020). Salient attributes of mobility apps: What does really matter for the citizen? In *Pacific Asia conference on information systems*. Dubai.
15. Vargo, S. L., & Lusch, R. F. (2017). Service-dominant logic 2025. *International Journal of Research in Marketing, 34*(1), 46–67.
16. Vargo, S. L., Maglio, P. P., & Akaka, M. A. (2008). On value and value co-creation: A service systems and service logic perspective. *European Management Journal, 26*(3), 145–152.
17. Nunes, A. A., Galvão, T., & Cunha, J. F. (2014). Urban public transport service co-creation: Leveraging passenger's knowledge to enhance travel experience. *Procedia - Social and Behavioral Sciences, 111*(5), 577–585.
18. Akaka, M. A., & Vargo, S. L. (2015). Extending the context of service: From encounters to ecosystems. *Journal of Services Marketing, 29*(6/7), 453–462.
19. Ballantyne, D., & Nilsson, E. (2017). All that is solid melts into air: The Servicescape in digital service space. *Journal of Services Marketing, 31*(3), 226–235.
20. Harris, L. C., & Goode, M. M. H. (2010). Online Servicescapes, trust, and purchase intentions. *Journal of Services Marketing, 24*(3), 230–243.
21. Kim, S. H., & Koh, J. (2007). *The effect of e-scape on internet shoppers' cognition, emotion, and behavior response*. In *International conference on information systems*. Montreal.
22. Bitner, M. J. (1992). Servicescapes: The impact of physical surroundings on customers and employees. *Journal of Marketing, 56*(2), 57–71.
23. Baker, J. (1987). The role of the environment in marketing services: The consumer perspective. In J. A. Czepiel, C. A. Congram, & J. Shanahan (Eds.), *The services challenge: Integrating for competitive advantage* (pp. 79–84). American Marketing Association.
24. Kang, H.-J., Kim, B., & Kwon, G. H. (2018). *The smart Servicescape framework in smart home healthcare service experience*. In *Academic design management conference*. London.
25. Roy, S. K., et al. (2019). The rise of smart consumers: Role of smart Servicescape and smart consumer experience co-creation. *Journal of Marketing Management, 35*(15–16), 1480–1513.
26. Nilsson, E., & Ballantyne, D. (2014). Reexamining the place of Servicescape in marketing: A service-dominant logic perspective. *Journal of Services Marketing, 28*(5), 374–379.
27. Harris, L. C., & Ezeh, C. (2008). Servicescape and loyalty intentions: An empirical investigation. *European Journal of Marketing, 42*(3/4), 390–422.
28. Luce, R. D., & Tukey, J. W. (1964). Simultaneous conjoint measurement: A new type of fundamental measurement. *Journal of Mathematical Psychology, 1*(1), 1–27.
29. Naous, D., & Legner, C. (2017). *Leveraging market research techniques in IS—A review of conjoint analysis in IS research*. In *International conference on information systems*. Seoul.

30. Hair, J. F., Jr., et al. (2014). *Multivariate data analysis*. Harlow.
31. Grison, E., Burkhardt, J.-M., & Gyselinck, V. (2017). How do users choose their routes in public transport? The effect of individual profile and contextual factors. *Transportation Research Part F: Traffic Psychology and Behaviour, 51*, 24–37.
32. Litman, T. (2008). Valuing transit service quality improvements. *Journal of Public Transportation, 11*(2), 43–63.
33. Kuhnimhof, T., et al. (2012). Men shape a downward trend in car use among young adults—Evidence from six industrialized countries. *Transport Reviews, 32*(6), 761–779.
34. Umweltbundesamt. (2019). *Veränderungen im Mobilitätsverhalten zur Förderung einer nachhaltigen Mobilität*.
35. Baltar, F., & Brunet, I. (2012). Social research 2.0: Virtual snowball sampling method using Facebook. *Internet Research, 22*(1), 57–74.
36. Kosinski, M., et al. (2015). Facebook as a research tool for the social sciences: Opportunities, challenges, ethical considerations, and practical guidelines. *American Psychologist, 70*(6), 543–556.
37. Bundesinstitut für Bevölkerungsforschung. *Durchschnittsalter der Bevölkerung in Deutschland (1871-2019)*. 2021 2021-08-03]; Available from: https://www.bib.bund.de/Permalink.html?id=10208850
38. Statistisches Bundesamt. *VGR des Bundes - Arbeitnehmerentgelt, Löhne und Gehälter*. 2019 18-02-2019]; Available from: https://www-genesis.destatis.de/genesis/online.
39. Ofungwu, J. (2014). *Statistical applications for environmental analysis and risk assessment*. John Wiley & Sons.
40. Schulz, T., et al. (2021). Smart mobility—An analysis of potential customers' preference structures. *Electronic Markets, 31*(1), 105–124.
41. Kanuri, V. K., Thorson, E., & Mantrala, M. K. (2014). Using reader preferences to optimize news content: A method and a case study. *International Journal on Media Management, 16*(2), 55–75.
42. Wlömert, N., & Eggers, F. (2016). Predicting new service adoption with conjoint analysis: External validity of BDM-based incentive-aligned and dual-response choice designs. *Marketing Letters, 27*(1), 195–210.
43. Chandler, J. D., & Vargo, S. L. (2011). Contextualization and value-in-context: How context frames exchange. *Marketing Theory, 11*(1), 35–49.
44. van Exel, N. J. A., & Rietveld, P. (2009). Could you also have made this trip by another mode? An investigation of perceived travel possibilities of car and train travellers on the main travel corridors to the City of Amsterdam, The Netherlands. *Transportation Research Part A: Policy and Practice, 43*(4), 374–385.
45. Circella, G., et al. (2017). *What affects millennials' mobility? PART II: The impact of residential location, individual preferences and lifestyles on young adults' travel behavior in California*.

International Promotion Patterns in the Smart City Literature: Exploring the Role of Geography in Affecting Local Drivers and Smart Cities' Outcomes

Filippo Marchesani , Francesca Masciarelli , and Andrea Bikfalvi

Abstract The rise of smart cities is a significant trend in urban development. However, only in recent years has the focus on the international promotion of these cities become prominent. Despite ongoing academic discussions on the impact of smart city development on urban environments, the global recognition of smart cities is uncertain due to their multidisciplinary nature. Therefore, we conducted a systematic literature review of articles published in top-tier peer-reviewed journals from 2008 to December 2021, providing a comprehensive analysis of existing literature. Specifically, by focusing on the influence of geographical location on cities' international promotion strategies, we highlight the local drivers and the outcomes of smart cities' urban trajectories in different geographical contexts. The paper concludes with a conceptual model aiming to contribute to smart city debates by providing further evidence of the role of geographical location in smart city trajectories.

Keywords Smart City · Internationalization · Systematic literature review · International promotion · Geography

F. Marchesani (✉)
University of "G. d'Annunzio" Chieti – Pescara, Pescara, Italy

Department of Business Administration and Product Design, University of Girona, Girona, Spain
e-mail: filippo.marchesani@unich.it; f.masciarelli@unich.it

F. Masciarelli
University of "G. d'Annunzio" Chieti – Pescara, Pescara, Italy

A. Bikfalvi
Department of Business Administration and Product Design, University of Girona, Girona, Spain
e-mail: andrea.bikfalvi@udg.edu

A. M. Braccini et al. (eds.), *Digital (Eco) Systems and Societal Challenges*, Lecture Notes in Information Systems and Organisation 72,
https://doi.org/10.1007/978-3-031-75586-6_11

1 Introduction

The role of smart cities in the urban panorama has gained great scholarly attention in recent decades as it directly influences a plethora of long-run objectives for the current cities, such as integrating and advancing economic, social and environmental areas [1]. Today, smart cities are capable of integrating both innovative models and technologies to optimize local processes and services, influencing the urban environment and playing a catalytic role in the urban landscape to becoming a context capable of attracting and retaining human and financial capital [2–4].

Although both scholars and practitioners believe that smart cities have the potential to shape the urban future, there is still an open discussion on the definition and conception of the smart city and their impact on the national and global level [5, 6]. Today, there is still an unclear conceptualization of the smart cities' implementation, combined with an academic gap on the role of geography in smart cities' initiatives worldwide [7, 8].

This state of art opens up different topics for discussion and emerging perspectives about the correct definition and implementation of smart cities. On the one hand, the implementation of "smart" in cities' development has led cities to a social, cultural, technological and economic environment suitable for citizens and stakeholders [9, 10]. However, on the other hand, it has created a new global competition to attract citizens, tourism, companies and financial capital by offering an internal context that considers its users at the center of urban development [8, 11]. In these trajectories, the needs of cities are different as they must consider the intrinsic development of the local context combined with the conceptualization of "smart" in cities.

Cities are becoming an entrepreneur of themselves and seek to acquire financial, human and institutional resources to reorganize their influence locally [12–15] and elevate their status on the international scene [11]. Therefore, the development and practices of smart cities' openness are essential to bypass the static vision of the city and move into a globalized and competitive context. However, this opening up of smart cities is still in a preliminary but recently has attracted a large stream of attention in the literature [8].

The promotion of cities through international promotion strategies follows the same strategic development process as the one implemented by companies and seeks to involve potential users by offering an urban context suitable for stakeholders, creating real global competition for urban contexts that aim to attract companies, innovative entrepreneurs, new citizens, but also increase tourism, and promote the financial flows [3, 16–18].

This work aims to systematically map the smart cities' literature in that interception by providing a holistic understanding of the development and implementation of smart cities in the global panorama. Specifically, we highlight how worldwide geographical areas adopt different international promotion strategies and development mechanisms driven by structural and strategic motivation (input) and smart cities' outcomes (output) according to their objectives and needs.

Thus, our research questions are: "*What are the relationships between the geographical area and the international promotion strategies of smart cities?*" and "*What are the local drivers and the smart city outcomes in the international promotion of smart cities?*"

To answer this question, our study is structured as follows. First, we delineate the conceptual boundaries useful to outline the research field and define the methodological and structural development of the review. Then, we define our research strategy by outlining the methods and the quality criteria to ensure a systematic and robust approach. The next section provides a descriptive overview of current research, followed by a thematic analysis of the findings. Specifically, in the first part, we highlight the publication trends, information, journal outlets, methodology applied, and research areas. In the second part, we analyze the geographical evolution of publications referring to academic production and the sampling of quantitative and qualitative articles on the subject, highlighting the different development trajectories and discussing the results on multiple levels such as macro-regions, countries, and cities level. Finally, we discuss practical and theoretical implications for academics and policymakers and suggest future research directions.

2 Conceptual Boundaries and Methodological Approach

To systematically analyze the literature on the interception between international promotion strategies and the development of smart cities, we adopt the systematic literature review methodology [8, 19]. This approach provides a method to identify, select, analyze, and synthesize existing literature based on a clear and repeatable protocol. We identify robust results and conclusions through an in-depth analysis of the area examined.

To assess this systematic literature review process, we establish the primary conceptual criteria to better outline our research area. In defining the keywords related to the international promotion strategies, we focus on the vision proposed by the international marketing research defined by the Journal of International Marketing that considers the concept of marketing in relation to the international arena where marketing activities occur beyond national and cultural boundaries [8].

Thus, we rely on the definition of marketing proposed by the American Marketing Association (2013): "the activity, set of institutions, and processes for creating, communicating, delivering, and exchanging offerings that have value for customers, clients, partners, and society at large" (AMA 2013). This definition allows us to evaluate the evolution of the studies related to the relationship between cities and various stakeholders from a global competition and development perspective. Cities are opening up and competing globally for human and financial capital, tourism, structural funds, and innovation [11, 20–23]. In this competitive environment, international promotion strategies allow cities to adapt to users and stakeholders in a customized manner, responding to their needs and becoming part of an increasingly competitive context [24]. In the past, local government regulation was considered one of the main obstacles to cross-border development, suggesting that legal restrictions in certain countries dictate modifications in products, prices, and promotional strategies for firms and local development. To survive, cities need to open up beyond the local context and be considered as companies operating in a globally competitive context. Consequently, cities must also outline their internal and international promotion strategies to develop and manage medium/long-term development plans [11].

In defining the keywords related to smart cities, we rely on the definitions of smart cities described in the literature [5] and on a more in-depth review of the reference literature published in the top international journals to select the most appropriate smart cities keywords [8, 25]. Today, the concept of smart cities can be analyzed according to different perspectives that consider different dimensions such as governance, environment, economy, people, living, and mobility [26]. This multidisciplinary area of intervention leads us to consider the city's evolution from a smart perspective based on the different declinations we considered in our set of keywords. In approaching these conceptual boundaries, we only consider international marketing and smart cities concepts, excluding studies that deal with the concept of smart cities but do not address this relationship. For this reason, papers concerning smart cities in terms of internal development are excluded from our sample.

2.1 Search Strategy

To deeply explore this research area, we have relied on EBSCOhost's Business Source Premier database as the primary source of research as it provides a solid level of coverage of the major reference journals. This database allows to evaluate the entire selection process thoroughly and reproduce the process by tracing the analysis steps methodically. As a common practice in literature reviews, we performed a three-level search considering keywords on titles, abstracts, and subject terms. Our selection of keywords is based on multiple qualitatively and contextually relevant factors, elaborating on an analysis of the previous literature reviews published in the main international reference journals. We considered the period ranging from January 2008 up to and including December 2021. We used January 2008 as the cutoff starting point, given that the first article matching the keywords appeared in 2008.

The usage of standard Boolean operators allowed for the creation of a single search algorithm. The keyword search algorithm performed by combining the concept of smart city and international marketing strategies was: *("marketing" OR "customer" OR "consumer" OR "export" OR "market" OR "entry" OR "internationalization" OR "internationalization" OR "network" OR "innovation" OR "product" OR "price" OR "promotion" OR "distribution" OR "channel" OR "brand" OR "Internet") AND ("Smart City" OR "Smart Cities" OR "Wired City" OR "Digital City" OR "Information City" OR "Intelligent City" OR*

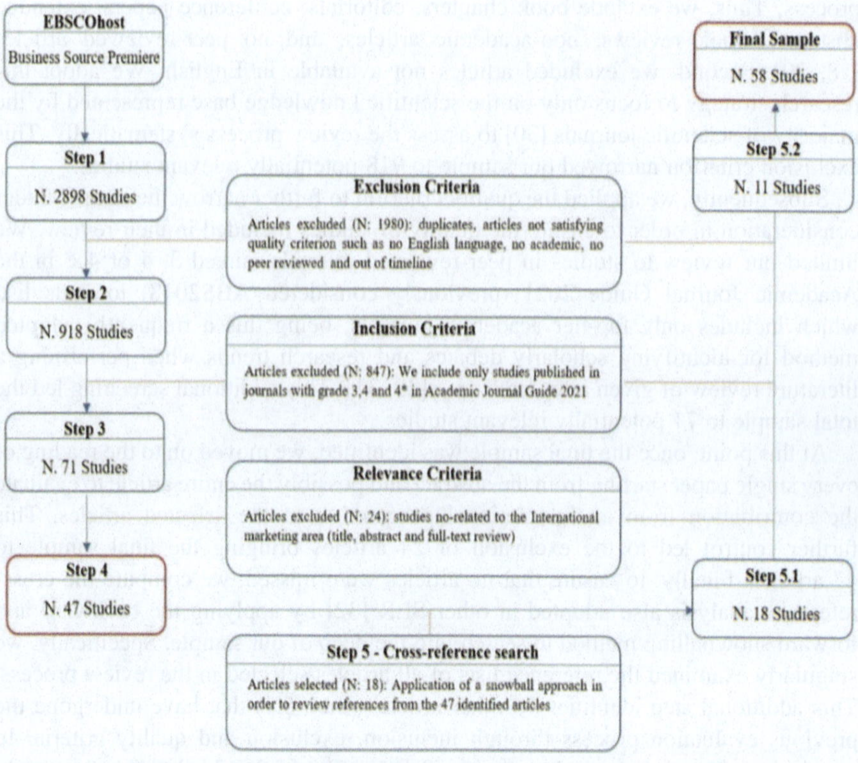

Fig. 1 Research strategy and boundaries

"Information City" OR "Information cities" OR "Knowledge-based City" OR "Knowledge City" OR "Knowledge cities" OR "Liveable City" OR "Liveable cities" OR "Ubiquitous City"). In this selection, we included the keywords related to the reference area according to the associated literature in the top journals regarding smart cities [8] and international marketing strategies [27].

After this screening process, 2898 studies relevant to this research area were selected. Subsequently, in order to have a more precise understanding of the role of international marketing strategies in Smart Cities, we decided not to consider studies focused on a national level and focusing only on the international dimension. Our research was thus structured to include studies that focused on the global vision of the smart city and the international marketing strategies (direct and indirect) used by the city to position itself globally. This process allows us to better understand the different dimensions of Smart Cities' development strategies on the international landscape.

Starting from this preliminary analysis, we applied exclusion and inclusion criteria to ensure the high as possible for the sample taken into consideration (See Fig. 1). First, to guarantee and high standard level, we excluded articles according to the quality academic criteria usually adopted in the systematic literature review process. Thus, we exclude book chapters, editorials, conference papers, extended abstracts, book reviews, non-academic articles, and no peer-reviewed articles [28, 29]. Second, we excluded articles not available in English. We adopt this research strategy to focus only on the scientific knowledge base represented by the majority of scientific journals [30] to assess the review process systematically. This exclusion criterion narrowed our sample to 918 potentially relevant studies.

Subsequently, we applied the quality criterion to further narrow the sample under consideration in order to ensure the quality of studies included in their review. We limited our review to studies in peer-reviewed journals ranked 3, 4 or 4 * in the Academic Journal Guide 2021 (previously considered ABS2018) journals list, which includes only top-tier academic journals, being this a frequently adopted method for identifying scholarly debates and research trends when performing a literature review of given a research area [29, 31]. This additional screening led the total sample to 71 potentially relevant studies.

At this point, once the final sample was identified, we moved on to the reading of every single paper starting from the abstract and possibly the entire article to evaluate the contribution from an international perspective of the selected articles. This further control led to the exclusion of 24 articles bringing the final sample to 47 articles. Finally, to ensure that no articles were missed, we compute the cross-reference analysis also adopted in other SLR [32] by applying the backward and forward snowballing method to search into the deep of our sample. Specifically, we singularly examined the reference lists of all articles selected in the review process. This additional step identifies 18 other articles (Step 5.1) that have undergone the previous evaluation process through inclusion, exclusion and quality criteria. In conclusion, 11 articles met the selection criteria (Step 5.2) added to the previously selected sample, bringing the final sample to 58 articles, as reported in Fig. 1.

Considering this final sample, we constructed an extraction table that considered the main details of the articles, such as the institution of author affiliation, methodology, sample, geographical information, and any relevant information such as theoretical and main results, practical implications, and future research to capture the geographical development of this research area. This allows us to systematically analyze the final sample and extract interpretive elements from it.

3 Results

3.1 Descriptive Analysis

Since 2008, the number of articles published every year had an increasing trend, as it can be observed in Fig. 2, with a generalized peak in the last 2 years that has shown an increasing trend compared to the recent development (2020 = 7 and 2021 = 12), highlighting the fact that is still growing and to a rapid degree. Specifically, the results show that academic output on the topic has increased exponentially over the past decade following the smart cities trajectories that have begun to move from a

Fig. 2 Evolution graph of the distribution of the number of publications per year

purely national context to a more global vision [33]. Moreover, it emerges that 42% of the scientific production of the last 13 years has been disseminated in publication outlets in the past 2 years, showing that the reviewed research area is quickly shifting into a more advanced stage. As we will also highlight later, this research has not remained anchored to the internal development of the city concept but is evolving, including practices and strategies that are ever closer to a competitive and managerial context.

The journals considered in this area are Urban Studies with 16 articles and Government Information Quarterly with 12 articles, covering more than 50% of the total sample. It is important to focus on this preponderance of articles because the sample shows different trends. On the one hand, there is a constant evolution from 2016 to 2020 of publications in Government Information Quarterly, mainly focused on governance and development policies considering theoretical and qualitative articles. On the other hand, a trend consolidated over the years in Urban Studies with a peak in the last year mainly focused on urban adaptation and development in cities. Other journals of note include Cambridge Journal of Regions, Economy and Society with 6 articles, California Management Review (3) and European Urban and Regional Studies, Technovation, Production Planning and Control and Public Management Review appear with 3 articles. The rest of the scientific production is distributed in different journals and thematic areas, as it can be interpreted from the text in the next paragraphs (See Table 1).

The thematic areas that emerge from our sample are various, as well as the conjunctions of this research area from a methodological perspective. However, consistently with the smart city concept, the emerging reference areas mainly concern urban study and the study of systems that support data-intensive applications. Table 2 show that the predominant subject area in this study is Regional Studies, Planning and Environment, which covers almost 50% of the total sample with 23 articles, followed by Information System with 12 articles. Other publications concern, Innovation (5), General Management, Ethics, Gender and Social Responsibility (3), Public Sector and Health Care (3), Operations and Technology Management (3), Operations Research and Management Science (2), Marketing (1) and Economics, Econometrics and Statistics (1). Deeply analyzing the final sample of the literature, several significant methodology-related trends emerge that evidence that

Table 1 Articles distribution in Academic Journals

Articles	Journals	AJG ranking
1	Research Policy	4*
3	Public Management Review	4
1	Production and Operations Management	4
1	Journal of Supply Chain Management	4
16	Urban Studies	3
12	Government Information Quarterly	3
6	Cambridge Journal of Regions, Economy and Society	3
5	California Management Review	3
3	European Urban and Regional Studies	3
3	Technovation	3
2	Production Planning and Control	3
1	IEEE Transactions on Systems, Man, and Cybernetics	3
1	Energy Economics	3
1	International Marketing Review	3
1	IEEE Transactions on Systems, Man, and Cyb.	3
1	Technological Forecasting and Social Change	3

Table 2 Methodology and subject area

	Methodology					
	Theor.	Empirical			Review	Total
Subject areas		Quantitative	Qualitative	Mixed-methods		
Econ, econometrics and statistics		1				1
General management, ethics, gender and social responsibility			3			3
Information systems	5	2	5	1	1	14
Innovation	2		2		1	5
Marketing					1	1
Operations and technology management	3					3
Operations research and management science	1		1			2
Public sector and health care				2	1	3
Regional studies, planning and environment	9		16	1		26
Total	20	3	27	4	4	58

the field is at an early stage and that the current advancement of this research trend is more theoretical than practical. This is confirmed by the study of applied methodologies which presented a large number of theoretical contributions (20) specifically referred to the first part of the timeline table and highlights how the study of the phenomenon has been addressed in this perspective first at a theoretical level and subsequently implemented in case studies and practical.

This is confirmed by the study of applied methodologies which presented a large number of theoretical contributions (20) specifically referred to the first part of the timeline table and highlights how the study of the phenomenon has been addressed in this perspective first at a theoretical level and subsequently implemented in case studies and practical. Moreover, great attention is concerned with the number of studies using a qualitative methodology approach. In particular, considering 34 empirical studies in our sample, 27 use a qualitative approach. Based on this qualitative contribution, a large part presents single or multi-case studies to analyze the phenomenon within a specific urban context or a nation. These results reveal how this phenomenon is still in an embryonic phase where various concepts, objectives and developments are still at an embryonic stage and not well fixed in the literature. The remaining empirical studies apply a mixed-methods approach (4 articles), and only 3 articles apply a quantitative approach.

Thus, the evolution of this research topic lacks an in-depth analysis and exploration in practices, an issue that future academics and practitioners should converge on and solve, as a profound analysis of the phenomenon will allow to build a strong theoretical foundation and further enhance the research area in theory and practices. The presence of 4 "review" articles related to governance [34–36] and marketing [8, 37] and highlights how there is a need to re-examine the current static and urban vision of the city into a (more) dynamic and global perspective.

3.2 *Geographical Distribution and Analysis*

The geographical analysis, placed at the centre of this systematic literature review, highlights important conjectures on the intersection between international marketing strategies and smart cities. Indeed, the expansion of cities outside the urban context is a phenomenon that mainly interests certain geographic areas. Below, we begin with an analysis of the authors, the geographical context, and the institution of the authors' affiliation. Then, we analyze the sample in-depth, evaluating the countries involved and the cities considered in the selected research.

Starting from the reference sample, we analyze the authorship of the publications in question, focusing on the number of authors, nations, and institutions to highlight the multi-project quality and cross-knowledge of the research. The number of authors is in line with the general academic context of reference, where most publications have 3 or more authors. In contradiction with this background, it is interesting to comment on the nature of these collaborations. The sample highlights that although the number of institutions involved is balanced (see Table 3), the reference nations involved in the various publications are strongly unbalanced to a single country (34 Articles) compared to the plurality of countries involving two (15 Articles) or three countries (9 Articles). This data contrasts with the study of international openness and strategies to promote the city at the international level.

Table 3 Authorship characteristics per authors, countries and institutions

	Numbers of authors (%)	Number of countries (%)	Number of institutions (%)
One	20.75	58.49	35.84
Two	28.3	26.41	30.18
Three or more	50.94	15.09	33.96

Table 4 First authors distribution

No.	Country	Macro-regions
11	United States	North America
9	United Kingdom	Europe and Central Asia
8	Spain	Europe and Central Asia
6	Italy	Europe and Central Asia
4	Canada	North America
2	China	East Asia and Pacific
2	Ireland	Europe and Central Asia
2	Netherlands	Europe and Central Asia
2	Australia	Europe and Central Asia
2	Chile	Latin America and Caribbean
2	UAE	Middle East and North Africa
1	India	South Asia
1	Korea	East Asia and Pacific
1	Kuwait	Middle East and North Africa
1	Denmark	Europe and Central Asia
1	Switzerland	Europe and Central Asia
1	Cyprus	Europe and Central Asia
1	Sweden	Europe and Central Asia
1	South Africa	Sub-Saharan Africa

However, the relatively young field of research and methodological developments (as seen above) suggests that in the future, the number of empirical research involving two or more countries will grow exponentially, as will the increase in the phenomenon studied.

Subsequently, by investigating the author's affiliations, we analyze this phenomenon's nature and interest worldwide following analyses at the national and macro-regions level. As it can be observed in Tables 4 and 5, scientific production on the subject is concentrated in Europe and Central Asia with 33 articles (57%) and North America with 15 articles (26%). In detail, we note that European scientific production is mainly developed in 3 countries (UK 9, Spain 8, and Italy 6), which alone cover the majority of the European scientific production on the subject. Moreover, Concerning North America, the publications are divided into 11 USA and 4 Canada. The rest of the scientific production originated in the remaining regions, specifically 3 in East Asia and Pacific (of which two in China and one in Korea), 3 in the Middle East and North Africa (2 in UAE and 1 in Kuwait), 2 in Latin America and Caribbean, 1 in Sub-Saharan Africa and 1 in South Asia. These results show how

Table 5 First authors' distribution per macro-regions

No.	Region
35	Europe and Central Asia
13	North America
3	East Asia and Pacific
3	Middle East and North Africa
2	Latin America and Caribbean
1	Sub-Saharan Africa
1	South Asia

Table 6 Sample geographical location of empirical papers per country, region and income group

No.	Country		Region	Income group
5	Italy	ITA	Europe and Central Asia	High income
4	Spain	ESP	Europe and Central Asia	High income
4	United States	USA	North America	High income
4	UK	GBR	Europe and Central Asia	High income
3	Canada	CAN	North America	High income
1	Austria	AUT	Europe and Central Asia	High income
2	Brazil	BRA	Latin Am. and Caribbean	Up/Md income
2	Chile	CHL	Latin Am. and Caribbean	High income
1	China	CHN	East Asia and Pacific	Up/Md income
1	Colombia	COL	Latin Am. and Caribbean	Up/Md income
1	Finland	FIN	Europe and Central Asia	High income
1	Germany	DEU	Europe and Central Asia	High income
1	Netherlands	NLD	Europe and Central Asia	High income
1	India	IND	South Asia	Lo/Md income
1	Portugal	PRT	Europe and Central Asia	High income
1	South Korea	KOR	East Asia and Pacific	High income
2	Sweden	SWE	Europe and Central Asia	High income
1	Taiwan	TWN	East Asia and Pacific	High income
1	Philippine	PHL	East Asia and Pacific	Lo/Md income
1	UAE	ARE	Midd. East and Nrt. Africa	High income

the academic interest in developing the smart city in a global landscape refers mainly to countries based on a vision of internationalization and openness to the outside world. While the strong technological component would suggest a greater development of these practices in Asia, with cities historically characterized by a robust implementation of big data and smart solutions [38], academic research on the development and promotion of the city in this intersection mainly concerns a trend of research in liberal and capitalist countries. A very particular case concerns the UK, which on the one hand, represents the main producer of academic articles on the subject (see Table 4); on the other hand, it is not strongly represented in the study sample (see Table 6), especially in the recent trend. This trend may be influenced by the "Brexit" that has influenced the trajectories of the development of smart cities

Table 7 Sample macro-regions distribution

No.	*Region*
20	Europe and Central Asia
7	North America
5	Latin America and Caribbean
4	East Asia and Pacific
1	South Asia
1	Middle East and North Africa
No.	*Income group*
32	High income
4	Upper middle income
2	Lower middle income

from a global perspective, widely represented in our sample in the pre-Brexit period [39], into a more urban and internal perspective.

Finally, we analyze the geographical distribution of the final sample and the cities considered as case studies. As Table 7 illustrates, the distribution is strongly unbalanced towards Europe (20) and North America (7), followed by Latin America (5) and finally by East Asia and Pacific (4), South Asia and the Middle East (1) and North Africa (1). The nations mainly considered in this field are Italy (5 articles), followed by Spain, the United States and the UK with 4 articles. This evidence may lead to different views. The first is the need to improve the collaboration between practitioners and academics to corroborate the geographical need, national policies and smart cities implementation. The second refers to the current policies related to the countries' openness regarding open data on smart cities' implementation and management. This transparency in management and investment allows for a detailed analysis of development strategies and trajectories, leading to a bilateral relationship between internal development and cities' international promotion.

It is also interesting to note that Latin America and Caribbean countries (5) also emerge in the sample, undergoing strong development from a smart point of view in recent years. These countries are surfing the smart city wave to solve internal problems and join a context that is not yet fully developed, as the case of Santiago de Chile presented in our final sample (see Table 8), which is to take a leap forward and catch up with more developed countries in terms of energy efficiency and environmental care [40, 41]. Moreover, to understand the level of development of the countries analyzed, we code our geographical sample using a three-group country classification that distinguishes between developing, emerging, and developed countries based on the World Bank's grouping of countries relative to annual gross national income (GNI) per capita. Accordingly, the developing group reunites low-income countries; the emerging group comprehends middle-income countries, and the developed category includes high-income countries. We decided to use the World Bank's classification based on the GNI per capita as it is widely used analytically to evaluate the country's development. This country coding allows us to rigorously determine the development of the countries examined by highlighting two considerations. The first is that the vast majority of the countries analyzed

Table 8 Cities considered in the case study

Sample City	
Code	City
ESP	Barcelona (3)
ITA	Milan (2)
BRA	Rio De Janeiro (2)
CHI	Santiago de Chile (2)
USA	Seattle
CAN	Vancouver
AUT	Vienna
GBR	London
DEU	Cologne
NLD	Amsterdam
PRT	PlanIT Valley
KOR	Songdo
SWE	Stockholm
TWN	Taipei
ITA	Naples
ARE	Dubai
PHL	Manila
CHI	Medellin
USA	Annapolis
PHI	New Clark City
CAN	Iqaluit
CAN	Nunavut

concern countries with a high income (32 articles), a sign that promoting the smart city in the global panorama is an elite concept involving more developed countries. The second is that the nature of publications in Upper middle income (4 articles) and Lower middle income (2 articles) countries is relatively recent, highlighting how this phenomenon motivates and pushes even less economically developed nations to draw on this phenomenon from a perspective of international development and promotion. This means that following or reproducing smart city models oriented to promoting the smart city into the global context in developed countries also serves as a model for less developed countries that aim at rising in the urban and geographical context of reference by boosting themselves in the urban environment and raising their status in the geographical area [8].

The city-level represents a large percentage of the empirical studies analyzed. Specifically, analyzing the sample of selected articles, 27 cities were used as case studies in the research. According to the sample, the main cities analyzed concern two European cities, Barcelona (3) and Milan (2), and two Latin American cities, Rio de Janeiro (2) and Santiago de Chile (2).

The precursor cities of this concept are mainly located in Europe. Barcelona (3 articles) has become a benchmark Smart City in the twenty-first century. Many studies start right from Barcelona to extend theories of reference globally, as to date, international competitiveness is driven by the innovativeness of cities [42]. Barcelona is a forerunner in this sector as it can provide a strongly smart context for the development and attraction of businesses and technology-based clusters [1, 43].

While European cities were precursors of the "smart" development of the city, it is interesting how cities such as Rio de Janeiro and Santiago de Chile are among the main cities analyzed. In this sense, cities in Latin America are striving to become global. According to Roy [44], the evolution toward a "smart" city in Latin America lies in the melting pot of development modernization projects, immigration, and neoliberal governance, which has led to a more global vision in recent years [40].

On the contrary, few projects concern the Asian continent, countries that have always been ahead of the smart city development but are not marginally included in the international promotion of the city. This evidence is configured in the different development trajectories of smart cities and will be discussed later to highlight a critical and theoretical framework of state of the art.

4 Discussion

This systematic literature review aims to characterize a link between smart cities and international promotion strategies in the global landscape. This procedure allows us to capture the direction of the link and the emerging geographical pattern in this relationship. The following conclusions result from this review. Large bodies of academic literature address smart cities and cities' development from an international perspective. However, literature documenting a clear linkage between the two is scant at the same time. In the intersection between international promotion strategies and smart city development, the geographic location plays a fundamental role by influencing internal drivers in developing smart cities, urban growth and development strategies at a national and international level. For example, if in certain geographic areas there is a "smart" implementation based on the citizen-centric perspective [9, 45], in other geographic areas, even they are considered "at the global vanguard" in smart city development [46, p. 71], the approach is mainly top-down (i.e. South Asia). Consequently, strategies and cities' development will differ according to their geographical and structural characteristics.

The lack of a direct connection in the literature is given not only by the (relative) recent development of the smart city concept [47] but also by a different vision of the same concept according to the geographical environment. This evolution leads governments and policymakers to approach the implementation of the smart city differently depending on the reference context and development objectives. In this article, we highlight how the geographical context influences the development trajectories of cities in relation to international promotion strategies (see Fig. 3). Specifically, it highlights how different inputs in the development of cities lead to substantial and well-defined outputs, which turn into different smart city trajectories linked to the geographical reference area. Thus, this review highlights three different approaches to the international promotion of cities: (1) the global-promotion

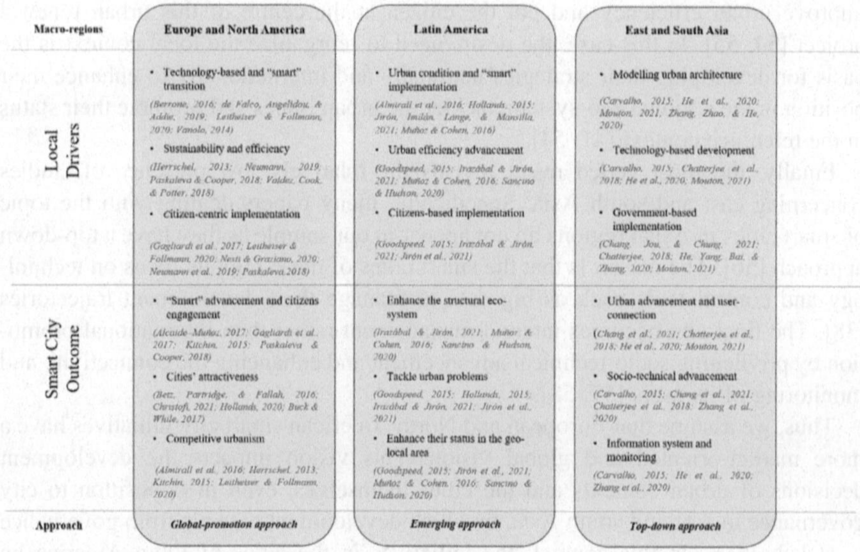

Fig. 3 Conceptual model

approach of cities located in Europe and North America, which aim to compete worldwide for innovation, tourism, and human and financial capital; (2) the emerging approach of cities in Latin America which aim to raise their status in the reference context and (3) the top-down approach of cities in East and South Asia focusing on urban advancement rather than global promotion.

The first approach concerns the cities located in Europe and North America, which compete globally and base their strategies on a capitalist perspective to attract tourism, human and financial capital, and companies. The smart evolution in those areas is driven by the technological and smart transition in services and processes that aim to improve the development of cities by placing the citizen and users at the centre of cities' strategies [48–50]. At the same time, the current need to be sustainable and efficient in medium-long term development leads cities to start and invest in this transformation process [16]. This evolution has impacted both internal and external perspectives and aims to evolve the static concept of cities towards a more comprehensive and global vision [6]. On the one hand, a global vision in cities development makes the city attractive to citizens and stakeholders and, on the other, enhances its status worldwide, useful for attracting human capital, talents and companies to compete locally and internationally [8, 51, 52].

The second approach focuses on the emerging trend in Latin American countries. These countries recently promoted smart city projects by initiating a "twinning relationship" with North American and European smart city projects (i.e., Rio, Santiago and Medellín whit Barcelona) to re-shape their own cities' trajectories due to the necessity to tackle internal problems in terms of a social and urban environment [40, 53]. The thrust of this transformation is given by the need to improve urban efficiency and put the citizen at the centre of this urban renewal project [54, 55]. In this case, the desire/need to reorganize the local context is the basis for developing their strategies nationally and internationally to enhance their position in the regional eco-system, tackler the urban issues and promote their status in the reference context [41, 54].

Finally, the most veiled result reveals the relatively low presence of studies concerning east and south Asia. Specifically, many papers dealing with the topic of smart cities in Asian regions do not appear in our sample as they have a top-down approach [56]. The reason is that the smart cities of these regions focus on technology and control tools such as big data to manage their development trajectories [38]. The final aim becomes internal management rather than international promotion by privileging socio-technical advancement and enhancing the connectivity and monitoring of its users [57, 58].

Thus, we assume that European and North American smart city initiatives have a more market-oriented and global vision. This vision impacts the development decisions of urban contexts and the cities themselves, even in opposition to city governance in east and south Asia, in which development extends from governance to stakeholders. In this context, the initiatives in the cities of Latin America lie between the two previous approaches. On the one hand, they aim to solve internal problems through the evolution of the city from a smart perspective. On the other, they plan to promote their position on the local and international scene.

5 Conclusion

In conclusion, the study, in addition to summarizing the geographical and urban contents on the specific topic through the approach of the SLR, systematically documents the recent research trends and the trajectories of the cities at the geographic level, showing different approaches to the concept of the smart city due to different technological, environmental, social, and evolutionary components.

The current results can be useful for both academics and practitioners from a strategic perspective. Specifically, from a theoretical view, we integrate new knowledge on the topic and support academics about the role of smart city initiatives in the urban environment. Furthermore, the different cities trajectories in morphologically, culturally, politically, and economically different countries influence the approaches and objectives of smart city projects, which can open up new theoretical developments on the practical evolution of smart cities from an international perspective [57]. Thus, we also map the literature on the global promotion of the city, providing new insights and theoretical evidence at a geographical level. An in-depth understanding of the geographical distribution would help the academics design a solid framework to promote and implement smart cities and generate a new flow of knowledge in the interplay between cities promotion, geographical area, and urban trajectories.

Finally, from a practical perspective, we support governance and policymakers in highlighting how different trajectories could modify the existing scenarios, reshaping a context that today is strictly focused on the operational objective of the smart city [59]. This perspective can offer insights into international promotion strategies and strengthen the current development trends in the different geographical areas highlighted in the literature.

Furthermore, these results open new research on the role of city promotion in the global context. The reduced number of empirical studies and the recent development of this research trend open to various studies on the subject. These studies can be traced horizontally by analyzing the reference context and the inputs and outputs required depending on the geographical area or vertically investigating the causes at the political and social levels. The international opening concert of smart cities continues to be underdeveloped. This feeds new lines of research on internal drivers and expected benefits (smart city outcome) in the international landscape.

To conclude, there are limitations that need to be acknowledged, consistent with all systematic literature reviews, which are related to the selection of the sample and the ongoing discourse within the references. Firstly, our choice of keywords and the utilization of EBSCOhost may have led to the inadvertent omission of pertinent literature. Secondly, our scope was centered exclusively on the international facet of the research, leading to a comprehensive analysis of the selected sample.

References

1. Camboim, G. F., Zawislak, P. A., & Pufal, N. A. (2019). Driving elements to make cities smarter: Evidences from European projects. *Technological Forecasting and Social Change, 142*(2017), 154–167.
2. Herrschel, T. (2013). Competitiveness AND sustainability: Can 'Smart City regionalism' square the circle? *Urban Studies, 50*(11), 2332–2348.
3. Tan, S. Y., & Taeihagh, A. (2020). Smart city governance in developing countries: A systematic literature review. *Sustain, 12*.
4. Marchesani, F., Masciarelli, F., & Bikfalvi, A. (2023). Smart city as a hub for talent and innovative companies: Exploring the (dis) advantages of digital technology implementation in cities. *Technological Forecasting and Social Change, 193*, 122636.
5. Albino, V., Berardi, U., & Dangelico, R. M. (2015). Smart cities: Definitions, dimensions, performance, and initiatives. *Journal of Urban Technology, 22*, 3–21.
6. de Falco, S., Angelidou, M., & Addie, J. P. D. (2019). From the 'smart city' to the 'smart metropolis'? Building resilience in the urban periphery. *European Urban and Regional Studies, 26*(2), 205–223.
7. Noori, N., de Jong, M., Janssen, M., Schraven, D., & Hoppe, T. (2021). Input-output modeling for Smart City development. *Journal of Urban Technology, 28*(1–2), 71–92.
8. Christofi, M., Iaia, L., Marchesani, F., & Masciarelli, F. (2021). Marketing innovation and internationalization in smart city development: A systematic review, framework and research agenda. *International Marketing Review, 38*(5), 948–984.
9. Paskaleva, K., & Cooper, I. (2018). Open innovation and the evaluation of internet-enabled public services in smart cities. *Technovation, 78*(July), 4–14.
10. Caragliu, A., & Del Bo, C. F. (2019). Smart innovative cities: The impact of Smart City policies on urban innovation. *Technological Forecasting and Social Change, 142*(2017), 373–383.

11. Taylor Buck, N., & While, A. (2017). Competitive urbanism and the limits to smart city innovation: The UK future cities initiative. *Urban Studies, 54*(2), 501–519.
12. Hollands, R. G. (2015). Critical interventions into the corporate smart city. *Cambridge Journal of Regions Economy and Society, 8*(1), 61–77.
13. Kummitham, R. K. R. (2019). Smart cities and entrepreneurship: An agenda for future research. *Technological Forecasting and Social Change, 149*(2018), 119763.
14. Kummitha, R. K. R., & Crutzen, N. (2017). How do we understand smart cities? An evolutionary perspective. *Cities, 67*, 43–52.
15. AlMalki, H. A., & Durugbo, C. M. (2022). *Systematic review of institutional innovation literature: Towards a multi-level management model*, no. 0123456789. Springer International Publishing.
16. Vanolo, A. (2014). Smartmentality: The Smart City as disciplinary strategy. *Urban Studies, 51*(5), 883–898.
17. Romão, J., Kourtit, K., Neuts, B., & Nijkamp, P. (2018). The smart city as a common place for tourists and residents: A structural analysis of the determinants of urban attractiveness. *Cities, 78*(2017), 67–75.
18. Marchesani, F. (2022). Exploring the relationship between digital services advance and smart tourism in cities : Empirical evidence from Italy. *Current Issues in Tourism*, 1–12.
19. Danese, P., Manfè, V., & Romano, P. (2018). A systematic literature review on recent lean research: State-of-the-art and future directions. *International Journal of Management Reviews, 20*, 579–605.
20. Spicer, Z., Goodman, N., & Olmstead, N. (2021). The frontier of digital opportunity: Smart city implementation in small, rural and remote communities in Canada. *Urban Studies, 58*(3), 535–558.
21. Marchesani, F., Masciarelli, F., & Doan, H. Q. (2022). Innovation in cities a driving force for knowledge flows: Exploring the relationship between high-tech firms, student mobility, and the role of youth entrepreneurship. *Cities, 130*, 103852.
22. Marchesani, F., Masciarelli, F., & Bikfalvi, A. (2023). City (r)evolution in the smart era: Smart mobility practices as a driving force for tourism flow and the moderating role of airport in cities. *International Journal of Tourism Cities, 9*, 1025–1045.
23. Marchesani, F., & Masciarelli, F. (2023). Does tourism flow in cities drive green practices in the current smart city trajectories? Empirical evidence from Italy. *International Journal of Tourism Cities*.
24. Um, T., & Chung, N. (2021). Does smart tourism technology matter? Lessons from three smart tourism cities in South Korea. *Asia Pacific Journal of Tourism Research, 26*(4).
25. Ruhlandt, R. W. S. (2018). The governance of smart cities: A systematic literature review. *Cities, 81*, 1–23.
26. Silva, B. N., Khan, M., & Han, K. (2018). Towards sustainable smart cities: A review of trends, architectures, components, and open challenges in smart cities. *Sustainable Cities and Society, 38*, 697–713.
27. Yang, M., & Gabrielsson, P. (2018). The Interface of international marketing and entrepreneurship research: Review, synthesis, and future directions. *Journal of International Marketing, 26*(4), 18–37.
28. Pisani, N., Kourula, A., Kolk, A., & Meijer, R. (2017). How global is international CSR research? Insights and recommendations from a systematic review. *Journal of World Business, 52*, 591–614.
29. Christofi, M., Vrontis, D., Thrassou, A., & Shams, S. M. R. (2019). Triggering technological innovation through cross-border mergers and acquisitions: A micro-foundational perspective. *Technological Forecasting and Social Change, 146*, 148–166.
30. Tranfield, D., Denyer, D., & Smart, P. (2003). Towards a methodology for developing evidence-informed management knowledge by means of systematic review. *British Journal of Management, 14*(3), 207–222.

31. Christofi, M., Vrontis, D., & Cadogan, J. W. (2019). Micro-foundational ambidexterity and multinational enterprises: A systematic review and a conceptual framework. *International Business Review*.
32. Wohlin, C. (2014). Guidelines for snowballing in systematic literature studies and a replication in software engineering. In *ACM International Conference Proceeding Series*.
33. Chatterjee, S., & Kar, A. K. (2015). Smart cities in developing economies: A literature review and policy insights. In *2015 International Conference on Advances in Computing, Communications and Informatics*, ICACCI 2015.
34. Alcaide-Muñoz, L., Rodríguez-Bolívar, M. P., Cobo, M. J., & Herrera-Viedma, E. (2017). Analysing the scientific evolution of e-Government using a science mapping approach. *Government Information Quarterly, 34*(3), 545–555.
35. Gil-Garcia, J. R., Dawes, S. S., & Pardo, T. A. (2018). Digital government and public management research: Finding the crossroads. *Public Management Review, 20*(5), 633–646.
36. Ullah, F., Qayyum, S., Thaheem, M. J., Al-Turjman, F., & Sepasgozar, S. M. E. (2020). Risk management in sustainable smart cities governance: A TOE framework. *Technological Forecasting and Social Change, 167*, 2021.
37. Bonakdar, A., & Audirac, I. (2020). City branding and the link to urban planning: Theories, practices, and challenges. *Journal of Planning Literature, 2*, 147–160.
38. Zhang, N., Zhao, X., & He, X. (2020). Understanding the relationships between information architectures and business models: An empirical study on the success configurations of smart communities. *Government Information Quarterly, 37*(2), 101439.
39. Contreras, G., & Platania, F. (2019). Economic and policy uncertainty in climate change mitigation: The London Smart City case scenario. *Technological Forecasting and Social Change, 142*, 384–393.
40. Irazábal, C., & Jirón, P. (2021). Latin American smart cities: Between worlding infatuation and crawling provincialising. *Urban Studies, 58*(3), 507–534.
41. Jirón, P., Imilán, W. A., Lange, C., & Mansilla, P. (2021). Placebo urban interventions: Observing Smart City narratives in Santiago de Chile. *Urban Studies, 58*(3), 601–620.
42. Bakici, T., Almirall, E., & Wareham, J. (2013). A Smart City initiative: The case of Barcelona. *Journal of the Knowledge Economy, 4*(2), 135–148.
43. Marchesani, F. (2023). *The global Smart City: Challenges and opportunities in the digital age*. Emerald Publishing Limited.
44. Roy, A. (2011). Urbanisms, worlding practices and the theory of planning. *Planning Theory, 10*(1), 6–15.
45. Morgan, K., & Webb, B. (2020). Googling the city: In search of the public interest on Toronto's 'smart' waterfront. *Urban Planning, 5*(1), 84–95.
46. Parasol, M. (2018). The impact of China's 2016 Cyber Security Law on foreign technology firms, and on China's big data and Smart City dreams. *Computer Law & Security Review*.
47. Almirall, E., et al. (2016). Smart cities at the crossroads: New tensions in city transformation. *California Management Review, 59*(1), 141–152.
48. Berrone, P., Ricart, J. E., & Carrasco, C. (2016). The open kimono: Toward a general framework for open data initiatives in cities. *California Management Review, 59*(1), 39–70.
49. Neumann, O., Matt, C., Hitz-Gamper, B. S., Schmidthuber, L., & Stürmer, M. (2019). Joining forces for public value creation? Exploring collaborative innovation in smart city initiatives. *Government Information Quarterly, 36*(4), 101411.
50. Nesti, G., & Graziano, P. R. (2020). The democratic anchorage of governance networks in smart cities: An empirical assessment. *Public Management Review, 22*(5), 648–667.
51. Betz, M. R., Partridge, M. D., & Fallah, B. (2016). Smart cities and attracting knowledge workers: Which cities attract highly-educated workers in the 21st century? *Papers in Regional Science, 95*(4), 819–842.
52. Kitchin, R. (2015). Making sense of smart cities: Addressing present shortcomings. *Cambridge Journal of Regions Economy and Society, 8*(1), 131–136.

53. Goodspeed, R. (2015). Smart cities: Moving beyond urban cybernetics to tackle wicked problems. *Cambridge Journal of Regions Economy and Society, 8*(1), 79–92.
54. Sancino, A., & Hudson, L. (2020). Leadership in, of, and for smart cities–case studies from Europe, America, and Australia. *Public Management Review, 22*(5), 701–725.
55. Muñoz, P., & Cohen, B. (2016). The making of the urban entrepreneur. *California Management Review, 59*(1), 71–91.
56. Leitheiser, S., & Follmann, A. (2020). The social innovation–(re)politicisation nexus: Unlocking the political in actually existing smart city campaigns? The case of SmartCity Cologne, Germany. *Urban Studies, 57*(4), 894–915.
57. Carvalho, L. (2015). Smart cities from scratch? A socio-technical perspective. *Cambridge Journal of Regions Economy and Society, 8*(1), 43–60.
58. Chatterjee, S., Kar, A. K., & Gupta, M. P. (2018). Success of IoT in Smart cities of India: An empirical analysis. *Government Information Quarterly, 35*(3), 349–361.
59. Shelton, T., Zook, M., & Wiig, A. (2015). The 'actually existing smart city'. *Cambridge Journal of Regions, Economy and Society, 8*(1), 13–25.

Intercepting Smart Policies to Foster High-Tech SMEs in Regional Environment

Ludovica Antenozio, Daniela Di Berardino, and Augusta Consorti

Abstract Regional environments are undergoing significant transformations, reshaping the geography of innovation, thanks to increasingly smart policies. In this study, we aim to examine the localization of high-tech SMEs in different local systems, focusing on the Italian landscape for an 8-year period (2013–2020). This research has been carried out on a heterogeneous sample of 250 high-tech SMEs from "startup.registrodelleimprese", employing descriptive analysis using T-test and U-test. Our findings demonstrate that the location decisions of high-tech SMEs are influenced by local policies that prioritize innovation and competitiveness. Moreover, they show the importance of SMEs in changing the entrepreneurial trait of regional environments. This contributes to the ongoing debate on the importance of smart policies in shaping the spatial distribution of high-tech SMEs and offers insights for policymakers, entrepreneurs, and stakeholders seeking to foster innovation-driven economic development in regional areas.

Keywords Smart policies · High-tech · SMEs · Digital innovation · Regional environment · Institutional theory

1 Introduction

The interrelation between industrial, organizational, institutional, social, temporal, and spatial features of different regional environment and the entrepreneurial innovation have been explored in literature. In recent years, some scholars have explored the positive role of institutional environment on technology entrepreneurship in the digital era [1–3]. Kummitha (2019) show that the innovative culture can foster the technology entrepreneurship and digital innovation [4]. High-tech small and medium enterprises (SMEs) are more sensitive to the external environment, due to

L. Antenozio (✉) · D. Di Berardino · A. Consorti
Department of Business Administration, University of Gabriele d'Annunzio Chieti-Pescara, Chieti, Italy
e-mail: ludovica.antenozio@unich.it; daniela.diberardino@unich.it; a.consorti@unich.it

A. M. Braccini et al. (eds.), *Digital (Eco) Systems and Societal Challenges*, Lecture Notes in Information Systems and Organisation 72,
https://doi.org/10.1007/978-3-031-75586-6_12

the rapid change of technology, to the networking effects of technology development, to the knowledge spillover linked to digitalization and to the rapid commercialization and industrialization of high technology [1, 5].

For these reasons, the regional and the urban environment have gained significant attention as a transformative approach to local development, characterized by the utilization of advanced technologies and data-driven solutions to enhance residents' quality of life, improve sustainability, and foster economic growth [6, 7]. Policymakers have recognized the potential of smart policies in shaping the landscape of high-tech SMEs and their impact on the localization of businesses [8, 9]. Smart policies serve as a guiding framework that provides strategic direction and incentives for the adoption of technologies and practices across various sectors [6]. These policies have become increasingly important in shaping the development of high-tech SMEs in less-developed areas [9]. Italy has experienced an increasing impact of smart policies on the evolutionary trajectory of high-tech SMEs and business location dynamics [10, 11]. The implementation of these policies offers an opportunity to leverage technology and innovation to drive economic growth [10], promote entrepreneurship [4, 12] and enhance the competitiveness of local areas [6, 13].

This paper contributes to the ongoing debate on the importance of high-tech SMEs, smart policies and regional environment [8, 12, 13] in shaping the localization and the growth of high-tech SMEs [9, 14]. By examining empirical evidence from Italy, we aim to explore the mechanisms by which smart policies shaping the spatial distribution of high-tech SMEs in Italian regions, thereby contributing to a better understanding of the dynamics of local development and its impact on regional economic growth, providing valuable insights for policymakers, entrepreneurs and stakeholders involved in fostering the growth of high-tech industries in these contexts.

The paper is structured as follows: Section 2 provides an overview of the importance of smart policies for high-tech SMEs in local environment. Section 3 outlines the research design and methodology used to gather and analyze data on the localization of high-tech SMEs in Italy. This section presents the empirical evidence on the localization of high-tech SMEs in different regions of Italy and explores how policies foster high-tech SMEs in different regional environment. Finally, Sect. 4 provides a discussion of the implications of the findings for policymakers and practitioners.

2 Theoretical Framework

2.1 The Institutional Theory

The theoretical link between the entrepreneurial activity and the contexts' features can be observed employing the Institutional theory [15], that examines how the environment affects the firm's structures and processes [16, 17]. Institutions are social structures <<composed of cultural-cognitive, normative, and regulative elements that, together with associated activities and resources, provide stability and meaning to social life>> [17].

A favorable institutional context fosters firms' innovation, internationalization, and competitiveness, especially in middle- and low-income countries [8, 11]. Additionally, some scholars show that the ICT development rate, the presence of venture capitals, the intense university-industry partnerships [18] and the presence of good human capital [12] are strong institutional drivers that influence the quality of entrepreneurial activity in a country. Many studies confirmed the positive role of normative, cognitive and regulatory aspects of institution in promoting entrepreneurship and innovation, especially at country-level [19, 20]. Conversely, few studies explore the relationships between the supportive or conducive aspects and the entrepreneurial activity of SMEs at local-level [2, 19]. The supportive or conductive aspect refers to the presence of qualified human capital, sophisticated infrastructures, such as ICT, dedicated financial resources, good universities with intense R&D activities, high-level of digital investments. These factors impact on innovation, affecting the formation and the attraction of high-tech ventures [12, 13]. Few scholars explored these impacts at regional-level or urban-level [21, 22] and they found positive association between the entrepreneurial innovation and these pillars: university-industry collaborations, investments in ICT, presence of dynamic entrepreneurial context and dynamic capital markets, human capital very skilled.

2.2 *High-Tech SMEs and Regional Environment*

The focus on the local environment, in innovation and entrepreneurship studies, has attracted increasing attention from scholars and policymakers, according to the rise of smart cities. Scholars and academics have identified regional environment as large markets [23] or as knowledge hubs [12, 13].

According to Marsal-llacuna [7], regional environment aim to achieve these goals by integrating ICT into various urban domains noting that smart initiatives typically rely on data, information, and IT to provide efficient services to citizens, monitor and optimize infrastructure, foster collaboration among stakeholders, and encourage innovation in both the public and private sectors.

On the edge of competitiveness and innovation, several studies have highlighted the importance of SMEs, including high-tech ones, in affecting the economic growth and job creation [8, 10]. These firms represent a fundamental component of the national and local innovation environment [8, 23], playing a critical role in the development and adoption of new technologies and business models [24]. In particular, SMEs are recognized for their ability to quickly adapt to changing market conditions [24], foster entrepreneurship [4] and local human capital [13, 25] and to promote social and environmental sustainability [26].

On the hand, digital start-ups and high-tech SMEs are the key factors in local and national development [5, 8, 10, 12]. Del Monte [27] conducted a study of Italian regions and showed that high tech firms and innovation are important drivers to foster the growth of local environment. The Italian regions with a higher level of SMEs and innovation grow faster than other regions. For this reason, some scholars argue that high-tech SMEs play an important role in in amplifying the positive effects of innovation on urban development [27–29], thereby enabling the implementation of smart strategies in different areas.

On the other hand, high-tech SMEs can benefit greatly from the regional's conducive factors, especially within smart areas, as it offers to innovative firms access to new sources of data, knowledge, and networking opportunities [22]. As noted by Kummitha [4], regional environment provides SMEs with the necessary infrastructure, resources, and support to develop and test their innovative solutions, and to scale them up to wider markets. This can lead to greater competitiveness and growth opportunities for SMEs [8], as well as better outcomes for citizens. Moreover, SMEs can leverage their proximity to other firms, research institutions, and knowledge-intensive organizations in the local environment to access valuable information and resources that can facilitate open innovation [27, 30, 31] and technology entrepreneurship [8, 18, 22]. This can help to build a innovation and economic growth with positive social and environmental outcomes for urban and regional areas and their citizens [23]. Therefore, it is crucial for smart policies and strategies to support the growth and development of high-tech SMEs, as they are key to developing the regional environment.

2.3 Smart Policies and High-Tech SMEs in the Regional Environment Context

Smart policies play a crucial role in shaping and guiding the local development. These policies aim to create an enabling environment that fosters innovation, collaboration, and sustainability. For example, the smart city is the innovative urban strategy that differs from other urban policies fort the pivotal role of innovation and technology [7]. A city is smart <<when investments in human and social capital and traditional and modern communication infrastructure fuel sustainable economic growth and a high quality of life, with a wise management of natural resources, through participatory governance>> [7, 32].

Vanolo [10] emphasizes that smart policies are instrumental in implementing and regulating the integration of ICT and data technologies within the local environment between the SMEs embedded within this setting. Smart policies can contribute to local competitiveness through innovation, fostering collaboration between businesses, academic institutions, and knowledge dissemination, providing several conducive factors [23]. Additionally, smart policies can enhance local services and infrastructure efficiency [10], attracting high-tech SMEs seeking supportive growth environments [4, 18, 33]. Moreover, these policies enable the competitiveness of local SMEs by improving their access to resources and markets [6, 34]. For these reasons, smart policies significantly influence location choices for high-tech SMEs [9, 35]. Furthermore, regional actions, such as grants for high-tech SMEs in development areas, have shown positive effects on business growth. Wu et al. (2019) demonstrated the positive impact of smart local environment schemes on high-tech company localization in the Pearl River Delta region of China [9]. Institutional factors, such as local entrepreneurship and innovation rate, knowledge networks, smart policies, resource availability, and awareness, also influence the entrepreneurial initiatives [14].

Despite the growing academic interest in the topic, smart policies are reshaping the dynamics of regional environment [6], including their economic growth, through the gradual localization of high-tech SMEs in specific territories [36]. However, the extent and clear evidence of the reconfiguration of high-tech SMEs' localization in response to smart policies remain unclear. Assuming the institutional theory, this study posits that these conductive aspects, such as the smart policies, affect the attraction of high-tech SMEs, contributing to the innovation at regional environment level, as follows:

Hp1 Smart policies support the formation and attraction of high-tech SMEs in regional environment

3 Methodology

3.1 Data Sample and Data Collection

This analysis is conducted using descriptive analysis, t-test, and Mann–Whitney U test to verify our hypotheses. Our sample consists of 250 high-tech SMEs located in the Italian territory selected from the "startup.registroimprese[1]" over 8 years ranging from 2013 to 2020. To guarantee the academic rigour, the analysis is based on the definition established by the EU (European Commission, 2003): small and medium enterprises are all firms that have less or equal than 250 employees and the turnover was less or equal than 50,000,000 € [37].

Figure 1 illustrates the geographical distribution of our sample considered across the country and highlights its size. The sample obtained displays a considerable degree of heterogeneity in terms of size and economic development. Notably, the northern part of the country demonstrates a higher level of heterogeneity compared to the southern part. The selection of those high-tech SMEs in Italy is due to a threefold motivation. First, the heterogeneity of the sample emerging by the

[1] the "startup.registroimprese" is the official Chambre of Commerce's database which contains all Italian high-tech SMEs registered in the specific special section of the business register as provided by Law 221/2012 and 33/2015.

Fig. 1 Geo-visualization of the sample of analysis

probability-proportional-to-size-sampling [38], representing the reference context, is characterized by enterprises located in North, Centre and South, medium-sized and large regions and less and well-developed according to the territorial identity considered in NUTS 2 of European Union policies (EU) and provided by European Commission in the plan for the "Cohesion Policy 2021–2027" project.[2] In the breakdown, less-developed are regions with GDP per capita below 75% of the EU average, regions in transition have GDP per capita between 75% and 90% and well-developed regions have a GDP per capita more than 90% of the EU average. We merged less developed and transition regions in our sample to oppose them to

[2] https://commission.europa.eu/funding-tenders/find-funding/funding-management-mode/2014-2020-european-structural-and-investment-funds_it

the developed ones and to highlight the different economic development between them, and we called the two sides "Less developed regions" and "Well developed regions". Second, the Italian context is a relevant test case with strong evidence of SMEs as these companies are an important and representative component of the business structure of the Country [39, 40] and are located throughout the Country. According to the European Commission, SMEs in Italy represent the basis of the economic system and are key to national and local development.[3] Third, a high level of high-tech SMEs creation significantly contributes to regional economic vitality and is a major sign of dynamic economy [8, 12]. Furthermore, observing SMEs embedded in specific regional environment is important because regional differences can influence the localization and the development of these firms [28, 41]. This level of observation is important to understand the challenges and opportunities in Italian entrepreneurial system for the digital transformation of firms.

The sample is highly significant in terms of contributing to the academic debate [26, 33, 40, 42].

3.2 Variables

The number of high-tech SMEs is our dependent variable called "High-tech SMEs" and represents the total number of innovative SMEs per Italian regions. It is a continuous variable measured by the logarithm of innovative SMEs in each region to the total number of firms in the respective region per year. This variable is usually used to assess the localization of SMEs for each region in the local context [31, 43, 44]. Firms in the region represent a measure of the attractiveness of local environment and a proxy of the regional development [45].

Our model includes four independent variables which represent the institutional smart policy investment at regional level for Innovation, R&D, firms' competitiveness, and the Digitalization. This institutional smart policies perspective is usually consistent with the notion that the access to tangible and intangible resources from both government and private individuals is a crucial enabler of entrepreneurial activity and to the firms' localization in one regional environment than others [6, 34], that permit us to examine the distribution of smart policies across the territory and how these policies drives the localization of high-tech SMEs [6, 10, 21].

The regional-level data to analyse institutional R&D investment was collected by the Italian National Institute of Statistics (ISTAT) and investment in Innovation, Digital, and firm's Competitiveness at regional level were collected data by Italian Government website in a special registered called "Opencoesione" which provide data on all implemented smart policies sorted by region and theme.[4] The data from

[3] European Commission, "European regional innovation scoreboard 2022 - Italy," 2021.

[4] https://opencoesione.gov.it/it/risorse_2014_2020/

Table 1 Description and operationalization of the variable

Variable	Description and measures
High-tech SMEs	High-tech SMEs per Italian regions measured as log to total firms in each region.
R&D	Supporting industrial research and development projects with universities and research centers, and strengthening research facilities and laboratories, standardized on GDP per capita.
Innovation services	Investment in innovation: support for innovative projects, technology transfer (districts/clusters), advanced innovation services for companies, standardized on GDP per capita.
Firms' competitiveness	Financial instruments, like guarantee funds and venture capital funds, support new and existing businesses. Other measures include program contracts for large enterprises and Integrated Facilitation Packages, standardized on GDP per capita.
Digital investments	The theme includes actions to improve infrastructure, connectivity, and services related to new technologies for citizens and businesses. It also covers initiatives for multimedia education, e-government, e-health, and e-inclusion services, standardized on GDP per capita.

Sources: startup.registroimprese.it; ISTAT (Italian National Institute of Statistics); Opencoesione.gov

this registry accurately analyse how regions allocated resources and promoted initiatives in the key areas of our study.

Table 1 reports all the description of the variables used to construct our analysis.

3.3 Results

This section discusses the results of exploration of regional-environment's smart policies in less and well-developed area and the localization of high-tech SMEs in the context of local disparities. Results are presented as follows.

Table 2 shows the descriptive analysis of variables and t-test of smart policies for R&D, innovation, firms' competitiveness, and digital investments for both less and well-developed areas. These factors are the conducive aspects of regional environment. The results suggest an overall positive role of adopting these smart policies in less developed areas, confirming the hypotheses of the study (Hp1). R&D investment and the total number of high-tech SMEs provide a more nuanced picture. If the contextual conditions within each regions are still crucial in guiding environment towards engaging in challenging policy agendas, the results suggest that less developed areas implement policies more in terms of high-tech innovation. Mean differences are statistically significant at least at the 95% level for all smart policies output measures. Interestingly, while the mean differences are quite substantial for the variables Innovation (less vs. well mean = 0.416), Competitiveness (less vs. well mean = 0.928) and Digital (less vs. well mean = 0.195), the opposite happens for the

Table 2 Descriptive and t-test

Variable	Obs	Mean	Std. Dev.	95% Conf. Interval		*p*-value
High-tech SMEs						
Total sample	1.814	2.059	1.319	19.990	21.205	
Less developed regions	674	1.357	1.012	12.793	14.356	
Well-developed regions	1.167	2.449	1.309	23.739	25.243	
Less vs. well	–	−1.091	−0.297	−11.999	−0.983	0.000***
R&D						
Total sample	2008	14.005	1.068	13.958	14.052	
Less developed regions	768	13.021	0.752	12.967	13.074	
Well-developed regions	1.24	14.615	0.726	14.574	14.655	
Less vs. well	–	−1.594	0.026	−16.611	−15.273	0.000***
Innovation services						
Total sample	1757	19.500	0.912	19.458	19.543	
Less developed regions	672	19.758	1.140	19.671	19.844	
Well-developed regions	1085	19.341	0.691	19.300	19.382	
Less vs. well	–	0.416	0.448	0.321	0.512	0.000***
Firms' competitiveness						
Total sample	1757	19.813	1.001	19.767	19.860	
Less developed regions	672	20.387	1.087	20.305	20.469	
Well-developed regions	1085	19.458	0.750	19.413	19.503	
Less vs. well	–	0.928	0.337	0.835	1.022	0.000***
Digital investments						
Total sample	1757	19.352	0.713	19.318	19.385	
Less developed regions	672	19.472	0.857	19.407	19.537	
Well-developed regions	1085	19.277	0.596	19.241	19.312	
Less vs. well	–	0.195	0.260	0.121	0.269	0.000***

Legenda: $*p < 0.05$; $**p < 0.01$; $***p < 0.001$

Table 3 Percentage mean differences less vs. well-developed urban areas

	Before SCP	From SCP	Delta
Less developed areas	33%	72%	**39%**
Well developed areas	47%	56%	**9%**

R&D investment variable (minus vs. average good = −1.594). In the latter case R&D investment is high in well-developed environment.

Clearly, there is still on average a localization of small and medium-sized high-tech enterprises in the most developed territories (well-developed mean = 2.449) but as can be seen from Table 3, increasing of high-tech SMEs after smart policies implementation is changing in Italy in favor of the territories that today are less developed. As we can see less-developed regional areas have a higher increase of high-tech SMEs after the incrementation of smart policies than well-developed ones.

Table 4 U-test

Two-sample Wilcoxon rank-sum (Mann-Whitney) test			
Year_group	Obs	Rank sum	Expected
Before smart policies (1)	160	71,762.5	51,600
From smart policies (2)	484	135,927.5	156,090
Total	644	207,690	207,690
Unadjusted variance	4,162,400.00		
Adjustment for ties	−91,115.69		

	4,071,284.31		
Ho: High-tech SMEs(year group==1) = High-tech SMEs (year group==2)			
z = 9.993			
Prob > |z| = 0.0000			

Indeed, these variables alone do not explain the totality of smart policies' investments since only business services investment has been taken into consideration, so we have considered the context variables, in order to operationalize the variables and provide a more comprehensive framework for the increasing growth of environments previously considered more underdeveloped than other areas commonly recognized as developed. This set of variables has been outlined in Tables 5 and 6 and they represent other conducive aspects of local environments that affect the smart policies.

This result is in line with the academic debate [9, 46], which implies that investing in smart policies may trigger innovative processes well beyond the relatively limited scope of the technologies directly involved in those policies and suggests that le smart policies drives the localization of high-tech SMEs.

To analyze the impact of smart policies in only less-developed regional areas we used the Two-sample Wilcoxon rank-sum (Mann-Whitney) test (Table 4) common used in the academic field [47, 48]. It is a non-parametric used to compare two independent sample when the distribution of the data may not be normal or when the assumptions of the t-test cannot be met and tests the null hypothesis that the two groups come from the same population.

This test compares the high-tech SMEs scores localized in less developed context between two groups, "Before smart policies" and "From smart policies", with 160 and 484 observations, respectively, and a total of 644 observations. The rank sum of the "Before smart policies" group was 71,762.5, and the rank sum of the "From smart policies" group was 135,927.5, with an expected rank sum of 51,600 and 156,090, respectively. The unadjusted variance was 4,162,400, and the adjustment for ties was −91,115.69, resulting in a total variance of 4,071,284.31. The null hypothesis, Ho: High-tech SMEs(year_group==1) = High-tech SMEs (year_group==2), was tested, resulting in a z-score of 9.993 and a two-tailed *p*-value of 0.0000, indicating a significant score between the two groups. This suggests that high-tech SMEs underwent a significant change from smart policies implementation.

This highlights how the context in which a new company settles depends on many factors, such as investments in innovation, digital networks that allow companies to work at their best, but it is also dictated by other factors such as the livability of the environment and the context, investments in education and employment as well as in administration and transportation, primary requirements for the establishment of small and medium-sized enterprises and their employees.

4 Discussion and Conclusion

The present study attempted to explore whether the conducive aspects of institution can affect the innovation and the entrepreneurial vivacity in the context. Specifically, this study has empirically verified whether the adoption of smart policies by regional environment (less or well-developed) would stimulate high-tech SMEs to locate themselves in one area than others. We are aware that smart policies, as specific conducive factors, favor local economic performance and growth the impact of regional innovation [6, 10]. In line with this finding, our results also suggest that if, on the one hand, the territories that are more developed have a good share of high-tech SMEs, we are witnessing a gradual migration of these high-tech SMEs to the territories less developed where, at the same time there is more investment in smart policies that stimulate innovation. These increase the stock of resources of regional areas and represent one of the main recognized drivers of economic growth [4, 7, 8, 12, 23]. On the other hands, the academic debate shows that high-tech SMEs play a key role in local environments' growth [8, 13]. This finding contributes to the institutional theory, suggesting that the interpretation of the relationship between innovative entrepreneurship and institutions needs to balance the *institutional logic* with the *institutional work perspective*, considering the transformative role of agents within the innovative ecosystems.

Our research offers several implications for both policymakers and firms. On one hand, policymakers should focus on creating comprehensive policy systems that promote the integration of advanced technologies, data-driven solutions and education. These policies should provide incentives and support mechanisms to attract and nurture high-tech SMEs in regional areas. On the other hand, for high-tech SMEs, it is of paramount importance to locate themselves in environments that invest in innovation development, as these SMEs struggle to grow without access to resources. This localization in developed areas that prioritize innovation and competitiveness can compensate for the limited resources of the enterprise in this regard. High-tech SMEs can benefit from these implications by creating growth opportunities, accessing resources and talent, collaborating with other organizations, expanding their market, and adopting sustainable practices. Maximizing the benefits of smart policies requires high-tech SMEs to adapt to the dynamics of the intelligent local environment and capitalize on the opportunities offered by such a context. Moreover, these results can be seen as a first step in clarifying the channels through which investing in policy initiatives based on the regional environment model can have a positive impact on regional localization of high-tech SMEs. In line with the academic debate, the firms are the main innovative actors [8], and innovative and entrepreneurial activity can and does take place in small and medium size cities, in suburbs even in rural areas [44]. From the other hand, attracting many high-tech SMEs can diversify the territorial context, industry, and entrepreneurial culture in the regional environment. Therefore, considering the relevance of high-tech SMEs for the Italian economy and the innovation [12, 13, 49], smart policy strategy needs to be developed engaging these innovative agents, often considered user and not driver of digitalization and innovation policies.

In conclusion, regional environment and smart policies can have a significant impact on high-tech SMEs and other way round. By providing a supportive context for entrepreneurship and innovation, regional environment can attract and retain high-tech SMEs that can contribute to the economic growth and development of the territories. It is important for smart cities planners and policymakers to ensure the efficacy of these policies.

Due to the quantitative nature of the analysis, and the complexity of the phenomenon of high-tech SMEs in local environment, this research presents intrinsic limitations related to the sample and variables used in the analysis, which open up opportunities for future investigations. The first limitation in conducting the research is the sample for analysis. Although it represents the development in the Italian and European contexts in terms of characteristics and structure, we focus on a single country. Future research could extend this sample to other countries with different policies, development plans, and social cultures to evaluate the impact of these results in various directions and balancing institutional logic [50] with institutional work perspective [51]. Although the regional context can be outlined, and a descriptive analysis of the various smart policies has been made, it should be investigated whether there is a relationship between SMEs, the nature and the degree of their innovation and the nature of smart policies in the local context. In addition, future research could consider alternative methodologies that could be explored to determine the causality of smart policies affecting high-tech SMEs, offering a different perspective on the influence of smart policies on high-tech SMEs and provide valuable insights for policymakers and scholars.

Appendix

Table 5 Contextual variables

Variable	Obs	Mean	Std. Dev.	95% Conf. Interval		*p*-value
Energy investment						
Total sample	1757	18.579	0.781	18.543	18.616	
Less developed regions	672	19.022	1.032	18.944	19.101	
Well-developed regions	1085	18.305	0.363	18.283	18.326	
Less vs. well	–	0.717	0.669	0.636	0.798	0.000***
Environment investment						
Total sample	1757	19.819	1.097	19.767	19.870	
Less developed regions	672	20.632	1.261	20.537	20.728	
Well-developed regions	1085	19.315	0.548	19.282	19.348	
Less vs. well	–	1.317	0.712	1.216	1.417	0.000***
Work investment						
Total sample	1757	19.707	0.622	19.678	19.736	
Less developed regions	672	19.471	0.759	19.414	19.529	
Well-developed regions	1085	19.853	0.463	19.826	19.881	
Less vs. well	–	−0.382	0.296	−0.445	−0.318	0.000***
Education investment						
Total sample	1757	19.855	0.786	19.818	19.892	
Less developed regions	672	19.870	1.042	19.791	19.949	
Well-developed regions	1085	19.846	0.574	19.811	19.880	
Less vs. well	–	0.024	0.468	−0.061	0.110	0.000***
Administration investment						
Total sample	1757	18.545	0.828	18.506	18.584	
Less developed regions	672	18.705	1.033	18.627	18.784	
Well-developed regions	1085	18.446	0.651	18.407	18.484	
Less vs. well	–	0.259	0.382	0.172	0.347	0.000***
Transport investment						
Total sample	1757	20.661	1.243	20.603	20.719	
Less developed regions	672	21.473	1.500	21.360	21.587	
Well-developed regions	1085	20.158	0.670	20.118	20.198	
Less vs. well	–	1.315	0.830	1.194	1.435	0.000***
Cultural investment						
Total sample	1757	18.861	1.173	18.80	18.916	
Less developed regions	672	19.471	1.169	19.382	19.559	
Well-developed regions	1085	18.484	1.00	18.424	18.544	
Less vs. well	–	0.986	0.163	0.879	1.093	0.000***
Social investment						
Total sample	1757	19.891	0.955	19.846	19.936	
Less developed regions	672	20.071	1.199	19.980	20.161	
Well-developed regions	1085	19.780	0.746	19.735	19.824	
Less vs. well	–	0.290	0.452	0.189	0.391	0.000***

Legenda: $*p < 0.05$; $**p < 0.01$; $***p < 0.001$

Table 6 Description of contextual variables

Variable	Description
Energy investment	The funded interventions involve building renewable energy plants, promoting energy efficiency in both the public and private sectors, developing cogeneration and trigeneration systems, and promoting tele-heating and tele-cooling
Environment investment	Interventions cover wastewater, waste management, and risk prevention measures such as defending residential areas and promoting biodiversity
Work investment	The theme covers labor market measures, lifelong learning in companies, and support for self-employment. It also includes measures to improve access to employment, increase women's participation, and reconcile work and private life
Education investment	The theme involves interventions to promote academic success and social inclusion, improve students' learning outcomes, and provide support to school personnel. It also includes adult education programs to prevent school dropout
Administration investment	The theme includes projects for public safety infrastructure and strengthening institutional capacities, improving policy and program development, statistical production, and technical assistance. It also involves evaluations, studies, communication, and information activities
Transport investment	The theme focuses on improving transportation infrastructure, including railway lines, road networks, and port connections, as well as promoting sustainable mobility and public transport in urban areas
Cultural investment	The theme focuses on preserving cultural heritage and promoting tourism through infrastructure interventions and service improvements
Social investment	Social inclusion interventions (job integration, social and healthcare infrastructure investments, housing policies, elderly care, active inclusion, and participation) are part of this theme to promote equal opportunities and improve the quality of life of disadvantaged groups

Sources: Opencoesione.gov
Note: All the variables in table are standardized on GDP per capita

References

1. Acs, Z. J., Estrin, S., Mickiewicz, T., & Szerb, L. (2018). Entrepreneurship, institutional economics, and economic growth: An ecosystem perspective. *Small Business Economics, 51*(2), 501–514. https://doi.org/10.1007/s11187-018-0013-9
2. Arabiyat, T. S., Mdanat, M., Haffar, M., Ghoneim, A., & Arabiyat, O. (2019). The influence of institutional and conductive aspects on entrepreneurial innovation: Evidence from GEM data. *Journal of Enterprise Information Management, 32*(3), 366–389. https://doi.org/10.1108/JEIM-07-2018-0165
3. Ge, J., Sun, H., & Chen, Y. (2020). Technology entrepreneurship of large state-owned firms in emerging economies. *Journal of Global Information Management, 28*(4), 120–134. https://doi.org/10.4018/JGIM.2020100107
4. Kummitha, R. K. R. (2019). Smart cities and entrepreneurship: An agenda for future research. *Technological Forecasting and Social Change, 149*, 119763. https://doi.org/10.1016/j.techfore.2019.119763.

5. Llach, J., Marquegrave, P., Bikfalvi, A., Simon, A., & Kraus, S. (2012). The innovativeness of family firms through the economic cycle. *Journal of Family Business Management, 2*(2), 96–109. https://doi.org/10.1108/20436231211261853
6. Caragliu, A., & Del Bo, C. F. (2019). Smart innovative cities: The impact of Smart City policies on urban innovation. *Technological Forecasting and Social Change, 142*, 373–383. https://doi.org/10.1016/j.techfore.2018.07.022
7. Marsal-llacuna, M., Colomer-llinàs, J., & Meléndez-frigola, J. (2015). Technological forecasting & social change lessons in urban monitoring taken from sustainable and livable cities to better address the Smart Cities initiative. *Technological Forecasting and Social Change, 90*, 611–622. https://doi.org/10.1016/j.techfore.2014.01.012
8. Adler, P., Florida, R., King, K., & Mellander, C. (2019). The city and high-tech startups: The spatial organization of Schumpeterian entrepreneurship. *Cities, 87*, 121–130. https://doi.org/10.1016/j.cities.2018.12.013
9. Wu, K., Wang, Y., Ye, Y., Zhang, H., & Huang, G. (2019). Relationship between the built environment and the location choice of high-tech firms: Evidence from the Pearl River Delta. *Sustainability*.
10. Vanolo, A. (2014). Smartmentality: The Smart City as disciplinary strategy. *Urban Studies, 51*(5), 883–898. https://doi.org/10.1177/0042098013494427
11. Abid, N., Marchesani, F., Ceci, F., & Masciarelli, F. (2023). Assessing capabilities to embrace digital transformation: The case of southern Italy. *Lecture Notes in Information Systems and Organisation, 59*, 169–182. https://doi.org/10.1007/978-3-031-15770-7_11
12. Marchesani, F., Masciarelli, F., & Bikfalvi, A. (2023). Smart city as a hub for talent and innovative companies: Exploring the (dis) advantages of digital technology implementation in cities. *Technological Forecasting and Social Change, 193*, 122636. https://doi.org/10.1016/j.techfore.2023.122636
13. Marchesani, F., Masciarelli, F., & Doan, H. Q. (2022). Innovation in cities a driving force for knowledge flows: Exploring the relationship between high-tech firms, student mobility, and the role of youth entrepreneurship. *Cities, 130*, 103852. https://doi.org/10.1016/j.cities.2022.103852
14. Sunny, S. A., & Shu, C. (2019). Investments, incentives, and innovation: Geographical clustering dynamics as drivers of sustainable entrepreneurship. *Small Business Economics, 52*(4), 905–927. https://doi.org/10.1007/s11187-017-9941-z
15. Abreu, M., Demirel, P., Grinevich, V., & Karataş-Özkan, M. (2016). Entrepreneurial practices in research-intensive and teaching-led universities. *Small Business Economics, 47*(3), 695–717. https://doi.org/10.1007/s11187-016-9754-5
16. DiMaggio, P. J., & Powell, W. W. (1983). *The Iron Cage Revisited Institutional Isomorphism and Collective Rationality, 47*(2), 147.
17. W. R. Scott, Institutions and organizations. 1995.
18. Kummitha, R. K. R. (2018). Entrepreneurial urbanism and technological panacea: Why Smart City planning needs to go beyond corporate visioning ? *Technological Forecasting and Social Change*, 0, 330–1. https://doi.org/10.1016/j.techfore.2018.07.010
19. Stenholm, P., Acs, Z. J., & Wuebker, R. (2013). Exploring country-level institutional arrangements on the rate and type of entrepreneurial activity. *Journal of Business Venturing, 28*(1), 176–193. https://doi.org/10.1016/j.jbusvent.2011.11.002
20. Urbano, D., & Alvarez, C. (2014). Institutional dimensions and entrepreneurial activity: An international study. *Small Business Economics, 42*(4), 703–716. https://doi.org/10.1007/s11187-013-9523-7
21. Audretsch, D. B., & Lehmann, E. E. (2005). Does the knowledge spillover theory of entrepreneurship hold for regions? *Research Policy, 34*(8), 1191–1202. https://doi.org/10.1016/j.respol.2005.03.012
22. Audretsch, D., Colombelli, A., Grilli, L., Minola, T., & Rasmussen, E. (2020). Innovative start-ups and policy initiatives. *Research Policy, 49*(10), 104027. https://doi.org/10.1016/j.respol.2020.104027

23. Caragliu, A., & Del Bo, C. F. (2018). Smart innovative cities: The impact of Smart City policies on urban innovation. *Technological Forecasting and Social Change*, 1–11. https://doi.org/10.1016/j.techfore.2018.07.022
24. Troise, C., Corvello, V., Ghobadian, A., & O'Regan, N. (2022). How can SMEs successfully navigate VUCA environment: The role of agility in the digital transformation era. *Technological Forecasting and Social Change, 174*, 121227. https://doi.org/10.1016/j.techfore.2021.121227
25. Zhang, F., & Zhu, L. (2021). Social media strategic capability, organizational unlearning, and disruptive innovation of SMEs: The moderating roles of TMT heterogeneity and environmental dynamism. *Journal of Business Research, 133*, 183–193. https://doi.org/10.1016/j.jbusres.2021.04.071
26. Denicolai, S., Zucchella, A., & Magnani, G. (2021). Internationalization, digitalization, and sustainability: Are SMEs ready? A survey on synergies and substituting effects among growth paths. *Technological Forecasting and Social Change, 166*, 120650. https://doi.org/10.1016/j.techfore.2021.120650
27. Del Monte, A., Moccia, S., & Pennacchio, L. (2022). Regional entrepreneurship and innovation: Historical roots and the impact on the growth of regions. *Small Business Economics, 58*(1), 451–473. https://doi.org/10.1007/s11187-020-00425-w
28. Del Monte, A., & Pennacchio, L. (2020). Historical roots of regional entrepreneurship: The role of knowledge and creativity. *Small Business Economics, 55*(1), 1–22. https://doi.org/10.1007/s11187-019-00139-8
29. Del Monte, A., & DeLuzenberger, R. (1989). The effect of regional policy on new firm formation in southern Italy. *Regional Studies, 23*(3), 219–230. https://doi.org/10.1080/00343408912331345432
30. Doh, S., & Kim, B. (2014). Government support for SME innovations in the regional industries: The case of government financial support program in South Korea. *Research Policy, 43*(9), 1557–1569. https://doi.org/10.1016/j.respol.2014.05.001
31. D'Angelo, A. (2012). Innovation and export performance: A study of Italian high-tech SMEs. *Journal of Management and Governance, 16*(3), 393–423. https://doi.org/10.1007/s10997-010-9157-y
32. Caragliu, A., del Bo, C., & Nijkamp, P. (2011). Smart cities in Europe. *Journal of Urban Technology, 18*(2), 65–82. https://doi.org/10.1080/10630732.2011.601117
33. Ardito, L., Raby, S., Albino, V., & Bertoldi, B. (2021). The duality of digital and environmental orientations in the context of SMEs: Implications for innovation performance. *Journal of Business Research, 123*, 44–56. https://doi.org/10.1016/j.jbusres.2020.09.022
34. Caragliu, A., & Del Bo, C. F. (2016). Do Smart Cities invest in smarter policies? Learning from the past, planning for the future. *Social Science Computer Review, 34*(6), 657–672. https://doi.org/10.1177/0894439315610843
35. Wu, A., Song, D., & Liu, Y. (2022). Platform synergy and innovation speed of SMEs: The roles of organizational design and regional environment. *Journal of Business Research, 149*, 38–53. https://doi.org/10.1016/j.jbusres.2022.05.016
36. Yang, J. S. (2017). The governance environment and innovative SMEs. *Small Business Economics, 48*(3), 525–541. https://doi.org/10.1007/s11187-016-9802-1
37. N.S.S. (1904). 'Commission". *Notes Queries, s10-I*(5), 88. https://doi.org/10.1093/nq/s10-I.5.88-c
38. Levy, P. S., & Lemeshow, S. (2013). *Sampling of populations: Methods and applications*. Wiley.
39. Cassetta, E., Monarca, U., Dileo, I., Di Berardino, C., & Pini, M. (2020). The relationship between digital technologies and internationalisation. Evidence from Italian SMEs. *Industry and Innovation, 27*(4), 311–339. https://doi.org/10.1080/13662716.2019.1696182
40. Scuotto, V., Santoro, G., Bresciani, S., & Del Giudice, M. (2017). Shifting intra- and inter-organizational innovation processes towards digital business: An empirical analysis of SMEs. *Creativity and Innovation Management, 26*(3), 247–255. https://doi.org/10.1111/caim.12221

41. Leonelli, S., Marchesani, F., & Masciarelli, F. (2022). Risk or opportunity? Exploring the relationship between entrepreneurial decision and the use of equity crowdfunding campaigns in less- and well-developed regions in Italy. *Contributions to Management Science*, 99–114. https://doi.org/10.1007/978-3-030-85950-3_6
42. Zoppelletto, A., Orlandi, L. B., Zardini, A., Rossignoli, C., & Kraus, S. (2023). Organizational roles in the context of digital transformation: A micro-level perspective. *Journal of Business Research, 157*, 113563. https://doi.org/10.1016/j.jbusres.2022.113563
43. Xu, J., & Li, J. (2019). The impact of intellectual capital on SMEs' performance in China: Empirical evidence from non-high-tech vs. high-tech SMEs. *Journal of Intellectual Capital, 20*(4), 488–509. https://doi.org/10.1108/JIC-04-2018-0074
44. Hervás-Oliver, J. L., Parrilli, M. D., Rodríguez-Pose, A., & Sempere-Ripoll, F. (2021). The drivers of SME innovation in the regions of the EU. *Research Policy, 50*(9), 104316. https://doi.org/10.1016/j.respol.2021.104316
45. Sternberg, R., & Arndt, O. (2001). The firm or the region: What determines the innovation behavior of European firms? *Economic Geography, 77*(4), 364–382. https://doi.org/10.1111/j.1944-8287.2001.tb00170.x
46. Gagliardi, L., & Percoco, M. (2011). Regional disparities in Italy over the long run: The role of human capital and trade policy. *Région et Développement, no. 33*.
47. Dasgupta, R., & Roy, A. (2023). International Journal of Intercultural Relations Moderation impact of national culture on international firm's environmental, social, governance and financial performance. *International Journal of Intercultural Relations, 92*, p. 101749. https://doi.org/10.1016/j.ijintrel.2022.101749.
48. Paoloni, M., Tutino, M., Paoloni, N., & Santolamazza, V. (2023). Financing innovation in agri-food industries: An analysis of the Italian micro, small and medium enterprises. *British Food Journal, 125*(13), 183–204. https://doi.org/10.1108/BFJ-04-2022-0342
49. Calignano, G., & Hassink, R. (2016). Increasing innovativeness of SMEs in peripheral areas through international networks? The case of southern Italy. *The Region, 3*(1), 25–42. https://doi.org/10.18335/region.v3i1.93
50. Friedland, R., & Alford, R. R. (1991). *Bringing society Back in: Symbols, practices, and institutional contradictions*.
51. Lawrence, T., & Suddaby, R. (2006). Institutions and institutional work. In *Handbook of organization studies* (pp. 215–254, 2nd ed.). Sage.

Microfounding Urban Big Data Infrastructure Through Multiplex Networks

Edgardo Bucciarelli, Alessia Regnicoli, and Aurora Ascatigno

Abstract A distinguishing feature of complex adaptive systems is that they can be viewed and described within a multileveled framework, rather than through a narrowly quantitative perspective. This is particularly relevant in cases where competing approaches, hypotheses, and data are concerned with emergent properties and human behaviour. When considered within this framework, the complexity and ubiquitous nature of today's urban areas, along with the data science and information-based strategies that drive them, has now reached the point where an integrated analysis of urban big data infrastructure (UBDI) can be outlined. Nevertheless, although there is more data and information than ever, it would be appropriate to refine and validate further assumptions, conjectures, and models that we have relied on. The primary objective of this work is not to advance the science, but rather to gain insight into the dimensions that have emerged from the state-of-the-art literature on big data infrastructure in urban contexts. This includes an understanding of the methodological challenges that arise in this nascent field. A second, and more original, objective is to propose a pre-analytical microfoundation of UBDI. This is achieved by representing an adjacency tensor of multiplex networks. Based on the above, UBDI is conceptualised as a novel hybrid organisational form, designed through the adoption of a unified and holistic perspective that considers all the critical dimensions contributing to the development of urban big data infrastructure within contemporary cities. The main focus is on the role of individuals in the urban ecosystem, seen as a complex adaptive research framework.

E. Bucciarelli (✉)
University of Chieti-Pescara, Pescara, Italy
e-mail: edgardo.bucciarelli@unich.it

A. Regnicoli
Half Lab Research, Pescara, Italy
e-mail: alessia.regnicoli@half-labresearch.eu

A. Ascatigno
School of Advanced Studies, University of Chieti-Pescara, Chieti, Italy
e-mail: aurora.ascatigno@unich.it

A. M. Braccini et al. (eds.), *Digital (Eco) Systems and Societal Challenges*, Lecture Notes in Information Systems and Organisation 72,
https://doi.org/10.1007/978-3-031-75586-6_13

Keywords Multi-faced data infrastructure · Multiplexity · Tensor-based framework

1 Introduction

In accordance with [1], a defining feature of complex systems is that they can be viewed and described within a framework of multiple perspectives on topics of interest. This is mainly the case when several frames of reference exist, that is, coordinate systems used to define space and the relations of entities within it. When viewed within this framework, the ubiquitous nature of today's urban areas, along with the science of data and information that drives them, has now reached the point where high expectations of better understanding and workable, evidence-based knowledge for researchers, practitioners, and policymakers appear to be accounted for and explained. In addition to containing more data and information than ever before, several assumptions, models, and methodological approaches that have been relied on in the past could be called into question by digital change. As part of the emerging debate, there is an agreed consensus on urban areas and their ecologies as complex systems. Among urban areas, contemporary cities are all-around representations of societies and infrastructure, but also institutions and networks that continuously generate data streams according to discrete and continuous events and ways of measuring phenomena.

As a consequence of the current investment in digital infrastructure, cities are becoming more complex and accessible to the population. In this context, significant improvements have been made in developing infrastructure for urban big data management and applications [2]. Concurrently, numerous research findings support the idea that big data supports a groundbreaking paradigm in urban infrastructure studies [3–7]. Specifically, these studies aim to improve operational decision-making in city management and services by utilising new data sources and computing methods [3, 8–13]. Nevertheless, the academic literature widely acknowledges the weaknesses of big data in this arena. Despite this ongoing academic debate, several governments around the world have included it in their policy and regulatory agendas. In the context of urban infrastructural limitations (see also [14, 15]), city administrations still lack the fundamental computing and database resources to support big data analytics. Consequently, the opportunities that cities—and urban areas in general—would attain from implementing big data and data sciences for analytics highlight the role of cities in filling the critical gaps. First, they *facilitate information flows and mechanisms of learning and coordination by heterogeneous individuals* (Bettencourt, [16], p. 12), and second, they help recognise favourable patterns of interaction *among seemingly unrelated knowledge and transform such information into new knowledge—and diagnose and evaluate urban development via qualitative and quantitative analysis* (Pan et al., [17], p. 173). Indeed, the connection and vital influence between infrastructure, information and data is not a recent phenomenon; what's new is the transformation of data infrastructure processes: digital, more intense, faster, scalable, and automated [18]. Furthermore, planning urban big data infrastructure (hereafter, UBDI) fulfils a crucial function in everyday cities. Traffic planners, urban planners, and geographers, among other multi-stakeholders, can rely on it to assess urban infrastructure functioning through models of individual daily urban activities using urban big data [19].

Building on the above literature, this work is motivated by two considerations. On the one hand, the new digital era substantially differs from the old ones, promoting a renovated interest in urban informatics (see more on [20]). On the other hand, we might have reason to believe that UBDI may be defined as a newly evolved and intricate form of organisation. As we explain in Sect. 2, these forms of organisation are primarily based on hierarchical structures shaped by elements of market power [21]. Therefore, the fundamental challenge is to develop a unified framework for UBDI that goes beyond the technological domain by considering the fuzzy relationship between urban big data, their sources and users, and decision-making (among others, see [22]). In light of these considerations, the social and human aspects of UBDI should provide a flexible approach that emphasises active participation in the urban development process with system data users. For these reasons, our work departs from previous literature by comprehensively investigating urban big data infrastructure. Similarly, we stress that novel hybrid organisational forms, such as UBDI, should be studied by adopting a holistic perspective, including the relationship between urban actors and physical/digital urban infrastructure. All things considered, the aim of this work is twofold: To understand which dimensions emerge from the state-of-the-art UBDI literature and, accordingly, to develop a microfoundation of UBDI by defining an adjacency-tensor of multiplex networks, focusing on the pivotal role of people in this research field. The latter aim explicitly relies on the representation of UBDI through adjacency tensors. This representation allows us to capture the structure and complexity typical of the UBDI network and translate it into relationships between the nodes of a multiplex network [23]. In this vein, following [24], the separation of layers within the multiplex network allows for the coupling of dynamical processes across and within layers: These processes are not achievable via traditional network representations [25]. Our work is structured as follows: Section 2 comprises a systematic literature review focusing on the recursive dimensions of UBDI. Section 3 contains a methodological approach to the study of UBDI through an adjacency-tensor representation of multiplex networks. Section 4 discusses some crucial aspects of UBDI. The ultimate goal of conducting further research on UBDI from both computational and experimental standpoints has been deferred to the future.

2 Urban Big Data Infrastructure: A Systematic Literature Review

As we move into the latest digital era, changing socioeconomic dynamics and new theoretical framework implications have highlighted a growing need to understand terms like urban big data infrastructure and what they mean. And herein lies part of the cause of today's confusion around terms like UBDI, driven primarily by concepts of urban performance, which are based on physical infrastructure and the availability/quality of knowledge sharing in social infrastructure [26]. In addition, the conceptualisation of UBDI differs significantly due to stakeholders, business alliances, and research institutions approaching the issue from different points of view. Against this background, common points emerge, especially in those relating to studies on the infrastructure of smart cities. Indeed, by browsing the literature, the key research topics in this arena deal with the implementation of Internet of Things (IoT) technology [27, 28] and big data analytics [17]. Other authors [29, 30] discuss how revealing factual information can foster smart city development and urban sustainability on the whole. As a result, the deployment of Information and Communications Technology (ICT), for instance, involves not only technological developments but also investments in social change and urban human capital (see more on [31]). In line with the above, the impact of human capital enhances the livability of cities in co-building urban infrastructure [18, 32–37]. Thus, we have reason to believe that much of this literature identifies de facto the urban infrastructure as an ecosystem of combined dimensions, recalling the holistic idea expressed by [38], who points out that urban infrastructure is the *connective tissue that knits people, places, social institutions and natural environment into coherent urban relations* (Graham & Marvin, [38], p. 43). Yet nowadays, this idea persists, embedding big data within the logic of urban infrastructure. In this regard, indeed, we identify different pathways in the existing literature landscape, which is mainly divided between authors who highlight the new digital processes in urban infrastructure (see [17, 19]) and those who stress the role of people in developing urban infrastructure (see, [39, 40]).

To discuss this topic in-depth, [18] characterises the typical conception of urban infrastructure as rooted in local public services and shared resources, such as public transport, electricity, water, and soil. Instead, the current conceptualisation of urban infrastructure is undergoing variations and innovations: The city is starting to be understood as a network connected by cables, sensors, display units, and related instruments. Accordingly, the systems that manage the big data through the elements that form the network need to be understood as urban infrastructure, too [18]. Recently, [2] clarified on UBDI that *the nature of Urban infrastructure should be interpreted broadly, as encompassing not only data, but also the software needed to handle the data, the people who possess the requisite skills, and the decision-makers and general public who make use of the products of urban big data and may also contribute data through crowd-sourcing* (Goodchild, [2], p. 543). However, despite the growing coexistence of big data mining technologies [41] and some initial successes in using advanced technologies (e.g., cloud computing and artificial intelligence) [30] in urban infrastructure (for further insights, [42–49]), many future challenges remain concerning urban big data efficient implementations (see, [50–53]). Some of the most debated questions arise from the heterogeneous nature and requirements of urban big data (see more on [54]), which differ from the traditionally understood data (see [40, 55–62]), especially in urban infrastructure integration. Given these details, we should also consider the security and privacy issues regarding urban big data [63, 64], especially when defining data ownership, in which open big data are structured and produced by IT infrastructure [54, 65].

In general, the difficulties associated with the lack of open-access data and the limit in accessing and using data also lead to further complications concerning the various sources of urban big data. To date, however, these sources can be represented by the technologies and digital assets [19, 35, 39, 62] through which urban big data are generated by smartphones [66–69], computers, sensors, cameras, global positioning systems [70], social networking sites [71–74], commercial transactions, games, monitoring objects and intelligent parking systems, software [75], while they can be represented in a broader context that includes the users interacting with these technologies and digital assets [76]. Hence, various solutions have been presented to provide optimum categorisation of sources, such as [22] suggested grouping big data sources according to the type of data providers. Data providers can be private (e.g., citizens and companies), public (e.g., governments and municipalities), or voluntary, in which providers generate their own data as they act as sensors themselves [77]. Nonetheless, the way of grouping private and public data uses the same technologies to realise big data generation and storage (e.g., Wi-Fi access) [4]. An alternative solution is provided by [78, 79], in which the group of volunteers generates their data through the sensors they have available (e.g., social networks). However, even in this scenario, the so-called volunteers only sometimes hold their own generated data, which are occasionally open access [22]. For instance, it is worth mentioning the relationship between public and volunteer data sources. Some cities adopt a system of small government agencies formed by volunteers, which support local decision-makers. Along these lines, analysing big data would make it possible to predict the changes and implications from a socio-economic and sustainable perspective (for further insights, see [76, 80, 81]). Therefore, small government agencies formed by volunteers are a clear example of how different sources operate in the same field of interest: Urban public policies. In short, there seems to be wide heterogeneity in the way of grouping sources. We can understand how these groupings, under which to include the different sources, can be multiple, broader, and more specific. Despite such heterogeneity, the literature shows that many of them include the same elements, though a taxonomy that allows scholars to agree on a standardised conceptual basis has yet to be consolidated. The same occurs when analysing the specifications between sources and the types of people who generate and/or use urban big data. As [58] point out, there exists a difference between data users and producers. These two figures sometimes coincide, sometimes not. The previous grouping source examples do not distinguish between data users or producers: They include people as an integral part of their group. These open issues reflect a broader set of concerns regarding the above distinction and how users sometimes act as products [22]. On the other hand, the question persists: [52] explore the concept of users as prosumers. From this point of view, users can be understood, at the same time, as producers and consumers of data. Among others, [17] also provide some examples concerning user groups in correspondence of five urban big data types. In this manner, these grouping proposals are primarily informed by the user community typically associated with each data type [76] and more importantly, they are not mutually exclusive or standardised (see [22]). Overall, *[i]t is important to recognize that these groups of people [users] are active in multiple roles in the entire ecosystem of urban big data, including the phases of data generation, maintenance, storage, and usage* (Xiao & Miller, [22], p. 548, brackets added).

In conclusion, our review broadly highlights the findings of recent studies, showing that the current literature is still nascent in demystifying big data in urban infrastructure and sketching the legal, policy, and normative questions surrounding its use. Within this interpretation and following [30], we suggest similar conclusions due to the inconsistency related to the lack of a unified research framework, yielding to fragmented analytic methods [30]). In particular, these fragmented analytic methods shed light on some cases to group urban big data, urban infrastructure, their sources and the related users to systematise some elements found in the literature of this research field. Properly, the limits of these groupings also highlight how the complexity of the topic in question reflects the manipulability manifested in the diminishing demarcation between the user, the data, sources, and the infrastructure as mere technological and digital assets [18]. Although we have summarised recent studies on urban big data infrastructure and closely related studies, there are major question marks over the state-of-the-art directions of their applications and research in this field. First, considering what the literature tells us about UBDI, can we define them as novel hybrid organisational forms? At this stage, as briefly anticipated in Sect. 1, UBDI may be defined as novel organisational forms that can be classified as external and internal hybrids [21]. Their hybrid nature derives from the changes occurring in several bargaining situations that involve the public sector, the market, and society [82]. Furthermore, according to [83], in the urban infrastructure arena, big data discussions are mainly based on economic aspects rather than the simultaneous organisation of different existing sectors or services [83]. These discussions are reinforced by the contemporary urban transformation, which reflects the considerable impact of private companies on the eventual planning and implementation of UBDI within contemporary cities [82]. This brings us to our second consideration. Since we have put forward that UBDI may be defined as novel organisational forms, is it convenient to also assume them as forms of digital ecosystem? Suppose it is undoubted that UBDI can include a robust digital component. In that case, it is not equally obvious to consider UBDI—as a form of digital ecosystems—an evolutionary step from a previous conception of urban infrastructure as an ecosystem of dimensions (see more on [84]). In a nutshell, in considering the concept of digital ecosystem, we note that it has been widely used in the literature on service-oriented architectures. This concept has been understood in this line of research to underline the notable interdependencies between those who provide services and those who use them in the field of information technologies [85, 86]. However, the term "digital ecosystem" has also been employed in a broader sense. For instance, it was used to represent self-organising capabilities and explain the concept of complexity, which envelops the strict relationship concerning the environment from technological and social perspectives [87]. Drawing on [52]'s insights, this work focuses mainly on understanding human beings' role in big data collection and analysing their decision-making: To further understand the interdependencies emerging from UBDI, a methodological approach will be proposed in Sect. 3 that helps to overcome typical limitations, such as that linked to the inter-dependence between urban big data, urban infrastructure, source, users, and dimensions of urban development. This approach involves microfounding UBDI through an adjacency-tensor representation of multiplex networks.

3 Studying a Multi-layer Network and Its Multiplexity

According to [88–91], the quantitative study of networks is crucial for the analysis of complex systems in both soft and hard sciences. For this reason, networks are employed in studying interactive systems, both natural and artificial, as complex systems that allow operators to control and monitor other systems. From a traditional analytical perspective, networks commonly consist of nodes connected through a single static edge that wraps around all connections between nodes. However, explaining networks from a traditional perspective simplifies the network concept because it fails to capture several aspects concerning complexity. Given the inescapable complexity, it is necessary to explore the characteristics of multiplexity [92] (e.g., the presence of multiple numbers of edges), including the coexistence of numerous types of various elements within the network [91]. Conversely, *the power of multilayer networks lies in their flexibility to characterize multiple types of interactions not possible using a traditional mono-layer network approach* (Kinsley et al., [25], p. 2). More specifically, nodes and edges form multilayer networks. The nodes are present within separate layers representing different types of interactions whose connections form the aspect. Along the lines of [25, 91, 93], the aspects can represent some types of interaction, space and time points, and portions of systems. We consider the intra and inter-layer connections between edges and nodes [25]. In general, it is also possible to consider some different types of multilayer networks. Among others, we might stress our attention on multiplex networks and interconnected networks [93, 94] and other different types of interlayer edges, which may configure different network slices [95, 96]. In the extant literature, although other approaches provide a robust framework to analyse urban infrastructure together with big data, they may need to consider the complexity that highly characterises urban informatics, particularly in the case of UBDI [25]. In several contexts, the role of different types of connection (e.g., different types of data, users, or interactions between users) can considerably impact our understanding of how UBDI can work and develop on the timeline using enduring formulas and principles of governing. As stated in Sect. 2, our proposal (introduced in Sect. 3.1) incorporates one of the advanced technologies mentioned in the literature. In this regard, urban computing is advantageous and still growing exponentially due to its use in managing crucial infrastructure facilities within the urban environment. Based on what has been created by many forerunner scholars and, most importantly, according to [97], a collection of smart computing technologies can help describe the recent concept that sees cities in a smart version. For this purpose, following [62], some centralised cloud-computing architectures have been developed and adopted in smart cities to increase efficiency in their processes. Therefore, we decided to exploit the urban computing approach in this work. Firstly, as confirmed in the above literature, it is believed that urban computing will be more widely used today and in the future. Secondly, through the development of urban computing, cities labelled as smart can store a considerable amount of data by providing applications that allow its use, including the transmission and protection of big data. As stated by [62], more than just cloud computing is required to address these ambitious challenges, not least because, over the years, there has been a heavy reliance on cloud computing in urban areas (see also [98]). But it is not enough if edge computing technologies are not also used. Edge computing, indeed, allows storing, processing, and analysing data at the ends of the network, close to the devices, and even offline. By doing so, the edges of the networks will be able to process the data and produce them in full compliance with the space-time and regulatory constraints. In particular, the three types of computer paradigms coexist within the internal network (cloud computing, edge computing, and mobile computing) [62]. In line with the above, we believe that the urban computing applied to multiplex networks may provide opportunities to redesign and expand decision-making efforts into urban public and private policies. Thus, according to [7], these opportunities might positively influence the provision and improvement of urban infrastructure. Moreover, the framework articulated in the literature [26, 99–108] is mainly focused on this direction, whereby the related literature explicitly addresses the review of urban areas in the wake of geometrical models to lay the foundations of modern regional science research. By and large, although different approaches and frameworks can be adopted in the reference literature to study the different types of multilayer networks [91], we adopt the approach based on multiplex networks in this work. To study and represent UBDI through multiplexes and temporal networks, it is essential to use a thorough analytical representation as the primary tool. As we will point out in the following subsection, we adopt the general approach of tensor algebra to represent UBDI.

3.1 Pre-analytical Representation of the Adjacency-Tensor of Multiplex Networks

We provide a pre-analytical microfoundation of UBDI by employing a supra-adjacency tensor to represent multiplex networks. As stated by [23], an interconnected network can be understood as a set of interconnected objects. From a mathematical perspective, a single-layer network can be represented through a graph defined as follows:

$$G = \{V, E\} \tag{1}$$

where the elements of the set $V = \{v_i\}_{i=1}^n$ refer to the vertices (or nodes) and represent the objects. In this work, the nodes symbolise human involvement in the urban context. As with other similar realities, such as digital ecosystems, the role of people is also quite fundamental in UBDI. People can be embedded in this setup and configured as end users, volunteer producers or developers, and they should be continually involved in the building process of UBDI. In this process, people provide upward feedback, improvement, and intrinsic need satisfaction by dynamically generating urban big data (see also [22]) through interactions displayed across digital platforms and devices. Based on the interactions between users, it is possible to trace back to all those work-related communications the presence of one of the basic primary social needs, interpersonal communication [88]. This communication via digital devices allows scholars to track human decisions and behaviour that emerge from the interactions. Scholars can consequently represent the complex networks related to human interactions also through multilayer frameworks [88]. Therefore, to include users' interactions when microfounding the UBDI network, we assume that users might be represented by the same physical and digital assets they use. In order to assume such a representation, the nodes of this work are (effectively) expressed by the mobile-computing platform, which is the sum of end users' mobile devices, while the platform can process data along with mobility (on this point, see specifically [109]). In this configuration, mobile devices can transmit the data to the central cloud through wireless networks [62]. In other words, through the pre-analytical representation in this sub-Section, we would like to enhance the role of people by transposing and repositioning their involvement in the mobile computing platform as the nodes of the multiplex network. Indeed, mobile computing implies a relationship and interaction between humans and computers in mobility. To further understand the concept of mobile computing, see [62]. At this stage, following [23], the elements of the set $E = V\mathrm{x}V$, designated as edges, represent the connections between the nodes. In our representation, the edges are represented by user data exchange, named edge computing sensors. Indeed, *[e]dge-computing sensors act as fixed data collectors with various computing powers depending on tasks assigned; for example, a higher edge-computing capacity enables handling analytics for a larger area, like a neighborhood. All data and processes can also be uploaded to the cloud's centralized computing, for extensive data processing and knowledge extraction or mining.* (Liu et al., [62], p. 762, brackets added). Therefore, it is possible to consider connecting edge computing platforms and mobile computing platforms within interactive applications. In analytical terms, we denote an edge from node v_i to node v_j. These nodes are related through the relation $v_i \rightarrow v_j$. Multiplex networks, for instance, can help model this kind of relations, identifying multiple connections, also denominated as layers, between some elements [23]. In this work, the layers are represented by the different dimensions (or axes) of what is defined in the literature as a smart city, following the approach found in [26]. Every single graph represents a specific layer containing the network elements within the same level. Grid computing represents the elements in each layer (see [62]) and, specifically designed, the graph also shows both the connections between the layers and the *[e]dges connecting nodes from different layers model the interactions between different layers* (El-Halouy et al., [23], p. 236, brackets added). Accordingly, the edge-computing sensors are connected to mobile computing from different smart city dimensions (represented by each layer of the multiplex network), composed of varying grid computing. Following the approach of [108], we consider two specific types of edges allowing the connection of node-layer pairs. Notably, we consider intra-layer edges and inter-layer edges. In this proceeding line, the layers are assumed to be aligned with nodes. Each layer contains a specific typology of each physical node representing a mobile device within the city areas (e.g., a quarter). The number of physical nodes is indicated with n, and the number of layers with L. In particular, *[e]ach copy of a physical node in any of the layers is called a node-layer pair* (Bergermann & Stoll, [108], p. 13, brackets added). We consider intra- and inter-layer edges. Thereby, we apply the intra-layer edges to connect node-layer pairs belonging to the same layer whenever the corresponding edge-computing sensor directly collects data from two mobile devices. Instead, inter-layer edges connect instances of the same physical nodes belonging to different layers whenever two edge-computing sensors collect data from the corresponding mobile device (precisely present in different smart city dimensions). In general, the multiplex networks can be sharped as the multilayer graph as follows:

$$G = \left(\tilde{\mathcal{V}}, \mathcal{E}^{(1)}, \ldots, \mathcal{E}^{(L)}, \tilde{\mathcal{E}}\right) \tag{2}$$

where $\tilde{\mathcal{V}}$, indicates a common vertex set for all layers; $\mathcal{E}^{(l)}$ indicates intra layer edge sets for all layers $l = 1, 2, \ldots, L$; $\tilde{\mathcal{E}}$ indicates the inter-layer edge set. Entirely in this vein, it is possible to adopt a supra-adjacency matrix representation, where this representation consists of a linear algebraic formulation typical of complex, multiplex networks (see particularly [93, 108, 110–112]). More precisely, the two types of edges are expressed by two different matrices.

First, following [108], we show the multilayer intra-layer adjacency matrix $\boldsymbol{A}_{intra} \in R^{nLxnL}$. This particular matrix type contains the edges characterising connections by an edge-computing platform. In addition, the matrix defines the block-diagonal matrix as follows (matrix 1):

$$\boldsymbol{A}_{intra} = blkdiag\left[\boldsymbol{A}^{(1)}, \ldots, \boldsymbol{A}^{(L)}\right] = \begin{bmatrix} \boldsymbol{A}^{(1)} & \boldsymbol{0} & \cdots & \boldsymbol{0} \\ \boldsymbol{0} & \boldsymbol{A}^{(2)} & \cdots & \boldsymbol{0} \\ \vdots & \vdots & \ddots & \vdots \\ \boldsymbol{0} & \boldsymbol{0} & \cdots & \boldsymbol{A}^{(L)} \end{bmatrix} \tag{3}$$

In matrix 1, $\boldsymbol{0} \in \mathrm{R}^{nxn}$ indicates the matrix of all zeros; $\boldsymbol{A}^{(l)} \in \mathrm{R}^{nxn}$ indicates each block-diagonal entry which in turn coincides to the adjacency matrix of layer l. Particularly, the block-diagonal incorporates the weight of the edge between the mobile device nodes i and j in layer l within entry $[\boldsymbol{A}^{(l)}]_{\mathrm{ij}}$. Otherwise, the value is zero if no edge is extant for $i, j \in \{1,2, \ldots, n\}$ and $l \in \{1,2, \ldots, L\}$. Secondly, we show inter-layer adjacency matrix $\boldsymbol{A}_{inter} \in \mathrm{R}^{nLxnL}$. This second matrix type encompasses the edges characterising possible data collection between edge-computing sensors. The matrix can be analytically defined as follows (matrix 2):

$$\mathbf{A}_{inter} = \begin{bmatrix} \mathbf{0} & \mathbf{O}^{(12)} & \cdots & \mathbf{O}^{(1L)} \\ \mathbf{O}^{(21)} & \mathbf{0} & \cdots & \mathbf{O}^{(2L)} \\ \vdots & \vdots & \ddots & \vdots \\ \mathbf{O}^{(L1)} & \mathbf{O}^{(L2)} & \cdots & \mathbf{0} \end{bmatrix} \tag{4}$$

where

$$\left[\mathbf{O}^{(lk)}\right]_{ij} = \begin{cases} 1, \textit{ if } i=j \textit{ and the physical node } x_i \textit{ is connected between } l \textit{ and } k \\ 0, \textit{ otherwise,} \end{cases}$$

In matrix 2, $l, k \in \{1,2,\ldots,L\}$ in order that $\mathbf{O}^{(lk)} \in \mathrm{R}^{nxn}$ encompasses ones only on a subgroup of its diagonal entries. Hence, inter-layer edges are conditional on whether the edge-computing sensors represented by layers l and k, both associated in a given physical node. Following [108], the block-diagonal of $\mathbf{A}_{\text{inter}}$ is set to zero matrices $\mathbf{0} \in \mathrm{R}^{nxn}$ because these entries would not embody a possible data collection of edge-computing sensors. In addition, it is necessary to consider that the above matrix specification of $\mathbf{A}_{\text{inter}}$ is more general compared to the specification provided by [108, 110–112]. In this regard, it is necessary to note that within their matrix specification, each $\mathbf{O}^{(lk)}$ is understood as a full identity matrix by encompassing all combinations of diagonal entries from zero to up n. Definitely, the matrix specification provided by [108, 110–112] allows each layer-layer pair to be coupled with a different weight and $\mathbf{A}_{\text{inter}}$ (as specificated in matrix 2) has no weights. Besides, the shaping of the constant transfer time between all the edge-computing sensors at all the mobile devices of the network can be realised by adding a parameter which allows the scaling of the inter-layer adjacency matrix. This parameter is given by ω. The specifications within matrices 1 and 2 allow us to describe the supra-adjacency matrix $\mathbf{A} \in \mathrm{R}^{nLxnL}$, by adding the parameter ω, as follows:

$$\mathbf{A} = \mathbf{A}_{intra} + \omega \mathbf{A}_{inter} \tag{5}$$

In Eq. 5, *$\omega \in R \geq 0$ is a scalar coupling parameter that trades of the relative importance of intra- and inter-layer weights* (Bergermann & Stoll, [108], p. 14). In addition, it is necessary to point out that, by following an undirected edges approach, $\mathbf{A} = \mathbf{A}^{\mathrm{T}}$. However, it could be argued that a considerable degree of sparsity delineates the supra-adjacency matrix $\mathbf{A}$ of our UBDI network. Admittedly, this delineation can emerge from matrices 1 and 2. In any case, our specification is edged by an additional scarcity as each edge computing sensor typically supports a small number of mobile devices enclosed within a specific, narrow urban space (e.g., a neighbourhood community). In this respect, it is noted that *most layers are approximately represented by chain graphs in which the number of edges is of the order of* *the number of non-isolated node-layer pairs* (Bergermann & Stoll, [108], p. 15). With regard to the main content of this subsection, it is necessary to consider that within the literature [91], different authors use different notations and terminologies to create adjacency matrices, including typical aspects and elements of complexity. Therefore, it is desirable that the way of creating and representing these matrices will be unified over time, thus reducing the degree of fuzziness in studying complex networks. This is why the way of representing these matrices should be unified, thus reducing the degree of fuzziness in studying these complex networks.

In summary, we preferred to introduce a holistic approach employing an urban computing framework to provide a pre-analytical representation of the adjacency tensor of multiplex networks. In this framework, each layer contains different types of urban big data, urban infrastructure, and their sources and users, as emerges in the theoretical foundations and reference disciplines used to account for the UBDI phenomenon (see Sect. 2). The subsequent stage of our proposal will concentrate on the distinctions between the various layers, with an analysis of urban big data conducted using computational tools.

4 Discussion and Future Research

The combination of UBDI dimensions as new organisational forms offers a novel perspective for addressing contemporary urban challenges holistically, driven by intrinsic reasons for complexity. Embracing a broad perspective of reality, particularly in relation to the infrastructure of urban big data, there is an opportunity to reconsider cities in the face of uncertainty. By recognising diverse research pathways and frameworks, this work is part of recent advances in the field of UBDI. In this context, the pre-analytical microfoundation proposed here concerns a possible, novel, holistically based approach to the recurring dimensions of the UBDI. However, it should be noted that our proposal does not address current limitations concerning urban big data infrastructure, especially those related to the issue of security and privacy (see Sects. 2 and 3). In any case, urban big data has demonstrated the potential to enhance our comprehension of the city and urban societies, thereby enabling more informed decision-making through the utilisation of human and data-rich resources (for further details, see [22]). Big data plays a central role in urban infrastructure, providing an extensive collection of databases and data sets (for further details, see [7]). In conclusion, our proposal aims to address some of the unresolved challenges in literature, which urban computing can potentially address, such as large-scale infrastructure, scalability, on-demand and hyperscaling, as suggested by [62]. Ultimately, it is also possible to help reduce some regional inequalities, at least potentially, since UBDI might contribute to the further development of smart cities and an urban environment that is relatively more able to meet the needs of all citizens. In the future, experimental evidence and computational analysis will be employed to inform data-driven decision-making in urban environments. This will be done with a clear understanding of the crucial role of humans in the urban ecosystem and with the implementation and monitoring of such decisions in real-time and with feedback.

References

1. Casti, J. L. (1984). Simple models, catastrophes and cycles. *Kybernetes, 13*(1), 213–229.
2. Goodchild, M. F. (2021). Introduction to urban big data infrastructure. In W. Shi, M. F. Goodchild, M. Batty, M. P. Kwan, & A. Zhang (Eds.), *Urban informatics* (pp. 543–545). Springer.
3. Kitchin, R. (2014). The real-time City? *Big Data and Smart Urbanism. GeoJournal, 79*(1), 1–14.
4. Kontokosta, C. E., & Johnson, N. (2017). Urban phenology: Toward a real-time census of the City using Wi-Fi data. *Computers, Environment and Urban Systems, 64*(1), 144–153.
5. Singleton, A. D., Spielman, S., & Folch, D. (2018). *Urban analytics*. Sage.
6. Van Meeteren, M., & Poorthuis, A. (2018). Christaller and "big data": Recalibrating Central place theory via the Geoweb. *Urban Geography, 39*, 122–148.
7. Strielkowski, W. (2019). *Social impacts of smart grids: The future of smart grids and energy market design*. Elsevier.
8. Batty, M. (2012). Smart cities, big data. *Environment and Planning B: Planning and Design, 39*(2), 191–193.
9. Bettencourt, L. M., & West, G. (2010). A unified theory of urban living. *Nature, 467*(7318), 912–913.
10. Ferreira, N., Lage, M., Doraiswamy, H., Vo, H., Wilson, L., Werner, H., Park, M., & Silva, C. (2015). Urbane: A 3d framework to support data driven decision making in urban development. In: *2015 IEEE conference on visual analytics science and technology (VAST)* (pp. 97–104). IEE, Piscataway.
11. Hong, B., Malik, A., Lundquist, J., Bellach, I., & Kontokosta, C. E. (2018). Applications of machine learning methods to predict readmission and length-of-stay for homeless families: The case of win shelters in New York City. *Journal of Technology in Human Services, 36*(1), 89–104.
12. Keller, S. A., Koonin, S. E., & Shipp, S. (2012). Big data and city living: What can it do for us? *Significance, 9*(4), 4–7.
13. Kontokosta, C. E., Hong, B., Johnson, N. E., & Starobin, D. (2018). Using machine learning and small area estimation to predict building-level municipal solid waste generation in cities. *Computers, Environment and Urban Systems, 70*(1), 151–162.
14. Alm, J. (2015). Financing urban infrastructure: Knowns, unknowns, and a way forward. *Journal of Economic Surveys, 29*(2), 230–262.
15. Glaeser, E. L., Kominers, S. D., Luca, M., & Naik, N. (2018). Big data and big cities: The promises and limitations of improved measures of urban life. *Economic Inquiry, 56*(1), 114–137.
16. Bettencourt, L. M. (2014). The uses of big data in cities. *Big Data, 2*(1), 12–22.
17. Pan, Y., Tian, Y., Liu, X., Gu, D., & Hua, G. (2016). Urban big data and the development of city intelligence. *Engineering, 2*(2), 171–178.
18. Tavmen, G. (2020). Data/infrastructure in the smart city: Understanding the infrastructural power of Citymapper app through technicity of data. *Big Data & Society, 7*(2), 1–15.
19. Strielkowski, W., Faminskaya, M., & Potekhina, E. (2021). Urban infrastructure via big data. In: *E3S web of conferences* (Vol. 301, pp. 1–9). EDP sciences, Les Ulis.
20. Shi, W., Cao, J., Zhang, Q., Li, Y., & Xu, L. (2016). Edge computing: Vision and challenges. *IEEE Internet of Things Journal, 3*(5), 637–646.

21. Foss, K., & Foss, N. J. (2005). *Simon on Problem-Solving: Implications for New Organizational Forms. Center for Strategic Management and Globalization*. SMG Working Paper No. 8/2005, 1–26.
22. Xiao, N., & Miller, H. J. (2021). Cultivating urban big data. In W. Shi, M. F. Goodchild, M. Batty, M. P. Kwan, & A. Zhang (Eds.), *Urban informatics* (pp. 547–565). Springer.
23. El-Halouy, S., Noschese, S., & Reichel, L. (2024). A tensor formalism for multilayer network centrality measures using the Einstein product. *Applied Numerical Mathematics, 200*, 236–253.
24. De Domenico, M., Sol'e-Ribalta, A., Cozzo, E., Kivelä, M., Moreno, Y., Porter, M. A., Gomez, S., & Arenas, A. (2013). Mathematical formulation of multilayer networks. *Physical Review X, 3*(4), 041022-1–041022-15.
25. Kinsley, A. C., Rossi, G., Silk, M. J., & VanderWaal, K. (2020). Multilayer and multiplex networks: An introduction to their use in veterinary epidemiology. *Frontiers in Veterinary Science, 7*(596), 1–13.
26. Caragliu, A., Del Bo, C., & Nijkamp, P. (2011). Smart cities in Europe. *Journal of Urban Technology, 18*(2), 65–82.
27. Murty, R. N., Mainland, G., Rose, I., Chowdhury, A.R., Gosain, A., Bers, J., & Welsh, M. (2008). CitySense: An urban-scale wireless sensor network and testbed. In: *Technologies for Homeland Security, 2008 IEEE conference* (pp. 583—588). IEEE, Waltham.
28. Atzori, L., Iera, A., & Morabito, G. (2010). The Internet of Things: A survey. *Computer Networks, 54*(15), 2787–2805.
29. Anejionu, O. C., Thakuriah, P. V., McHugh, A., Sun, Y., McArthur, D., Mason, P., & Walpole, R. (2019). Spatial urban data system: A cloud-enabled big data infrastructure for social and economic urban analytics. *Future Generation Computer Systems, 98*(1), 456–473.
30. Kong, L., Liu, Z., & Wu, J. (2020). A systematic review of big data-based urban sustainability research: State-of-the-science and future directions. *Journal of Cleaner Production, 273*(123142), 1–16.
31. Neirotti, P., De Marco, A., Cagliano, A. C., Mangano, G., & Scorrano, F. (2014). Current trends in Smart City initiatives: Some stylised facts. *Cities, 38*(1), 25–36.
32. Berry, C. R., & Glaeser, E. L. (2005). The divergence of human capital levels across cities. *Papers in Regional Science, 84*(3), 407–444.
33. Harrison, C., & Donnelly, I. A. (2011). A theory of smart cities. In: *Proceedings of the 55th Annual Meeting of the ISSS-2011* (pp. 1–15). Hull.
34. Kharrazi, A., Qin, H., & Zhang, Y. (2016). Urban big data and sustainable development goals: Challenges and opportunities. *Sustainability, 8*(1293), 1–6.
35. De, S., Zhou, Y., Larizgoitia Abad, I., & Moessner, K. (2017). Cyber–physical–social frameworks for urban big data systems: A survey. *Applied Sciences, 7*(1017), 1–26.
36. Villegas-Ch, W., Palacios-Pacheco, X., & Luján-Mora, S. (2019). Application of a smart city model to a traditional university campus with a big data architecture: A sustainable smart campus. *Sustainability, 11*(2857), 1–28.
37. Liu, C., Wu, H., Wang, J., & Wang, M. (2020). A unified fourth-order tensor-based smart community system. *Sensors, 20*(5990), 1–13.
38. Graham, S., & Marvin, S. (2001). *Splintering urbanism: Networked infrastructures, technological mobilities and the urban condition*. Routledge.
39. Hashem, I. A. T., Chang, V., Anuar, N. B., Adewole, K., Yaqoob, I., Gani, A., Ahmed, E., & Chiroma, H. (2016). The role of big data in smart city. *International Journal of Information Management, 36*(5), 748–758.
40. Goodchild, M. F. (2022). Elements of an infrastructure for big urban data. *Urban Informatics, 1*(3), 1–5.
41. Wu, X., Zhu, X., Wu, G. Q., & Ding, W. (2013). Data mining with big data. *IEEE Transactions on Knowledge and Data Engineering, 26*(1), 97–107.
42. Witten, I. H., & Frank, E. (2002). Data mining: Practical machine learning tools and techniques with Java implementations. *ACM SIGMOD Record, 31*(1), 76–77.

43. Howe, J. (2006). The rise of crowdsourcing. *Wired Magazine, 14*(6), 1–4.
44. Kloch, C., Petersen, E. B., & Madsen, O. B. (2011). Cloud based infrastructure, the new business possibilities and barriers. *Wireless Personal Communications, 58*(1), 17–30.
45. Chen, C. P., & Zhang, C. Y. (2014). Data-intensive applications, challenges, techniques and technologies: A survey on Big Data. *Information Sciences, 275*(1), 314–347.
46. Golov, N., & Ronnback, L. (2017). Big data normalization for massively parallel processing databases. *Computer Standards & Interfaces, 54*(1), 86–93.
47. Reichstein, M., Camps-Valls, G., Stevens, B., Jung, M., Denzler, J., & Carvalhais, N. (2019). Deep learning and process understanding for data-driven Earth system science. *Nature, 566*(7743), 195–204.
48. Xu, C., Du, X., Fan, X., Giuliani, G., Hu, Z., Wang, W., Liu, J., Wang, T., Yan, Z., Zhu, J., Jiang, T., & Guo, H. (2022). Cloud-based storage and computing for remote sensing big data: a technical review. *International Journal of Digital Earth, 15*(1), 1417–1445.
49. Zhang, X., Zhou, Y. N., & Luo, J. (2022). Deep learning for processing and analysis of remote sensing big data: A technical review. *Big Earth Data, 6*(4), 527–560.
50. Marx, V. (2013). The big challenges of big data. *Nature, 498*(7453), 255–260.
51. Cai, L., & Zhu, Y. (2015). The challenges of data quality and data quality assessment in the big data era. *Data Science Journal, 14*(2), 1–10.
52. Chauhan, S., Agarwal, N., & Kar, A. K. (2016). Addressing big data challenges in smart cities: a systematic literature review. *info, 18*(4), 73–90.
53. Lim, C., Kim, K. J., & Maglio, P. P. (2018). Smart cities with big data: Reference models, challenges, and considerations. *Cities, 82*(1), 86–99.
54. Günther, W. A., Mehrizi, M. H. R., Huysman, M., & Feldberg, F. (2017). Debating big data: A literature review on realizing value from big data. *The Journal of Strategic Information Systems, 26*(3), 191–209.
55. Gupta, R., Gupta, H., & Mohania, M. (2012). Cloud computing and big data analytics: What is new from databases perspective? In S. Srinivasa & V. Bhatnagar (Eds.), *Big data analytics: First international conference, BDA 2012* (Lecture notes in computer science) (Vol. 7678, pp. 42–61). Springer.
56. Demchenko, Y., Grosso, P., De Laat, C., & Membrey, P. (2013). Addressing big data issues in scientific data infrastructure. In: *2013 International conference on collaboration technologies and systems (CTS)* (pp. 48–55). IEEE.
57. Hu, W., Gao, Y., Ha, K., Wang, J., Amos, B., Chen, Z., Pillai, P. & Satyanarayanan, M. (2016). Quantifying the impact of edge computing on mobile applications. In: *Proceedings of the 7th ACM SIGOPS Asia-Pacific workshop on systems* (pp. 1–8). Association for Computing Machinery, Hong Kong.
58. Cai, J. X., Huang, B., & Song, Y. M. (2017). Using multi-source geospatial big data to identify the structure of polycentric cities. *Remote Sensing of Environment, 202*(1), 210–221.
59. Zhu, X., & Guo, D. S. (2017). Urban event detection with big data of taxi OD trips: A time series decomposition approach. *Transactions in GIS, 21*(3), 560–574.
60. Song, Y., Huang, B., Cai, J., & Chen, B. (2018). Dynamic assessments of population exposure to urban greenspace using multi-source big data. *Science of the Total Environment, 634*(1), 1315–1325.
61. Alipour, M., & Harris, D. K. (2020). A big data analytics strategy for scalable urban infrastructure condition assessment using semi-supervised multi-transform self-training. *Journal of Civil Structural Health Monitoring, 10*(1), 313–332.
62. Liu, Q., Gu, J., Yang, J., Li, Y., Sha, D., Xu, M., Shams, I., Yu, M., & Yang, C. (2021). Cloud, edge, and mobile computing for smart cities. In W. Shi, M. F. Goodchild, M. Batty, M. P. Kwan, & A. Zhang (Eds.), *Urban informatics* (pp. 757–795). Springer.
63. Matturdi, B., Zhou, X., Li, S., & Lin, F. (2014). Big data security and privacy: A review. *China Communications, 11*(14), 135–145.

64. Henze, M., Hermerschmidt, L., Kerpen, D., Häußling, R., Rumpe, B., & Wehrle, K. (2016). A comprehensive approach to privacy in the cloud-based Internet of Things. *Future Generation Computer Systems, 56*(1), 701–718.
65. Madsen, A. K. (2015). Between technical features and analytic capabilities: Charting a relational affordance space for digital social analytics. *Big Data & Society, 2*(1), 1–15.
66. Tu, W., Cao, J., Yue, Y., Shaw, S. L., Zhou, M., Wang, Z., Chang, W., Xu, Y., & Li, Q. (2017). Coupling mobile phone and social media data: A new approach to understanding urban functions and diurnal patterns. *International Journal of Geographical Information Science, 31*(12), 2331–2358.
67. Tu, W., Cao, R., Yue, Y., Zhou, B., Li, Q., & Li, Q. (2018). Spatial variations in urban public ridership derived from GPS trajectories and smart card data. *Journal of Transport Geography, 69*(1), 45–57.
68. Sulis, P., Manley, E., Zhong, C., & Batty, M. (2018). Using mobility data as proxy for measuring urban vitality. *Journal of Spatial Information Science, 16*(1), 137–162.
69. Jiang, J., Li, Q., Tu, W., Shaw, S. L., & Yue, Y. (2019). A simple and direct method to analyse the influences of sampling fractions on modelling intra-city human mobility. *International Journal of Geographical Information Science, 33*(3), 618–644.
70. Zhou, M., Wang, D., Li, Q., Yue, Y., Tu, W., & Cao, R. (2017). Impacts of weather on public transport ridership: Results from mining data from different sources. *Transportation Research Part C: Emerging Technologies, 75*(1), 17–29.
71. Kim, K. S., Kojima, I., & Ogawa, H. (2016). Discovery of local topics by using latent spatio-temporal relationships in geo-social media. *International Journal of Geographical Information Science, 30*(9), 1899–1922.
72. Jendryke, M., Balz, T., McClure, S. C., & Liao, M. (2017). Putting people in the picture: Combining big location-based social media data and remote sensing imagery for enhanced contextual urban information in Shanghai. *Computers, Environment and Urban Systems, 62*(1), 99–112.
73. Liu, X., He, J., Yao, Y., Zhang, J., Liang, H., Wang, H., & Hong, Y. (2017). Classifying urban land use by integrating remote sensing and social media data. *International Journal of Geographical Information Science, 31*(8), 1675–1696.
74. Martí, P., Serrano-Estrada, L., & Nolasco-Cirugeda, A. (2019). Social media data: Challenges, opportunities and limitations in urban studies. *Computers, Environment and Urban Systems, 74*(1), 161–174.
75. Gómez Romero, C. D., Díaz Barriga, J. K., & Rodríguez Molano, J. I. (2016). Big data meaning in the architecture of IoT for smart cities. In: *Data mining and big data: First international conference proceedings 1* (pp. 457–465). Springer.
76. Thakuriah, P., Tilahun, N. Y., & Zellner, M. (2017). Big data and urban informatics: Innovations and challenges to urban planning and knowledge discovery. In P. Thakuriah, N. Y. Tilahun, & M. Zellner (Eds.), *Seeing cities through big data: Research, methods and applications in urban informatics* (pp. 11–45). Springer Geography.
77. Goodchild, M. F. (2007). Citizens as sensors: The world of volunteered geography. *GeoJournal, 69*(1), 211–221.
78. Gao, S., Liu, Y., Kang, Y., & Zhang, F. (2021). User-generated content: A promising data source for urban informatics. In W. Shi, M. F. Goodchild, M. Batty, M. P. Kwan, & A. Zhang (Eds.), *Urban informatics* (pp. 503–522). Springer.
79. Tu, W., Li, Q., Zhang, Y., & Yue, Y. (2021). User-generated content and its applications in urban studies. In W. Shi, M. F. Goodchild, M. Batty, M. P. Kwan, & Zhang (Eds.), *Urban informatics* (pp. 523–539). Springer.
80. Bayulgen, O. (2020). Localizing the energy transition: Town-level political and socio-economic drivers of clean energy in the United States. *Energy Research & Social Science, 62*(101376), 1–12.
81. Seijas, A., & Gelders, M. M. (2021). Governing the night-time city: The rise of night mayors as a new form of urban governance after dark. *Urban Studies, 58*(2), 316–334.

82. Wu, F. (2018). Planning centrality, market instruments: Governing Chinese urban transformation under state entrepreneurialism. *Urban Studies, 55*(7), 1383–1399.
83. Ersoy, A., & Chaves Alberto, K. (2019). Understanding urban infrastructure via big data: The case of Belo Horizonte. *Regional Studies, Regional Science, 6*(1), 374–379.
84. Ma, Y., Wright, J., Gopal, S., & Phillips, N. (2020). Seeing the invisible: From imagined to virtual urban landscapes. *Cities, 98*(102559), 1–10.
85. Vargo, S. L., Maglio, P. P., & Akaka, M. A. (2008). On value and value co-creation: A service systems and service logic perspective. *European Management Journal, 26*(3), 145–152.
86. Lusch, R. F., & Nambisan, S. (2015). Service innovation: A service-dominant logic perspective. *MIS Quarterly, 39*(1), 155–176.
87. Lazazzara, A., Ricciardi, F., & Za, S. (2020). Introduction to digital ecosystem. In A. Lazazzara, F. Ricciardi, & S. Za (Eds.), *Exploring digital ecosystems: Organizational and human challenges* (pp. 1–7). Springer International Publishing.
88. Boccaletti, S., Latora, V., Moreno, Y., Chavez, M., & Hwang, D. U. (2006). Complex networks: Structure and dynamics. *Physics Reports, 424*(4–5), 175–308.
89. Newman, M. E. J. (2010). *Networks: An introduction*. Oxford University Press.
90. Estrada, E. (2012). *The structure of complex networks: Theory and applications*. Oxford University Press.
91. De Domenico, M., Granell, C., Porter, M. A., & Arenas, A. (2016). The physics of spreading processes in multilayer networks. *Nature Physics, 12*(10), 901–906.
92. Wasserman, S., & Faust, K. (1994). *Social network analysis: Methods and applications*. Cambridge University Press.
93. Kivela, M., Arenas, A., Barthelemy, M., Gleeson, J., Moreno, Y., & Porter, M. (2014). Dynamical and spectral properties of complex networks. *Journal of Complex Networks, 2*(3), 203–271.
94. Silk, M. J., Finn, K. R., Porter, M. A., & Pinter-Wollman, N. (2018). Can multilayer networks advance animal behavior research? *Trends in Ecology Evolution, 33*(6), 376–378.
95. Gomez, S., Diaz-Guilera, A., Gomez-Gardenes, J., Perez-Vicente, C. J., Moreno, Y., & Arenas, A. (2013). Diffusion dynamics on multiplex networks. *Physical Review Letters, 110*(2), 1–6.
96. Sole-Ribalta, A., De Domenico, M., Kouvaris, N. E., Diaz-Guilera, A., Gomez, S., & Arenas, A. (2013). Spectral properties of the Laplacian of multiplex networks. *Physical Review E, 88*(3), 032807-1–032807-6.
97. Washburn, D., Sindhu, U., Balaouras, S., Dines, R. A., Hayes, N., & Nelson, L. E. (2009). Helping CIOs understand "smart city" initiatives. *Growth, 17*(2), 1–17.
98. Etro, F. (2015). The economics of cloud computing. In *Cloud technology: Concepts, methodologies, tools, and applications* (pp. 2135–2148). IGI Global.
99. Porta, S., Crucitti, P., & Latora, V. (2006a). The network analysis of urban streets: A dual approach. *Physica A: Statistical Mechanics and its Applications, 369*(2), 853–866.
100. Batty, M. (2008). The size, scale, and shape of cities. *Science, 319*(5864), 769–771.
101. Barthélemy, M., & Flammini, A. (2008). Modeling urban street patterns. *Physical Review Letters, 100*(13), 138702-1–138702-4.
102. Barthélemy, M. (2011). Spatial networks. *Physics Reports, 499*(1–3), 1–101.
103. Courtat, T., Gloaguen, C., & Douady, S. (2011). Mathematics and morphogenesis of cities: A geometrical approach. *Physical Review E, 83*(3), 036106-1–036106-12.
104. Chan, S. H., Donner, R. V., & Lammer, S. (2011). Urban road networks—spatial networks with universal geometric features? A case study on Germany's largest cities. *The European Physical Journal B, 84*(1), 563–577.
105. Barthelemy, M., Bordin, P., Berestycki, H., & Gribaudi, M. (2013). Self-organization versus top-down planning in the evolution of a city. *Scientific Reports, 3*(1), 2153.
106. Barthelemy, M. (2016). *The structure and dynamics of cities*. Cambridge University Press.
107. Sharifi, A. (2019). Resilient urban forms: A review of literature on streets and street networks. *Building and Environment, 147*(1), 171–187.

108. Bergermann, K., & Stoll, M. (2021). Orientations and matrix function-based centralities in multiplex network analysis of urban public transport. *Applied Network Science, 6*(1), 1–33.
109. Akherfi, K., Gerndt, M., & Harroud, H. (2018). Mobile cloud computing for computation offloading: Issues and challenges. *Applied Computing and Informatics, 14*(1), 1–16.
110. Taylor, D., Myers, S. A., Clauset, A., Porter, M. A., & Mucha, P. J. (2017). Eigenvector- based centrality measures for temporal networks. *Multiscale Modeling & Simulation, 15*(1), 537–574.
111. Taylor, D., Porter, M. A., & Mucha, P. J. (2019). Supracentrality analysis of temporal networks with directed interlayer coupling. In P. Holme & J. Saramaki (Eds.), *Temporal network theory* (pp. 325–344). Springer.
112. Taylor, D., Porter, M. A., & Mucha, P. J. (2021). Tunable eigenvector-based centralities for multiplex and temporal networks. *Multiscale Modeling Simulation, 19*(1), 113–147.

Exploring the Evolution of the Circular Economy Debate

Michele Cipriano, Stefano Za, and Francesco Virili

Abstract This study takes into the NextGeneration EU plan with regard to the project entitled "ECOSISTER: Ecosystem for Sustainable Transition in EmiliaRomagna" by the Italian "Piano Nazionale Ripresa e Resilienza" (PNRR). This research refers to the sub-area of the project focused on circular economy. Specifically, the aim of this research is to explore the current state of the art of the circular economy debate by performing a bibliometric analysis of the literature. To this end, we extracted 1060 papers published from 2007 to 2023 using the Scopus database. Then, we apply the bibliometric methods in carrying on performance analysis and science mapping investigations. The outcome of this work is twofold: (i) to quantitatively describe the existing research and its evolution by considering refereed journals in the business domain; (ii) to recognise the main topics characterising the discourse by performing a co-word analysis. This preliminary study seeks to pave the groundwork to provide a quantitative overview of the thematic evolution and conceptual structures concerning circular economy research. These findings are building a knowledge base to define a theoretical and methodological position for the next research steps in the context of the ECOSISTER project: development of models and evaluation systems based on organisational factors and HR practices to implement sustainability and the circular economy in industries operating in the Emilia Romagna region (Italy).

Keywords Circular economy · Taxonomy EU · Ecosister · Bibliometric analysis

M. Cipriano (✉) · F. Virili
Catholic University of the Sacred Heart, Piacenza, Italy
e-mail: michele.cipriano@unicatt.it; francesco.virili@unicatt.it

S. Za
University "G. D'Annunzio" of Chieti-Pescara, Pescara, Italy
e-mail: stefano.za@unich.it

A. M. Braccini et al. (eds.), *Digital (Eco) Systems and Societal Challenges*, Lecture Notes in Information Systems and Organisation 72,
https://doi.org/10.1007/978-3-031-75586-6_14

1 Introduction

The Italian region Emilia Romagna is characterised by one of the most relevant innovation ecosystems in Europe, structured as a live network of resources, institutions, organisations, and projects. The regional innovation ecosystem acts as an innovation powerhouse towards regional growth for Italy and beyond by encouraging collaboration, backing R&D, and supporting entrepreneurship [1, 2].

In this context, it was recently approved and launched the Ecosister project (Ecosystem for Sustainable Transition in Emilia-Romagna), backed by the NextGeneration EU plan, through the Italian national plan "Piano Nazionale Ripresa e Resilienza" (PNRR). This flagship research project involves all the most important research institutions in the region, including six universities, four public research centres and 13 private research and innovation centres, participating with more than 800 researchers, investing 110,000,000 (€) granted funding in 3 years.

The project aim is to leverage the innovation ecosystem to support the productive system of Emilia-Romagna, which is strong and highly competitive, towards a sustainable transition. Specifically, the research activities focus on materials for sustainability and ecological transition, production, storage, and saving of clean energy, green manufacturing for a sustainable economy, intelligent solutions for mobility, housing, and zero-carbon emission energy, circular economy and blue economy, ecological transition based on high-performance computing and data technology.

This research refers to the sub-area of the Ecosister project focused on circular economy. Among other definitions of circular economy provided by the literature, Murray et al. [3] define circular economy as an economic model aimed to maximise ecosystem functioning and human well-being in a sustainable way. Specifically, a model based on the design and management of planning, resourcing, procurement, production and reprocessing the entire network of production from both process and output perspectives [3]. In this regard, some scholars have examined practical and political traits related to the circular economy [4]. Others have focused on the three pillars of sustainability (economic, environmental, and social), investigating how this model could be leveraged to develop sustainable businesses and achieve sustainable development goals [5, 6]. Further researchers have studied innovations and digitalisation of processes, focusing on digital technologies and strategies for carrying sustainable output [7, 8].

Thus, this study intends to explore the current state of the art of the circular economy debate by performing a bibliometric analysis of the literature. The underlying question of this exploratory analysis is: What are the most relevant research topics, contributions, and streams in the evolving debate about the circular economy? The answer to this question is preliminary to setting a cumulative contribution in order to identify and bridge a specific gap in theory and practice while targeting and designing the Ecosister aims.

The paper unfolds as follows. The next section provides the methodological underpinnings and the literature search protocol. The performance and science mapping analyses are provided in the results section. Final remarks and conclusions close the paper.

2 Approach and Research Method

Among many statistical techniques useful to analyse the literature, the bibliometric approach is particularly apt to systematically study scientific publications in relation to a given domain [9–13]. This approach is often used by scholars [14, 15] for quantitatively exploring the history, development, and general state of the art of a research field, as well as topics over a long period [16, 17]. Precisely, this technique consists of collecting bibliographic material from online databases [17, 18]. Then, bibliometric data could be examined through basic descriptive analyses (i.e., performance analysis) [19, 20] and more accurate ones for investigating a scientific field and exploring an area in relation to its knowledge structure and evolution (i.e., science mapping) [21, 22].

Hence, this preliminary study adopts a bibliometric approach to examine the state of the art of the literature concerning the circular economy discourse [23]. We apply performance analysis and science mapping methods [17] in exploring the structure and characteristics of topics through the study of selected scientific publications [24, 25]. Our aim is to examine the research hotspots in related fields and the trend of circular economy research, as well as uncover links between concepts through term co-occurrences [10, 26]. In particular, we attempt to start a co-word analysis by developing the authors' keyword co-occurrences network to investigate the main concepts debated in scientific research and the interactions between them [17]. The co-word analysis is aimed at developing an actual representation of an article's content [27] and then supporting researchers in understanding the conceptual structure of the research field [17].

In doing so, we first analyse and describe the distribution of publications among different sources. Afterwards, among many approaches and available data, we chose to work exclusively with the keywords defined by the authors of the papers (i.e. excluding "indexed keywords" generated by the online databases). This choice is based on the assumption that the keywords defined by the original author(s) of a paper are thought to represent such contribution closely, in accordance with the authors' standpoint [28]. Then, we identify the most widely used keywords by the authors of the papers in our dataset. Accordingly, we propose the authors' keyword co-occurrences network recognising clusters of the author's keywords [29–31]. In comparison to other analyses that indirectly construct the relation between papers (such as citation or co-authorship analysis), the co-word analysis leverages the co-occurrences of two words in the same paper to create a similarity measure based on the actual content of a paper [10, 24]. According to Lamboglia et al. [10], the co-occurrence of two words represents an indicator of how these two concepts are related to each other [32]. That is, the analysis of the keywords co-occurrence supports the investigation of the connections between the main topics

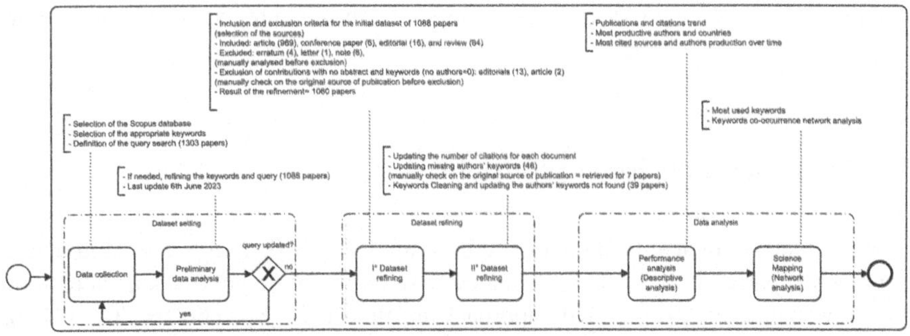

Fig. 1 Research protocol adapted from Za and Braccini [33]

discussed in the papers of our dataset. In this regard, the resulting network is a graphical representation of how each keyword has been mentioned together with another one. So, if two keywords have been mentioned together in a paper, there is a tie between them (co-occurrence). Observing the connections among the keywords in the networks makes it possible to recognise clusters of the keywords co-occurrence [24]. Thus, we locate keyword networks strongly linked to each other [27], presenting the resulting diagram. Next, we describe the research protocol of this study (see Fig. 1) that we tailored from Za and Braccini [33].

For this study, we developed a research protocol based on three steps: (Ist) dataset setting, (IInd) dataset refining, and (IIIrd) data analysis. As a first step, we identified the Scopus database for collecting the dataset by considering that academics and practitioners of social studies widely use such an indexing platform [34]. Then, we defined and refined the research query several times to retrieve a comprehensive dataset with regard to our objectives. We initially searched for the term "circular economy" in the authors' keywords, title and abstract papers fields, restricting the search to papers written only in English. At the same time, the query was also set in the "ISSN" field, which is the "International Standard Serial Number" of a journal. Specifically, the whole set of ISSNs of the journals ranked in the Academic Journal Guide (AJG2021)[1] was included. The AJG is released by the Chartered Association of Business Schools (CABS),[2] and assesses the quality of journals, determines the excellence of business research, and the relative status of different business specialisations [35]. Among a set of 22 distinct fields of study, this guide ranks journals into five categories (i.e. 4*, 4, 3, 2, 1), where 4* is the top-level [34]. This is to quantitatively describe the debate on the circular economy while considering the general recognition of leading research journals in the business domain based on citations and impact. As a result, the query retrieved 1303 publications. However, we refined the query by restricting the search to the title and abstract paper fields

[1] https://charteredabs.org/academic-journal-guide-2021/
[2] https://charteredabs.org/

Table 1 Sample of the refined set of author's keywords

Original author's keywords	The adopted keywords
Circular economy	Circular economy
Circular economy (ce)	
The circular economy	
Circular economies	
Ce	
Life cycle assessment	Life cycle assessment
Life cycle assessment (lca)	
Life-cycle assessment (lca)	
Life-cycle assessment	

(excluding the authors' keyword field) since we noticed that some papers included keywords that did not represent the actual aim of a contribution (compared to the abstract and title of the same paper) from a manual check.

By running the revised query, we collected an initial dataset of 1088 publications covering a period automatically established from the search (last updated 6th June 2023). Still, we performed two main refinements of the dataset in the IInd step. We first defined the sources to be included. By exploring the different sources of the publications (automatically established by the platform), we included journal articles, conference papers, editorials, and reviews. In contrast, we excluded erratum, letters, and notes (after analysing these papers). Moreover, we excluded the publications missing the author(s)' name and both abstract and keywords after a manual check on the source page of the publications. After this selection, we had a refined dataset of 1060 papers.

In the second round of refinement, we updated the number of citations for each document, also checking for publications missing information for this field. Furthermore, focusing on the bibliometric data concerning the author's keywords, we cleaned and updated some of the author's keywords since we noticed that different keywords representing the same topic overlapped among the papers (i.e. synonyms and periphrases). In other words, by seeking to keep the authors' closest perspective, we homogenised objectively and theoretically similar keywords (i.e., acronyms, singular or plural spelling variations, abbreviations, and etymologically equivalent keywords). We refined an initial author's keywords set of 3071 (different occurrences) to a homogenised one composed of 2920 by adopting the most recurrent among the group of similar ones (see an example in Table 1). Also, since we identified 46 papers missing the author's keywords but were apt for the analysis, we first attempted to manually collect the missing keywords on the source page of the publications. In doing this, we retrieved the keywords for seven papers while we selected and added a set of representative keywords for each of the remaining papers. Specifically, we added only homogenised keywords after reading the papers. Thus, the final dataset consisted of 1060 papers, comprising the complete bibliometric data set.

In the IIIrd and last step of this protocol, we performed the bibliometric analysis by using the software R-studio with Bibliometrix package [36, 37] and VOS viewer

[38, 39] and Ghepi [40, 41] to create the keywords co-occurrences network. Thus, we examined the publications and citations trend [33, 42], exploring the most productive authors and countries. Then, we developed the authors' keyword co-occurrences network, focusing on the most used author's keywords and their co-occurrences [16, 32].

3 Results

This section refers to two sub-sections in line with the aims of the study. The first sub-section is based on the results of the performance analysis. It provides the trend of publications and citations by focusing on the most relevant sources, countries, authors, and citations of the publications in the final dataset. The second carries on a preliminary science mapping analysis, investigating the most influential topics discussed in the publications of our dataset based on the most recurring keywords used by authors. Specifically, it focuses on the trend of the most 21 used keywords (with at least 20 occurrences), the authors' keywords co-occurrences and the resulting network.

3.1 Performance Analysis

We performed this analysis at the beginning of June 2023, focusing on the final dataset of 1060 papers (see Fig. 1) distributed over 188 sources. Concerning the document type the search has automatically established, the dataset comprises 968 articles, 6 conference papers, 3 editorials, and 83 reviews. Figure 2 depicts the

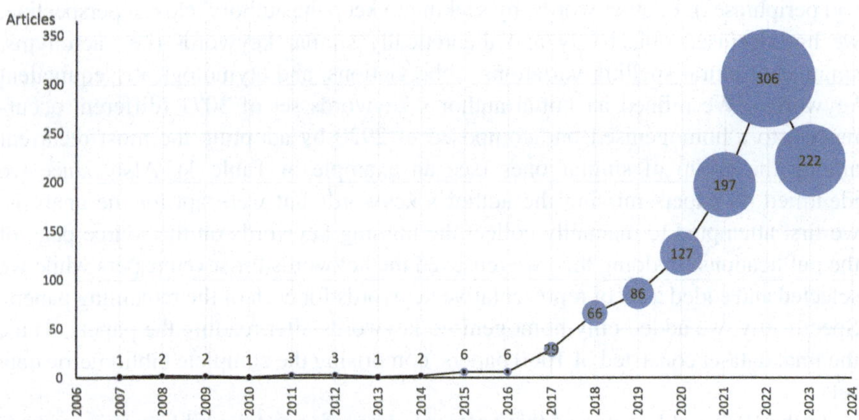

Fig. 2 Annual scientific production of the circular economy debate from 2007

annual scientific publication trend of the circular economy debate since 2007, described subsequently.

Looking at Fig. 2, the publication trend of the debate focused on circular economy covers the period from 2007 to date. However, the publication trend appears remarkably scant and regular until 2015, when scientific production slightly increments, with six publications overall as well as in 2016. Specifically, no more than three papers per year have been previously published. In comparison, the number of publications has increased significantly every year since 2017. The trend confirms the reasonably recent interest in the specific research domain with almost exponential growth starting from the 2020s (also considering the new policies related to the NextGeneration EU plan launched around those years). Also, although 2023 is assigned 222 publications in early June, the number of publications for this year may likely grow beyond 2022, considering the general trend. Anyway, the last 3 years (2021, 2022, 2023) represent the most productive ones, collecting almost 70% of the total publications in the dataset.

By examining the most relevant sources, we noticed that the publications are distributed over various specialisations, developing a multidisciplinary discussion. In particular, it appears that among 188 different sources, 101 published one paper and 38 two papers. Concerning the remaining 49 sources, 16 out of 49 published three papers, 5 published four, 4 published five, 2 published six, and three others published 7, 8, and 9, respectively. In comparison, Table 2 shows the remaining top 19 sources published at least 10 papers each (see Number of Publication). Moreover, Table 2 also provides information concerning the field of study of these journals and the related ranks in accordance with the AJG2021 (see Ch. 2). Also, Appendix 1 provides the list of the whole set of the field of study of the AJG list, including the tag used in the following descriptions. Overall, the *Journal of Environmental Management* is the most prolific, with 193 publications, followed by two others that published more than 100 papers each: the *Business Strategy and The Environment Journal* and the *Journal of Industrial Ecology*.

Afterwards, we focused on the contributions that received more attention among scholars by developing a preliminary citation analysis [33, 42, 43]. We perform this analysis to draw a first overview of the papers published in a specific discipline, where the number of citations represents the popularity and influence of a paper in the scientific community. Overall, 50 publications in our dataset (of 1060 papers) received at least 100 citations, followed by a further 80 collecting at least 50. Also, while 756 publications received less than 50 citations over time, 153 papers did not yet receive any citations. In comparison, we report the 23 most cited papers collecting more than 200 citations in Appendix 2, including the specific field of study (F.of.S.) in accordance with the AJG2021, the Total Citations (TC) and Total Citation per Year (TCpY.) for each publication. In this regard, Murray et al. [3] received the most significant number of citations (1282) over time, more than double those received by Govindan & Hasanagic [44], which is the second most cited paper in the dataset (591). In addition to those two publications, only 10 out of 23 gathered more than 300 citations. It is also interesting to note that 14 out of 23 most cited papers are published by journals assigned to the field of Social Science in the

Table 2 Top 19 most relevant sources

Source	N. of P.	Field of study and Rank (AJG2021)
Journal of Environmental Management	193	SOCSCI—(3)
Business Strategy and The Environment	149	SOCSCI—(3)
Journal of Industrial Ecology	116	SOCSCI—(2)
International Journal of Production Research	43	OPS&TECH—(3)
Environmental Science and Technology	38	SOCSCI—(3)
Production Planning and Control	26	OPS&TECH—(3)
Corporate Social Responsibility and Environmental Management	24	RSP&ENV—(1)
International Journal of Logistics Management	20	OPS&TECH—(1)
Management of Environmental Quality	20	SOCSCI—(1)
Annals of Operations Research	16	OR&MANSCI—(3)
International Journal of Productivity and Performance Management	16	OPS&TECH—(1)
International Journal of Logistics Research and Applications	15	OPS&TECH—(1)
Operations Management Research	15	OPS&TECH—(1)
Benchmarking	14	OPS&TECH—(1)
European Planning Studies	12	RSP&ENV—(2)
Building Research and Information	11	SOCSCI—(2)
Environmental Science and Policy	11	SOCSCI—(3)
Built Environment Project and Asset Management	10	RSP&ENV—(1)
Thunderbird International Business Review	10	IB&AREA—(2)

AJG2021. Those journals are the *Journal of Industrial Ecology* (10 out of 14), the *Economy and Society* Journal (1), the *Business Strategy and the Environment* Journal (2), and the *Local Economy* Journal (1). Interestingly, by considering the aims of these journals, it is possible to develop a preliminary understanding concerning the themes and issues that this research community is particularly interested in debating. For example, considering the *Journal of Industrial Ecology*, research is mainly progressing about "environmental impacts and drivers of the stocks and flows of material, energy and other resources in production and consumption activities". In comparison, the *Economy and Society* journal focuses on "economic relations and governance, progressive politics, and life science". The *Business Strategy and the Environment* journal promotes the understanding concerning "business strategies for improving the natural (green) environment", and the *Local Economy* Journal is concerned with "place-based policies for economic development, regeneration, and human development".

A further metric that could be relevant to the aim of this study is represented by the most productive countries. By exploring the bibliometric field concerning the authors' affiliation, it is possible to analyse the number of contributions assigned for each country based on the authors' affiliation in a dataset. In doing that, we plot the result of this analysis in Fig. 3, considering the countries collecting at least

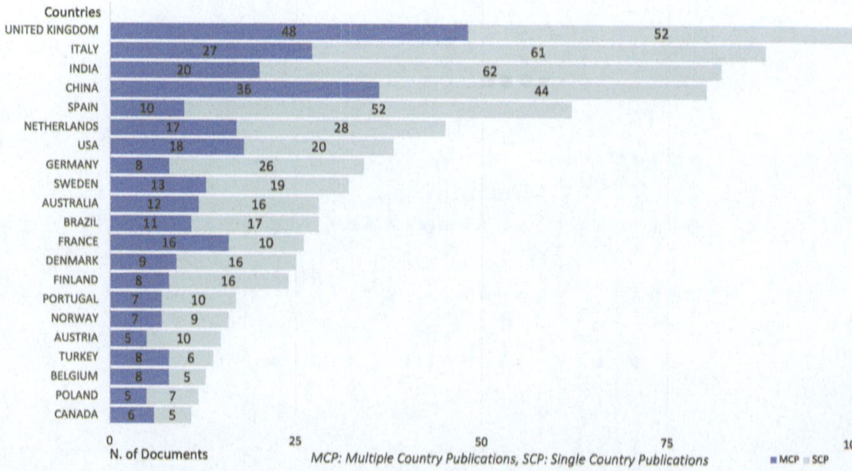

Fig. 3 Most productive countries (with at least 10 publications) included in the local dataset

10 publications. Additionally, the diagram makes it possible to distinguish the publications whose authors belong to a single country (SCP) or multiple countries (MCP).

In other words, Fig. 3 also shows the countries whose authors usually publish by collaborating with colleagues from different countries. By looking at Fig. 3, it appears that the circular economy debate has been significantly developed in the United Kingdom, with 100 contributions overall. Italy (88), India (82), and China (80) follow with slightly fewer publications, anyway more significant than the remaining countries. Notably, Italy represents the most productive country among the countries belonging to the European Union, conceivably depending on the many scholars involved in the NextGeneration EU and PNRR plans. In this regard, Italy presents a number of SCP almost double the one concerning MCP, as in the cases of India, Spain, and Germany. Similarly, the Netherlands, Denmark, Finland, and Austria likewise collect an SCP slightly greater than the MCP. In contrast, France, Turkey, Belgium, and Canada are the countries with an MCP level (16, 8, 8, and 6 publications, respectively) greater than the SCP (10, 6, 5, and 5 publications, respectively). Moreover, regardless of the publication rate, the United Kingdom, China, USA, Australia, Portugal, Norway, and Poland show almost equal levels of the number of publications for SCP and MCP.

Then, we focused on the authors' production over time, considering the authors with at least six publications in the local dataset. Adopting this threshold, we identified the 24 most productive authors over time, showing the results in Fig. 4. For each author, the dot size represents the number of published articles, while the intensity of the colour defines the total citations per year.

Exploring the number of papers in Fig. 4 contributed, Kumar A. is the most productive author, with 13 articles published in different journals between 2020 and

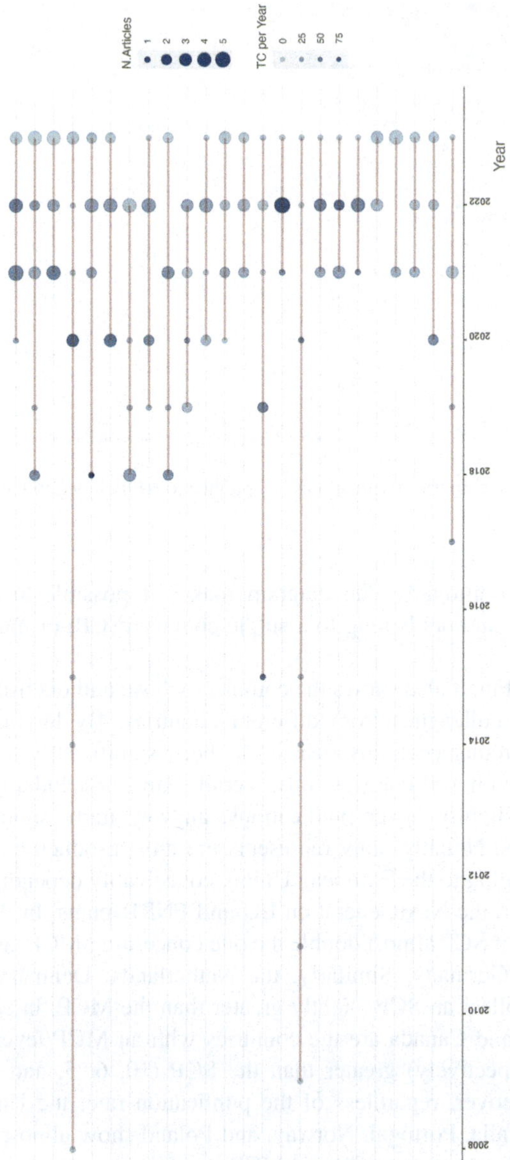

Fig. 4 Top authors' production over time in relation to the most 24 authors

2023. Garza-Reyes JA. follows with 12 contributions between 2018 and 2023. Moreover, Kazancoglu Y. and Sarkis J. contributed 11 publications between 2021–2023 and 2008–2023. Besides, Sarkis J. could be considered one of the pioneers in the circular economy debate, with one publication in 2008, in the early days of this stream of research (see Fig. 2). Similarly, it is the case of Zhu Q. contributed with seven papers between 2009 and 2023. Next, considering nine publications are Govindan K., Iraldo F., and Van Wassenhove LN., between 2018–2023, 2020–2023, and 2018–2022, respectively. Moreover, Daddi T., Kumar V., Lopes De Sousa Jabbour AB., Sehnem S., and Singh RK. contributed each with eight publications in different years between 2018 and 2023. Similarly to Zhu Q., with seven publications contributed, Mangla SK., Wiedenhofer D., and Yu Z., while the remaining eight authors contributed with six publications, especially between 2021 and 2023.

Regarding these authors' impact on literature, 3 out of 24 most productive authors also belong to the list of authors receiving at least 200 citations for one of their publications. In particular, Govindan K. received a total of 881 citations over his nine publications (in different journals), whose 591 for a co-authored publication in the *International Journal of Production Research* [44]. The other two authors received 206 citations for one of their papers, which is co-authored with a third author. Interestingly, these two authors are mentioned as pioneers since they started debating circular economy in 2008 and 2009 (yet the number of citations is not related to publications concerning these 2 years). Specifically, Sarkis J. received a total of 429 citations over his nine publications (in different journals). In comparison, Zhu Q. received a total of 426 citations for her seven publications (in other Journals). For both authors, 206 citations are assigned to their co-authored publication in the *Production Planning & Control* Journal [45]. Concerning Kumar A., the most productive author in the local dataset, he received 357 citations among 13 different publications with no significant rate for one of them. To be thorough about the already discussed authors, we report the number of citations each received hereafter. That is, Garza-Reyes JA. received a total of (408) citations, Kazancoglu Y. (209), Iraldo F. (311), Van Wassenhove LN. (297), Daddi T. (289), Kumar V. (392), Lopes De Sousa Jabbour AB. (265), Sehnem S. (112), Singh RK (97), Mangla SK. (98), Wiedenhofer D. (824), and Yu Z. (315).

3.2 Science Mapping

Focusing on the science mapping methods, we sought to start investigations of co-word analysis by developing the authors' keyword co-occurrences network. In particular, we focused on the most recurring keywords used by authors in the local dataset with the aim of exploring the most important topics related to the circular economy debate. By developing this analysis, we are able to recognise some insights regarding the content and the relations between the topics discussed in our dataset [17]. Moreover, we set a minimum threshold of 20 occurrences in selecting the authors' keywords for developing the following analysis. As a result, we obtained

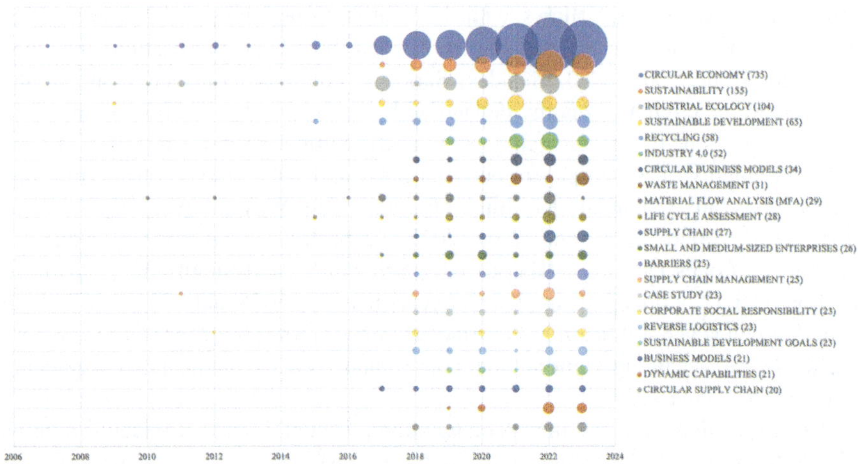

Fig. 5 Authors' keywords distribution over the years

21 keywords that we recognised as the top 21 most used by the authors discussing circular economy from 2007 to date, so we analysed their related trends.

By examining such 21 most used keywords, we developed Fig. 5, showing the related trends over the last 16 years. Looking at the graph, it is not surprising that *circular economy* is the most frequent keyword, represented by 735 occurrences. *Sustainability* and *industrial ecology* follow with significantly fewer occurrences, 155 and 104, yet greater compared to all the others. Also, with less frequency, *sustainable development*, *recycling*, *industry 4.0*, *circular business models*, and *waste management* are the other keywords with at least 30 occurrences (65, 58, 52, 34, 31, respectively). In general, Fig. 5 shows that the frequency of the 21 keywords appears toughly regular over the years, considering that the research proliferation on circular economy intensified precisely from 2017 to date. Accordingly, this period shows a higher concentrated level of occurrences concerning multidisciplinary topics related to the circular economy stream of research. Focusing on 2017 in particular, the keywords *business models*, *small and medium-sized enterprises*, *life cycle assessment* and *material flow analysis (MFA)* represent the main topics and aspects used in discussing the leading subjects represented by the first five keywords (as in Fig. 5). Among those keywords, it is interesting to note that *material flow analysis (mfa)* is one of the few keywords already used in previous years (i.e., in 2010, 2012 and 2016), while *life cycle assessment* was used for the first time in 2015. Likewise peculiar are the keywords *supply change management* and *corporate social responsibility*, used in 2011 and 2012 for the first time.

Focusing on the first six most frequent keywords with at least 50 occurrences (representing the leading topics related to the circular economy), we can see that *industry 4.0* has been used since 2019, *sustainability* since 2017, as in the case of *recycling* (instead used for the first time in 2015). Also, scholars have been growingly using the keywords *sustainability* and *sustainable development* since 2017,

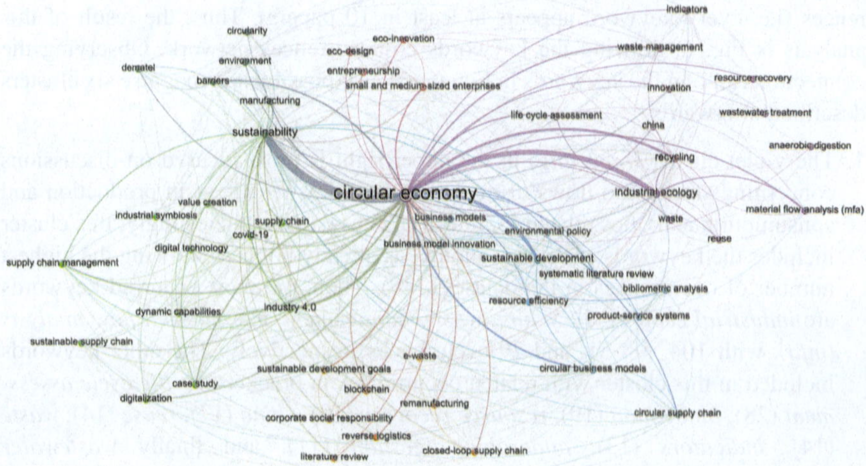

Fig. 6 Author's keywords co-occurrences network

although the latter keyword was used for the first time in 2009. However, *industrial ecology* is the only keyword that appears to be used regularly with the leading *circular economy* since the early days of such a debate. In particular, those two keywords were used together for the first time in 2007, as well as in 2009, 2011, 2012, 2014, and 2015, and consistently since 2017. Then, while the keyword *circular economy* was also used in 2013 and 2016, *industrial ecology* was used together with *material flow analysis (mfa)* in 2010.

These preliminary results seem to support the purpose of this paper partially, highlighting some of the most frequent aspects debated by scholars concerning the circular economy debate. Figure 5 clearly outlines the specific focus of the discussion in different years, where heterogeneous keywords could represent linked topics. Accordingly, we then performed the keywords co-occurrence analysis [24, 46] in order to investigate the connections among the main topics discussed in the local dataset.

Starting from the 21 most recurring keywords, we created the co-occurrence network (see Fig. 6). For this purpose, we used the software VOS viewer [38, 39] and Ghepi [40, 41] to create a graph which displays the resulting network. Thus, we locate keyword networks strongly linked to each other [27], presenting the resulting diagram. In particular, such a network is a graphical representation of how each (author's) keyword has been mentioned together with another one. In Fig. 6, each node (and its label) in the graph identifies one keyword. The more the thickness of a keyword, the more the number of connections between such keyword and other keywords in the network (occurrence of a keyword). Hence, if two keywords have been mentioned together in a publication, there is a tie between them (co-occurrence). Moreover, the thickness of a tie represents the number of contributions including the pair of keywords. For this study, the keywords' drawn in the graph respect a threshold set of 10 concerning the minimum number of occurrences (i.e. every keyword appears at least in 10 papers). Thus, the result of this analysis is Fig. 6, drawing the keywords co-occurrences network. Observing the connections among the keywords in Fig. 6 makes it possible to recognise six clusters described afterwards.

1. The violet cluster (*recycling*) in the upper right is most focused on discussions concerning stocks and flows of material, as well as resources in production and consumption activities related to industrial ecosystems. Interestingly, this cluster includes the keywords circular economy, as already noticed, showing the highest number of occurrences in the dataset (735). Then, the most occurred keywords are *industrial ecology*, *recycling*, *waste management* and *material flow analysis (mfa)*, with 104, 58, 31, and 29 occurrences, respectively. The other keywords included in this cluster with related occurrences in brackets are *life cycle assessment* (28), *innovation* (19), *resource recovery* (19), *china* (17), *reuse* (14), *waste* (14), *indicators* (13), *anaerobic digestion* (11), and finally *wastewater treatment* (11).
2. The pink cluster (entrepreneurship) in the middle top is related to business strategies for improving environmental impacts and some aspects concerning ecological initiatives, especially regarding small and medium-sized enterprises. In particular, this cluster is based on four keywords overall. The most recurring keyword is small and medium-sized enterprises, with (26) occurrences, followed by eco-innovation (15), eco-design (19), and entrepreneurship (10).
3. The grey cluster (*sustainability*) in the upper left focuses on broader discussions concerning environmental impacts and drivers characterising manufacturing and related sustainability practices. As a manner of fact, *sustainability* is the most recurring keyword for this cluster, with (155) occurrences. This cluster also comprises the keywords *barriers* with (25) occurrences, followed by *manufacturing* (17), *dematel* (14), *environment* (13), and *circularity* (12).
4. The green cluster (*supply chain*) in the bottom left is related to the discussions focused on the impact and adoption of digital technologies for transforming processes and activities through ecological and sustainable change management. From an academic point of view, the keyword *case study* represents particular scholarly attention on empirical investigations related to these topics. For this cluster, the most occurred keyword is *industry 4.0,* with (51) occurrences. Then, the other keywords included in this cluster with related occurrences in brackets are *supply chain* (27), *supply chain management* (25), *case study* (23), *dynamic capabilities* (21), *covid-19* (16), *digitalization* (14), *digital technology* (13), *industrial symbiosis* (11), *value creation* (11), and finally, *sustainable supply chain* (10).
5. The orange cluster (*corporate social responsibility*) in the middle bottom is focused on discussions concerning economic and human development innovation processes upon the circular economy umbrella, such as regenerate, share, optimise, loop, virtualise, and exchange. Then, the most occurred keywords are *sustainable development goals*, *reverse logistics*, and *corporate social*

responsibility, with 23, 23, and 22 occurrences, respectively. The other keywords included in this cluster with related occurrences in brackets are *remanufacturing* (18), *closed-loop supply chain* (18), *blockchain* (17), *e-waste* (14), and *literature review* (11).

6. The light blue cluster (*efficiency*) in the bottom right is related to discussions concerning economic relations, business model redesign, governance, and policy aspects. Considering some of the keywords included in this cluster, it emerges that particular scholarly attention is given to systematic and structured literature analysis that explores such topics. For this cluster, the most occurred keywords are *sustainable development*, *circular business models*, *business models* and *circular supply chain*, with 65, 34, 21, and 20 occurrences, respectively. Then, the remaining keywords included in this cluster with related occurrences in brackets are *resource efficiency* (19), *systematic literature review* (17), *business model innovation* (15), *bibliometric analysis* (13), *environmental policy* (12) and *product-service systems* (11).

By exploring the author's keyword co-occurrences, this analysis provides a first overview of the topics mainly debated in the discussion focusing on circular economy. To further investigate the topics discussed in the dataset and their relevance, starting from the co-occurrence network of all keywords, it could be interesting to progress the investigation by developing a thematic map [17] in a further step.

4 Discussion and Conclusions

This study intends to build a knowledge base to define a theoretical and methodological position for the following research steps in the context of the *Ecosister* project. To identify and bridge a specific gap in theory and practice while targeting the *Ecosister* aims, we adopted bibliometric methods to examine the circular economy debate. For this purpose, we developed performance and science mapping investigations based on 1060 papers. The performance analysis depicts the growing interest in research on circular economy starting from 2017, showing a significant increase of almost 70% of the total publications in the last 3 years. Considering the different analyses we performed, among other factors, this trend is likely to be particularly affected by many policies and plans defined by the European Union in the same years. Afterwards, we developed the author's keywords' co-occurrence networks, intending to pave the groundwork for co-word analysis. We analysed the 21 most frequent keywords and described the network of the co-occurrences of such keywords in relation to six clusters.

As a result, this paper recognises multiple research topics (represented by the different keywords) describing the advancement of the circular economy discourse over the years. In particular, the keywords co-occurrences network identifies six clusters that could represent specific sub-areas of interest and might support the design and development of further comprehensive analyses. In this regard, although we provided a thorough descriptive analysis with respect to the science mapping exploration, this preliminary quantitative study presents the traits of the debate on the circular economy, providing interest for further investigations.

Thus, the six clusters identified here (*recycling*, *entrepreneurship, sustainability, supply chain, corporate social responsibility,* and *efficiency*) can be (in further extensions) compared and integrated with the major themes and patterns identified in extant literature, particularly in existing literature reviews. Accordingly, we propose some of the potentially interesting lines of future development based on three of the most cited literature reviews appearing in our dataset hereafter.

Specifically, in Lüdeke-Freund et al. [47], the focus of the literature review is on Circular Economy Business Models (CEBM). Six major CEBM patterns are identified: *repair and maintenance*, *reuse and redistribution*, *refurbishment and remanufacturing, recycling*, *cascading and repurposing*, and *organic*.

In Panchal et al. [48], the research articles were classified according to the Sustainable Development Goals (SDGs) addressed, industries involved, key areas of circular economy, pillars of sustainability, circular economy principles (R-Imperatives and Systems perspective), type of cycle in CE, and transversality (generic, product-specific, and sector-specific). The most relevant area of CE is waste management in the context of performance evaluation. Furthermore, innovation and investments are critical to other areas of the circular economy value chain. In the technical cycle, maximum work is done in the metals and mining industry, whereas the pulp and paper industry is the least explored.

In addition, Bag and Pretorius [49], an integrative review focusing on antecedents of circular economy capabilities, identifies interesting and promising theoretical constructs relevant to developing circular economy capabilities, including institutional pressures and digital resources.

The different focus areas, research objectives, and theoretical perspectives of the exemplary reviews sketched here open several patterns for future developments. Precisely, it could be interesting to extend and deepen the major classification area of extant research debate, consider alternative focus areas for more in-depth investigations, and unveil potentially fruitful theoretical frameworks for investigating antecedents for the diffusion and development of the circular economy. For example, additional empirical research could simultaneously examine the relationships between characteristics and implications related to different industrial ecosystems, the type of circularity practices contributing to the transition from linear to circular business models, and potential innovations fostered by the organisations under investigation.

As a contribution, this research investigated the scientific production related to the circular economy by considering the list of journals included in the AJG2021. Accordingly, our analyses strictly refer to the general recognition of refereed journals in the business domain based on citations and impact. Then, this review could support further researchers in progressing this line of inquiry, as well as in developing additional studies concerning circular economy.

Besides, this paper has some limitations. First, this research is based only on Scopus and does not integrate the input dataset with collections from other databases (e.g. Web of Science). Second, we provided a preliminary citation analysis. In a future step, it could be interesting to extend such research by identifying the most cited publication for each most productive author. Then, this could be useful for designing and conducting a complete citation and co-citation analysis that in-depth describes the evolution of citation patterns and the theoretical building blocks through the co-citation networks [33].

Moreover, we discussed the author's keywords co-occurrences network, providing a preliminary understanding of the conceptual structure, evolution, and relations between the important topics debated in our dataset. As a further step, we could perform a complete co-word analysis by developing a thematic map to represent a set of research themes mapped into a (two-dimensional) strategical diagram as a synthetic representation of such a network [17]. Hence, we could explore the publications assigned to each cluster in the thematic map and examine the most relevant themes and relations among multiple topics and issues being debated. For example, further comprehension could be developed regarding the theoretical relevance and the degree of development of the different themes assigned to each cluster. At the same time, we could further analyse the publications related to each quadrant of the thematic map, focusing on the field of studies defined by the AJG2021. In other words, we might develop an understanding of how the different themes evolved, considering the specific area, the research community, or the group of interest with regard to fields of studies and the scopes of various journals. Finally, since this research primarily relies on analysing the authors' keywords, it could be helpful to perform a computational literature review as a complementary approach for integrating the study of the abstracts of the corpus.

Acknowledgements This study was funded by the "National Recovery and Resilience Plan (NRRP), Mission 04 Component 2 Investment 1.5 – NextGenerationEU, Call for tender n. 3277 dated 30/12/2021, Award Number: 0001052 dated 23/06/2022".

Disclosure of Interests The authors have no competing interests to declare that are relevant to the content of this article.

Appendices

Appendix 1 List of the Whole Set of Fields of Study Defined in the AJG2021

Field of study defined in the AJG2021	Tag
Accounting	ACCOUNT
Business and Economic History	BUS HIST & ECON HIS
Economics, Econometrics and Statistics	ECON
Entrepreneurship and Small Business Management	ENT-SBM
Finance	FINANCE
General Management, Ethics, Gender and Social Responsibility	ETHICS-CSR-MAN
Human Resource Management and Employment Studies	HRM&EMP

(continued)

Field of study defined in the AJG2021	Tag
Information Management	INFOMAN
Innovation	INNOV
International Business and Area Studies	IB&AREA
Management Development and Education	MDEV&EDU
Marketing	MKT
Operations and Technology Management	OPS&TECH
Operations Research and Management Science	OR&MANSCI
Organisational Studies	ORGSTUD
Psychology (General)	PSYCH (GENERAL)
Psychology (Organisational)	PSYCH (WOP-OB)
Public Sector and Health Care	PUBSEC
Regional Studies, Planning and Environment	RSP&ENV
Sports, Leisure, Tourism and Sector Studies	SECTOR
Social Sciences	SOCSCI
Strategy	STRAT

Appendix 2 Top 23 Most Cited Papers with at least 200 Citations

Paper	F.of.S.	TC	TCpY.
Murray, A., Skene, K., & Haynes, K. (2015). The Circular Economy: An Interdisciplinary Exploration of the Concept and Application in a Global Context. In Journal of Business Ethics (Vol. 140, Issue 3, pp. 369–380). Springer Science and Business Media LLC. https://doi.org/10.1007/s10551-015-2693-2	MDEV&EDU	1282	183,14
Govindan, K., & Hasanagic, M. (2018). A systematic review on drivers, barriers, and practices towards circular economy: a supply chain perspective. In International Journal of Production Research (Vol. 56, Issues 1–2, pp. 278–311). Informa UK Limited. https://doi.org/10.1080/00207543.2017.1402141	OPS&TECH	591	98,50
Haas, W., Krausmann, F., Wiedenhofer, D., & Heinz, M. (2015). How Circular is the Global Economy?: An Assessment of Material Flows, Waste Production, and Recycling in the European Union and the World in 2005. In Journal of Industrial Ecology (Vol. 19, Issue 5, pp. 765–777). Wiley. https://doi.org/10.1111/jiec.12244	SOCSCI	570	63,33
Blomsma, F., & Brennan, G. (2017). The Emergence of Circular Economy: A New Framing Around Prolonging Resource Productivity. In Journal of Industrial Ecology (Vol. 21, Issue 3, pp. 603–614). Wiley. https://doi.org/10.1111/jiec.12603	SOCSCI	566	80,86
	OR&MANSCI	563	93,83

(continued)

Paper	F.of.S.	TC	TCpY.
Lopes de Sousa Jabbour, A. B., Jabbour, C. J. C., Godinho Filho, M., & Roubaud, D. (2018). Industry 4.0 and the circular economy: a proposed research agenda and original roadmap for sustainable operations. In Annals of Operations Research (Vol. 270, Issues 1–2, pp. 273–286). Springer Science and Business Media LLC. https://doi.org/10.1007/s10479-018-2772-8			
Schroeder, P., Anggraeni, K., & Weber, U. (2018). The Relevance of Circular Economy Practices to the Sustainable Development Goals. In Journal of Industrial Ecology (Vol. 23, Issue 1, pp. 77–95). Wiley. https://doi.org/10.1111/jiec.12732	SOCSCI	550	110,00
Zink, T., & Geyer, R. (2017). Circular Economy Rebound. In Journal of Industrial Ecology (Vol. 21, Issue 3, pp. 593–602). Wiley. https://doi.org/10.1111/jiec.12545	SOCSCI	482	68,86
Lüdeke-Freund, F., Gold, S., & Bocken, N. M. P. (2018). A Review and Typology of Circular Economy Business Model Patterns. In Journal of Industrial Ecology (Vol. 23, Issue 1, pp. 36–61). Wiley. https://doi.org/10.1111/jiec.12763	SOCSCI	431	86,20
Gregson, N., Crang, M., Fuller, S., & Holmes, H. (2015). Interrogating the circular economy: the moral economy of resource recovery in the EU. In Economy and Society (Vol. 44, Issue 2, pp. 218–243). Informa UK Limited. https://doi.org/10.1080/03085147.2015.1013353	SOCSCI	365	40,56
McDowall, W., Geng, Y., Huang, B., Barteková, E., Bleischwitz, R., Türkeli, S., Kemp, R., & Doménech, T. (2017). Circular Economy Policies in China and Europe. In Journal of Industrial Ecology (Vol. 21, Issue 3, pp. 651–661). Wiley. https://doi.org/10.1111/jiec.12597	SOCSCI	347	49,57
Mathews, J. A., & Tan, H. (2011). Progress Toward a Circular Economy in China. In Journal of Industrial Ecology (Vol. 15, Issue 3, pp. 435–457). Wiley. https://doi.org/10.1111/j.1530	SOCSCI	330	25,38
den Hollander, M. C., Bakker, C. A., & Hultink, E. J. (2017). Product Design in a Circular Economy: Development of a Typology of Key Concepts and Terms. In Journal of Industrial Ecology (Vol. 21, Issue 3, pp. 517–525). Wiley. https://doi.org/10.1111/jiec.12610	SOCSCI	312	44,57
Rosa, P., Sassanelli, C., Urbinati, A., Chiaroni, D., & Terzi, S. (2019). Assessing relations between Circular Economy and Industry 4.0: a systematic literature review. In International Journal of Production Research (Vol. 58, Issue 6, pp. 1662–1687). Informa UK Limited. https://doi.org/10.1080/00207543.2019.1680896	OPS&TECH	273	68,25
De Angelis, R., Howard, M., & Miemczyk, J. (2018). Supply chain management and the circular economy: towards the circular supply chain. In Production Planning & Control (Vol. 29, Issue 6, pp. 425–437). Informa UK Limited. https://doi.org/10.1080/09537287.2018.1449244	OPS&TECH	265	44,17

(continued)

Paper	F.of.S.	TC	TCpY.
Bressanelli, G., Perona, M., & Saccani, N. (2018). Challenges in supply chain redesign for the Circular Economy: a literature review and a multiple case study. In International Journal of Production Research (Vol. 57, Issue 23, pp. 7395–7422). Informa UK Limited. https://doi.org/10.1080/00207543.2018.1542176	OPS&TECH	233	46,60
Nobre, G. C., & Tavares, E. (2017). Scientific literature analysis on big data and internet of things applications on circular economy: a bibliometric study. In Scientometrics (Vol. 111, Issue 1, pp. 463–492). Springer Science and Business Media LLC. https://doi.org/10.1007/s11192-017-2281-6	INNOV	230	32,86
Linder, M., Sarasini, S., & van Loon, P. (2017). A Metric for Quantifying Product-Level Circularity. In Journal of Industrial Ecology (Vol. 21, Issue 3, pp. 545–558). Wiley. https://doi.org/10.1111/jiec.12552	SOCSCI	228	32,57
Moreau, V., Sahakian, M., van Griethuysen, P., & Vuille, F. (2017). Coming Full Circle: Why Social and Institutional Dimensions Matter for the Circular Economy. In Journal of Industrial Ecology (Vol. 21, Issue 3, pp. 497–506). Wiley. https://doi.org/10.1111/jiec.12598	SOCSCI	220	31,43
Hazen, B. T., Mollenkopf, D. A., & Wang, Y. (2016). Remanufacturing for the Circular Economy: An Examination of Consumer Switching Behavior. In Business Strategy and the Environment (Vol. 26, Issue 4, pp. 451–464). Wiley. https://doi.org/10.1002/bse.1929	SOCSCI	217	31,00
Centobelli, P., Cerchione, R., Chiaroni, D., Del Vecchio, P., & Urbinati, A. (2020). Designing business models in circular economy: A systematic literature review and research agenda. In Business Strategy and the Environment (Vol. 29, Issue 4, pp. 1734–1749). Wiley. https://doi.org/10.1002/bse.2466	SOCSCI	211	52,75
Zeng, X., Mathews, J. A., & Li, J. (2018). Urban Mining of E-Waste is Becoming More Cost-Effective Than Virgin Mining. In Environmental Science & Technology (Vol. 52, Issue 8, pp. 4835–4841). American Chemical Society (ACS). https://doi.org/10.1021/acs.est.7b04909	SOCSCI	209	34,83
Kouhizadeh, M., Zhu, Q., & Sarkis, J. (2019). Blockchain and the circular economy: potential tensions and critical reflections from practice. In Production Planning & Control (Vol. 31, Issues 11–12, pp. 950–966). Informa UK Limited. https://doi.org/10.1080/09537287.2019.1695925	OPS&TECH	206	51,50
Andrews, D. (2015). The circular economy, design thinking and education for sustainability. In Local Economy: The Journal of the Local Economy Policy Unit (Vol. 30, Issue 3, pp. 305–315). SAGE Publications. https://doi.org/10.1177/0269094215578226	RSP&ENV	203	22,56

References

1. Catala, B., Savall, T., & Chaves-Avila, R. (2023). From entrepreneurial and innovation ecosystems to the social economy ecosystem. *Journal of Business Research, 163*, 113932. https://doi.org/10.1016/j.jbusres.2023.113932
2. Mosconi, F., & D'Ingiullo, D. (2023). Institutional quality and innovation: Evidence from Emilia-Romagna. *Economics of Innovation and New Technology, 32*, 165–197. https://doi.org/10.1080/10438599.2021.1893140
3. Murray, A., Skene, K., & Haynes, K. (2015). The circular economy: An interdisciplinary exploration of the concept and application in a global context. *Journal of Business Ethics, 140*, 369–380. https://doi.org/10.1007/s10551-015-2693-2
4. Fadeeva, Z., & Van Berkel, R. (2021). Unlocking circular economy for prevention of marine plastic pollution: An exploration of G20 policy and initiatives. *Journal of Environmental Management, 277*, 111457. https://doi.org/10.1016/j.jenvman.2020.111457
5. Geissdoerfer, M., Savaget, P., Bocken, N. M. P., & Hultink, E. J. (2017). The circular economy—A new sustainability paradigm? *Journal of Cleaner Production, 143*, 757–768. https://doi.org/10.1016/j.jclepro.2016.12.048
6. Korhonen, J., Honkasalo, A., & Seppälä, J. (2018). Circular economy: The concept and its limitations. *Ecological Economics, 143*, 37–46. https://doi.org/10.1016/j.ecolecon.2017.06.041
7. Chauhan, C., Parida, V., & Dhir, A. (2022). Linking circular economy and digitalisation technologies: A systematic literature review of past achievements and future promises. *Technological Forecasting and Social Change, 177*, 121508. https://doi.org/10.1016/j.techfore.2022.121508
8. Marsh, A. T. M., Velenturf, A. P. M., & Bernal, S. A. (2022). Circular economy strategies for concrete: Implementation and integration. *Journal of Cleaner Production, 362*, 132486. https://doi.org/10.1016/j.jclepro.2022.132486
9. Scornavacca, E., Paolone, F., Za, S., & Martiniello, L. (2020). Investigating the entrepreneurial perspective in smart city studies. *International Entrepreneurship and Management Journal*. published. https://doi.org/10.1007/s11365-019-00630-4
10. Lamboglia, R., Lavorato, D., Scornavacca, E., & Za, S. (2021). Exploring the relationship between audit and technology. A bibliometric analysis. *Meditari Accountancy Research, 29*, 1233–1260. https://doi.org/10.1108/MEDAR-03-2020-0836
11. Cobo, M. J., Jürgens, B., Herrero-Solana, V., Martínez, M. A., & Herrera-Viedma, E. (2018). Industry 4.0: A perspective based on bibliometric analysis. *Procedia Computer Science, 139*, 364–371. https://doi.org/10.1016/j.procs.2018.10.278
12. Bracarense, N., Bawack, R., Wamba, S. F., & Carillo, K. D. A. (2022). Artificial intelligence and sustainability: A bibliometric analysis and future research directions. *Pacific Asia Journal of the Association for Information Systems, 14*, 136–159. https://doi.org/10.17705/1pais.14209
13. Za, S., & Spagnoletti, P. (2013). Knowledge creation processes in information systems and management: Lessons from simulation studies. In: *Lecture notes in information systems and organisation* (pp. 191–204). https://doi.org/10.1007/978-3-642-37228-5_19.
14. Chinotaikul, P., & Vinayavekhin, S. (2020). Digital transformation in business and management research: Bibliometric and co-word network analysis. In: *2020 1st international conference on big data analytics and practices (IBDAP)* (pp. 1–5). IEEE. https://doi.org/10.1109/IBDAP50342.2020.9245456
15. Kraus, S., Durst, S., Ferreira, J. J., Veiga, P., Kailer, N., & Weinmann, A. (2022). Digital transformation in business and management research: An overview of the current status quo. *International Journal of Information Management., 63*, 102466. https://doi.org/10.1016/j.ijinfomgt.2021.102466
16. Za, S., Ghiringhelli, C., & Virili, F. (2020). Organizational change and learning: An explorative bibliometric-based literature analysis. In: *Lecture Notes in Information Systems and Organisation* (pp. 429–442). https://doi.org/10.1007/978-3-030-23665-6_31.

17. Cobo, M. J., López-Herrera, A. G., Herrera-Viedma, E., & Herrera, F. (2011). An approach for detecting, quantifying, and visualizing the evolution of a research field: A practical application to the Fuzzy Sets Theory field. *Journal of Informetrics, 5*, 146–166. https://doi.org/10.1016/j.joi.2010.10.002
18. Donthu, N., Kumar, S., & Pattnaik, D. (2020). Forty-five years of Journal of Business Research: A bibliometric analysis. *Journal of Business Research, 109*, 1–14. https://doi.org/10.1016/j.jbusres.2019.10.039
19. White, H. D., & McCain, K. W. (1998). Visualizing a discipline: An author co-citation analysis of information science, 1972–1995. *Journal of the American Society for Information Science., 49*, 327–355. https://doi.org/10.1002/(SICI)1097-4571(19980401)49:4<327::AID-ASI4>3.0.CO;2-W
20. Aria, M., Misuraca, M., & Spano, M. (2020). Mapping the evolution of social research and data science on 30 years of social indicators research. *Social Indicators Research, 149*, 803–831. https://doi.org/10.1007/s11205-020-02281-3
21. Small, H. (1999). Visualizing science by citation mapping. *Journal of the American Society for Information Science, 50*, 799–813. https://doi.org/10.1002/(SICI)1097-4571(1999)50:9<799::AID-ASI9>3.0.CO;2-G
22. Börner, K., Chen, C., & Boyack, K. W. (2005). Visualizing knowledge domains. *Annual Review of Information Science and Technology., 37*, 179–255. https://doi.org/10.1002/aris.1440370106
23. Castriotta, M., Loi, M., Marku, E., & Naitana, L. (2019). What's in a name? Exploring the conceptual structure of emerging organizations. *Scientometrics, 118*, 407–437. https://doi.org/10.1007/s11192-018-2977-2
24. Zupic, I., & Čater, T. (2015). Bibliometric methods in management and organization. *Organizational Research Methods., 18*, 429–472. https://doi.org/10.1177/1094428114562629
25. Ferreira, M. P., Santos, J. C., de Almeida, M. I. R., & Reis, N. R. (2014). Mergers & acquisitions research: A bibliometric study of top strategy and international business journals, 1980–2010. *Journal of Business Research., 67*, 2550–2558. https://doi.org/10.1016/j.jbusres.2014.03.015
26. Ali, I., Balta, M., & Papadopoulos, T. (2023). Social media platforms and social enterprise: Bibliometric analysis and systematic review. *International Journal of Information Management, 69*, 102510. https://doi.org/10.1016/j.ijinfomgt.2022.102510
27. Callon, M., Courtial, J. P., & Laville, F. (1991). Co-word analysis as a tool for describing the network of interactions between basic and technological research: The case of polymer chemistry. *Scientometrics, 22*, 155–205. https://doi.org/10.1007/BF02019280
28. Callon, M., Courtial, J.-P., Turner, W. A., & Bauin, S. (1983). From translations to problematic networks: An introduction to co-word analysis. *Social Science Information, 22*, 191–235. https://doi.org/10.1177/053901883022002003
29. Caputo, A., Marzi, G., Maley, J., & Silic, M. (2019). Ten years of conflict management research 2007-2017. *International Journal of Conflict Management, 30*, 87–110. https://doi.org/10.1108/IJCMA-06-2018-0078
30. Marzi, G., Caputo, A., Garces, E., & Dabic, M. (2020). A three decade mixed-method bibliometric investigation of the IEEE transactions on engineering management. *IEEE Transactions on Engineering Management, 67*, 4–17. https://doi.org/10.1109/TEM.2018.2870648
31. Huang, J.-H., Duan, X.-Y., He, F.-F., Wang, G.-J., & Hu, X.-Y. (2021). *A historical review and bibliometric analysis of research on weak measurement research over the past decades based on Biblioshiny*. 1–19.
32. Cambrosio, A., Limoges, C., Courtial, J. P., & Laville, F. (1993). Historical scientometrics? Mapping over 70 years of biological safety research with coword analysis. *Scientometrics, 27*, 119–143. https://doi.org/10.1007/BF02016546
33. Za, S., & Braccini, A. M. (2017). Tracing the roots of the organizational benefits of IT services. In: *Exploring services science* (pp. 3–11). https://doi.org/10.1007/978-3-319-56925-3_1

34. Rahal, A., & Zainuba, M. (2019). The rating dilemma of academic management journals: Attuning the perceptions of peer rating. *Advances in Business Research, 9*, 26–45.
35. Walker, J., & Wood, G. (2021). Methodology. *Academic Journal Guide 2021*. https://charteredabs.org/wp-content/uploads/2021/06/Academic_Journal_Guide_2021-Methodology.pdf. https://doi.org/10.36548/jitdw.2021.2
36. Aria, M., & Cuccurullo, C. (2017). Bibliometrix: An R-tool for comprehensive science mapping analysis. *Journal of Informetrics, 11*, 959–975. https://doi.org/10.1016/j.joi.2017.08.007
37. Aria, M., Cuccurullo, C.: Comprehensive science mapping analysis, (2022).
38. Perianes-Rodriguez, A., Waltman, L., & van Eck, N. J. (2016). Constructing bibliometric networks: A comparison between full and fractional counting. *Journal of Informetrics, 10*, 1178–1195. https://doi.org/10.1016/j.joi.2016.10.006
39. van Eck, N. J., & Waltman, L. (2014). Visualizing bibliometric networks. In: *Measuring scholarly impact* (pp. 285–320). Springer International Publishing. https://doi.org/10.1007/978-3-319-10377-8_13
40. Bastian, M., & Heymann, S. (2014). *Gephi: An open source software for exploring and manipulating networks*, 4–6. https://doi.org/10.13140/2.1.1341.1520
41. Bastian, M., Heymann, S., & Jacomy, M. (2009). Gephi: An open source software for exploring and manipulating networks. BT - International AAAI Conference on Weblogs and Social. In: *International AAAI Conference on Weblogs and Social Media* (pp. 361–362).
42. Baier-Fuentes, H., Merigó, J. M., Amorós, J. E., & Gaviria-Marín, M. (2019). International entrepreneurship: A bibliometric overview. *International Entrepreneurship and Management Journal, 15*, 385–429. https://doi.org/10.1007/s11365-017-0487-y
43. Merigó, J. M., Mas-Tur, A., Roig-Tierno, N., & Ribeiro-Soriano, D. (2015). A bibliometric overview of the Journal of Business Research between 1973 and 2014. *Journal of Business Research, 68*, 2645–2653. https://doi.org/10.1016/j.jbusres.2015.04.006
44. Govindan, K., & Hasanagic, M. (2018). A systematic review on drivers, barriers, and practices towards circular economy: A supply chain perspective. *International Journal of Production Research, 56*, 278–311. https://doi.org/10.1080/00207543.2017.1402141
45. Kouhizadeh, M., Zhu, Q., & Sarkis, J. (2020). Blockchain and the circular economy: Potential tensions and critical reflections from practice. *Production Planning & Control., 31*, 950–966. https://doi.org/10.1080/09537287.2019.1695925
46. Za, S., Pallud, J., Agrifoglio, R., & Metallo, C. (2020). Value co-creation in online communities: A preliminary literature analysis. In: *Lecture Notes in Information Systems and Organisation* (pp. 33–46). https://doi.org/10.1007/978-3-030-23665-6_4
47. Lüdeke-Freund, F., Gold, S., & Bocken, N. M. P. (2019). A review and typology of circular economy business model patterns. *Journal of Industrial Ecology, 23*, 36–61. https://doi.org/10.1111/jiec.12763
48. Panchal, R., Singh, A., & Diwan, H. (2021). Does circular economy performance lead to sustainable development?—A systematic literature review. *Journal of Environmental Management, 293*, 112811. https://doi.org/10.1016/j.jenvman.2021.112811
49. Bag, S., & Pretorius, J. H. C. (2022). Relationships between industry 4.0, sustainable manufacturing and circular economy: Proposal of a research framework. *International Journal of Organizational Analysis, 30*, 864–898. https://doi.org/10.1108/IJOA-04-2020-2120

How Social Communication and New Media Have Reshaped the Way People Deal with Religion? A Systematic Literature Review

Johana Hajdini and **Lea Iaia**

Abstract Religion can be seen as a driver of social change in both individual and collective behavior. With the emergence of interactive technologies and the new media, the way religion is perceived has experienced changes and evolved to be present also in virtual spaces. To understand the promotion of religious beliefs and organizations, it could be approached to digital marketing research, as an increasing number of religious organizations are making use of the opportunities digital marketing provides to reach out to believers and bring religious lessons to a wider audience. This article aims to investigate the role and influence of digital communication and social media in the religious context of research to understand how technology has reshaped religion and affected social change, to provide some guidelines for organization that must handle with. We developed a systematic review of two databases, covering technology and social sciences, as well as top journals that publish in religious studies. We found several internal (e.g., attitude towards the usefulness of internet, length of time as a user, individuals' religious beliefs, etc.) and external drivers (e.g., affordance of social media, persuasive messages, sacred and secular influences, etc.) of adoption of new media when considering a religious context, as well as evidenced the existence of both positive (e.g., empowerment, promotion of norms and values, etc.) and negative outcomes (mis-, and dis-information, divided online public sphere, protest stimulating, etc.) for individuals, organizations and society. While research has experienced increased attention, the findings of this study suggest there is still room for future research to expand from existing findings and drive attention to less investigated constructs or adopt different methodological perspectives.

Keywords Digital communication · Social media · Mobile · Religion · Systematic review

J. Hajdini (✉)
University "Gabriele d'Annunzio" of Chieti-Pescara, Pescara, Italy

L. Iaia
University of Turin, Turin, Italy

A. M. Braccini et al. (eds.), *Digital (Eco) Systems and Societal Challenges*, Lecture Notes in Information Systems and Organisation 72,
https://doi.org/10.1007/978-3-031-75586-6_15

1 Introduction

The relevance of technological innovations is mostly related to their ability to continuously disrupt rules and address new ones [1], affecting boundaries and dynamics of economies, markets and society as well as reshaping social theories and paradigms [2].

The pervasiveness of digital technologies, such as digital, social media and mobile platforms, has an impact on society. It is evident in the new ways customers interact, and companies reach them, looking for strategies able to catch their attention, in a dynamic and volitive environment. In fact, new technologies are evolving the ways marketing deals with digital technologies, thus reshaping the field. The digital marketing research has moved from the study of the simplest usage of digital channels in companies' marketing strategies, to a whole investigation of the process that consider the usage of digital technologies to stimulate the interaction with customers, collaborators, competitors, context, and company [3]. Along with technologies, religion can be seen as driver of social change in both individual and collective behavior [4], as it influences the 84% of people [5, 6] in their wisdom, morality and ethics [7, 8]. If "religion is everywhere" [9], "religious media are found in houses of worship, but also in one's own home. Religious conversations can be face-to-face, but they're often mediated" [10]. Those statements summarize two studies' perspectives in the relationship between religion and media [11, 12], where the "mediation" approach investigates the communication process using media [13, 14], and the "mediatization" approach examines the results of the usage of media into social and cultural life, in terms of changes [15].

The combination of new technologies with religion has brought authors to question the influence and challenges of the cyberspace in communicating religion [16, 17], the online religion framework through the website [18] and the emerging techno-spiritual practices that "are important for the ways in which they highlight alternate paradigms for technology creation, deployment, consumption and resistance, as well as pointing to different communities, practices and habits that could be supported" [19]. Nowadays, articles treat the religious-oriented mobile media and applications [20–22], the measurement of the impact of those religious apps on society [23] and religious experience [15, 24], as well as the usage of new digital toll as the crowdfunding platform [25]. This growing interest in the context of social communication, new media, and religion have created a niche in the Internet studies known as "digital religion" [26–29]. The complexity of the "religion" construct and its intricacy with other cultural constructs caused the unsolved attempt of authors toward a common definition [6, 30] resulting in a deep fragmentation of studies in several literature fields that highlight its under-investigation [31, 32].

In addition, the impact of COVID-19 pandemic has further disrupted people's paradigms, including the way they used to deal with DSMM platforms [33], as well as with religion [34], increasing a need to explore the emerging paradigms.

To the best of our knowledge, this would be the first systematic review investigating the role and influence of digital, social media, and mobile (DSMM) technologies in the religious context of research. Even though recently relevant research has been developed in the field of digital religion, there is a great potential in investigating the phenomena from multiple perspectives, to not include merely the investigation of digitalization of religion, but provide a comprehensive understanding of how digital technology and culture impact religious practice and beliefs, and the way it is being presented, accepted and consumed in the digital space [35]. Therefore, through this investigation we aim at providing a holistic understanding of the emerging paradigms resulting from the binomial of digital technologies and religion, through the analysis of DSMM marketing studies, to understand the consumption of religion in everyday life. Inspired by the framework of digital marketing for the analysis of the research in DSMM marketing field, properly interpreted for this analysis, we will focus on the relationship between the usage of such digital technologies and religion, with the aim at achieving a wider understanding how technology has reshaped the way religion is communicated and consumed, affecting social change. Through the "Antecedents-Phenomenon-Consequences" logic [36, 37], and the adoption of the framework for research in Digital Marketing [3], we will carry out a systematic literature review on those topics, aiming to: (i) review the extant research, (ii) generate a multi-dimensional framework based on religion, digital communication and social media for academics and practitioners, (iii) find the relevant theoretical insights and knowledge gaps, which could draw the path for (iv) future research carried out by scholars, (v) as well as to find guidelines, that represent the empirical implications useful to practitioners.

2 Methodology

The present article is a systematic literature review aiming to explore extant research in the domain. A systematic literature review is a robust procedure used to make sense of large and often complex bodies of knowledge [38, 39]. The systematic review relies on a scientific and replicable procedure, a research protocol made of several steps that guides the entire review [40, 41]. Following this specific protocol and the careful report of it makes the procedure transparent and replicable in future research [42, 43].

2.1 Review Questions

With the development of technologies, social media and online interfaces have found a broad usage in several fields of everyday life, not leaving behind religion, its expression and consumption. Social media is gaining increased attention as a mean in mobilizing religious practices [44]. Messages of religious content are being shared in different social media platforms, while online entities are trying to construct a public image and reach and attract believers through the dissemination of the word of God [45, 46]. On the other hand, as social media cannot be detached from public debates of religious features, it employs a certain effect on the understanding of religiosity among believers and non-believers [47, 48].

While there is an increased attention to social media platforms for the communication of religious content [46, 49], extant research fails to provide a comprehensive understanding of the way social media is shaping how people experience and cope with religion in everyday life [50]. The intellectual composition of literature is very fragmented, and contradictions surround the debate on the topic. Moreover, previous research calls for an investigation of religion in tandem with marketing [51]. Therefore, this systematic literature review aims to respond to the call for research and provide a better understanding of the role that DSMM marketing plays in the consumption of religion in everyday life. Also considering that "a domain advances when literature in that domain is logically synthesized" [52], this research finds motivation.

Therefore, this systematic literature review aims to answer the following questions:

RQ1: What is the publication trend of religion and DSMM research?
RQ2: What are the top publications and countries for religion and DSMM research?
RQ3: What are the antecedents and consequences of the phenomenon?

2.2 Search Protocol

In this literature review we follow the Scientific Procedures and Rationales for Systematic Literature Reviews (SPAR-4-SLR) protocol [52]. Following the protocol, the systematic literature review methodology consists of three stages, respectively: assembling, arranging, and assessing the literature [52]. The protocol itself guides to some inclusion and exclusion criteria for the publications in the development of the sample, that can fit or get adapted easily to different research topics.

Assembling Stage
The first stage, namely the assembling stage, consists of two sub-stages [52]: identification and acquisition. Starting with the identification, this review identifies publications that are related to "religion and DSMM" *(domain)* to gain insights on the performance of religion and digital, social media, mobile marketing (DSMM) research (RQ1 to RQ3). Specifically, the review is interested in journal articles that appear in SCImago Journal Ranking, as considered in extant research [53, 54]. Regarding the source quality, the aim of including a measure to the quality is to ensure that high quality journals requiring rigorous research, will improve the quality of articles in our sample [55, 56]. We consider the SCImago Journal Ranking, which ranks journals by their average prestige per article, in order to evaluate the importance of a journal within a field of study [53, 54]. This is done to ensure a better inclusivity of high-quality journals publishing within the domain.

Coming to the second sub-stage, the acquisition, for this systematic literature review we considered the combination of two databases Scopus and EBSCOhost, with a search conducted on specific top journals [57] publishing in the field of religious studies. The indicated top journals based on their impact factor (IF) and publishing in the field of religious studies that were searched are the following: *International Journal of Islamic and Middle Eastern Finance and Management*, *Journal for the Scientific Study of Religion*, *Sociology of Religion*, *Politics and Religion*, *Review of Religious Research*, *Journal of Beliefs and Values*, *Religion and Education*, *British Journal of Religious Education*, *The International Journal for the Psychology of Religion*, *Psychology of Religion and Spirituality*, and *Review of Religion and Health*.

Broadening our search to all the above explained search mechanisms is justified by the need to cover all relevant publications. Extant research suggests that social media plays an important role in religion since it may be useful to reach and build religious communities and to keep believers informed, involved, and engaged with their content. Research reports individuals, religious leaders, and congregations using Facebook, Twitter and other platforms to strengthen religious participation [58]. Therefore, in order to understand the beginning and the evolving of the discussion over time, we considered publications starting from January 1990, corresponding to the time when World Wide Web was born [59], till December 2022, corresponding to the time when the databases were accessed and searched. A set of keywords were collected from a careful assessment of the literature. We identified keywords related to "religion" [51, 60–64] and keywords related to "digital, social media and mobile marketing" [3, 65–68]. Considering a combination of both set of keywords and upon agreement, the following search query was approved:

("religion" OR "religious" OR "religiosity" OR "religiousness" OR "religious belief" OR "spiritual" OR "spirituality" OR "spiritualism" OR "faith" OR "priest" OR "church" OR "mosque" OR "synagogue" OR "temple" OR "Christian" OR "Catholic" OR "Muslim" OR "Islam" OR "Jewish" OR "Protestant" OR "Hindu" OR "Sikh" OR "Buddhism") AND ("Electronic marketing" OR "e-marketing" OR "internet marketing" OR "electronic marketplace" OR "e-marketplace" OR "electronic word of mouth" "e-WOM" OR "social web" OR "social media" OR "Web 2.0" OR "social networks" OR "digital marketing" OR "mobile marketing" OR "user-generated content" OR "Facebook" OR "YouTube" OR "Twitter" OR "online retailing" OR "search advertising" OR "banner advertising" OR "Linked In" OR "LinkedIn" OR "Instagram" OR "Tik Tok" OR "TikTok" OR "online commerce" OR "electronic commerce" OR "e-commerce" OR "app" OR "application").

This query was used to search on title, abstract and keywords and returned a total number of 1433 publications in the assembling stage.

Arranging Stage

As the assembling stage of the review, also the arranging stage consists of two sub-stages [52]: organization and purification. For the organization, we relied on several filters available both in Scopus and EBSCOhost in the advanced search option of both databases, and choose to consider language of publication, document type, source type and subject area, as recommended by [52]. Regarding the framework on which the results will be organized, we considered the Antecedents-Phenomenon-Consequences framework [36, 37], as it is suitable to a deeper understanding of the phenomenon.

Following with the purification of results, we considered the inclusion of "articles" written in "English" language and published in "journals", in two areas: (1) "business, management and accounting", and (2) "religious studies", as the topic of interest is in the intersection of these two areas of research. The purification sub-stage developed as above is also recommended by [52]. Yet, to ensure the quality of the publications, we included only publications in journals SJR ranked Q1, Q2, as done in other literature reviews [54]. Out of the results 8 articles were extracted as duplicates, to leave in our sample only original articles in English language and published in the top ranked journals. This procedure in the arranging stage returned a total of 63 documents to be included in our sample for further analysis.

Assessing Stage

As with the previous stages, also the assessing stage of the protocol consists of two sub-stages [52]: evaluation and reporting. A total of 63 publications were evaluated in terms of their performance and their contribution to religion and DSMM research. The descriptive analysis is a performance analysis aimed to evaluate the publication trend during the years, the most contributing countries, and most prominent citations, consisting of important building blocks of the domain, thus answering to two of our research questions (RQ1, RQ2). Next, an organization of the articles in our sample in the adopted framework of antecedents-phenomenon-consequences, provides deep investigation to the preconditions that gave rise to the phenomenon of interest (digital religion), as well as the evolution and consequences that come along with it for a comprehensive understanding.

For the reporting of results, a combination of figures, tables, and words were used to carefully report and interpret the results in the light of all the possible limitations of the study. While the study is not exhaustive of the literature, it provides some important insights for a comprehensive understanding of the phenomenon and the evolution of the research domain, at the same time identifying gaps and making recommendations for future investigations that will bring research forward. The protocol is reported in Fig. 1.

Assembling

- *Identification*
  - Research questions: Performance of religion and digital, social media, mobile marketing (DSMM) research (RQ1 to RQ3).
  - Domain: Religion and DSMM.
  - Source type: Journals.
  - Source quality: SCImago Journal Ranking.
- *Acquisition*
  - Search mechanism and material acquisition: Scopus, EBSCOhost and top journals publishing in the field of religious studies.
  - Search period: January 1990 - December 2022
- Search keywords: ("religion" OR "religious" OR "religiosity" OR "religiousness" OR "religious belief" OR "spiritual" OR "spirituality" OR "spiritualism" OR "faith" OR "priest" OR "church" OR "mosque" OR "synagogue" OR "temple" OR "Christian" OR "Catholic" OR "Muslim" OR "Islam" OR "Jewish" OR "Protestant" OR "Hindu" OR "Sikh" OR "Buddhism") AND ("Electronic marketing" OR "e-marketing" OR "internet marketing" OR "electronic marketplace" OR "e-marketplace" OR "electronic word of mouth" "e-WOM" OR "social web" OR "social media" OR "Web 2.0" OR "social networks" OR "digital marketing" OR "mobile marketing" OR "user-generated content" OR "Facebook" OR "YouTube" OR "Twitter" OR "online retailing" OR "search advertising" OR "banner advertising" OR "Linked In" OR "LinkedIn" OR "Instagram" OR "Tik Tok" OR "online commerce" OR "electronic commerce" OR "e-commerce" OR "app" OR "application").
- Total documents returned from assembling stage: 1433 documents.

Arranging

- *Organization*
  - Organization codes: Language, document type, source type, and subject area.
  - Organizing frameworks: Antecedents-Phenomenon-Consequences.
- *Purification*
  - Language: English.
  - Document type: Articles.
  - Source type: Journals.
  - Subject area: The intersection of business, management, and accounting with religious studies.
  - Source quality: SJR ranked Q1, Q2.
- Total documents retained from arranging stage: 63 documents.

Assessing

- *Evaluation*
  - Total documents for analysis: 63 articles
  - Performance analysis: Analysis of the publication trend (RQ1), publication outlets, authors, countries, institutions, and most prominent citations (RQ2) to evaluate the performance of digital, social media and mobile marketing on religious research
  - Science mapping: Authorship characteristics and country analysis to enrich insights on contribution in the domain (RQ2) and an analysis of antecedents and consequences to improve the understanding of the phenomenon of interest.
  - Software: Microsoft Excel.
  - Future research agenda: Identified methodological gaps and unanswered questions (RQ4)
- *Reporting*
  - Convention: Figures, tables, and words.
  - Sources of support: No financial support received for this research.

Fig. 1 Search protocol

Assembling

- *Identification*
  - Research questions: Performance of religion and digital, social media, mobile marketing (DSMM) research (RQ1 to RQ3).

(continued)

- Domain: Religion and DSMM.
- Source type: Journals.
- Source quality: SCImago Journal Ranking.

- *Acquisition*
  - Search mechanism and material acquisition: Scopus, EBSCOhost and top journals publishing in the field of religious studies.
  - Search period: January 1990–December 2022

- Search keywords: ("religion" OR "religious" OR "religiosity" OR "religiousness" OR "religious belief" OR "spiritual" OR "spirituality" OR "spiritualism" OR "faith" OR "priest" OR "church" OR "mosque" OR "synagogue" OR "temple" OR "Christian" OR "Catholic" OR "Muslim" OR "Islam" OR "Jewish" OR "Protestant" OR "Hindu" OR "Sikh" OR "Buddhism") AND ("Electronic marketing" OR "e-marketing" OR "internet marketing" OR "electronic marketplace" OR "e-marketplace" OR "electronic word of mouth" "e-WOM" OR "social web" OR "social media" OR "Web 2.0" OR "social networks" OR "digital marketing" OR "mobile marketing" OR "user-generated content" OR "Facebook" OR "YouTube" OR "Twitter" OR "online retailing" OR "search advertising" OR "banner advertising" OR "Linked In" OR "LinkedIn" OR "Instagram" OR "Tik Tok" OR "online commerce" OR "electronic commerce" OR "e-commerce" OR "app" OR "application").
- Total documents returned from assembling stage: 1433 documents.

Arranging

- *Organization*
  - Organization codes: Language, document type, source type, and subject area.
  - Organizing frameworks: Antecedents-Phenomenon-Consequences.

- *Purification*
  - Language: English.
  - Document type: Articles.
  - Source type: Journals.
  - Subject area: The intersection of business, management, and accounting with religious studies.
  - Source quality: SJR ranked Q1, Q2.

- Total documents retained from arranging stage: 63 documents.

(continued)

Assessing

- *Evaluation*
  - Total documents for analysis: 63 articles
  - Performance analysis: Analysis of the publication trend (RQ1), publication outlets, authors, countries, institutions, and most prominent citations (RQ2) to evaluate the performance of digital, social media and mobile marketing on religious research
  - Science mapping: Authorship characteristics and country analysis to enrich insights on contribution in the domain (RQ2) and an analysis of antecedents and consequences to improve the understanding of the phenomenon of interest.
  - Software: Microsoft Excel.
  - Future research agenda: Identified methodological gaps and unanswered questions (RQ4)
- *Reporting*
  - Convention: Figures, tables, and words.
  - Sources of support: No financial support received for this research.

3 Mapping Extant Research

3.1 Publication Trend Over the Years

We analyzed the n. 63 papers in our sample and found that there is a growing attention to research in the last years. Even though the time frame for this search was 1990–2022, the first relevant publication in our sample starts from the year 2004. A possible interpretation for that can be the fact that religion was for long considered strictly related to the tangible and the sacred place was an important component of worship [69]. The publication trend experiences several up and downs during the period 2004–2022, to reach a peak in 2021 with N = 16 publications, which may be attributable to the mandatory changes and increased attention to digital channels following the COVID-19 pandemics [70–72]. What should be noted is the fact that more than half of the papers in our sample (53.9%) have been published over the last 4 years (2019–2022), which is evidence of the growing research attention in the domain. Table 1 shows the evolution of research over the years, starting from 2004 till 2022, for a total of 63 publications in our sample.

These findings confirm that the intersection of religion and DSMM, despite being a promising research domain, has started to gain attention only in the last decade, steaming from the possibility of detaching religion from the religious place, while offering a greater attention to new ways of experiencing religion and spirituality [73–76].

Table 1 Publication trend over the years

Publication outlet	2004	2005	2011	2012	2013	2014	2015	2016	2017	2018	2019	2020	2021	2022	Total
Journal of Broadcasting & Electronic Media									1						1
The Communication Review										1					1
American Behavioral Scientist							1								1
American Sociological Review				1											1
Anatolia		1													1
Anthropological Quarterly							1								1
British Journal of Religious Education						1							1		2
Cyberpsychology, Behavior, and Social Networking						1									1
Electronic Commerce Research and Applications	1														1
Information, Communication & Society			3		1				1			1	3	1	10
Information Technology & People										1					1
International Journal of Islamic and Middle Eastern Finance and Management														1	1
Journal for the Scientific Study of Religion			1				1		1				1		4
Journal of Advertising													1		1
Journal of Communication Inquiry							2			2					4
Journal of Consumer Marketing							1								1
Journal of Information Science													1		1
Journal of Islamic Marketing													1	2	3
Journal of Macromarketing								1							1
Journal of Public Relations Research													2		2

Journal of Public Policy and Marketing														1	1
Journal of Religion and Health												1	1		2
Journalism & Mass Communication Quarterly													1		1
Organization Studies												1			1
Politics and Religion											1	1	1		3
Public Relations Review											1				1
Religion and Education										1			1		2
Review of Religious Research											1	1	1	2	5
Sociological Perspectives								1							1
Sociology of Religion					1									2	3
The Communication Review									1	1					2
The International Journal of Press/Politics													1	1	2
Total	1	1	4	1	2	2	6	2	4	6	3	5	16	10	63

Note: The rows include information about the journals, while the columns include information about the years of publication

3.2 Country Description and Prominent Citations

We have identified a total of 127 authors in our sample from universities and institutions in 21 countries (see Table 2). As it is evident from the table, our sample is dominated by authors from USA (n = 21 publications), followed by contributions from Israel and Canada (n = 6 publications each), UK (n = 4 publications), Malaysia and Sweden (n = 3 publications each), and Germany, Indonesia, Norway, The Netherlands, and Turkey (n = 2 publications each). The remaining countries in our sample provide one single publication each.

Next, Table 3 presents the most impactful publications on the topic using as a measure the total citations. This is a common measure in terms of quality, because

Table 2 First author's geographical location

First author's geographical location	Count of publications
USA	21 publications
Israel, Canada	6 publications each
UK	4 publications
Malaysia, Sweden	3 publications each
Germany, Indonesia, Norway, Netherlands, Turkey	2 publications each
Costa Rica, Czech Republic, France, India, Jordan, Kenya, Kuwait, Pakistan, Poland, and New Zealand	1 publication each
Total	63 publications

Table 3 Most prominent citations

Studies	Citations	Publication details
(Bail, 2012)	314	Bail, C. A. (2012) 'The Fringe Effect: Civil Society Organizations and the Evolution of Media Discourse about Islam since the September 11th Attacks', American Sociological Review, 77(6), pp. 855–879. doi: 10.1177/0003122412465743.
(Zainul, Osman and Mazlan, 2004)	100	Zainul, N., Osman, F. and Mazlan, S. H. (2004) 'E-Commerce from an Islamic perspective', Electronic Commerce Research and Applications, 3(3), pp. 280–293. doi: 10.1016/j.elerap.2004.01.002.
(Hutchings, 2011)	82	Hutchings, T. (2011) 'Contemporary Religious Community and the Online', Society, (March 2012), pp. 37–41.
(Bobkowski and Pearce, 2011)	66	Bobkowski, P. S. and Pearce, L. D. (2011) 'Baring their souls in online profiles or not? Religious self-disclosure in social media', Journal for the Scientific Study of Religion, 50(4), pp. 744–762. doi: 10.1111/j.1468-5906.2011.01597.x.
(Lundby, 2011)	60	Lundby, K. (2011) 'PATTERNS OF BELONGING IN ONLINE / OFFLINE INTERFACES OF RELIGION', Information, Communication & Society, (November 2011), pp. 37–41.

the times an article was cited in other research publications provides an insight to the accumulation, as well as the development of knowledge [77]. Total citations were extracted from Google Scholar on 30 March 2022. Regarding to the citations, the five most cited studies in our sample are authored by Bail (2012; Citations, 314), Zainul, Osman and Mazlan (2004; Citations, 100), Hutchings (2011; Citations, 82), Bobkowski and Pearce (2011; Citations, 66), Lundby (2011; Citations, 60).

These articles only highlight the broad range of research on the topic, where mostly particular interest is given to religious discourse in digital, social media, online interfaces, and the effect it has on religious activities, self-disclosure, and identity with the several usages it is given that consider both the positive (e.g., engagement, promotion, information dissemination, community building, etc.) [78–81] and the negative effects (e. g. hate speech, dissident behavior, religious extremism and radicalization, etc.) [45, 47, 82–84].

4 Results and Data Synthesis

Important insights of this literature review can derive from a thematic analysis of the articles in our sample. To develop the thematic analysis we draw on the framework of digital marketing [3], which helps the understanding of research in the digital marketing (DM) field. With the evolution of the DM initially from "the marketing of products and services using digital channels—to an umbrella term describing the process of using digital technologies [. . .]" [3], this approach aims the identification of important touchpoints to evidence the interaction of digital technologies with the five C's—customers, collaborators, competitors, context, and company [3].

According to the framework we first analyzed the environment, where the main considerations are the role of customers, with context, collaborators, as well as competitors. In the environment we can include platforms, search engines, two-sided markets, user-generated content, consumer behavior and contextual interactions. Summarizing, here we represent the concepts, entities (institutions or individuals) and the structures as we investigate the interaction of each with digital technologies.

Considering *environment* analysis as a starting point, we develop the analysis of *the company*. The development and advancement of digital technologies is providing companies with new opportunities to reach target audiences, add value to products or services with the exploration of networks and digital marketplaces or completely shifting to digital services. When analyzing the company, an important consideration should be given to the 4 Ps' model and *marketing research*. Lastly, according to the framework we collect information useful to develop *marketing strategies*. An evaluation of company's actions should be considered for the investigation of *outcomes*, to highlight how value is created for customers, what is the customer lifetime value and the firm value.

Given these points, we are provided with a holistic approach to deeply investigate the capabilities of digital technologies in any context. Moreover, the "Antecedents—

Phenomenon—Consequences" framework was adopted to organize the publications in our sample. To conclude the reclassification of articles in our sample according to Antecedents-Phenomenon-Consequences and the DM framework, we aim to identify how digital marketing strategies provide a support for religious practice, while deeply crafting the role of digital technologies and their interactions in religious consumption. Considering it under the religion perspective, the framework is useful to comprehend the interaction of technologies with the religious practices, in the light of the way religious entities gain popularity, disseminate religious information, reach believers, make decisions, and develop specific behaviors related to their religious identity, and not only.

4.1 Antecedents

Considering the adopted framework, we collected in the "antecedent" category all the drivers of introducing DSMM into the Religion consumption. Therefore, this category includes both internal and external factors that affect the adoption and usage of DM in religious practices.

Moving from the adopted framework of digital marketing, we will consider all the changes in competitive environment. Due to evolution of digital technologies, religious practice should also consider the adoption and acceptance of such technologies for better outcomes. The aspect is studied by several articles in our sample moving from different theoretical perspectives.

The first DM theme in this category is the analysis of environment. Using the cognitive fit theory and the elaboration likelihood model, [85] investigates drivers of halal cosmetics purchase intention and finds that attitude towards halal cosmetics mediates the relationship of drivers of e-WOM on purchase intention. Another study is the one by [86] that investigates the significant and formative relationships in children's spirituality and their influence and finds social friendships to be valuable to children while enhancing the important role of technology and social media in these relationships. Drawing on the Habermas' theory of communicative action [87] explores patterns of belonging in the religious context, considering both online and offline interfaces and their interaction and finds the new media environment not antithetical to being religious. Drawing on a Muslim country context and considering the tenets of secularization theory, [50] investigate the effects of religiosity on internet consumption finding that increasing religiosity is related to decrease in Internet consumption, which is contrary to the previous study that suggests that new media context is not antithetical to religiosity [87]. Other studies in the environment analysis investigate religious implications of social media in education [88], social media effect on Islamic women behavior of wearing a veil (hijab) [89], religious social media influencers drawing on public relations theory and Ledingham's general theory of relationship management [81], bridging the research-practice gap on Facebook drawing on a data of posts shared on a Facebook page for religious education teachers [90], the likelihood of being a disordered social media user drawing of the theory of religious orientation [91], the effect of religiosity on the digital divide drawing on secularization theory and sociological theory of religion [92], religious tourism and the tourists' perception of a religious heritage site [93], and the social media usage to find and verify information according to halal food products [94].

The second DM theme regards company and considers the use of digital technologies and Internet, the channel, platform/two-side markets and marketing research. In this category the authors employ different theories to investigate important opportunities for companies such as new channels, platforms or two-sided markets and marketing research. In his study [95] draws on the theory of pluralism and theory of intergenerational religious momentum to investigate the usage of social network site (SNS) effect on religious beliefs and religious service attendance. SNS are also considered in the study by [75] where the authors investigate membership and usage of SNS under influence of religiousness. Lastly, drawing on resource mobilization theory [48] investigate physical protest and digital debate on SNS and find diverse political and cultural discourses that shape rituals in urban space.

The third and last DM theme encountered for the antecedent category regards marketing strategies. In summary, the articles included here employ a range of theories such as psychological theories, Olsonian theory of joining, advertising theory, network theory and relationship theory, to investigate how is religious language used on Twitter by Members of Congress (MOC) [73], the Christian Right Agenda [96], megachurches' audience-centric advertising strategies on social media [97], and the role of social media platforms in stakeholder engagement strategy [79]. Overall, the findings suggest usage of religious language on Twitter and better outcomes from tweets with religious appeals compared to non-religious tweets [73], message flexibility in composing communications as a concern about good faith representation [96], the usage of persuasive messages to increase online engagement [97], and a shift from one-way to two-way communication strategies with the prioritization of digital connections due to COVID-19 pandemics [79]. The findings in the marketing strategies section offer useful insights to marketers to provide the preconditions for the achievement of the desired outcomes.

4.2 Phenomenon

In the phenomenon category are included studies pertaining to four main themes of the investigation in intersection with DM.

In the analysis of the environment, [98] highlighted the role of perceived religious obligations in online decision making when consumers face dilemmas related to religious rules and faith. Authors draw on social identity theory and conclude that consumers online act based on perceived religious obligations, rather than making decisions based on their own wellbeing. Other authors analyzed the religious self-disclosure in social media while using sociological theories of religion to suggest a relationship between believing that religion is a public matter, and the religiosity of profile owners' friendship group with religious identification and self-disclosure. Other studies investigate the selfie-phenomenon while drawing on adaptive structuration theory and technology appropriation theory, to understand how dual cultural identity is exhibited and reaffirmed by this mean [99], or investigate the Islamophobic discourse on Twitter after Brexit, moving from the agonistic theory and finding that the majority frame Islam negatively [47]. The article of [100] investigates the selfie-nationalism of Modi as a socially mediated form of governance and finds a role of it in India's plural religious traditions. Finally, the article of [76] explores the prevalence of different types of digital religion practices in Canada and finds it a phenomenon present among Millennials, mostly in the form of digital content consumption, as well as a connection to in-person practices.

The second DM theme is mostly concerned with the use of digital technologies and the Internet as a channel for achieving the desired outcomes. Studies included here identify online channels providing service in the context of emerging online churches [101], as well as visual communication through Instagram as a channel to serve a public relations function [78].

Also in the third DM theme, which relates to company's choice, the channel, promotion, and marketing research are considered important to reach the desired outcomes. Here we should mention the choice of e-commerce as a new way of doing business encouraged by Islam in coexistence with the Islamic principles of doing business [102].

The last DM theme to be considered is related to marketing strategies. Drawing on construal theory, the study by [46] investigates religious authority on social media and finds the existence of strategic management of social, spatial, affective, and hypothetical distance.

4.3 Consequences

In this category a complete analysis of the outcomes achieved by Religion through the usage of DSMM is provided. A reclassification of them in compliance with the DM themes, brings the emersion of several clusters.

The first theme identified here refers to marketing strategy, represented by five articles and employing three theories. The first one is the study by [103] that identifies an avoidance of advertising in traditional and digital media related to religiousness. Another article included here is the one by [104] that moves from critical race theory and blog theory and to investigate the intersection between race and religion within a digital counter public. Next, [105] draws on social identity theory and finds that Muslim advocacy organizations rely on empowerment strategies to reach the desired outcomes in American muslin minorities. The last article included in this category is the article by [106], that draws on probability theory and proposes a measure called Christian Religiosity Revealed by Search, that performs better than the previously used Gallup Poll and World Values Survey religiosity scores.

The second group of articles regards the achievable outcomes. The first article [107] while investigating religious hashtag activism finds both positive and negative outcomes, starting from islamophobia to cross-cultural identity and promotion of diversity of the Muslim community. Another article [108] found interesting positive outcomes from connecting religious self-identification with improved levels of civility among Latter-Day Saint (LDS) Twitter users. A more recent study [49] through a systematic literature review aiming to synthetize the representation of Islam in social media again found both positive (1—Islam as a liberal religion; 4—Islam as a religion of collective identity; 5—Islam as a humane religion) and negative (2—Islam as a religion of extremism and terrorism; 3—Islam as a religion of gender discrimination) representations. Considering the recent event of the pandemics [109] investigates the interconnection between online and offline in the context of virtual prayer during the COVID-19 pandemics enhancing the transition from the physical space to the virtual one as challenging the performance of rituals. Yet, the author suggests that it is a solution for crisis, but for long-term it is not a good option. In the same line with [49] is also the study by [110], that again finds positive and negative reactions to Islam while investigating the online reactions to Muhammad cartoons and employing Resnick's normalization theory, concluding for a highly divided public sphere in relation to Islam. The study by [82] moves from the probability theory of Bayes and identifies hate speech over Twitter platform, and [83] found that Internet plays a role in networking, radicalization and inducing foreign travel as well as planning and selecting targets for attack. We evidence again the adoption of social identity theory by [111] in his investigation of (ir)-religious identities contribution to online interreligious polarization, and finds interreligious polarization online for moral authority. Other studies included in this category find the depiction of Muslims as enemies from angry and fearful fringe organizations [112], a role of social media on protest stimulation conditioned by beliefs about religious political authority [45], and a double-edged sword effect for the advancement of religious literacy while considering the spread of information in social media [113]. Interesting positive outcomes are reported in the studies by [78] that finds the usage of Instagram related to a public relations function, [80] that finds a universal shared experience used to bring together religious and non-religious audiences, [44] that employ gatekeeping theory and find the development of a collective identity and the protector role, [114] that employ actor-network theory and find that a mantra facilitate materialization of a Buddhist NGO's ethos, and finally [115] finding a transformation of contemporary religiosity that promotes a ready-made and easily accessible set of norms and values.

These findings informed the development of a multi-dimensional framework based on religion, digital and social media communication for academics and practitioners (see Fig. 2).

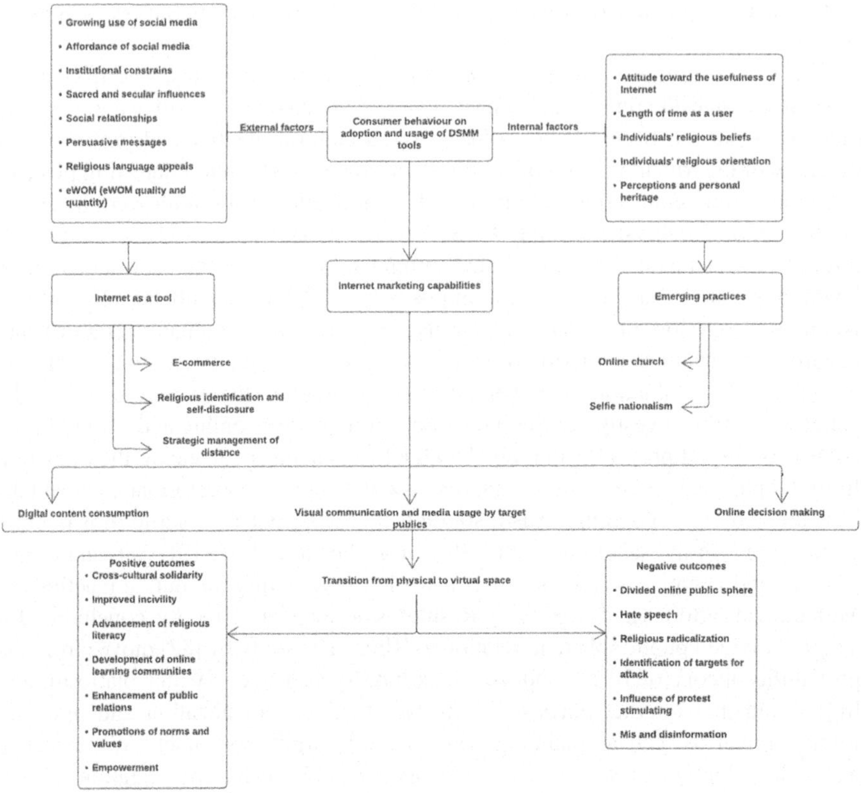

Fig. 2 Integrated framework of research

5 Conclusions and Future Research

We tried to understand the complex intersection of religion and new media while developing a careful synthesis of the literature, with the aim to provide an integrative framework, which would be most of use in bringing research forward. This article develops a descriptive and thematic analysis of a sample of 63 articles to respond to the main research questions.

This systematic review demonstrated that there is a broad range of research on the topic which is gaining increased attention in the last decade with higher number of publications, as well as diverse research perspectives considering both positive and negative effects of the usage of new media in religion consumption. To add to that, we found several internal (e.g., attitude towards the usefulness of internet, length of time as a user, individuals' religious beliefs, etc.) and external drivers (e.g., affordance of social media, persuasive messages, sacred and secular influences, etc.) for the adoption of new media when considering a religious context, as well as evidenced the existence of both positive (e.g., empowerment, promotion of norms and values, improved incivility, etc.) and negative outcomes (mis and disinformation, divided online public sphere, protest stimulating, etc.) for individuals, organizations and society as a whole.

While this review is not exhaustive of the literature, its findings can be further complemented with new perspectives or new findings in the domain. Considering the debate on the topic and considering this literature review at the intersection of religion and marketing, it's findings may be limited due to the sample size, which can be further improved in future research with the integration of other databases.

This article provides an important starting point to future research, contributing to the advancement of the domain through development of future research to respond to unanswered questions.

From a methodological perspective, the articles in our sample call for future research employing:

- *Longitudinal measurement methods*—as suggests the study by [116] for the dialogic, developing nature of self-disclosure over time; the study by [117] to track evolution in perception when considering the usage of social media platforms; the study by [89] for the development of a religiosity index that can be used for a broad range of countries and a long time frame.
- *Case study methodology*—as suggests the study by [73] on how a religious member (Buddhist, Muslim, or Hindu) approaches religion on SNS.
- *Comparative studies*—as suggests the study by [45] to investigate the role of religion in different countries with varying levels of democracy and freedom in media
- *Quantitative methods*—as suggest the studies by [79] to develop knowledge on the OPR goals and practices of church communications, [117] to confirm the correlations between exposure to the 'others' and individual views of social and cultural differences
- *Qualitative methods*—as suggests the study by [49] with the employment of interview data to gather deeper insight on activities on social media and motivations for posting.

Despite the methodological perspective, through a careful collection of unanswered questions we developed a list to be considered for future research (see Table 4).

In terms of unanswered questions, there is a broad range of opportunities to future investigations, in exploring dilemmas and practices to religious identity change, how social media may help or hinder the promotion of cultural and religious values through selfies or other forms used to self-express the religious identity of individuals, and how theological variables affect behaviors, trying to understand the usage of social media networks by different faith groups. Other important investigations should focus on the online-offline interplay, aiming to explore the extent to which online encounters shape attitudes and behaviors in the offline context. Another very important unanswered question should try to delve into the understanding of the type of religious content available in social media, how it is made accessible and who is responsible to make it available. From a market perspective it can be interesting to explore how religion-oriented Internet sources may affect the relationship between

Table 4 Unanswered questions

Unanswered question	Representative references
What dilemmas and practices would we find if we looked at the opposite process of identity change, namely, Muslim women who are becoming less religious?	(Agbarya and John, 2021)
Has the mainstreaming of anti-Muslim political discourse strengthened individuals' attachments to a Muslim American collective identity? Does overt anti-Muslim political discourse aid or hinder the process of Muslim American integration and political participation? How do Muslims and their organized groups confront, contest, and subvert this discourse and to what effects?	(Cury, 2019)
How and to what extent selfies or other forms of social media-based self-expression reflect acculturation towards global consumer culture and/or promote or inhibit cross-cultural interaction?	(Dey et al., 2018)
How theological variables affect behaviors? How faith groups use social networks, practice public relations, and understand organization-public relationships?	(Golan, Morehouse and English, 2021)
How online religious encounters shape offline intergroup attitudes and courses of behavior?	(Grigoropoulou, 2020)
What content is available on social media platform? How do users find this content? Who uploads the content and how is it presented?	(Henry, 2021)
How a number of other types of religion-oriented Internet sources, such as blogs, forums, community building websites, news sites, and religious organization websites, have the potential to change the relationship between markets and consumers?	(Kamarulzaman et al., 2016)
How do "sacralization and secularization processes" (Edgell 2012: 257) work out in the SNS realm?	(Miller, Mundey and Hill, 2013)
How members of the public experience a sense of belonging into congregational political communities and what is the role of these communities in various electoral outcomes?	(Siles et al., 2021)
Can an activity (social media influencers) that brings so much personal benefit really be labeled as altruistic, especially when those engaging in the activity display egoistic behaviors (i.e., building networks, seeking self-validation, etc.)?	(Smith et al., 2021)
How are imams using Facebook and guiding Muslim communities online? Are Christians hiding or downplaying religious identity in heterogeneous online spaces? How do Jewish learners find strength to express their religious beliefs on Twitter in the face of antisemitism?	(Woodward and Kimmons, 2018)
How social media and other technologies impact people's attitudes and behaviors? How social norms may differ among countries with strong cultural and/or religious traditions and how social networking technology use affects attitudes and behaviors among people in those countries?	(Young et al., 2014)
How cultural representations in social media platforms such as Facebook, Twitter, Snapchat, and TikTok allow access to and promote shared interpretations of religious ritual revision?	(Kapoor et al., 2022)
How spiritual leaders practiced pandemic spiritual leadership in different religious context in comparison?	(Taylor & Benac, 2022)
To what extent is digital religion finding support among new segments of populations (i. e., Gen Z) that are not followers of more conventional forms of organized religion?	(Wilkins-Laflamme, 2022)

markets and consumers. Lastly, important questions should investigate how social media is used by different religious public figures, how different cultural and religious traditions in different countries affect the way social media is used, as well as the understanding of religious social media influencers and how it is reconciled the personal benefit with the religious values of altruism, etc. Therefore, future research should take in consideration both the methodological gaps identified in the literature by this systematic literature review, as well as the yet unanswered questions that will improve and complement understanding of how social communication and new media have reshaped the way people deal with religion.

References

1. Ferreira, J. J. M., et al. (2019). To be or not to be digital, that is the question: Firm innovation and performance. *Journal of Business Research, 101*, 583–590. https://doi.org/10.1016/j.jbusres.2018.11.013
2. Ossewaarde, M. (2019). Digital transformation and the renewal of social theory: Unpacking the new fraudulent myths and misplaced metaphors. *Technological Forecasting and Social Change, 146*, 24–30. https://doi.org/10.1016/j.techfore.2019.05.007
3. Kannan, P. K., & Li, H. (2017). "Alice": Digital marketing: A framework, review and research agenda. *International Journal of Research in Marketing, 34*(1), 22–45. https://doi.org/10.1016/j.ijresmar.2016.11.006
4. Cohen, O., et al. (2013). The conjoint community resiliency assessment measure as a baseline for profiling and predicting community resilience for emergencies. *Technological Forecasting and Social Change, 80*(9), 1732–1741. https://doi.org/10.1016/j.techfore.2012.12.009
5. Hackett, C., et al. (2012). *The global religious landscape*. DC Pew Res. Cent.
6. Orellano, A., et al. (2020). The Influence of Religion on Sustainable Consumption: A Systematic Review and Future Research Agenda. *Sustainability., 12, 19*, 7901. https://doi.org/10.3390/su12197901
7. Finlay, V., & Palmer, M. (2003). Faith in conservation. *The World Bank*. https://doi.org/10.1596/0-8213-5559-7
8. Rice, G. (2006). Pro-environmental Behavior in Egypt: Is there a Role for Islamic Environmental Ethics? *Journal of Business Ethics, 65*(4), 373–390. https://doi.org/10.1007/s10551-006-0010-9
9. Mazur, E. M., & McCarthy, K. (2001). *God in the details: American religion in popular culture*. Psychology Press.
10. Stout, D. A. (2013). *Media and religion*. Routledge. https://doi.org/10.4324/9780203148112.
11. Couldry, N., & Hepp, A. (2013). Conceptualizing Mediatization: Contexts, Traditions. *Arguments. Commun. Theory., 23*(3), 191–202. https://doi.org/10.1111/comt.12019
12. Fornäs, J. (2014). Mediatization of popular culture. In *Mediatization of Communication* (pp. 483–504). Walter de Gruyter GmbH. https://doi.org/10.1515/9783110272215.483
13. Meyer, B. (2011). Mediation and immediacy: Sensational forms, semiotic ideologies and the question of the medium. *Social Anthropology, 19*, 1–39. https://doi.org/10.1111/j.1469-8676.2010.00137.x
14. Meyer, B. (2020). *Religion as Mediation. Entangled Relig., 11*, 3. https://doi.org/10.46586/er.11.2020.8444
15. Nwankwo, A. O. (2020). Connectivity and communion: The mobile phone and the Christian religious experience in Nigeria. *New Media Soc*, November, 1–18. https://doi.org/10.1177/1461444820970180.

16. Grieve, G. P. (1995). Imagining a Virtual Religious Community: Neo-Pagans and the Internet. *Chicago Anthropol. Exch., 7, 98*, 132.
17. O'Leary, S. D. (1996). Cyberspace as Sacred Space: Communicating Religion on Computer Networks. *Journal of the American Academy of Religion, 64*(4), 781–808.
18. Helland, C. (2005). Online religion as lived religion. Methodological issues in the study of religious participation on the internet. *Online-heidelb. J. Relig. Internet.* https://doi.org/10.11588/rel.2005.1.380
19. Bell, G. (2006). No More SMS from Jesus: Ubicomp, Religion and Techno-spiritual Practices. In P. Dourish & A. Friday (Eds.), *UbiComp 2006: Ubiquitous Computing* (pp. 141–158). Springer. https://doi.org/10.1007/11853565_9
20. Bellar, W. R., et al. (2019). The Intersection of Religion and Mobile Technology. *Presented at the September*. https://doi.org/10.4018/978-1-5225-7598-6.ch070
21. Campbell, H. (2010). *When religion meets new media*. Routledge.
22. Campbell, H. A., et al. (2014). There's a religious app for that! A framework for studying religious mobile applications. *Mob. Media Commun., 2*(2), 154–172. https://doi.org/10.1177/2050157914520846
23. Wagner, R. (2013). You are what you install: Religious authenticity and identity in mobile apps. *Digit. Relig., 199–206.*
24. Bragge, J., et al. (2019). Unveiling the intellectual structure and evolution of external resource management research: Insights from a bibliometric study. *Journal of Business Research, 97*(January), 141–159. https://doi.org/10.1016/j.jbusres.2018.12.050
25. Copeland, A. J. (2015). Crowdfunding a new church: A multimodal analysis of faith-related giving rhetoric on Indiegogo. *Online-heidelb. J. Relig. Internet., 9.*
26. Campbell, H. A. (2012). *Digital religion: Understanding religious practice in new media worlds*. Routledge.
27. Helland, C. (2016). Digital religion. In: *Handbook of Religion and Society* (pp. 177–196). Springer.
28. Hoover, S. M., & Kim, S. S. (2016). *Handbook of religion and society*. Springer International Publishing. https://doi.org/10.1007/978-3-319-31395-5.
29. Song, B., & Wen, J. (2020). (Taylor): Online corporate social responsibility communication strategies and stakeholder engagements: A comparison of controversial versus noncontroversial industries. *Corporate Social Responsibility and Environmental Management, 27*(2), 881–896. https://doi.org/10.1002/csr.1852
30. Emmons, R. A., & Paloutzian, R. F. (2003). The Psychology of Religion. *Annual Review of Psychology, 54*(1), 377–402. https://doi.org/10.1146/annurev.psych.54.101601.145024
31. Engelland, B. T. (2014). Religion, humanism, marketing, and the consumption of socially responsible products, services, and ideas: Introduction to a special topic section. *Journal of Business Research, 67*(2), 1–4. https://doi.org/10.1016/j.jbusres.2013.03.005
32. Mottner, S., & Ford, J. B. (2010). International Journal of Nonprofit and Voluntary Sector Marketing: special issue on marketing and religion. *International Journal of Nonprofit and Voluntary Sector Marketing, 15*(4), 301–304. https://doi.org/10.1002/nvsm.395
33. Vargo, D., et al. (2021). Digital technology use during COVID-19 pandemic: A rapid review. *Hum. Behav. Emerg. Technol., 3*(1), 13–24.
34. Djupe, P. A., & Burge, R. P. (2020). The Prosperity Gospel of Coronavirus Response. *Politics and Religion, 1–22*, 552–573. https://doi.org/10.1017/S175504832000053X
35. Tsuria, R., & Campbell, H. A. (2021). Introduction to the study of digital religion. In: *Digital religion* (pp. 1–21). Routledge.
36. Narayanan, V. K., et al. (2011). The cognitive perspective in strategy: An integrative review. *J. Manage., 37*(1), 305–351. https://doi.org/10.1177/0149206310383986
37. Pisani, N., & Ricart, J. E. (2016). Offshoring of Services: A Review of the Literature and Organizing Framework. *Management International Review, 56*(3), 385–424. https://doi.org/10.1007/s11575-015-0270-7

38. Denyer, D., & Tranfield, D. (2009). Producing a systematic review. In *The Sage handbook of organizational research methods* (pp. 671–689). Sage Publications Ltd. https://psycnet.apa.org/record/2010-00924-039
39. Gaur, A., & Kumar, M. (2018). A systematic approach to conducting review studies: An assessment of content analysis in 25 years of IB research. *Journal of World Business, 53*(2), 280–289. https://doi.org/10.1016/j.jwb.2017.11.003
40. Christofi, M., et al. (2021). Marketing innovation and internationalization in smart city development: a systematic review, framework and research agenda. *Int. Mark. Rev. ahead-of-p, 38*, ahead-of-print–ahead-of-pr984. https://doi.org/10.1108/IMR-01-2021-0027
41. Tranfield, D., et al. (2003). Towards a Methodology for Developing Evidence-Informed Management Knowledge by Means of Systematic Review. *British Journal of Management, 14*(3), 207–222. https://doi.org/10.1111/1467-8551.00375
42. Christofi, M., et al. (2017). *Marketing research on mergers and acquisitions: a systematic review and future directions*. https://doi.org/10.1108/IMR-03-2015-0100
43. Vrontis, D., & Christofi, M. (2019). R&D internationalization and innovation: A systematic review, integrative framework and future research directions. J. Bus. Res. 128. *March, 2021*, 812–823. https://doi.org/10.1016/j.jbusres.2019.03.031
44. de Vries, M., et al. (2017). Digital contestation in protracted conflict: The online struggle over al-Aqsa Mosque. *The Communication Review, 20*(3), 189–211. https://doi.org/10.1080/10714421.2017.1362814
45. Buckley, D. T. et al. (2021). Is religion the opiate of the digital masses? Religious authority, social media, and protest. *Information, Communication Society*, 1–17. https://doi.org/10.1080/1369118X.2021.1971279.
46. Golan, O., & Martini, M. (2020). The Making of contemporary papacy: manufactured charisma and Instagram. *Information, Communication & Society, 23*(9), 1368–1385. https://doi.org/10.1080/1369118X.2019.1567803
47. Evolvi, G. (2019). #Islamexit: inter-group antagonism on Twitter. *Information, Communication & Society, 22*(3), 386–401. https://doi.org/10.1080/1369118X.2017.1388427
48. Fader, A., & Gottlieb, O. (2015). Occupy Judaism: Religion, Digital Media, and the Public Sphere. *Anthropological Quarterly, 88*(3), 759–793. https://doi.org/10.1353/anq.2015.0032
49. Hashmi, U. M., et al. (2021). The representation of Islam within social media: a systematic review. *Information, Communication & Society, 24*(13), 1962–1981. https://doi.org/10.1080/1369118X.2020.1847165
50. Hesapci Sanaktekin, O., et al. (2013). The effects of religiosity on internet consumption: A study on a Muslim country. *Information, Communication & Society, 16*(10), 1553–1573. https://doi.org/10.1080/1369118X.2012.722663
51. Kumar, S. et al. (2022). Religion as a social shaping force in entrepreneurship and business: Insights from a technology-empowered systematic literature review. *Technological Forecasting and Social Change, 175*, November 2021. https://doi.org/10.1016/j.techfore.2021.121393
52. Paul, J., et al. (2021). Scientific procedures and rationales for systematic literature reviews (SPAR-4-SLR). *International Journal of Consumer Studies, 45*, 1–16. https://doi.org/10.1111/ijcs.12695
53. Agostino, I. R. S., et al. (2020). Forecasting models in the manufacturing processes and operations management: Systematic literature review. *Journal of Forecasting, 39*(7), 1043–1056. https://doi.org/10.1002/for.2674
54. Hungara, A., & Nobre, H. (2021). A consumer culture theory perspective of the marketplace: An integrative review and agenda for research. *International Journal of Consumer Studies, 45*(4), 805–823. https://doi.org/10.1111/ijcs.12670
55. Xiao, Y., & Watson, M. (2017). Guidance on Conducting a Systematic Literature Review. *Journal of Planning Education and Research, 39*(1), 93–112. https://doi.org/10.1177/0739456X17723971

56. Yang, L., et al. (2021). Quality Assessment in Systematic Literature Reviews: A Software Engineering Perspective. *Information and Software Technology, 130*, 106397. https://doi.org/10.1016/j.infsof.2020.106397
57. Resurchify. *Top Journals in Religious studies*. Available at: https://www.resurchify.com/impact/category/Religious-studies
58. Brubaker, P. J., & Haigh, M. M. (2017). The religious Facebook experience: Uses and gratifications of faith-based content. *Soc. Media+ Soc., 3, 2*, 2056305117703723.
59. Oppitz, M., Tomsu, P. (2018). World Wide Web. In *Inventing the cloud century* (pp. 229–266). Springer.
60. AbdAleati, N. S., et al. (2016). Religiousness and mental health: Systematic review study. *Journal of Religion and Health, 55*(6), 1929–1937.
61. Adamczyk, A., et al. (2017). Religion and crime: A systematic review and assessment of next steps. *Sociology of Religion, 78*(2), 192–232.
62. Hope, M. O., et al. (2020). Black Caribbean emerging adults: A systematic review of religion and health. *Journal of Religion and Health, 59*(1), 431–451.
63. Rizvi, M. A. K., & Hossain, M. Z. (2017). Relationship between religious belief and happiness: A systematic literature review. *Journal of Religion and Health, 56*(5), 1561–1582. https://doi.org/10.1007/s10943-016-0332-6
64. Tracey, P. (2012). Religion and organization: A critical review of current trends and future directions. *The Academy of Management Annals, 6*(1), 87–134.
65. Knoll, J. (2016). Advertising in social media: a review of empirical evidence. *International Journal of Advertising, 35*(2), 266–300. https://doi.org/10.1080/02650487.2015.1021898
66. Lamberton, C., & Stephen, A. T. (2016). A thematic exploration of digital, social media, and mobile marketing: Research evolution from 2000 to 2015 and an agenda for future inquiry. *Journal of Marketing, 80*(6), 146–172. https://doi.org/10.1509/jm.15.0415
67. Ngai, E. W. T. (2003). Internet marketing research (1987-2000): a literature review and classification. *European Journal of Marketing, 37*(1/2), 24–49. https://doi.org/10.1108/03090560310453894
68. Salo, J. (2017). Social media research in the industrial marketing field: Review of literature and future research directions. *Industrial Marketing Management, 66*, 115–129. https://doi.org/10.1016/j.indmarman.2017.07.013
69. Mazumdar, S., & Mazumdar, S. (2004). Religion and place attachment: A study of sacred places. *Journal of Environmental Psychology, 24*(3), 385–397. https://doi.org/10.1016/j.jenvp.2004.08.005
70. Kapoor, V., et al. (2022). Ritual revision during a crisis: The case of Indian religious rituals during the COVID-19 pandemic. *Journal of Public Policy & Marketing, 07439156221081485*, 277–297. https://doi.org/10.1177/07439156221081485
71. Kühle, L., & Larsen, T. L. (2021). 'Forced'online religion: Religious minority and majority communities' media usage during the COVID-19 lockdown. *Religions, 12*(7), 496.
72. Singarimbun, K. (2021). E-Church as a virtual service communities during COVID-19 pandemics. *J. Komun. Ikat. Sarj. Komun. Indones., 6*(1), 96–106.
73. Bramlett, B. H., & Burge, R. P. (2021). God talk in a digital age: How members of congress use religious language on Twitter. *Politics and Religion, 14*(2), 316–338. https://doi.org/10.1017/S1755048320000231
74. MacWilliams, M. W. (2002). Virtual Pilgrimages on the Internet. *Religion, 32*(4), 315–335. https://doi.org/10.1006/reli.2002.0408
75. Miller, B. J., et al. (2013). Faith in the age of facebook: Exploring the links between religion and social network site membership and use. *Sociology of Religion A Q. Rev., 74*(2), 227–253. https://doi.org/10.1093/socrel/srs073
76. Wilkins-Laflamme, S. (2021). Digital Religion Among U.S. and Canadian Millennial Adults. *Review of Religious Research, 0123456789*, 225–248. https://doi.org/10.1007/s13644-021-00463-0

77. Crossan, M. M., & Apaydin, M. (2010). A multi-dimensional framework of organizational innovation: A systematic review of the literature. *Journal of Management Studies, 47*, 1154–1191. https://doi.org/10.1111/j.1467-6486.2009.00880.x
78. Al-Kandari, A. A., et al. (2019). An Arab perspective on social media: How banks in Kuwait use instagram for public relations. *Public Relations Review, 45, 3*, 101774. https://doi.org/10.1016/j.pubrev.2019.04.007
79. Golan, G., et al. (2021). Building relationships with the faithful: examining church communicators perceptions of social media influencers in their OPR strategy. *Journal of Public Relations Research, 33*(4), 250–266. https://doi.org/10.1080/1062726X.2021.2011729
80. Hutchings, T. (2017). "We are a united humanity": Death, emotion and digital media in the Church of Sweden. *Journal of Broadcasting & Electronic Media, 61*(1), 90–107. https://doi.org/10.1080/08838151.2016.1273930
81. Smith, B. G., et al. (2021). Social media conversion: lessons from faith-based social media influencers for public relations. *Journal of Public Relations Research, 33*(4), 231–249. https://doi.org/10.1080/1062726X.2021.2011728
82. Aljarah, I., et al. (2021). Intelligent detection of hate speech in Arabic social network: A machine learning approach. *Journal of Information Science, 47*(4), 483–501. https://doi.org/10.1177/0165551520917651
83. Levin, B. (2015). The original web of hate: Revolution Muslim and American Homegrown Extremists. *The American Behavioral Scientist, 59*(12), 1609–1630. https://doi.org/10.1177/0002764215588815
84. Pintak, L., et al. (2021). Influencers, amplifiers, and icons: A systematic approach to understanding the roles of islamophobic actors on Twitter. *Journalism & Mass Communication Quarterly*. https://doi.org/10.1177/10776990211031567
85. Anubha (2021). Mediating role of attitude in halal cosmetics purchase intention: an ELM perspective. *Journal of Islamic Marketing*, ahead-of-p, ahead-of-print. https://doi.org/10.1108/JIMA-04-2021-0112
86. Birkinshaw, S. (2015). Spiritual friends: An investigation of childrens spirituality in the context of British urban secondary education. *British Journal of Religious Education, 37*(1), 83–102. https://doi.org/10.1080/01416200.2014.902806
87. Lundby, K. (2011). Patterns of belonging in online/offline interfaces of religion. *Information, Communication & Society*, November 2011, 37–41.
88. Woodward, S., & Kimmons, R. (2019). Religious implications of social media in education. *Religious Education, 46*(2), 271–293. https://doi.org/10.1080/15507394.2018.1510249
89. Young, S. D., et al. (2014). The influence of social networking technologies on female religious veil-wearing behavior in Iran. *Cyberpsychology, Behavior, and Social Networking, 17*(5), 317–321. https://doi.org/10.1089/cyber.2013.0338
90. Aukland, K. (2021). Bridging the research–practice gap on Facebook: a study of online communication between RE teachers and researchers. *British Journal of Religious Education, 00*(00), 1–12. https://doi.org/10.1080/01416200.2021.1920366
91. Buzdar, M. A., et al. (2020). Effects of religious orientations on the prevalence of social media disorder among Muslim University Students in Pakistan. *Journal of Religion and Health, 59*(6), 3247–3256. https://doi.org/10.1007/s10943-019-00915-6
92. Dilmaghani, M. (2018). Religiosity and the digital divide in Canada. *The Communication Review, 21*(3), 181–211. https://doi.org/10.1080/10714421.2018.1468184
93. Gvili, Y., & Poria, Y. (2005). Online mass customization: The case of promoting heritage tourist websites. *Anatolia, 16*(2), 194–206. https://doi.org/10.1080/13032917.2005.9687177
94. Kamarulzaman, Y., et al. (2016). Religion, markets, and digital media: Seeking halal food in the U.S. *Journal of Macromarketing, 36*(4), 400–411. https://doi.org/10.1177/0276146715622243
95. McClure, P. K. (2016). Faith and facebook in a pluralistic age: The effects of social networking sites on the religious beliefs of emerging adults. *Sociological Perspectives, 59*(4), 818–834. https://doi.org/10.1177/0731121416647361

96. Wilson, A. R., & Djupe, P. A. (2020). Communicating in good faith? Dynamics of the Christian Right agenda. *Politics and Religion, 13*(2), 385–414. https://doi.org/10.1017/S1755048319000543
97. Morehouse, J., & Saffer, A. J. (2021). Promoting the faith: Examining Megachurches' audience-centric advertising strategies on social media. *Journal of Advertising, 50*(4), 408–422. https://doi.org/10.1080/00913367.2021.1939202
98. Agbarya, A., & John, N. (2021). Online tie and content management and changing religious identity among Muslim Arab women in Israel. *Information, Communication & Society*, 1–16. https://doi.org/10.1080/1369118X.2021.1942956.
99. Dey, B. L., et al. (2018). Selfie appropriation by young British South Asian adults: Reifying, endorsing and reinforcing dual cultural identity in social media. *Information Technology and People, 31*(2), 482–506. https://doi.org/10.1108/ITP-08-2016-0178
100. Rao, S. (2018). Making of selfie nationalism: Narendra Modi, the paradigm shift to social media governance, and crisis of democracy. *Journal of Communication Inquiry, 42*(2), 166–183. https://doi.org/10.1177/0196859917754053
101. Hutchings, T. (2011). Community and the Online. *Society*, March 2012, 37–41.
102. Zainul, N., et al. (2004). E-Commerce from an Islamic perspective. *Electronic Commerce Research and Applications, 3*(3), 280–293. https://doi.org/10.1016/j.elerap.2004.01.002
103. Ketelaar, P. E., Konig, R., Smit, E. G., & Thorbjørnsen, H. (2015). "In ads we trust": religiousness as a predictor of advertising trustworthiness and avoidance. *Journal of Consumer Marketing, 32*(3), 190–198.
104. Boutros, A. (2015). Religion in the Afrosphere. *Journal of Communication Inquiry, 39*(4), 319–337. https://doi.org/10.1177/0196859915608916
105. Cury, E. (2019). Contesting islamophobia and securing collective rights: Muslim American Advocacy in the 2016 Elections. *Politics and Religion, 12*(4), 710–735. https://doi.org/10.1017/S1755048318000469
106. Yeung, T. Y. C. (2019). Measuring Christian Religiosity by Google Trends. *Review of Religious Research, 61*(3), 235–257. https://doi.org/10.1007/s13644-019-00379-w
107. Pennington, R. (2018). Making space in social media: #MuslimWomensDay in Twitter. *Journal of Communication Inquiry, 42*(3), 199–217. https://doi.org/10.1177/0196859918768797
108. Kimmons, R., et al. (2017). Religious identity, expression, and civility in social media: Results of data mining Latter-Day Saint Twitter accounts. *Journal for the Scientific Study of Religion, 56*(3), 637–657. https://doi.org/10.1111/jssr.12358
109. Ben-Lulu, E. (2021). Zooming in and out of virtual jewish prayer services during the COVID-19 pandemic. *Journal for the Scientific Study of Religion, 60*(4), 852–870. https://doi.org/10.1111/jssr.12746
110. Al-rawi, A. (2022). Online reactions to the Muhammad Cartoons: YouTube and the Virtual Ummah Author (s): Ahmed Al-Rawi Published by: Wiley on behalf of Society for the Scientific Study of Religion Stable URL: https://www.jstor.org/stable/24644340 Online Reactions to the. 54, 2, 261–276.
111. Grigoropoulou, N. (2020). Discussing God: The effect of (ir)religious identities on topic-sentiment polarization in online debates. *Review of Religious Research, 62*(4), 533–561. https://doi.org/10.1007/s13644-020-00425-y
112. Bail, C. A. (2012). The Fringe effect: Civil society organizations and the evolution of media discourse about Islam since the September 11th Attacks. *American Sociological Review, 77*(6), 855–879. https://doi.org/10.1177/0003122412465743
113. Henry, A. M. (2021). Religious literacy in social media: A need for strategic amplification. *Religious Education, 48*(1), 89–101. https://doi.org/10.1080/15507394.2021.1876507
114. Brummans, B. H. J. M., et al. (2020). Recycling stories: Mantras, communication, and organizational materialization. *Organization Studies, 41*(1), 103–126. https://doi.org/10.1177/0170840618819033

115. Sisler, V. (2011). Cyber counsellors: Online fatwas, arbitration tribunals and the construction of Muslim identity in the UK. *Information, Communication & Society, 14*(8), 1136–1159. https://doi.org/10.1080/1369118X.2011.579140
116. Bobkowski, P. S., & Pearce, L. D. (2011). Baring their souls in online profiles or not? Religious self-disclosure in social media. *Journal for the Scientific Study of Religion, 50*(4), 744–762. https://doi.org/10.1111/j.1468-5906.2011.01597.x
117. Lev-On, A., & Lissitsa, S. (2018). Facilitating cross-cleavage communication online: Findings from interviews with ultra-Orthodox, religious, and secular participants. *The Communication Review, 21*(3), 212–227. https://doi.org/10.1080/10714421.2018.1495434

Smart Inclusive Cities Advancing

Mauro Romanelli

Abstract As smart communities, cities of the future aim at becoming inclusive cities using the potential of technologies to drive citizen-centric development by adopting a smarty city strategy and vision in urban planning to promote and shape inclusive urban growth and communities, improving the quality of life, and developing the city as an inclusive community. Inclusive urban development relies on smart cities and communities. Cities support collaborative and inclusive urban spaces, selecting a smart city view towards urban development. Smart cities shape the city as an inclusive community.

Keywords Inclusive cities · Smart cities · Smart communities · Urban future

1 Introduction

Cities of tomorrow are re-planning the urban future to shape smart and inclusive urban communities. Cities contribute to continuous urban change, constructing a wealthy urban future, employing technologies to drive innovation-led and socially inclusive urban growth and communities, improving the quality of life and promoting community-driven social innovations [1–3]. Cities are building a smart city strategic framework for urban development, fostering a collaborative model, combining top-down and community-driven approaches, promoting multi-actor and collaborative processes [4, 5]. As nodes of innovation smart cities help create inclusive cities, empowering citizens as co-designers and co-producers of services [6, 7]. As smart communities, cities develop cooperative and collaborative processes for innovation [8]. As engines of innovation, cities improve urban competitiveness and contribute to ensuring an enhanced quality of life for communities in the long-term horizon [6, 9]. Smart cities support urban communities to drive inclusive growth, empowering citizens as co-producers of services and social value [10].

M. Romanelli (✉)
Department of Business and Economics, University of Naples Parthenope, Naples, Italy
e-mail: mauro.romanelli@uniparthenope.it

A. M. Braccini et al. (eds.), *Digital (Eco) Systems and Societal Challenges*, Lecture Notes in Information Systems and Organisation 72,
https://doi.org/10.1007/978-3-031-75586-6_16

Planning future urban development relies on adopting a smart city strategy as a vision for driving inclusive cities and communities, following a prepositive approach, by designing socially inclusive cities by promoting collaborative urban processes and involving citizens and communities [11–13] coherently with a strategic smart urban planning design adopted by ordinary cities in Europe in order to transform the city into a smart city [14], driving social and inclusive innovation [15], and providing solutions for sustainable urban, social and economic development [13]. Smart urbanism leads to more inclusive cities [16]. As smart inclusive communities, cities put people first, and foster human and social capital at the heart of sustainable smart urban development [2]. Cities adopt a smart city vision to support inclusive urban growth. Smart inclusive urban development relies on citizen-centric smart cities that strengthen collaborative processes [17], by aligning human, social, cultural, economic and environmental factors by reinforcing stakeholder engagement [18]. Thus, as intelligent communities, cities become spaces for social and inclusive innovation in order to improve quality of life and drive sustainable urban communities [19, 20].

Smart inclusive cities allow technology and digital applications to support urban communities to confront and solve problems and improve the quality of life, focusing on the proactive role of citizens in tackling technology to better enhance urban spaces [21]. Inclusive cities support sustainable urban development, strengthening a collaborative and participatory space of action and strategy among public/private actors and urban stakeholders who support city continuity with change, stressing urban citizenship [22, 23].

Open and bottom-up cities promote inclusive growth, providing social and economic opportunities, thereby reinforcing community participation [24]. Smart cities focus on citizens and drive the city as a smart community [25]. The future of cities is smart in terms of defining policies for driving socially inclusive urban growth [26]. Smart cities contribute to shaping inclusive urban communities and growth [2, 27]; the city is viewed as an informative, organisational and interactive space [28] and as a net action and inclusive space [29]. Smart cities contribute to collaborative processes that involve citizens, companies, and public authorities through digital spaces, taking a smart human-centric view towards urban development [30]. A smart city supports social quality of life enrichment and helps improve social and economic issues within urban communities, shaping the city of the future [31]. Smart cities improve quality of life, shaping citizen-centred, co-production-led platforms and collaboration-oriented and innovation-led communities, engaging the wider community and transforming management and services within smart sustainable urban ecosystems [5, 6, 32, 33].

The future of urban development hinges on smart cities and smart communities. Cities are rethinking urban planning, following a sustainability-oriented and smart strategy, involving the stakeholders and citizens, strengthening participation and multi-actor decision-making, and driving inclusive urban growth through collaboration among urban stakeholders for smart city/community innovation [34, 35]. The research gap requires identifying smart cities and communities as drivers of innovation and social inclusion within urban communities. There are still few studies that focus on the smart city as a driver of innovative and inclusive cities and urban communities. The smart city view supports the city as an engine of social innovation and inclusion within urban communities. The research question refers to how cities are rethinking the urban future, adopting a smart vision by designing smart inclusive communities as engines of sustainable urban development. The aim of this study is to clarify how a smart city vision helps drive smart inclusive cities and communities. The contribution of the study is to elucidate that smart city planning and strategy help shape the city as a community that drives urban innovation and social inclusion. Crucially, smart inclusive cities construct a wealthy future for urban communities. The paper is compiled as follows. After the introduction and the methodological section, in the third section, cities are presented as inclusive communities while in the fourth section, the smart inclusive city vision that helps drive the city to support future development is discussed. In the fifth section, three case studies (Paris, Vienna and Florence) elaborate on the smart city vision and planning that is driving smart inclusive cities. Finally, the discussion and conclusions are outlined.

2 Methodological Section

The study, which is qualitative, descriptive and exploratory, analyses how cities are rethinking their future development as inclusive, smart and sustainable communities. While cities are planning to transform urban environments into smart cities as urban policy priorities, they are rediscovering the smart city as an opportunity to drive the city as an inclusive community. The research involves document analysis. Some European smart strategy frameworks related to Florence [36], Paris [37] and Wien [38] are identified. The study centres on exploring three case studies (Paris, Florence and Wien) that refer to cities that are adopting a smart city vision to urban development, redesigning the future of urban communities coherently with a positivist approach to urban planning [11], by adopting a smart city strategy as a vision for driving inclusive and collaborative urban processes, and designing socially inclusive cities by involving citizens and communities [12, 13]. The cities' sample was selected by considering how some European cities are managing urban development, selecting a smart view of the social growth of urban communities. The phenomenon of cities adopting a smart view towards urban development to shape inclusive and sustainable communities is emerging and ongoing contemporarily. These illustrative cases are used to explore a phenomenon that is still underway. The smart city frameworks discussed shed light on the attempt to shape a smart inclusive city as an innovative and emerging phenomenon, and enable cities to evolve as inclusive communities. The study employs a multiple case study methodology and analysis [4, 39]. Specifically, smart city framework and strategy provide a means for urban planning that serves urban development solutions refers to research concerning the relationships between the issues drawn by smart city framework planning and the impact on urban development and benefits for communities. The research methods involved case selection and data collection from policy documents. In particular, smart city frameworks adopted by the municipalities of Paris, Florence and Wien as policy documents are considered information sources to collect to analyse data and information and investigate how some European cities are rethinking and planning urban future development coherently with a smart city view by designing a smart and inclusive community as an engine of urban innovation and social growth. Descriptive case study research was employed for the qualitative analysis of the smart city strategy adopted by municipalities to make the city smart city and community [15, 40–42].

3 Inclusive Cities and Communities

The future of cities expects inclusive urban communities coherently with the *UN 2030 Agenda for Sustainable Development* [43]. In the *New Urban Agenda* building inclusive cities and communities contribute to driving economic, social and healthy growth, promoting social cohesion and integration [44]. As socially inclusive urban communities, cities improve the quality of life, developing the well-being of the whole community, enabling cooperation and interactivity among public and private sectors [45]. Urban social and community-driven innovations anticipate multi-actor collaboration and partnerships leading to pathways for social inclusion and change [46]. Cities are planning their urban development, integrating social, economic, environmental and territorial dimensions [47]. As inclusive spaces and platforms for collaborative innovations, cities support private, public, no profit actors and citizens in collaborating in interactive arenas to engender new solutions that benefit urban communities [48]. Socially inclusive, sustainable and prosperous cities contribute to urban development and innovation [49], strengthening the community and social capital [50]. Inclusive cities shape human-oriented inclusive urban communities and development by underpinning collaborative, participatory and multi-actor urban innovation, promoting the wellbeing of people, thus avoiding entering decline [22]. As social incubators of urban change and innovation, open and bottom-up cities are engines of economic and social growth and belong to the people [20, 24]. Cities are socially sustainable communities, focusing on people, and shaping urban spaces for social interaction and participation within urban networks by driving community-led initiatives and leading to socially inclusive urban spaces [51, 52].

4 Towards Smart Inclusive Cities

Smart inclusive cities are advancing in order to shape smart and wealthy urban communities. In the information age, smart cities and communities support social and community inclusion, and urban open innovation [5, 30]. The idea underlying the vision of smart cities is to design inclusive and sustainable urban communities, achieving social and technological issues [2]. Moreover, building smart cities of the future relies on shaping social and respectful relationships that involve citizens and communities [6]. As a positive condition within communities, social sustainability implies social cohesion and refers to healthy and liveable communities [53]. Smart cities contribute to achieving social sustainability and inclusion, encouraging a collaborative planning approach and stakeholder engagement [54]. Smart and truly inclusive cities improve quality of life and focus on citizen empowerment to drive long-term urban sustainability and inclusive growth [6]. The smart city model helps to provide a social response to social issues concerning urban growth perspectives [14]. The aim of smart cities is to contribute to socially inclusive and open innovative urban communities [6]: smart cities contribute to shaping the social pillar for quality of life improvement [55]. The future of urban development hinges on driving smart inclusive growth and designing smart cities that contribute to enhancing human capital and urban stakeholder collaboration. Smart cities support urban planning and contribute to bettering the quality of life enhancing human and social capital [56], and, as engines of public value creation [57], smart cities and communities contribute to developing inclusive growth. A smart city is a smart community that can promote the wellbeing of all its members, enabling collaborative processes within urban spaces [27, 58]. A smart city view supports community development for urban change and open innovation [6, 59]. Cities develop smart and sustainable solutions, fostering collaboration among all urban stakeholders to drive urban innovation and achieve social sustainability [3, 45, 54]. Smart cities employ information technology strategically and extensively to improve the quality of life within urban communities [25, 60], meeting the needs of the future without compromising the rights of future generations [61]. In addition, smart and inclusive communities support the social dimension of the city, connecting the human, institutional and technological components of urban environments [62], creating sustainable as well as inclusive and people-centered communities [21]. Cities will become smart communities, sustainable, healthy, and exciting places to live and work, and open collaborative spaces for the active participation of all urban stakeholders [2]. Smart cities support a collaboration-led and human-centred view of urban development [8, 48]. Smart city initiatives aid community engagement and enhance citizen participation in urban governance [63]. The smart community develops collaboration, cooperation and partnership among voluntary, educational, private and public organisations, and citizens [64]. Cities adopt a smart vision to drive sustainable and inclusive growth and support innovation [34]. As engines of inclusive urban growth, smart cities and communities enable multi-level and multi-sectoral interactions, fostering co-designed innovative solutions [49]. Building smart cities helps to shape socially innovative and inclusive communities [65] and bolsters sustainable urban growth through efficient resource management for knowledge and innovation assets [66]. Cities adopt and implement a smart strategy by developing community, technology and policy for sustainable and inclusive urban growth by empowering the citizens to work for urban and social value creation [10], following a human-centric driven view for technological and social innovation. Smart inclusive cities shape human-centred, intelligent, digital and socially-driven urban communities to encourage diverse stakeholder participation in urban growth, fostering collaboration and social networking [67, 68]. Furthermore, smart city visions focus on human and social capital and stakeholder engagement [69]. Smart cities contribute to improving and extending the wealth of people within inclusive urban communities that proceed towards sustainable urban development [70, 71], empowering users and citizens for more informed and intelligent behaviour [72]. Smart cities contribute to shaping socially inclusive urban communities by promoting private-public partnerships and collaboration, abandoning a techno-centric view, and tracking a pathway for engendering dialogue and confrontation on future urban growth, enhancing a human-oriented vision of smart city building [73]. Building inclusive smart cities relies on encouraging the actors to foster a quadruple helix to support digital innovation hubs [74]. Thus, shaping inclusive smart cities supports citizen-led smart urban interventions [75] and fosters urban vitalism that relies on driving community-led initiatives and innovations that contribute to improving the quality of life [76].

5 Smart Inclusive Cities as Future Urban Communities Advancing

In this research three case studies are presented and analysed. The smart vision planning of some European cities helps us understand how cities are rethinking their urban future in terms of sustainable and inclusive growth. Smart inclusive cities put people as the first actor of human and civil progress. The cities adopt a smart vision in order to drive collaborative processes and spaces, improve the quality of life of their citizens and shape inclusive and sustainable cities of the future.

In the *Firenze Smart City Plan* [36] the city is a living organism comprising people within the context of digital urban transformation that enables intelligent communities. Citizens play a proactive role in identifying the pathway of urban development by enhancing the quality of life for each and every citizen living in an urban metropolitan environment. In particular, planning a smart urban vision helps drive the city as a community of people and an engine of meaning creation, culture production, creativity, and thinking. Promoting smartness requires using technology to make cities more intelligent, sustainable and capable of driving innovation, and reinforce social relationships within the urban community. A smart city refers to a city that is changing and constructing new social, urban, and economic responses to environmental and historical pressures. The smart city plan is an open space for debate, confrontation, collaboration, and exchange of information and knowledge among all urban stakeholders (public administration, research centers, cultural institutions, businesses, associations, groups, citizens) involved to support urban, social, and economic development. Consequently, a smart city master plan helps the city to drive continuous urban innovation, to improve the quality of life within the community and develop sustainable urban planning that relies on clear and strong distributed and collective leadership and vision. Hence, information technology is a critical successful factor and facilitator of all smart city actions and initiatives. A smart city strategy depends on open innovation to ensure stakeholder involvement by embracing the four *Is*: *integration* of all possible aspects and sectors in charge of a municipality's competences and background; *innovation* means the development of innovative services and approaches, and relies on the potential offered by digital and interactive information technology; *involvement* is conceived as a means to urge stakeholders to identify, plan, share, and implement strategic, long-term vision and goals more ambitious than the current; and *information* is related to the use of information technology as a way to reinforce the relationships between the municipality and citizens regarding the monitoring of the implementation of smart urban strategy and policies.

In the *Smart City Wien Framework Strategy* [37] the 2050 vision utilises some key concepts: quality of living, sustainability, prosperity, opportunities for education and workplaces. The role of information and communication technology is to simplify the lives of individuals and contribute to a better quality of life. Promoting smartness supports urban change processes. As smart communities, cities do not let anybody down and integrate the social component into the development process, focus on initiatives for social inclusion and ensure quality of living, enabling people's participation. A smart and sustainable city strategy relies on rethinking urban governance models, strengthening co-ordination and cooperation as means of constructing shared, collaborative and multi-actor processes that involve all the stakeholders within the urban community, consolidating the cooperation on smart city issues with universities and research centres and institutions to stimulate social innovation vision and engender opportunities for experimenting with new opportunities for urban value creation. Developing a smart strategy relies on establishing the participation possibilities of citizens and experts, promoting co-determination and management by considering the needs of all residents, meeting the needs of many different population groups, recognising this diversity, maintaining both high levels of safety and social security, leisure quality and culture, openness and maintaining high standards of public services and healthcare system, bolstering co-determination and participation to democratically ensure modes of governance that support urban development and drive social innovations. The Wien smart city supports social inclusion, stimulating social innovations and sustaining both social and technological developments more strongly inspired by the needs of citizens, and taking particular account of the interaction between individuals and organisations.

In the Paris smart city framework *Paris Smart and Sustainable looking ahead to 2020 and beyond* [38] the role of a city using technology for becoming a smart and sustainable community is to improve the quality of life. The smart and sustainable city acts as a platform that is open, innovation-oriented and future-driven. Smartness is a means to drive the city towards a sustainable future related to quality of life improvement. Developing the city of the future means bringing together social, technological and organisational aspects and relies on three pillars: the *connected city* (the tool) relies on constantly changing infrastructures such as communication networks and continually integrating technological advances; the *open city* (the method) relies on stimulating citizen participation and collaborative projects, exchanging, sharing and co-creating with researchers, scientists and academics, strengthening innovation ecosystem and promoting public innovation by transforming public administration, simplifying processes, and improving public services through city employees who contribute to reinventing the administration with their ideas and practices; and the *sustainable city* (the goal) is a place where the technology serves the people, improving their inclusion in city life by allowing them to be involved in creating public services and policy decision-making processes. Smart cities are places where technologies support people and help include them in city life, bridging the gap between new public services and policymaking. In particular, a smart and sustainable city relies on the intelligent work of citizens and enables people to face global challenges and play a proactive role in building the urban future.

6 Discussion and Conclusions

Shaping smart inclusive cities helps drive cities as inclusive communities. A smart city strategy and vision supports the pathway towards urban social sustainability [19, 21, 22]. and contributes to ensuring a high quality of life, making wealthy urban communities collaborative spaces and *loci* of innovation and empowering citizens as co-producers of policies and services. Planning smart inclusive cities strengthens the potential of information technology to develop smart urban communities that drive inclusive social growth, identifying a pathway to future urban social and sustainable development by empowering citizens and driving open innovation, and relying on human and social capital building [6, 53, 56]. Smart city visions and applications contribute to shaping future urban development. Smart, open and inclusive cities contribute to continuous urban development and innovation, ensuring better quality of life within urban communities. Cities are planning a smart urban vision to support social inclusion within urban spaces and facilitate technology-enabled communities that support urban collaborative spaces. The smart city planning of three European cities supports the processes of social innovation and inclusion, shaping urban collaborative spaces where private and public actors, and citizens contribute to services co-production, innovative and creative solutions for sustainability and value creation within urban communities.

The Paris sustainable city vision enables the role of technology as a means to make the city a connected and inclusive community shaping an organisational and informational space by engaging citizens and developing the open city as an engine of collaborative processes, strengthening participatory policy-making processes and services to drive social and inclusive growth. In the Wien smart city framework, the use of technology supports community development and helps drive the city as an inclusive community opening up to collaborative processes that support urban value creation and innovation processes. Technology is a means to enhance co-participation and co-decision-making and support social inclusion as a strategic and organisational view to sustainable urban development. In the Florence smart city

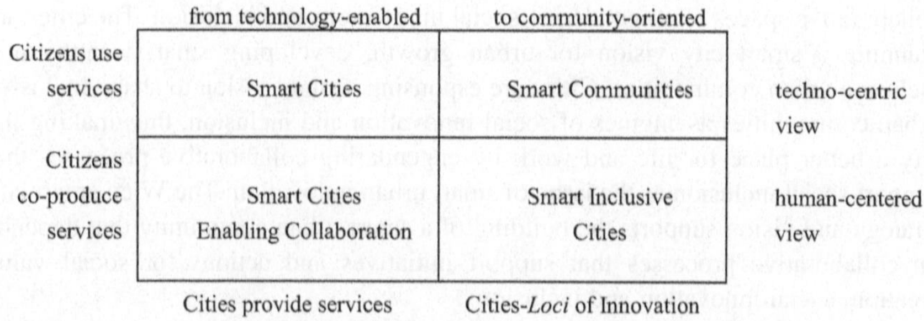

Fig. 1 Towards smart innovative and inclusive urban communities

plan the focus relies on using information technology to ensure information and improve integration to support citizen and community involvement to drive urban innovation. Developing a smart city depends on fostering stakeholder participation and engagement, shaping inclusive and innovative urban communities. Hence, technology enables citizen participation and community development in urban value creation processes, innovation and sustainability.

As engines of innovation, cities are planning smart city development, moving from a technology-enabled to a community-oriented and human-centric vision that relies on collaborative processes that involve all the urban stakeholders: adopting a human-centred or techno-centric view to smart urban social growth and favouring an information-driven or participative-oriented vision in the co-construction and co-innovation of a smart and sustainable urban pathway; putting the people first, focusing on human and social capital, and community; shaping urban collaborative spaces to drive continuous social and economic innovation, empowering citizens as co-producers of services than merely users of urban services, and strengthening stakeholders' participation and involvement as key drivers of urban change within the city as a collaboration-oriented, inclusion-driven and innovation-led community.

While traditional smart cities depend on citizens as users of services provided by the city coherently with a techno-centric view, smart communities employ human resources and technological infrastructures to shape the urban spaces as engines and *loci* of innovation. As human-centred and community-oriented *loci* of innovation that empower citizens as co-producers of services, cities are planning a smart city vision that supports the development of smart innovative and inclusive communities. As technology-enabled and human-centred providers of services, cities are proposing a smart view in transitioning towards smart cities as collaborative communities that value the role of citizens as co-producers of services. As collaborative urban communities, cities are going smart to put the people first and support stakeholder involvement and participation in city development and innovation. The framework of analysis is illustrated in Fig. 1.

The Paris smart city vision supports a pathway that necessitates technology as a driver of cooperative and open processes that involve all urban stakeholders to collaborate to proceed towards a sustainable socially innovative and inclusive city. The aim of the Florence smart city framework is to facilitate organisational and collaborative spaces for engendering social innovations and inclusion. The cities are planning a smart city vision for urban growth, developing smart wealthy and inclusive urban communities. Cities are espousing a smart vision to shape inclusive urban communities as engines of social innovation and inclusion, thus making the city a better place for life and work by engendering collaborative processes that support social inclusion as the issue of smart urban innovation. The Wien smart city strategy and vision supports the building of a smart urban community that depends on collaborative processes that support initiatives and actions for social value creation, social innovation and inclusion.

As smart inclusive communities, cities drive continuous social innovation, strengthening stakeholder involvement and participation. Smart inclusive cities contribute to future urban development, identifying a community-oriented vision, assuming a human-centred view and promoting collaborative processes for co-construction and co-innovation of smart and sustainable urban pathways. Smart inclusive cities and communities advocate a human-centred and participation-oriented view to urban growth, dealing with technology, making the city a better place for engendering collaborative and open processes that empower citizens and support services' co-production, social innovation and inclusion within urban environments.

In the study theoretical, organisational, managerial and social implications are observed. Smart inclusive cities contribute to human-led and community-centred cooperative processes that drive open and socially innovative urban communities. Smart solutions support social inclusion and equipe the city as an open collaborative space for urban innovation and value creation. A smart inclusive city stresses the city as an open organisational space and engine of social and economic growth and innovation, and requires citizen empowerment and development of managerial skills and competences.

However, there are some limitations to the study. Particularly, the study is exploratory. Only three illustrative case studies are considered. In the analysis the adoption of a smart city vision and planning supports inclusive urban communities. As smart communities, cities adopt a smart vision to support socially inclusive and collaborative spaces and shape a sustainable urban future in the long-term horizon. Future research perspectives imply investigating how the discourse about planning and designing the smart city vision is leading to designing and developing inclusive and sustainable cities and communities within the context of Italian cities.

References

1. Yigitcanlar, T. (2021). Smart city beyond efficiency: Technology–policy–Community at play for sustainable urban futures. *Housing Policy Debate, 31*, 88–92.
2. Eger, J. M. (2005). Smart communities, universities, and globalization: Educating the workforce for tomorrow's economy. *Metropolitan Universities, 16*(4), 28–38.
3. Kummitha, R. K. R., & Critzen, N. (2017). How do we understand smart cities? An evolutionary perspective. *Cities, 67*, 43–52.

4. Mora, L., Deakin, M., & Reid, A. (2019). Strategic principles for smart city development: A multiple case study analysis of European best practices. *Technological Forecasting and Social Change, 142*, 70–97.
5. Sørensen, E., & Törfing, J. (2018). Co-initiation of collaborative innovation in urban spaces. *Urban Affairs Review, 54*, 388–418.
6. Paskaleva, K. A. (2011). The smart city: A nexus for open innovation? *Intelligent Buildings International, 3*, 153–171.
7. Granier, B., & Kudo, H. (2016). How are citizens involved in smart cities? Analysing citizen participation in Japanese 'smart communities'. *Information Polity, 21*(1), 61–76.
8. Andreani, S., Kalchschmidt, M., Pinto, R., & Sayegh, A. (2019). Reframing technologically enhanced urban scenarios: A design research model towards human centered smart cities. *Technological Forecasting and Social Change, 142*, 15–25.
9. Appio, F. P., Lima, M., & Paroutis, S. (2019). Understanding smart cities: Innovation ecosystems, technological advancements, and societal challenges. *Technological Forecasting and Social Change, 142*, 1–14.
10. Martin, C. J., Evans, J., & Karvonen, A. (2018). Smart and sustainable? Five tensions in the visions and practices of the smart-sustainable city in Europe and North America. *Technological Forecasting and Social Change, 133*, 269–278.
11. Joss, S. (2016). Smart city: A regressive agenda. In *Proceedings of the Society for the History of Technology Annual Meeting, Singapore* (pp. 23–28).
12. Nielsen, B. F., Baer, D., & Lindkvist, C. (2019). Identifying and supporting exploratory and exploitative models of innovation in municipal urban planning; key challenges from seven Norwegian energy ambitious neighborhood pilots. *Technological Forecasting and Social Change, 142*, 142–153.
13. Mora, L., & Bolici, R. (2017). How to become a smart city: Learning from Amsterdam. In *International conference on smart and sustainable planning for cities and regions* (pp. 251–266). Springer.
14. Mora, L., & Bolici, R. (2015). Urban regeneration in the digital era: How to develop smart city strategies in large European cities. *Techne. Journal of Technology fro Architecture and Environment, 5*(2), 110–119.
15. Anttiroiko, A. V., Valkama, P., & Bailey, S. J. (2014). Smart cities in the new service economy: Building platforms for smart services. *AI & SOCIETY, 29*(3), 323–334.
16. Odendaal, N. (2021). Everyday urbanisms and the importance of place: Exploring the elements of the emancipatory smart city. *Urban Studies, 58*(3), 639–654.
17. Malek, J. A., Lim, S. B., & Yigitcanlar, T. (2021). Social inclusion indicators for building citizen-centric smart cities: A systematic literature review. *Sustainability, 13*, 376.
18. Mora, L., Deakin, M., Reid, A., & Angelidou, M. (2019). How to overcome the dichotomous nature of smart city research: Proposed methodology and results of a pilot study. *Journal of Urban Technology, 26*, 89–128.
19. Martinez, J., Mikkelsen, C. A., & Phillips, R. (2021). Introduction: Quality of life and sustainability, socio-spatial, and multidisciplinary perspectives. In J. In Martinez, C. A. Mikkelsen, & R. Phillips (Eds.), *Handbook of quality of life and sustainability* (pp. 1–14). Springer.
20. Newman, P., & Jennings, J. (2008). *Cities as sustainable ecosystems. Principles and practices*. Island Press.
21. Chang, J. I., Choi, J., An, H., & Chung, H. Y. (2022). Gendering the smart city: A case study of Sejong City, Korea. *Cities, 120*, 103422.
22. Varma, S., & Gill, H. (2010). Development strategies for inclusive cities. In P. In Singh & S. Varma (Eds.), *Organizing and managing in the era of globalization* (pp. 368–387). SAGE Publications India Pvt Ltd.
23. Turnbull, S. (2007). A framework for designing sustainable urban communities. *Kybernetes, 36*(9–10), 1543–1557.

24. Sennett, R. (2017). The open city. In *The post-urban world: Emergent transformation of cities and regions in the innovative global economy* (Vol. 97).
25. Yigitcanlar, T. (2017). Smart cities in the making. *International Journal of Knowledge-Based Development, 8*(3), 201–205.
26. Visvizi, A., Lytras, M. D., Damiani, E., & Mathkour, H. (2018). Policy making for smart cities: Innovation and social inclusive economic growth for sustainability. *Journal of Science and Technology Policy Management, 9*(2), 126–133.
27. Lara, A. P., Da Costa, E. M., Furlan, T. Z., & Yigitcanlar, T. (2016). Smartness that matters: Towards a comprehensive and human-Centred characterisation of smart cities. *Journal of Open Innovation: Technology, Market and Complexity, 2*(2), 1–13.
28. Knox, H. (2010). Cities and organisation: The information city and urban form. *Culture and Organization, 16*(3), 185–195.
29. Czarniawska, B. (2002). Remembering while forgetting: The role of automorphism in City Management in Warsaw. *Public Administration, 62*(2), 63–173.
30. Komninos, N. (2014). Introduction: The age of intelligent cities. In N. Komninos (Ed.), *The age of intelligent cities. Smart environments and innovation-for-all strategies* (pp. 1–9). Routledge.
31. Lazariou, G. C., & Roscia, M. (2012). Definition methodology for the smart cities model. *Energy, 47*(1), 326332.
32. Palumbo, R., Manesh, M. F., Pellegrini, M. M., Caputo, A., & Flamini, G. (2021). Organizing a sustainable smart urban ecosystem: Perspectives and insights from a bibliometric analysis and literature review. *Journal of Cleaner Production, 297*, 126662.
33. Nam, T., & Pardo, T. A. (2011). Smart city as urban innovation with dimensions of technology, people and institutions. In *Proceedings of the 5th international conference on theory and practice of electronic governance* (pp. 185–194). ACM.
34. European Commission: Smart cities and communities—European Innovation Partnership, C (2012) 4701 final, Brussels, 10.7.2012 (2012).
35. Yigitcanlar, T., & Teriman, S. (2015). Rethinking sustainable urban development: Towards an integrated planning and development process. *International journal of Environmental Science and Technology, 12*(1), 341–352.
36. Comune di Firenze: Firenze Smart City plan (2015).
37. Vienna City Administration: Smart City Wien Framework Strategy (2014).
38. Mairie de Paris: Paris smart and sustainable looking ahead to 2020 and beyond (2015).
39. Eisenhardt, K. M. (2009). Building theories from case study research. *Academy of Management Review, 14*(4), 532–550.
40. Angelidou, M. (2014). Smart city policies: A spatial approach. *Cities, 41*, S3–S11.
41. Angelidou, M. (2017). The role of smart city characteristics in the plans of fifteen cities. *Journal of Urban Technology, 24*(4), 3–28.
42. Sancino, A., & Hudson, L. (2020). Leadership in, of, and for smart cities–case studies from Europe, America, and Australia. *Public Management Review, 22*(5), 701–725.
43. United Nations: Transforming our world: The 2030 agenda for sustainable development, A/RES/ 70/1, on 25–27 September 2015, New York, NY (2015).
44. United Nations: The new urban agenda. United Nations conference on housing and sustainable urban development (habitat III), Quito, Ecuador, 20 October 2016 (2017).
45. Stren, R. E., & Polèse, M. (2000). Understanding the new sociocultural dynamics of cities: comparative urban policy in a global context. In R. E. Stren & M. Polèse (Eds.), *The social sustainability of cities: diversity and the management of change* (pp. 3–38). University of Toronto Press.
46. Lord, J., & Hutchinson, P. (2007). *Pathways to inclusion. Building a new story with people and communities*. Captus Press.
47. European Union: Cities of tomorrow. Challenges, visions, ways forward (2011).
48. Meijer, A. J., & Thaens, M. (2018). Urban technological innovation: Developing and testing a sociotechnical framework for studying smart city projects. *Urban Affairs Review, 54*(2), 363–387.

49. European Commission: Report from the Commission to the Council on the Urban Agenda for the EU, COM(2017) 657 final, 20.11.2017 (2017).
50. Haapio, A. (2012). Towards sustainable urban communities. *Environmental Impact Assessment Review, 322*, 165–169.
51. Giddings, B., Hopwood, B., Mellor, M., & O'Brien, G. (2006). Back to the City: A route to urban sustainability. In M. Jenks & N. Dempsey (Eds.), *Future forms and design for Sustainable Cities* (pp. 13–30). Architectural Press.
52. Dempsey, N., Bramley, G., Power, S., & Brown, C. (2011). The social dimension of sustainable development: Defining urban social sustainability. *Sustainable Development, 19*(5), 289–300.
53. McKenzie, S. (2004). Social sustainability: Towards some definition.
54. Freestone, R., & Favaro, P. (2022). The social sustainability of smart cities: A conceptual framework. *City, Culture and Society, 29*, 100460.
55. Silva, B. N., Khan, M., & Han, K. (2018). Towards sustainable smart cities: A review of trends, architectures, components, and open challenges in smart cities. *Sustainable Cities and Society, 38*, 697–713.
56. Neirotti, P., De Marco, A., Cagliano, A. C., Mangano, G., & Scorrano, F. (2014). Current trends in Smart City initiatives: Some stylised facts. *Cities, 38*, 25–36.
57. Pardo, T. A., Gil-Garcia, J. R., Gascó-Hernández, M., Cook, M. E., & Choi, I. (2021). Creating public value in cities: A call for focus on context and capability. In *Smart cities and smart governance: towards the 22nd century sustainable city* (pp. 119–139).
58. Gil-Garcia, J. R., Pardo, T. A., & Nam, T. (2016). A comprehensive view of the 21 century city: Smartness as technologies and innovation in urban contexts. In J. R. Gil-Garcia et al. (Eds.), *Smarter as the new urban agenda. A comprehensive view of the 21st century, City* (pp. 1–21). Public Administration and Information Technology, Springer.
59. Stratigeia, A. (2012). The concept of 'smart cities' Towards Community Development? *Networks and Communication Studies, 36*(3–4), 375–388.
60. Giffinger, R., Fertner, C., Kramar, H., Kalasek, R., Pichler-Milanovic, N., & Meijers, E. (2007). Smart cities. Ranking of European medium-sized cities, Final Report, Centre of Regional Science, Vienna UT.
61. Peris-Ortiz, M., Bennett, D. R., & Yábar, D. P. B. (2017). *Sustainable smart cities. Innovation, technology, and knowledge management*. Springer.
62. Nam, T., & Pardo, T. A. (2011). Conceptualizing smart city with dimensions of technology, people and institutions. In *Proceedings of the 12th annual international digital government research conference: Digital government innovation in challenging times* (pp. 282–291). ACM.
63. Chourabi, H., Gil-Garcia, J. R., Pardo, T. A., Nam, T., Mellouli, S., Scholl, H. J., Walker, S., & Nahon, K. (2012). Understanding Smart Cities: An integrative framework. In *45th Hawaii International Conference on System Sciences*.
64. Lindskog, H. (2004). Smart communities initiatives. Proceedings of the 3rd ISOneWorld Conference (Vol. 16).
65. European Economic and Social Committee Opinion of the European Economic and Social Committee on 'Smart cities as drivers for development of a new European industrial policy', C383/24 (2015).
66. Bătăgan, L. (2011). Smart cities and sustainability models. *Informatica Economică, 15*(3), 80–87.
67. Liang, D., De Jong, M., Schraven, D., & Wang, L. (2021). Mapping key features and dimensions of the inclusive city: A systematic bibliometric analysis and literature study. *International Journal of Sustainable Development & World Ecology, 29*, 1–20.
68. Komninos, N., & Tsarchopoulos, P. (2013). Toward intelligent Thessaloniki: From an agglomeration of apps to smart districts. *Journal of the Knowledge Economy, 4*(2), 149–168.
69. Fernandez-Anez, V., Fernández-Güell, J. M., & Giffinger, R. (2018). Smart City implementation and discourses: An integrated conceptual model. The case of Vienna. *Cities, 78*, 4–16.

70. Angelidou, M., Psaltoglou, A., Komninos, N., Kakderi, C., Tsarchopoulos, P., & Panori, A. (2017). Enhancing sustainable urban development through smart city applications. *Journal of Science and Technology Policy Management, 9*(2), 146–169.
71. Ahvenniemi, H., Huovila, A., Pinto-Seppä, I., & Airaksinen, M. (2017). What are the differences between sustainable and smart cities? *Cities, 60*, 234–245.
72. Komninos, N., & Mora, L. (2018). Exploring the big picture of smart city research. *Scienze Regionali, 17*(1), 15–38.
73. Vanolo, A. (2014). Smartmentality: The smart city as disciplinary strategy. *Urban Studies, 51*(5), 883–898.
74. Lepore, D., Testi, N., & Pasher, E. (2023). Building inclusive smart cities through innovation intermediaries. *Sustainability, 15*(5), 4024.
75. Kummitha, R. K. R., & Crutzen, N. (2019). Smart cities and the citizen-driven internet of things: A qualitative inquiry into an emerging smart city. *Technological Forecasting and Social Change, 140*, 44–53.
76. Nederhand, J., Avelino, F., Awad, I., De Jong, P., Duijn, M., Edelenbos, J., et al. (2023). Reclaiming the city from an urban vitalism perspective: Critically reflecting smart, inclusive, resilient and sustainable just city labels. *Cities, 137*, 104257.

Sustainability-Oriented Information Systems to Support a Network's Sustainability Transition: Lights and Shadows

Alessia Zoppelletto, Sabrina Bonomi, and Paolino Fierro

Abstract This article aims to understand how network SMEs engage in the transition toward sustainability, leveraging information systems to support sustainable management of their networks.

The present study analyzes a 3-year in-depth longitudinal case study of an Italian business network orchestrated by the "Brun Gelmino" Company. The leading firm developed sustainability-oriented network information systems with the collaboration of "Feelera", an intermediary operating in the industry of sustainability-oriented information systems and platforms development.

The results provide insights into the implementation of a sustainable shift of a business network by leveraging sustainability-oriented information systems to develop a network sustainability platform. Indeed, a sustainability-oriented information system may be a key driver to increase a business network's understanding of sustainability-related issues, improving the network's sustainability performance, and fostering a network's sustainability transition through the implementation of new organizational practices.

However, the implementation of a sustainability-oriented information system may also generate negative dynamics, resulting in a series of tensions between the network leading firm, the network firms, and external stakeholders such as clients or institutions.

Keywords Sustainability-oriented information systems · Business network · Digital platform · Sustainability transition · Sustainability

---

A. Zoppelletto (✉)
University of Verona, Verona, Italy
e-mail: alessia.zoppelletto@univr.it

S. Bonomi
eCampus University, Novedrate, Italy
e-mail: sabrina.bonomi@uniecampus.it

P. Fierro
PEGASO Telematic University, Naples, Italy
e-mail: paolino.fierro@unipegaso.it

A. M. Braccini et al. (eds.), *Digital (Eco) Systems and Societal Challenges*, Lecture Notes in Information Systems and Organisation 72,
https://doi.org/10.1007/978-3-031-75586-6_17

1 Introduction

Due to the pressing global challenges, there is a growing need for companies in traditional industries to reevaluate their existing strategies and business models and actively participate in the sustainability transition [1].

Aggregations of organizations, such as business networks and ecosystems, relying on participatory architectures, collaboration, and cooperative behaviors seem more resilient in facing grand societal challenges and shaping their sustainability transition [2]).

For instance, Ghisetti et al. [3] found that businesses achieve higher environmental performance levels when they engage in external collaboration agreements. Indeed, an organization's relations with its stakeholders are essential in advancing firm flexibility, organizational adaptability, stimulating creativity and problem-solving capabilities [2]).

To this extent, digital transformation offers many opportunities. Indeed, through digital technologies, organizations can easily adopt participatory digital architectures such as digital platforms to promote network coordination and agility [4], also with sustainability-oriented purposes ([5], [6]).

Using digital technologies for sustainability-focused purposes is not easily accomplished by companies, particularly small and medium-sized enterprises (SMEs). Various studies indicate that simply adopting digital technologies does not guarantee the development of a sustainable strategy rooted in data. [7]. To address this purpose, companies need to improve both their digital architectures and their internal knowledge and culture.

To this extent, information systems that can collect, manage, and analyze data related to sustainability are becoming pivotal tools for adopting and managing more sustainable practices and improving the organizations' sustainability performance.

At the same time, the organization's sustainability performance needs to consider the environmental and sustainable practices of a range of stakeholders [8], such as its supply chain partners.

The sustainability-related data of companies' stakeholders needs to be collected across the supply chain. According to De Camargo Fiorini and Chiappetta Jabbour [9], organizations seeking to improve their sustainability performance need a considerable amount of data from their partners.

Dedicated information systems can map companies' sustainability performance across the value chain and share sustainability-oriented data among business partners operating on the same supply chain.

Studies on the potential of digital transformation to enhance sustainability performance tend to focus on the firm level despite this evidence (e.g., [10], [11–13]).

Conversely, literature on digital transformation's potential to enhance the sustainable transition of organizational architectures (e.g., business networks, business ecosystems, platform ecosystems) is still underdeveloped. Indeed, at the inter-organizational level of analysis, studies investigating the relationship between sustainability and digitalization focus mainly on supply chains [14, 15], and we can spot limited contributions addressing the issue of sustainability-oriented information systems [16]. Navigating the sustainability transition and tackling grand challenges [17] remains an under-investigated topic in relation to architectures such as business networks as they endeavor to develop information systems focused on sustainability.

Therefore, the study's research question is: how are network SMEs involved in sustainability transition using information systems to support sustainable network management?

The paper is structured as follows. The next section provides the theoretical framework of the research. Section 3 explains the empirical setting, the case study selection, and the methodology adopted in the study. Section 4 shows the results, whereas in Sect. 5, we discuss the research findings, practical implications, limitations, and suggestions for future research venues.

2 Literature Review

External pressures from customers, business partners, supply chain partners, suppliers, or policymakers may drive organizations' transition toward sustainability[1] [19]. Organizations face requests from external stakeholders related to various environmental pressures such as regulations, competition, and stakeholder expectations. These demands require them to address grand challenges like sustainability and environmental responsibility [17].

For organizations to successfully undergo a sustainable transition and meet the needs of external stakeholders, it is crucial to leverage digital transformation as a tool [20]. Companies are increasingly able to use digital technologies to gather information on environmental or social concerns [21]. These technologies can be utilized to collect data for purposes such as reducing a firm's carbon footprint, developing more environmentally friendly products or services, and optimizing the usage of raw materials or natural resources.

As companies navigate toward their sustainable transition and respond to their stakeholders' pressures, they need significant information and data from their partners to support the implementation of sustainable practices across their value chain [22].

To this extent, companies need to move from an organization-centric perspective towards a multi-stakeholder perspective of sustainability transitions since sustainability-related challenges cross multiple organizational boundaries [17]. Indeed, the organization's sustainability performance must also take into account the environmental and sustainable practices of various stakeholders contributing to the same product or service (Sharma & Henriques, 2005) to enable the adoption of sustainable value chain practices.

[1] Sustainability transition refers to a form of progress that meets the needs of the present without endangering the capacity of future generations to fulfill their own needs [18].

Digital technologies facilitate the uptake of sustainable value chain practices by allowing companies to share a large volume of information with their partners, spanning organizational boundaries and influencing the behaviors of organizations within the same value chain [23].

To do so, organizations need to comprehend how to integrate digital and sustainability-oriented information systems across their value chain to enhance overall sustainability practices [9]).

Firms are required not only to collect sustainability-related information but also to dedicate time and resources towards effective utilization and associated strategies to promote innovative and more sustainable production processes and business models to enhance the sustainable transition of their value chain [24].

Indeed, according to De Camargo Fiorini and Chiappetta Jabbour [9], information systems can be a crucial resource for addressing environmental issues if organizations understand how to integrate them with sustainability-oriented initiatives to identify sustainable practices and improve sustainability performance.

The capitalization of sustainability-related data collected through dedicated information systems results in more effective decision-support tools with accurate and reliable data able to predict and prevent unsustainable practices [9]) also across the supply chain [25]. Indeed, as shown by Pozzebon et al. [26], sustainability-oriented information systems are able to improve the alignment of sustainable data and information with company practices, showing that information systems can facilitate the development of sustainable processes, services, and products.

The role of information systems in supply chain management has been extensively studied. Still, the potential benefits they offer to sustainable supply chain management have only been sporadically addressed in the literature [25]. The available studies focus on supply chains and the environmental sustainability domain. Conversely, there seems to be a lack of empirical studies exploring how these information systems are implemented and managed in other organizational architectures (e.g., business networks) to handle a sustainability transition by considering all three sustainability domains (environmental, social, and economic).

As suggested by Jämsä et al. [19], when considering SMEs, a network is the context where business activities and business relationships take place in the form of various interdependent and intertwined nets formed by these relationships. Therefore, our study seeks to develop a more comprehensive understanding of the role and impact of sustainability-oriented information systems between firms belonging to the same business network. In doing so, we are particularly concerned with a better understanding of how sustainability-oriented information systems affect network firms in terms of their understanding of and adaptation to the sustainability transition. Therefore, we engaged in an empirical, qualitative case study.

Table 1 Sustainability-oriented information systems and platforms

Intermediary	Main stakeholder considered	The main focus of the sustainability-oriented data generated through information systems
Connecting food	B2C	Communication & Consumer Engagement
Genuine way	B2C	Communication & Consumer Engagement
Trusty	B2C	Communication & Consumer Engagement
FoodChain	B2C	Communication & consumer engagement
Circularize	B2B /supply chain	Logistic
Wenda	B2B /supply chain	Logistic
Feelera	B2B & B2C	Supply chain, Communication & Consumer Engagement
Sourcemap	B2B	Supply chain, Communication & Consumer Engagement
Equovadis	B2B /supply chain	Formal practices: Certification

3 Methodology

3.1 Empirical Setting and Case Study Selection

The empirical setting of this study is focused on the intermediaries[2] operating in Italy that offer sustainability-oriented information systems and platforms. Digital intermediary platforms and their most significant features are summarized in Table 1.

Researchers have collected this data and then validated it through an interview with a specialist in the sector.

Considering stakeholders' orientation, the available intermediaries in Italy are mostly focused on the valorization of the company's sustainability-oriented data (collected through dedicated information systems) towards consumers (i.e., B2C) or towards the other companies of a particular supply chain (i.e., B2B). Among these two groups of intermediaries, one (i.e., Feelera) is oriented towards both groups of stakeholders, collecting data with the purpose of communicating to consumers the company's sustainability performance and sharing sustainability-oriented data across business partners operating on the supply chain.

Among the above-mentioned intermediaries, Feelera is a startup focused on the creation of platforms and solutions for transparency and traceability of the supply chain. Feelera created a cloud platform to track and tell the story of products and the sustainability of their supply chain. Feelera allows visibility "end to end" in the production chain and generates the digital passport of a product, thus demonstrating its authenticity and conformity with the specifications and regulations. The supply chain leader can thus collect, organize, and share data and documents throughout the

[2]The intermediaries collected in the present study are firms with strong digital core competencies able to help network SMEs in developing sustainability-oriented information systems and platforms. These intermediaries support SMEs in data collection, analysis, reporting and communication of their sustainability data.

production process of the supply chain and integrate multimedia content for cross-cutting and effective communication through intuitive and attractive interfaces, both B2 B and B2C, natively integrated [27].

3.2 *Case Study Selection and Description of the Digital Platform: The Feelera-Brun Gelmino Digital Platform*

Brun Gelmino S.r.l. Brun Gelmino is a company expert in the processing and processing of vegetables, founded in 1983 with headquarters in Verona, Italy. It operates in all the agri-food centers of Northern Italy and in some national Retailers with the brands “Brun Gelmino”, “La Regina”, “Gli Orti del Re”, “El Duca” and “Piccolo Lord”. The leading firm, Brun Gelmino, is certified as a Global Gap Chain of Custody, as well as all associated companies. Therefore, several controls are carried out on the labeling of products, product analyses, and other controls concerning food health regulations. The product’s passion, care, quality, and seriousness distinguish Brun Gelmino and make it one of the leading companies in the Italian fruit and vegetable sector [28].

Regarding the dimension of the companies belonging to the Brun Gelmino’s network, more than half have between 10 and 49 employees, more than 2/3 are fruit and vegetable producers, and 70% of the network companies have other sub-suppliers for the products sold to the Brun Gelmino’s company.

Feelera and Brun Gelmino worked together to create a sustainability-oriented digital platform to calculate an aggregate sustainability score for the whole business network, starting from each company’s score.

Figure 1 shows the digital platform created by the Feelera intermediary.

A survey was conducted among the companies belonging to the business network to calculate these scores. The development of this sustainability-oriented survey started with the integration of mainstream methodologies, first of all, GRI (the most widespread international framework for non-financial performance and the principles of Civil Economy [29].

The result is a matrix in which on the horizontal axis are listed six domains of value taken from the keywords of Civil Economy [29], (participatory democracy, community and circular subsidiarity, common goods, relational goods and happiness, meritocracy and rewarding, inclusion and fraternity).

Conversely, on the vertical axis, five corporate areas (which correspond to the organizational functions) are included: (1) Governance, Strategy, environment, (2) Human Resources, (3) Supply Chain, and (4) Marketing [30].

In the cells of the grid of the resulting Matrix, there are 40 socio-environmental indicators, which can be used as a “company dashboard” because they evaluate sustainability in all three dimensions (economic, social, and environmental). For each indicator, scores have been developed and normalized in the same range from 0 to 100 to aggregate and compare indicators that measure impacts of different types,

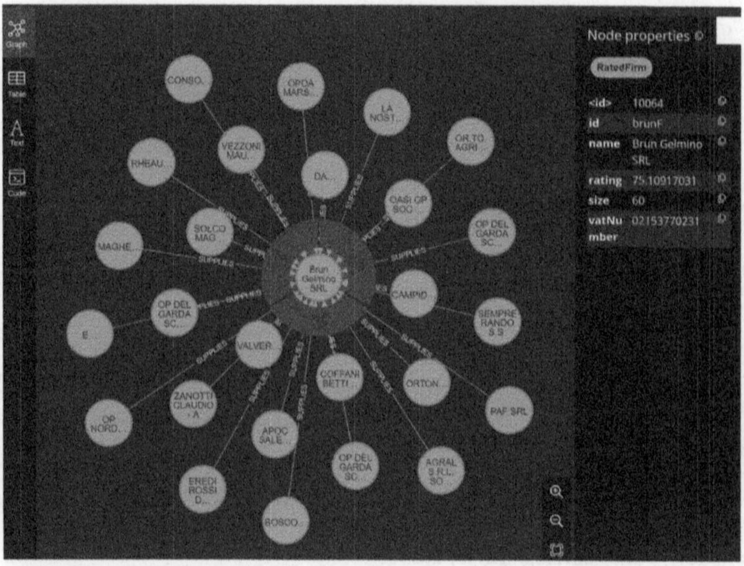

Fig. 1 The digital network platform

calculated from the data available in the company. Eventually, the indicators have been linked to the Sustainable Development Goals (SDGs), to quantify the contribution of each organization towards these objectives recognized as standard at the macroeconomic and international level [27].

3.3 *Data Collection and Analysis*

Since research in the selected context is limited, this study aims to investigate the integration of sustainability-oriented information system technologies with a more in-depth, qualitative approach, as suggested by Ozkan-Ozen et al. [15].

A case study is conducted following Eisenhardt's [31] and Yin's [32] recommendations for using case studies in the initial stages of theory development. The longitudinal case study analyzes the phenomena of the formation of a digital platform ecosystem in which the development of a business sustainability goal plays a key role.

The data collection lasted 3 years, starting in 2020, until 2023. Data was collected from participation, participant observation, workshops, seminars, and personal interviews. Written material was collected both online and offline (e.g., published official documents such as internal documents, newspaper articles, and company brochures) (see Table 2).

Both academic-practitioner interaction and interview discussion were conducted in Italian, as it is the mother tongue of both researchers and founders. Then, all the

Table 2 Longitudinal data collection

Period	Collected data	Note
November 2019	Idea development	A first draft of the project with Feelera's founder
April 2020	First draft of the project	Final draft of the project with Feelera's founder and the other stakeholders
August/ September 2020	Project submission	
December 2020	Approval of the financing of the project	Cariverona Bank financed the project
March 2021	Interview	Interview with the Feelera's founder
March 2021	Interview	Interview with the Brun Gelmino's founder
May 2021	A first draft of the questionnaire	
July 2021	The final version of the questionnaire	
December 2021	Survey data	Data from each SME of Brun Gelmino's network has been collected
January–May 2022	Code development for the platform	
June–September 2022	Beta testing of the platform & participant observation	
September 2022–January 2023	The final release of the platform interviews & participant observation	
February 2023	Final meeting with all the Project's stakeholders	Seminar on the developed project. All the Project's stakeholders were hosted by the University of Verona to discuss the developed project.
May 2023	Internal summary document	Report on the developed project
April 2023	Interview with the Feelera's founder	Interview to better understand the structure of the market and the main competitors (other players/intermediaries). The interview lasted about 1 h
June 2023	Public document	Book on the developed project

materials were translated into English. The quotes we cited from the interviews were translated by one author, and then the other authors checked to ensure conceptual equivalence.

To check the validity of data, written materials have been triangulated with official reports, press reports, and interviews, following the classical guidelines of qualitative research [32]. Moreover, by collecting data in more continuous and varied opportunities in time, action research offered the opportunity to triangulate findings by using a cyclical data collection [33], thus observing events, the development of social processes, and the reports of each participant, and investigating how these change in time [34]. Data was highlighted and coded by using Nvivo.

Finally, the key themes emerging from the collected material were categorized into different codes by following the Gioia methodology [35].

4 Findings

In what follows, we organized our results by highlighting the emerging themes regarding the approach to the sustainability transition developed by the Brun Gelmino business network through the implementation of sustainability-oriented information systems.

The process of reaching an agreement through analysis involved three distinct rounds, during which researchers compared their data analysis results and ultimately reached a consensus on the coding scheme (see Appendix 1).

4.1 *Business Network's Understanding of Sustainability*

The network's awareness of sustainability-related issues increased progressively through collaboration with the intermediary. Indeed, the leading firm, Brun Gelmino, increased his understanding of sustainability-related issues, highlighting the most important goals in terms of *social* and *environmental* sustainability:

> Among the sustainability initiatives, the most important for network firms are the reduction of processing waste and waste in general and the reduction of discrimination, child labor, and unethical working conditions. Indeed, the most exposed processes to sustainability issues are production, its planning, and transport. [27]

By stating the main sustainability goals for the network and starting the implementation of the sustainability-oriented information systems, the network was able to assess its starting point. Indeed, before starting the project in 2020, there was scarce availability of data concerning sustainability, poor information system integration, and data exchange of the network on sustainability-related issues:

> Before this project began [i.e., 2020], it was low the number of companies that share IT and information systems to gather data on sustainability-related issues within the other actors of the supply chain. [27]

Later, in 2022, after the first sustainability assessment was made through a survey of all the business network firms, the awareness of sustainability performance increased together with the control on the network sustainability level. Indeed, the leading firm increased its awareness of social sustainability-related issues regarding the business network through the new data available on the information system. By using the words of the Feelera's Business Analyst:

> From the sustainability-oriented information system and by reading the scores obtained by the companies, it emerges that for communication and transparency, about half of the companies communicate their sustainability strategies internally, while they are less engaged

in communication with external stakeholders. In fact, as we can see, only three companies have compiled environmental, social, or sustainability reports, while most do not answer the question. Regarding the promotion of legality, almost all adopt regular contracts and electronic invoicing, and six of them are engaged in the fight against illegal employment. (Feelera's Business Analyst)

4.2 Network Information Systems to Foster Sustainability

To face the sustainability transition, the network adopted sustainability-oriented information systems to gather the necessary information to increase the (current and future) network's sustainability performance. Indeed, as explained by the CEO of Brun Gelmino, the new information systems supported a greater environmental and economic sustainability performance for the whole network:

> The new information systems defined clearer methods and procedures. Creating a collaboration with clearer methods and procedures has helped every company in the network to better organize the planning, from the withdrawal to the warehouse up to the B2B intra-network sales. Less waste means both greater environmental sustainability of our operations and greater economic sustainability because it improves the margins of all the companies in the network. (CEO of Brun Gelmino)

However, up to now, the developed platform is managed and controlled by the leading firm, which can stimulate individual companies to undertake specific sustainability-oriented actions to improve their sustainability performance. Despite this, according to the CEO, to have an effective future development of the information systems as a network platform for sustainability, network firms also need to interact and participate in the platform:

> The only network manager is Brun Gelmino. The leading firm has all the visibility on the network's sustainability performance. Therefore, the leading firm can stimulate the individual company to do something or not. The companies among them do not have a reciprocal influence: maybe they don't even know each other, but they can make the assessment, but they do not exchange the results among themselves. The exploitation of knowledge is, therefore, lacking at this stage. Surely, it should be placed in a stage of greater maturity of the platform. (CEO of Brun Gelmino)

Despite its strengths, information systems also have some limitations. Indeed, according to the Intermediary CEO, the sustainability performance has been conceived as a sum of the single sustainability scores even though an organizational structure as a business network has a multiplier effect in terms of sustainability:

> It is difficult for the information systems to capture all the synergies between the companies of the network. We can see the single organization's score and the sum/average sustainability score at the network level. But the network has a multiplier effect given by the network itself, and there is a limit because this is not visible now. (Feelera's CEO)

4.3 Sustainability Transition Through New Practices

Through the partnership with Feelera and the implementation of the sustainability-oriented information system, we found that the Brun Gelmino leading firm is fostering a sustainability-oriented culture in the network, both at the single organizational level and at the whole network level:

> We are struggling to enhance the sustainability-oriented culture inside each organization belonging to the Brun Gelmino business network. (CEO of Brun Gelmino)
>
> We try to innovate by bringing the Civil Economy sustainable paradigm into our business network. (CEO of Brun Gelmino)

The attempt to spread the sustainability-oriented culture in the network characterizes a phase in which the leading firm is learning how to manage and boost the network's sustainable transition. This learning process allowed the network to achieve improvements in terms of social sustainability for workers:

> Now, through the new information systems, there is greater control over legality and transparency. I am thinking, for example, of accident and risk prevention. From the analysis that we made on the net, we immediately see if the companies are not compliant. This reduces the opportunistic behaviors. This work moves towards greater worker safety and control over workers' exploitation and the issue of illegal work. (CEO of Brun Gelmino)

Moreover, also the single firms belonging to the network are developing their learning process by leveraging the data available in the sustainability-oriented information systems:

> Now, most of the companies share decisions supported by information with upstream and downstream actors in the supply chain, as well as performance targets. (CEO of Brun Gelmino)

This phase also led to a new awareness: the sustainable performance of the network needs a collaborative approach involving external partners—such as Authorities—able to control and validate the sustainability data:

> In terms of legality, it is important that these platforms are connected to the Authorities because complaints are often not heard. Control bodies/Authorities do not perceive the benefits of these information systems. (CEO of Brun Gelmino)

4.4 Development of Tensions During the Sustainability Transition

The experience of implementing a sustainability-oriented information system gained through the partnership with Feelera generated adverse side effects.

In particular, we collected data on the tensions between the leading network firms and the network firms in implementing sustainability-oriented information systems. Indeed, some network firms perceived risk in the grown transparency brought by the sustainability-oriented information systems:

For some firms, sharing knowledge is a risk more than a strength. Some firms don't perceive it as a virtuous step that raises the bar of sustainability-oriented culture for all the companies of the network. (Feelera's Business Analyst)

Companies belonging to the network perceive as a risk too much transparency for the competitive environment. They are afraid they can no longer sell the same product at a higher price in their territory. (Purchasing Manager of Brun Gelmino)

Besides this, the leading firm also understood the importance of conducting some activities aimed at sensitizing its client's culture regarding sustainability since the leading network's client (Retailer) perceived a risk in the network's investment in sustainability information systems. By using the words of the Brun Gelmino's Account Manager:

Buyers of large retailers do not understand anything of sustainability. They understand their specific vertical and a traditional logic that goes on for a hundred years. (Account Manager of Brun Gelmino)

Moreover, the learning path needed to build a stronger commitment in terms of sustainability-oriented actions also needs to develop a sustainability-oriented mentality. Unfortunately, not all the firms were able to adapt quickly to such a path and cultural tensions:

Not all companies can understand this transition. They say, "Why do we have to fill out questionnaires? It's time-consuming". Farmers have different levels of sustainability culture. (Commercial Manager of Brun Gelmino)

Eventually, from the point of view of the leading firm, by looking to the future, latent tensions may arise from the network's firms, particularly regarding the management of the network in relation to the sustainability score:

This platform can allow the manual simulation of the change of the aggregate rating to vary the input parameters. The next step after the weighted calculation of scores would be the development of simulations to identify minor changes to the supply chain to improve the aggregate score. Alternatively, there are simulation procedures that automatically calculate the aggregate rating as the attributes of nodes and relationships change. The simulations aim to find which characteristics of the supply chain allow for an improvement of the aggregate rating, trying to select, for a given target score, the configurations with the minimum changes compared to the initial configuration. [27]

Brun Gelmino can then have leverage to keep or take a company off the sustainable network based on its score. Who operates the platform can decide who is inside and who is outside based on the sustainability score. The platform thus becomes not only a sustainability-oriented tool but also a validator that becomes enabling to remain in the network. (Feelera CEO)

5 Discussion and Conclusion

The present study aims to understand how SMEs and their network firms face the sustainability transition by using information systems to support sustainable network management.

Our findings highlight how to reach this purpose, a business network adapts its organizational processes, decision-making procedures, and sustainability strategy during its sustainability transition by leveraging sustainability-oriented information systems to develop a network sustainability platform.

The sustainability-oriented information system is a crucial driver in increasing a business network's understanding of sustainability-related issues, expanding the network's sustainability practices, and fostering a network's sustainability transition (see Table 3). New practices to promote sustainability involve nurturing a culture focused on sustainability within the network, boosting overall sustainability performance, and encouraging a collaborative approach with a focus on sustainability.

This study emphasizes the growing awareness among network firms about their role in addressing social and environmental issues. It recognizes the interconnected nature of digital and sustainable transitions as interlinked goals to achieve [20], where data from digital tools serves both to evaluate sustainability performance and adjust a company's sustainability agenda.

However, despite these positive effects, the implementation of a sustainability-oriented information system may also generate negative side effects. In particular, the present study highlights how implementing the sustainability-oriented information system at the network level generated a series of tensions.

Indeed, tensions arose between the network firms and the leading firms in implementing sustainability-oriented information systems.

Besides this, the practical implementation of the information system opens a series of future critical issues and tensions between companies, which are now latent. Indeed, in the future, the leading firm may choose to collaborate with a network firm based on its sustainability score.

This study responds to Vial's [36] call to further investigate the impact of digital transformation by connecting it with sustainability literature from a theoretical perspective. The study examines the potential of digital transformation to improve the sustainable evolution of organizational architectures (business networks) from a theoretical perspective. To do so, it adopts an inter-organizational perspective, which has received less attention in sustainability literature [37]. Moreover, the present study also contributes to the limited number of studies addressing the issue of how digital transformation and digital technologies may have side effects on sustainability outcomes.

The study contributes to the literature on information systems and their benefits for sustainable management of organizational architectures, which tends to focus on supply chains and environmental sustainability. The contribution explores the implementation and sustainability-oriented management of these systems in business networks, adopting a broader concept of sustainability that includes both environmental and social domains.

From a practical standpoint, our study has significant implications as it brings new insights into the opportunities for companies through digital technologies, encouraging both businesses and institutions to invest in activities that enhance firms' digital knowledge.

Table 3 Coding structure

First order concepts	Second order themes	Aggregate dimensions
Understanding of the most critical issues in terms of social sustainability	Understanding of sustainability-related issues and the low availability of data	Business Network's understanding of sustainability
Understanding of the most essential issues in terms of environmental sustainability		
Assessment of the starting point: Poor information system integration and data exchange of the network on sustainability-related issues		
Institutional data highlighting the leading firm's increased awareness of social sustainability-related issues regarding the business network through the new data available on the information system	Increased control on the level of sustainability	
Statements regarding the fact that new information systems support a more significant environmental and economic sustainability performance for the whole network	New information systems increase the network's sustainability performance	Network information systems to foster sustainability
The future evolution of the information system may be the exploitation by all the network firms of the platform	Future development of the information systems as a network platform for sustainability	
The design of the sustainability scores has limitations: It is only a sum of the firm's scores	Current information system limitations	
The leading firm enhances the sustainability-oriented culture both at the single organizational level and at the whole network level	Fostering sustainability-oriented culture in the network	Sustainability transition through new practices
Improvements gained in terms of social sustainability for workers	Increased sustainability performance	
Business network learning process by developing sustainable solutions		
The necessity of external partners' collaboration (e.g., policymakers, authorities) to share data for sustainability transition	Promoting a sustainability-oriented collaborative approach	
Risk perceived from the network firms towards transparency promoted by the sustainability-oriented information systems	Tensions towards the leading firm for the implementation of sustainability-oriented information systems	Development of tensions during the sustainability transition
Risk perceived from the network's client (retailers) towards investing		

(continued)

Table 3 (continued)

First order concepts	Second order themes	Aggregate dimensions
in sustainability information systems		
Cultural tensions for the implementation of sustainability-oriented information systems		
Future dynamics between network firms and the leading firms may involve tensions concerning the sustainability score of network firms	Latent future tensions may come from network firms	

Moreover, the study was conducted in Italy, where SME networks are particularly developed. By supporting Italian networks to become digitally mature, institutions may also support the reinforcement of their sustainability performance. To assess the external validity of this study, similar case studies can be conducted also in different country's socio-economic systems.

The present work has other limitations that should be considered when interpreting its results. The paper focuses on the Italian food industry, specifically the horticulture industry. Therefore, our results should be tested in other business sectors with different peculiarities.

Additionally, another relevant limitation is related to the qualitative methodology employed since the results coming from the data at our disposal may not be generalizable.

Funding The research project was financed by the Cariverona Foundation

Appendix 1 The coding table

Aggregate Dimension	Second order themes	First order concepts	Quote	Source
Business Network's understanding of sustainability	Understanding of sustainability-related issues and the low availability of data	Understanding of the most critical issues in terms of *social* sustainability	*"Among the sustainability initiatives, the most important for network firms are [...] the reduction of discrimination, child labor and*	Rossignoli et al. [27]

(continued)

Aggregate Dimension	Second order themes	First order concepts	Quote	Source
			unethical working conditions."	
		Understanding of the most essential issues in terms of *environmental* sustainability	*"Among the sustainability initiatives, the most important for network firms are the reduction of processing waste and waste in general and the reduction [. . .]. Indeed, the most exposed processes to sustainability issues are production, planning, and transport."*	Rossignoli et al. [27]
		Assessment of the starting point: Poor information system integration and data exchange of the network on sustainability-related issues	*"Before this project began, the number of companies that share IT and information systems was low to gather data on sustainability-related issues within the other actors of the supply chain."*	*Interview: CEO of Brun Gelmino*
	Increased control on the level of sustainability	Institutional data highlighting the leading firm's increased understanding of social sustainability-related issues regarding the business network through the new data available on the *information system*	*"From the sustainability-oriented information system and by reading the scores obtained by the companies, it emerges that for communication and transparency, about half of the companies communicate their sustainability strategies*	*Interview: Feelera's business analyst*

(continued)

Aggregate Dimension	Second order themes	First order concepts	Quote	Source
			internally, while they are less engaged in communication with external stakeholders. As we can see, only three companies have compiled environmental, social, or sustainability reports, while most have not answered the question. Regarding, instead, the promotion of legality, almost all adopt regular contracts and electronic invoicing, and six of them are engaged in the fight against illegal employment."	
Network information systems to foster sustainability	New information systems increase the network's sustainability performance	Statements regarding the fact that new information systems support a greater environmental and economic sustainability performance for the whole network	*"The new information systems defined clearer methods and procedures. Creating a collaboration with clearer methods and procedures has helped every company in the network to better organize the planning, from the withdrawal to the warehouse up to the B2B intra-network sales. Less waste means both greater*	*Interview: CEO of Brun Gelmino*

(continued)

Aggregate Dimension	Second order themes	First order concepts	Quote	Source
			environmental sustainability of our operations and greater economic sustainability because it improves the margins of all the companies in the network."	
	Future development of the information systems as a network platform for sustainability	The future evolution of the information system may be the exploitation by all the network firms of the platform	*"The only network manager is Brun Gelmino. The leading firm has all the visibility on the network's sustainability performance. Therefore, the leading firm can stimulate the individual company to do something or not. The companies among them do not have a reciprocal influence: Maybe they don't even know each other, but they can make the assessment, but they do not exchange the results among themselves. The exploitation of knowledge is, therefore, lacking at this stage. Surely, it should be placed in a stage of greater maturity of the platform."*	*Interview: Feelera CEO (intermediary)*
	Current information system limitations	The design of the sustainability scores has limitations: It is only	*"It is difficult for the information systems to capture all the*	*Interview: Feelera CEO (intermediary)*

(continued)

Aggregate Dimension	Second order themes	First order concepts	Quote	Source
		a sum of the firm's scores	*synergies between the network companies. We can see the single organization's score and the sum/average sustainability score at the network level. But the network has a multiplier effect given by the network itself, and there is a limit because this is not visible now."*	
Sustainability transition through new practices	Fostering sustainability-oriented culture in the network	The leading firm enhances the sustainability-oriented culture both at the single organizational level and at the whole network level	*"We try to innovate by bringing the civil economy sustainable paradigm into our business network."*	*Interview: CEO of Brun Gelmino*
			"Moreover, we are struggling to enhance the sustainability-oriented culture inside each organization belonging to the Brun Gelmino business network."	*Interview: CEO of Brun Gelmino*
	Increasing sustainability performance	Improvements gained in terms of social sustainability for workers	*"Now, through the new information systems, there is greater control over legality and transparency. I am thinking, for example, of accident and risk prevention. From the analysis that we made on the net, we*	*Interview: CEO of Brun Gelmino*

(continued)

Aggregate Dimension	Second order themes	First order concepts	Quote	Source
			immediately see if the companies are not compliant. This reduces the opportunistic behaviors. This work moves towards greater worker safety and control over workers' exploitation and the issue of illegal work."	
		Business network learning process by developing sustainable solutions	*"Now, most of the companies share decisions supported by information with upstream and downstream actors in the supply chain, as well as performance targets."*	*Interview: CEO of Brun Gelmino*
	Promoting a sustainability-oriented collaborative approach	The necessity of *external* partners' collaboration (e.g., policymakers, authorities) to share data for sustainability transition	*"In terms of legality, it is important that these platforms are connected to the authorities because complaints are often not heard. Control bodies/ authorities do not perceive the benefits of these information systems."*	*Interview: CEO of Brun Gelmino*
Development of tensions during the sustainability transition	Tensions towards the leading firm for the implementation of sustainability-oriented information systems	Risk perceived from the network firms towards transparency promoted by the sustainability-oriented information systems	*"For some firms, sharing knowledge is a risk more than a strength. Some firms don't perceive it as a virtuous step that raises the bar of sustainability-*	*Interview: Feelera's business analyst*

(continued)

Aggregate Dimension	Second order themes	First order concepts	Quote	Source
			oriented culture for all the network companies."	
			"Companies belonging to the network perceive as a risk too much transparency for the competitive environment. They are afraid they can no longer sell the same product at a higher price in their territory."	*Interview: Account manager of Brun Gelmino*
		Risk perceived from the network's client (retailers) towards investing in sustainability information systems	*"Buyers of large retailers do not understand anything about sustainability. They understand their specific vertical and traditional logic well, which has been going on for a hundred years."*	*Interview: Sales manager of a network firm*
			"Buyers of large retailers are doing a lot of greenwashing activities, but buyers are focused only on margins and on the economic side of the balance sheet. If our clients do not understand	*Interview: Sales manager of Brun Gelmino*

(continued)

Aggregate Dimension	Second order themes	First order concepts	Quote	Source
			our efforts to improve our sustainability, then it becomes only an increased cost to the retailer."	
		Cultural tensions for the implementation of sustainability-oriented information systems	*"Not all companies can understand this transition. They say, "why do we have to fill out questionnaires? It's time-consuming:" farmers have different levels of sustainability culture."*	*Interview: Commercial manager of Brun Gelmino*
	Latent future tensions may come from network firms	Future dynamics between network firms and the leading firms may involve tensions concerning the sustainability score of network firms	*"This platform can simulate manually the change of the aggregate rating to vary the input parameters. The next step after the weighted calculation of scores would be the development of simulations to identify minor changes to the supply chain to improve the aggregate score. Alternatively, simulation procedures automatically calculate the aggregate rating as the attributes of nodes and relationships change. The aim of the simulations is to find*	Rossignoli et al. [27]

(continued)

Aggregate Dimension	Second order themes	First order concepts	Quote	Source
			which characteristics of the supply chain allow for an improvement of the aggregate rating, trying to select, for a given target score, the configurations with the minimum changes compared to the initial configuration."	
			"Brun Gelmino can then have leverage to keep or take a company off the sustainable network based on its score. Who operates the platform can decide who is inside and who is outside based on the sustainability score. The platform thus becomes not only a sustainability-oriented tool but also a validator that becomes enabling to remain in the network."	*Interview: Feelera CEO (intermediary)*

References

1. George, G., Howard-Grenville, J., Joshi, A., & Tihanyi, L. (2016). Understanding and tackling societal grand challenges through management research. *Academy of Management Journal, 59*(6), 1880–1895.
2. Ortiz-de-Mandojana, N., & Bansal, P. (2016). The long-term benefits of organizational resilience through sustainable business practices. *Strategic Management Journal, 37*, 1615–1631.
3. Ghisetti, C., Marzucchi, A., & Montresor, S. (2015). The open eco-innovation mode. An empirical investigation of eleven European countries. *Research Policy, 44*(5), 1080–1093. https://doi.org/10.1016/j.respol.2014.12.001
4. Constantinides, P., Henfridsson, O., & Parker, G. G. (2018). Introduction—platforms and infrastructures in the digital age. *Information Systems Research, 29*(2), 381–400. https://doi.org/10.1287/isre.2018.0794
5. Ramezani, J., & Camarinha-Matos, L. M. (2020). Approaches for resilience and antifragility in collaborative business ecosystems. *Technological Forecasting and Social Change, 151*, 119846. Elsevier. November 2019.
6. Zoppelletto, A., Bullini Orlandi, L., & Rossignoli, C. (2020). Adopting a digital transformation strategy to enhance business network commons regeneration: An explorative case study. *The TQM Journal, 32*(4), 561–585. https://doi.org/10.1108/TQM-04-2020-0077
7. Cainelli, G., Mazzanti, M., & Zoboli, R. (2011). Environmental innovations, complementarity and local/global cooperation: Evidence from north-east Italian industry. *International Journal of Technology, Policy and Management, 11*(3–4), 328–368.
8. Sharma, S., & Henriques, I. (2005). Stakeholder influences on sustainability practices in the Canadian forest products industry. *Strategic Management Journal, 26*, 159–180. https://doi.org/10.1002/smj.439
9. De Camargo Fiorini, P., & Chiappetta Jabbour, C. J. (2017). Information systems and sustainable supply chain management towards a more sustainable society: Where we are and where we are going. *International Journal of Information Management, 37*(4), 241–249. https://doi.org/10.1016/j.ijinfomgt.2016.12.004
10. Baumgartner, R. J., & Ebner, D. (2010). Corporate sustainability strategies: Sustainability profiles and maturity levels. *Sustainable Development, 18*(2), 76–89. https://doi.org/10.1002/sd.447
11. El Hilali, W., El Manouar, A., & Janati Idrissi, M. A. (2020). Reaching sustainability during a digital transformation: A PLS approach. *International Journal of Innovation Science, 12*, 52–79. https://doi.org/10.1108/IJIS-08-2019-0083
12. Ghobakhloo, M., Iranmanesh, M., Grybauskas, A., Vilkas, M., & Petraitė, M. (2021). Industry 4.0, innovation, and sustainable development: A systematic review and a roadmap to sustainable innovation. *Business Strategy and the Environment, 30*(8), 4237–4257. https://doi.org/10.1002/bse.2867
13. Gupta, S., Meissonier, R., Drave, V. A., & Roubaud, D. (2020). Examining the impact of cloud ERP on sustainable performance: A dynamic capability view. *International Journal of Information Management, 5*, 102028.
14. Nica, E. (2019). Cyber-physical production networks and advanced digitalization in industry 4.0 manufacturing systems: Sustainable supply chain management, organizational resilience, and data-driven innovation. *Journal of Self-Governance and Management Economics, 7*(3), 27. https://doi.org/10.22381/JSME7320194
15. Ozkan-Ozen, Y. D., Kazancoglu, Y., & Kumar Mangla, S. (2020). Synchronized barriers for circular supply chains in industry 3.5/industry 4.0 transition for sustainable resource management. *Resources, Conservation and Recycling, 161*, 104986. https://doi.org/10.1016/j.resconrec.2020.104986
16. Plumpton, D. (2019). Cyber-physical systems, internet of things, and big data in industry 4.0: Digital manufacturing technologies, business process optimization, and sustainable

organizational performance. *Economics, Management, and Financial Markets, 14*(3), 23. https://doi.org/10.22381/EMFM14320193
17. Ferraro, F., Etzion, D., & Gehman, J. (2015). Tackling grand challenges pragmatically: Robust action revisited. *Organization Studies, 36*(3), 363–390.
18. Baker, S. (2006). *Sustainable development*. Routledge.
19. Jämsä, P., Tähtinen, J., Ryan, A., & Pallari, M. (2011). Sustainable SMEs network utilization: The case of food enterprises. *Journal of Small Business and Enterprise Development, 18*(1), 141–156.
20. Montresor, S., & Vezzani, A. (2022). Digital technologies and eco-innovation. Evidence of the twin transition from Italian firms. DRUID22, Copenhagen Business School, Copenhagen, Denmark June 13–15.
21. Antonioli, D., Cecere, G., & Mazzanti, M. (2018). Information communication technologies and environmental innovations in firms: Joint adoptions and productivity effects. *Journal of Environmental Planning and Management, 61*(11), 1905–1933.
22. Perl, E., & Vorbach, S. (2009). Environmental information for sustainable supply chains. *Progress in Industrial Ecology: An International Journal, 6*(1), 44–67.
23. Lyytinen, K., Yoo, Y., & Boland, R. J., Jr. (2016). Digital product innovation within four classes of innovation networks. *Info Systems Journal, 26*, 47–75. https://doi.org/10.1111/isj.12093
24. Rossi, M., Cappelletti, F., & Germani, M. (2022). Design for environmental sustainability: Collect and use company information to design green products. *Procedia CIRP, 105*, 823–828. https://doi.org/10.1016/j.procir.2022.02.136
25. O'Rourke, D. (2014). The science of sustainable supply chains. *Science, 344*(6188), 1124–1127.
26. Pozzebon, M., Petrini, M., de Mello, R. B., & Garreau, L. (2011). Unpacking researchers' creativity and imagination in grounded theorizing: An exemplar from IS research. *Information and Organization, 21*(4), 177–193.
27. Rossignoli, C., Bazzani, C., Bulllini Orlandi, L., Bonomi, S., Cantele, S., Confente, I., Corezzola, F., Gaudenzi, B., Giorgetti, A., Leonarduzzi, M. F., Lovato, A., Pelosi, S., Ricci, E. C., Russo, I., Zardini, A., & Zoppelletto, A. (2023). *Tracciabilità digitale di filiera: Creare relazioni aziendali collaborative per lo sviluppo sostenibile del territorio*. Franco Angeli. ISBN 9788835152644.
28. Brun Gelmino. (2023). About us. Retrieved in February 2023, from https://brungelmino.it/azienda/
29. Bruni, L., & Zamagni, S. (2004). Economia civile: Efficienza, equità, felicità pubblica, il Mulino, Bologna.
30. Zovko, V. (2018). Management in the Year 2050. *Interdisciplinary Description of Complex Systems, Scientific Journal, 16*(3–B), 417–426.
31. Eisenhardt, K. M. (1989). Building theories from case study research. *Academy of Management Review, 14*(4), 548.
32. Yin, R. K. (1984). *Case study research: Design and methods*. Sage Publications.
33. Eden, C., & Huxham, C. (1996). Action research for the study of organizations. In S. Clegg, C. Hardy, & W. R. Nord (Eds.), *Handbook of organizational studies* (pp. 526–542). Sage.
34. Glaser, B. G., & Strauss, A. L. (1967). *The discovery of grounded theory*. Chicago.
35. Gioia, D. A., Corley, K. G., & Hamilton, A. L. (2013). Seeking qualitative rigor in inductive research: Notes on the Gioia methodology. *Organizational Research Methods, 16*(1), 15–31. https://doi.org/10.1177/1094428112452151
36. Vial, G. (2019). Understanding digital transformation: A review and a research agenda. *Journal of Strategic Information Systems, 28*(2), 118–144.
37. Dyllick, T., & Muff, K. (2016). Clarifying the meaning of sustainable business: Introducing a typology from business-as-usual to true business sustainability. *Organization & Environment, 29*(2), 156–174.

To Ban, or Not to Ban, this Is the D(AI)lemma: An Analysis of Ecosystem Landscapes

Francesco Bolici, Alberto Varone, and Gabriele Diana

Abstract The relationship between innovation diffusion and privacy is often controversial. On March 31th 2023, the Italian Data Protection Authority (GPDP) determined the temporary suspension of ChatGPT in Italy on account of illicit data collection and processing practices. This study uses the Twitter debate as a proxy to examine how the Italian landscape responded to the suspension of ChatGPT, and its perception on the innovation-privacy trade-off. Our findings reveal that the intervention of the GPDP sparked an active and socially engaged reaction. Both popular and less popular users played significant roles in the flow of information, with popular users being more central in terms of connections and less popular users demonstrating stronger brokering capabilities. The suspension of ChatGPT had an impact on the sentiment and content of the debate, with the majority of users expressing negative opinions in their contributions. However, contributions mentioning VPN and alternatives to ChatGPT generally showed a more positive sentiment compared to those emphasizing privacy. This suggests that users' negative sentiment was mainly connected with the inaccessibility of ChatGPT rather than to privacy concerns. Consequently, the Italian landscape viewed the GPDP intervention more as a restriction rather than a protective measure, prioritizing innovation diffusion over privacy considerations.

Keywords AI · Privacy · Ecosystem · SNA · Social media

1 Introduction

The relationship between innovation diffusion and privacy is often controversial [1].

The rapid diffusion of AI-powered systems is expected to have profound economic and social impacts, as 80% of the US labor force could have at least 10% of their work tasks affected by their introduction [2]. ChatGPT is a chatbot relying on a

F. Bolici (✉) · A. Varone · G. Diana
University of Cassino and Southern Lazio, Loc. Folcara, Cassino, Italy
e-mail: f.bolici@unicas.it; alberto.varone@unicas.it; gabriele.diana@unicas.it

A. M. Braccini et al. (eds.), *Digital (Eco) Systems and Societal Challenges*, Lecture Notes in Information Systems and Organisation 72,
https://doi.org/10.1007/978-3-031-75586-6_18

generative AI algorithm released by OpenAI in November 2022. This is able to support (more or less successfully) humans in creative writing, essay writing, prompt writing, code writing, and answering questions [3]. ChatGPT is already described as evolutionary, revolutionary [4], and destined to inevitably spread [5]. Evidence supporting these claims can be easily grasped. First, only in January 2023, the ChatGPT webpage registered over 9 million interactions from users in Italy; this accounted for a 300% increase compared to the preceding month [6]. Second, within the first 5 months of 2023, more than 400 academic documents were indexed on Scopus containing the string "ChatGPT" within the title, keywords or abstract. These span more than 20 subject areas, denoting a multi-disciplinary range of applications. Third, from November 30th 2022 to May 27th 2023, we detected approximately 16 million of contributions posted on Twitter containing the word "ChatGPT" (one per second on average).

On March 30th 2023, the Italian Data Protection Authority (GPDP) imposed on OpenAI a temporary limitation to treat Italian users' personal data. This determined the inaccessibility of ChatGPT in Italy on March 31st. The GPDP decision was grounded on the following claims: i. OpenAI provided ChatGPT users with no information notice on how data is collected and processed for training the underlying algorithm; ii. an appropriate legal basis for the collection and processing of personal data used to train ChatGPT was lacking; iii. the processing of personal data was found to be inaccurate, as the information provided by ChatGPT did not always correspond to the real data; iv. no user age verification was detected, whereas the use of ChatGPT is reserved to individuals who are at least 13 years old according to the terms published by OpenAI [7]. Exploring the social dynamics connected to the suspension of ChatGPT in Italy, this article aims at analyzing the public debate in a particular moment where innovation diffusion and privacy issues are in conflict.

According to the landscape ecology theory, ecosystems within a spatially heterogeneous area can be structurally, functionally and dynamically related. These relations explain how energy, materials, and species are distributed and flow across ecosystems [8]. Social media like Twitter represent a valid proxy to measure diffusion processes and how these are socially influenced [9]. Starting from the assumption that users participating in the Twitter debate belong to a mosaic of different but interrelated ecosystems, we argue that analyzing the Twitter debate it is possible to gather a bird-eye view on the social dynamics affecting innovation diffusion at the landscape level. Analyzing approximately 15,000 Twitter contributions, this work combines Social Network and Sentiment Analysis techniques to answer the following research questions: which are the characteristics exhibited by the public debate when a potential conflict between speed of innovation diffusion and privacy issues exist? How does the public debate evolve from the pre- to post-ban phase of a public intervention limiting innovation diffusion?

2 Literature Review

2.1 *Innovation Diffusion and Social Network Theory*

Innovation can be defined as an idea, practice, or object that is perceived as new by its adopters, where newness can be expressed in terms of knowledge, persuasion, or a decision to adopt [10]. Innovation diffusion refers to "the process by which an innovation is communicated through certain channels over time among the members of a social system" [10]. Accordingly, social networks represent influential channels for the diffusion of ideas, innovations and behaviors [11, 12]. Important social factors affecting the speed of innovation diffusion are contagion, structural equivalence, prestige, spatial proximity, culture and social pressure [11, 13–15]. Social contagion underlies the process through which attitudes and behaviors spread within social systems, particularly via spatial proximity [15]. In the realm of innovation diffusion, social contagion represents a mechanism to manage uncertainty: when adopters and non-adopters are spatially proximate, the latter can gather information about an innovation, observe the consequences of its adoption and feel increasing pressure to embrace it [11]. This process is incremental: as an innovation spreads within a social system, the number of adopters increases following a S-shaped distribution [10, 13]. Social contagion positively relates to the concept of structural equivalence, describing the extent to which the members of a community share the same connections with the same individuals. Indeed, structurally equivalent individuals have been found to "attend" and mutually influence each other's behavior [11, 15]. Cultural similarity and prestige represent two conduits for innovation diffusion respectively relying upon common values and status [15]. These are closely connected to the ideas of opinion leaders and knowledge (or opinion) brokers. Opinion leaders are actors influencing other individuals' behaviors with relative frequency, and generally exhibit high mass media exposure, great social participation and high social status [10]. As indicated in [14] opinion leaders differ from opinion brokers as their primary function is filling structural holes within a social structure and integrating information from different communities. Being exposed to heterogeneous groups, opinion brokers are influenced by diverse perspectives, represent a source of social capital for the network and are more likely to have ideas perceived as valuable by others [16, 17]. Both opinion leaders and opinion brokers influence the rate of innovation diffusion within social networks [10, 12, 18, 19].

2.2 *Data Privacy*

Data privacy is defined in [20] as the degree of control that an individual has over the release of his personal information, including its collection, use, access, and correction of errors. The dramatic technological evolution of the last decades has significantly enhanced the extent to which personal data can be collected and processed [21]. This trend reconceptualized persistent surveillance from being a prevalently military practice to a product feature [21], while making existing privacy frameworks obsolete [22, 23]. Accordingly, data privacy was classified among the most critical ethical issues in the information age [20].

The work of [24] identified four primary dimensions of individuals' concerns over data privacy: collection, unauthorized secondary use, improper access and error. Similarly, in [23], a taxonomy of four groups of activities potentially harmful to privacy protection were detected. These included i. information collection, ii. information processing, iii. Information dissemination, and iv. invasion (i.e., the use of personal data to intrude into one's personal life and interfere with her/his decisions).

Although the disclosure of personal data can influence emotions, thoughts and behaviors at the individual, consumer and citizen level, research shows that people are generally unaware of the information they share and how it can be used [1]. Moreover, the relationship between individuals' attitudes and behaviors in the domain of data protection is paradoxical [25, 26]. This is known as the privacy paradox, and describes how individuals claiming to be concerned with the way their personal data is collected and used are generally willing to trade it for relatively small rewards [25] [25]. attempted to resolve the privacy paradox using five research streams: privacy calculus, social theory, cognitive biases and heuristics; bounded rationality, incomplete information, and information asymmetries; and quantum theory. From this, it emerges that individuals may be willing to disclose personal data: when the perceived gains are greater than the expected losses; to engage in social relationships; biasedly believing to be unlikely to experience negative consequences; on account of information incompleteness, asymmetry and the cognitive inability to perceive the associated risks; on account of dynamic preferences, which change over time and depend upon the time at which the actual decision is made.

Data privacy concerns are influenced by anthropomorphism [27]: the exhibition of human-like characteristics from non-human agents [28]. shown that users are both less concerned with the disclosure of personal information and more inclined to follow chatbots recommendation when these express friendliness or socialness [29]. analyzed conversational AI systems and found that technology adoption is affected by privacy concerns and consumers' trust (i.e. the beliefs regarding the integrity, benevolence, and ability of the service provider to safeguard their interests). Indeed, the work of [30] suggests that AI technologies cannot be trusted, but only relied upon. This is justified by the fact that human-made objects cannot be held responsible for their actions and does not have emotions towards the trustor. On the other hand, consumers should trust the organizations developing and using them. In this vein, [31] identified a set of eight privacy design strategies to help IT architects to support privacy by design early in the software development life cycle. These rely upon: i. minimizing the amount of personal data to be processed; ii. designing the system to hide information that spontaneously emerges from the use of a system (or keep them confidential when this is legitimately collected, stored or processed);

iii. Aggregating data at the highest level; iv. keeping separate data sources in separate databases, while processing personal data in a distributed fashion v. providing data subjects with control over their data; vi. informing data subjects whenever their personal data are processed; vii. Ensuring that the designed system is compliant with privacy policies; viii. Demonstrating the compliance of data processing practices with policies and legal requirements.

Despite their relevance, the design of privacy policies is problematic. First, privacy policies should be flexible enough to evolve with the complexity of the information age, while at the same time providing adequate protection to often naïve, uncertain, and vulnerable individuals [1]. Second, in the digital era, data is a valuable resource. Regulations limiting data transfer may negatively affect the development rate of AI technologies, which can jeopardize economic growth at the country level [32].

As the need for privacy is socially created, privacy cannot be understood independently from society [23]. Twitter data have been frequently used to monitor the social response to events concerned with data privacy. For instance, [33] analyzed the public reaction to the Cambridge Analytica scandal, identifying a difference among responsibility attribution between English and Spanish speaking users. The work of [34] analyzed the Twitter debate on the Equifax data breach, highlighting high levels of anger and frustration especially connected to the fear of future losses and indignation for the Equifax communication strategy. The study of [35] analyzed the data breach at Ticketfly, showing that cybersecurity was not perceived as a big issue by US Twitter users, even during a conspicuous attack of that kind.

3 Research Method

The aim of this article is to analyze the public response to the temporary suspension of ChatGPT in Italy under a structural, emotional and social standpoint. The research methodology adopted in this study exploits two analytical techniques (Social Network Analysis and Sentiment Analysis) and two data sources (Google Trends and Twitter).

3.1 Analytical Techniques

Social Network Analysis (SNA) is an interdisciplinary technique developed under the influences of mathematics and computer science [36]. Adopting a quantitative approach, SNA focuses on the study of information exchanges and patterns of relationships within social networks [19]. As the diffusion of innovation can be described as a social phenomenon [12], SNA has been extensively employed to study such dynamics [9, 12, 18, 37]. In this respect, social media like Twitter were found to play a central role in the study of diffusion processes [38]. For these reasons, we employ SNA to analyze the Twitter debate concerned with the innovation-privacy controversy addressed in this study.

Sentiment analysis (or opinion mining) is an analytical methodology using natural language processing techniques to analyze textual information and determine the writer's polarity towards a topic [39]. Opinions have been constructed as a four-dimensional concept, underlined by an holder believing a claim about a topic and associating a (positive, neutral or negative) sentiment with that belief [40]. As a basic trait of human behaviors, opinions are socially influenced and shape individuals' decisions [39–42]. By allowing people to reach large audiences, Twitter has been extensively used to analyze people's opinions towards different topics and how these are shaped by social interactions [9, 40]. In this work, we adopt the algorithm for sentiment and emotion classification provided in [43], specifically trained on Italian Tweets. This utilizes the Italian BERT model (UmBERTo), fine-tuned by sampling and labeling 1000 tweets each day from August 20th to October 12th 2020 on daily trending topics. According to the authors, this approach improved the robustness of the algorithm, which was trained on a range of different topics across a considerable timespan. The resulting model proved to effectively classify input data according to their (positive or negative) sentiment, obtaining state-of-the-art performances on the current benchmark for Italian sentiment analysis algorithms [43].

3.2 Data Sources

Google Trends is a freely accessible platform providing access to a large and unfiltered sample of search requests made via the Google Search Engine, available in an anonymized, categorized and aggregated manner [44, 45]. Google Trends showed to adequately support the exploration of innovation diffusion dynamics [46], and to be predictive of human behaviors in multiple domains, such as finance, migration and tourism [47–50]. Providing access to a pool of queries and topics associated with a search request, Google Trends can also represent a source of relational data [48].

Twitter is a famous social media site allowing users to post messages up to 280 characters (tweets) and interact with others through mentions, replies and retweets [51]. On account of its global reach, large user base and data openness, Twitter represents a relevant source of relational data, especially in the fields of diffusion processes and emergent behaviors [42]. Twitter and Google Trends data are often used in conjunction [52, 53], and were found to be comparable in terms of trending topics and searched queries [54]. Their combined use effectively supported the analysis of the public debate in the domain of technological innovation, both in terms of diffusion [53] and emotional perspectives [52].

3.3 Data Collection and Modeling

We designed our data collection and modeling process in three phases. Taking advantage of the Google Trends platform, the first phase allowed us to identify the keywords pertinent to our analysis. The second phase was concerned with the acquisition of Twitter data. The third phase focused on modeling such data to create the social network representing the public debate we analyzed.

Phase one: keywords identification. Using as a reference point the date at which the GPDP announced on Twitter the suspension of ChatGPT and the service became unavailable in Italy (i.e. March 31st), we split the timeframe of analysis in two equal parts: the pre-ban period (March 24th—March 30th) and the post-ban period (March 31st—April 6th). Through the Google Trends platform, we used a snowball mining approach to collect the most closely related queries and topics associated with the debate we address. This was performed in two stages. In the first, we collected the queries and topics directly associated with the search term "ChatGPT", obtaining a list of first-order associated keywords. Then, using the latter as new search terms, we repeated the process to obtain second-order associated keywords. Together, this provided a detailed picture of the themes surrounding web searches on ChatGPT before and after the ban. The relationships emerging from this process were arranged in four networks: i. pre-ban query network; ii. post-ban query network; iii. pre-ban topics network and iv. post-ban topics network. For each of these, we adopted the community detection algorithm designed in [55] to identify the most relevant classes of keywords searched in concomitance with the suspension of ChatGPT. This algorithm provides an unsupervised method based on modularity optimization to efficiently identify communities in large networks, where modularity reflects the density of connections within a community as compared to connections between communities. This process led to the definition of the inclusion rule to mine Twitter data. The selected keywords were: Italia, Privacy, Garante, GPDP, #data, #dati, VPN, Proxy, Opera, Ban, Blocco, Blocca, Bloccato, Bloccare, Funziona, Disabilita, Alternativa, Alternative, Bard, POE, PizzaGPT, Bing, Chatsonic, midjourney, DALL-E, #ai, #ia.

Phase two: Twitter data collection. By accessing the Twitter APIs, we mined all of the Twitter contributions satisfying the following requirements: i. being posted within March 24th and April 6th; ii. being written in Italian; and iii. Containing at least one of the following keywords (ChatGPT, GPT, OpenAI, #ai, #ia) in combination with at least one of the following ones (Italia, Privacy, Garante, GPDP, #data, #dati, VPN, Proxy, Opera, Ban, Blocco, Blocca, Bloccato, Bloccare, Funziona, Disabilita, Alternativa, Alternative, Bard, POE, PizzaGPT, Bing, Chatsonic, midjourney, DALL-E, #ai, #ia). The presence of #ai and #ia on both sides of the rule permitted to consider both the interaction between AI and the ban, and on ChatGPT and AI. 2176 contributions only contained #ai, #ia or #ai & #ia, and were eliminated in the data cleaning stage. The final dataset is composed of 14,898 Twitter contributions.

Phase three: modeling the social network. Each user represents a node in the network. Edges represent users' interactions, and are both weighted and directed. Weights represent the number of interactions between two users, while the direction identifies the source and target nodes of the information flow. Four kinds of interactions were identified: retweets (originating from the retweeting user and directed towards the tweet author); replies (originating from the replying user and directed to the receiver); quoted tweets (originating from the quoting user and directed to the quoted one); quoted replies (represented by two edges: one originating from the replying user and directed to the quoted one, and another originating from the replying user and directed to the receiver of the reply; each quoted reply represents one contribution and two interactions). Users whose tweets did not gather engagement within the network are shown as isolated nodes. We use the generic term "contribution" when generally discussing tweets, retweets, replies, quoted tweets and quoted replies as an aggregate.

In 1.5% of the collected interactions, data on quoted authors were not available as their contributions did not satisfy our inclusion rule. Despite this, eliminating these relationships and representing the quoting authors as isolated nodes was not reflective of the social pattern emerging from the public debate. Accordingly, we filled this gap by creating a RoW (rest of the world) node accounting for the interactions between users within our network quoting users outside it. As the number of interactions following within these contingencies was marginal, this strategy permitted the representation of the network with higher fidelity while not significantly impacting the results of our analysis. In this work, we consider the number of interactions to be marginal if eliminating the involved nodes or representing them in a RoW-aggregate is substantially indifferent in terms of main results obtained (Fig. 1).

4 Results

Our analysis begins with the examination of the complete network, with a specific focus on the differences between the pre- and post-ban characteristics of the debate. Subsequently, we compare two sub-networks that emerged as particularly relevant in the discussion: the first being concerned with privacy and the second with VPN & ChatGPT alternatives.

4.1 Analysis of the Complete Network

Following the approach described in Sect. 3.3, Fig. 2 provides a graphical representation of the Twitter debate before and after the intervention of the GPDP. In the networks, nodes represent Twitter users. These are colored based on their community of belonging, and their size represents their degree centrality, that is the number

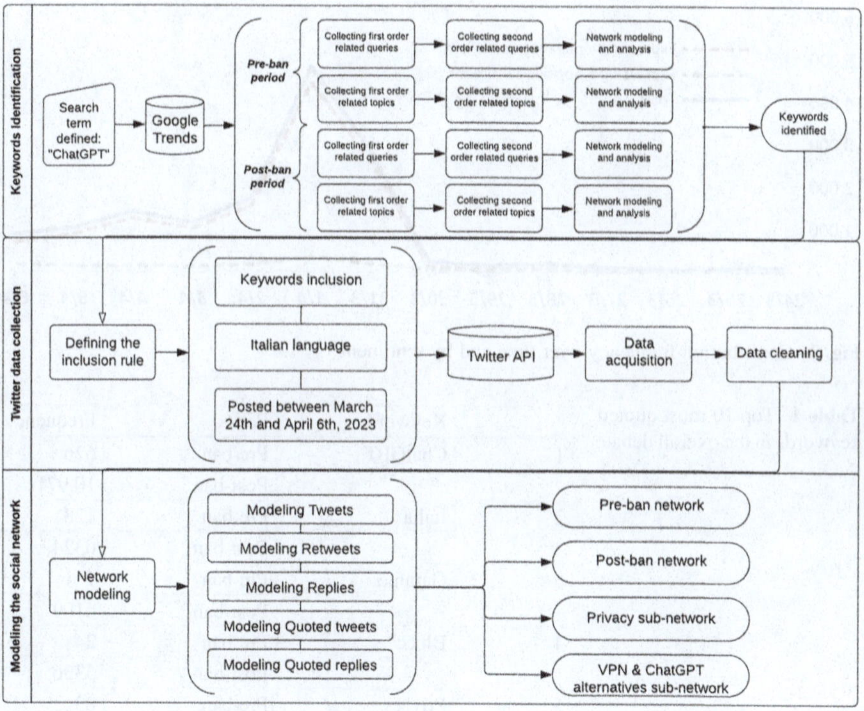

Fig. 1 Data collection and modeling process

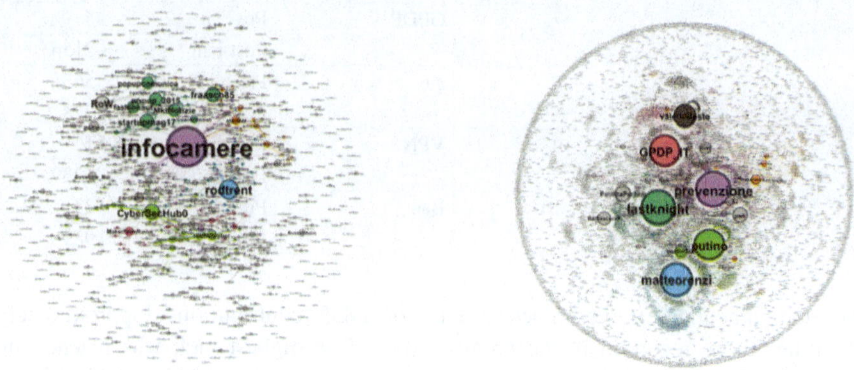

Fig. 2 Pre-ban network (left) and post-ban network (right)

of other users they interacted with. As anticipated in the methodology section, nodes are connected by directed and weighted edges, representing interactions in the forms of retweets, replies, quoted tweets and quoted replies.

As shown in Fig. 3, the intervention of the GPDP had a relevant influence over the number of contributions posted. In particular, on March 31st 2023 (when ChatGPT

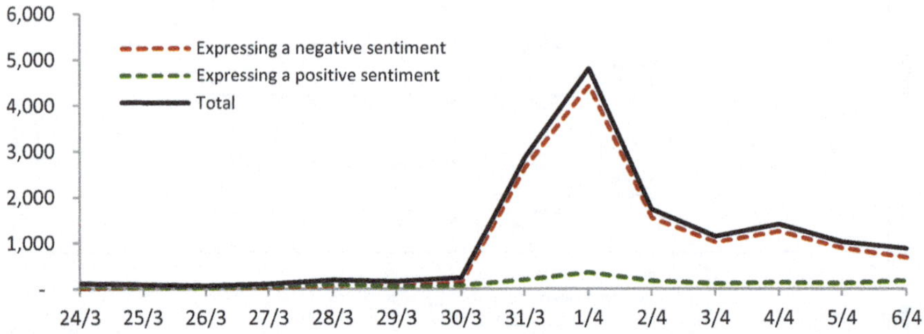

Fig. 3 Contribution frequency over time and by sentiment

Table 1 Top 10 most quoted keywords in the overall debate

	Keyword	Period	Frequency
1	ChatGPT	Pre-ban	626
		Post-ban	10,971
2	Italia	Pre-ban	128
		Post-ban	6324
3	Garante	Pre-ban	1
		Post-ban	6109
4	Blocc*	Pre-ban	24
		Post-ban	5336
5	Privacy	Pre-ban	83
		Post-ban	4935
6	OpenAI	Pre-ban	200
		Post-ban	4095
7	GPDP	Pre-ban	5
		Post-ban	2156
8	#ai	Pre-ban	565
		Post-ban	728
9	VPN	Pre-ban	1
		Post-ban	1239
10	Ban	Pre-ban	33
		Post-ban	989

became unavailable), we mined a total of 2855 contributions (approximately 12 times those recorded in the previous day). The highest pick was reached on April first, when 4813 contributions were collected (almost 20 times the volume registered on March 30th). Although in the following 2 days the number of contributions posted was descending, a trend inversion was recorded on April 4th. On this day, the GPDP announced a meeting with OpenAI to address the claims previously advanced. Overall only 999 of the collected contributions were posted before the ban, while 13,899 were posted after it.

The discussions before and after the ban show significant differences in the topics being debated, as shown in Table 1. Out of the top 10 most frequently mentioned

Table 2 Structural characteristics of the pre- and post- ban networks

	Pre-ban network	Post-ban network	Rate of variation
Users	692	7762	10.2
Tweets	522	3925	6.52
Clusters	115	345	2
Diameter	3	14	3.7

keywords before the ban, five (#ia, #data, midjourney, Bard, and Bing) were replaced in the subsequent period by Garante, Blocc* (including blocco, blocca, bloccare, bloccato), GPDP, VPN, and Ban.

As shown in Table 2, the network diameter is remarkably higher in the post-ban debate. On one hand, this is likely the consequence of a larger network size. On the other, it may indicate higher levels of resonance within the discussion, allowing information to be disseminated more extensively. Adopting the community detection algorithm developed in [55], essentially outlined in the methodology section of this paper, we identified 115 communities in the pre-ban network, and 345 in the post-ban. Clusters containing a single isolated node were not considered in this count. The information flow expressed in the post-ban network appeared as significantly more centralized than in the pre-ban, as the ten most populated communities accounted altogether for about 50% of the nodes in the network (against 29% accounted by the ten most populated communities in the pre-ban network).

Users participated in the process of information diffusion both actively (i.e. posting tweets) and socially (i.e. mainly through retweets and replies). The network analysis reveals a large difference in the number of published tweets, from 522 in the pre-ban to 3925 in the post-ban period. The post-ban debate shows increased user engagement, expressed as both a higher average number of retweets per tweet (from 0.79 to 1.74) and higher average number of replies per tweet (from 0.09 to 0.73).

Both the pre- and post-ban debates saw the participation of users with heterogeneous levels of popularity. Using as a reference the number of followers, we classified users in the four classes: micro popular (from 0 to 100 followers); limitedly popular (from 101 to 1000 followers); popular (from 1001 to 10,000 followers); macro popular (more than 10,000 followers). A fifth class accounted for users for which followers count was not available. Compared to the pre-ban, the post-ban network exhibited a higher share of micro and limitedly popular nodes (respectively 27% versus 21% and 40% versus 33%).

The analysis of degree centrality highlighted the presence of nodes having the characteristics of opinion leaders. These were bloggers, politicians, academics, journalists, news pages and AI enthusiasts (Table 3). Most of them took part in the discussion playing a dual role, as both sources and recipients in the information flow. The analysis also shows that the most central users in terms of degree centrality were not always among the most popular within the debate; an exception is @matteorenzi (former Italian prime minister) who is the third most popular user and the third most central node in terms of degree centrality.

Table 3 Top 10-degree central nodes within the overall debate

	Id	Followers	Degree	Description
1	prevenzione	3785	404	DPO; blogger
2	lastknight	30,065	397	Academic; blogger
3	matteorenzi	3,379,591	381	Italian politician
4	GPDP_IT	10,744	357	GPDP account
5	putino	13,724	352	Journalist
6	valeriodeste	6204	253	Academic
7	PoliticaPerJedi	58,496	177	News page
8	pwk	3314	164	Entrepreneur
9	BarbascuraX	87,518	144	Blogger
10	mentecritica	102,522	137	Tech. Enthusiast

Table 4 Top 10 broker nodes within the overall debate

	Id	Followers	Betweenness centrality	Description
1	prevenzione	3785	651,207	DPO; blogger
2	lastknight	30,065	285,674	Academic; blogger
3	putino	13,724	268,295	Journalist
4	FabioA	296	162,292	Personal profile
5	gabrielepx	1222	105,273	Personal profile
6	Luke_like	3071	82,468	AI enthusiast
7	pwk	3314	77,298	Entrepreneur
8	AlexFondi	138	70,330	AI enthusiast
9	vitalbaa	31,715	64,419	Journalist
10	mrk4m1	5279	63,032	Personal profile

Our results also indicated the presence of broker nodes (Table 4): users filling structural holes within the social network and permitting the connection among otherwise limitedly connected communities. Four of the ten users with the highest brokering capacity were also among the most central in terms of degree centrality. However, the remaining six were also generally less popular, highlighting the relevance of common users in the diffusion of information and opinions within the emerging social structure.

As shown in Fig. 2, the GPDP intervention clearly affected the sentiment of the debate. In the pre-ban period, the portion of contributions expressing positive and negative sentiment was almost the same. More specifically, on March 25th, 26th, 29th and 30th negative contributions prevailed, respectively accounting for 51%, 53%, 66% and 64% of the daily contributions mined. On the opposite, On March 24th, 27th and 28th contributions expressing a positive polarity prevailed, representing respectively 65%, 62% and 56% of the daily contributions collected. This parity is not observed in the post-ban period, where contributions expressing a negative sentiment always prevailed, ranging from 93% to 79% of the daily contributions analyzed. Negative was also the predominant sentiment expressed by the contributions of the most degree and betweenness central nodes, underlying that the social debate might have been influenced by their opinion.

4.2 Sub-Networks Analysis: VPN & ChatGPT Alternatives Vs Privacy

Following the approach described in Sect. 3.3, Fig. 4 provides a graphical representation of the Twitter debate concerned with VPN & ChatGPT alternatives (which includes the keywords VPN, Alternativa, Alternative, Bard, POE, PizzaGPT, Bing and Chatsonic), and on Privacy (including the keyword Privacy). As in Fig. 2, nodes represent Twitter users. These are colored based on their community of belonging, and their size represents their degree centrality, that is the number of other users they interacted with. Nodes are connected by directed and weighted edges, representing interactions in the forms of retweets, replies, quoted tweets and quoted replies.

The two sub-networks appeared different under both the structural and emotional dimensions. The size of the privacy sub-network is more than twice that of the VPN & ChatGPT alternatives one, accounting respectively for 3495 versus 1509 nodes. Among these, 704 participated in both discussions. Overall, the tone expressed when participating in the VPN & ChatGPT alternatives sub-network was relatively more positive. Out of the 704 users who participated in both debates, 47 users showed a predominantly positive sentiment when discussing privacy, while 105 users displayed a predominantly positive sentiment when discussing VPN and alternatives to ChatGPT. This trend is confirmed when extending the analysis to the whole sub-network: the interactions mentioning ChatGPT alternatives and VPNs were comparably less negative than those mentioning privacy (79% against 93% of negative polarization).

In both sub-networks the information flow is centered around journalists, bloggers and technology enthusiasts. However, in the privacy debate we observed

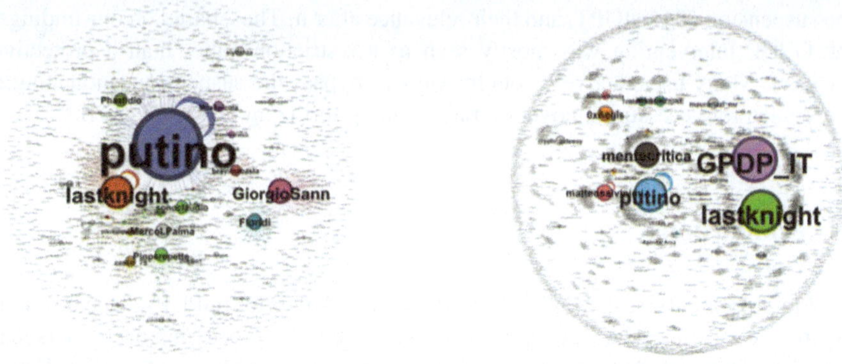

Fig. 4 VPN & ChatGPT alternatives sub-network (left) and Privacy sub-network (right)

a higher centrality of institutional users such as politicians and the GPDP Twitter profile. Despite being remarkably smaller in size, the VPN & ChatGPT alternatives sub-network was characterized by longer paths of information diffusion, emphasized by a greater network diameter (10 versus 7 in the privacy sub-network).

5 Discussion

In line with several studies, the relationship between rapid innovation diffusion and privacy emerges as complex and controversial [20, 22, 28, 56]. Using as a proxy the Twitter debate, our analysis indicated that the Italian landscape became actively and vocally engaged when confronted with a conflict between innovation diffusion and privacy. This was underlined by the involvement of numerous and heterogeneous users differing in popularity and interests. The increased sociality registered in the post-ban phase reinforces this claim.

The analysis identified the presence of potential opinion leaders and opinion brokers within the debate. The partial mismatch between users' centrality and popularity supports the claim that influence within the social structures is not solely determined by follower counts, but also by the structural characteristics of the debate and specific users' attributes (e.g. the nature of their posting activity). Indeed, users with high brokering capacities were generally less popular than the most degree central ones. The sentiment analysis revealed a significant escalation of negative contributions after the intervention of the GPDP. The expression of negative sentiment by highly central nodes (both in terms of degree and betweenness centrality) might have favored the diffusion of negative perceptions on the topic.

The sub-network analysis supported the hypothesis that users' negative perceptions were mainly related to the unavailability of ChatGPT rather than to privacy concerns. Indeed, when discussing VPNs & ChatGPT alternatives (which are ways to circumvent the unavailability of ChatGPT) users expressed a more positive sentiment if compared to discussions only pertaining privacy considerations. This thesis is supported by the substantial absence of contributions quoting VPN before the suspension of ChatGPT, and their relevance after it. Thus, based on our findings, the GPDP intervention was mostly seen as a restriction rather than a protective measure. Many users actively sought ways to bypass the suspension, indicating a preference for accessing innovation rather than prioritizing privacy concerns.

6 Conclusions

On March 30th 2023, the Italian Data Protection Authority (GPDP) detected illicit practices concerning the way OpenAI was collecting and processing users' personal data through ChatGPT. This determined its suspension on March 31st 2023. Using as a proxy the Twitter debate, this study analyzed the suspension of ChatGPT to gather a bird-eye view on the controversial relationship between innovation diffusion and privacy at the ecological landscape level.

The suspension of ChatGPT generated substantial growth in the number of users and interactions included in the emerging network. This was connected to a relevant variation in the topics discussed, especially emphasizing a growing interest in VPNs. At the user level, the debate was participated by individuals differing in terms of popularity and typology (e.g., journalists, bloggers, politicians, technology enthusiasts, etc.). The most degree central users were generally more popular, while less popular users showed higher brokering capabilities. Both participated in the debate mainly expressing a negative sentiment, which has likely influenced the whole debate.

Our analysis suggested that users' negativity was prevalently connected with the inaccessibility of ChatGPT rather than with concerns over the illicit use of personal data. Analyses at the sub-network level revealed that contributions quoting VPN or ChatGPT alternatives expressed a more positive sentiment than those mentioning privacy. In conclusion, our analysis suggests that the Italian landscape viewed the suspension of ChatGPT more as a restriction rather than a protective measure. This highlighted a preference for promoting innovation diffusion over prioritizing privacy concerns.

7 Theoretical and Practical Implications

This study contributes to the ongoing debate on balancing innovation diffusion and privacy protection, prompting society to reflect on its preferences and values. The negative sentiment attached to the GPDP intervention highlights the growing relevance of AI-powered services in modern life. In accordance with studies adopting a more micro-level perspective, the analysis of individuals' behaviors at the landscape level emphasized a more generalized tendency to prioritize convenience over privacy concerns. This aspect offers avenues for further research on the complex interplay between technology, privacy, innovation, and user perceptions at the societal level, contributing to the literature on privacy behaviors, attitudes and privacy paradox.

This study also provides a set of implications relevant for businesses operating with users' data. The analysis of the ChatGPT suspension suggests prioritizing transparency in data collection and processing practices in order to avoid possible controversies and regulatory actions. Other than transparent, such practices should adhere to the legal requirement of the jurisdictions in which such organizations operate. This aspect is challenging on account of the novelty of technologies such as AI and the consequent gaps in regulations and potential inconsistencies across different national jurisdictions and authorities. When such interventions are operated, this study highlights the relevance of crisis management strategies, promoting effective communication with regulators, customers and other stakeholders to solve them. Thus, more in general, organizations must weigh the benefits of innovative offerings against potential privacy-related aspects, making informed decisions on how to merge these elements in their business strategies.

8 Limitations and Future Research

One limitation of our work is connected to the absence of a neutral class in the sentiment analysis algorithm we adopted. Future studies may develop and apply new sentiment analysis algorithms to better classify ambiguous contributions not expressing a clear polarity. Moreover, the use of a RoW node accounting for the relationship between users within the network quoting users outside it should be carefully considered. As anticipated in the methodology session, the adoption of this strategy is advisable only if the variations generated in the SNA measures do not substantially affect the results of the analysis.

Future research may extend the timeframe of analysis to also consider how the Italian ecological landscape responded to the ban removal. This, together with the insights presented in this paper, may provide a more complete picture of the event under analysis. Our study focused on Tweets written in Italian. Accordingly, future research may encompass the analysis of contributions in other languages to explore how the GPDP intervention was perceived internationally. Lastly, further research may inquire on whether (and eventually how) the ban influenced user behaviors over a more prolonged time period, as the immediate reaction to the intervention might have been affected by impulsiveness and emotional factors.

References

1. Acquisti, A., Brandimarte, L., & Loewenstein, G. (2015). Privacy and human behavior in the age of information. *Science, 347*, 509–514. https://doi.org/10.1126/science.aaa1465
2. Eloundou, T., Manning, S., Mishkin, P., & Rock, D. (2023). GPTs are GPTs: An early look at the labor market impact potential of large language models. http://arxiv.org/abs/2303.10130.
3. Taecharungroj, V. (2023). "What can ChatGPT do?" Analyzing early reactions to the innovative AI Chatbot on twitter. *BDCC, 7*, 35. https://doi.org/10.3390/bdcc7010035
4. Gordijn, B., & Have, H. T. (2023). ChatGPT: Evolution or revolution? *Medicine, Health Care and Philosophy, 26*, 1–2. https://doi.org/10.1007/s11019-023-10136-0
5. van Dis, E. A. M., Bollen, J., Zuidema, W., van Rooij, R., & Bockting, C. L. (2023). ChatGPT: Five priorities for research. *Nature, 614*, 224–226. https://doi.org/10.1038/d41586-023-00288-7
6. Statista: Number of interactions with OpenAI.com and ChatGPT among internet users in Italy from October 2022 to January 2023. (2023). https://www.statista.com/statistics/1379705/italy-openai-chatgpt-engagement/
7. GPDP: Provvedimento del 30 marzo 2023 [9870832]. Accessed April 04, 2023, from https://www.garanteprivacy.it:443/home/docweb/-/docweb-display/docweb/9870832
8. Turner, M. G. (1989). Landscape ecology: The effect of pattern on process. *Annual Review of Ecology, Evolution, and Systematics, 20*, 171–197.

9. Bolici, F., Acciarini, C., Marchegiani, L., & Pirolo, L. (2020). Innovation diffusion in tourism: How information about blockchain is exchanged and characterized on twitter. *TQM*. https://doi.org/10.1108/TQM-01-2020-0016
10. Rogers, E. M. (1983). *Diffusion of innovations*. Free Press; Collier Macmillan.
11. Burt, R. S. (1987). Social contagion and innovation: Cohesion versus structural equivalence. *American Journal of Sociology, 92*, 1287–1335. https://doi.org/10.1086/228667
12. Valente, T. W. (1996). Social network thresholds in the diffusion of innovations. *Social Networks, 18*, 69–89. https://doi.org/10.1016/0378-8733(95)00256-1
13. Abrahamson, E., & Rosenkopf, L. (1997). Social network effects on the extent of innovation diffusion: A computer simulation. *Organization Science, 8*, 289–309. https://doi.org/10.1287/orsc.8.3.289
14. Aula, P., & Parviainen, O. (2012). Communicating connections: Social networks and innovation diffusion. In H. Melkas & V. Harmaakorpi (Eds.), *Practice-based innovation: Insights, applications and policy implications* (pp. 49–63). Springer. https://doi.org/10.1007/978-3-642-21723-4_4
15. Strang, D., & Soule, S. A. (1998). Diffusion in organizations and social movements: From hybrid corn to poison pills. *Annual Review of Sociology, 24*, 265–290. https://doi.org/10.1146/annurev.soc.24.1.265
16. Bohlmann, J. D., Calantone, R. J., & Zhao, M. (2010). The effects of market network heterogeneity on innovation diffusion: An agent-based modeling approach: The effects of market network heterogeneity on innovation diffusion. *Journal of Product Innovation Management, 27*, 741–760. https://doi.org/10.1111/j.1540-5885.2010.00748.x
17. Burt, R. S. (2004). Structural holes and good ideas. *American Journal of Sociology, 110*, 349–399. https://doi.org/10.1086/421787
18. Beni Houd, Y., & El Amrani, M. (2022). Social network analysis: A useful tool for studying innovation diffusion processes. *Economia agro-alimentare, 1*, 1–59. https://doi.org/10.3280/ecag2022oa12059
19. Haythornthwaite, C. (1996). Social network analysis: An approach and technique for the study of information exchange. *Library & Information Science Research, 18*, 323–342. https://doi.org/10.1016/S0740-8188(96)90003-1
20. Willems, J., Schmid, M. J., Vanderelst, D., Vogel, D., & Ebinger, F. (2022). AI-driven public services and the privacy paradox: Do citizens really care about their privacy? *Public Management Review, 25*, 1–19. https://doi.org/10.1080/14719037.2022.2063934
21. Bartneck, C., Lütge, C., Wagner, A., & Welsh, S. (2021). Privacy issues of AI. In *An introduction to ethics in robotics and AI* (pp. 61–70). Springer International Publishing. https://doi.org/10.1007/978-3-030-51110-4_8
22. Raab, C. D. (2020). Information privacy, impact assessment, and the place of ethics. *Computer Law & Security Review, 37*, 105404. https://doi.org/10.1016/j.clsr.2020.105404
23. Solove, D. J. (2006). A taxonomy of privacy. *University of Pennsylvania Law Review, 154*, 477. https://doi.org/10.2307/40041279
24. Smith, H. J., Milberg, S. J., & Burke, S. J. (1996). Information privacy: Measuring individuals' concerns about organizational practices. *MIS Quarterly, 20*, 167. https://doi.org/10.2307/249477
25. Kokolakis, S. (2017). Privacy attitudes and privacy behaviour: A review of current research on the privacy paradox phenomenon. *Computers & Security, 64*, 122–134. https://doi.org/10.1016/j.cose.2015.07.002
26. Zafeiropoulou, A. M., Millard, D. E., Webber, C., & O'Hara, K. (2013). Unpicking the privacy paradox: Can structuration theory help to explain location-based privacy decisions? In *Proceedings of the 5th annual ACM web science conference* (pp. 463–472). ACM, Paris France. https://doi.org/10.1145/2464464.2464503
27. Kronemann, B., Kizgin, H., Rana, N., Dwivedi, K., & Y. (2023). How AI encourages consumers to share their secrets? The role of anthropomorphism, personalisation, and privacy

concerns and avenues for future research. *SJME, 27*, 2–19. https://doi.org/10.1108/SJME-10-2022-0213
28. Ischen, C., Araujo, T., Voorveld, H., Van Noort, G., & Smit, E. (2020). Privacy concerns in Chatbot interactions. In A. Følstad, T. Araujo, S. Papadopoulos, E. L.-C. Law, O.-C. Granmo, E. Luger, & P. B. Brandtzaeg (Eds.), *Chatbot research and design* (pp. 34–48). Springer International Publishing. https://doi.org/10.1007/978-3-030-39540-7_3
29. Vimalkumar, M., Sharma, S. K., Singh, J. B., & Dwivedi, Y. K. (2021). 'Okay google, what about my privacy?': User's privacy perceptions and acceptance of voice based digital assistants. *Computers in Human Behavior, 120*, 106763. https://doi.org/10.1016/j.chb.2021.106763
30. Ryan, M. (2020). In AI we trust: Ethics, artificial intelligence, and reliability. *Science and Engineering Ethics, 26*, 2749–2767. https://doi.org/10.1007/s11948-020-00228-y
31. Hoepman, J.-H. (2014). Privacy design strategies. In N. Cuppens-Boulahia, F. Cuppens, S. Jajodia, A. Abou El Kalam, & T. Sans (Eds.), *ICT systems security and privacy protection* (pp. 446–459). Springer. https://doi.org/10.1007/978-3-642-55415-5_38
32. Mazurek, G., & Małagocka, K. (2019). Perception of privacy and data protection in the context of the development of artificial intelligence. *Journal of Management Analytics, 6*, 344–364. https://doi.org/10.1080/23270012.2019.1671243
33. González, F., Yu, Y., Figueroa, A., López, C., & Aragon, C. (2019). Global reactions to the Cambridge Analytica scandal: A cross-language social media study. In *Companion proceedings of the 2019 world wide web conference* (pp. 799–806). ACM, San Francisco USA. https://doi.org/10.1145/3308560.3316456
34. Novak, A. N., & Vilceanu, M. O. (2019). "The internet is not pleased": Twitter and the 2017 Equifax data breach. *The Communication Review, 22*, 196–221. https://doi.org/10.1080/10714421.2019.1651595
35. Vogler, D., & Meissner, F. (2020). How users tweet about a cyber attack: An explorative study using machine learning and social network analysis. *Journal of Digital Media & Policy, 11*, 195–214. https://doi.org/10.1386/jdmp_00016_1
36. Otte, E., & Rousseau, R. (2002). Social network analysis: A powerful strategy, also for the information sciences. *Journal of Information Science, 28*, 441–453. https://doi.org/10.1177/016555150202800601
37. Van Der Valk, T., & Gijsbers, G. (2010). The use of social network analysis in innovation studies: Mapping actors and technologies. *Innovations, 12*, 5–17. https://doi.org/10.5172/impp.12.1.5
38. Kumar, S., Morstatter, F., & Liu, H. (2014). *Twitter data analytics*. Springer. https://doi.org/10.1007/978-1-4614-9372-3
39. Nandwani, P., & Verma, R. (2021). A review on sentiment analysis and emotion detection from text. *Social Network Analysis and Mining, 11*, 81. https://doi.org/10.1007/s13278-021-00776-6
40. Taboada, M. (2016). Sentiment analysis: An overview from linguistics. *Annual Review of Linguistics, 2*, 325–347. https://doi.org/10.1146/annurev-linguistics-011415-040518
41. Liu, B. (2012). *Sentiment analysis and opinion mining*. Springer.
42. Steinert-Threlkeld, Z. C. (2018). *Twitter as data*. Cambridge University Press. https://doi.org/10.1017/9781108529327
43. Bianchi, F., Nozza, D., & Hovy, D. (2021). FEEL-IT: Emotion and sentiment classification for the Italian language. Proceedings of the Eleventh Workshop on Computational Approaches to Subjectivity, Sentiment and Social Media Analysis (pp. 76–83).
44. Google: FAQ about Google Trends data. Accessed May 20, 2023, from https://support.google.com/trends/answer/4365533?hl=en&ref_topic=6248052
45. Rogers, S. (n.d.). What is Google Trends data — and what does it mean? Accessed May 20, 2023, from https://medium.com/google-news-lab/what-is-google-trends-data-and-what-does-it-mean-b48f07342ee8
46. Dos Santos, M. J. P. L. (2018). Nowcasting and forecasting aquaponics by Google trends in European countries. *Technological Forecasting and Social Change, 134*, 178–185. https://doi.org/10.1016/j.techfore.2018.06.002

47. Dastgir, S., Demir, E., Downing, G., Gozgor, G., & Lau, C. K. M. (2019). The causal relationship between bitcoin attention and bitcoin returns: Evidence from the copula-based granger causality test. *Finance Research Letters, 28*, 160–164. https://doi.org/10.1016/j.frl.2018.04.019
48. Pan, B., Chenguang Wu, D., & Song, H. (2012). Forecasting hotel room demand using search engine data. *Journal of Hospitality and Tourism Technology, 3*, 196–210. https://doi.org/10.1108/17579881211264486
49. Wladyka, D. (2017). Queries to Google search as predictors of migration flows from Latin America to Spain. *JPSS, 25*, 312–327. https://doi.org/10.25133/JPSSv25n4.002
50. Zhang, W., Wang, P., Li, X., & Shen, D. (2018). Quantifying the cross-correlations between online searches and bitcoin market. *Physica A: Statistical Mechanics and its Applications, 509*, 657–672. https://doi.org/10.1016/j.physa.2018.06.073
51. Schuster, J., & Kolleck, N. (2020). The global diffusion of social innovations—An analysis of twitter communication networks related to inclusive education. *Frontiers in Education, 5*, 492010. https://doi.org/10.3389/feduc.2020.492010
52. Bian, J., Yoshigoe, K., Hicks, A., Yuan, J., He, Z., Xie, M., Guo, Y., Prosperi, M., Salloum, R., & Modave, F. (2016). Mining Twitter to Assess the Public Perception of the "Internet of Things". *PLoS One, 11*, e0158450. https://doi.org/10.1371/journal.pone.0158450
53. Philippas, D., Rjiba, H., Guesmi, K., & Goutte, S. (2019). Media attention and bitcoin prices. *Finance Research Letters, 30*, 37–43. https://doi.org/10.1016/j.frl.2019.03.031
54. Giummole, F., Orlando, S., & Tolomei, G. (2013). Trending topics on twitter improve the prediction of Google hot queries. In *2013 international conference on social computing* (pp. 39–44). IEEE. https://doi.org/10.1109/SocialCom.2013.12
55. Blondel, V. D., Guillaume, J.-L., Lambiotte, R., & Lefebvre, E. (2008). Fast unfolding of communities in large networks. *Journal of Statistical Mechanics, 2008*, P10008. https://doi.org/10.1088/1742-5468/2008/10/P10008
56. Saura, J. R., Ribeiro-Soriano, D., & Palacios-Marqués, D. (2022). Assessing behavioral data science privacy issues in government artificial intelligence deployment. *Government Information Quarterly, 39*, 101679. https://doi.org/10.1016/j.giq.2022.101679

Does AI Reflect Human Behaviour? Exploring the Presence of Gender Bias in AI Translation Tools

Marco Smacchia, Stefano Za, and Alvaro Arenas

Abstract Natural language processing tools are becoming more and more important in our daily life, enabling us to perform many tasks in a timely and efficient manner. However, as the utilisation of these tools growth, so does the risk of unexpected consequences due to the presence of bias. This study investigates the presence of gender bias within the most popular neural machine translation and large language model tools. We defined a set of Italian sentences concerning ten specific jobs, where the gender of the subjects is not explicitly mentioned. Employing those AI tools, we translated the sentences from Italian to English, requiring the gender to be explicitly mentioned. Afterwards, we developed a survey to obtain human translations for the same sentences, allowing us to compare the differences between the responses generated by the tools and those from individuals. Results show a high presence of gender bias especially for the jobs associated with a male gender and demonstrate a consistency between the outcome obtained by the tools and the results of the survey. These findings serve as a starting point for exploring the origins of gender bias within natural language processing tools and how they reflect gender distributions in our society and human behaviour regarding job occupations.

Keywords Natural language processing · Neural machine translation · Large language models · Gender bias · Artificial intelligence bias

---

M. Smacchia (✉) · S. Za
University "G. D'Annunzio" of Chieti-Pescara, Pescara, Italy
e-mail: marco.smacchia@unich.it; stefano.za@unich.it

A. Arenas
IE Business School, Madrid, Spain
e-mail: alvaro.arenas@ie.edu

A. M. Braccini et al. (eds.), *Digital (Eco) Systems and Societal Challenges*, Lecture Notes in Information Systems and Organisation 72,
https://doi.org/10.1007/978-3-031-75586-6_19

1 Introduction

In the last few years, artificial intelligence (AI) has gained much attention from both scholars and practitioners, with a particular focus on societal aspects [1]. Within this context, natural language processing (NLP) tools, such as chatbots, translators and speech recognition, have witnessed a surge in popularity because they allow users to interact without using machine language [2]. NLP, a subfield of AI, encompasses the development of machine algorithms capable of understanding human language, consisting of two main branches: natural language understanding and natural language generation [2, 3]. The first branch is related to the study of linguistics and to the understanding of human language, while the second is focused on the process of producing such language [2]. NLP finds application in various tasks, such as automatic summarisation, discourse analysis, speech recognition, machine translations, and many others (ibid.). In the last few years, this technology gained popularity due to the introduction of neural networks and large language models (LLM) that are able to solve many NLP tasks without having specific training data for a given job (zero-shot tasks) [4–6]. Machine translation (MT) is one of the NLP fields significantly impacted by this transition [6].

MT allows a machine to translate natural language sentences, providing an instant translation of words, sentences, documents and even of speeches [7, 8]. In the past, MT primarily relied on a set of predetermined translation rules and linguistic knowledge. However, nowadays state-of-the-art MT systems implement neural networks that use a training dataset of parallel texts to translate an input sentence to a target output by using the information acquired during its training [9]. MT serve as a useful tool that simplifies the way we communicate with people that speak other languages by providing large volumes of translated text or speech in a few seconds [10]. As the industry value continues to growth, so does the number of tools available in the market that are used worldwide by companies and individuals for many tasks[1,2] Since this technology is broadly used, unexpected results such as mistranslations or biases could have severe implications. Vieira et al. [8] conducted a review in which they explore MT bias across legal and medical fields. They reported interesting examples such as the low accuracy of Google Translate for translating medical instructions to patients suffering from diabetes. Additionally, they discuss an incident in which Google Translate was used by a police officer to obtain consent during inspections, which later faced challenges during the court audience due to concerns about overcoming language barriers. In both cases, the translation tools

[1] Global Market Insights. (April 6, 2017). Machine translation market size worldwide, from 2016 to 2024 (in million U.S. dollars) [Graph]. In Statista. Retrieved May 14, 2023, from https://www.statista.com/statistics/748358/worldwide-machine-translation-market-size/.

[2] Stanford University. (April 15, 2023). Number of commercial machine translation (MT) programs available globally from 2017 to 2022 [Graph]. In Statista. Retrieved May 14, 2023, from https://www.statista.com/statistics/1378793/mt-translation-programs-number/.

outcomes can cause serious damage to the individuals involved, underscoring the paramount importance of addressing these kinds of issues.

In this study, we focus on examining the presence of gender bias within AI translation tools. Specifically, we selected five jobs mostly done by women and five jobs mostly done by men (on the basis of relevant reports). We then we constructed sentences involving these jobs and translated them from Italian to English using the API of five different AI translation tools (Google Translate, Deepl, Microsoft Azure, GPT 3.5 and Text DaVinci). All the original sentences in Italian did not include a subject (the gender was not made explicit). Since in Italian it is possible omitting the subject in a sentence, our experiment aims at measuring the gender bias in English translations where, on the other hand, the subject must always be made explicit. To compare the results obtained from an AI with those of human beings, we also developed a questionnaire that we submitted to a sample of Italian individuals.

The purpose of this study is to address the limitations identified in the literature by investigating the presence of gender bias in the outcome of five different AI tools when sentences without subject are presented. More specifically, we aim to answer the following questions:

1. *To what extent does gender bias occur inside the most common AI translation tools?*
2. *Related to gender bias, are there differences in the output of a translation depending on how the query is formulated?*
3. *Concerning the translation output, which jobs are most likely to be biased?*
4. *What are the results of a comparison between the results obtained from an AI with those obtained by Human beings?*

The contribution of this study is structured as follows. In the next section, we provide a theoretical background about the gender bias inside MT along with the limitations detected and outline the methodology we used to perform our research. We subsequently present the results obtained together with the discussion. Finally, in the conclusion section, we state the theoretical and practical contribution together with the limitations and avenues for future research.

2 Theoretical Background

Inside the AI debate, research focusing on identifying, investigating, and addressing biases has become increasingly relevant [11]. Although AI and its subfields bring enormous potentialities and advantages in many domains, the presence of biases could bring dangerous and unpleasant consequences [12]. Since AI is used worldwide by private, public and governmental organisations to support the decision-making process of many activities, its outcome influences many people simultaneously [13]. Bias inside data and resources used to train the AI model or inside the algorithm could cause and amplify issues such as discrimination, inequality, and lack of privacy and trust [12, 14–17].

Among the possible biased outcomes concerning AI technology, the presence of gender bias inside neural MT tools has a significant relevance [18–20]. Gender bias occurs when one gender is preferred or prejudiced with respect to the others. NLP algorithms or training datasets, on which machine translation tools are based, could reinforce or amplify damaging gender stereotypes [17]. There are many real-world cases related to this issue, from resume filtering giving preference to male candidates, to credit applications refused to women even if they have a higher score than a male applicant [17, 21].

Gender bias in MT tools based on AI could be attributed to different factors. For example, behaviours or habits embedded in society described by the training data could affect the outcome of a translator. Technical issues in the data or the algorithm used to develop the artefact could lead to some forms of gender bias. Finally, since AI tools are capable of learning, different use in various contexts could influence the behaviour of the MT [22].

The presence of gender bias inside neural MT tools is not a new topic. There are many press articles that underlined sexist behaviour in online translators[3],[4] In addition, several articles also tried to inspect and also address this issue. Stanovsky et al., [18] propose an evaluation method for gender bias inside MT tools based on morphological analysis. They analysed six MT tools both industrial and academic and detected the presence of translation errors related to gender. Another study focuses on reducing gender bias by training a neural MT tool and applying several automated techniques to address the issue. Results indicate that when these techniques are used to reduce the gender bias in a neural MT tool, the performances are worse with respect to the baseline system. Among the methods used only domain adaptation provides better results after a model is trained [19]. Bernagozzi et al., [20], used a method proposed by Srivastava et al., [23] to evaluate the presence of gender bias in MT tools that could be used by third parties. Moreover, through a questionnaire, they inspect the impact that such biases have on people and how this issue is perceived. Schiebinger [24] underlines the necessity to analyse gender bias inside MT tools as she notes their trend to translate with a default masculine form.

Although this phenomenon has been studied several times, there are some aspects that still need to be addressed. The language source of multiple datasets used to perform the research is English [18, 20]. Many studies have not considered the fact that in some languages sentences without a subject are valid while, in other languages, the subject must be outlined [23]. Moreover, some contributions use a limited number of tools to make comparisons and simple sentences [20, 23]. To carry out the research we adapted the framework of Srivastava et al., [23] to assess

[3]Parmy Olson, The Algorithm That Helped Google Translate Become Sexist, Forbes. Available at: https://www.forbes.com/sites/parmyolson/2018/02/15/the-algorithm-that-helped-google-translate-become-sexist/.

[4]Shivali Best, Is Google Translate SEXIST? Users report biased results when translating gender-neutral languages into English, Daily Mail. Available at: https://www.dailymail.co.uk/sciencetech/article-5136607/Is-Google-Translate-SEXIST.html.

the presence of gender bias inside MT tools without having access to their source code or training data.

In the next section, we describe the process adopted to conduct our research. Starting from studies on gendered language concerning the reinforcement of gender stereotypes in job titles [25, 26] and from statistics about the occupations mostly performed by a specific gender, we developed a set of sentences to translate. Every phrase is related to a specific job that could be used to identify both men and women (gendered-language free). We avoided referring to occupations that could be related specifically to masculine or feminine forms to avoid possible bias due to gendered language.

3 Methodology

This contribution adopts an exploratory design as the main aim is to *seek new insights* into the evaluation of gender bias inside AI translation tools [27]. Our primary goal was to assess the presence of bias in translators when a sentence with no subject (a common practice in some languages) is translated into a sentence in which the subject must be mandatorily made explicit. To this end, we have developed a set of sentences in Italian in which the subject has not been made explicit and which can be attributed to either a male or a female and then we translated them in English. Each sentence focuses on ten particular jobs, which we chose by searching within Eurostat databases[5, 6] in World Bank Group[7] and U.S. Bureau of Labor Statistics[8] reports. More specifically, we selected the five jobs mostly done by women and just as many held mostly by men. In order to be selected, the name of the job had to be impersonal in Italian (not attributable to a male or female audience). We developed three sentences for each job, the first one quite simple, while the other two more elaborate. Since all sentences have been translated in English, we arranged for the first sentence to contain only personal pronouns, while the other two contained both personal pronouns and possessive adjectives. As an example, the following three sentences are those already translated in English and referring to carer (in bold the words concerning the gender):

[5] European Jobs Monitor 2021: Gender gaps and the employment structure. Available at: https://www.aranagenzia.it/attachments/article/12440/European%20Jobs%20Monitor%202021-Gender%20gaps%20and%20the%20employment%20structure.pdf.

[6] Jobs still split along gender lines. Available at: https://ec.europa.eu/eurostat/web/products-eurostat-news/-/EDN-20180307-1.

[7] Gender-based Employment Segregation: Understanding Causes and Policy Interventions. Available at: https://documents1.worldbank.org/curated/en/483621554129720460/pdf/Gender-Based-Employment-Segregation-Understanding-Causes-and-Policy-Interventions.pdf.

[8] Labor Force Statistics from the Current Population Survey. Available at: https://www.bls.gov/cps/cpsaat39.htm.

- ***She*** *said* ***she*** *works as a carer in the home of an elderly person.*
- ***She*** *started* ***her*** *job as a carer after an elderly person requested assistance.*
- *After losing* ***her*** *job as a carer,* ***she*** *thought of changing life.*

In the next step, we selected the tools used to perform our study. We chose them according to two parameters: the popularity of the translator and the availability of the APIs. After a screening, we chose three of the most used neural MT tools in the market: Google Translate, DeepL, and Microsoft Azure. Since LLM models are becoming more and more relevant inside the debate and are also trained on much bigger datasets than translators, we decided to add to the current list, the models GPT 3.5 turbo and Text-DaVinci 003 on which Chat GPT is based [5, 28]. We referred to the API documentation of these MT tools to write a Python script in which we translated the 30 sentences in three different ways, first, we translated the entire text corpus (all sentences at once), then we translated all the corpus from an external document and finally, we translated the sentences one by one. The results, consisting of 90 translations per tool, were listed in an Excel sheet and labelled according to the gender that was made explicit in the English translation (M for male, F for female and N for neutral) and job. Depending on the output of the translation we classified the results as *biased* when the output reflects the underlying data used to develop the sentences, *converging biased* when the output is influenced by the previous translations (underlying data) and converges towards the same result and *unbiased* when the output is translated using in a neutral way or the translation path doesn't reflect a biased behaviour.

We then analysed the results measuring the presence of bias in the translation considering each tool both individually and in aggregated form. Then we compared the results with those obtained from the questionnaire for each job. Lastly, we consider the translation trend between the different responses to the last question concerning the aim of the study.

To better explain the processes on which the research is based we graphically represented our research protocol (Fig. 1) that we adapted from the model of Srivastava et al., [23] to assess the presence of bias inside MT tools by third parties. Moreover, to assess the presence of bias, we take into account the statistics concerning the gender gap inside the selected jobs. To make the model clearer and more reproducible we used the business process modelling notation (BPMN).

In this study, we also developed a questionnaire to compare the results obtained by AI tools with those obtained by humans. More specifically, our aim is to understand whether gender bias is still present in the way people think in our society.

The questionnaire reported the 30 sentences in Italian translated into English, to which all references regarding gender (pronouns and adjectives) were appropriately removed, by asking the respondent to complete the sentences giving them a proper meaning (fill in the blank questions). All the sentences were presented in the same order they were submitted to the AI tools. At the beginning and at the end of the form were also asked demographic questions. The first question was related to the English level to assess the familiarity of the respondents with the language. After completing the 30 questions related to the translated sentences, respondents were asked: the

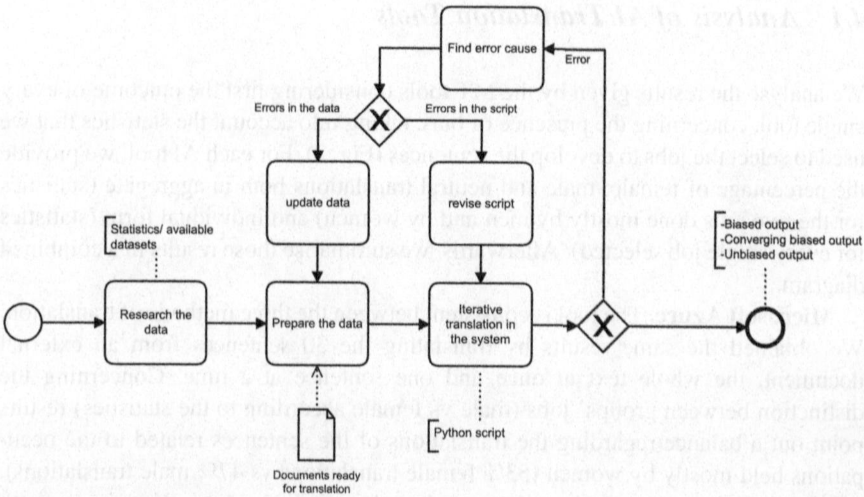

Fig. 1 Research protocol

gender they identify with, their Italian region of origin, their age, and their educational qualification. All the demographic questions, although mandatory had the option "I prefer not to answer" or "other". Finally, we added a further question asking the respondent to explain in a few words what was in her/his opinion the main aim of this study. After the questionnaire was completed, we provided information about the objective of the research.

We decided to use the fill in the blank structure for various reasons. First, letting people translate all the sentences would have gone beyond our purposes and would have led to possible errors and a difficult analysis of the outcomes, caused by an excessive amount of noise within the dataset. Then, we wanted to make the questionnaire available for the people that are not proficient in the English language, by reducing the possibility of mistakes due to their lack of expertise.

We submitted the questionnaire to a random sample of 100 Italian speakers. The respondents were 53. Of these responses, 11 were discarded because they were inconsistent with what was required within the questionnaire. The data concerning the 42 questionnaires, was collected from late April to early June 2023. To develop the survey, we used the tool Jotform. Further information about the sample is discussed in paragraph 4.2.

4 Results

In this section we present the results obtained by the analysis conducted on the translation tools first and then the outcome of the questionnaire.

4.1 Analysis of AI Translation Tools

We analyse the results given by the MT tools considering first the outcome of every single tool, concerning the presence of bias, taking into account the statistics that we used to select the jobs to develop the sentences (Fig. 2). For each AI tool, we provide the percentage of female, male and neutral translations both in aggregate (statistics for the five jobs done mostly by men and by women) and individual form (statistics for every single job selected). Afterwards, we summarise those results in a combined diagram.

Microsoft Azure. The tool is consistent between the three methods of translation. We obtained the same results by translating the 30 sentences from an external document, the whole text at once and one sentence at a time. Concerning the distinction between groups' jobs (male vs female according to the statistics) results point out a balance regarding the translations of the sentences related to the occupations held mostly by women (53% female translations vs 47% male translations). While the tool obtains good results regarding the previous group, when it comes to the one populated by jobs done mostly by men the outcome becomes highly biased. In this group, all the translations are in the masculine form (0% female translations vs 100% male translations). By looking at single jobs, almost all of them are always translated using the masculine or the feminine form. The only exception is represented by kindergarten teacher (67% female translations vs 33% male translations). Finally, the only two occupations translated with the feminine form are carer (translated by the tool as caregiver) and secretarial assistant. All the other jobs are translated always using male adjectives and pronouns.

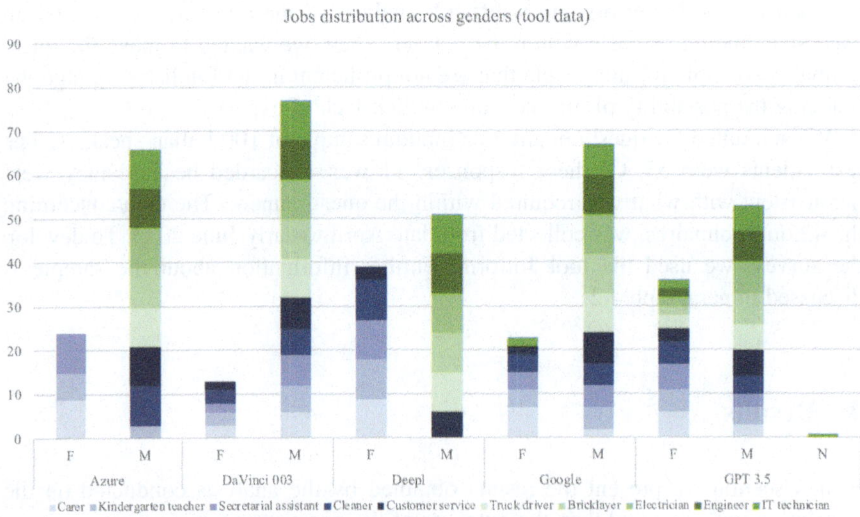

Fig. 2 Jobs distribution across genders (tools taken separately)

DeepL. This tool presents a few differences between the methods of translation. Taking into account the outcome obtained by translating all the text from an external document, there is a perfect distinction between the female group job (100% female translations vs 0% male translations) and the male group job (0% female translations vs 100% male translations). Considering the methods of translating the whole text at once and one sentence at a time, the results are consistent for the occupations held mostly by men (0% female translations vs 100% male translations). While for the female group job, there is a small component translated with the masculine form (80% female translations vs 20% male translations). Concerning the single occupations, we have a clear distinction for the jobs done mostly by women (carer, kindergarten teacher, secretarial assistant and cleaner, 100% female translations vs 0% male translations) and the jobs done mostly by men (truck driver, bricklayer, electrician, engineer and IT technician, (0% female translations vs 100% male translations). The only exception is represented by customer service (33% female translations vs 67% male translations).

Google Translate. This translator has substantial differences between the outcome obtained by translating all the text from an external document and the other two methods. By looking at the results of the first method, all the sentences are translated using the masculine form for both female group job (6% female translations vs 100% male translations) and male group job (0% female translations vs 100% male translations), the only exception is represented only by the first sentence (a simple phrase with the job carer). Concerning the other two methodologies, results indicate a degree of variation in translations related to works carried out by a female majority (66% female translations vs 33% male translations) and almost no variation regarding the male group job (6% female translations vs 94% male translations). Looking at the overall results of the three translation methods, there is almost an equality between masculine and feminine forms in the women's group of jobs (47% female translations vs 53% male translations), while in the male group, there is almost a total trend in translations using the masculine form (4% female translations vs 96% male translations). By analysing the single jobs, it can be noted a variation for all the occupations contained in the female group. Kindergarten teacher, secretarial assistant and cleaner are equal with 44% of translations using feminine forms and 56% using a masculine form. Also, carer (78% female translations vs 22% male translations) and customer service (22% female translations vs 78% male translations) are translated using different forms. Regarding the men group, the only job that has outcome translated with the feminine form is IT technician (22% female translations vs 78% male translations).

Text DaVinci-003. In the tool analysis, we have found consistency between the translation from an external document and the whole text at once. In particular, through these two methods, we obtained a one-way outcome, consisting of all sentences translated with the masculine form for both groups (0% female translations vs 100% male translations). Things change by translating the statements one by one only regarding the female group job (87% female translations vs 13% male translations). Overall, there is an overwhelming majority of the male form of translation, with the female counterpart only present in the third method of translation (14%

female translations vs 86% male translations). Concerning the single jobs there is a variation only regarding the female group. Carer, kindergarten teacher and cleaner are translated 33% of the time with a female form and 67% with a male form. While customer service and secretarial assistant sentences are translated using a feminine form (22%) and using a masculine form (78%).

GPT 3.5 Turbo. The last tool has a difference from the others as it is an LLM tool which the primary function is the generation of textual content and not only translation. Since it doesn't support the translation from an external document, we have opted instead for a continuous interaction (hit and run talk) where we submitted the sentences one by one without resetting the chat. Starting from the method just described results indicate the prevalence of feminine form for the translation of the sentences in both groups of jobs. Only the last sentences in the men group have been translated with a male form and the last one with a neutral form (73% female translations, 20% male translations, 7% neutral translations). Taking into consideration the method regarding the whole text translated at once, all the translations have been made using the male pronouns and adjectives (0% female translations vs 100% male translations). Finally, when the chat was reset for each sentence, we had as a result a small variation between male and female forms in the women group job (67% female translations vs 33% male translations) and a univocal translation concerning men group (0% female translations vs 100% male translations). By looking at the jobs, it could be noted that all the occupations present a variation (carer and secretarial assistant 67% female, 33% male, cleaner and kindergarten teacher 56% female, 44% male, customer service and truck driver 33% female, 67% male, bricklayer, electrician and engineer 22% female, 78% male and IT technician 22% female, 67% male and 11% neutral).

Overall results. After inspecting each tool, we decided to take into consideration the results in aggregated form. Results highlight a substantial difference between the female group job (54% female translations vs 46% male translations) and the male group job (6% female translations, 94% male translations, 0.4% neutral translations). Concerning the jobs (Fig. 3), all occupations related to the men's group are translated almost exclusively using male adjectives and pronouns (truck driver 7% female, 93% male, bricklayer, electrician and engineer 4% female, 96% male and IT technician 9% female, 89% male and 2% neutral). As regards jobs done mainly by women, there is much more variation (carer 76% female, 24% male, kindergarten teacher 60% female, 40% male, secretarial assistant 67% female, 33% male, cleaner 47% female, 53% male and customer service 22% female, 78% male).

4.2 Analysis of the Survey

On the basis of the demographic information gathered from the survey, 57% (24) of the respondents identify themselves as woman while 43% (18) as men. The majority of the respondents are between 26–35 years old (55%); the other group is represented by people whose age is between 18 and 25 (40%) and 55–65 (5%).

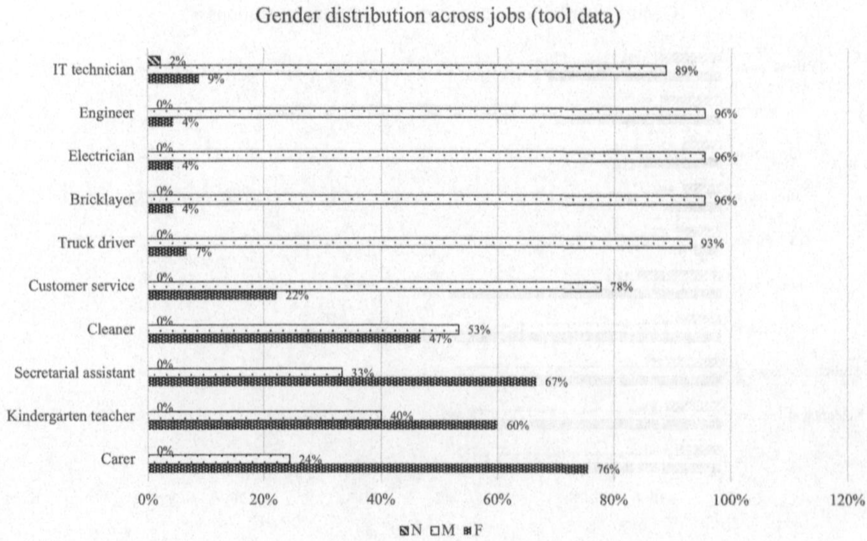

Fig. 3 Gender distribution across jobs taken singularly (tool aggregate data)

Regarding the Italian region of origin, most of the people who answered the questionnaire came from Lazio (26%) and Abruzzo (43%) (central part of the country). As for the educational background, almost all the respondents have a bachelor's or a master's degree (74%), other participants have a PhD (12%) and a high school diploma (12%), only one preferred not to say his background. Finally, 12% of the participants have a C2 knowledge of the English language, while the 31%, 29%, 23% and 5% have respectively C1, B2, B1 and A2 knowledge. Considering the data in aggregate form it can be distinguished a similar pattern to that observed for data collected from the tools (female group job: 55% female translations, 37% male translations, 8% neutral translations, male group job: 14% female translations, 79% male translations, 7% neutral translations). Concerning the single jobs there is also consistency between tool data and questionnaire data with slight differences regarding cleaner and engineer. Figure 4 display the results concerning the differences in translation between the selected jobs. We have more variation concerning the occupations held mostly by women (carer 62% female, 32% male, 6% neutral, kindergarten teacher 56% female, 36% male, 8% neutral, secretarial assistant 55% female, 38% male, 7% neutral, cleaner 65% female, 29% male, 6% neutral and customer service 39% female, 49% male, 12% neutral) than the men's group of jobs (truck driver 4% female, 90% male, 6% neutral, bricklayer 8% female, 87% male, 6% neutral, electrician 11% female, 83% male, 6% neutral, engineer 24% female, 67% male, 9% neutral and IT technician 25% female, 66% male and 10% neutral).

As the sample is still too small, we decided to compare only the answers of male and female respondents. There is no noticeable difference between the answers, although male individuals (female group job: 46% female translations, 47% male

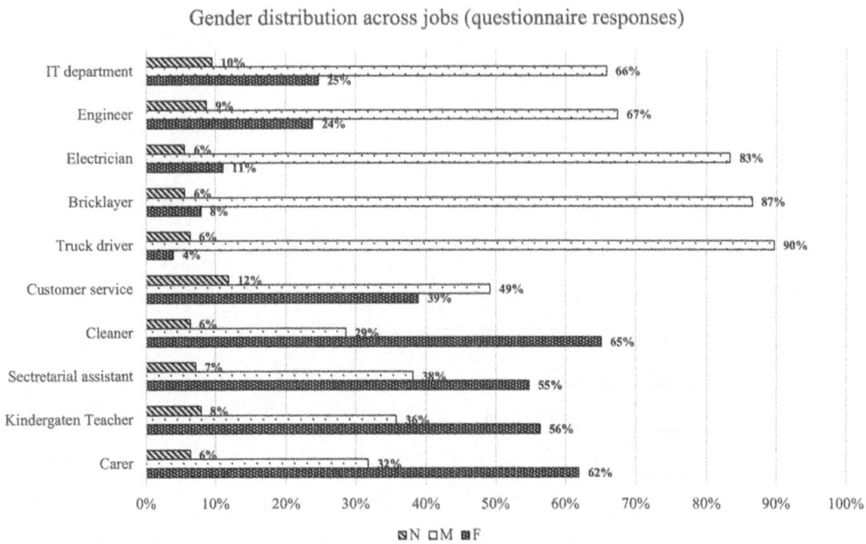

Fig. 4 Gender distribution across jobs taken singularly (questionnaire data)

translations, 8% neutral translations and male group job: 18% female translations, 74% male translations, 8% neutral translations) are less biased than female ones (female group job: 63% female translations, 29% male translations, 8% neutral translations and male group job: 12% female translations, 82% male translations, 6% neutral translations). Afterwards, taking into consideration the further question concerning the perceived object of this research, it was possible to see how much awareness of the nature of the analysis had an impact on the responses.

We divided the answers to the question by categorising them with "*unaware*" (16 participants) if there is no awareness from the respondent concerning the aim of the research, "*almost aware*" (7 participants) if there is partial awareness and "*aware*" (19 participants) if there is total awareness. Looking at the data (Fig. 5), the answers appear very similar regardless of the level of awareness the survey participant has. Respondents belonging to the category "*unaware*" (female group job: 44% female translations, 48% male translations, 8% neutral translations and male group job: 10% female translations, 83% male translations, 7% neutral translations) appear to be less biased on the female job group than respondents belonging to category "*almost aware*" (female group job: 57% female translations, 40% male translations, 3% neutral translations and male group job: 19% female translations, 78% male translations, 3% neutral translations) and "*aware*" (female group job: 62% female translations, 28% male translations, 10% neutral translations and male group job: 17% female translations, 74% male translations, 9% neutral translations), but more biased regarding the men's job group.

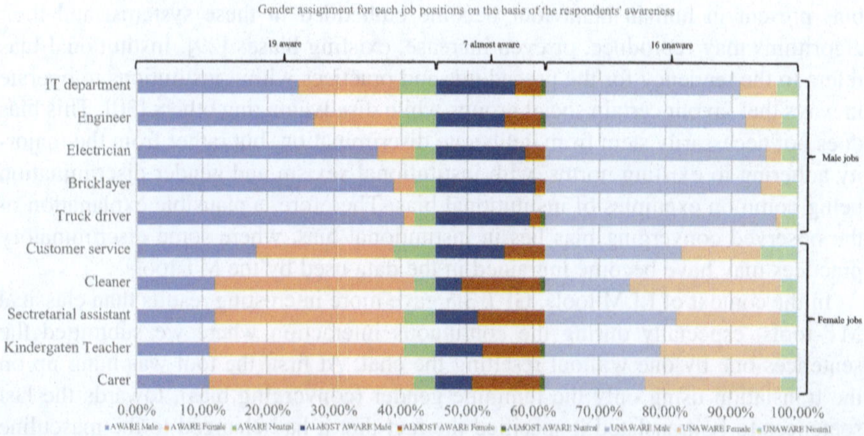

Fig. 5 Gender distribution across jobs, based on the respondent awareness of the research aim

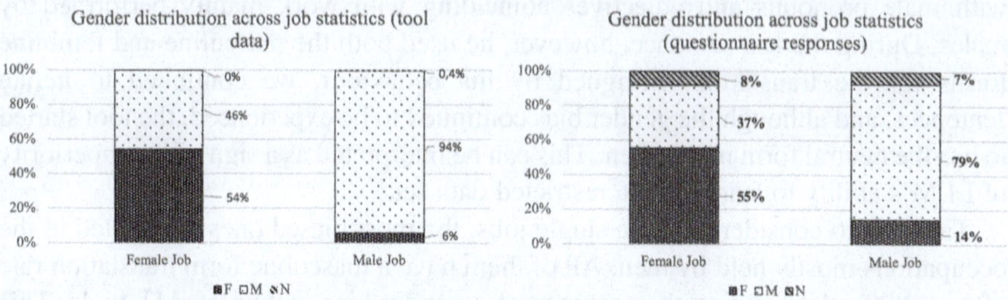

Fig. 6 Gender distribution across male and female group jobs (tools vs questionnaire)

5 Discussion

Based on the gathered data, our objective was to extract the necessary information to address our research questions. In examining the individual translation generated by the MT tools, we identified two primary biases. The first bias occurs mostly when the data is translated from an external document (DeepL, Google, DaVinci) or when the sentences are submitted all at once (DaVinci, GPT). We called this behaviour *converging bias* because the tool is influenced by the first translation output and remains consistent from the beginning until the end of the task. The second bias pertains to the inclination towards a specific gender when it becomes necessary to explicitly state the subject of a sentence during translation. In instances where the occupation is predominantly associated with women, there exists some diversity in the form (masculine or feminine) used for translation. However, concerning occupations predominantly associated with men, the outputs reveal a presence of significant gender bias, as depicted in Fig. 6.

Data used in AI, as it is the case of MT tools, is sourced from user-generated content or collected through other systems developed by humans. Consequently, any bias present in human behaviour become embedded in these systems, and their algorithms may reproduce, or even increase, existing biases [29]. Institutional bias refers to the tendency for the procedures and practices within institutions to operate in ways that favour certain social groups while disadvantaging others [30]. This bias does not necessarily stem from deliberate discrimination, but rather from the majority adhering to existing norms, with institutional sexism and gender discrimination being common examples of institutional bias. Therefore, a plausible explanation of the observed converging bias lies in institutional bias, where some discriminatory practices may have become ingrained in the data used by the MT tools.

In the context of LLM tools, GPT 3.5 gave more interesting results than classical MT tools, especially during the continuous interaction where we submitted the sentences one by one without resetting the chat. At first, the tool was hung up on the translation using only the feminine gender (converging bias), towards the last sentences to be translated it specified the fact that it had changed to the masculine pronoun as the gender of the worker was not specified in Italian. This behaviour represents a form of gender bias in the underlying data as the tool began to translate with male pronouns and adjectives coinciding with work mainly performed by males. During the last sentence, however, he used both the masculine and feminine forms for the translation. Intrigued by his behaviour, we continued to iterate sentences, and although the gender bias continued to be experienced, the tool started to use the neutral form more often. This can be interpreted as a sign of the superiority of LLM's ability to learn from a restricted data set.

Taking into consideration the single jobs, the most biased ones are related to the occupations mostly held by men. All of them have a masculine form translation rate of over 89%, determining the presence of a gender bias within the MT tools. This trend is not explainable by the converging bias, as the translation always began with the female job group. Regarding the occupations mostly detained by women, the most biased job seems to be the carer, followed by the secretarial assistant and the kindergarten teacher. The cleaner is the job that has almost gender equality among the translations, while customer service is biased more on the male side. Finally, IT technician is the only job that was translated using a neutral form (Fig. 3).

When comparing the results of the translation and the results of the questionnaire, no major differences emerge. Looking at Fig. 6, it is interesting to note that the ratio is similar between the two outcomes, although the results of the survey appear to be less biased, especially by looking at the fact that there are more neutral translations in which both male and female pronouns and adjectives are used. The same trend is noted by taking into account the single jobs. With the exception of cleaner, all the jobs appear to be less biased presenting a more equal distribution between genders. Truck driver, bricklayer and electrician, however, are still heavily biased.

Social constructionist theory posits that gender is a socially constructed concept shaped by cultural, societal, and historical factors [31], and may serve as a theoretical explanation for the similar results provided by the MT tools and the questionnaire. As mentioned before, bias in AI can arise when the training data used to develop AI systems reflects and perpetuates societal biases and stereotypes. Hence, if the training data contains gender imbalances or reinforces gender stereotypes, the AI system may learn and perpetuate those biases in its outputs.

After an aggregate analysis, we further inspected the data gathered from the survey. More specifically, we divided the responses according to gender and according to awareness about the research scope. From this analysis not emerged substantial differences, both in terms of gender difference and awareness of the purpose of the research (Fig. 5). However, the male respondents seem to be less biased with respect to the female respondents, while the participants that had no awareness about the aim of the study are less biased for what concerns the female job group.

Previous research has identified three approaches for bias mitigation [32]. Firstly, pre-processing methods concentrate on the data, with the aim of generating a "balanced" dataset that can be utilised by any learning algorithm. The underlying concept behind these approaches is that by ensuring fairness in the training data, the resulting model will exhibit reduced discrimination. Secondly, in-processing methods centre around the ML algorithm itself, where the classification problem is reformulated by explicitly incorporating the model's discriminatory behaviour into the objective function through regularization or constraints. Thirdly, post-processing methods focus on the ML model by either modifying its internal mechanisms (white-box approaches) or adjusting its predictions (black-box approaches).

6 Conclusion

This study aims to investigate gender bias within some of the most widely used neural machine translation and large language model tools. To conduct this research, we carefully selected a set of thirty Italian sentences related to ten specific gender-neutral occupations that can be expressed in both masculine and feminine forms. In our translations, we intentionally omitted the explicit mention of gender. These sentences were then translated from Italian to English using various AI tools. Additionally, we designed a survey to gather translations of the same sentences from human participants. The purpose of this survey was to compare the responses obtained from the AI tools with those provided by human translators.

The results reveal the existence of two distinct biases. The first one, called converging bias, describes the tendency of the translation tool to utilise the same form of translation for all occurrences in the dataset, based on the initial translation. The second bias, known as gender bias, signifies a preference for a specific translation form (either male or female) over the other. In our dataset, gender bias is highly associated with occupations held mostly by men, while jobs which are statistically done by a female majority have more variation. We also determined the more biased jobs according to the group selected and investigated the discrepancies arising from different input modalities (full text, external document, one sentence at a time). Lastly, the results of the survey are consistent with the outcomes obtained from the translations of the tools. Notably, there is no significant difference in the outcomes based on the gender of the respondents or their awareness of the research objectives. This research serves as an initial exploration into the presence of gender-related biases within AI translation tools.

In the research, the observed gender bias could have different implications in society. For example, bias could reinforce the behaviour already embedded in the people by perpetuating the stereotypes about jobs and societal roles. Moreover, such issues could under-represent a determined gender leading to translation and non-recognition problems (women or men are not taken into consideration in determined translation concerning a specific job, for example). Under-representation issues in a specific tool could also affect gender representation across different cultures [22].

This paper has both theoretical and practical contributions. From a theoretical point of view, we contributed to the literature concerning AI bias derived from the data used to train the models by inspecting the occurrence of bias inside translations made by AI tools. Specifically, we described and implemented a method to assess the presence of gender bias inside MT and LLM tools and compare their performances with human behaviour and tendencies. We focused on translating sentences from a language that allows the omission of the subject in sentences to a language that requires the subject to be made explicit. To this end, we adapted the framework given by Srivastava et al., [23] to better represent the process of developing and translating the dataset occurrences and assessing the presence of bias. We discovered the presence of a converging bias in which the outcome is influenced by previous translations. Overall, our research methodology could be used to obtain preliminary insights into the phenomena under investigation.

From a practical point of view, this article can assist developers and designers to better identify the presence of gender bias inside translation tools. While the presence of gender bias within these tools has been discussed both in scientific literature and press articles [18], there is still considerable work to be done to address this issue and enhance the fairness of these AI tools. There is also the need to establish standardised and unbiased ways to measure and identify such biases inside MT tools to rigorously evaluate their outcome and give suggestions on which issues should be addressed. Moreover, as highlighted by Tomalin et al. [19], it is not always necessary to address the bias in the underlying data before the training of the algorithm, as this may lead to a worse outcome in certain cases. Our results indicate that these kinds of bias are embedded inside the society and are subsequently transferred to AI tools. For this reason, it is crucial to address societal behaviour by raising awareness among individuals regarding these issues. In this scenario, governments, firms, and policymakers should play a central role in nudging people to give more attention to these aspects and, hence, in changing their behaviour. Additionally, it would be interesting to further explore how to evaluate a biased behaviour, particularly in the context of determining the right translation for each sentence.

The study also presents some limitations. First, the dataset used in this research comprise only ten jobs and thirty sentences. Future studies could increase the dataset in order to explore gender bias across a broader range of occupations and also assess the presence of gender bias in more complex sentence structures. Moreover, concerning the usage of AI online tools, it would be interesting to investigate if the geographical location from which the translation request is performed (e.g., using a VPN connection) could affect the final outcome. Culture traits characterizing a specific geographical zone could influence the results as well as the iterative nature of translation requests. Additionally, the current study focused solely on Italian to English translations. Future studies could use more languages that allow subject omission in the construction, such as Spanish or Persian. Finally, concerning the survey, the sample used could be improved by increasing the number and demographic variety of the respondents in order to have more meaningful insights from the collected data.

References

1. Smacchia, M., & Za, S. (2022). Artificial intelligence in organisation and managerial studies: A computational literature review. In *ICIS 2022 Proceedings* (Vol. 6, pp. 0–17).
2. Khurana, D., Koli, A., Khatter, K., & Singh, S. (2023). Natural language processing: State of the art, current trends and challenges. *Multimedia Tools and Applications, 82*, 3713–3744. https://doi.org/10.1007/s11042-022-13428-4
3. Young, T., Hazarika, D., Poria, S., & Cambria, E. (2017). Recent trends in deep learning based natural language processing. *IEEE Computational Intelligence Magazine, 13*, 55–75.
4. Chowdhery, A., Narang, S., Devlin, J., Bosma, M., Mishra, G., Roberts, A., Barham, P., Chung, H. W., Sutton, C., Gehrmann, S., Schuh, P., Shi, K., Tsvyashchenko, S., Maynez, J., Rao, A., Barnes, P., Tay, Y., Shazeer, N., Prabhakaran, V., et al. (2022). PaLM: Scaling Language Modeling with Pathways. *Journal of Machine Learning Research, 24*(240), 1–113.
5. Qin, C., Zhang, A., Zhang, Z., Chen, J., Yasunaga, M., & Yang, D. (2023). Is ChatGPT a general-purpose natural language processing task solver? arXiv preprint arXiv:2302.06476.
6. Stahlberg, F. (2020). Neural machine translation: A review. *Journal of Artificial Intelligence Research, 69*, 343–418.
7. Tan, Z., Wang, S., Yang, Z., Chen, G., Huang, X., Sun, M., & Liu, Y. (2020). Neural machine translation: A review of methods, resources, and tools. *AI Open, 1*, 5–21. https://doi.org/10.1016/j.aiopen.2020.11.001
8. Vieira, L. N., O'Hagan, M., & O'Sullivan, C. (2021). Understanding the societal impacts of machine translation: a critical review of the literature on medical and legal use cases. *Information, Communication & Society, 24*(11), 1515–1532. https://doi.org/10.1080/1369118X.2020.1776370
9. Castilho, S., Moorkens, J., Gaspari, F., Calixto, I., Tinsley, J., & Way, A. (2017). Is neural machine translation the new state of the art? *The Prague Bulletin of Mathematical Linguistics, 108*, 109–120. https://doi.org/10.1515/pralin-2017-0013
10. Doherty, S. (2016). The impact of translation technologies on the process and product of translation. *International Journal of Communication, 10*, 23.
11. Smacchia, M., & Za, S. (2023). Exploring artificial intelligence bias, fairness and ethics in organisation and managerial studies. In *ECIS 2023 research papers* (p. 362).
12. van Giffen, B., Herhausen, D., & Fahse, T. (2022). Overcoming the pitfalls and perils of algorithms: A classification of machine learning biases and mitigation methods. *Journal of Business Research, 144*, 93–106. https://doi.org/10.1016/j.jbusres.2022.01.076

13. Zuiderwijk, A., Chen, Y. C., & Salem, F. (2021). Implications of the use of artificial intelligence in public governance: A systematic literature review and a research agenda. *Government Information Quarterly, 38*, 101577. https://doi.org/10.1016/j.giq.2021.101577
14. Hoffmann, A. L. (2019). Where fairness fails: Data, algorithms, and the limits of antidiscrimination discourse. *Information, Communication & Society, 22*, 900–915. https://doi.org/10.1080/1369118X.2019.1573912
15. Mehrabi, N., Morstatter, F., Saxena, N., Lerman, K., & Galstyan, A. (2021). A survey on bias and fairness in machine learning. *ACM Computing Surveys, 54*, 1–35. https://doi.org/10.1145/3457607
16. O'Neil, C. (2016). *Weapons of math destruction: How big data increases inequality and threatens democracy*. Broadway Books.
17. Sun, T., Gaut, A., Tang, S., Huang, Y., Elsherief, M., Zhao, J., Mirza, D., Belding, E., Chang, K.-W., & Wang, W. Y. (2020). Mitigating gender bias in natural language processing: Literature review. In *ACL 2019-57th Annual Meeting of the Association for Computational Linguistics, Proceedings of the Conference* (pp. 1630–1640).
18. Stanovsky, G., Smith, N. A., & Zettlemoyer, L. (2019). Evaluating gender bias in machine translation. In *Proceedings of the 57th Annual Meeting of the Association for Computational Linguistics* (pp. 1679–1684).
19. Tomalin, M., Byrne, B., Concannon, S., Saunders, D., & Ullmann, S. (2021). The practical ethics of bias reduction in machine translation: Why domain adaptation is better than data debiasing. *Ethics and Information Technology, 23*, 419–433. https://doi.org/10.1007/s10676-021-09583-1
20. Bernagozzi, M., Srivastava, B., Rossi, F., & Usmani, S. (2021). Gender bias in online language translators: Visualization, human perception, and bias/accuracy tradeoffs. *IEEE Internet Computing, 25*, 53–63. https://doi.org/10.1109/MIC.2021.3097604
21. Kelley, S., Ovchinnikov, A., Hardoon, D. R., & Heinrich, A. (2022). Antidiscrimination Laws, artificial intelligence, and gender bias: A case study in nonmortgage Fintech lending. *Manufacturing and Service Operations Management, 24*, 3039–3059. https://doi.org/10.1287/msom.2022.1108
22. Savoldi, B., Gaido, M., Bentivogli, L., Negri, M., & Turchi, M. (2021). Gender bias in machine translation. *Transactions of the Association for Computational Linguistics, 9*, 845–874. https://doi.org/10.1162/tacl
23. Srivastava, B., & Rossi, F. (2018). Towards composable bias rating of AI services. In *AIES 2018- Proceedings of the 2018 AAAI/ACM Conference on AI, Ethics, and Society* (pp. 284–289). Association for Computing Machinery, Inc. https://doi.org/10.1145/3278721.3278744
24. Schiebinger, L. (2014). Scientific research must take gender into account. *Nature, 507*, 9–9. https://doi.org/10.1038/507009a
25. Liben, L. S., Bigler, R. S., & Krogh, H. R. (2002). Language at work: Children's gendered interpretations of occupational titles. *Child Development, 73*, 810–828. https://doi.org/10.1111/1467-8624.00440
26. Bigler, R. S., & Leaper, C. (2015). Gendered language: Psychological principles, evolving practices, and inclusive policies. *Policy Insights From the Behavioral and Brain Sciences, 2*, 187–194. https://doi.org/10.1177/2372732215600452
27. Makri, C., & Neely, A. (2021). Grounded theory: A guide for exploratory studies in management research. *International Journal of Qualitative Methods, 20*, 16094069211013654. https://doi.org/10.1177/16094069211013654
28. King, M. R. (2023). A conversation on artificial intelligence, chatbots, and plagiarism in higher education. *Cellular and Molecular Bioengineering, 16*(1), 1–2. https://doi.org/10.1007/s12195-022-00754-8
29. Karimi, F., Génois, M., Wagner, C., Singer, P., & Strohmaier, M. (2018). Homophily influences ranking of minorities in social networks. *Scientific Reports, 8*, 11077. https://doi.org/10.1038/s41598-018-29405-7

30. Henry, P. J. (2010). Institutional bias. In *The Sage handbook of prejudice, stereotyping and discrimination* (pp. 426–440). SAGE Publications.
31. Brickell, C. (2006). The sociological construction of gender and sexuality. *The Sociological Review, 54*, 87–113.
32. Ntoutsi, E., Fafalios, P., Gadiraju, U., Iosifidis, V., Nejdl, W., Vidal, M. E., Ruggieri, S., Turini, F., Papadopoulos, S., Krasanakis, E., Kompatsiaris, I., Kinder-Kurlanda, K., Wagner, C., Karimi, F., Fernandez, M., Alani, H., Berendt, B., Kruegel, T., Heinze, C., Broelemann, K., Kasneci, G., Tiropanis, T., & Staab, S. (2020). Bias in data-driven artificial intelligence systems—An introductory survey. *Wiley Interdisciplinary Reviews: Data Mining and Knowledge Discovery, 10*, 1–14. https://doi.org/10.1002/widm.1356

A Systems Integration view on Data Ecosystems

Federica Ceci and Andrew Davies

Abstract Ecosystems comprise complex webs of affiliated entities, characterized by multilateral connections that transcend bilateral relationships, encompassing dependencies across dimensions. Participants in ecosystems are interconnected through resource dependencies and product/service offerings, fostering collaboration, innovation, and knowledge generation. A crucial aspect of digital ecosystems is the continuous data interaction and exchange. Collaboration among actors in these networks drives innovation, value creation, and new business establishment by discovering, storing, publishing, consuming, and reusing data. Technology plays a pivotal role in ecosystem formation, as digital data proliferation and advancements reinforce their significance beyond administrative support. Data have become pervasive resources for knowledge acquisition and action in response to challenges. In the current landscape of data ecosystems, integrating technologies, processes, and data presents increasingly complex challenges. Examining this phenomenon through the systems integration literature offers valuable insights for managing interdependencies and complexities within data ecosystems.

Keywords Data ecosystems · Systems integration

1 Introduction

The diffusion of digital technologies has significantly reshaped the way firms operate, blurring the boundaries between internal and external elements. This phenomenon has been extensively explored in the ecosystem literature, which delves into the intricate networks of interconnected organizations [1–7]. Ecosystems are

F. Ceci (✉)
Department of Business Administration, University G.d'Annunzio, Chieti-Pescara, Italy
e-mail: f.ceci@unich.it

A. Davies
Science Policy Research Unit, University of Sussex Business School, Brighton, UK
e-mail: Andrew.Davies@sussex.ac.uk

A. M. Braccini et al. (eds.), *Digital (Eco) Systems and Societal Challenges*, Lecture Notes in Information Systems and Organisation 72,
https://doi.org/10.1007/978-3-031-75586-6_20

complex webs of affiliated entities characterized by multilateral connections that extend beyond bilateral relationships, encompassing dependencies across various dimensions. While ecosystems generally lack hierarchical management structures, there has been a lack of extensive research on the regulations that govern membership and relationships within them. Participants in ecosystems are interconnected through dependencies on resources and product/service offerings, which provide unique benefits and promote collaboration, resulting in innovation and the generation of knowledge.

One crucial aspect of digital ecosystem is the continuous interaction and exchange of data. The interconnectedness of actors within an ecosystem provides a competitive advantage that can shape the dominance of a particular ecosystem design, thereby influencing the future trajectory of the market. In such networks, actors collaborate to discover, store, publish, consume, and reuse data, driving innovation, value creation, and the establishment of new businesses. To gain a comprehensive understanding of ecosystems, it is essential to contemplate how technology plays a role in their formation. With the proliferation of digital data and advancements in data technologies, their traditional roles as tools for administrative support and organizational rationalization are reinforced. In various domains, data are no longer secondary components but have become pervasive resources and mediums through which organizations gain knowledge and take action in response to the challenges they face.

Therefore, in the current landscape of data ecosystems, actors face increasingly complex challenges. The integration of technologies, processes, and data has become more demanding than ever before. To better comprehend this intricate phenomenon, we propose examining it through the lens of systems integration literature. Systems integration, a field that has traditionally dealt with coordinating and integrating complex systems, offers valuable insights into managing the interdependencies and complexities inherent in data ecosystems. By leveraging the knowledge and understanding gained from systems integration literature, we can navigate the intricacies of integrating technologies, processes, and data within data ecosystems, enabling us to address the challenges effectively and achieve successful outcomes.

The paper is structured as follows: Section 2 provides a comprehensive review of the existing literature on data ecosystems, exploring their key characteristics and dynamics. In Sect. 3, we delve into the concept of systems integration and its relevance in the context of data ecosystems, drawing insights from established literature in the field. Section 4 introduces our research strategy, presenting an overview of the Gaia X project as a case study to examine the complexities of systems integration within data ecosystems. Building upon this foundation, Sect. 5 identifies and analyzes the challenges associated with systems integration in the context of data ecosystems, offering valuable insights for practitioners and researchers. Finally, in the discussion and conclusion section, we synthesize the key findings, highlight their implications, and suggest potential avenues for future research, contributing to a deeper understanding of the intricacies and opportunities within data ecosystems.

2 Literature Review on Data Ecosystems

The diffusion of connectivity services and software enables firms to restructure their environment, blurring the boundaries between internal and external elements. This phenomenon has been extensively examined within the ecosystem literature, exploring the intricate networks of interconnected organizations [1, 3, 4, 8–10]. Ecosystems are complex webs of affiliated entities, characterized by multilateral connections that extend beyond bilateral relationships and involve dependencies across various dimensions [11]. While ecosystems are typically not hierarchically managed, there has been limited research on the rules governing membership and relationships [12]. Participants within ecosystems are linked by resource and product/service dependencies that confer distinct advantages, fostering innovation and knowledge creation through active collaboration [13].

The continuous interaction and exchange of data within an ecosystem provide a competitive advantage that can shape the dominance of a particular ecosystem design, influencing the future trajectory of the market [14]. In complex networks, actors collaborate to discover, store, publish, consume, and reuse data, driving innovation, value creation, and the establishment of new businesses (Oliveira et al., [15]). To facilitate the interconnection of actors through data exchange, ecosystems develop various roles with different functions [16]. A notable role is the "keystone" actor, often embodied by a firm that successfully leverages innovative developments and shapes the market design [5]. The emergence of a dominant design is a crucial phase that significantly influences firms' strategies and performance, emphasizing the importance of shaping the technological trajectory to outperform competitors [17, 18]. Co-evolution, characterized by simultaneous cooperative and competitive relationships (also known as coopetition), is a shared characteristic among ecosystem concepts [11, 19].

To gain a comprehensive understanding of ecosystems, it is essential to contemplate how technology plays a role in their formation. This involves examining various elements such as data management systems, modular architectures, application programming interfaces (APIs), and boundary technologies that facilitate the exchange of data, services, data links, and data-based services among different organizations. In the realm of data ecosystems, the evolution of the digital economy in conjunction with data has driven the advancement and development of business concepts [20].

When examining digital ecosystems, it is crucial to explore and conceptualize the pivotal role of data as the primary element that organizes the entire ecosystem [21, 22]. Given that all actors within the ecosystem generate vast amounts of data continuously, it is crucial to capture and analyze this data from multiple perspectives. Integrating data derived from modern technologies with existing lower-grade technology services presents an effective approach to achieve digital transformation and foster sustainable societies [20, 23]. Actors within the ecosystem, based on their respective roles, contribute diverse forms of data and business analytics as valuable resources that can be transformed into assets. These assets serve to connect firms with users, promote collaboration, and facilitate the co-creation of value [24].

The concept of "data as a natural resource" represents a commitment to establishing a system that promotes accountability, trust, transparency, enforcement, and sustainability in a world where data is increasingly valuable and traded across generations [25]. With the proliferation of digital data and advancements in data technologies, their traditional roles as tools for administrative support and organizational rationalization are reinforced. In various domains, data are no longer secondary components but have become pervasive resources and mediums through which organizations gain knowledge and take action in response to the challenges they face [26].

Therefore, in the current landscape of data ecosystems, actors face increasingly complex challenges. The integration of technologies, processes, and data has become more demanding than ever before. To better comprehend this intricate phenomenon, we propose examining it through the lens of systems integration literature. Systems integration, a field that has traditionally dealt with coordinating and integrating complex systems, offers valuable insights into managing the interdependencies and complexities inherent in data ecosystems. By leveraging the knowledge and understanding gained from systems integration literature, we can navigate the intricacies of integrating technologies, processes, and data within data ecosystems, enabling us to address the challenges effectively and achieve successful outcomes.

3 Systems Integration in the Data Ecosystem Domain

The concept of systems integration emerged during the 1950s and 1960s to facilitate the coordination of complex systems design and integration in the aerospace and defense industry. It quickly became a fundamental aspect of the newly established field of systems engineering [27–29]. Since then, complex systems have relied on systems integrators to define the overall design, component parts, and interfaces of a system. This includes coordinating a network of component and subsystem suppliers throughout various phases, such as design, production, integration, commissioning, and handover to operations [30–33]. While early literature explored systems integration as a novel form of organization and process for managing large system-based projects like the Polaris ballistic missile and Apollo moon landing programs, it was not until the 1990s that scholars in management and innovation studies recognized its crucial role in the management of large technology projects ([28]), complex products and systems ([30, 34]; [32, 33]) and implantation of IT architecture [31, 35, 36].

Systems integration revolves around the effective coordination of resources, such as technologies, components, software, and knowledge. It encompasses technical, strategic, and organizational capabilities and holds significant importance, particularly in high-tech firms, as a core strategic concept [32, 37, 38]. The capability of systems integration involves managing outsourcing, joint sourcing, and insourcing to leverage the advantages of both outsourcing and vertical integration throughout various phases of the product life cycle [33, 38]. Systems integration exhibits "two faces"[32]. The first face involves the development and integration of inputs within an organization to create a new product. The second face encompasses the activities required to integrate components from external firms, including suppliers, partners, start-ups, and even competitors, collaborating to produce innovative solutions. This external network expands the capabilities and range of components that can be combined to deliver value to customers [39–41]. A systems integrator is the pioneering organization responsible for designing and integrating modular products, services, or components to realize a system that can be brought to the market. It stands in contrast to vertically integrated companies that produce and sell all products and services internally [36, 42, 43].

Therefore, we see how systems integration goes beyond being a mere technical skill; it is a core strategic capability that enables firms to determine their position within the industry, identify competitors, select partners, and pursue vertical integration up and downstream [32, 44, 45]. It is closely linked to decisions regarding in-house production, outsourcing, and collaboration in both production and competition [36, 46, 47]. The challenge of effective system integration lies in successfully composing the various parts within the value network to create innovative solutions. System integrators must possess the knowledge to manage open or networked innovation. As technologies and competencies become increasingly complex, firms need access to new knowledge, resources, and innovation networks. In line with this reasoning, the diffusion and adoption of the digital ecosystem paradigm have led to a shift from competition to collaboration among actors in digital fields.

The networked nature of data ecosystems gives a paramount role to systems integration, where it involves the process of combining different components, subsystems, software applications and knowledge into a cohesive and unified system. The goal of systems integration in information systems is to enable seamless communication, data exchange, and interoperability between various elements within an IT infrastructure. In information systems, the complexity of integrating diverse technologies, applications, and data sources can be substantial. And each different technologies, applications, and data sources requires a different body of knowledge the must be managed to successfully achieve the integration.

From a technical viewpoint, different actors in ecosystems often rely on multiple software systems, databases, and platforms that may operate independently and use different data formats or protocols. Systems integration helps overcome these challenges by establishing connections and enabling data flow between these disparate systems. For instance, one area where systems integration is particularly critical in information systems is enterprise resource planning (ERP). ERP systems consolidate various business functions, like finance, HR, supply chain management, and CRM, into a unified system. This integration streamlines processes, improves data accuracy, and enhances decision-making [31, 48]. Systems integration is also vital in cloud computing and hybrid IT environments, where cloud-based services need to integrate with on-premises systems and legacy applications. It ensures seamless integration, data consistency, security, and efficient operations [49]. Data integration from multiple sources is another aspect of systems integration. Organizations gather data from internal and external sources, including customer databases, IoT devices, social media, and third-party systems. Integrating these diverse data sources provides a comprehensive view, supports data-driven decisions, and extracts valuable insights [50].

Also, in not-technical domain data ecosystems present significant challenges when it comes to systems integration. Ecosystems involve a multitude of interconnected parts that need to be coordinated, aligned, and seamlessly integrated with each other. This process involves bringing together diverse knowledge and components, which can be both tangible and intangible in nature [33]. Systems integration encompasses the collaborative efforts undertaken across organizational boundaries in interorganizational projects to effectively integrate the systems delivered by these projects.

Building upon the work by Whyte and Davies [51], we are proposing an overview of the following 4 approaches to systems integration in complex interorganizational projects, applying those concepts to the specificities represented in the data ecosystems domain:

3.1 Systems Integration as a Phase

System integration is often viewed as a project phase that occurs in the later stages, encompassing testing, verification, and validation. This process follows an iterative approach, where decomposition and integration occur at various levels. In the domain of data ecosystems, system integration can be seen in the phase of the development of a data analytics platform. After the platform has undergone decomposition into different components and functionalities, system integration becomes a project phase in the later stages. This involves testing, verification, and validation of the integrated platform, following an iterative approach to ensure its effectiveness and reliability.

3.2 Systems Integration as a Cross-Cutting Specialist Engineering Function

In the realm of software and control systems, which can exhibit significant cyber-physical complexity spanning multiple subprojects, system integration is sometimes narrowly focused. This narrower perspective involves extensive testing and commissioning to ensure seamless integration. Within data ecosystems, system integration can focus on the integration of various data sources and processing systems. For example, in a smart city project, system integration may involve the integration of sensors, data collection platforms, and analytics systems across multiple subprojects. Extensive testing and commissioning are necessary to ensure the seamless flow and processing of data, considering the cyber-physical complexities involved.

3.3 Systems Integration as a Project-level Technical Process

The technical aspect of systems integration necessitates a multidisciplinary approach, leveraging diverse technological capabilities. It revolves around systems architectures and entails collaborating with the supply chain upstream to manage technical coordination and changes at the component, subsystem, and system levels [32, 52]. This responsibility may be assigned to a single entity, known as the systems integrator, or it can be a distributed activity. In the context of data ecosystems, systems integration requires a multidisciplinary approach to handle diverse technological capabilities. For instance, in the development of a data marketplace, integration activities may involve collaborating with data providers, data consumers, and technology partners. This collaboration ensures technical coordination and accommodates changes at different levels, such as integrating data sources, defining data formats, and establishing secure data exchange mechanisms.

3.4 Systems Integration as a Program-Wide Strategic Function

Systems integration, also referred to as metasystems integration [34], involves making decisions regarding the division of labor, project governance, and coordination with project sponsors, operators, and users. It requires active engagement with operators and users to seamlessly integrate project deliverables into existing operating systems. Systems integration in data ecosystems includes decision-making regarding the division of labor, data governance, and coordination with various stakeholders. For instance, in the implementation of a data sharing platform for healthcare, system integration involves engaging with healthcare providers, patients, and regulatory bodies. This engagement ensures the seamless integration of data sharing capabilities into existing healthcare systems, respecting privacy regulations and meeting the needs of different stakeholders.

4 Research Strategy

4.1 Overview of the Empirical Context, the GaiaX Project

GAIA-X is a European project aimed at creating a federated and secure data infrastructure for Europe. It is an initiative driven by various organizations, including governments, businesses, and research institutions, with the goal of establishing a trustworthy and sovereign data ecosystem.

It represents a unique research context due to the variety of stakeholders involved: it comprises more than 340 members composed by startups as well as well-established corporations, operating in a variety of industrial contexts and in more than 20 countries. Further information provided in Table 1.

The Gaia-X organizational structure is composed by three bodies: the Gaia-X Association, the national Gaia-X Hubs and the Gaia-X Community. The Gaia-X Association develop regulatory frameworks, ensure that necessary services are made available, consolidate, and facilitate the work and collaboration within the Gaia-X community, represent the members of Gaia-X and promote international cooperation; Gaia-X Hubs develop ecosystems, bundle national initiatives, and provide a central contact point to interested parties in their respective countries. The network of Gaia-X Hubs supports the growth of a dynamic ecosystem from a bottom-up approach, from a national level to a European and international level. Finally, Gaia-X support an open-source software community. As stated by the website, the main decision makers are the members that can participate in the working group and provides ideas and contribute to decisions that are then ratified by the board of directors.

The project's primary objective is to address the current challenges related to data sovereignty, data availability, and data sharing. It aims to provide a framework that enables secure data sharing and interoperability across different industries and sectors while maintaining data protection and privacy. GAIA-X promotes the development of a federated data infrastructure based on common rules and standards. It focuses on the concept of "data spaces," which are virtual environments where data providers and users can exchange and collaborate on data in a trusted manner. These data spaces are designed to facilitate data sharing while respecting data ownership and control.

Table 1 Overview of the GaiaX network

Industries involved	Aerospace, Agriculture, Tourism, Education, Energy, Finance, Geoinformation, Health, Manufacturing, Media, Mobility, Public Sector, Smart Cities, Smart Living, Construction and Logistics
National hubs (Countries involved)	Austria, Belgium, California, Finland, France, Germany, Greece, Hungary, Italy, Japan, Luxembourg, Netherlands, Poland, Portugal, Romania, Slovakia, Slovenia, South Korea, Spain, Texas, Washington DC

At the moment of the data collection (June 2023), Gaia-X featured ten lighthouse projects.

5 Data Collection and Methodological Approach

This study employed a qualitative research approach to gain insights into the phenomenon under investigation. Specifically, data were collected from public documents, such as reports, articles, podcast and publications, which were readily accessible to the general public. This ensured transparency and openness in the data collection process. The research followed an inductive approach, allowing for the emergence of themes and patterns from the collected data. This approach is particularly suitable for exploring new areas, as it enables researchers to develop theoretical frameworks and concepts based on the observed data [53–56].

5.1 Identification of the Challenges of Systems Integration in Data Ecosystems

Systems integration in data ecosystems presents several challenges that organizations must navigate to ensure successful integration. The analysis of the data regarding the GAIA-X project lead to the identification of the following challenges:

a. *Heterogeneity of Data System*

Data ecosystems typically consist of diverse data systems with varying formats, structures, and technologies. Integrating these disparate systems to enable seamless data exchange and interoperability can be challenging. For example, GAIA-X aims to integrate data across different sectors and industries, such as healthcare, manufacturing, and finance, which have their own specific data systems and standards. Harmonizing and aligning these systems to facilitate smooth integration poses a significant challenge.

b. *Data Governance and Privacy.*

Data ecosystems involve the sharing and exchange of sensitive information among multiple stakeholders. Ensuring data governance, privacy, and compliance with regulations like GDPR (General Data Protection Regulation) becomes crucial. GAIA-X addresses this challenge by establishing a trusted framework that enables secure and privacy-preserving data sharing and processing while complying with legal and regulatory requirements. This involves implementing robust data protection mechanisms and standardized data governance practices across the ecosystem.

c. *Data Scalability and Interoperability.*

Data ecosystems often need to handle large volumes of data generated by multiple sources. Achieving scalability and ensuring interoperability among different data systems are critical challenges. GAIA-X aims to address this challenge by establishing a federated data infrastructure that enables scalable data processing and seamless integration across various cloud and edge computing environments.

d. *Data Quality and Consistency.*

Integrating data from diverse sources may introduce challenges related to data quality and consistency. Data may have inconsistencies, errors, or lack standardization, making it difficult to integrate and derive meaningful insights. GAIA-X tackles this challenge by promoting data quality frameworks and standards that encourage data providers to maintain high-quality data and ensure consistency across the ecosystem.

e. *Collaboration and Governance Models.*

Establishing effective collaboration and governance models among ecosystem participants is essential for successful systems integration. In GAIA-X, various stakeholders, including data providers, data consumers, and service providers, need to collaborate and agree on common standards, protocols, and governance mechanisms. Developing a shared understanding of roles, responsibilities, and decision-making processes is crucial to address the challenges of collaboration and governance.

f. *Complex Data Transformation.*

Integrating data from various sources often involves complex data transformation processes. Data may need to be standardized, cleansed, or transformed to ensure compatibility and consistency. In the GAIA-X project, organizations face the challenge of transforming data from different domains, such as healthcare records or manufacturing sensor data, into a unified format that can be effectively integrated and analyzed.

g. *Legacy System Integration.*

Many organizations have legacy systems that were developed using outdated technologies or have custom-built components. Integrating these legacy systems with modern data ecosystems can be challenging due to differences in data structures, protocols, or compatibility issues. In the GAIA-X project, organizations face the task of integrating existing legacy systems with the new data ecosystem, requiring careful planning and implementation strategies.

h. *Change Management and Organizational Culture.*

Systems integration in data ecosystems often requires significant changes in processes, workflows, and organizational culture. Organizations may need to adapt their internal practices, roles, and responsibilities to align with the collaborative nature of data ecosystems. GAIA-X emphasizes the need for change management strategies that facilitate smooth organizational transitions and promote a culture of data sharing and collaboration.

i. *Security and Trust.*

Data ecosystems involve sharing and exchanging sensitive information, raising concerns about data security and trust. Organizations must establish robust security measures to protect data throughout the integration process and ensure that all participants adhere to data privacy and security regulations. GAIA-X addresses this challenge by emphasizing security and trust as core principles, promoting secure data sharing and access controls within the ecosystem.

j. *Scalable Infrastructure.*

As data ecosystems grow and evolve, scalability becomes a critical challenge. Organizations must ensure that the underlying infrastructure can handle the increasing volume, velocity, and variety of data. GAIA-X focuses on building a scalable infrastructure that can accommodate the growing demands of data integration, storage, and processing across multiple cloud and edge computing environments.

6 Bridging Challenges and Approaches

Table 2 provides an overview of different approaches to systems integration and the associated challenges. In the first approach, systems integration is considered as a phase within a project, with challenges related to data governance and privacy, as well as ensuring data quality and consistency. It typically occurs in the later stages and involves testing, verification, and validation. The focus is on ensuring the smooth integration of different systems and components. These challenges highlight the importance of establishing robust data management practices and ensuring the integrity and compliance of data throughout the integration process.

Table 2 Overview of different approaches to systems integration and the associated challenges

Approach	Challenges
Systems integration as a phase	Data Governance and Privacy Data Quality and Consistency.
Systems integration as a cross-cutting specialist engineering function	Heterogeneity of Data System Data Scalability and Interoperability Complex Data Transformation Legacy System Integration.
Systems integration as a project-level technical process	Collaboration and Governance Models Scalable Infrastructure. Security and Trust.
Systems integration as a program-wide strategic function	Change Management and Organizational Culture.

The second approach views systems integration as a cross-cutting specialist engineering function, involving challenges such as dealing with heterogeneous data systems, ensuring data scalability and interoperability, managing complex data transformations, and integrating legacy systems. These challenges emphasize the need for managing data heterogeneity, scalability, interoperability, and complex transformations to enable effective integration across different systems. The focus is on leveraging specialized expertise and tools to handle the technical complexities involved in integrating diverse data systems effectively.

The third approach sees systems integration as a project-level technical process, with challenges in terms of establishing effective collaboration and governance models, building scalable infrastructure, and ensuring security and trust. It involves coordinating and managing the integration efforts across different systems, subsystems, and components. These challenges highlight the importance of establishing effective collaboration mechanisms, building scalable infrastructure, and implementing robust security measures throughout the integration project.

Lastly, systems integration as a program-wide strategic function brings challenges related to change management and organizational culture. These challenges emphasize the significance of change management, addressing organizational culture, and driving strategic alignment to ensure successful integration efforts that span across the entire program. Integrating systems often brings significant organizational changes. These challenges require effective change management strategies, stakeholder engagement, and leadership to drive the integration program and ensure organizational alignment.

7 Conclusions

The concept of systems integration in the context of data ecosystems plays a pivotal role in managing the complexities and interdependencies of interconnected organizations. Systems integration, which originated as a means to coordinate complex systems design and integration in industries such as aerospace and defense, has evolved into a fundamental aspect of managing large technology projects, complex products and systems, and IT architecture implementation. The different approaches to systems integration in the data ecosystem domain provide valuable insights into the integration challenges faced by organizations.

Systems integration is not merely a technical skill but a core strategic capability that enables firms to position themselves within the industry, identify competitors, select partners, and pursue vertical integration. It involves decision-making at various stages, ranging from design and implementation to maintenance and evolution. By understanding and applying the four proposed approaches to systems integration—modularization, standardization, coordination, and adaptation—organizations operating within data ecosystems can effectively manage the complexities, dependencies, and interconnections involved.

The empirical context of the GAIA-X project provides a valuable opportunity to further explore the challenges and opportunities related to systems integration in data ecosystems. By studying the GAIA-X project, researchers can gain practical insights into the implications of systems integration and its role in realizing the objectives of data ecosystems.

This paper contributes to the understanding of data ecosystems and highlights the significance of systems integration in managing the complexities inherent in these ecosystems. The proposed approaches to systems integration offer a comprehensive framework for organizations to effectively integrate technologies, processes, and data within data ecosystems. By embracing systems integration principles, organizations can navigate the challenges of data exchange, collaboration, and innovation, ultimately driving value creation and shaping the future trajectory of the market in the digital era. The insights gained from this research can inform practitioners and policymakers in their efforts to harness the potential of data ecosystems and unlock their benefits for society as a whole.

References

1. Alaimo, C., Kallinikos, J., & Valderrama, E. (2019). Platforms as service ecosystems: Lessons from social media. *Journal of Information Technology, 35*(1), 25–48. https://doi.org/10.1177/0268396219881462
2. Bogers, M., Sims, J., & West, J. (2019). What is an ecosystem? Incorporating 25 years of ecosystem research. *Academy of Management Proceedings, 2019*(1), 11080.
3. De Simone, C., Ceci, F., & Alaimo, C. (2022). Data ecosystem and data value chain: An exploration of drones technology applications. In *Sustainable digital transformation: Paving the way towards smart organizations and societies* (pp. 203–218). Springer.
4. Kapoor, R., & Agarwal, S. (2017). Sustaining superior performance in business ecosystems: Evidence from application software developers in the iOS and Android smartphone ecosystems. *Organization Science, 28*(3), 531–551.
5. Kapoor, R., Iansiti, M., & Levien, R. (2004). Ecosystems: broadening the locus of value creation. *Harvard Business Review, 82*(1), 12.
6. Passiante, G. (2010). In G. Passiante (Ed.), *Evolving towards the internetworked enterprise*. Springer US. https://doi.org/10.1007/978-1-4419-7279-8_9
7. Subramaniam, M., Iyer, B., & Venkatraman, V. (2019). Competing in digital ecosystems. *Business Horizons, 62*(1), 83–94.
8. Baldwin, C. Y. (2012). Organization design for business ecosystems. *Journal of Organization Design, 1*(1).
9. Um, S., Yoo, Y., & Wattal, S. (2015). The evolution of digital ecosystems: A case of Word Press from 2004 to 2014.
10. Weill, P., & Woerner, S. L. (2015). Thriving in an increasingly digital ecosystem. *MIT Sloan Management Review, 56*(4), 27–34.
11. Jacobides, M. G., Cennamo, C., & Gawer, A. (2018). Towards a theory of ecosystems. *Strategic Management Journal, 39*(8), 2255–2276.
12. Gulati, R., Puranam, P., & Tushman, M. (2012). Meta-organization design: Rethinking design in interorganizational and community contexts. *Strategic Management Journal, 33*(6), 571–586.

13. Pappas, I. O., Mikalef, P., Giannakos, M. N., Krogstie, J., & Lekakos, G. (2018). Towards digital transformation and sustainable societies. *Information Systems and e-Business Management, 16*(3), 479–491. https://doi.org/10.1007/s10257-018-0377-z
14. Blijleven, V., Angeren, J. Van, Jansen, S., & Brinkkemper, S. (2013). An evolutionary economics approach to ecosystem dynamics. *August 2015*. https://doi.org/10.1109/DEST.2013.6611323.
15. Oliveira, M. I. S., Barros Lima, G. D. F., & Lóscio, B. F. (2019). Investigations into data ecosystems: A systematic mapping study. *Knowledge and Information Systems, 61*, 1–42.
16. Hanssen, G. K. (2012). A longitudinal case study of an emerging software ecosystem: Implications for practice and theory. *Journal of Systems and Software, 85*(7), 1455–1466. https://doi.org/10.1016/j.jss.2011.04.020
17. Abernathy, W. J., & Utterback, J. M. (1978). Patterns of industrial innovation. *Technology Review, 80*(7), 40–47.
18. Tushman, M. L., & Anderson, P. (1986). Technological discontinuities and organizational environments. *Administrative Science Quarterly, 31*(3), 439–465.
19. Rong, K., Lin, Y., Li, B., Burström, T., Butel, L., & Yu, J. (2018). Business ecosystem research agenda: More dynamic, more embedded, and more internationalized. *Asian Business and Management, 17*(3), 167–182. https://doi.org/10.1057/s41291-018-0038-6
20. George, G., Haas, M. R., & Pentland, A. (2014). From the editors: Big data and management. *Academy of Management Journal, 57*(2), 321–326. https://doi.org/10.5465/amj.2014.4002
21. Alaimo, C., & Kallinikos, J. (2021). Managing by data: Algorithmic categories and organizing. *Organization Studies, 42*(9), 1385–1407.
22. Alaimo, C., & Kallinikos, J. (2022). Organizations decentered: Data objects, technology and knowledge. *Organization Science, 33*(1), 19–37.
23. Alaimo, C. (2021). From people to objects: The digital transformation of fields. *Organization Studies, 43*(7), 1091–1114. https://doi.org/10.1177/01708406211030654
24. Xie, K., Wu, Y., Xiao, J., & Hu, Q. (2016). Value co-creation between firms and customers: The role of big data-based cooperative assets. *Information and Management, 53*(8), 1034–1048. https://doi.org/10.1016/j.im.2016.06.003
25. Aaltonen, A., Alaimo, C., & Kallinikos, J. (2021). The making of data commodities: Data analytics as an embedded process. *Journal of Management Information Systems, 38*(2), 401–429.
26. Alaimo, C., Kallinikos, J., & Aaltonen, A. (2020). Data and value. In *Handbook of digital innovation*. Edward Elgar Publishing.
27. Davies, A. (2017). *Projects: A very short introduction*. Oxford University Press.
28. Hughes, T. P. (1998). *Rescuing prometheus*. Pantheon Books.
29. Johnson, S. B. (2003). Systems integration and the social solution of technical problems in complex systems. *The Business of Systems Integration*, 35–55.
30. Brusoni, S., Prencipe, A., & Pavitt, K. L. R. (2001). Knowledge specialization and the boundaries of the firm: Why do firms know more than they make? *Administrative Science Quarterly, 46*(4), 597–621.
31. Ceci, F., Masini, A., & Prencipe, A. (2019). Impact of IT offerings strategies and IT integration capability on IT vendor value creation. *European Journal of Information Systems, 28*(6), 591–611. https://doi.org/10.1080/0960085X.2019.1627488
32. Hobday, M., Davies, A., & Prencipe, A. (2005). Systems integration: A core competence of the modern corporation. *Industrial and Corporate Change, 14*(6), 1109–1143.
33. Prencipe, A., Davies, A., & Hobday, M. (2003). *The business of systems integration*. Oxford University Press.
34. Davies, A., & Mackenzie, I. (2014). Project complexity and systems integration: Constructing the London 2012 Olympics and Paralympics Games. *International Journal of Project Management, 32*(5), 773–790. https://doi.org/10.1016/j.ijproman.2013.10.004

35. Ceci, F., & Prencipe, A. (2008). Configuring capabilities for integrated solutions: Evidence from the IT sector. *Industry and Innovation, 15*(3), 277–296. https://doi.org/10.1080/13662710802040879
36. Ceci, F., & Prencipe, A. (2016). Division of labour, supplier relationships, and knowledge integration. In *Managing knowledge integration across boundaries* (p. 106).
37. Pavitt, K. (2003). Specialization and systems integration: where manufacture and service still meet. In A. Prencipe, A. Davies, & M. Hobday (Eds.), *The business of system integration*. Oxford University Press.
38. Sako, M. (2003). Modularity and outsourcing: The nature of co-evolution of product architecture and organization architecture in the global automotive industry. In A. Prencipe & M. Hobday (Eds.), *The business of systems integration*. Oxford University Press.
39. Davies, A. (2004). Moving base into high-value integrated solutions: A value stream approach. *Industrial and Corporate Change, 13*(5), 727–756.
40. Galbraith, J. (2002). *Designing organizations: An executive guide to strategy, structure, and process*. Jossey-Bass, Wiley.
41. Miraglia, S., & Davies, A. (2009). Learning dynamics within the solutions network. In *Dynamic learning networks* (pp. 75–93). Springer US.
42. Ceci, F., & Masini, A. (2011). Balancing specialized and generic capabilities in the provision of integrated solutions: Empirical evidence from the IT sector. *Industrial and Corporate Change, 20*(1), 91–132. https://doi.org/10.1093/icc/dtq069
43. Eloranta, V., & Turunen, T. (2016). Platforms in service-driven manufacturing: Leveraging complexity by connecting, sharing, and integrating. *Industrial Marketing Management, 55*, 178–186.
44. Geleilate, J.-M. G., Parente, R. C., & Talay, M. B. (2021). Can systems integration lead to improved performance? The role of strategic alliances. *Industrial Marketing Management, 95*, 17–28.
45. Huikkola, T., & Kohtamäki, M. (2017). Solution providers' strategic capabilities. *Journal of Business & Industrial Marketing, 32*(5), 752–770.
46. Ceci, F., & Prencipe, A. (2013). Does distance hinder coordination? identifying and bridging boundaries of offshored work. *Journal of International Management, 19*(4), 324–332. https://doi.org/10.1016/j.intman.2013.04.001
47. Mackenzie, I., & DeCusatis, C. (2013). Sustaining innovation when outsourcing components in multi-technology, multi-component systems. *Innovation: Management, Policy and Practice, 15*(1), 2–16. https://doi.org/10.5172/impp.2013.15.1.2
48. Umapathy, K., Purao, S., & Barton, R. R. (2008). Designing enterprise integration solutions: effectively. *European Journal of Information System, 17*(5), 518–527. https://doi.org/10.1057/ejis.2008.39
49. Purao, S., Bolloju, N., & Tan, C. H. (2018). A modeling language for conceptual design of systems integration solutions. *ACM Transactions on Management Information Systems, 9*(2), 1–25. https://doi.org/10.1145/3185046
50. Whyte, J., Stasis, A., & Lindkvist, C. (2016). Managing change in the delivery of complex projects: Configuration management, asset information and "big data". *International Journal of Project Management, 34*(2), 339–351. https://doi.org/10.1016/j.ijproman.2015.02.006
51. Whyte, J., & Davies, A. (2021). Reframing systems integration: A process perspective on projects. *Project Management Journal, 52*(3), 237–249.
52. Davies, A., & Hobday, M. (2005). *The business of projects*. Cambridge University Press.
53. Darke, P., Shanks, G., & Broadbent, M. (1998). Successfully completing case study research: Combining rigour, relevance and pragmatism. *Information Systems Journal, 8*(4), 273–289. https://doi.org/10.1046/j.1365-2575.1998.00040.x
54. Eisenhardt, K. M. (1989). Building theories from case study research. *Academy of Management Review, 14*(4), 532–550. https://doi.org/10.5465/amr.1989.4308385
55. Stake, R. E. (1995). *The art of case study research*. Sage.
56. Yin, R. K. (2009). *Case study research: Design and methods*. Sage Publications.

Green Recommendation Systems for Smart and Sustainable Cities: A Proof-of-Concept on the City of Milan

Matteo Spinazzola, Dario Cottafava, and Marco Pironti

Abstract This work contributes to the study of Green Information Systems (GIS) for the transition to smarter and more sustainable cities, as well as drivers of innovation and entrepreneurship. The literature on GIS has primarily focused on the use of sensory data, neglecting the role of information systems to provide other types of data-driven services, such as knowledge or partnership recommendations. To address this gap, this paper offers a first conceptualization for the use of Green Recommendation Systems (GRS) and a first preliminary application to the Italian city of Milan. This was achieved by reviewing existing literature on GIS and recommendation systems, and particularly on professional social matching. From there, an original framework presenting the functioning of a GRS for Smart and Sustainable Cities (GRS3C) was designed. This was then tested by simulating its usage for the city of Milan, focusing on the recommendation of academic knowledge and actors specialized on air pollution. Preliminary results show that a GRS3C may support policymakers and entrepreneurs in understanding the complexity of current issues, as well as in identifying local actors with relevant expertise. Doing so, this paper expands the concept of GIS and provides a new application of professional social matching concepts, thus contributing to both research areas. As a proof-of-

M. Spinazzola (✉)
Department of Economics and Statistics "Cognetti de Martiis", University of Turin, Turin, Italy
e-mail: matteo.spinazzola@unito.it

D. Cottafava
Department of Economics and Statistics "Cognetti de Martiis", University of Turin, Turin, Italy

Departament d'Empresa Campus Bellaterra, Facultat d'Economia i Empresa, Universitat Autonoma de Barcelona, Barcelona, Spain

Centre for Entrepreneurship and Social Innovation Research, Universitat Autonoma de Barcelona, Barcelona, Spain
e-mail: dario.cottafava@unito.it

M. Pironti
Department of Computer Science, University of Turin, Turin, Italy
e-mail: marco.pironti@unito.it

A. M. Braccini et al. (eds.), *Digital (Eco) Systems and Societal Challenges*, Lecture Notes in Information Systems and Organisation 72,
https://doi.org/10.1007/978-3-031-75586-6_21

concept, it may motivate the development of actual GRSs which could foster innovation and entrepreneurship for smart and sustainable cities.

Keywords Green information systems · Smart and sustainable cities · Green recommendation system

1 Introduction

This work contributes to the study of Green Information Systems (GIS) as key assets for the transition to smarter and more sustainable cities, as well as drivers of innovation and entrepreneurship [1, 2]. The literature on GIS, however, has primarily focused on the use of big data produced by sensors, neglecting the role of information systems to provide other types of data-driven services, such as knowledge or partnership recommendations [3, 4]. To address this gap, the current paper offers a first conceptualization for the use of Green Recommendation Systems (GRS) and a first preliminary application to the Italian city of Milan.

This was achieved by reviewing existing literature on GIS and recommendation systems and their potential value for smarter and more sustainable cities [5, 6]. Instead of providing a comprehensive review of all available publications, however, it synthetizes just enough material on GIS and recommendation systems to point at the synergies between them [7]. Next, following an iterative approach [8], it connects the two streams in an original framework [9] introducing the functioning of a GRS for Smart and Sustainable Cities (GRS3C).

This framework was then tested by simulating its usage for the City of Milan, focusing on the recommendation of relevant academic knowledge and actors specialized on the issue of air pollution. Partially drawing on the concept of Digital Urban Acupuncture (DUA) [10], preliminary results show that a GRS3C may support policymakers and entrepreneurs in understanding the complexity of social, environmental, and economic issues, as well as in identifying local actors which may contribute to the development of adequate solutions. Doing so, this paper expands the concept of GIS beyond its traditional focus on sensory data and provides a smart and sustainable application of professional social matching concepts thus contributing to both research areas.

As a proof-of-concept, it may motivate policymakers to develop actual GRSs, which could foster innovation and entrepreneurship for the development of innovative solutions for smart and sustainable cities. The following section provides the literature background concerning GIS, recommendation systems and professional social matching, as well as DUA. Next, in the methodological section, a brief overview of the proposed GRS3Cs framework is presented as well a description of its preliminary application to the city of Milan. Preliminary results from this application are provided in the subsequent, fourth, section. Last, the main theoretical and practical implications are drawn.

2 Background

2.1 Green Information Systems

Green information systems (GIS) are networks of hardware, software, and procedures designed to reduce environmental impacts. By supporting real time human-machine or machine-machine interactions, they increase operational efficiency, provide real-time, data-driven insights, and open opportunities for new products and services, ultimately accelerating the adoption of sustainable practices [11–13]. GIS have long been used to improve the environmental performance of individual organizations, but are increasingly recognized as fundamental also for the adoption of advanced solutions for sustainability challenges beyond the organizational boundaries [14].

One such example is the use of GIS for managing water, air quality, or road traffic, by municipalities. While local administrations have traditionally used GIS to collect data in silos and for sole monitoring purposes, more proactive and open data approaches have been adopted in the last decade [15–17]. Indeed, the shift towards smart and sustainable cities is revolutionizing the use of GIS to collect and use big data, changing how cities operate and will operate in the future [18]. On the one hand, by utilizing a combination of key novel technologies such as the internet-of-things, blockchain, artificial intelligence, and cloud computing, local governments are increasingly able to measure and monitor environmental factors and human behaviors in real time and with improved accuracy [19]. On the other hand, they are employing information systems to make these data accessible across their departments and to external factors such as universities, businesses, startups, and citizens [20, 21]. Other than favoring coordination among government branches, this approach recognizes the value of the local ecosystem in which multiple diverse actors collaborate with complementary activities, from research and development to the commercialization of new product or service [3, 22]. Hence, the expanded use of GIS in smart and sustainable cities may meaningfully impact the ability of society to address the most pressing environmental and social issues, all while improving transparency towards citizens and favoring entrepreneurship and innovation [2, 23, 24].

While this topic has been great interest to academic and practitioners in urban development, management, and governance, as of today it has received only limited attention from the information systems community [24]. Even more so, the literature on GIS has neglected the role of information systems to provide other types of data-driven services, such as knowledge or partnership recommendations.

2.2 Recommendation Systems and Professional Social Matching

As a response to the overabundance of information and Big Data [25], recommendation systems have emerged in recent decades [26]. Particularly to recommend books, movies, and products from online shops, or as streaming platforms, they have been incredibly common [27, 28]. These systems typically implement a combination of two logics: first "consumer preferences", as people are assumed to be interested in products similar to those they already own, have bought, or have searched for; second "homophily", by assuming that consumers may be interested in products similar to those of other consumers with similar preferences or with whom they are socially connected [29]. More recently, recommendation systems have shifted their focus from products and services to actual "people" recommendations, such as in social networks (e.g. Facebook) and dating apps (e.g. Tinder) [30]. Indeed, social matching systems such as these are also based on the idea that people with similar interests or connections are more likely to be compatible with each other and possess similar preferences.

Accordingly, professional social matching is simply a vocational application of social matching systems to the professional context [26], as the success of professional social networks (e.g. LinkedIn) increased the interest of both the academic and business communities to this topic [29]. As such, it emerged in the information systems literature as a tool to recommend professionally relevant matches of people or organizations based on their professional characteristics, such as skills, experience, interests, sector, or location [30]. Typical applications include the identification of new employers for a specific team or company [31], or of ideal partnering organizations for innovation purposes [32], or of academic co-authors and experts [32].

Focusing on the scientific and innovation domain, several approaches and tools for professional social matching have been studied and developed, mostly based on bibliometric and patent data [33]. As a non-exhaustive list: synthetic indicators of organizations' innovation and collaboration propensity have been used to match and prioritize potential partners [34]; citations and collaboration information have been employed to map networks of collaborating organizations or individuals, using link prediction algorithms and triadic closure principles to predict future partnerships based on historical interaction [35, 36]; patents and scholarly articles have been mined with Natural Language Processing to extract insights and recommend collaborations based on content similarity or complementarity [37, 38]. Recently, these methodologies have been combined to account for network structure, actor thematic affinity, and innovation roles [39, 40].

Though believed to boost networking, collaboration, and innovation [33], many barriers and limitations remain. First, factors intrinsic to the data like gender, race, and socioeconomic status may bias recommendation algorithms, with multiple consequences [41]. Professional social matching could end up creating excessively homogenous networks, since most recommendation systems use homophily to suggest new recommendations, which may reinforce existing patterns rather than create new opportunities and paths [41, 42]. Consequently, the creation of homogeneous 'bubbles' may provoke an extreme polarization and a lack of diversity, with detrimental consequences for both inclusion and innovation [42, 43]. On the user side, additional issues may emerge. Professional social matching platforms require users to share sensitive personal and professional information, opening privacy and data security concerns. Cyberattacks, data breaches, and misuse can compromise trust, especially when information may be scraped from the web, a practice whose legality is still in question [44], and privacy could be broken even if data is anonymized [45]. In addition, the accuracy of recommendations could be questioned and cause distrust in the system [26]. Last, until now existing systems have mainly focused on maximizing individual-level matchings rather than working at a community- or ecosystem-level, thus potentially generating sub-optimal results [5, 46].

2.3 *Digital Urban Acupuncture*

A primal application of GRSs would include the support to policy- and decision-makers [47] and the provision of transparent and easily accessible information to any other actor within the ecosystem [2, 48]. Analyzing an (innovation) ecosystem from the point of view of the underlying relationships, indeed, may be used by policy-makers to develop specific and targeted instruments, including 'nudges' [49]. Even more, as described by Iaconesi and Persico (2017), they could support the development of micro-interventions within the framework of DUA. Similarly, to the medical acupuncture, this concept refers to micro and very specific interventions based on granular data about citizens, businesses or actors' interactions within the urban ecosystem, to maximize effectiveness and efficiency.

By looking at cities as living ecosystems, hence: "it is possible to take into consideration the myriads of microhistories of all of its members to identify flows of information, communication, knowledge, emotion, opinion, activation, and their patterns over geography and time" [10]. Such microhistories, or pressure points "can be activated to creatively provoke engagement, interconnection, relation, and the breaking of undesired loops and patterns. This allows for both a dynamic definition—and polyphonic—of the well-being of the city" [10]. For example, by analyzing such microhistories or pressure points, administrators could concentrate on unhealthy locations and plan to redesign them in a regenerative way by considering natural and man-made locations that are valued by the community, such as small court gardens or fountains, which have positive effects on community health but are typically underappreciated from the decision-makers' point of view [50]. Similarly, they may take advantage of large and complex analysis of relationships among every actor within the innovation or cultural ecosystem of a city to plan proper policies and micro-interventions as for in the innovation ecosystem of Kansas City or the cultural ecosystem of Rome in Italy [10]. Such micro-histories could, and should, be punctually stimulated with ad-hoc information system such as the case study First Life web-platform, used to stimulate active citizens' participation in co-design entire neighbourhood in the City of Turin [51].

Similar interventions would be crucial to fully capitalize on all the knowledge available within a specific urban ecosystem, as previous studies have shown that addressing complex sustainability challenges often requires to leverage dispersed expertise and to organize actors in equally complex governance arrangements [2, 52]. While addressing these challenges, knowledge would nurture the local entrepreneurial and innovation ecosystem allowing local businesses and research organizations to efficiently exploit it [53, 54]. Indeed, previous evidence has found that organizations highly benefit from the availability of material and immaterial resources not only from within [55] but also from outside [4, 56] their boundaries, and even from beyond the boundaries of their local ecosystem [57]. Accordingly, the being able to identify relevant knowledge and knowledge holders would be fundamental to boost innovation and entrepreneurship [3, 46, 58].

3 Methodology

Drawing on existing literature on GIS and professional social matching, an original framework for a GRS3C was designed. An overview of its key functions and features is here provided, remanding the reader to the existing literature for more detailed discussions of individual components and to the following section for an empirical example. As in similar works, information on local actors can be retrieved from common repositories such as Scopus, Web of Science, the European Patent Office, Business Registries, and so on. These data sources must be processed, homogenized and merged into a unitarian database. Actors are univocally identified and associated with information such as their organization type, their location, size, industrial sector. Then, with social network analysis techniques, collaborations are mapped to assess actors' centrality in existing networks (eg. in co-authorship networks when analyzing academic papers), as well as their propensity to collaborate. Last, available textual material (eg. abstracts from academic papers) is analyzed with topic modelling tools to identify common themes beyond disciplinary silos and identify for each actor its area of expertise [33, 46]. This structured information is then stored in a database feeding the GRS3C, which policymakers, enterprises or other actors can interrogate via a web interface. Differentiating itself from other recommendation systems [58], the GRS3C would be structured around three steps that users would progressively navigate through (a simplified flowchart is presented in Fig. 1):

1. Users interact with the GRS3C to identify their main topic of interest; this is achieved by following a decision tree from the most general to the most-specific topic, avoiding information overload. The decision tree is based on a hierarchical topic clustering obtained from existing textual material [59].

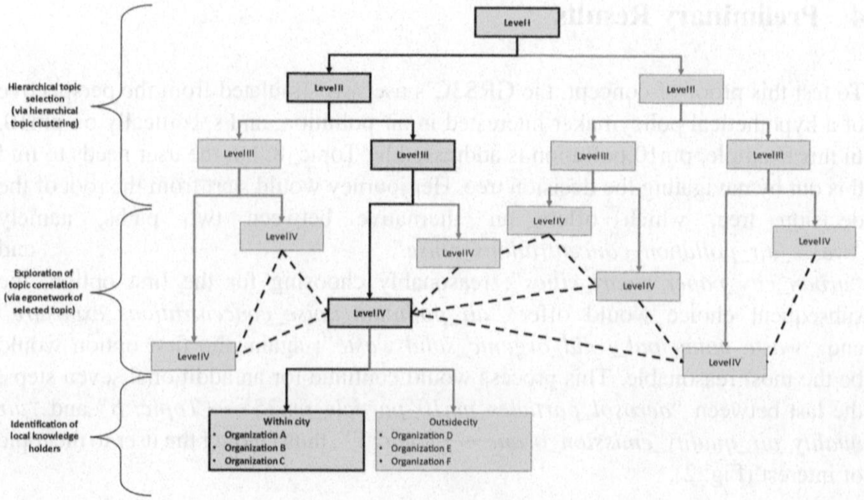

Fig. 1 Green Recommendation System for Smart and Sustainable Cities, users' navigation. Text in bold and black highlights a user's journey (Own work)

2. Once a specific sub-topic is selected, the platform provides an exploration of the other topics most associated with the topic of interest. This allows to obtain a more comprehensive understanding of the specific sub-topic in its relations with other topics. Here users also have the opportunity to focus on alternative sub-topics. This exploration is enabled by an ego-network based on the dissimilarity matrix produced in the topic modelling activity [39, 60].
3. Last, based on the sub-topic chosen, users are provided with a list of actors most experienced at working on it, possibly distinguishing between locally operating actors and geographically distant ones, as well benefitting on additional information such as actors' centrality in existing networks [33].

The city of Milan was selected to offer a proof-of-concept of the GRS3C as it constitutes one of the most advanced smart and sustainable cities in the country [61]. First, a database was constructed collecting articles published on the topic of smart and sustainable cities. This was achieved by employing the Scopus' pre-made query for SDG.11 "Sustainable cities and communities", limiting results to English articles published in Italy since 2003. This leveraged a total of 19,956 articles ranging across physical, social, and life sciences [62]. Second, this dataset was cleaned and processed to extract key information on authoring organizations [63]. Third, the state-of-the-art sentence-embedding model BERTopic was used to inductively identify 98 topics from the abstracts contained in the dataset [64]. These topics were then clustered in a hierarchical form, to provide the hierarchical structure used in step 1, and a topic dissimilarity matrix was generated to inform the construction of the topic-correlation network which informed step 2 [65]. Last, for every sub-topic, the list of the most active organization operating within the city of Milan was extracted, thus delivering the ultimate output required by step 3 [33, 46].

4 Preliminary Results

To test this proof-of-concept, the GRS3C's use was simulated from the perspective of a hypothetical policymaker interested in air pollution, and specifically on pm10. In this example, pm10 pollution is addressed by Topic_8, but the user needs to find this out by navigating the decision tree. Her journey would start from the root of the decision tree, which offers an alternative between two paths, namely *"waste_air_pollution_concentrations_noise"* and *"urban_city_paper_smart_cities"*; reasonably choosing for the first option, the subsequent choice would offer *"air_pollution_noise_concentrations_exposure"* and *"waste_municipal_solid_organic_solid waste"*; again, the first option would be the most reasonable. This process would continue for an additional seven steps, the last between *"aerosol_particles_pm10_particle_pm25 — Topic: 8"* and *"air quality_air_quality_emission_ozone — Topic: 7"*, thus landing the user to the topic of interest (Fig. 2).

Fig. 2 Hierarchical topics decision tree, simplified version. From top to bottom, the text in bold and underlined highlights path to Topic_8 (Own work)

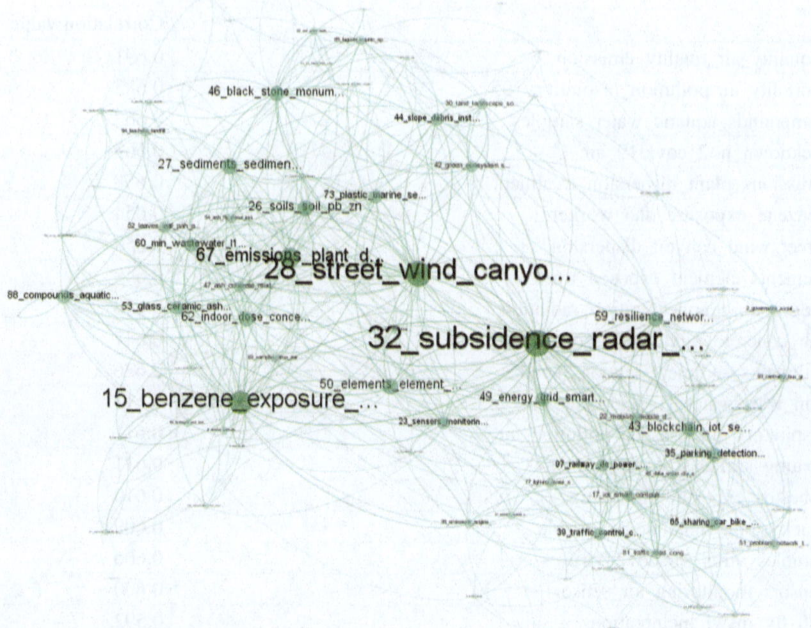

Fig. 3 Topic network visualization (Own work)

Once the specific sub-topic has been identified, the policymaker has the opportunity to explore how it is connected to other topics and, more broadly, how issues are connected to each other. This is achieved via a network visualization of topics' dissimilarity. In Fig. 3 node and label size represent the node degree, but other metrics can be used such as the betweenness centrality [66], authority [67] or page-rank [68], depending on the aim. First, this allows to obtain a more comprehensive understanding of the issues that must be faced by cities. In the current example Topic_28, which relates to the formation of anthropogenic canyons that affect winds and pollutants' dispersion, emerges as a highly central node. This centrality indicates that Topic_28 could be fundamental to address many issues at once, and is quite reasonable given the dispersing effect that wind may have on many different pollutants [69]. Second, Fig. 3 allows to identify the topics that are most connected to Topic_8. Some of them are obvious, such as *"7_air quality_air_quality_emission"* and *"13_mortality_air pollution_respiratory_95"*, while others are more surprising, such as *"15_benzene_exposure_dna_workers"*, *32_subsidence_radar_deformation_images"*, or *"96_green_roofs_heat_thermal"*, just to mention a few (Table 1). These connections between topics would further support the policymakers in the identification of connections between issues at the city level, bringing to the spotlight areas for priority policy intervention [60, 70].

Table 1 Topics most connected to Topic_8

Topic	Correlation value
7_air quality_air_quality_emission	0.691
13_mortality_air pollution_respiratory_95	0.683
88_compounds_aquatic_water_samples	0.663
70_lockdown_no2_covid19_air	0.663
67_emissions_plant_dispersion_treatment	0.658
15_benzene_exposure_dna_workers	0.654
28_street_wind_canyon_dispersion	0.650
50_elements_element_exposed_trace	0.648
62_indoor_dose_concentration_radiation	0.648
47_ash_concrete_mixtures_aggregates	0.647
27_sediments_sediment_lagoon_metal	0.626
60_min_wastewater_l1_degradation	0.613
66_respiratory_diseases_air pollution_air	0.611
87_coating_surfaces_stone_properties	0.611
95_asbestos_exposure_mm_lung	0.610
46_black_stone_monuments_marble	0.609
69_samples_virus_sarscov2_viruses	0.606
23_sensors_monitoring_air_sensor	0.600
54_ash_fly_mswi_incineration	0.592
53_glass_ceramic_ash_ashes	0.590
26_soils_soil_pb_zn	0.588
73_plastic_marine_sea_debris	0.587
52_leaves_leaf_pah_pahs	0.587
84_hydrogen_port_energy_ships	0.582
38_emissions_engine_diesel_emission	0.577
56_drug_wastewater_drugs_alcohol	0.576
0_waste_solid_waste management_collection	0.551
32_subsidence_radar_deformation_images	0.548
75_wastewater_biomass_removal_nutrient	0.545
90_ship_port_ships_emissions	0.542

After exploring the relationship with other topics, the user has the opportunity to identify organizations possessing relevant expertise in the specific topic of interest. Table 2 shows that the city of Milan is relatively well positioned, as local organizations have published 19 papers on pm10 pollution according to the available material. Specifically, these organizations include universities, such as the University of Milan (5 publications), the University of Milano-Bicocca (3), and the Polytechnic University of Milan (2), public hospitals and research institutions such as the Policlinico Hospital of Milan (5) and Italian National Research Council (2), as well as a consultancy firm such as Arianet Srl (2). Accordingly, this list of actors can be employed by the policymaker to identify adequate partners for the development and rollout of holistic solutions to deal with pm10 pollution in the city

Table 2 Italian cities with the highest number of publications on pm10

City	Number of publications
Rome	29
Milan	19
Florence	16
Cassino	7
Lecce	5
Genoa	4
Venice	4
Campobasso	4
Bologna	4

[6, 70]. Moreover, though not performed here due to the short list of alternatives and the proof-of-concept nature of this study, additional criterial could be employed to identify the best-fitting organization to collaborate with: examples include the possession of complementary knowledge and resources [71], or the positioning in existing collaboration networks at the local or global level [36], or synthetic indicators of collaboration propensity and effectiveness [37], or a mix of these techniques [33].

5 Discussion and Conclusion

This paper presents several limitations. On the one hand, the articles selected for the analyses only constitute a small sample of all available articles produced on smart and sustainable cities, and relying on SDG11 is a proxy for this concept as well. Hence, the prosecution of this work would certainly require to expand the articles' selection to obtain a more comprehensive perspective on existing literature. Moreover, to maximize the benefits that such a platform may provide, including additional sources of data, such as data on businesses and their services, as well as on relevant technologies for smart and sustainable cities [39, 72] would be recommended. On the other hand, the design of a GRS3C would necessarily require a participatory and collaborative approach [70], so as to enable final users (such as policymakers or entrepreneurs) to contribute to the definition of its key features, as the ultimate goal of recommendation systems is to simplify operations [26, 29].

Nonetheless, this paper already contributes to the study of GIS and their application in smart and sustainable cities. As a proof-of-concept, it shows that a GRS3C could be constructed to support policy-makers and other potential users: first, it shows that such a system could be affectively used to provide an intuitive tree-like representation could be used to organize and navigate knowledge available in a city and to identify a specific topic of interest [59]; second, it shows that a network representations could be used to provide a more comprehensive picture of other related topics, offering users an opportunity to further expand their knowledge and understanding of the issue of interest [39, 60]; third, it shows that once a final topic is chosen a list of organizations could be provided and ranked to identify potential partners [33].

Accordingly, the preliminary findings suggest that a GRS3C could assist decision-makers in better comprehending the complexities of social, environmental, and economic problems, as well as in locating actors who might contribute to the formulation of suitable solutions. Hence, by lowering exploration and interaction costs, a GRS3C could be fundamental to engage a multiplicity of local actors in the development of adequate solutions to the most pressing environmental challenges [57, 73]. This would facilitate the flow of tangible and intangible resources among actors, boosting innovation and entrepreneurship at the city level [2, 74] by exploiting the relational dimensions of all actors within an local and punctual ecosystem. In this sense, the use of large dataset with a relational component—i.e., with information about collaborations, relationships, interactions—recalling the concept of DUA may facilitate the design of micro-interventions or policies [50]. Accordingly, this paper contributes to the expansion of GIS and professional social matching concepts, opening for more research at the intersection of these two literature streams. Moreover, as a proof-of-concept it may motivate the development of actual GRS3Cs which could facilitate the development of innovative solutions for smart and sustainable cities, and support policymakers dealing with complex challenges [52].

Disclosure of Interests The authors have no competing interests to declare that are relevant to the content of this article.

References

1. Carayannis, E. G., Grigoroudis, E., Campbell, D. F. J., Meissner, D., & Stamati, D. (2018). The ecosystem as helix: An exploratory theory-building study of regional co-opetitive entrepreneurial ecosystems as quadruple/quintuple helix innovation models. *R and D Management, 48*, 148–162. https://doi.org/10.1111/radm.12300
2. Cillo, V., Farronato, N., Scuotto, V., Pironti, M., Pisano, P., & Del Giudice, M. (2020). Torino City Lab, an open innovation participatory ecosystem. The city works with entrepreneurial universities in shaping the smart city ecosystem. In: Grand challenges: companies and universities working for a better society. Sinergie Italian Journal of Management.
3. Corbett, J., & Mellouli, S. (2017). Winning the SDG battle in cities: How an integrated information ecosystem can contribute to the achievement of the 2030 sustainable development goals. *Information Systems Journal, 27*, 427–461. https://doi.org/10.1111/isj.12138
4. Addo, A. (2022). Orchestrating a digital platform ecosystem to address societal challenges: A robust action perspective. *Journal of Information Technology, 37*, 359–386. https://doi.org/10.1177/02683962221088333
5. Olsson, T., Huhtamäki, J., & Kärkkäinen, H. (2020). Directions for professional social matching systems. *Communications of the ACM, 63*, 60–69. https://doi.org/10.1145/3363825
6. Archer, M., & Zytko, D. (2019). Social matching systems for research collaboration: A profile page design for University Faculty. In *Conference companion publication of the 2019 on computer supported cooperative work and social computing* (pp. 146–150). Association for Computing Machinery. https://doi.org/10.1145/3311957.3359459
7. Van de Ven, A. H. (1989). Nothing is quite so practical as a good theory. *Academy of Management Review, 14*, 486–489. https://doi.org/10.5465/amr.1989.4308370

8. Weick, K. E. (1989). Theory construction as disciplined imagination. *Academy of Management Review, 14*, 516–531. https://doi.org/10.5465/amr.1989.4308376
9. Gilson, L. L., & Goldberg, C. B. (2015). Editors' comment: So, what is a conceptual paper? *Group & Organization Management, 40*, 127–130. https://doi.org/10.1177/1059601115576425
10. Iaconesi, S., & Persico, O. (2017). Digital urban acupuncture. In *Digital urban acupuncture* (pp. 123–147). Springer International Publishing. https://doi.org/10.1007/978-3-319-43403-2_9
11. Kossahl, J., Busse, S., & Kolbe, L. M. (2012). The evolvement of energy informatics in the information systems community: A literature analysis and research agenda. *Proceedings*.
12. Jenkin, T. A., Webster, J., & McShane, L. (2011). An agenda for 'green' information technology and systems research. *Information and Organization, 21*, 17–40. https://doi.org/10.1016/j.infoandorg.2010.09.003
13. Hanelt, A., Busse, S., & Kolbe, L. M. (2017). Driving business transformation toward sustainability: Exploring the impact of supporting IS on the performance contribution of eco-innovations. *Information Systems Journal, 27*, 463–502. https://doi.org/10.1111/isj.12130
14. Zeiss, R., Ixmeier, A., Recker, J., & Kranz, J. (2021). Mobilising information systems scholarship for a circular economy: Review, synthesis, and directions for future research. *Information Systems Journal, 31*, 148–183. https://doi.org/10.1111/isj.12305
15. Danzinger, J. N., Kraemer, K. L., & King, J. L. (1978). An assessment of computer technology in U.S. local governments. *Urban Systems, 3*(1), 21–37.
16. Page, B., & Voigt, K. (2003). Recent history and development of environmental information systems and databases in Germany. *Online Information Review, 27*, 37–50. https://doi.org/10.1108/14684520310462554
17. Wong, P. F., Chia, F. C., Kiu, M. S., & Lou, E. C. W. (2022). Potential integration of blockchain technology into smart sustainable city (SSC) developments: A systematic review. *Smart and Sustainable Built Environment, 11*, 559–574. https://doi.org/10.1108/sasbe-09-2020-0140
18. Adepetu, A., Arnautovic, E., Svetinovic, D., & de Weck, O. L. (2014). Complex urban systems ICT infrastructure modeling: A sustainable city case study. *IEEE Transactions on Systems, Man, and Cybernetics: Systems, 44*, 363–374. https://doi.org/10.1109/tsmc.2013.2257744
19. Brauer, B., Eisel, M., & Kolbe, L. (2015). The state of the art in smart city research – A literature analysis on green IS solutions to Foster environmental sustainability. Pacific Asia Conference on Information Systems.
20. Ganapati, S. (2011). Uses of public participation geographic information systems applications in E-government. *Public Administration Review, 71*, 425–434. https://doi.org/10.1111/j.1540-6210.2011.02226.x
21. Chourabi, H., Nam, T., Walker, S., Gil-Garcia, J. R., Mellouli, S., Nahon, K., Pardo, T. A., & Scholl, H. J. (2012). Understanding smart cities: An integrative framework. In *2012 45th Hawaii International Conference on System Sciences* (pp. 2289–2297). https://doi.org/10.1109/HICSS.2012.615
22. Walravens, N., Breuer, J., & Ballon, P. (2014). Open data as a catalyst for the smart city as a local innovation platform. https://papers.ssrn.com/abstract=2636315
23. Pereira, G. V., Macadar, M. A., Luciano, E. M., & Testa, M. G. (2017). Delivering public value through open government data initiatives in a Smart City context. *Information Systems Frontiers, 19*, 213–229. https://doi.org/10.1007/s10796-016-9673-7
24. Kitsios, F., & Kamariotou, M. (2022). Digital innovation and entrepreneurship transformation through open data hackathons: Design strategies for successful start-up settings. *International Journal of Information Management, 69*, 102472. https://doi.org/10.1016/j.ijinfomgt.2022.102472
25. Allam, Z., & Dhunny, Z. A. (2019). On big data, artificial intelligence and smart cities. *Cities, 89*, 80–91. https://doi.org/10.1016/j.cities.2019.01.032
26. Terveen, L., & McDonald, D. W. (2005). Social matching. *ACM Transactions on Computer-Human Interaction (TOCHI), 12*, 401–434. https://doi.org/10.1145/1096737.1096740

27. Olakanmi, O. O., & Odeyemi, K. O. (2021). A collaborative 1-to-n on-demand ride sharing scheme using locations of interest for recommending shortest routes and pick-up points. *International Journal of Intelligent Transportation Systems Research, 19*, 285–298. https://doi.org/10.1007/s13177-020-00234-1
28. Khan, U. A., Memon, F. A., Bhutto, M. A., & Arain, A. A. (2022). Recommending products based on visual similarity using machine learning. In *A fusion of artificial intelligence and internet of things for emerging cyber systems* (pp. 261–268). Springer International Publishing. https://doi.org/10.1007/978-3-030-76653-5_14
29. Bobadilla, J., Ortega, F., Hernando, A., & Gutiérrez, A. (2013). Recommender systems survey. *Knowledge-Based Systems, 46*, 109–132. https://doi.org/10.1016/j.knosys.2013.03.012
30. Nayak, R., Zhang, M., & Chen, L. (2010). A social matching system for an online dating network: A preliminary study. In *2010 IEEE international conference on data mining workshops*. IEEE. https://doi.org/10.1109/icdmw.2010.36
31. Faliagka, E. K. (2012). Application of machine learning algorithms to an online recruitment system. In *The Seventh International Conference on Internet and Web Applications and Services*.
32. Cai, Y., Ferrer, B. R., & Lastra, J. L. M. (2019). Building university-industry co-innovation networks in transnational innovation ecosystems: Towards a transdisciplinary approach of integrating social sciences and artificial intelligence. *Sustainability, 11*(17), 4633. https://doi.org/10.3390/su11174633
33. Qi, Y., Zhang, X., Hu, Z., Xiang, B., Zhang, R., & Fang, S. (2022). Choosing the right collaboration partner for innovation: A framework based on topic analysis and link prediction. *Scientometrics, 127*, 5519–5550. https://doi.org/10.1007/s11192-022-04306-9
34. Geum, Y., Lee, S., Yoon, B., & Park, Y. (2013). Identifying and evaluating strategic partners for collaborative R&D: Index-based approach using patents and publications. *Technovation, 33*, 211–224. https://doi.org/10.1016/j.technovation.2013.03.012
35. Yan, E., & Guns, R. (2014). Predicting and recommending collaborations: An author-, institution-, and country-level analysis. *Journal of Informetrics, 8*, 295–309. https://doi.org/10.1016/j.joi.2014.01.008
36. Chen, W., Qu, H., & Chi, K. (2021). Partner selection in China interorganizational patent cooperation network based on link prediction approaches. *Sustainability, 13*, 1003. https://doi.org/10.3390/su13021003
37. Jeon, J., Lee, C., & Park, Y. (2011). How to use patent information to search potential technology partners in open innovation. *Journal of Intellectual Property Rights, 16*(5), 385–393.
38. Wang, X., Wang, Z., Huang, Y., Liu, Y., Zhang, J., Heng, X., & Zhu, D. (2017). Identifying R&D partners through subject-action-object semantic analysis in a problem & solution pattern. *Technology Analysis & Strategic Management, 29*, 1167–1180. https://doi.org/10.1080/09537325.2016.1277202
39. Park, I., Jeong, Y., Yoon, B., & Mortara, L. (2015). Exploring potential R&D collaboration partners through patent analysis based on bibliographic coupling and latent semantic analysis. *Technology Analysis & Strategic Management, 27*, 759–781. https://doi.org/10.1080/09537325.2014.971004
40. Ding, J. D., & Guo, J. (2021). Mining potential author cooperative relationships based on the similarity of content and path. *Information Studies: Theory & Application, 44*(1), 124–128.
41. Li, J., Stones, R. J., Wang, G., Li, Z., Liu, X., & Xiao, K. (2016). Being accurate is not enough: New metrics for disk failure prediction. In *2016 IEEE 35th symposium on reliable distributed systems (SRDS)*. IEEE. https://doi.org/10.1109/srds.2016.019
42. Kubin, E., & von Sikorski, C. (2021). The role of (social) media in political polarization: A systematic review. *Annals of the International Communication Association, 45*, 188–206. https://doi.org/10.1080/23808985.2021.1976070

43. Orsatti, G., Quatraro, F., & Pezzoni, M. (2020). The antecedents of green technologies: The role of team-level recombinant capabilities. *Research Policy, 49*, 103919. https://doi.org/10.1016/j.respol.2019.103919
44. Mancosu, M., & Vegetti, F. (2020). What you can scrape and what is right to scrape: A proposal for a tool to collect public Facebook data. *Social Media+ Society, 6*, 205630512094070. https://doi.org/10.1177/2056305120940703
45. Kalidien, S., Choenni, S., & Meijer, R. (2010). Crime statistics online: Potentials and challenges of the 11th Annual International Digital .... https://doi.org/10.5555/1809874.1809900.
46. Spinazzola, M., Farronato, N., Murray, A., & Pironti, M. (2023). Unlocking the potential of professional social matching in innovation ecosystems: A conceptual framework and research agenda to Foster local interactions in global networks. In Rediscovering local roots and interactions in management. Sinergie Italian Journal of Management.
47. Porru, S., Misso, F. E., Pani, F. E., & Repetto, C. (2020). Smart mobility and public transport: Opportunities and challenges in rural and urban areas. *Journal of Traffic and Transportation Engineering (English Edition), 7*, 88–97. https://doi.org/10.1016/j.jtte.2019.10.002
48. Chamoso, P., González-Briones, A., De La Prieta, F., Venyagamoorthy, G. K., & Corchado, J. M. (2020). Smart city as a distributed platform: Toward a system for citizen-oriented management. *Computer Communications, 152*, 323–332. https://doi.org/10.1016/j.comcom.2020.01.059
49. Poch, M., Aldao, C., Godo-Pla, L., Monclús, H., Popartan, L. A., Comas, J., Cermerón-Romero, M., Puig, S., & Molinos-Senante, M. (2023). Increasing resilience through nudges in the urban water cycle: An integrative conceptual framework to support policy decision-making. *Chemosphere, 317*, 137850. https://doi.org/10.1016/j.chemosphere.2023.137850
50. Cottafava, D. (2019). Big data, social networks and well-being. In E. Naboni & L. Havinga (Eds.), *Regenerative design in digital practice. A handbook for the built environment* (pp. 85–91). Eurac Research.
51. Antonini, A., et al. (2016). First life, the neighborhood social network: A collaborative environment for citizens. In *Proceedings of the 19th ACM conference on computer supported cooperative work and social computing companion* (pp. 1–4).
52. Spinazzola, M., & Cavalli, L. (2022). The 2030 agenda for sustainable development and the WEF nexus. In *Connecting the sustainable development goals: The WEF nexus* (pp. 3–12). Springer International Publishing. https://doi.org/10.1007/978-3-031-01336-2_1
53. Bertello, A., Battisti, E., De Bernardi, P., & Bresciani, S. (2022). An integrative framework of knowledge-intensive and sustainable entrepreneurship in entrepreneurial ecosystems. *Journal of Business Research, 142*, 683–693. https://doi.org/10.1016/j.jbusres.2021.12.054
54. Grande, S., Bertello, A., De Bernardi, P., & Ricciardi, F. (2022). Enablers of explorative and exploitative intellectual capital in entrepreneurial ecosystems. *Journal of Intellectual Capital, 24*(1), 35–69. https://doi.org/10.1108/jic-07-2021-0197
55. Shehzad, M. U., Zhang, J., Dost, M., Ahmad, M. S., & Alam, S. (2023). Linking green intellectual capital, ambidextrous green innovation and firms green performance: Evidence from Pakistani manufacturing firms. *Journal of Intellectual Capital, 24*, 974–1001.
56. Scuotto, V., Del Giudice, M., Bresciani, S., & Meissner, D. (2017). Knowledge-driven preferences in informal inbound open innovation modes. An explorative view on small to medium enterprises. *Journal of Knowledge Management, 21*, 640–655. https://doi.org/10.1108/jkm-10-2016-0465
57. Farronato, N., Spinazzola, M., Scuotto, V., & Pironti, M. (2022). Trans-city data integration platforms: An explorative study on smart Dublin and Torino City lab. In *Proceedings of the Open Living Lab Days Conference 2022*.
58. Oksanen, K., & Hautamäki, A. (2015). Sustainable innovation: A competitive advantage for innovation ecosystems. *Technology Innovation and Management Review, 5*, 24–30. https://doi.org/10.22215/timreview/934

59. Govender, P., & Sivakumar, V. (2020). Application of k-means and hierarchical clustering techniques for analysis of air pollution: A review (1980–2019). *Atmospheric Pollution Research, 11*, 40–56. https://doi.org/10.1016/j.apr.2019.09.009
60. Wang, M.-Y., Fang, S.-C., & Chang, Y.-H. (2015). Exploring technological opportunities by mining the gaps between science and technology: Microalgal biofuels. *Technological Forecasting and Social Change, 92*, 182–195. https://doi.org/10.1016/j.techfore.2014.07.008
61. Cassinadri, E., Gambarini, E., Nocerino, R., & Scopelliti, L. (2019). Sharing cities: From vision to reality. A people, place and platform approach to implement Milan's Smart City strategy. *IJSEPM, 24*. https://doi.org/10.5278/ijsepm.3336
62. Pranckutė, R. (2021). Web of science (WoS) and Scopus: The titans of bibliographic information in today's academic world. *Publications, 9*, 12. https://doi.org/10.3390/publications9010012
63. Kathuria, A., Gupta, A., & Singla, R. K. (2021). A review of tools and techniques for preprocessing of textual data. In *Computational methods and data engineering* (pp. 407–422). Springer Singapore. https://doi.org/10.1007/978-981-15-6876-3_31
64. Sharifian-Attar, V., De, S., Jabbari, S., Li, J., Moss, H., & Johnson, J. (2022). Analysing longitudinal social science questionnaires: Topic modelling with BERT-based embeddings. In *2022 IEEE international conference on big data (big data)*. IEEE. https://doi.org/10.1109/bigdata55660.2022.10020678
65. Grootendorst, M. P. (n.d.). BERTopic. Accessed May 31, 2023, from https://maartengr.github.io/BERTopic/index.html
66. Brandes, U. (2001). A faster algorithm for betweenness centrality. *Journal of Mathematical Sociology, 25*, 163–177. https://doi.org/10.1080/0022250x.2001.9990249
67. Kleinberg, J. M. (1999). Hubs, authorities, and communities. *ACM Computing Surveys, 31*, 5. https://doi.org/10.1145/345966.345982
68. Brin, S., & Page, L. (2012). Reprint of: The anatomy of a large-scale hypertextual web search engine. *Computer Networks, 56*, 3825–3833. https://doi.org/10.1016/j.comnet.2012.10.007
69. Vardoulakis, S., Fisher, B. E. A., Pericleous, K., & Gonzalez-Flesca, N. (2003). Modelling air quality in street canyons: A review. *Atmospheric Environment, 1994*(37), 155–182. https://doi.org/10.1016/s1352-2310(02)00857-9
70. Cottafava, D., & Corazza, L. (2021). Co-design of a stakeholders' ecosystem: An assessment methodology by linking social network analysis, stakeholder theory and participatory mapping. *Kybernetes, 50*, 836–858. https://doi.org/10.1108/k-12-2019-0861
71. Song, B., Seol, H., & Park, Y. (2016). A patent portfolio-based approach for assessing potential R&D partners: An application of the Shapley value. *Technological Forecasting and Social Change, 103*, 156–165. https://doi.org/10.1016/j.techfore.2015.10.010
72. Xu, G., Wu, Y., Minshall, T., & Zhou, Y. (2018). Exploring innovation ecosystems across science, technology, and business: A case of 3D printing in China. *Technological Forecasting and Social Change, 136*, 208–221. https://doi.org/10.1016/j.techfore.2017.06.030
73. Huhtamäki, J., & Olsson, T. (2018). Digital social matching ecosystem for knowledge work. In *Proceedings of the 10th International Joint Conference on Knowledge Discovery, Knowledge Engineering and Knowledge Management*. SCITEPRESS – Science and Technology Publications. https://doi.org/10.5220/0006950301940199
74. Spinazzola, M., Scuotto, V., Farronato, N., & Pironti, M. (2022). Identifying synergies and barriers to the adoption of disruptive technologies for sustainable societies – An innovation ecosystem perspective. In *2022 IEEE International Conference on Technology Management, Operations and Decisions (ICTMOD)* (pp. 1–6). https://doi.org/10.1109/ICTMOD55867.2022.10041880

Studying the Distribution of Strategies in the Two-Scenario Snowdrift Game

Edgardo Bucciarelli, Shu-Heng Chen, Aurora Ascatigno, and Alfredo Colantonio

Abstract The Snowdrift Game, a commonly adopted model for studying cooperation in a competitive scenario, serves as a framework in this work. Computer simulations are used to investigate how variations in the payoff structure affect the strategies adopted by players. Two scenarios with distinct payoff parameters are explored. Players engage in strategies aligned with game theory principles. The distribution of these strategies is examined through an ecological perspective. The findings of the work are in line with the mixed strategy Nash equilibrium, implying a higher prevalence of cooperation in the scenario offering greater rewards for mutual cooperation. These results demonstrate the significant influence of payoff manipulation on cooperative behaviour within the game.

Keywords Social dilemmas · Computational economics · Strategies

1 Introduction

The evolution of cooperation among individuals has been a subject of interest to scholars across various research fields. This fascination has led to decades of investigation, primarily through two complementary approaches: Experimentation

E. Bucciarelli (✉)
University of Chieti-Pescara, Pescara, Italy
e-mail: edgardo.bucciarelli@unich.it

S.-H. Chen
National Chengchi University, Taipei, Taiwan
e-mail: chchen@nccu.edu.tw

A. Ascatigno
School of Advanced Studies, University of Chieti-Pescara, Chieti, Italy
e-mail: aurora.ascatigno@unich.it

A. Colantonio
International Telematic University Uninettuno, Rome, Italy
e-mail: a.colantonio@students.uninettunouniversity.net

A. M. Braccini et al. (eds.), *Digital (Eco) Systems and Societal Challenges*, Lecture Notes in Information Systems and Organisation 72,
https://doi.org/10.1007/978-3-031-75586-6_22

with living organisms [1] and computer simulations [2]. As reviewed by [3], this multifaceted exploration has drawn upon various strategic constructs. Notably, the Snowdrift Game has become a prominent framework for analysing potential conflict and competition scenarios between individuals. The game, also known as the Hawk-Dove or Chicken Game [4–7], presents a classic social dilemma within game theory [8]. Players face a binary choice—to cooperate or defect. This framework crosses the boundaries of standard game theory, finding significant applications in evolutionary game theory as well [4]. Within this domain, the Snowdrift Game serves as a valuable tool for understanding the evolution of cooperation among interacting entities in natural ecosystems. The entities in question can range from human societies to diverse life forms such as animals, cells, and bacteria. It is essential to clarify that this work does not explore cooperation within the context of natural ecosystems. Instead, we focus on computer simulations made up of fictitious players whose behavioural strategies remain constant over time. This work, specifically, presents key findings from computer simulations that contribute to the ongoing discourse within the existing literature on the Snowdrift Game. Two distinct scenarios are developed within the related framework to deepen our understanding of how strategy distributions and payoffs evolve, particularly from an ecological perspective. It is worth noting that this perspective remains largely unexplored in Snowdrift Game research.

As previously noted by [7], the Snowdrift Game has demonstrated potential for investigating individual conflicts and competition, but it has received relatively little scholarly attention in recent decades. This underrepresentation in the literature served as a critical foundation for our work, particularly in light of the potential to further bridge the gap between the Prisoner's Dilemma and the Snowdrift game. To investigate possible variations in expected payoffs among fictitious players within the Snowdrift game, we conducted computer simulations, all viewed through an ecological lens. The specific Game Theory strategies operated in our simulations are based on those outlined by [9]. Based on the above, we believe that the outcomes of tournaments conducted in the Prisoner's Dilemma and those in the Snowdrift game can be meaningfully compared using these strategies (see [9]). The juxtaposition promises to reveal intriguing dynamics within the related strategic constructs, particularly from an ecological viewpoint.

Therefore, building upon the paper of [9], whose strategies can be adapted to categorise human behaviour and facilitate inter-subject comparisons during experiments [10], we focus on fictitious players whose behaviour is governed by pre-defined strategies. As outlined by [11], furthermore, these strategies encompass two unconditional options: *Cooperator* and *Defector*. Three conditional strategies, *TitForTat*, *Suspicious TitForTat*, and *Anti TitForTat*, are also included. The primary objective of the simulation conducted is to compare the interaction outcomes of the two unconditional strategies and identify any differences in their expected payoffs. This comparison serves as a foundation for introducing supplementary strategies and assessing how they influence expected payoff variations. Upon closer inspection, the comparison above aims to validate the mixed strategy Nash equilibrium of the Snowdrift Game [12].

This work investigates whether modifications to the payoff parameters of the Snowdrift Game, as outlined in [13], affect the expected payoffs of fictitious players. Section 2 provides a thorough explanation of the payoffs (T, R, S, and P) used in the simulations carried out. Precisely, Scenario 1 uses payoffs of $T = 5$, $R = 3$, $S = 1$, and $P = 0$, while Scenario 2 uses $T = 4$, $R = 3$, $S = 2$, and $P = 0$. We further explore potential variations in expected payoffs across scenarios for fictitious players adopting different strategies in each iteration. Following the approach of [14], the simulation of each scenario was repeated for no. 200 tournaments.

From an ecological point of view, following [15], we identify the dominant strategies that persist within each scenario and potentially translate into success in the other. By examining strategy combinations across no. 1000 simulated tournaments, we build an ecological environment based on the payoffs achieved by each player type. Our simulations further bridge two of Axelrod's seminal papers, namely [14, 15]. The bridge is established through three key aspects: First, we adopt the standard number of tournaments commonly used for this type of simulation, as outlined in [14]. This ensures consistency and facilitates comparison with other studies. Second, we incorporate the widely used *TitForTat* strategy, as discussed in both [14, 15]. This strategy allows us to analyse player interactions within the Snowdrift Game, drawing parallels to its application in the Prisoner's Dilemma. Third, we examine the interactions within an ecological framework, similar to the approach proposed in [15]. Emergent ecology sheds light on how the strategies adopted by the fictitious players influence their success in the simulated environment.

Beyond this introductory section, this work is structured as follows: Sect. 2 introduces the Snowdrift Game and provides an in-depth description of its payoff parameters. Section 3 illustrates the strategies used in the computer simulations and explains the ecological environment. Section 4 outlines the methods we used to run the simulations. We thus divide Section 4 into two sub-Sections, each reporting the results obtained from each scenario. Section 5 provides a comprehensive discussion of the results, presenting our stances and potential avenues for further research while contributing to the ongoing debate.

2 The Snowdrift Game

As highlighted by [16], the Snowdrift Game (hereafter SG) is a well-established model for investigating potential conflicts and competitive scenarios between individuals. The game is often represented by two drivers stranded by a snow avalanche [16]. Both drivers could not continue their journey until the snow had been removed. As described in [7], each driver must simultaneously decide whether to cooperate by shovelling the snow or to defect by not helping. The individual decisions of each driver then lead to specific payoffs. As mentioned above, SG traditionally uses four payoffs: T, R, S, and P, where $T > R > S > P$ holds.

In this framework, P is the payoff for mutual defection. If neither driver chooses to cooperate by shovelling snow from one part of the road to the other, both drivers are stuck and receive a payoff of P. Conversely, the payoff for mutual cooperation is represented by R. If both drivers share the effort and cost of shovelling (represented by R), they can both continue their journeys. The temptation to defect is captured by T, i.e. the payoff received by a driver who shirks responsibility while the other shovels (who receives the so-called sucker payoff, S). It is worth considering, albeit briefly, the relative values of T and S. The driver who cooperates by shovelling snow receives S, a lower payoff than the driver who defects to receive T. While both drivers can continue once the snow is cleared, the cooperating driver bears a more significant cost.

A 2x2 symmetric payoff matrix can represent SG based on [16]. Players can choose between C (cooperation) and D (defection). The payoff can be determined by combining pure strategies as follows:

$$\begin{array}{cc} & \begin{array}{cc} C & D \end{array} \\ \begin{array}{c} C \\ D \end{array} & \begin{pmatrix} R & S \\ T & P \end{pmatrix} \end{array}$$

According to [17], the following condition characterises the payoffs of SG: T > R > S > P. Changing this condition allows configurations for other non-cooperative games, such as the Prisoner's Dilemma, the Stag Hunt Game, and the Harmony Game (among others, see [12]). In addition, it should be noted that there are only two Nash equilibria in SG, namely (C, D) and (D, C), *[…] in which the players adopt opposite pure strategies, but these cannot be reached without introducing correlations between the players. Therefore, the best solution is a mixed strategy Nash equilibrium […]* (Correira & Stoof, [18], p. 2, brackets added).

In particular, to calculate the mixed strategy Nash equilibrium, it is necessary to specify two parameters: B and C. These parameters are obtained from the payoffs of SG. B and C are subject to the conditions B > 0 and C < 0, respectively. In this regard, the parameter B is determined by the difference between S and P, while the parameter C is defined by the difference between R and T. According to [12], we can calculate the proportion of cooperators (P_c) as follows:

$$P_C = \frac{|B|}{(|B| - |C|)} \tag{1}$$

The proportion of cooperators is given in Eq. 1 by dividing the absolute value of B by the difference between parameters B and C (in absolute value). The proportion of defectors (P_d) can be calculated as follows:

$$P_d = 1 - P_c \tag{2}$$

Specifically, by subtracting the proportion of cooperators from the unit, the proportion of defectors is determined, as indicated in Eq. 2.

In this sense, [7] suggests that SG is a kind of anti-coordination game with partial cooperation. In the case of players adopting pure strategies opposite to the Nash equilibrium, partial cooperation can occur. As stated by [7], turn-taking (alternating opposite decisions between players) is a Pareto-efficient solution. However, considering a repeated variant of SG, the turn-taking behaviour *is not an equilibrium state in finitely repeated games, i.e. players are permanently tempted to reject this solution* (Stark, [7], p. 2459). This temptation is a potential cause for a cooperation dilemma or, more generally, a social dilemma (see [19]).

The mixed strategy Nash equilibrium can be determined by solving Eqs. 1 and 2. In sub-Sects. 4.1 and 4.2, we explain the results of implementing Eqs. 1 and 2 for the specified payoff parameters in each scenario. As previously stated, each scenario is characterised by specific payoff parameters: T = 5, R = 3, S = 1, and P = 0 in the first scenario. The parameters indicate that if both players fold, they receive a payoff of 0. Cooperation between the two players results in a payoff of 3. Finally, if one player cooperates and the other defects, the defector receives a payoff of 5, while the cooperator receives a payoff of 1. In the second scenario, the following payoff parameters apply: T = 4, R = 3, S = 2, and P = 0. In this scenario, in accordance with [13], we have reduced the temptation payoff (T) by one unit (from 5 to 4) and increased the sucker payoff (S) by one unit (from 1 to 2). Upon first inspection, it may appear that players are less inclined to pursue a defection strategy. This may be due to a perceived reduction in the incentive to defect. As discussed below, embracing a purely ecological perspective is crucial to defining the winning strategies that persist over time. Accordingly, we will explore the differences in winning strategies between 200 and 1000 tournaments.

3 Strategies and Ecological Environment

The SG, designed as a two-player, two-strategy framework, allows players to choose between cooperation and defection. To investigate the potential outcomes of these choices, we resort to established game theory strategies as in [9] in order to explore the expected payoffs of fictitious players. Our preliminary objective is to assess whether these Prisoner's Dilemma strategies could effectively adapt to the SG context. Purposely, we set the following strategies: *Defector, Cooperator, TitForTat, Suspicious TitForTat*, and *Anti TitForTat.*

In keeping with [11], the first two strategies (*Defector* and *Cooperator*) are defined as unconditional. Regardless of what other players do, an unconditional cooperator or unconditional defector will always cooperate or defect. Instead, the other three strategies are defined as conditional in nature (e.g., *TitForTat, Suspicious TitForTat,* and *Anti TitForTat*). The strategies are conditioned (i.e., conditional) because the choices made by the individual player at time t + 1 are influenced by those made by the opponent at time t.

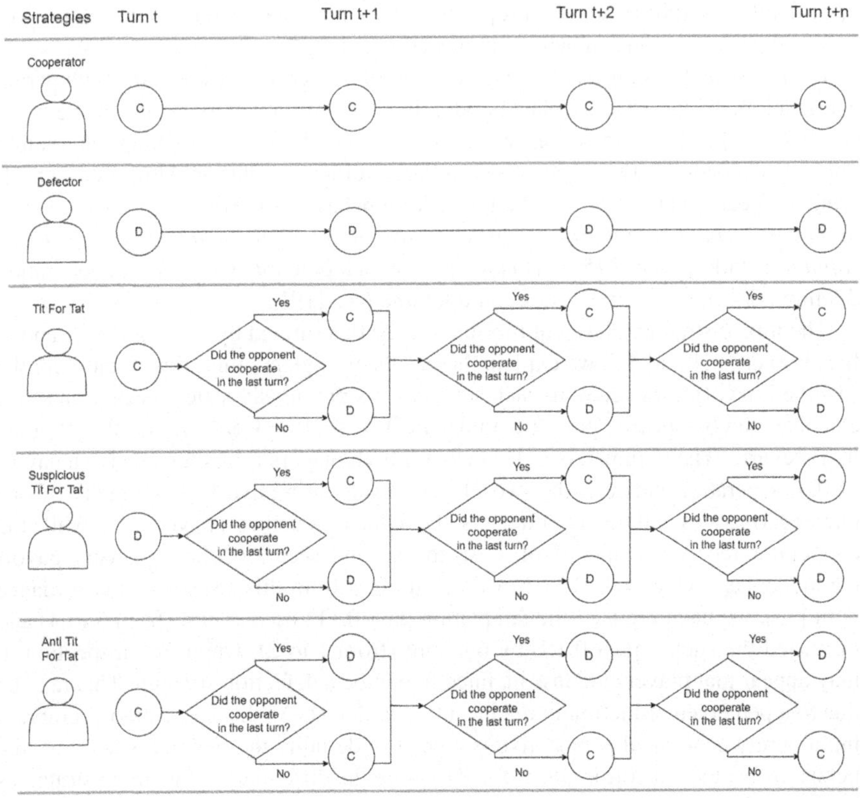

Fig. 1 A representation of the strategies adopted in the simulations

Figure 1 visually represents the strategies employed in the computer simulations. The time is expressed in turns. Firstly, we observe the unconditional strategy, *Cooperator*, which is distinguished for each turn by persistent cooperation (C). Secondly, we observe another unconditional strategy, i.e. *Defector*, distinguished for each turn by persistent defection (D). Thirdly, the first conditional strategy, *TitForTat*, is characterised by cooperation (C) in the first turn. In subsequent turns, it is characterised by cooperation (C) if the opponent cooperated in the previous turn. The strategy is instead characterised by defection (D) in the following turns. Fourthly, we observe the second conditional strategy, *Suspicious TitForTat*, characterised by defection (D) in the first turn. Similarly to *TitForTat*, the *Suspicious TitForTat* is characterised by cooperation (C) in the following turns if the opponent has cooperated in the previous turn. In contrast, the *Anti TitForTat* is characterised by defection (D) in the subsequent turns. Finally, we consider the third conditional strategy, *Anti TitForTat*, which is characterised by cooperation (C) in the initial turn.

Unlike the *TitForTat* strategy, the *Anti TitForTat* involves a persistent defection (D) if the opponent cooperated in the previous turn. Conversely, if the opponent did not cooperate, this strategy is characterised by cooperation in the following turns. In the simulations carried out, we set the behaviour of fictitious players based on the strategies previously described and grouped as follows:

(1) *Cooperator* and *Defector*;
(2) *Cooperator*, *Defector* and *TitForTat*;
(3) *Cooperator*, *Defector*, *TitForTat*, and *Suspicious TitForTat*;
(4) *Cooperator*, *Defector*, *TitForTat*, *Suspicious TitForTat*, and *Anti TitForTat*.

Each scenario is associated with a distinct set of strategies. By sequentially introducing one strategy at a time, one can observe the differences in expected payoffs resulting from fictitious player interactions.

In accordance with the approach of [15], we created an environment called ecosystem using the Axelrod Python library [20] for each scenario. This environment was generated using a purely ecological approach based on the payoff matrix generated during tournaments (e.g., the repetition of interaction among fictitious players). In this specific environment, *if one [strategy] gets twice as high a tournament score in the initial round as another [strategy], then it will be twice as well-represented in the next round. This creates a simulated second generation of the tournament in which the average score achieved by a [strategy] is the weighted average of its score with each of the [strategies], where the weights are proportional to the success of the other [strategies] in the initial generation* (Axelrod, [15], p. 398, brackets added).

Therefore, we adopted Axelrod's [15] approach to investigate the evolutionary stability of each strategy included in the environment thus constructed. From an ecological perspective, [15] suggests that the changing distribution of (some) strategies can be studied, but not their evolution over time. This is because fictitious players cannot change their behaviour over time while playing in tournaments. From this perspective, therefore, we cannot help but observe a winning strategy that persists over time, resulting from unchangeable behaviour. Nevertheless, we are interested in examining whether there are variations in the winning strategy between the 200 and 1000 tournaments.

4 Methods and Results

This section outlines the principal methods used in conducting computer simulations in both scenarios. The two sub-sections provide a detailed exposition of the results obtained. We present results derived from calculating the mixed strategy Nash equilibrium in each scenario.

The primary objective of the simulation below is to examine the changing distribution of strategies by analysing the expected payoffs that arise from the interaction of grouped strategies within each scenario. The grouped strategies were explained in Sect. 3. Four simulations were conducted for each scenario to study the evolution and potential differences in expected payoffs resulting from the grouped strategies. First, the grouped strategies (group no. 1, see Sect. 3) were included. Subsequently, to explore the results from interactions among the five-game theory strategies, the other grouped strategies (groups no. 2-3-4) were included (see [9]). To investigate the interactions between the fictitious players who adopt the previously defined strategies, no. 200 tournaments were conducted to iterate the game, following the methodology outlined in [14]. The same universe was employed in both scenarios to ensure comparable and reproducible results. The Axelrod library [20] was used to run computer simulations working with Python 3.

4.1 Scenario 1

The approach conducted in [13] is adopted to set the payoff parameters for SG in the current first scenario: T = 5, R = 3, S = 1, and P = 0. Based on [18], only two Nash equilibria exist in this game's standard version. The two Nash equilibria emerging from this scenario are (1,5) and (5,1), respectively. In contrast, a mixed strategy Nash equilibrium is the only equilibrium that allows defectors and cooperators to coexist. Equation 1 can be used to determine the proportion of cooperators. In this scenario, the proportion of cooperators is $P_c = 0.3333$. The proportion of defectors is obtained by difference (see Eq. 2) and equals $P_d = 0.6667$. This scenario is characterised by a mixed strategy Nash equilibrium of 0.667 and 0.333. The main phases of the computer simulations and the results obtained are reported below. The SG was initially defined by setting the parameters based on this first scenario. The Axelrod library [20] was employed to determine the strategies of fictitious players. In the figures below, warm shades of colour (e.g., yellow) represent high payoffs, while cool shades of colour (e.g., blue) represent low payoffs.

In the initial simulation, as anticipated above, the two unconditional strategies, *Cooperator* and *Defector* (group no. 1, see Sect. 3), were included. The command was launched to start tournaments (i.e., iterations). Through the iterations, the results inherent to the winning strategy were obtained. The winning strategy is determined by the highest payoffs achieved in all tournaments. It was observed that the *Defector* strategy (scores = 1000) yielded the highest payoff compared to the *Cooperator* strategy (scores = 200). Figure 2 displays these results. When players interact by adopting the two unconditional strategies, *Defector* yields a relatively higher payoff.

Subsequently, the third strategy, *TitForTat* (group no. 2), was included in the analysis. It was observed that the *Defector* (scores = 1005) remained the winning strategy when compared to the *Cooperator* (scores = 800) and *TitForTat* (scores = 601). These results can be seen in Fig. 3. Despite including a conditional strategy in this simulation, the *Defector* strategy allows the player to achieve a relatively higher payoff, as evidenced by the results. Furthermore, the fourth strategy, the *Suspicious TitForTat*, has been implemented. The winning strategy is

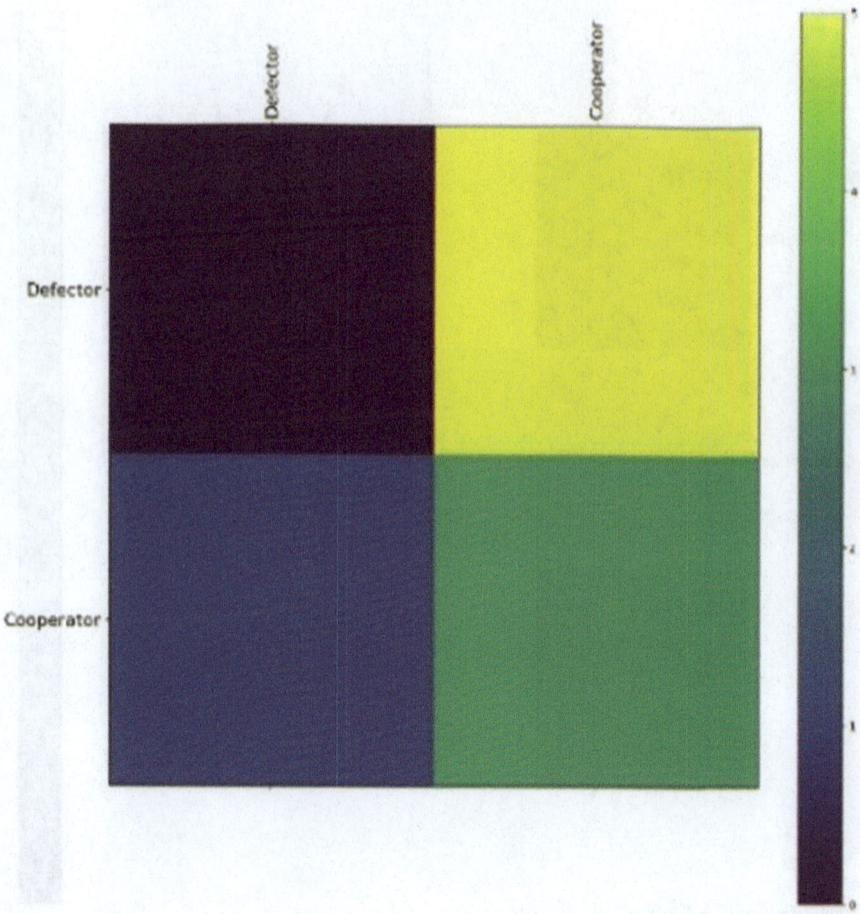

Fig. 2 Scenario 1: Matrix of expected payoff from the interaction between strategies (group no. 1)

Cooperator (scores = 1398) against *Suspicious TitForTat* (scores = 1202), *TitForTat* (scores = 1201) and *Defector* (scores = 1005). Figure 4 illustrates the results. Compared to previous simulations, a reversal of the observed trend occurred. It can be seen that *Cooperator* can achieve a higher payoff by incorporating the strategy *Suspicious TitForTat*. By contrast, the *Defector* has a lower payoff than the other strategies.

Ultimately, the fifth strategy, *Anti TitForTat* (4), was included in the analysis. This strategy was found to be the most effective against *Defector* (scores = 2005), *Suspicious TitForTat* (scores = 1652), *TitForTat* (scores = 1651) and *Cooperator* (scores = 1600). The results are presented in Fig. 5: They suggest that the conditional strategy *Anti TitForTat* allows the player to achieve a higher payoff than other

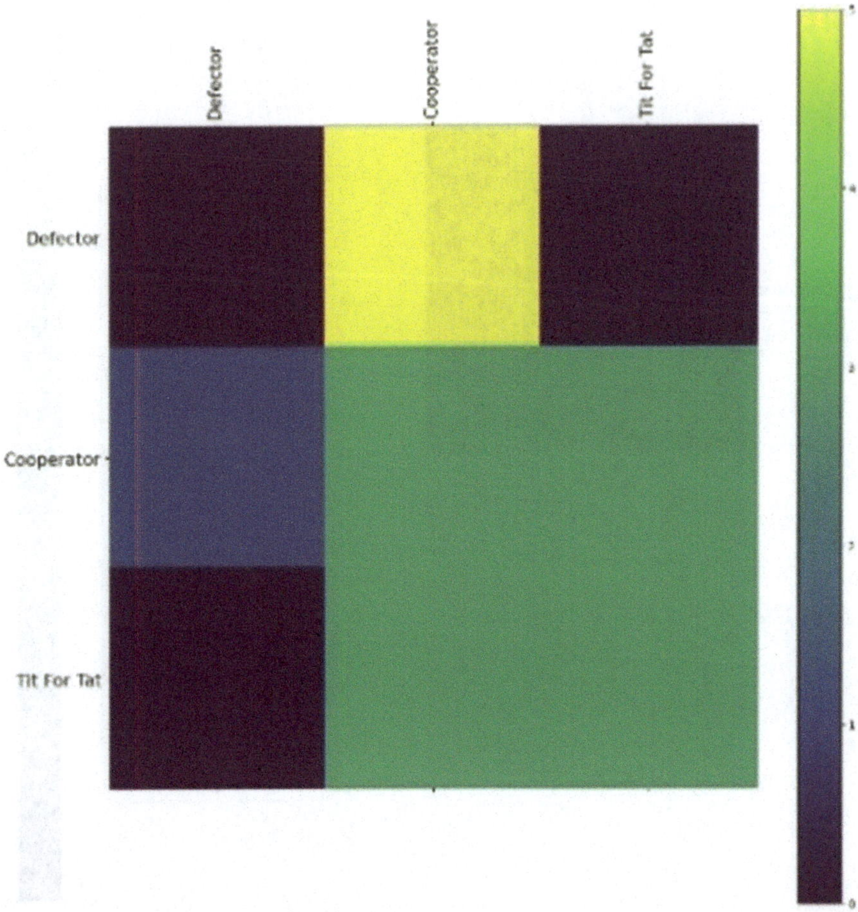

Fig. 3 Scenario 1: Matrix of expected payoff from the interaction among strategies (group no. 2)

strategies. Compared to the previous simulation, including the conditional strategy *Anti TitForTat* results in a trend reversal.

An ecological ecosystem was constructed using the approach that emerged in [15] and the Axelrod library [20]. The ecosystem was replicated with 1000 iterations for each group of strategies (e.g., (1),(2),(3),(4)). The simulation results are shown in Figs. 6, 7, 8, 9. Significantly, after 1000 iterations, the distributions of strategies that persist over time in each simulation were observed to be: (1) *Defector* and *Cooperator*; (2) *Defector* and *Cooperator*; (3) *Defector* and *Cooperator*; (4) *Defector* and *Anti TitForTat*.

The results indicate that unconditional strategies have a better chance of survival over time, particularly when interactions are repeated for 1000 iterations, replacing conditional strategies. The *TitForTat* strategy is also unsuccessful in any simulation,

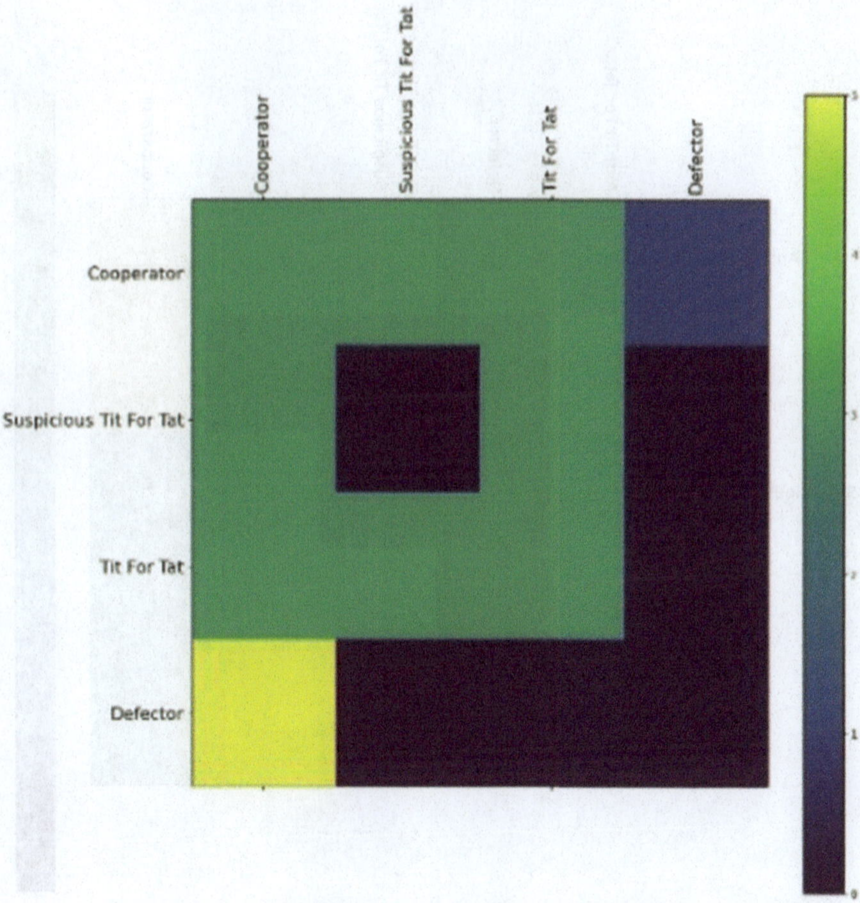

Fig. 4 Scenario 1: Matrix of expected payoff from the interaction among strategies (group no. 3)

unlike the typical outcome observed in other social dilemmas, such as the Prisoner's Dilemma (see [14, 21]).

4.2 Scenario 2

The payoff parameters in SG are T = 4, R = 3, S = 2, and P = 0 in the second scenario. The temptation payoff was reduced by one unit (from 5 to 4), and the sucker payoff increased by one unit (from 1 to 2). According to [18], on the one hand, the standard version of this game has only two Nash equilibria, which, in this scenario, are (4,2) and (2,4), respectively. In the same scenario, on the other hand, a mixed strategy Nash equilibrium exists and determines the coexistence of defectors

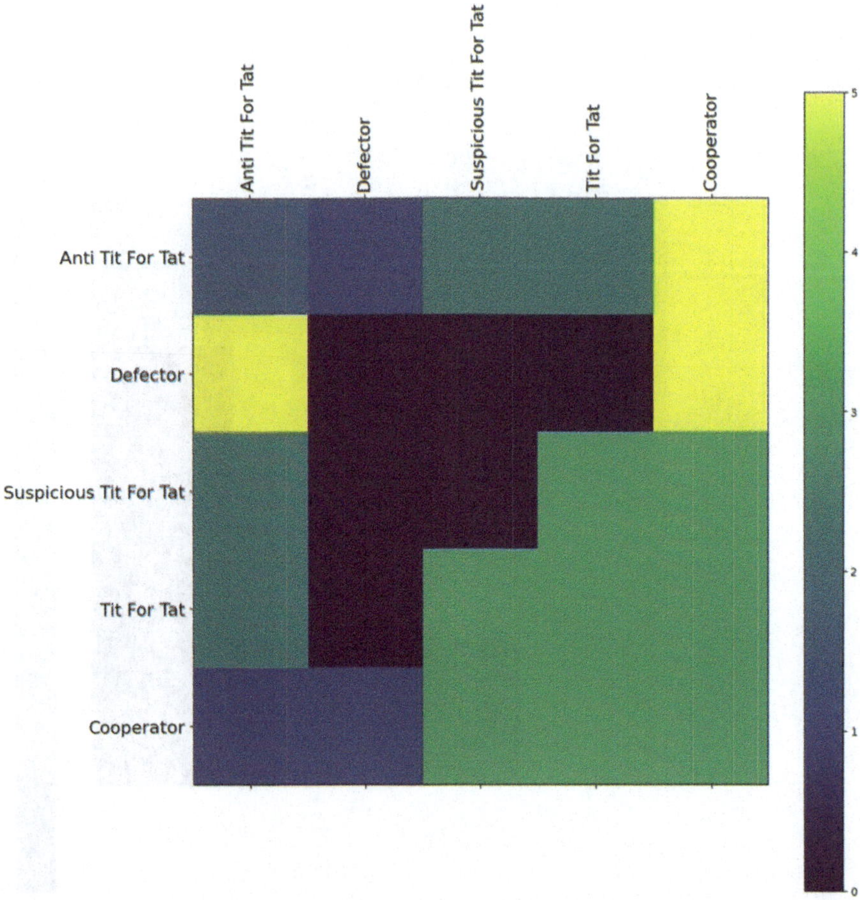

Fig. 5 Scenario 1: Matrix of expected payoff from the interaction among strategies (group no. 4)

and cooperators. As specified in Eq. 1, the proportion of cooperators is $P_c = 0.667$, while the proportion of defectors is $P_d = 0.333$. At a glance, it becomes evident that the proportion of cooperators and defectors differs significantly from that of the previous scenario. Strategies that emphasise greater cooperation are more likely to result in higher payoffs than those involving more defection. It is hypothesised that strategies involving more cooperation are more likely to survive over time. Following the same computer simulation phases as the first scenario, those methods and computational approaches have been adopted. In the figures below, warm colour tones (e.g., the yellow one) depict relatively higher payoffs, similar to the first scenario. Conversely, cool shades of colour (e.g., the blue one) are employed to represent relatively lower payoffs.

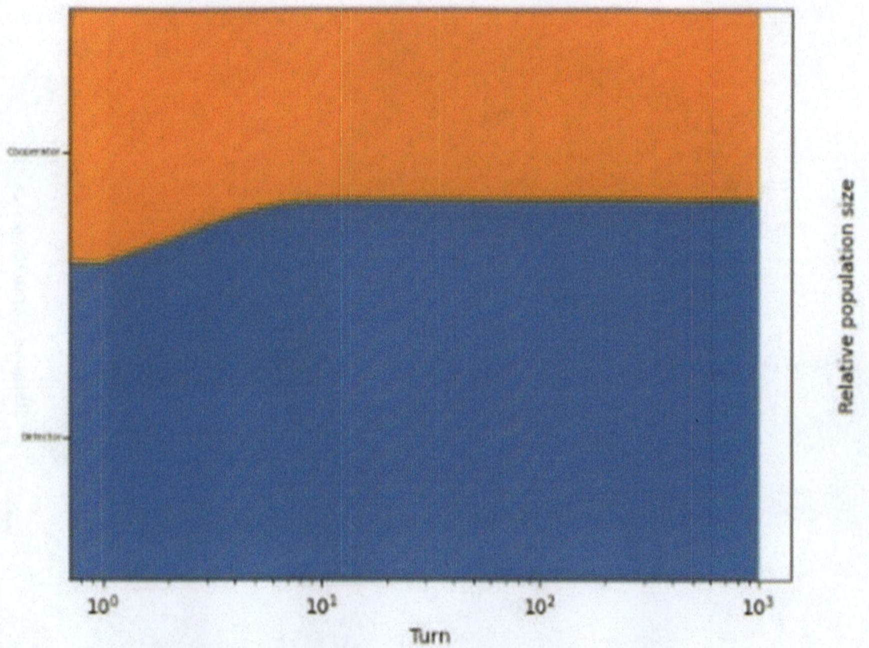

Fig. 6 Scenario 1: Distribution of winning strategies in the ecosystem environment (group no. 1)

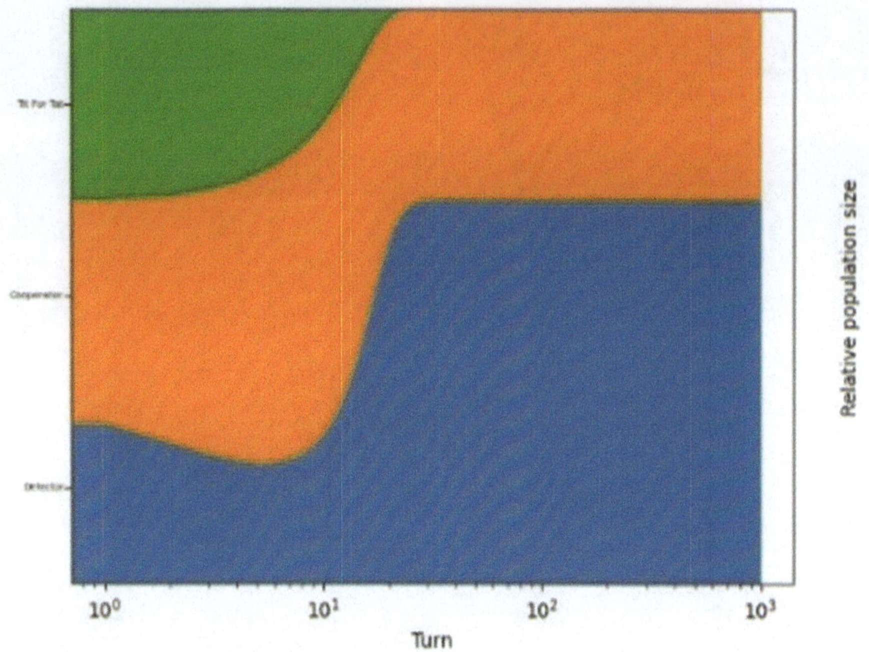

Fig. 7 Scenario 1: Distribution of winning strategies in the ecosystem environment (group no. 2)

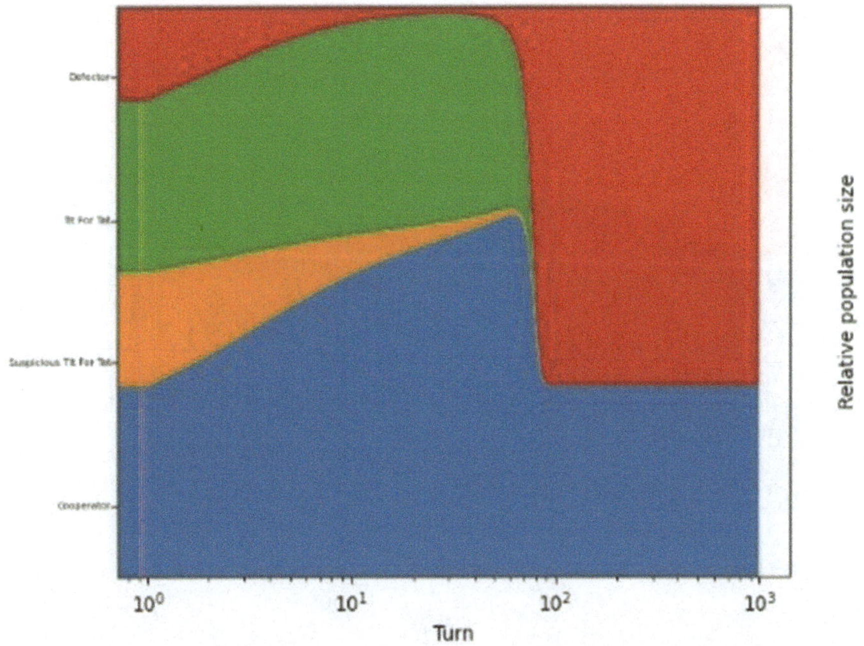

Fig. 8 Scenario 1: Distribution of winning strategies in the ecosystem environment (group no. 3)

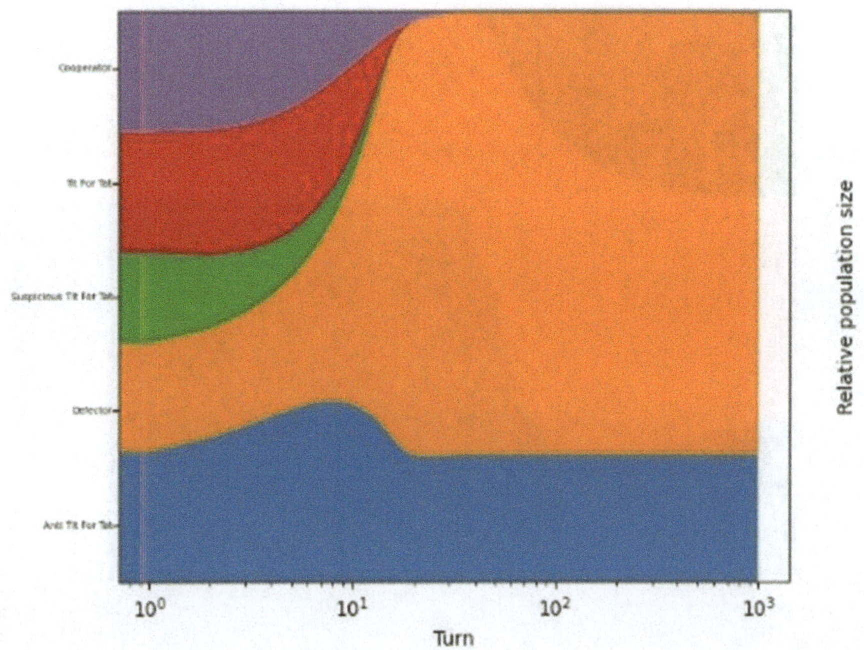

Fig. 9 Scenario 1: Distribution of winning strategies in the ecosystem environment (group no. 4)

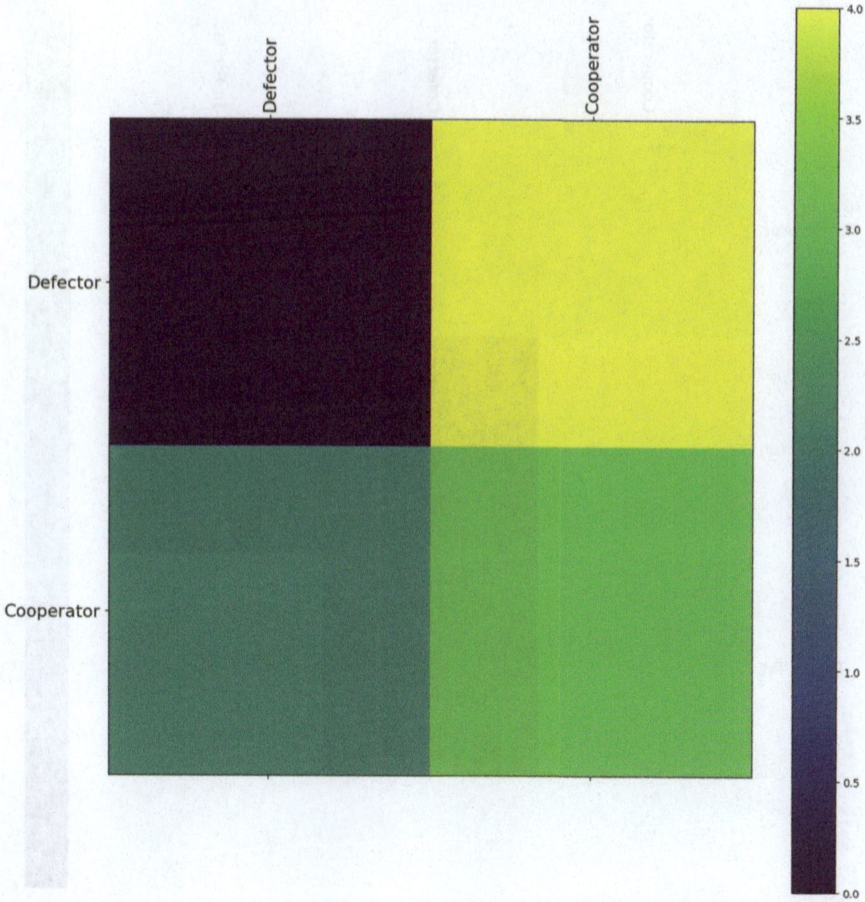

Fig. 10 Scenario 2: Matrix of expected payoff from the interaction between strategies (group no. 1)

The two unconditional strategies, *Cooperator* and *Defector* (group no. 1), were used in the initial simulation. The command was launched to activate the tournament (iterations) and obtain results related to the winning strategy. It was observed that the winning strategy was *Defector* (scores = 800) compared to *Cooperator* (scores = 400). Figure 10 illustrates the results that are consistent with Scenario 1. When players interact with two specific unconditional strategies, the *Defector* receives a relatively higher payoff, as evidenced by the results.

Similarly to Scenario 1, a third strategy, *TitForTat* (group no. 2), was included. The results showed that the winning strategy was *Cooperator* (scores = 1000) against *Defector* (scores = 804) and *TitForTat* (scores = 602). Figure 11 shows these results accordingly: They support our preliminary belief that by reducing the temptation payoff, players are discouraged from adopting strategies that lead to

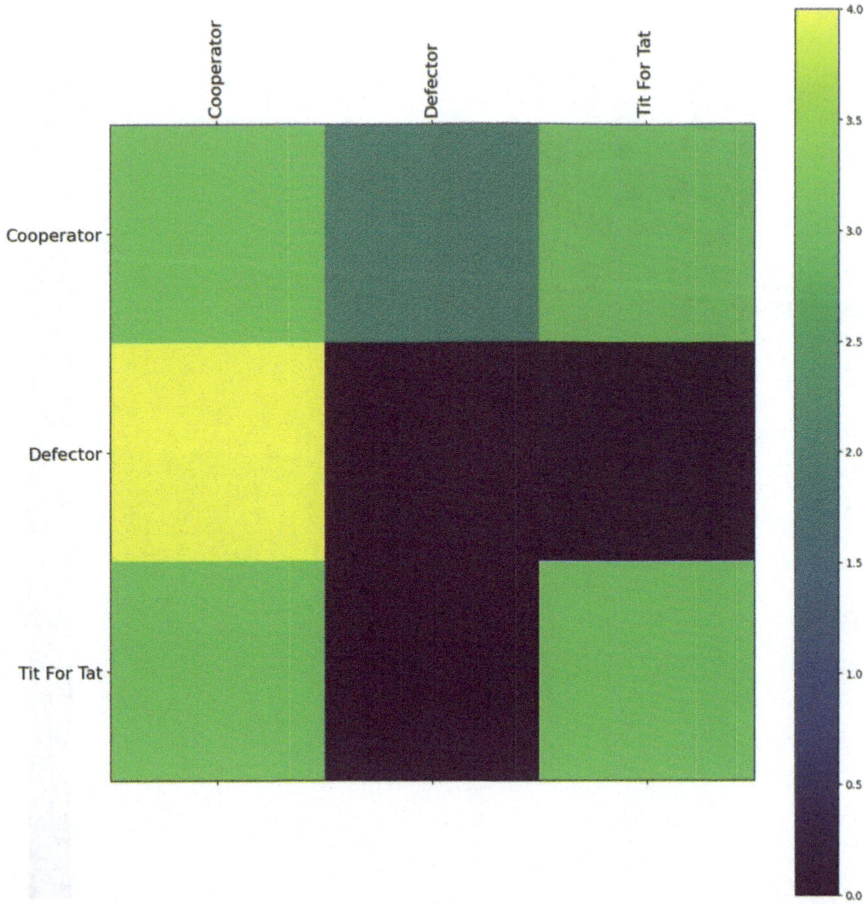

Fig. 11 Scenario 2: Matrix of expected payoff from the interaction among strategies (group no. 2)

more defection. Consequently, it is more likely to observe players behaving cooperatively.

We included a fourth strategy, the *Suspicious TitForTat* (group no. 3). The winning strategy is *Cooperator* (scores = 1599) against *TitForTat* (scores = 1202), *Suspicious TitForTat* (scores = 1201), and *Defector* (scores = 804). The results can be seen in Fig. 12. Despite the introduction of a further conditional strategy, *Cooperator* remains the winning strategy. The results are, in part, consistent with Scenario 1. While the winning strategy is identical, the second and third-best strategies are in opposition to Scenario 1.

Finally, a fifth strategy, i.e. *Anti TitForTa*t (group no. 4), was added to the existing strategies. It was observed that the winning strategy was *Anti TitForTat* (scores = 2099) against *Cooperator* (scores = 2000), *TitForTat* (scores = 1652), *Suspicious TitForTat* (scores = 1651) and *Defector* (scores = 1604). The results are

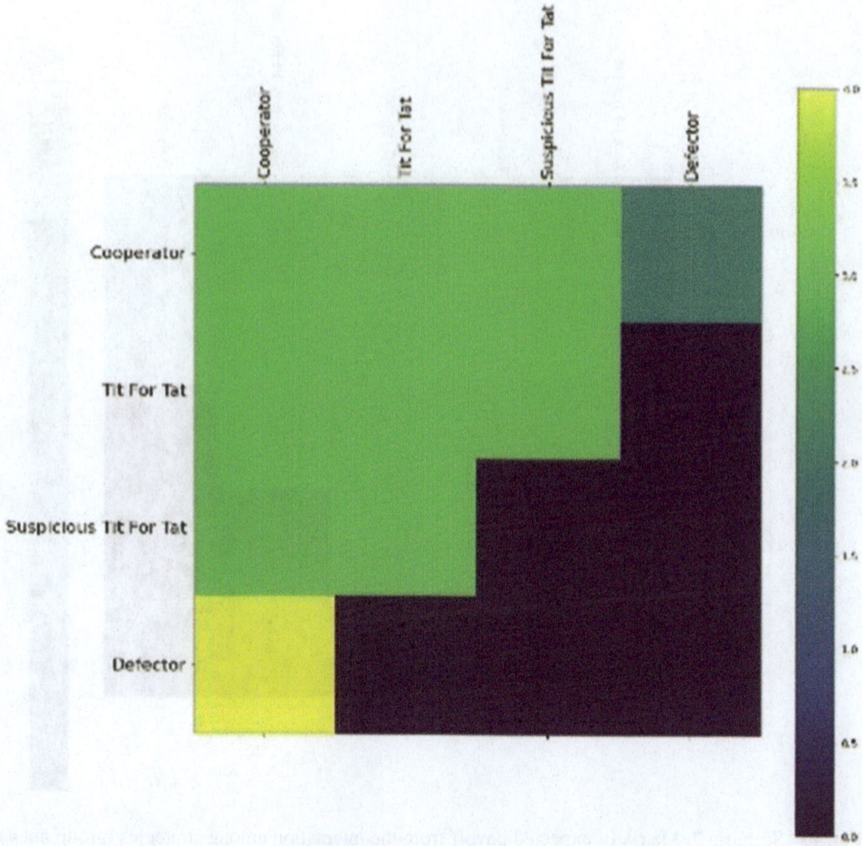

Fig. 12 Scenario 2: Matrix of expected payoff from the interaction among strategies (group no. 3)

presented in Fig. 13. They are consistent with the first scenario and similar to the previous simulation. In the second scenario, the second-best strategy is *Cooperator*, while in the first scenario, *Defector* is the second-best.

Furthermore, an ecosystem was created that repeats 1000 iterations for each group of strategies. Figures 14, 15, 16, 17 illustrate the results obtained. The distributions of strategies that persist over time after 1000 iterations are as follows: (1) *Cooperator* and *Defector*; (2) *Cooperator* and *Defector*; (3) *Cooperator* and *TitForTat*; (4) *Anti TitForTat*, *Cooperator* and *Defector*.

The simulation results provide insight into how unconditional strategies are more resilient over time, replacing conditioned ones, particularly when the interactions are repeated 1000 times. Cooperative strategies are dominant in the second scenario. The *TitForTat* strategy is not a winner in any simulation, as it was in the first scenario, even after 1000 iterations.

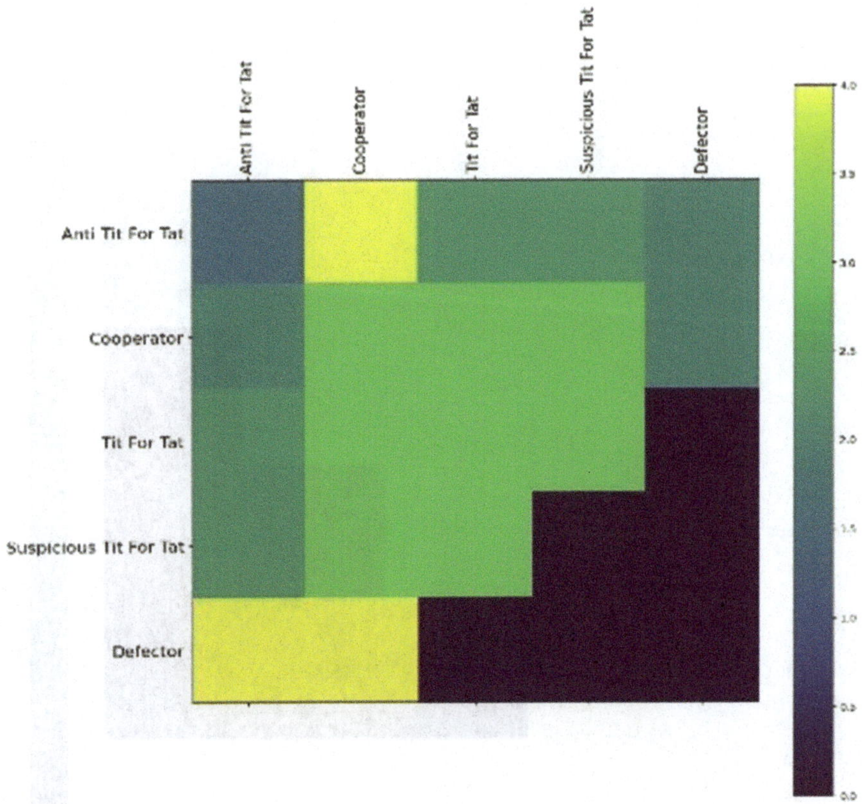

Fig. 13 Scenario 2: Matrix of expected payoff from the interaction among strategies (group no. 4)

5 Discussion and Future Research

This work has examined the SG in its repeated version, taking into account the different results regarding the expected payoff when combining particular strategies. To this end, we draw some conclusions by briefly discussing the main results of the simulations conducted. In that regard, we distinguish some characteristics between the two scenarios considered. The outcomes derived from 1000 iterations align closely with the mixed strategy Nash equilibria calculated for each scenario. A coexistence of defectors and cooperators is observed. Notably, the first scenario exhibits a higher prevalence of defectors, whereas the second scenario portrays a higher prevalence of cooperators. From an ecological perspective, it becomes evident that subtle adjustments in the Snowdrift game's payoff parameters can significantly influence the expected payoffs arising from the combination of strategies. An increase in the expected payoffs potentially impacts the long-term survivability of specific strategies. Our observations reveal a higher propensity towards cooperation

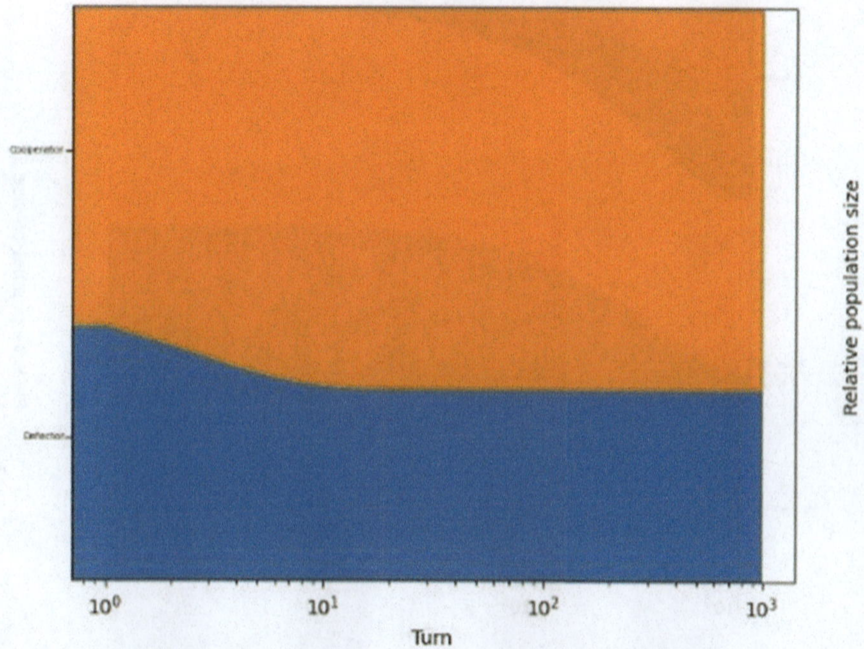

Fig. 14 Scenario 2: Distribution of winning strategies in the ecosystem environment (group no. 1)

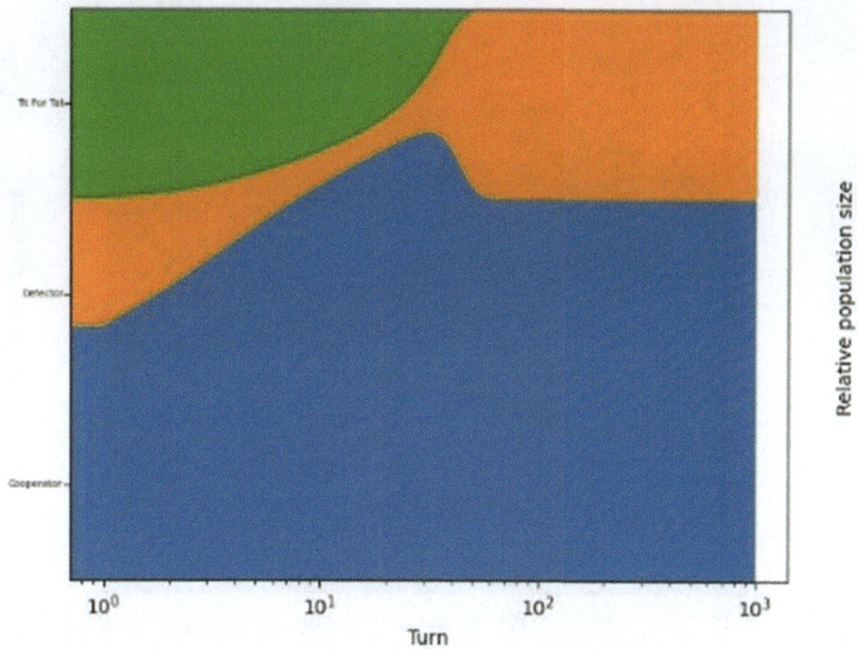

Fig. 15 Scenario 2: Distribution of winning strategies in the ecosystem environment (group no. 2)

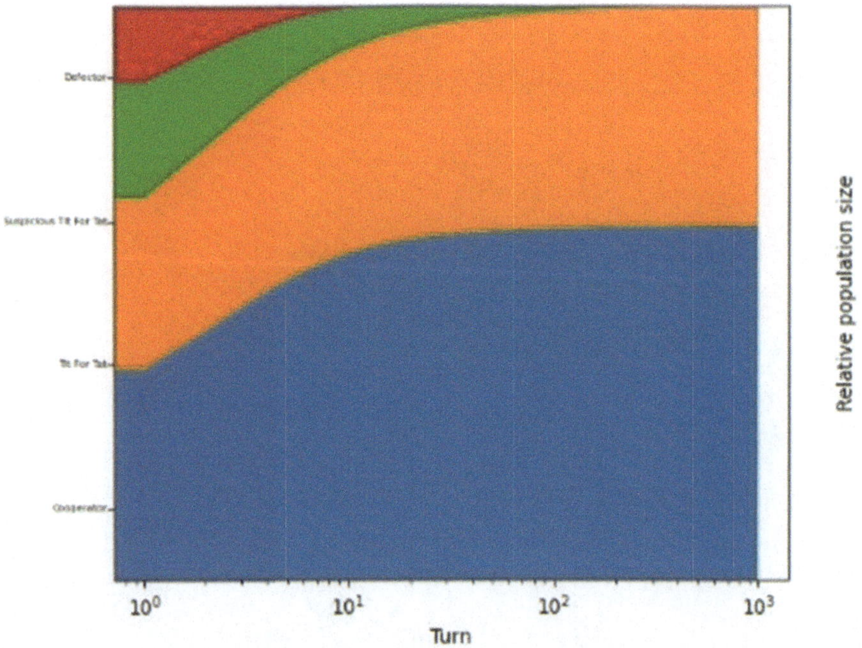

Fig. 16 Scenario 2: Distribution of winning strategies in the ecosystem environment (group no. 3)

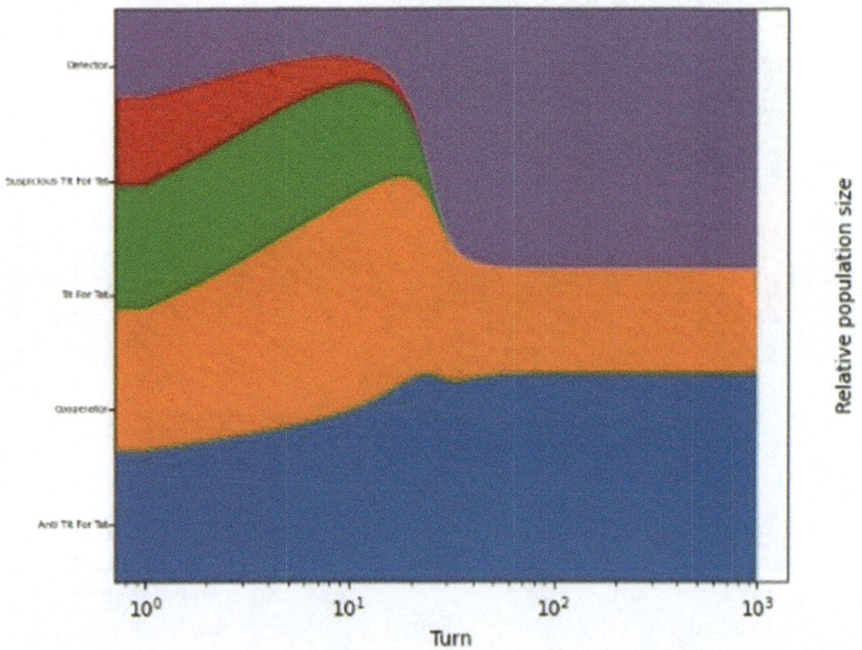

Fig. 17 Scenario 2: Distribution of winning strategies in the ecosystem environment (group no. 4)

in Scenario 2 compared to Scenario 1. This shift towards cooperative strategies becomes more pronounced when the temptation to defect decreases and the sucker payoff increases. Our findings diverge from those of [13], but this divergence can be attributed to their examination of the Snowdrift Game in a spatial structure rather than an ecological ecosystem. As stated by [7], the Snowdrift Game presents an enthralling strategic construct that has received little attention in the literature. In the future, we intend to delve deeper into the Snowdrift Game, adopting an evolutionary game theory approach through both computer simulations and experimentation with human subjects. In keeping with [10], the insights gleaned from our simulations can also facilitate comparisons between the behaviour of fictitious players and human experimental subjects. Doing so makes it possible to classify experimental subjects based on their utilised strategies. We can further compare experimental results with post-experiment simulations on fictitious players.

Our research aims to contribute to the ongoing debate within the existing literature concerning SG. The findings of our study could potentially catalyse future research. These studies could expand the scope of SG, incorporating well-established methods employed to explore other social dilemmas, such as the Prisoner's Dilemma. In this vein, it would be beneficial to encourage further research on SG from an ecological perspective. Last but not least, being able to use different methodologies, including human experimentation and computer simulations, to investigate social dilemmas emerging from standard game theory has the potential to reinforce the integration of computational and experimental aspects within this research domain. This integration would facilitate the establishment of a more coherent nexus between computational and experimental economics.

References

1. Jiang, L. L., Perc, M., & Szolnoki, A. (2013). If cooperation is likely punish mildly: Insights from economic experiments based on the snowdrift game. *PLoS One, 8*(5), 1–7.
2. Sasaki, T., & Okada, I. (2015). Cheating is evolutionarily assimilated with cooperation in the continuous snowdrift game. *Biosystems, 131*(1), 51–59.
3. Gore, J., Youk, H., & Van Oudenaarden, A. (2009). Snowdrift game dynamics and facultative cheating in yeast. *Nature, 459*(7244), 253–256.
4. Maynard Smith, J. (1982). *Evolution and the theory of games*. Cambridge University Press.
5. Sugden, R. (1986). *The economics of rights, co-operation and welfare*. Basil Blackwell.
6. Doebeli, M., & Hauert, C. (2005). Models of cooperation based on the prisoner's dilemma and the snowdrift game. *Ecology Letters, 8*(7), 748–766.
7. Stark, H. U. (2010). Dilemmas of partial cooperation. *Evolution, 64*(8), 2458–2465.
8. von Neumann, J., & Morgenstern, O. (1944). *Theory of games and economic behaviour*. Princeton University Press.
9. Hilbe, C., Nowak, M. A., & Traulsen, A. (2013). Adaptive dynamics of extortion and compliance. *PLoS One, 8*(11), 1–9.
10. Albert, M., Güth, W., Kirchler, E., & Maciejovsky, B. (2007). Are we nice(r) to nice (r) people?—An experimental analysis. *Experimental Economics, 10*(1), 53–69.
11. Ramazi, P., & Cao, M. (2020). Global convergence for replicator dynamics of repeated snowdrift games. *IEEE Transactions on Automatic Control, 66*(1), 291–298.

12. Helbing, D., & Johansson, A. (2010). Cooperation, norms, and revolutions: A unified game-theoretical approach. *PLoS One, 5*(10), 1–15.
13. Ziaukas, P., Ragulskis, T., & Ragulskis, M. (2014). Communication scheme based on evolutionary spatial 2×2 games. *Physica A: Statistical Mechanics and its Applications, 403*(1), 177–188.
14. Axelrod, R. (1980a). Effective choice in the prisoner's dilemma. *Journal of Conflict Resolution, 24*(1), 3–25.
15. Axelrod, R. (1980b). More effective choice in the prisoner's dilemma. *Journal of Conflict Resolution, 24*(3), 379–403.
16. Souza, M. O., Pacheco, J. M., & Santos, F. C. (2009). Evolution of cooperation under N-person snowdrift games. *Journal of Theoretical Biology, 260*(4), 581–588.
17. McAvoy, A., & Hauert, C. (2015). Asymmetric evolutionary games. *PLoS Computational Biology, 11*(8), 1–26.
18. Correia, A. D., & Stoof, H. T. (2019). Nash equilibria in the response strategy of correlated games. *Scientific Reports, 9*(1), 1–8.
19. Dawes, R. M. (1980). Social dilemmas. *Annual Review of Psychology, 31*(1), 169–193.
20. Knight, V., Campbell, O., Marc Gaffney, T., Shaw, E., Reddy Janga, V., Glynatsi, N., Campbell, J., Langner, K. M., Singh, S., Rymer, J., Campbell, T., Young, J., Hakem, M., Palmer, G., Glass, K., Mancia, D., Argenson, E., Martin, J., Kjurgielajtis Murase, Y., et al. (n.d.). Axelrod-Python/Axelrod: v4.12.0 [Computer software]. Accessed April 8, 2023, from https://github.com/Axelrod-Python/Axelrod
21. Sigmund, K., & Nowak, M. A. (1999). Evolutionary game theory. *Current Biology, 9*(14), R503–R505.

Bargaining, Inequality, and Willingness to Bribe: A Novel Experimental Design

Edgardo Bucciarelli, Umberto Masotti, and Aurora Ascatigno

Abstract Recent decades have seen a surge in experimental research on collective action problems. These problems, which include bargaining and cooperation situations, often result in free-riding and corruption, especially when the initial resources that people have at their disposal are unequal. These typical real-world situations can be stylised using specific experimental games to study human competitive and cooperative behaviour. In the wake of the above, this work proposes a novel, three-stage experimental design that endogenously determines initial endowments, starting from the Ultimatum Bargaining Game. The outcome of the Ultimatum Bargaining Game serves as the initial endowment for a real-effort Public Goods Game. The outcome of the Public Goods Game then serves as the basis for a subsequent Bribery Game, in which the willingness to engage in bribery is assessed. A reduction in final earnings is applied when the bribery threshold has been exceeded. The experimental design involves treatment and control groups to investigate the conditions under which individuals contribute to local and global public goods. This design offers a novel opportunity to study the provision of public goods, incorporating elements of novelty that hold promise for advancing our understanding of collective action.

Keywords Experimental economics · Design research · Algorithmic social sciences research

E. Bucciarelli (✉) · U. Masotti
University of Chieti-Pescara, Pescara, Italy
e-mail: edgardo.bucciarelli@unich.it; umberto.masotti@unich.it

A. Ascatigno
School of Advanced Studies, University of Chieti-Pescara, Chieti, Italy
e-mail: aurora.ascatigno@unich.it

A. M. Braccini et al. (eds.), *Digital (Eco) Systems and Societal Challenges*, Lecture Notes in Information Systems and Organisation 72,
https://doi.org/10.1007/978-3-031-75586-6_23

1 Introduction

The past few decades have witnessed a significant surge in experimental studies to understand collective action problems. In this vein, this paper focuses on bargaining, cooperation, and corruption issues. In this field, scholars have employed various experimental paradigms to investigate human economic behaviour. These paradigms have yielded valuable contributions to the existing literature, fostering rapid growth. One prominent feature of these experimental paradigms is the inclusion of emergent social dilemmas. In these experiments, participants are placed in situations where their decisions have a reciprocal effect on the entire group (e.g., [1]). Researchers often give participants unequal initial resources to ensure that the results are more realistic. These resources can originate from previous bargaining processes, which serve as an analogy for market dynamics where economic agents drive downstream inequality. It is important to note that within this context, "inequality" refers specifically to the uneven distribution of resources and, thus, capabilities among members of a given community. In simpler terms, it signifies disparities in individual resources leading to varying levels of contribution potential. Resource inequalities are commonplace in everyday life, manifesting across diverse situations and contexts. Therefore, this study aims first to capture and stylise scenarios where individuals with unequal resources engage in negotiation, followed by decisions concerning contribution.

Building on the above, this work proposes a novel experimental design conceived as a continuation of [2], in which the authors first introduced the idea of combining the Ultimatum Bargaining Game and the Voluntary Contribution Mechanism. This work is conceived as a continuation of that initial paper and, in that wake, proposes a novel experimental design combining the Ultimatum Bargaining Game, the Public Goods Game, and the Bribery Game. As discussed below, the initial phase of the experimental design comprises an Ultimatum Bargaining Game conducted between an artificial agent and human experimental subjects per the approach outlined in [3]. The subsequent phase of the experimental design is comprised of two sequential treatments. The initial treatment involves experimental subjects in a basic Public Goods Game version configured as a real-effort task (as described in [4]). The second treatment, known as the Bribery Game [5], includes the possibility of receiving pecuniary punishment from the experimenter (e.g., [6]). Following the approach proposed by [2], our experimental design combines three games by concatenating them. The payoff obtained in the preceding game serves as the initial endowment in the subsequent game, starting with the Ultimatum Bargaining Game. The control of certain experimental variables, such as the endogenous creation of the initial endowment used in the Public Goods Game, can be improved by adopting this approach. Our experimental design lets us simultaneously study the decisions and choices made by participants in the Ultimatum Game and the Public Goods Game. In most studies referenced in the literature, these two experimental paradigms are usually carried out separately. In most cases, the initial endowment is provided by the experimenter exogenously.

As described below, the initial endowment in our experimental design is endogenous. It is important to note that the optimal payoff level in a Public Goods Game scenario is not uniform for every participant. This level is influenced by the perceptions, preferences, and motives of each participant, which motivates them to make specific choices over others (see [7, 8]). It is also worth noting that other scholars have employed the Ultimatum Game and the Public Goods Game in their experimental designs to study human behaviour (see [9–11]). However, the two games were not combined in their experimental designs. Moreover, other scholars have conducted experiments in which subjects were initially endowed with unequal resources (e.g., [12–20]). However, in these studies, the initial endowments were not determined endogenously based on the payoffs received in the Ultimatum Bargaining Game.

In general, the proposed experimental design allows for the conduct of either an Internet experiment or a lab-in-the-field experiment using a digital platform. However, conducting a lab-in-the-field experiment, as [21] noted, can present challenges due to increased complexity. This complexity arises from the difficulties in controlling some extraneous variables, with the anonymity of the experimental subjects representing a notable issue (e.g., issues related to social distance, as discussed by [22]). As the authors in [23] suggest, opting for a different type of experiment can yield different results, and these differences can be attributed to the distinct characteristics that set apart these two types of experiments. Internet experiments offer better anonymity protection since participants cannot see each other (see [24]). In contrast, lab-in-the-field experiments may compromise anonymity due to social distance since participants might recognise others' typical attributes, potentially influencing their decisions. To address this issue, a possible solution is to conduct a parallel experiment using the same pool of experimental subjects and compare the results.

The experimental design proposed is intended to test null hypotheses derived from the existing literature. In particular, the following null hypotheses will be tested:

H.1: The majority of human beings adopt a conditional contribution strategy (e.g., [25, 26]). Experimental subjects' contribution decisions are influenced by the contributions of others, leading to a tendency to imitate.

H.2: It has been observed that experimental subjects tend to reduce their contributions to the common fund over time (e.g., [6, 27]).

H.3: It can be reasonably assumed that those who cooperate are unlikely to offer a bribe, whereas those who defect are more likely to do so (see, [5]).

These hypotheses are based on experimental findings by previous authors and are well-documented in the current literature. Notably, these hypotheses challenge existing theories because, from a standard economic perspective, experimental subjects should consistently exhibit selfish behaviour throughout the experiment. In this context, [28] notes that, from a standard economic perspective, it is expected that experimental subjects will exhibit a lack of cooperative behaviour, resulting in unequal pie distribution in the Ultimatum Bargaining Game and non-contribution to the common fund in the Public Goods Game. However, as we will observe, most experimental results from other studies deviate from these expectations. Consequently, the experimental approach provides valuable insights into understanding human behaviour in bargaining and cooperation settings.

In detail, our work is structured as follows: Sect. 1 introduces the key topics to be covered. Section 2 discusses the Ultimatum Bargaining Game and the Public Goods Game, examining their characteristics, purposes, and recurrent findings in the literature. Section 3 outlines the experimental design, methods, and procedures to be followed for the experimentation. This section further provides a detailed explanation of each treatment in its respective sub-sections. Furthermore, we emphasise the significance of a crucial variable, namely conditional contribution, which has been extensively studied in the existing literature [26]. By manipulating this variable, we aim to investigate the impact of others' contributions on the experimental subject's contributions in a Public Goods Game. We will randomly assign the entire subject pool into treatment and control groups, following the approach detailed in [29], to investigate the phenomenon of conditional contribution. The initial random assignment of subjects to one of the two groups will be maintained throughout the experiment. In this spirit, *[r]andomization to treatment is fundamental to statistical control in the design of experiments* (Harrison et al., [30], p. 498, brackets added). To conclude, Section 4 discusses various aspects of experimental design and suggests further research and study on this topic, such as the possibility of conducting pilot experiments in this context. These pilot experiments can be used to validate null hypotheses and to evaluate the success of the experiment. Conducting pilot experiments can help to refine and improve the experimental design.

2 Ultimatum Game and Public Goods Game

Over the past few decades, the existing literature has seen an influx of primary evidence from experimental studies. Among the myriad of issues explored in these studies, collective action problems have received particular attention, extending beyond the laboratory walls [31].

According to [32, 33], it can be traced back to the work of [34], one of the first attempts to analyse the Ultimatum Bargaining Game (hereafter UBG) experimentally. The bilateral version of the UBG involves two parties: The proposer and the responder. These two parties negotiate the division of a certain amount of money or tokens, denoted by x. The proposer's task is to divide x between themselves and the responder. The proposer makes an offer, i, between 0 and x. After receiving and evaluating the proposer's offer, the responder decides whether or not to accept it. In the case of acceptance, the responder receives the offered amount, i, while the proposer receives the difference between the total amount, x, and the amount given to the responder (x—i). Conversely, if the responder declines the offer, both parties receive nothing.

According to [33], proposers typically offer, on average, about 45% of the total amount, and responders usually accept such offers. Most UBG experiments use human participants. However, in our experimental design, we use an artificial agent as the proposer and a human participant as the responder, as we will discuss further.

In the second part of the experiment, participants will be required to make decisions about contributions to a public goods game. It is important to note that the Voluntary Contribution Mechanism (hereafter, VCM) represents one of the most prominent institutional frameworks employed in the context of the Public Goods Game [35]. The VCM is a system that allows members of a society to provide public goods voluntarily. In the VCM, individuals allocate their initial resources to contribute to creating public goods voluntarily. From a standard economic perspective, individuals should adopt a dominant strategy in the VCM. The reason for adopting this dominant strategy is that the marginal returns from producing public goods are inferior to those from producing private goods. The dominant strategy suggests that individuals should act as free riders, not contributing their resources to the public good (e.g., [36–39]).

Over time, the potential application of the VCM for experimental investigations concerning the provision of public goods has piqued the interest of numerous scholars. As more scholars have been drawn to its appeal, the VCM has been embraced as an institution within the context of the Public Goods Game (hereafter, PGG). The early adoption of the PGG as an experimental paradigm has increased the contribution to the literature on this topic. In this context, numerous scholars have researched specific aspects to identify the factors and motivations that drive humans to deviate from what is expected from the standard economic approach. Among these aspects, we can highlight the role of intrinsic motivations guiding the decision-making of experimental subjects. These motivations may lead experimental subjects to contribute to the common fund in a manner that differs from the theoretical expectations. The motivations above are underpinned by altruism and other social preferences. Upon examination of the literature on the PGG, it becomes evident that many findings recur regularly. One of the most persistently observed findings is that experimental subjects frequently allocate a considerable portion of their initial resources to the common fund. This observation diverges from the predominant hypothesis, which prescribes that experimental subjects should behave as free riders [28]. In contrast to the expectations of the dominant strategy, the average contribution to the common fund stands at approximately 50% of the initial endowment. Voluntary contributions to the common fund typically fluctuate between 40 to 60% of the initial endowment [40]. The attainment of experimental results in contrast to the dominant strategy has piqued the interest of numerous scholars, prompting them to delve deeper into research in this direction. Several experimental results have revealed a number of factors and phenomena that influence contributions to the common fund. In this context, the conditional contribution is considered a key explanatory factor for generous contributions. The concept of conditional contribution encompasses an experimental subject's awareness of the contributions made by others to the common fund, influencing their own contribution decisions. In this context, [26] examined the role of conditional contribution in the PGG in its linear and one-shot forms and found that approximately 50% of the total subject pool exhibited characteristics of conditional contributors. The experimental design proposed in this work, among other things, seeks to explore conditional contribution. Furthermore, the study aims to investigate other phenomena, including corruption and pecuniary punishment. A detailed description of the experimental design is provided in the Section below.

3 Experimental Design

The UBG represents a functional tool in the experimental design proposed here to generate disparities in initial endowments within the PGG following [2]. In this regard, experimental subjects participating in the experiment will utilise the UBG payoffs as their initial PGG endowments. At the commencement of the experiment, we will randomly assign each experimental subject to either the treatment or control group. In the treatment group, experimental subjects will be informed about the contribution decisions made by others in previous rounds of the PGG. A table will display the average contributions of earlier rounds on their screens. As per [26], the contributions of the treatment group are conditional.

Conversely, in the control group, experimental subjects will not be aware of the contribution decisions made by others. Consequently, the contributions made by the control group are unconditional. Regardless of the group assignment, all experimental subjects will be subjected to all the treatments in our experimental design. The general configuration of the experimental design is as follows: For an algorithmic representation, please see, https://drive.google.com/file/d/1dUIVqBglp0rtWH0YBMZPgfayQU3Wux2/view.

The following section provides a more detailed explanation of each treatment within the experimental design. Firstly, we will briefly introduce standard procedures that every experimental subject must follow. Each experimental subject will need to access the experiment platform by clicking a link provided by the experimenters via email after connecting to the internet using their smartphone, PC, or tablet. Upon entering the platform, each experimental subject will be prompted to select a language (e.g., Italian or English) and complete the registration process. This process involves completing a virtual form with personal details such as name, surname, email, gender, age, city of residence, level of education, and occupation. Following successful registration, experimental subjects will receive credentials comprising a username and password necessary for logging in. Both registration and login must be completed to participate in the initial phase of the experiment (UBG) on the platform. A random number generator system will assign each experimental subject to either the control or treatment group, and they will be assigned a unique ID code. The experimenters will only have access to the ID code, thus ensuring the anonymity of experimental subjects. No communication will be allowed between experimental subjects. Before the commencement of each experimental task, instructions will be displayed on the screen, outlining the experiment's dynamics and the number of repetitions. As previously noted by [41], the revelation of the number of repetitions may influence the expectations of experimental subjects. This revelation can be seen as a signal that helps us understand emerging social norms in the experiment. Notably, the instructions do not specify the inequality of initial endowment levels, which experimental subjects will gradually realise over time. Furthermore, as we conduct repeated experiments, several factors may influence the expectations of experimental subjects. Factors such as reputation, beliefs, and trust in others can play a significant role. These factors contribute to the growing evidence of reciprocity and imitation behaviours among experimental subjects, particularly when experiments are repeated with the same subject pool (see [41, 42]).

The initial phase of the experiment comprises a one-shot UBG. In this game, an artificial agent (proposer) will offer a specific sum of money to the human participant (responder), who must decide whether to accept or reject the offer. The responder's decision will determine their subsequent payoff. Subsequently, each experimental subject will engage in the PGG with a real-effort task for 16 rounds, with the initial endowment equal to the payoff from the UBG. Subsequently, each participant will participate in the Bribery Game (hereafter, PGGB) for 16 rounds. The PGGB incorporates a centralised and exogenous punishment system designed to penalise experimental subjects under specific conditions. In total, each experimental subject will be involved in 33 experimental tasks.

After the experiment, all tokens earned by the experimental subjects will be converted into euros at a rate of 1 token = 0.30 euros, as per [43]. Subsequently, the converted amount in euros will be credited to each experimental subject's current account.

3.1 Ultimatum Bargaining Game

The UBG is based on a study previously proposed by [3], in which the authors analyse human behaviour and emotional responses to artificial agents. The following Section provides a detailed explanation of how the UBG is configured. Each experimental subject logs in to the platform using their credentials to complete the experimental task. Alternatively, they must register and then log in. Once logged in, human experimental subjects read the instructions and confirm their understanding. Once the experimental subject has confirmed that the instructions are clear, the artificial agent makes an offer displayed on the subject's mobile device or PC screen. At this point, the experimental subject (responder) decides whether to accept or reject the offer made by the artificial agent.

Now, let us introduce X and Y, where X represents an artificial agent (proposer), and Y represents a human experimental subject (responder). They must divide a positive quantity, denoted as ω, consisting of 10 tokens at time $t = 1$ (UBG one-shot). The payoff functions for the proposer, x_p, and the responder, y_r, can be represented as follows:

$$x_p = (\omega - S)c \text{ with } c = \{0, 1\} \tag{1}$$

$$y_r = \begin{cases} S \text{ if } c=1 \\ 4 \text{ if } c=0 \end{cases} \tag{2}$$

Within Eqs. 1 and 2, $\omega = 10$ indicates the number of tokens to be divided; S represents the offer made by the proposer to the responder with $0 \leq S \leq \omega$; $c = \{0,1\}$ is a parameter that can assume a value equal to 0 or 1. Suppose the responder accepts the offer, $c = 1$. The proposer's payoff (x_p) equals the difference between omega and the offer, S. The responder's payoff (y_r) equals the accepted offer S. Suppose the responder rejects the offer, $c = 0$. The responder's payoff (y_r) is equal to 4. In this regard, within Eq. 2, we have included an integer number, 4. The responder will be given four tokens as a payoff if they reject the offer.

According to [44], proposers typically offer an average of 40% of the initial endowment, as indicated in number 4. Notably, the responder is initially unaware that they will receive a payoff of 4 if they reject the offer. However, their participation in the UBG allows them to discover this, as suggested by [45]. As previously mentioned, our experimental design is concatenated. To allow responders who reject the offer to participate in the PGG, they can receive a payoff of 4. According to [44], the artificial agent (proposer) will be programmed to imitate human behaviour, especially regarding the average amount offered. Thus, the artificial agent randomly proposes offers to the experimental subjects greater than or equal to 2 and less than 8, $2 \leq S < 8$.

The initial endowment utilised in the PGG will be determined by multiplying the total payoff obtained in the UBG by the human responder by a factor of three. This multiplication marks the conclusion of the initial phase of the experiment.

3.2 Public Goods Game

The PGG is a real-effort task based on [4], which allows experimental subjects to cooperate or defect. In this version, experimental subjects perform image recognition tasks derived from the CIFAR-10 dataset [46]. The CIFAR-10 dataset comprises 60,000 32×32 colour images, allowing the experimenter to create image recognition tasks based on specific classes (e.g., automobiles, dogs, trucks, and more). For instance, the experimenter may ask the experimental subjects to recognise particular image classes among a set of images.

At the commencement of the PGG, the experimental subjects begin with unequal initial endowments based on the total payoff obtained in the UBG. In the real-effort task PGG, experimental subjects contribute to the public good by performing an individual task. Instructions provided during the PGG initialisation phase will include performance details. Each subject will be prompted to answer "Would you like to contribute?" on their mobile device or PC screen by selecting either "yes" or "no".

To contribute to the common fund, experimental subjects must correctly solve the image recognition tasks created from CIFAR-10. Successful task completion results in an increase of one token to the subject's initial endowment, while a 1.2 tokens increase is applied to the common fund. If the tasks are solved incorrectly or left incomplete, the subject's initial endowment remains unchanged. In the event of an incorrect or incomplete solution in over 60% of the rounds, a monetary penalty of a two-token reduction is applied to the subject's initial endowment. Participants in the control group can only view their payoff from the last completed round. In contrast, participants in the treatment group can view the payoff from the previous completed round and the average number of contributions made by other subjects.

In PGG, the payoff functions for each round can be represented by a system of two equations as follows:

$$\pi_i^2 = \begin{cases} y_r + e_i + \omega \sum_{j=1}^{n} e_j \text{ if } e_i = 1 \\ y_r + \omega \sum_{j=1}^{n} e_j \text{ if } e_i = 0 \end{cases} \tag{3}$$

The payoff of the experimental subject i is represented by π_i^2, while y_r is the initial endowment deriving from the UBG, and e_i is a parameter that can have two values. $e_i = 1$ when the experimental subject correctly solves the task. $e_i = 0$ occurs when the experimental subject, i, does not contribute by either not solving the task correctly or not completing the task. $\omega = 1.2$ is the marginal per capita return (MPCR) from the group account; $\sum_{j=1}^{n} e_j$ is the sum of the correct answers given to the task by the experimental subjects j (members of the group, including the experimental subject i).

The total payoff function of the non-punished experimental subject is as follows:

$$\pi_{tot}^2 \sum_{t=1}^{16} \pi_i^2 \text{ if } e_{tot} \geq e_{max} \frac{60}{100} \tag{4}$$

Where π_{tot}^2 is the total payoff of the non-punished experimental subject; t indicates the time (rounds); $e_{tot} = \sum_{t=1}^{16} e_i$ (including both $e_i = 1$ and $e_i = 0$) indicates the sum of all correct and wrong answers provided by the experimental subject i during all 16 rounds. Finally, $e_{max} = \sum_{t=1}^{16} e_i$ (including only $e_i = 1$) indicates the maximum value of correct answers that experimental subject i can obtain (16).

Instead, the total payoff function of the punished experimental subject is as follows:

$$\pi_{\text{totp}}^2 \sum_{t=1}^{16} \pi_i^2 - c \text{ if } e_{\text{tot}} < e_{\max} \frac{60}{100} \tag{5}$$

Where π_{tot}^2 is the total payoff of the punished experimental subject; t indicates the time (rounds); c = 2 is the cost of the punishment.

As outlined by [47], when the private fund MPCR exceeds the common fund MPCR, experimental subjects should not contribute according to the Nash equilibrium of the game. In contrast, the [48] approach indicates that the common fund MPCR in our PGG is higher than the private fund MPCR. Consequently, our PGG addresses an unusual scenario not frequently encountered in the existing literature, as noted by [49]. In the existing literature, the private fund MPCR is often equal to 1, and the common fund MPCR is frequently equal to 1.2. In contrast, in our PGG, the private fund MPCR is 1, and the common fund MPCR is 1.2. In this context, [48] suggests that the hypothesis of contributing the maximum amount to the common fund is associated with maximising payoff in this unusual scenario. This hypothesis, which is often overlooked from the perspective of standard economics, requires further in-depth analysis.

3.3 Bribery Game

In the PGGB, the experimental subjects must complete a real-effort task identical to those in the PGG. However, the PGGB is structured based on the Bribery Game proposed by [5]. Each round of the PGGB consists of two phases. During the first phase, each experimental subject performs image recognition tasks. After the first phase, the second phase involves participating in the Bribery Game for each round. The specifics of these two phases are delineated below. At the beginning of the PGGB, the experimental subjects commence with disparate initial endowments, which are determined by the total payoff obtained in the PGG. These initial endowments are renewed for each round. In the initial phase, participants are tasked with solving image recognition tasks created by the experimenter based on images from the CIFAR-10 dataset. During the initial phase of each PGGB round, a choice prompt will be displayed on each experimental subject's mobile device or PC screen. In line with the PGG, the experimental subject must click the "yes" or "no" button to respond to the question, "Would you like to contribute?". Experimental subjects contribute to the public good by performing a real-effort task. The instructions during the initialisation phase of the PGGB will provide details regarding the performance of each experimental subject in the PGGB. In more detail, the experimental subject must successfully solve the image recognition tasks based on CIFAR-10 to contribute to the common fund. If the tasks are solved correctly, the subject's initial endowment increases by one token, and the common fund increases by 1.2 tokens. However, if the tasks are solved incorrectly or left incomplete, the subject's initial endowment does not increase. In contrast to the PGG, the PGGB includes a second phase for each round.

During the second phase, each experimental subject participates in the Bribery Game. In this phase, the experimental subject has two options: (1) to bribe others or (2) to be bribed by others to limit contributions to the common fund. The decision to bribe others results in a reduction of two tokens in the experimental subject's payoff, whereas being bribed by others increases their payoff by two tokens. However, if the experimental subject chooses to bribe others for more than 50% of the rounds, they will incur a penalty of eight tokens, directly reducing their total payoff.

In the PGGB, the single-period payoff functions are as follows:

$$\pi_i^3 = \begin{cases} \pi_{tot}^2 + e_i + \omega \sum_{j=1}^{n} e_j + (b-2); \quad b = \{0,2,4\} \ \ if \ \ e_i = 1 \\ \pi_{tot}^2 + \omega \sum_{j=1}^{n} e_j + (b-2); \quad b = \{0,2,4\} \ \ if \ \ e_i = 0 \end{cases} \tag{6}$$

The payoff of the experimental subject i is represented by π_i^3; the endowment deriving from the PGG is represented by π_{tot}^2, and e_i is a parameter that can take two values. $e_i = 1$ when the experimental subject correctly solves the task. $e_i = 0$ occurs when the experimental subject, i, does not contribute by either not solving the task correctly or not completing the task. $\omega = 1.2$ is the marginal per capita return (MPCR) from the common fund; $\sum_{j=1}^{n} e_j$ is the sum of the correct answers given to the task by the experimental subjects j (members of the group, including the experimental subject i). b = {2,4,0} is a parameter that can assume the value of 2 (not to bribe and not to be bribed), 4 (to be bribed) or 0 (to bribe).

The total payoff function of the non-punished experimental subject is as follows:

$$\pi_{\text{tot}}^3 \sum_{t=1}^{16} \pi_i^3 \ \text{if} \ \alpha_{\text{tot}} \leq \alpha_{\text{max}} \frac{50}{100} \tag{7}$$

In Eq. 7, we included the parameter α to indicate how many times each experimental subject has been bribed. In particular, $0 \leq \alpha_{\text{tot}} \leq 16$ and $\alpha_{\text{max}} = 16$.

Instead, the total payoff function of the punished experimental subject is as follows:

$$\pi_{\text{totp}}^3 \sum_{t=1}^{16} \pi_i^3 - c \ \text{if} \ \alpha_{\text{tot}} \geq \alpha_{\text{max}} \frac{50}{100} \tag{8}$$

Where c = 8 indicates the cost of punishment inflicted by the experimenter.

In summary, the proposed experimental design exhibits two distinctive features that differentiate it from those commonly found in the literature. The first noteworthy feature is the concatenated nature of the experimental design. Each experimental subject's initial endowment at the start of a new game is contingent upon the decisions they made in the preceding game, with the UBG employed as the primary source of initial endowment inequality.

The second feature pertains to the endogenous creation of the initial endowment, which is internally generated within the experiment. In contrast to a scenario where the experimenter bestows the initial endowment upon the experimental subject, it is internally generated within the experiment in our experimental design. This feature is accentuated by the fact that both the PGG and the PGGB necessitate real effort on the part of the experimental subjects.

The following Section will examine potential applications and extensions of the experimental design proposed here.

4 Discussion and Future Research

The experimental design presented in this work can be adopted in various experimental settings to study human behaviour in bargaining and cooperative contexts. The experimental design that was previously presented is versatile and suitable for conducting Internet and lab-in-the-field experiments. We briefly discussed some significant differences observed in both types of experiments, such as the impact of anonymity on experimental results. Nonetheless, web-based platforms, such as oTree [50], can be utilised for conducting both types of experiments. Open-source web platforms, such as oTree, enable experimental subjects to interact through mobile devices with internet connectivity, as is widely recognised. In this context, [51] suggests that these web platforms facilitate experiments with a large number of participants and expedite the data collection process compared to experiments that do not utilise them. Consequently, by employing these platforms, the experimental results would likely exhibit increased robustness.

It is important to note that experimental subjects can be categorised as either volunteers or pseudo-volunteers, regardless of the type of experiment adopted [52]. highlights a significant distinction between these two categories of subjects. The term volunteers refers to randomly recruited individuals who voluntarily participate in experiments. In contrast, pseudo-volunteers are individuals recruited quasi-randomly and join as part of a specific group, which may include schoolchildren, university students, employees, or company management. As [52] suggests, inconsistencies in results can arise when comparing experimental data collected from experiments involving two different types of volunteers. Conducting the same experiment with both types of volunteers and comparing the results could provide valuable insights into these inconsistencies.

The experimental approach allows for studying specific collective action problems related to common and public goods. Extensive literature exploration reveals that many scholars have been captivated by the experimental study of producing public goods from local and global perspectives [53] defines local public goods as those designed to meet the needs of small and organised societal groups, such as a city. Local public goods include street lighting, national defence programmes, regulations, public education, and public health. Conversely, [54] defines global public goods as encompassing ideas, products, services, policies, and issues that impact all living beings without regard to national or natural borders. This definition highlights the global and cross-border scope of global public goods. Examples of global public goods include, but are not limited to, vaccination campaigns to prevent the spread of diseases, corruption, cyberbullying, and environmental and ecological issues, particularly in climate change and other initiatives concerning the safeguarding of the natural ecosystem (see [14, 55]).

In conclusion, our experimental design can be employed to study socio-economic phenomena in contexts involving both small and large groups of individuals. In the future, our goal is to conduct the experiment presented in this work and design more experiments focused on global issues, enhancing the current literature debate.

References

1. Dawes, R. M. (1980). Social dilemmas. *Annual Review of Psychology, 31*(1), 169–193.
2. Bucciarelli, E., Chen, S.-H., Cinosi, S., & Zenone, S. (forthcoming). Advancing cognitive design research in economics: A novel approach to studying two experimental paradigms. In E. Bucciarelli, S.-H. Chen, J. Parra, & J. M. Corchado (Eds.), *Decision economics: Reckoning with radical uncertainty and its multifarious forms*. Springer-Nature.
3. Swiderska, A., Krumhube, E. G., & Kappas, A. (2019). Behavioral and physiological responses to computers in the ultimatum game. *International. Journal of Technology and Human Interaction, 15*(1), 33–45.
4. Hackel, J., Yamamoto, H., Okada, I., Goto, A., & Taudes, A. (2021). Asymmetric effects of social and economic incentives on cooperation in real-effort-based public goods games. *PLoS One, 16*(4), 1–11.
5. Buffat, J., & Senn, J. (2018). *Corruption, norm enforcement and cooperation* (pp. 1–31). University of Zurich, Department of Economics., Working Paper No. 260, Revised version, Available at SSRN. https://doi.org/10.2139/ssrn.3018606
6. Fehr, E., & Gächter, S. (2000). Cooperation and punishment in public goods experiments. *American Economic Review, 90*(1), 980–994.
7. Irwin, J. R., McClelland, G. H., McKee, M., Schulze, W. D., & Norden, N. E. (1998). Payoff dominance vs. cognitive transparency in decision making. *Economic Inquiry, 36*(2), 272–285.
8. Smith, V. L., & Walker, J. M. (1993). Monetary rewards and decision cost in experimental economics. *Economic Inquiry, 31*(2), 245–261.
9. Henrich, J., & Smith, N. (2004). Comparative experimental evidence from Machiguenga, Mapuche, Huinca, and American populations. In J. Henrich et al. (Eds.), *Foundations of human sociality, economic experiments and ethnographic evidence from fifteen small-scale societies* (pp. 125–167). Oxford University Press.
10. Ensminger, J., & Cook, K. (2014). Prosociality in rural America: Evidence from dictator, ultimatum, public goods, and trust games. In E. J. Jean & J. Henrich (Eds.), *Experimenting with social norm: Fairness and punishment in cross-cultural perspective* (pp. 445–464). Russel Sage Foundation.
11. Fraser, S., & Nettle, D. (2020). Hunger affects social decisions in a multi-round public goods game but not a single-shot ultimatum game. *Adaptive Human Behavior and Physiology, 6*(1), 334–355.
12. Buckley, E., & Croson, R. (2006). Income and wealth heterogeneity in the voluntary provision of linear public goods. *Journal of Public Economics, 90*(4–5), 935–955.

13. Kingsley, D. C. (2016). Endowment heterogeneity and peer punishment in a public good experiment: Cooperation and normative conflict. *Journal of Behavioral and Experimental Economics, 60*(1), 49–61.
14. Tavoni, A., Dannenberg, A., Kallis, G., & Löschel, A. (2011). Inequality, communication, and the avoidance of disastrous climate change in a public goods game. *PNAS, 108*(29), 11825–11829.
15. Weis, J., Cadigan, J., Schmitt, P., & Swope, K. (2017). Endowment effects and contribution strategies in public good experiments. *Archives of Psychology, 1*(1), 1–17.
16. Gächter, S., Mengel, F., Tsakas, E., & Vostroknutovd, A. (2017). Growth and inequality in public good provision. *Journal of Public Economics, 150*(1), 1–13.
17. Antinyan, A., Corazzini, L., & Neururer, D. (2015). Public good provision, punishment, and the endowment origin: Experimental evidence. *Journal of Behavioral and Experimental Economics, 56*(1), 72–77.
18. Heap, S. P. H., Ramalingam, A., & Stoddard, B. V. (2016). Endowment inequality in public goods games: A re-examination. *Economics Letters, 146*(1), 4–7.
19. Keser, C., Märkstadter, A., & Schmidt, M. (2017). Mandatory minimum contributions, heterogenous endowments and voluntary public-good provision. *Games and Economic Behavior, 101*(1), 291–310.
20. van den Berg, P., Dewitte, P., Aertgeerts, I., & Wenseleers, T. (2020). How the incentive to contribute affects contributions in the one-shot public goods game. *Nature, Scientific Reports, 10*(18732), 1–5.
21. List, J. A., & Price, M. K. (2013). *Handbook on experimental economics and the environment*. Edward Elgar Publishing.
22. Charness, G., & Gneezy, U. (2008). What's in a name? Anonymity and social distance in dictator and ultimatum games. *Journal of Economic Behavior & Organization, 68*(1), 29–35.
23. Charness, G., Haruvy, E., & Sonsino, D. (2007). Social distance and reciprocity: An internet experiment. *Journal of Economic Behavior & Organization, 63*(1), 88–103.
24. Anderhub, V., Müller, R., & Schmidt, C. (2001). Design and evaluation of an economic experiment via the internet. *Journal of Economic Behavior & Organization, 46*(2), 227–247.
25. Vogelsang, M., Jensen, K., Kirschner, S., Tennie, C., & Tomasello, M. (2014). Preschoolers are sensitive to free riding in a public goods game. *Frontiers in Psychology, 5*(729), 1–9.
26. Fischbacher, U., Gächter, S., & Fehr, E. (2001). Are people conditionally cooperative? Evidence from a public goods experiment. *Economics Letters, 71*(1), 397–404.
27. Harbaugh, W. T., & Krause, K. (2000). Children's altruism in public good and dictator experiments. *Economic Inquiry, 38*(1), 95–109.
28. Saijo, T. (2008). Spiteful behavior in voluntary contribution mechanism experiments. In C. R. Plott & V. L. Smith (Eds.), *Handbook of experimental economics results* (Vol. 1, pp. 802–816). Elsevier.
29. List, J. A., Sadoff, S., & Wagner, M. (2011). So you want to run an experiment, now what? Some simple rules of thumb for optimal experimental design. *Experimental Economics, 14*(1), 439–457.
30. Harrison, G. W., Lau, M. I., & Rutström, E. E. (2009). Risk attitudes, randomization to treatment, and self-selection into experiments. *Journal of Economic Behavior & Organization, 70*(3), 498–507.
31. Olson, M. (1971). *The logic of collective action. Public goods and the theory of groups*. Harvard Economic Press. [1965].
32. Thaler, R. H. (1988). Anomalies: The ultimatum game. *Journal of Economic Perspectives, 2*(4), 195–206.
33. Houser, D., & McCabe, K. (2014). Experimental economics and experimental game theory. In P. W. Glimcher & E. Fehr (Eds.), *Neuroeconomics* (2nd ed., pp. 19–34). Academic, Elsevier.
34. Güth, W., Schmittberger, R., & Schwarze, B. (1982). An experimental analysis of ultimatum bargaining. *Journal of Economic Behavior & Organization, 3*(4), 367–388.

35. Lappalainen, O. (2018). Cooperation and strategic complementarity: An experiment with two voluntary contribution mechanism games with interior equilibria. *Games, 9*(3), 1–24.
36. Isaac, R., Walker, J. M., & Thomas, S. H. (1984). Divergent evidence on free-riding: An experimental examination of possible explanations. *Public Choice, 43*(1), 113–149.
37. Kinukawa, S., Saijo, T., & Una, M. (2000). Partial communication in a voluntary-contribution-mechanism experiment. *Pacific Economic Review, 5*(3), 411–428.
38. Sigmund, K. (2010). *The calculus of selfishness*. Princeton University Press.
39. Dong, Y., Zhang, B., & Tao, Y. (2016). The dynamics of human behaviour in the public goods game with institutional incentives. *Nature, Scientific Reports, 28809*(6), 1–7.
40. Marwell, G., & Ames, R. E. (1981). Economists free ride, does anyone else? Experiments on the provision of public goods, IV. *Journal of Public Economics, 15*(3), 295–310.
41. Hoffman, E., McCabe, K. A., & Smith, V. L. (1998). Behavioral foundations of reciprocity: Experimental economics and evolutionary psychology. *Economic Inquiry, 36*(3), 335–352.
42. Vanberg, C. (2008). Why do people keep their promises? An experimental test of two explanations. *Econometrica, 79*(6), 1467–1480.
43. Khadjavi, M., & Lange, A. (2013). Prisoners and their dilemma. *Journal of Economic Behavior & Organization, 92*(1), 163–175.
44. Oosterbeek, H., Sloof, R., & van de Kuilen, G. (2004). Cultural differences in ultimatum game experiments: Evidence from a meta-analysis. *Experimental Economics, 7*(1), 171–188.
45. Madsen, D. Ø., & Stenheim, T. (2015). Experimental methods in economics and psychology: A comparison. *Procedia-Social and Behavioral Sciences, 187*(1), 113–117.
46. Krizhevsky, A. (2009). Cifar-10 dataset. Accessed April 26, 2023, from https://www.cs.toronto.edu/~kriz/cifar.html
47. Boulu-Reshef, B. H., Brott, S., & Zylbersztejn, A. (2017). Does uncertainty deter provision of public goods? *Revue économique, 5*(68), 785–791.
48. Baker, R. J., II, Walker, J. M., & Williams, A. W. (2009). Matching contributions and the voluntary provision of a pure public good: Experimental evidence. *Journal of Economic Behavior & Organization, 70*(1–2), 122–134.
49. Cadigan, J., Wayland, P. T., Schmitt, P., & Swope, K. (2011). An experimental dynamic public goods game with carryover. *Journal of Economic Behavior & Organization, 80*(3), 523–531.
50. Chen, D. L., Schonger, M., & Wickens, C. (2016). oTree—An open-source platform for laboratory, online, and field experiments. *Journal of Behavioral and Experimental Finance, 91*, 88–97.
51. Wissink, J., van Beest, I., Pronk, T., & van de Ven, N. (2022). The online coalition game: A tool for online interactive coalition formation research. *Behavior Research Methods, 54*(3), 1078–1091.
52. Eckel, C. C., & Grossman, P. J. (2000). Volunteers and pseudo-volunteers: The effect of recruitment method in dictator experiments. *Experimental Economics, 3*(1), 107–120.
53. Stiglitz, J. E. (1982). *The theory of local public goods twenty-five years after Tiebout: A perspective* (Vol. w0954, pp. 17–53). National Bureau of Economic Research.
54. Kaul, I., Grunberg, I., & Stern, M. (1999). *Global public goods: International cooperation in the 21st century*. Oxford University Press.
55. Hasson, R., Löfgren, Å., & Visser, M. (2020). Climate change in a public goods game: Investment decision in mitigation versus adaptation. *Ecological Economics, 70*(2), 331–338.

Correction to: Digital (Eco) Systems and Societal Challenges

Alessio Maria Braccini, Francesca Ricciardi, and Francesco Virili

Correction to:
A. M. Braccini et al. (eds.), *Digital (Eco) Systems and Societal Challenges*, Lecture Notes in Information Systems and Organisation 72,
https://doi.org/10.1007/978-3-031-75586-6

The original version of the chapters were inadvertently published with the following corrections:

In chapter 1:

1. The chapter titles mentioned within the text were incorrect.
2. In a few cases, the term [REF] was retained.

These changes have now been corrected.

In chapter 7:

The author's names were misspelled as Balzani Luca and Corsi Katia; and they have been corrected to Luca Balzani and Katia Corsi.

The updated version of these chapters can be found at
https://doi.org/10.1007/978-3-031-75586-6_1
https://doi.org/10.1007/978-3-031-75586-6_7

A. M. Braccini et al. (eds.), *Digital (Eco) Systems and Societal Challenges*, Lecture Notes in Information Systems and Organisation 72,
https://doi.org/10.1007/978-3-031-75586-6_24

The manufacturer's authorised representative in the EU is Springer Nature Customer Service Centre GmbH, Europaplatz 3, 69115 Heidelberg, Germany. If you have any concerns regarding our products, please contact ProductSafety@springernature.com

Printed and bound by CPI Group (UK) Ltd, Croydon, CR0 4YY
30/09/2026
02225561-0014